Embedded/ Real-Time Systems: Concepts, Design and Programming

Black Book™

Dr. K. V. K. K. Prasad

Published by:

dreamtech PRESS

ISBN: 978-81-7722-461-0

Reprint 2019

Printed at: Nisha Enterprises

Preface

We are surrounded by embedded computing devices—at home, in the office, even while we are traveling in a car or an aircraft. Nearly 99% of the processors that are manufactured go into these embedded systems. Just about 1% of the processors are used on the desktops, workstations and mainframe computers. "Ubiquitous computing" and "pervasive computing" are the two important phrases that reflect the omni-presence of embedded systems.

Last few years, saw tremendous growth in the technology of embedded systems—the processor speed increased manifold, new development tools are paving way for fast and easier development of the embedded software and the applications of embedded systems are witnessing an exponential growth. As a result, the demand for professionals with expertise in embedded system design also increased manifold in recent years. Due to the shortage of skilled human resources in this area, embedded system engineers are the most sought-after professionals and their salaries are skyrocketing. Surprisingly, people with knowledge of embedded systems design are very few despite the fact that the embedded system development is one of the fastest growing areas.

Embedded system development continues to be a very challenging task mainly because it requires specialized skills—good knowledge of hardware platforms, good exposure to the latest tools and techniques for software development and knowledge of the application domain. Those equipped with these skills have the potential of becoming good embedded system designers.

Welcome to the World of Embedded Systems

We are surrounded by embedded systems. Wherever we go—home, hospital, hotel, factory, shopping mall and so on—embedded systems are around. Even while we are on the move—in a car or in an aircraft, we are amidst embedded systems. The embedded systems do their jobs silently, and their presence is not obvious unlike desktop computers! Though embedded systems have been around for many decades, the last decade of the 20th century has seen many exciting developments in this arena.

The processor speeds have increased manifold. In addition to 8-bit and 16-bit processors, 32-bit and even 64-bit processors are used in many embedded systems paving way for very powerful applications. Powerful Digital Signal Processors are available making audio and video processing much easier. All this is leading to an era of multimedia communication using mobile devices. Mobile phones and palmtops are becoming more and more powerful and provide wireless Internet access. This is leading to the revolution of anywhere anytime communication.

With the advent of the networked information appliances, we are now witnessing a revolution. Even tiny embedded systems can be network-enabled and they can get connected to the Internet. A remarkable feature that makes the embedded systems highly useful is that these can be accessed from anywhere on the earth using a normal web browser. Therefore, their important role in networked information appliances can be easily visualized. Examples of such applications are remote monitoring of factory equipment, real-time weather monitoring, security systems etc.

Another innovation in the embedded system arena is in the software development. Earlier, developing embedded systems involved writing in assembly language and hence it was a highly specialized activity. Nowadays, with the availability of powerful development tools, programming can be done in high-level languages such as C, C++ and Java; the software can be tested on desktops and then ported on to the embedded systems. As a result, development time has been drastically reduced and the software maintenance has become very easy.

Well, all these developments are paving way for a brave new world of embedded systems—the power of desktop computers is now available on our palmtops, the mobile phone can be used not just for voice calls, but also for multimedia communication while on the move. And, the network-enabled embedded systems can be accessed through the Internet. In short, embedded systems are redefining the information, communication and entertainment technologies. They are providing a great impetus to the developments in every industrial sector—office automation, manufacturing, transportation, telecommunications, finance, healthcare, entertainment, etc.

It is not an exaggeration to say that we are lucky enough to be in the midst of such exciting developments. And, can we stay away from being a part of such a great revolution being brought forth by embedded systems? No, and this book will put you in the midst of that electrifying action.

About the Book

Embedded system development involves teamwork among three different sets of people: hardware engineers, software engineers and application domain experts. In most of the embedded systems projects, the software engineer and the hardware engineer do not understand the jargon of each other; both also find it difficult to communicate with the application domain experts. It is mainly due to these communication gaps, many embedded system projects get into trouble. The objective of this book is to lay the necessary foundation in hardware building blocks and software development tools and techniques. It also aims at giving exposure to representative application domains so that you can take up embedded systems development in any application area of your choice.

This book is addressed to the software engineers who would like to take up embedded system development as their career. The best way of starting work on embedded systems is to work on the evaluation boards of popular micro-controllers/processors and write the software that works on these boards. Accordingly, the architectures of popular micro-controllers and processors are discussed and software development using the evaluation boards is covered in detail. Even if you do not have access to an evaluation board, you can learn the embedded software development by experimenting with the code on your desktop computer. After gaining the necessary knowledge of the hardware to write the firmware, you will be in a position to comfortably communicate with a hardware engineer in her jargon. Embedded system designers have a wide variety of processors to choose from, but if you are comfortable with one processor, it is not at all difficult to switch over to another processor.

Again, a large number of operating systems are used in embedded systems. In this book, the concepts of embedded/real-time operating systems are presented with illustrative examples written in C code using open source operating systems. These operating systems are becoming very popular and also access to them is free. An overview of the commercial operating systems is also given. If you get a good grasp of one or two embedded/real-time operating systems, it is not difficult to switch over to another operating system of your choice.

In embedded software development, C programming language continues to play a major role, though C++ and Java are catching up. Development in C for embedded systems is much more involved than application software development and hence the finer aspects of system programming in C are covered in detail with illustrative examples. Development of applications in C++ and Java are also covered with case studies from a variety of application domains.

As Digital Signal Processor-based embedded systems are gaining lot of practical importance, particularly due to advances in multimedia communication over mobile networks, one chapter in this book focuses on DSP theory and practice. Most of the books on DSP cover lot of mathematics without explaining the physical concepts. In this book, a totally different approach is taken—more emphasis is on gaining a deep understanding of the physical significance of the mathematics of DSP. DSP programming using MATLAB is also covered.

Though a number of books are available on embedded systems, most of them focus either on theory alone or on programming aspects alone. This book provides the necessary balance between theory and practice by covering the concepts with illustrative practical examples. Emphasis is also given to the design of embedded systems, and the process of embedded system design is discussed in detail.

The programming of embedded systems is illustrated through a number of case studies in different application domains such as consumer electronics, data communication, mobile computing, RFID etc. Working on these case studies will give you the necessary breadth and depth in embedded software development using the latest tools.

At the end of each chapter, questions and exercises are given to test your comprehension. The solutions to selected exercises are also provided.

Target Audience and Prerequisites for Reading the Book

This book is addressed to the undergraduate/graduate students of computer/electronics engineering. Knowledge of basics of digital electronics and microprocessor architecture is all that is required to start reading this book. In view of the recent trends in embedded system development, the emphasis is not on use of assembly language programming. It is assumed that you have a basic knowledge of high-level languages (C, C++ or Java).

If you are a software professional with experience in application software development, and if you want to switch over to embedded software development; or if you are a computer science/electrical engineering student with special interest in embedded systems development, this book is for you.

If you are a project manager and now your new assignment is to manage an embedded system development project; this book will give you all the necessary ammunition to make your project a success.

Organization of the Book

This book is organized into 22 chapters.

Chapter 1 gives an introduction to embedded systems. The important features and specialties of embedded systems are discussed and a simplified architecture of an embedded system is presented. Various categories of embedded systems are discussed and recent trends in embedded system development are presented.

Chapter 2 gives the details of embedded system architecture. The building blocks of the hardware of an embedded system are presented. An overview of the software architecture—operating system, communication software and application software—is also given. The process of creating an executable image is discussed. The tools required for development and testing of embedded systems are listed.

Chapter 3 deals with programming for embedded systems. As C language continues to be the most widely used language for embedded software development, system level programming aspects of C are discussed with illustrative code examples. Development tools such as debuggers, profilers and revision control system are discussed. The importance of C++ and Java as programming languages for embedded software development is also highlighted.

Chapter 4 focuses on the process of embedded system development. To develop quality embedded systems, a systematic procedure has to be defined and this procedure is explained in this chapter. The various stages in software development process viz., requirements engineering, design, implementation, integration and testing, and maintenance are discussed. The issues involved in managing embedded system development project are also discussed. Some of the major fiascos in embedded system development have been presented which teach us very important lessons. The various issues to be considered for choosing a processor and operating system are also listed.

Chapter 5 deals with hardware platforms. The platforms used for embedded system are discussed. The details of custom-built platforms using 89C51 and AVR micro-controller are given with detailed circuit schematics. This chapter gives an insight into the hardware design of micro-controller based boards.

Chapter 6 deals with communication interfaces. The details of communication interfaces such as RS232/UART, RS422/RS485, IEEE 1394, USB, Ethernet, IEEE 802.11 wireless LAN interface, Infrared and Blutooth are discussed. Both hardware aspects and protocol architecture for these interfaces are presented.

Chapter 7 presents the concepts of embedded/real-time operating systems. The various services provided by the operating systems are discussed. Task scheduling algorithms and inter-task communication are explained. This chapter's emphasis is on the theoretical aspects of embedded/real-time operating systems.

Chapter 8 gives an overview of the off-the-shelf operating systems. Non-real-time embedded operating systems such as Embedded NT, Windows XP Embedded and

Embedded Linux are reviewed. QNX Neutrino, VxWorks, MicroC/OS-II and RTLinux real-time operating systems are also reviewed. The salient features of handheld/mobile operating systems viz., Palm OS, Symbian OS, Windows CE and Windows CE.NET are presented. The important commonalities and differences in features of the off-the-shelf operating systems are listed.

Chapter 9 describes through case studies the process of creating the target image that includes the operating system and the application software.

Chapter 10 gives the architectures of representative embedded systems. The architectures of digital thermometer, handheld computer, navigation system, IP Phone, Software-Defined Radio, Smart cards and RF tags are presented to bring out the diversity in embedded system development.

Chapter 11 focuses on embedded software development in Linux environment. An overview of the Linux commands and shell programming is presented followed by the system-level programming in Linux. Through illustrative examples and programs, the function calls to access operating system services are discussed. The programming aspects of task management and inter-task communication are presented.

Chapter 12 focuses on embedded software development in RTLinux environment. Intricacies of real-time operating system function calls are discussed with examples.

Chapters 13 to 20 focus on various case studies. The complete source code for developing a variety of applications is given to enable the reader get a deep understanding of embedded system development.

Chapter 13 presents a case study of development of a navigation system. The location information obtained from a GPS receiver is displayed on a digitized map. GPS simulator software is also given for those who do not have access to a GPS receiver.

Chapter 14 gives the implementation details of development of a protocol converter that converts Ethernet packets to RS232 format. The intricacies in designing packet formats and network programming are also revealed in this case study.

Chapter 15 presents a case study on development of embedded database application using embedded Visual Basic for Pocket PC. For those who have been working in application software development but want to get on to the bandwagon of embedded software development, this is the best chapter to start off.

Chapter 16 gives the details of development of mobile applications using J2ME. Details of two projects viz., an electronic city guide and electronic voting through mobile phone are presented.

Chapter 17 gives the details of development of embedded applications using 89C51-based development board. The use of cross-development platform tools are explained followed by the application development in C language.

Chapter 18 presents the details of development of embedded applications using AVR micro-controller based development board. The use of cross-platform development tools for AVR micro-controllers is presented followed by application development on this board.

Chapter 19 gives the details of development of embedded applications using Intel

StrongARM development board. A variety of applications are presented to illustrate development of high-end applications on this board. These applications include parallel communication, interfacing a stepper motor, JPEG encoder, MP3 decoder, file transfer and interfacing IrDA card.

Chapter 20 deals with RFID systems. RFID application development is illustrated through programming of RFID reader in C++. This chapter also discusses the issues involved in embedded system programming using C++. The advantages of object-oriented programming are discussed and the salient features of embedded C++ are given.

Chapter 21 deals with DSP-based embedded systems. The fundamentals of digital signal processing are presented and the process of developing embedded systems using digital signal processors is discussed in detail. The various application areas of DSP are explained. MATLAB programs for signal processing applications are also presented.

Chapter 22 gives the glimpses of future developments in the area of embedded systems. The concept of ubiquitous computing and pervasive computing is discussed and the possible applications are discussed.

If you want to be a "complete" embedded system engineer with an interest in both hardware and software, you can read all the chapters in sequence. If your interest is only in hardware, the suggested sequence is Chapters 1, 2, 4, 5, 6, 9, 10 and 17 to 22. If only software interests you, then the suggested sequence is Chapters 1 to 4, 7 to 16, 20 to 22. If you have interest in programming only in C/C++, you can skip Chapters 15 and 16. If you are a project manager interested in getting a bird's eye view of embedded systems, you can go through the Chapters 1, 2, 4, 8, 10, 21 and 22.

Appendix A gives glossary, with explanation of important terms. If you want to quickly become familiar with the jargon used in embedded systems, this is the place to start reading the book.

Appendix B gives a list of acronyms and abbreviations commonly encountered in embedded system literature.

Appendix C gives the solutions to selected exercises.

Appendix D gives the list of reference books and Internet resources.

Appendix E gives the information about the Online Content.

Now, let us begin our journey to unravel the mysteries of the embedded systems!

Credits

Chapter 19 has been contributed by Aspire Communication Pvt. Ltd., Bangalore.

The following engineers of Innovation Communications Systems Ltd., Hyderabad contributed to the software development in various chapters of this book: Mr. A. Veerraju, Mr. V. Satish Chandra, Mr. K.V.P.S. Raju, Mr. A. Srinivasa Varma, Ms. P.U.N.V. Padmavathi, Mr. Darshan Mehta, Mr. Sachin Bhayare, Mr. Jijo Jacob and Mr. P. Pratap Reddy.

Contents at a Glance

Table of Contents

Chapter 1

Introduction to Embedded Systems

CHAPTER OBJECTIVES

After reading this chapter, you will be able to:

- Understand what is an embedded system
- List the various application areas in which embedded systems are used
- Categorize embedded systems
- Gain knowledge of the architecture of an embedded system
- Understand the requirements of embedded systems
- Learn about the recent trends in embedded system development

Embedded systems are omnipresent. We find them everywhere—at our homes, in our offices, in shopping malls, in hospitals, in cars, in aircraft and so on. In this introductory chapter, we will define an embedded system and study the various market segments for the embedded systems. We will study how the embedded systems can be divided into different categories based on their functionality. We will discuss the architecture of an embedded system and the special requirements of these systems. We will also discuss the recent trends in embedded system development.

1.1 What is an Embedded System?

An embedded system can be defined as a computing device that does a specific focused job. Appliances such as the air-conditioner, VCD player, DVD player, printer, fax machine, mobile phone etc. are examples of embedded systems. Each of these appliances will have a processor and special hardware to meet the specific requirement of the application along with the embedded software that is executed by the processor for meeting that specific requirement. The embedded software is also called "firmware".

The desktop/laptop computer is a general purpose computer. You can use it for a variety of applications such as playing games, word processing, accounting, software development and so on. In contrast, the software in the embedded systems is always fixed.

Embedded systems are characterized by some special features listed below:

- Embedded systems do a very specific task, they cannot be programmed to do different things.
- Embedded systems have very limited resources, particularly the memory. Generally, they do not have secondary storage devices such as the CDROM or the floppy disk.
- Embedded systems have to work against some deadlines. A specific job has to be completed within a specific time. In some embedded systems, called real-time systems, the deadlines are stringent. Missing a deadline may cause a catastrophe—loss of life or damage to property.
- Embedded systems are constrained for power. As many embedded systems operate through a battery, the power consumption has to be very low.
- Embedded systems need to be highly reliable. Once in a while, pressing ALT-CTRL-DEL is OK on your desktop, but you cannot afford to reset your embedded system.
- Some embedded systems have to operate in extreme environmental conditions such as very high temperatures and humidity.
- Embedded systems that address the consumer market (for example, electronic toys) are very cost-sensitive. Even a reduction of $0.1 is lot of cost saving, because thousands or millions systems may be sold.
- Unlike desktop computers in which the hardware platform is dominated by Intel and the operating system is dominated by Microsoft, there is a wide variety of processors and operating systems for the embedded systems. So, choosing the right platform is the most complex task.

In Brief...

An embedded system is a computing device that does a specific job. Both the hardware and software in an embedded system are optimized for that specific job.

1.2 Application Areas

Nearly 99 per cent of the processors manufactured end up in embedded systems. The embedded system market is one of the highest growth areas as these systems are used in very market segment—consumer electronics, office automation, industrial automation, biomedical engineering, wireless communication, data communication, telecommunications, transportation, military and so on.

Consumer appliances: At home we use a number of embedded systems which include digital camera, digital diary, DVD player, electronic toys, microwave oven, remote controls for TV and air-conditioner, VCD player, video game consoles, video recorders etc. Today's high-tech car has about 20 embedded systems for transmission control, engine spark control, air-conditioning, navigation etc. Even wristwatches are now becoming embedded systems. The palmtops are powerful embedded systems using which we can carry out many general-purpose tasks such as playing games and word processing.

Office automation: The office automation products using embedded systems are copying machine, fax machine, key telephone, modem, printer, scanner etc.

Industrial automation: Today a lot of industries use embedded systems for process control. These include pharmaceutical, cement, sugar, oil exploration, nuclear energy, electricity generation and transmission. The embedded systems for industrial use are designed to carry out specific tasks such as monitoring the temperature, pressure, humidity, voltage, current etc., and then take appropriate action based on the monitored levels to control other devices or to send information to a centralized monitoring station. In hazardous industrial environment, where human presence has to be avoided, robots are used, which are programmed to do specific jobs. The robots are now becoming very powerful and carry out many interesting and complicated tasks such as hardware assembly.

Medical electronics: Almost every medical equipment in the hospital is an embedded system. These equipments include diagnostic aids such as ECG, EEG, blood pressure measuring devices, X-ray scanners; equipment used in blood analysis, radiation, colonoscopy, endoscopy etc. Developments in medical electronics have paved way for more accurate diagnosis of diseases.

Computer networking: Computer networking products such as bridges, routers, Integrated Services Digital Networks (ISDN), Asynchronous Transfer Mode (ATM), X.25 and frame relay switches are embedded systems which implement the necessary data communication protocols. For example, a router interconnects two networks. The two networks may be running different protocol stacks. The router's function is to obtain the data packets from incoming ports, analyze the packets and send them towards the destination after doing necessary protocol conversion. Most networking equipments, other than the end-systems (desktop computers) we use to access the networks, are embedded systems.

Telecommunications: In the field of telecommunications, the embedded systems can be categorized as subscriber terminals and network equipment. The subscriber terminals such as key telephones, ISDN phones, terminal adapters, web cameras are embedded systems. The network equipment includes multiplexers, multiple access systems, Packet Assemblers Disassembers (PADs), satellite modems etc. IP phone, IP gateway, IP gatekeeper etc. are the latest embedded systems that provide very low-cost voice communication over the Internet.

Wireless technologies: Advances in mobile communications are paving way for many interesting applications using embedded systems. The mobile phone is one of the marvels of the last decade of the 20th century. It is a very powerful embedded system that provides voice communication while we are on the move. The Personal Digital Assistants and the palmtops can now be used to access multimedia services over the Internet. Mobile communication infrastructure such as base station controllers, mobile switching centers are also powerful embedded systems.

Instrumentation: Testing and measurement are the fundamental requirements in all scientific and engineering activities. The measuring equipment we use in laboratories to measure parameters such as weight, temperature, pressure, humidity, voltage, current etc. are all embedded systems. Test equipment such as oscilloscope, spectrum analyzer, logic analyzer, protocol analyzer, radio communication test set etc. are embedded systems built around powerful processors. Thanks to miniaturization, the test and measuring equipment are now becoming portable facilitating easy testing and measurement in the field by field-personnel.

Security: Security of persons and information has always been a major issue. We need to protect our homes and offices; and also the information we transmit and store. Developing embedded systems for security applications is one of the most lucrative businesses nowadays. Security devices at homes, offices, airports etc. for authentication and verification are embedded systems. Encryption devices are

In Brief...

Nearly 99 per cent of the processors that are manufactured end up in embedded systems. Embedded systems find applications in every industrial segment—consumer electronics, transportation, avionics, biomedical engineering, manufacturing, process control and industrial automation, data communication, telecommunication, defence, security etc.

used to encrypt the data/voice being transmitted on communication links such as telephone lines. Biometric systems using fingerprint and face recognition are now being extensively used for user authentication in banking applications as well as for access control in high security buildings.

Finance: Financial dealing through cash and cheques are now slowly paving way for transactions using smart cards and ATM (Automatic Teller Machine, also expanded as Any Time Money) machines. Smart card, of the size of a credit card, has a small micro-controller and memory; and it interacts with the smart card reader/ATM machine and acts as an electronic wallet. Smart card technology has the capability of ushering in a cashless society.

Well, the list goes on. It is no exaggeration to say that eyes wherever you go, you can see, or at least feel, the work of an embedded system!

1.3 Categories of Embedded Systems

Based on functionality and performance requirements, embedded systems can be categorized as:

- Stand-alone embedded systems
- Real-time systems
- Networked information appliances
- Mobile devices

In Brief...

Embedded systems can be categorized as: (a) stand-alone systems (b) real-time systems (c) networked information appliances, and (d) mobile devices.

1.3.1 Stand-alone Embedded Systems

As the name implies, stand-alone systems work in stand-alone mode. They take inputs, process them and produce the desired output. The input can be electrical signals from transducers or commands from a human being such as the pressing of a button. The output can be electrical signals to drive another system, an LED display or LCD display for displaying of information to the users. Embedded systems used in process control, automobiles, consumer electronic items etc. fall into this category. In a process control system, the inputs are from sensors that convert a physical entity such as temperature or pressure into its equivalent electrical signal. These electrical signals are processed by the system and the appropriate electrical signals are produced using which an action is taken such as opening a valve. A few embedded systems used at home are shown in Fig. 1.1

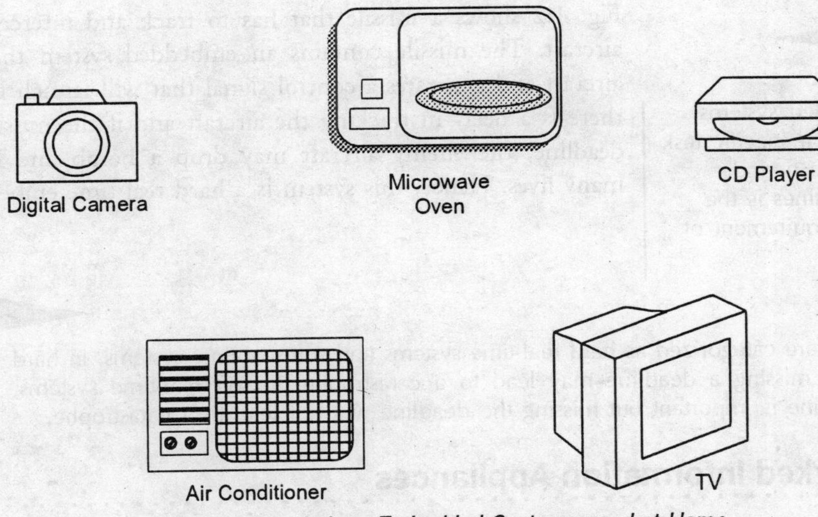

Fig. 1.1: Stand-alone Embedded Systems used at Home

1.3.2 Real-Time Systems

Embedded systems in which some specific work has to be done in a specific time period are called real-time systems. For example, consider a system that has to open a valve within 30 milliseconds when the humidity crosses a particular threshold. If the valve is not opened within 30 milliseconds, a catastrophe may occur. Such systems with strict deadlines are called hard real-time systems. In some embedded systems, deadlines are imposed, but not adhering to them once in a while may not lead to a catastrophe. For example, consider a DVD player. Suppose, you give a command to the DVD player from a remote control, and there is a delay of a few milliseconds in executing that command. But, this delay won't lead to a serious implication. Such systems are called soft real-time systems.

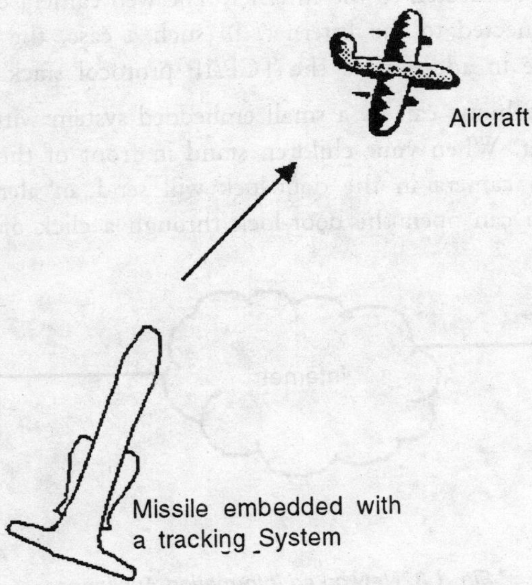

Fig. 1.2: Hard Real-Time Embedded System

In Brief...

Real-time embedded systems have to complete a specific task in a specified time period. Meeting the deadlines is the most important requirement of real-time systems.

Fig. 1.2 shows a missile that has to track and intercept an enemy aircraft. The missile contains an embedded system that tracks the aircraft and generates a control signal that will launch the missile. If there is a delay in tracking the aircraft and if the missile misses the deadline, the enemy aircraft may drop a bomb and cause loss of many lives. Hence, this system is a hard real-time embedded system.

Notes...

Real-time systems are categorized as hard real-time systems and soft real-time systems. In hard real-time systems, missing a deadline may lead to a catastrophe. In soft real-time systems, meeting the deadline is important but missing the deadline will not lead to a catastrophe.

1.3.3 Networked Information Appliances

Embedded systems that are provided with network interfaces and accessed by networks such as Local Area Network or the Internet are called networked information appliances. Such embedded systems are connected to a network, typically a network running TCP/IP (Transmission Control Protocol/ Internet Protocol) protocol suite, such as the Internet or a company's Intranet. These systems have emerged in recent years. These systems run the protocol TCP/IP stack and get connected either through PPP or Ethernet to a network and communicate with other nodes in the network. Here are some examples of such systems:

- A networked process control system consists of a number of embedded systems connected as a Local Area Network. Each embedded system can send real-time data to a central location from where the entire process control system can be monitored. The monitoring can be done using a web browser such as the Internet Explorer.
- A web camera can be connected to the Internet. The web camera can send pictures in real-time to any computer connected to the Internet. In such a case, the web camera has to run the HTTP server software in addition to the TCP/IP protocol stack.
- The door-lock of your home can be a small embedded system with TCP/IP and HTTP server software running on it. When your children stand in front of the door-lock after they return from school, the web camera in the door-lock will send an alert to your desktop over the Internet and then you can open the door-lock through a click of the mouse.

Fig. 1.3: Networked Information Appliance

Fig. 1.3 shows a weather monitoring system connected to the Internet. TCP/IP protocol suite and HTTP web server software will be running on this system. Any computer connected to the Internet can access this system to obtain real-time weather information. The networked information appliances need to run the complete TCP/IP protocol stack including the application layer protocols. If the appliance has to provide information over the Internet, HTTP web server software also needs to run on the system.

1.3.4 Mobile Devices

Mobile devices such as mobile phones, Personal Digital Assistants (PDAs), smart phones etc. are a special category of embedded systems. Though the PDAs do many general-purpose tasks, they need to be designed just like the 'conventional' embedded systems. The limitations of the mobile devices—memory constraints, small size, lack of good user interfaces such as full-fledged keyboard and display etc.—are same as those found in the embedded systems discussed above. Hence, mobile devices are considered as embedded systems. However, the PDAs are now capable of supporting general-purpose application software such as word processors, games, etc.

1.4 Overview of Embedded System Architecture

Every embedded system consists of custom-built hardware built around a Central Processing Unit (CPU). This hardware also contains memory chips onto which the software is loaded. The software residing on the memory chip is also called the 'firmware'. The embedded system architecture can be represented as a layered architecture as shown in Fig. 1.4. The operating system runs above the hardware, and the application software runs above the operating system. The same architecture is applicable to any computer including a desktop computer. However, there are significant differences. It is not compulsory to have an operating system in every embedded system. For small appliances such as remote control units, air-conditioners, toys etc., there is no need for an operating system and you can write only the software specific to that application. For applications involving complex processing, it is advisable to have an operating system. In such a case, you need to integrate the application software with the operating system and then transfer the entire software on to the memory chip. Once the software is transferred to the memory chip, the software will continue to run for a long time and you don't need to reload new software.

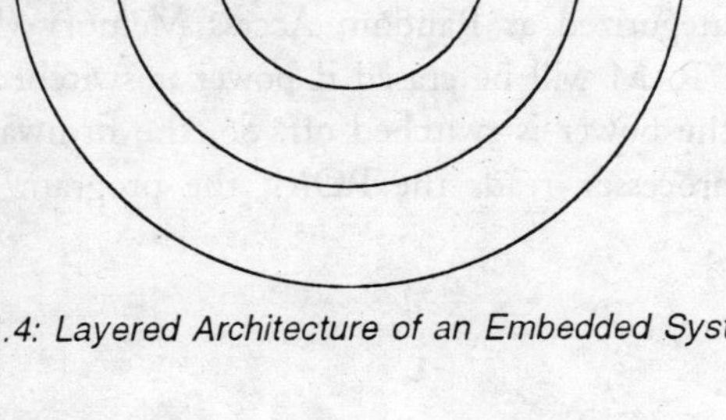

Fig. 1.4: Layered Architecture of an Embedded System

Now, let us see the details of the various building blocks of the hardware of an embedded system. As shown in Fig. 1.5, the building blocks are:

- Central Processing Unit (CPU)
- Memory (Read-only Memory and Random Access Memory)
- Input Devices
- Output devices
- Communication interfaces
- Application-specific circuitry

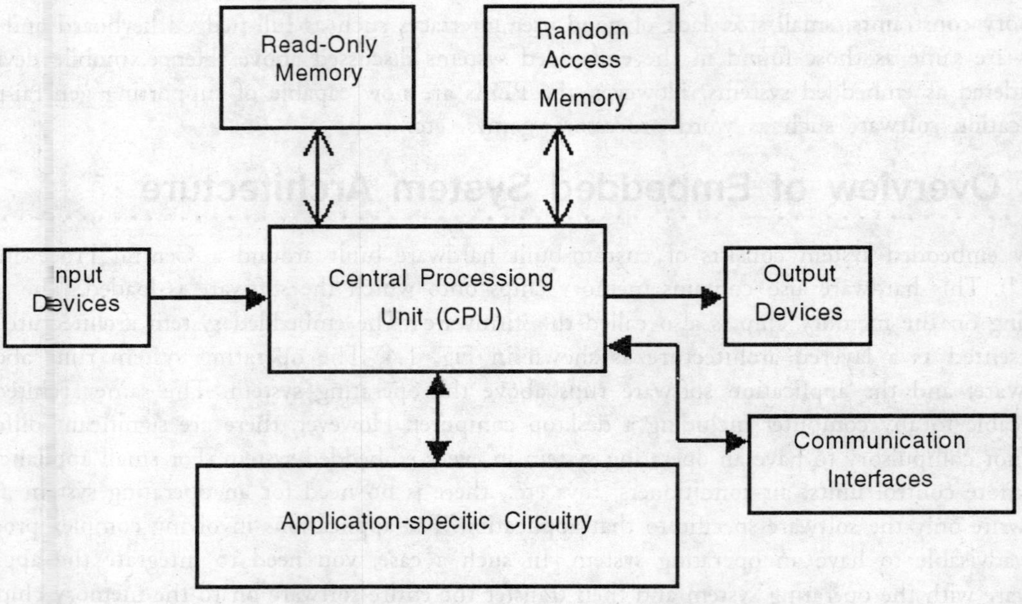

Fig. 1.5: Simplified Hardware Architecture of an Embedded System

Central Processing Unit (CPU): The Central Processing Unit (processor, in short) can be any of the following: micro-controller, microprocessor or Digital Signal Processor (DSP). A micro-controller is a low-cost processor. Its main attraction is that on the chip itself, there will be many other components such as memory, serial communication interface, analog-to-digital converter etc. So, for small applications, a micro-controller is the best choice as the number of external components required will be very less. On the other hand, microprocessors are more powerful, but you need to use many external components with them. DSP is used mainly for applications in which signal processing is involved such as audio and video processing.

Memory: The memory is categorized as Random Access Memory (RAM) and Read Only Memory (ROM). The contents of the RAM will be erased if power is switched off to the chip, whereas ROM retains the contents even if the power is switched off. So, the firmware is stored in the ROM. When power is switched on, the processor reads the ROM, the program is transferred to RAM and the program is executed.

Input devices: Unlike the desktops, the input devices to an embedded system have very limited capability. There will be no keyboard or a mouse, and hence interacting with the embedded system is no easy task. Many embedded systems will have a small keypad—you press one key to give a specific command. A keypad may be used to input only the digits. Many embedded systems used in process control do not have any input device for user interaction; they take inputs from sensors or transducers and produce electrical signals that are in turn fed to other systems.

Output devices: The output devices of the embedded systems also have very limited capability. Some embedded systems will have a few Light Emitting Diodes (LEDs) to indicate the health status of the system modules, or for visual indication of alarms. A small Liquid Crystal Display (LCD) may also be used to display some important parameters.

Communication interfaces: The embedded systems may need to interact with other embedded systems or they may have to transmit data to a desktop. To facilitate this, the embedded systems are provided with one or a few communication interfaces such as RS232, RS422, RS485, Universal Serial Bus (USB), IEEE 1394, Ethernet etc.

Application-specific circuitry: Sensors, transducers, special processing and control circuitry may be required for an embedded system, depending on its application. This circuitry interacts with the processor to carry out the necessary work.

The entire hardware has to be given power supply either through the 230 volts main supply or through a battery. The hardware has to be designed in such a way that the power consumption is minimized.

We will discuss each of these building blocks in greater detail in the next chapter.

In Brief...

The building blocks of an embedded system's hardware are: Central processing Unit, memory, input/output devices, communication interfaces and application-specific circuitry.

Notes...

The CPU of an embedded system can be: (a) micro-controller, (b) microprocessor, or (c) Digital Signal Processor.

A micro-controller is the best choice for small embedded systems because it has memory and peripherals in the same chip as the CPU and hence very few extra components are required. Digital Signal Processors are the best choice if the application demands signal processing such as audio/video processing.

1.5 Specialities of Embedded Systems

As compared to desktop computers, workstations or mainframes, embedded systems have many specialities. Developers need to keep these specialities in mind while designing embedded systems.

1.5.1 Reliability

When we use a desktop, sometimes the system 'hangs' and we need to reset the computer. Generally, this does not cause any problem. However, this is not the case with the embedded systems used in mission-critical applications. They must work with high reliability.

Reliability is of paramount importance in embedded systems. They should continue to work for thousands of hours without break. Many embedded systems used in industrial control are inaccessible. They are hidden in some other large-sized equipment; hence there will not be a reset button on such systems! So, the design of the embedded system should be such that in case the system has to be reset, the reset should be done automatically. Special hardware/software needs to be built into the system to take care of it. This special module is known as watchdog timer.

Many embedded systems used in industrial automation and defence equipment need to work in extreme environmental conditions such as very high/low temperatures, high humidity. Besides, they should be able to withstand bump and vibrations. Hence, very stringent environmental specifications have to be met by such systems. The ability to work reliably in extreme environmental conditions is known as ruggedness. Not only the military equipment, even the consumer appliances such as the mobile phone need to be very rugged. Many people keep dropping their mobile phone on the floor, but still it works because it is very rugged.

1.5.2 Performance

Many embedded systems have time constraints. For instance, in a process control system, a constraint can be: "if the temperature exceeds 40 degrees, open a valve within 10 milliseconds." The system must meet such deadlines. If the deadlines are missed, it may result in a catastrophe. You can imagine the damage that can be done if such deadlines are not met in a safety system of a nuclear plant.

1.5.3 Power Consumption

Most of the embedded systems operate through a battery. To reduce the battery drain and avoid frequent recharging of the battery, the power consumption of the embedded system has to be very low. To reduce power consumption such hardware components should be used that consume less power. Besides, emphasis should be on reducing the components count of the hardware. To reduce component count, the hardware designers have the option of using Programmable Logic Devices (PLDs) and Field Programmable Gate Arrays (FPGAs). Reducing the component count apart from reducing the power consumption also increases the reliability of the system.

1.5.4 Cost

For embedded systems used in safety applications of a nuclear plant or in a spacecraft, cost may not be a very important factor. However, for embedded systems used in consumer electronics or office automation, the cost is of utmost importance. Suppose you designed a toy in which the electronics will cost US$20. By a careful analysis of the design, if you can find a way to reduce the cost to US$19, it will be a great job. Don't underplay the importance of that one dollar because when you sell 10 million toys the cost reduction is $10 million! Not surprisingly, the hardware engineers debate on component selection to reduce even $0.1.

1.5.5 Size

Size is certainly a factor for many embedded systems. We do not like a mobile phone that has to be carried on our backs. The size and the weight are important parameters in embedded systems used in aircraft, spacecraft, missiles etc. because in such cases, every inch and every gram matters. To reduce the size and the weight, again the hardware engineers have to design their boards by reducing the component count to the maximum possible extent. During the initial development of mobile phones based on GSM (Global System for Mobile Communication), GSM was expanded as "God, Send Mobiles" because of the complexity of the mobile phone. Today, the mobile phones go into our pockets, thanks to developments in microelectronics.

1.5.6 Limited User Interface

Unlike desktops, which have full-fledged input/output devices, embedded systems do not have sophisticated interfaces for input and output. Some embedded systems do not have any user interface at all. They take electrical signals as input and produce electrical signals as output. In many embedded systems, the input is through a small function keypad or a set of buttons. The output is displayed either on a set of LEDs or a small LCD. For example, the mobile phone has a small display of 4 lines x 16 characters. The input is through a keypad and composing a small text message is not and easy task. Developing a user friendly interface with limitation of the input/output devices is a challenging task for firmware developers.

1.5.7 Software Upgradation Capability

Embedded systems are meant for a very specific task. So, once the software is transferred to the embedded system, the same software will run throughout its life. However, in some cases, it may be necessary to upgrade the software. Consider the example of a Public Call Office (PCO). At the PCO, an embedded system is used which displays the amount to be paid by a telephone user. The amount is calculated by the firmware, based on the calling number and the duration of the call. From time to time, the telecom operator will change the algorithm for the calculation of the bill amount. So, every time there is a tariff change, the PCO operator has to replace the program stored in the memory of the embedded system with new program. This is very cumbersome, considering that a memory chip will have to be replaced in thousands of PCOs. Nowadays, software upgradation is done by downloading the software onto the embedded system through a network connection. In future, such an upgradation may become mandatory for many embedded systems.

In Brief...

While designing embedded systems, the following aspects need to be considered by the developers: reliability, performance, power consumption, cost, size, limited user interface and software upgradation capability.

Notes...

By using PLDs and FPGAs, the number of components in an embedded system can be reduced. Reducing the component count increases the system's reliability and also reduces the power consumption.

1.6 Recent Trends in Embedded Systems

In good old days, developing embedded systems was confined to a very few 'specialists'. Most of the embedded software was written only in assembly language and hence writing, debugging and maintaining the code were very difficult and time consuming. With the availability of powerful processors and advanced development tools, embedded software development is no longer 'rocket science'. In this section, we will review the advances in embedded systems.

1.6.1 Processor Power

The growing importance of embedded systems can be gauged by the availability of processors. About 150 varieties of processors are available from around 50 semiconductor vendors. Powerful 8-bit, 16-bit, 32-bit and 64-bit micro-controllers, and microprocessors are available to cater to the different market segments. The clock speed and the memory addressing capability of these processors are also increasing. Very powerful Digital Signal Processors are also available for real-time analysis of audio and video signals. As a result, the power of desktop computers is now available on palmtops.

1.6.2 Memory

The cost of memory chips is reducing day by day. As a result, the embedded systems can be made functionally rich by incorporating additional features such as networking protocols and even graphical user interfaces. The cost of memory chips used to discourage developers from porting an operating system onto the target hardware. As the memory chips are becoming cheaper, porting an operating system is no longer an issue. Now, wristwatches with embedded Linux operating system are available.

1.6.3 Operating Systems

Unlike the desktops on which the options for an operating system are limited (predominantly, Windows), a variety of operating systems are available which can be ported onto the embedded system. The main advantage of embedding an operating system is that the software development will be very fast and maintaining the code is very easy. The software can be developed in a high-level language such as C. So, time to market the system gets reduced. If real-time performance is required, a real-time operating system can be used. In addition to many commercial embedded/real-time operating systems, open source software campaign led to development of many open source operating systems. The attraction of open source software is that it is free and also the complete source code is available to customize the software as per your application needs.

1.6.4 Communication Interfaces and Networking Capability

With the availability of low-cost chips, embedded systems can be provided networking capability through communication interfaces such as Ethernet, 802.11 wireless LAN, and Infrared. Network-enabling of an embedded system has many advantages: it can be accessed over a network for remote control or monitoring. Besides, upgrading the embedded software is very easy as the new version can be uploaded through the network interface. Due to the enhanced memory capacities of the embedded systems, TCP/IP protocol stack and the HTTP server software can also be ported onto the system and such systems can be accessed over the Internet from anywhere on the earth.

1.6.5 Programming Languages

Development of embedded software was done mostly in assembly languages. However, due to the availability of cross-compilers, most of the development is now done in high level languages such as C. The object-oriented languages, like C++ and Java, are now catching up. The main attraction of Java is its platform independence. In fact, the development of Java programming language was initiated mainly to address the embedded system market. Many exciting applications are possible by having a Java Virtual Machine in an embedded system. In enables the system download Java applets from a server and execute them. Microsoft's embedded visual tools can be used for development of embedded software applications. People with experience in Microsoft Visual Studio can become embedded software developers with very little training.

1.6.6 Development Tools

Availability of a number of tools for development, debugging and testing as well as for modelling the embedded systems is now paving way for fast development of robust and reliable systems. Development tools such as MATLAB and Simulink can be used to model an embedded system as well as to generate code, substantially reducing the development time. Development tools such as BREW (Binary Runtime Environment for Wireless), Java 2 Micro Edition (J2ME) development tools, Wireless Application Protocol (WAP) development tools facilitate easy development of applications for mobile devices. The entire application can be developed and tested on desktop computers, and then deployed in the field.

In Brief...

Advances in processor power, memory devices, operating systems, networking interfaces, programming languages, development tools and programmable hardware are paving way for very powerful embedded systems and also faster and easier development as compared to olden days.

1.6.7 Programmable Hardware

Programmable Logic Devices (PLDs) and Field Programmable Gate Arrays (FPGAs) pave the way for reducing the components on an embedded system, leading to small, low-cost systems. After developing the prototype of an embedded system, for mass production, an FPGA can be developed which will have all the functionality of the processor, peripherals as well as the application-specific circuitry. "System-on-Chip" is the catchword that reflects the current developments in programmable hardware—a single chip is the embedded system!

Summary

This chapter presented an overview of embedded systems. An embedded system can be defined as a computing device that does a very specific job. Embedded systems find applications in every industrial segment—entertainment, consumer electronics, industrial automation, healthcare, transportation, aviation, defence etc. Embedded systems can be categorized as stand-alone systems, real-time systems, networked information appliances and mobile devices. An embedded system consists of hardware, an operating system and the application software. The hardware consists of a processor, memory, input/output devices, communication interfaces and application-specific circuitry. The operating system and the application software are integrated and transferred to the memory of the embedded system. The important considerations for designing an embedded system are: reliability, performance, low power consumption, low cost, small size, limited user interface and capability to upgrade software in the field. The recent developments in embedded systems arena—processor power, memory, operating systems, communication interfaces and networking capability, programming languages, development tools and programmable hardware—are also reviewed. In this chapter, the jargon of embedded systems is introduced; we will explore the details in the subsequent chapters.

Questions

1. What is an embedded system? Differentiate between a general purpose computing system and an embedded system.
2. List the various application areas of embedded systems and give examples for each application area.
3. List the important building blocks of an embedded system.
4. What are the different categories of embedded systems? Give examples of each category.
5. Differentiate between hard real-time system and soft real-time system.
6. What are the special considerations in designing embedded systems?

Exercises

1. Can mobile devices be categorized as embedded systems? Discuss.
2. List the embedded systems used in the military applications.
3. List the major manufacturers of micro-controllers and microprocessors.
4. List the major manufacturers of digital signal processors.
5. It is not possible to provide full-fledged keyboard withn a small palmtop computer. Therefore, it is difficult to input text in these devices. In this case what options can be provided to the uses for easy typing of text

Chapter 2

Architecture of Embedded Systems

CHAPTER OBJECTIVES

After reading this chapter, you will be able to:

- Learn the hardware architecture of an embedded system
- Gain knowledge of the software architecture of an embedded system
- Get an overview of the TCP/IP protocol architecture
- Understand the process of creating an executable image for the embedded system
- Grasp the details of cross-platform development
- Know about the various tools required for hardware/software development.

In this chapter, we will study the details of the architecture of embedded systems. In desktop computers, the hardware platform is dominated by Intel and the software platform is dominated by Windows. But, for embedded systems development, we have a wide variety of processors and operating systems. However, without getting bogged down with the specifics of a processor, we will study the general architecture of the hardware and discuss the details of various building blocks. We will also study the software architecture—the services provided by the operating system, the communication software and the application software that need to be integrated into the embedded system. We will discuss how the software developed on a host system is transferred to the embedded system. The tools required for development and testing of embedded systems are also discussed briefly.

2.1 Hardware Architecture

The simplified architecture of an embedded system was presented in Chapter 1. In this section, we will discuss this architecture in more detail. Needless to say, this section does not make you a great designer of hardware, but it will give you the necessary foundation to take up the hardware development. While discussing the hardware details, representative Integrated Circuit (IC) numbers are given. Going through the data sheets of these ICs will be of immense help in appreciating the hardware details. Even if your focus is on firmware development, a good understanding of the hardware details presented in this section is a must.

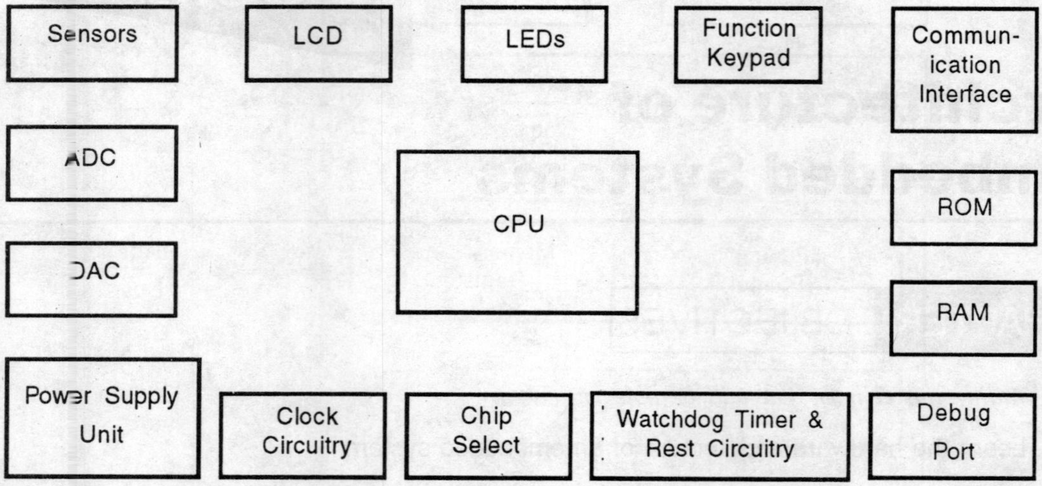

Fig. 2.1: Building Blocks of the Hardware in an Embedded System

In Brief...

The various building blocks of the hardware of an embedded system are: Central Processing Unit, Read-Only Memory and Random Access Memory, input devices such as sensors, analog-to digital converter and keypad; output devices such as digital-to-analog converter, LEDs, LCD; debug port, communication interfaces and power supply unit.

The various building blocks of embedded system hardware are shown in Fig. 2.1. These building blocks are explained in the following subsections.

2.1.1 Central Processing Unit

The Central Processing Unit (CPU) used in an embedded system can be one of the following two categories:

- General Purpose Processor (GPP)
- Digital Signal Processor (DSP)

The GPPs are further classified as micro-controllers and microprocessors. As mentioned in the previous chapter, a micro-controller has memory and other peripherals on the chip itself; hence, it is the best choice for small embedded systems. On the other hand, a microprocessor is more powerful but requires a large number of external components. The internal architecture of processor is shown in Fig. 2.2.

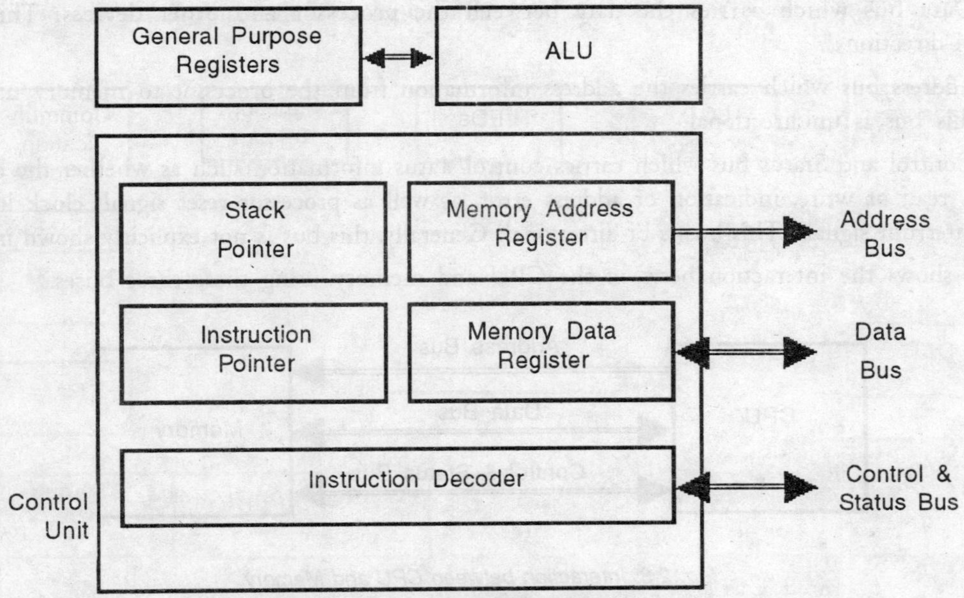

Fig. 2.2: Internal Architecture of a Processor

The CPU consists of

- Arithmetic Logic Unit (ALU) which performs arithmetic and logic operations (such as add, multiply, subtract, etc.)
- General purpose registers. These registers constitute the processor's internal memory. The number of registers varies from processor to processor. Registers contain the current data and operands that are being manipulated by the processor. When a processor is referred to as of 8-bits, 16-bits etc., it refers to the width of the registers.
- Control unit that fetches the instructions from memory, decodes them and executes them. A control unit consists of
  - o Instruction Pointer that points to the next instruction to be executed. Instruction Pointer is also called Program Counter.
  - o Stack Pointer that points to the stack in the memory. In the external memory, the processor implements a stack. When required, the contents of registers are transferred to this stack. The processor keeps track of the next free location in the stack through stack pointer.
  - o Instruction Decoder that decodes the instructions.
  - o Memory Address Register and Memory Data Register.

Processor Architectures

In addition to manipulating data, a processor's job is to read data and instructions from memory, read and write data to memory, write data to output devices, and read data from input devices. To do these functions, the processor communicates with other devices using three buses, a bus being a group of signals. These buses are:

- Data bus which carries the data between the processor and other devices. This bus is bi-directional.
- Address bus which carries the address information from the processor to memory, and hence this bus is unidirectional.
- Control and Status bus which carries control/status information such as whether the operation is read or write, indication of address error, as well as processor reset signal, clock input and interrupt signals. This bus is bi-directional. Generally, this bus is not explicitly shown in figures.

Fig. 2.3 shows the interaction between the CPU and memory using these three buses.

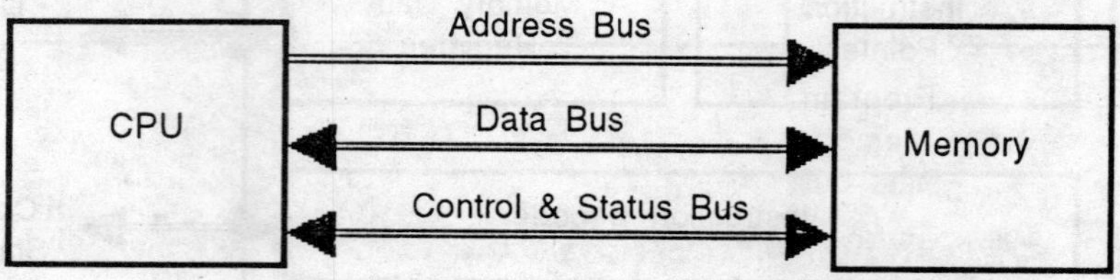

Fig. 2.3: Interaction between CPU and Memory

Based on the number of memory and data buses used, there are three types of architectures for the processors. These are:

- Von Neumann Architecture
- Harvard Architecture
- Super Harvard Architecture

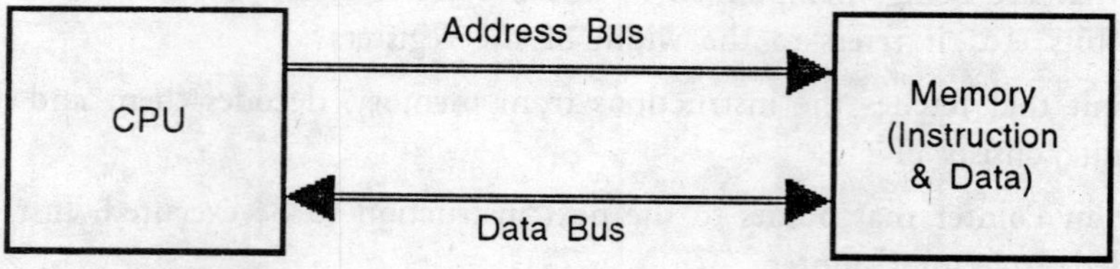

Fig. 2.4: von Neumann Architecture

The von Neumann architecture is the most widely used architecture. As shown in Fig. 2.4, this architecture, has one memory chip which stores both instructions and data. The processor interacts with the memory through address and data buses to fetch instructions and data.

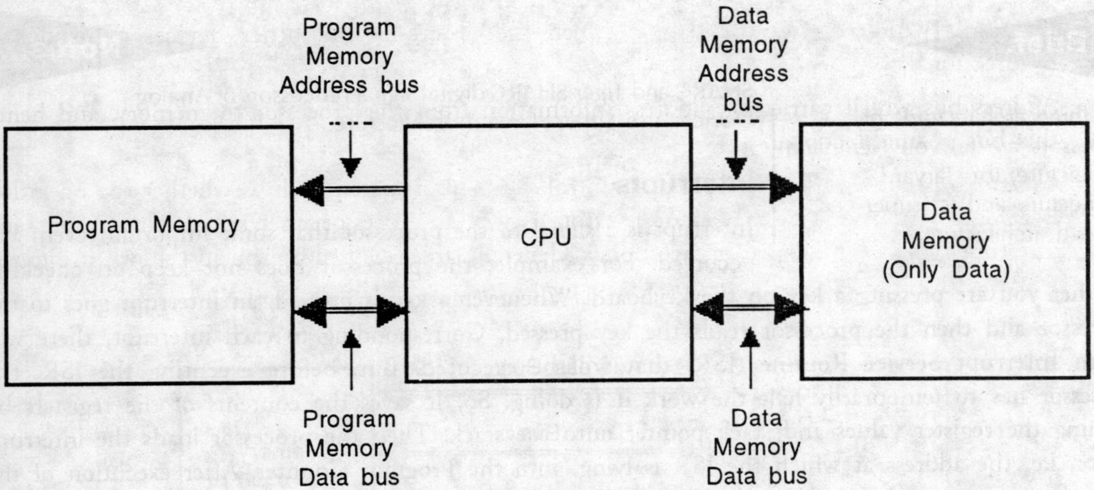

Fig. 2.5: Harvard Architecture

The Harvard architecture is shown in Fig. 2.5. In this architecture, there are two separate memory blocks—one is program memory and the other is data memory. Program memory stores only instructions and data memory stores only data. Two pairs of data buses are used between the CPU and the memory blocks. Program memory address bus and program memory data bus are used to access the program memory. Data memory address bus and data memory data bus are used to access the data memory. Certainly, this architecture is much more efficient because accessing the instructions and data will be very fast.

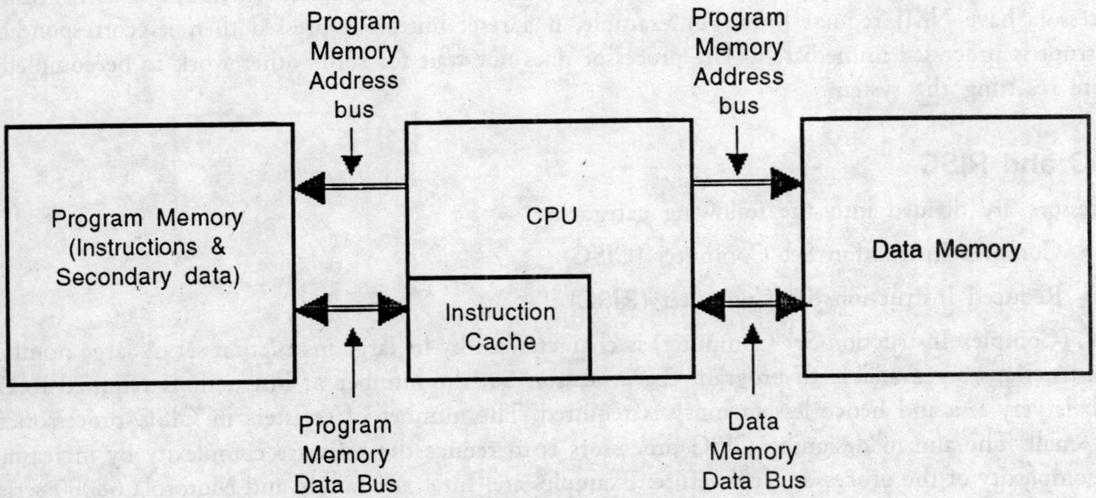

Fig. 2.6: Super-Harvard Architecture

The super Hardvard Architecture (SHARC) a slight but significant modification of the Harvard architecture. It is shown in Fig. 2.6. In Harvard architecture, the data memory is accessed more frequently than the program memory. Therefore, in SHARC, provision has been made to store some secondary data in the program memory to balance the load on both memory blocks. This sarchitecture, proposed by Analog Devices, is used extensively in Digital Signal Processors.

In Brief...

The three architectures of processors are (a) von Neumann architecture; (b) Harvard architecture and (c) super-Harvard architecture.

Notes...

SHARC and Tiger SHARC digital signal processors of Analog Devices use Super-Harvard architecture.

Interrupts

Interrupt is a signal to the processor that some important event has occurred. For example, the processor does not keep on checking whether you are pressing a key on the keyboard. Whenever a key is pressed, an interrupt goes to the processor and then the processor reads the key pressed. Corresponding to each interrupt, there will be an Interrupt Service Routine (ISR) that will be executed. But, before executing the ISR, the processor has to temporarily halt the work it is doing. So, it saves the contents of the registers by pushing the register values and stack pointer onto the stack. Then the processor loads the interrupt vector, i.e. the address at which the ISR is lying, into the Program Counter. After execution of the ISR, the processor reloads the registers and the stack pointer, and resumes the previous execution. There may be more than one interrupt to the processor. Hence, priorities are assigned to the interrupts so that the processor executes the highest priority interrupt.

A Programmable Interrupt Controller (PIC) interfaces with the CPU to handle external devices and decide which interrupt has to be processed. An interrupt table contains the details of various interrupts such as interrupt number (IRQ), the memory location where the ISR is stored (interrupt vector), priority of the interrupt and the frequency with which the interrupt is likely to occur.

Interrupt that has to be processed immediately is called Non-Maskable Interrupt (NMI). Many processors have NMI request lines. For example, if a reset button is pressed then its corresponding interrupt is processed immediately. The processor does not wait for some other work to be completed before resetting the system.

CISC and RISC

Processors are divided into the following categories:

- Complex Instruction Set Computer (CISC)
- Reduced Instruction Set Computer (RISC)

CISC (Complex Instruction Set Computer) is characterized by its large instruction set. A large number of instructions are available to program the processor. So, the number of instructions required to do a job is very less and hence less memory is required. The number of registers in CISC processors is very small. The aim of designing CISC processors is to reduce the software complexity by increasing the complexity of the processor architecture. Examples are: Intel x86 family and Motorola 68000 series processors.

RISC (Reduced Instruction Set Computer) is characterized by its limited number of instructions. A complex instruction is obtained as a sequence of simple instructions. So, in RISC processors, the software is complex but the processor architecture is simple. However, large number of registers are required in RISC processors, which are of small size and consume less power. Another feature of RISC processors is the pipelined instruction execution. While one instruction is being executed, second instruction is decoded and the third instruction is fetched leading to faster execution of the program. Embedded systems generally use RISC processors. Examples are ARM, ATMEL AVR, MIPS, Microchip PIC, Power PC and Sun SPARC.

There are nearly 150 processors manufactured by about 50 semiconductor manufacturers. The specifications of these processors differ significantly. We will study the details of Intel family and AVR family micro-controllers and Intel StrongARM microprocessor in this book. While evaluating the processor, the following specifications are to be considered:

- Clock speed
- Length of the registers
- Width of data bus and address bus
- Number of registers
- Internal RAM
- Internal ROM
- On-chip peripherals such as timer, UART, ADC, DAC
- Interrupt lines
- Number of programmable I/O lines

In Brief...

Processors are broadly categorized as RISC processors and CISC processors. Intel x86 and Motorola 68000 family processors are examples of CISC processors. ATMEL AVR, MIPS, Microchip PIC, PowerPC and SunSPARC are examples of RISC processors.

2.1.2 Memory

The memory is divided into two categories: program memory and data memory. The program memory stores the firmware permanently whereas data memory contents are erased when power is switched off. Both program memory and data memory can be internal to the processor (as in the case of a micro-controller) or it can be external memory.

In a micro-controller, both program memory and data memory are on chip. However, if the capacity of the internal memory is not sufficient, you can use external memory chips to increase the memory capacity.

Memory chips are classified as:

- Random Access Memory (RAM)
- Read-Only Memory (ROM)
- Hybrid Memory

Random Access Memory (RAM)

In RAM, the memory locations can be accessed randomly. RAM is a read-write chip as you can perform both read and write operations on it. RAM is of two types: Static RAM (SRAM) and Dynamic RAM (DRAM). SRAM loses its contents the moment power is switched off to the chip. DRAM retains its contents for a fraction of a second even if power is supplied continuously to the chip. To keep its contents intact, DRAM has to be refreshed periodically. A DRAM controller is used to carry out this operation. SRAM is faster and consumes less power. The main attraction of DRAM is that it is very cheap and hence it is used when a high-capacity RAM is required but the chip has to be of low cost.

In Brief...

The two types of RAM are: Static RAM and Dynamic RAM. SRAM loses its contents when power is switched off. DRAM needs to be refreshed periodically to retain its contents. SRAM is faster and consumes less power, but DRAM is cheaper.

DRAM is used in handheld computers.

Hundai HM 62256 BLP-7 is an SRAM chip with 32 KB capacity and an access time of 70 nanosec.

Read Only Memory (ROM)

ROM is used to store the firmware in embedded systems because it retains its contents even if power is switched off. But then, how do you write data into the ROM chip first time? Some ROMs are fused in the factory, i.e. data is written in the factory and then shipped. A variety of ROMs are available with different capabilities. These are: Programmeble ROM and Erasable Programmable ROM.

Programmable ROM (PROM): PROM devices can be programmed only once. When your firmware is ready, put it on the PROM and then mount the device on your embedded system. Well, if your firmware has a bug, you need to throw that PROM.

Erasable Programmable ROM (EPROM): EPROM can be programmed many times. To write data into EPROM, you need an EPROM Programmer. Also, you need a tool called EPROM Eraser to erase the contents. An EPROM Eraser applies Ultra Violet (UV) radiation to the device to erase the contents.

As compared to RAM, ROMs are slower.

Hybrid memory devices

Electrically Erasable PROM (EEPROM): EEPROM is similar to EPROM but its contents can be erased by applying electrical signal to one of the pins of the device.

Non-Volatile RAM: Non-Volatile RAM is SRAM with a battery backup. So, even if power is switched off, the battery will ensure that the contents are not erased.

Flash memory: Flash memory is type of EEPROM. These low-cost chips are characterized by their fast read quality (but not fast write). The memory is divided into sectors or blocks. Typical sector size is 256 bytes to 16 KB. Each sector is an erasable unit. When erased, the bits in that sector are set to 1 (i.e. byte = 0xff). As it is electrically erasable, contents of the Flash memory can be updated in the embedded system. Flash memory is nowadays extensively used in embedded systems for storing the firmware.

The main attraction of Flash is that it can be used as a 'disk' by developing a Flash file system, so that data can be accessed through file names rather than through memory addresses.

Remember, a sector in a Flash memory chip can last about one million erase cycles. It appears a big number but may not be sufficient for some embedded applications.

ATMEL's AT25080 (1 KB), AT25160 (2KB), AT25320 (4 KB), AT25640 (8KB) are the EEPROMs. AMD's AM29F010 is a Flash device of 128 KB capacity.

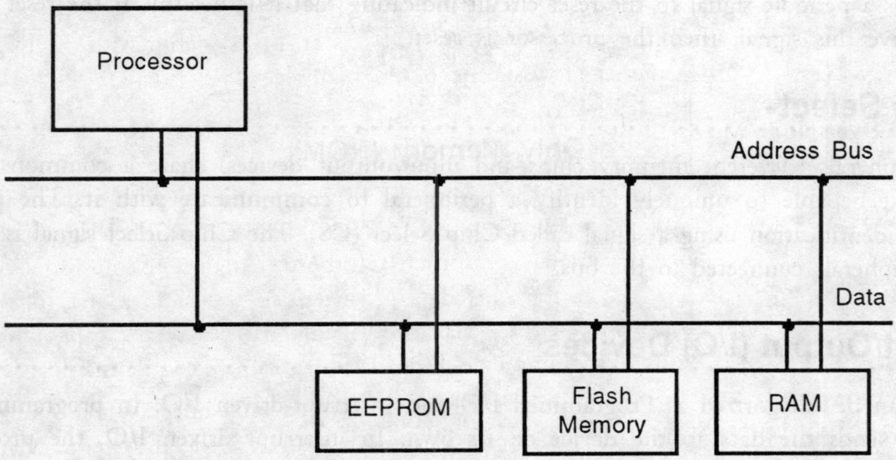

Fig. 2.7: Memory in Embedded Systems

As shown in Fig. 2.7, an embedded system can contain different types of memory such as RAM, EEPROM and Flash.

In Brief...

EEPROM and Flash are the most widely used memory chips because they are in-circuit programmable.

2.1.3 Clock Circuitry

The processor has to be given the clock input to one of the pins. To generate the clock signal, a crystal and oscillator are required. For some processors, the oscillator circuitry is in-built, only external crystal has to be added to generate the clock signal. Real Time Clock (RTC) keeps track of the date and time.

All processor events are related to the clock. The higher the clock frequency, the higher the speed of the processor. However, different processors cannot be compared based on clock speed alone. One processor may take one clock cycle for executing an instruction, whereas another processor may take 16 clock cycles to execute the same instruction.

Notes...

Real-Time Clock (RTC) is used in embedded systems to provide "real" time including the date.

2.1.4 Watchdog Timer/Reset Circuitry

In Brief...

Watchdog timer is used to reset the processor automatically if it does not receive a signal periodically from the processor indicating its healthy status. This mechanism obviates the need for a reset button on the embedded system.

Most embedded systems do not have a reset button. Due to some software or hardware error, a need may arise to reset the processor. The watchdog timer does the resetting. A timer is set to a large value and it is decremented slowly. If the timer value reaches zero, the processor is reset through a reset-signal. If everything is going on fine, intermittently, the timer value is again set to the large value.

If a reset button is provided in an embedded system, on pressing the button, a reset signal is sent to the processor. Alternatively, the processor sends a periodic signal to the reset circuit indicating that it is healthy. If the reset circuitry does not receive this signal, then the processor is reset.

2.1.5 Chip Select

As many peripherals (different memory chips and input/output devices) share a common bus, the processor must be able to uniquely identify a peripheral to communicate with it. The processor performs this identification using a signal called Chip Select (CS). The Chip Select signal is available to all the peripherals connected to the bus.

2.1.6 Input/Output (I/O) Devices

I/O devices can be categorized as Programmed I/O and Interrupt-driven I/O. In programmed I/O, the processor sends the data to the device on its own. In interrupt driven I/O, the processor is interrupted by an interrupt signal and the ISR is executed. ISR transfers the data from the input device to the memory or memory to output device.

Dynamic Memory Access (DMA)

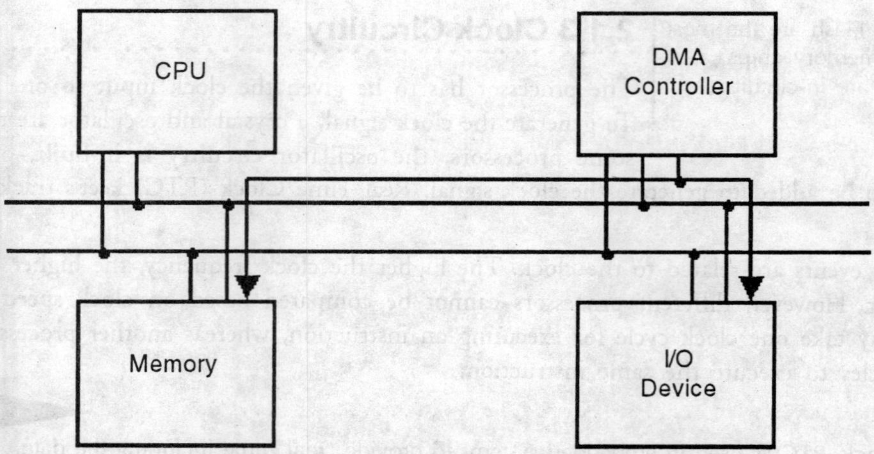

Fig. 2.8: Dynamic Memory Access

In Brief...

Dynamic Memory Access facilitates transfer of data between the input/output device and the memory directly without the intervention of the processor.

Generally, data transfer between the I/O device and the memory is coordinated by the CPU. In cases where handling of the I/O device by the processor is not efficient, data transfer between the I/O device and the memory can take place directly, which is known as DMA. A special device called DMA controller does the job. DMA controller takes the control of the buses and transfers data between the I/O device and the memory. This is depicted in Fig. 2.8.

Sensors and Transducers

Embedded systems need to convert real-life information into equivalent electrical signals. This is achieved through sensors and transducers. Some important sensors and transducers are listed below:

- Temperature sensors convert the temperature into an equivalent electrical voltage. The output of the sensor is a signal whose voltage level is proportional to the temperature. Measurement of temperatures in air-conditioners, boilers, coffins etc. is done through this sensor. Analog Devices' AD22100, AD22103 and Dallas Semiconductors' DS 18B20 are examples of temperature sensors.
- Light sensors convert the light intensity into an equivalent electrical voltage. The output of the sensor, the voltage level, is proportional to the light incident on the sensor. The light is sensed through a photodiode, and an in-built amplifier amplifies the voltage level. An example is Texas Advanced Optical Solutions' TAOS TSL250R.
- Accelerometer converts the acceleration into voltage. The voltage is proportional to the acceleration of a vehicle. ADXL 150/250 does this job.
- Pressure sensors convert the pressure level to voltage level. Pressure sensors are used in blood pressure equipment, and to measure altitude of aircraft, ocean depth etc. MPXA 6115A is an example.
- **Microphone and speakers:** Microphone converts the acoustic energy into a voltage signal. When you speak into a microphone, the output of the microphone is an electrical signal with continuously varying amplitude. The speakers convert the electrical signal back into acoustic waves.
- **Video camera and monitor:** The real-life image or scenery is converted into electrical signal using a video camera. The video camera output is a continuously varying electrical signal. The electrical signal is converted back to the image on a monitor.

In Brief...

Sensors and transducers convert the real-life information into equivalent electrical signals. These analog signals are converted into digital format to be processed by the processor.

Note that the electrical signals produced by these sensors and transducers are analog signals. Their amplitude varies continuously with time. However, the computing devices are digital. They can process only digital data. Hence, we need to convert the analog signals into digital signals.

ADC and DAC

The analog signals produced by sensors and transducers have one important characteristic: bandwidth. The bandwidth of a signal is the highest significant frequency component present in the signal. For instance, voice signals have a bandwidth of 4 KHz, i.e. the frequency components above 4 KHz are insignificant.

The analog signal can be converted into digital format in two stages: sampling and quantization. In sampling, the amplitude levels of the signal are measured at regular intervals as shown in Fig. 2.9. In quantization, the sampled value is converted into a number. The sample value shown in Fig. 2.9 lies between 250 and 251. So, the sample value is approximated to 250.

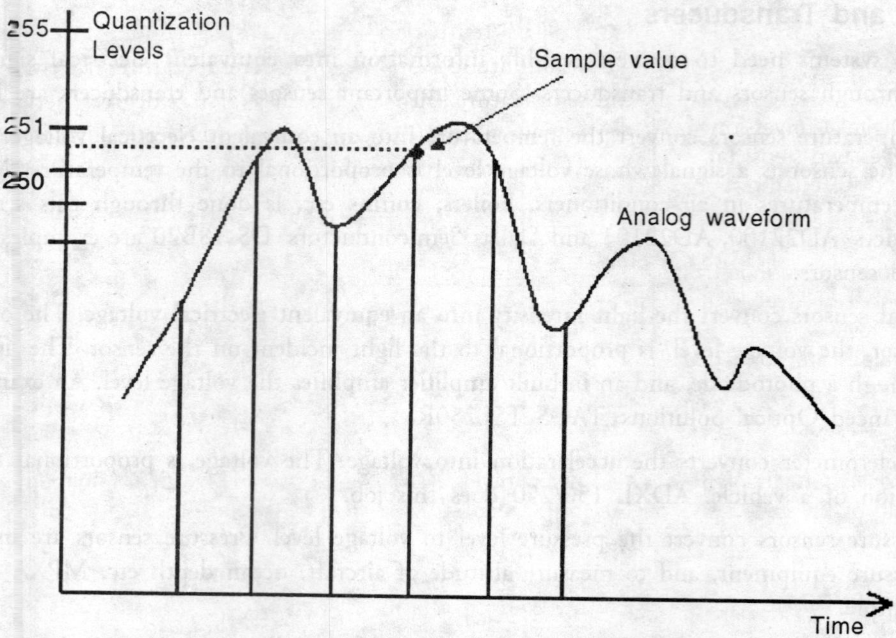

Fig. 2.9: Analog-to-Digital Conversion

How many samples are required to correctly represent an analog signal? Nyquist theorem provides the answer. If the bandwidth of a signal is B Hz, the number of samples required per second (called the sampling rate) should be at least 2B. So, for voice signals with a bandwidth of 4 KHz, the minimum sampling rate is 8000 samples per second. These samples are quantized by dividing the complete range of amplitudes into say 256 levels. These levels are called quantization levels. To represent the 256 levels, 8 bits are required. Hence, to represent each sample value, 8 bits are required. To represent 4096 levels, 12 bits are required.

This process of sampling and quantization is done through Analog-to-Digital Converter (ADC) chips. The reverse process of converting the digital signal to analog signal is done through Digital-to-Analog Converter (DAC).

Note that analog-to-digital conversion introduces error because each sample value is rounded off to its nearest quantization level. This error is known as quantization error. By increasing the number of quantization levels, the quantization error can be reduced. Another important aspect in analog-to-digital conversion is the sampling rate. If the sampling is done at a rate lower than the Nyquist sampling rate, then the analog signal is not represented correctly and the effect is known as aliasing. So, while choosing the ADC and DAC chips, the two important characteristics are:

- Sampling rate
- Resolution

Consider the voice signals again. In telephone networks, the voice signals are considered to have a bandwidth of 4 KHz and the resolution is 8 bits. In CD audio, the bandwidth is considered to be 44.1 KHz and 16-bit resolution is used and hence the quality of CD audio is very high. In DVD audio, the bandwidth is considered as 48 KHz, and the resolution is 24 bits.

In Brief...

Analog-to-Digital Conversion (ADC) involves two steps: (a) sampling; and (b) quantization. The analog signal is sampled at regular intervals and the sampled values are rounded off to fixed number of levels called quantization levels. These quantized values are converted into bit stream.

Consider a temperature sensor that produces an electrical signal whose amplitude is proportional to temperature. If we want to measure the temperature with an accuracy of 0.5 degrees between 0 and 50 degrees, we need 100 levels. So, an ADC of 7 bits is enough. As 7-bit ADC's are not available, we choose an 8-bit ADC.

Many micro-controllers have on-chip ADC. If the on-chip ADC does not serve your purpose, you can have an external ADC. An example of ADC is MAX 1245. MAX 525 is a 12-bit DAC. Analog Devices AD 9772 is an example of high-end ADC with a sampling rate of 150 Mega Samples Per Second (MSPS) and 14-bit resolution.

Notes...

According to Nyquist theorem, a signal of bandwidth B has to be sampled with a minimum sampling rate of 2B so that the signal can be reconstructed without any distortion.

Function keypad

Fig. 2.10: Function Keypad for Tape-Recorder Functionality

Based on the application, an embedded system has to be provided with a function keypad to input data and/or commands. A representative function keypad is shown in Fig. 2.10. This keypad has been designed to do the functions of controlling a tape recorder. It has various buttons for play, record, pause, fast forward, go to first file, go to last file etc. Based on the application needs, you need to design your keypad and interface it to the processor circuitry.

In Brief...

In embedded systems, the function keypads are used to facilitate limited inputs to the system. These function keypads have to be custom-designed for the specific application.

Light Emitting Diodes (LEDs)

LEDs are the most widely used output devices in embedded systems. Red, green and yellow LEDs are used for status display as well as for indications of visual alarms for such events as power supply failure. Blue and white LEDs are also available, but they are very expensive.

Liquid Crystal Display (LCD)

In LCD, liquid-crystal solution is sandwiched by two sheets for polarizing material. LCD is used to display the status information or to display prompts to the user. The display can be as small as 1 line with 8 characters. Other displays used in embedded systems can be of 6.4 inch or 8.4 inch etc. The diagonal distance is indicated as display size. Resolution can be 640 * 480 or 1024 * 768 etc. The display driver circuitry is connected to the processor.

Display technology is changing very fast. Thin Film Transistor (TFT) displays provide very high-resolution display. TFT displays are used in mobile phones. Another innovation is 3-dimensional displays in which two LCDs are used to give the 3-dimensional effect.

In Brief...

LCD, TFT and OLED displays of different sizes and resolutions are used to display status information and prompts.

Another type of display that is now making inroads is Organic Light Emitting Diode (OLED) display in which any organic light-emitting polymer is placed between anode and cathode. When a voltage is applied between anode and cathode, the organic material glows. OLED gives a much brighter display as compared to LCD and is now being used on mobile phones and PDAs.

Serial Peripheral Interface (SPI)

SPI was developed by Motorola. Peripheral devices such as memory chips, potentiometers, ADCs and DACs, Real-Time Clock etc. are provided with SPI interface so that they can be interfaced to the processor. The processor generates the clock and the peripheral uses the clock to synchronize its acquisition of the data.

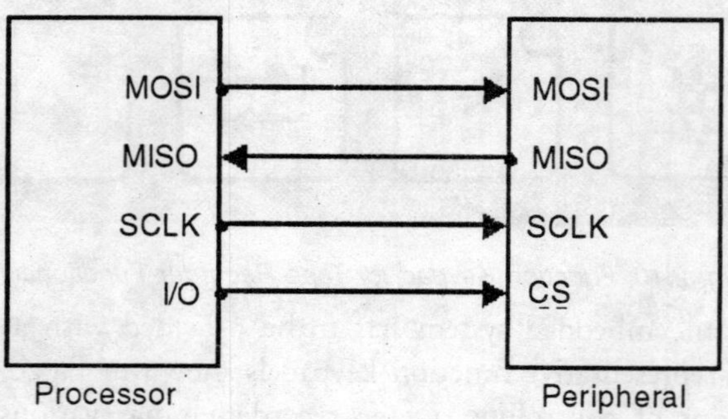

Fig. 2.11: Serial Peripheral Interface

SPI users four type of signals for interfacing peripherals to the processor

- Master Out Slave In (MOSI)
- Master In Slave Out (MISO)
- Serial Clock (SLCK)
- Chip Select (CS) for the peripheral

SPI is based on the master-slave protocol. The processor acts as the master and the peripheral acts as the slave. As shown in Fig. 2.11, the processor and the peripheral are connected using these 4 signals. Both the master and the slave contain shift registers. The master sends a byte to the slave on MOSI line, and the slave sends its register contents on MISO line. Both write and read can be done simultaneously. If the master has to read a byte from the slave, it has to write a dummy byte to initialize the slave for transmission. This is a synchronous protocol for communication between the processor and the peripheral.

In Brief...

Serial Peripheral Interface (SPI) uses a set of 4 signals for interfacing peripherals to the processor. RTC, EEPROMs, Flash memory etc. can be interfaced using SPI.

DS 1305 Real Time Clock (RTC), AD 5203 digital potentiometer, ATMEL AT45DB161 2MB serial data flash, AT25640 EEPROM 8KB, AT25080 1KB, AT25160 2KB, AT25320 4 KB EEPROMs can also be interfaced using SPI pins.

Inter-Integrated Circuit (I^2C) Bus

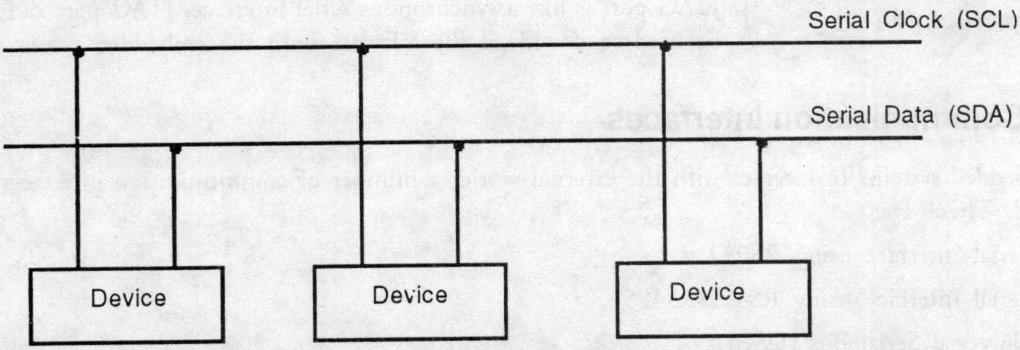

Fig. 2.12: Inter-Integrated Circuit Bus

I^2C bus uses 2 wires for connecting devices, as shown in Fig. 2.12. The bus is bi-directional and synchronous to a common clock. Micro-controllers with built-in I^2C are available. Data rates of 100 Kbps (standard mode) and 400 kbps (fast mode) are supported.

In Brief...

Inter-Integrated Circuit bus is used to interface a number of devices to the processor using master-slave protocol. Each device is given a unique address of 7-bits or 10-bits and hence 128 or 1024 devices can be connected on to the bus.

The bus consists of two lines—Serial Clock (SCL) and Serial Data (SDA). Both lines remain high when not in use. A device using the bus drives the line low. Each device has a unique address of 7-bits or 10-bits. If 7 bits are used, 128 devices can be connected to the bus. A device can act as a master or slave. Transmitting device is the master and the receiving device is the slave. The same line is used for master transmission and slave response. I^2C bus—is a multi-master bus, more than one device can act as master.

You can interface a RTC such as Philips PCF8353, a display of Matrix Orbital VFD2041 of 80 characters by 4 lines to the processor using I^2C bus.

2.1.7 Debug Port

Debugging a processor-based board is very difficult. Earlier, many processor manufacturers used to provide proprietary interfaces to do the debugging. Joint Test Access Group (JTAG) standardized a mechanism for providing the debugging through a port called JTAG port. JTAG port provides access to the internals of the processor. The standard IEEE 1149.1a-1993 (Standard Test Access Port and Boundary Scan Architecture) gives the details of the protocols used in JTAG port.

Using a technique known as Boundary Scan, the connections between the processor and the memory/peripherals can be probed by given appropriate signals at the output pins and reading the response from input pins.

In Brief...

Joint Test Access Group (JTAG) port is a standardized port to access the internal circuitry of the processor. JTAG port is used for debugging as well as to download the software on to the embedded system.

JTAG port consists of 4 signals:

- Test Data Input (TDI)
- Test Data Output (TDO)
- Test Mode Select (TMS)
- Test Clock (TCK)

JTAG port is like a synchronous serial interface. JTAG port can also be used to download the software onto the embedded system.

2.1.8 Communication Interfaces

For embedded systems to interact with the external world, a number of communication interfaces are provided. These are:

- Serial interface using RS232
- Serial interface using RS422/RS485
- Universal Serial Bus (USB)
- Infrared
- Ethernet
- Wireless interface based on IEEE 802.11 Wireless LAN standard
- Bluetooth radio interface

We will discuss the details of communication interfaces in Chapter 6.

2.1.9 Power Supply Unit

An embedded system operates either through a 230 V mains supply or through a battery. Since the components in the embedded system require different DC voltages such as +12 volts, -12 volts, +5 volts, +3.3 volts etc., a Power Supply Unit (PSU) is required which provides stable DC voltages from the mains or battery. An AC adapter converts the mains supply to +5volts to +12 volts DC supply giving a current up to 500 mA. The batteries give different voltages, but the output is not stable and the power supply unit has to derive the necessary voltages from this DC voltage. Voltage regulators are used for this purpose. The input to a voltage regulator is a range of DC voltages and the output is a stable fixed voltage.

DC-DC converters convert an unregulated voltage to a constant DC voltage. There are two types of DC-DC converters used in embedded systems.

- Linear regulators
- Switching regulators

In linear regulators, the output voltage is less than the input voltage. They need less number of components, hence these regulators cost less and give low noise. But they are less efficient and waste more power. The IC LM78xx series are examples of linear regulators.

Switching regulators step-up or step-down the input voltage level, or invert the voltage level. For instance, switching regulator can produce 5 volt DC by taking 3.6volt input from a battery. They are more efficient as they waste less power during conversion, but more components are required and hence these regulators are more noisy, occupy more space, and costly. LM78xx series, Maxim's MAX 603, 604, 1615, 724 are examples.

For designing the PSU of an embedded system, the power supply requirement for different components has to be identified and the total current rating has to be estimated. Note that some devices, particularly the processors, take more power during startup. Flash devices draw high current during write operations. These considerations need to be kept in mind while working out the power supply requirements. Reducing the power consumption is very important. Some of the important steps in this direction are:

- Use low power devices
- Processors and peripherals such as UART, memory devices to be put into low power mode when they are not in use.
- If the hardware contains lot of ICs such as gates, flip flops etc., the component count can be reduced using PLDs or FPGAs.

In Brief...

DC-DC converters are divided into linear regulators and switching regulators. The linear regulators are less noisy, but less efficient as compared to switching regulators.

2.2 Software Architecture

The software in an embedded system consists of an operating system and the application software. The operating system is optional; if it is not present, you need to write your own software routines to access the hardware.

As embedded systems are constrained for memory, we cannot use an operating system such as Windows or Unix on them. But still, we need the services provided by an operating system. We will discuss the services provided by an operating system and then discuss the requirements of the embedded operating systems.

2.2.1 Services Provided by an Operating System

Every computing device, whether it is a mainframe, desktop computer or an embedded system, needs a piece of software using which the user interacts with the hardware. This software is the operating system (OS). When the computer is switched on, first the OS is loaded into the main memory (RAM). When we invoke an application, say, word processing software, this application is loaded into the RAM.

We can use the computer for doing different things simultaneously—such as word processing, downloading the email etc. Each job is done by invoking an application software package. To write an application software package, we divide the job into different smaller jobs, write the code for each smaller job and then combine the entire code. In case of a desktop system, each job is called a "process" and in an embedded system, each job is called a "task". Each task needs memory and needs to access I/O devices. Managing these multiple tasks is done by the OS. An OS has to do the following functions:

- Process/task management
- Memory management
- Input/Output management including managing the file system
- Providing services to the applications
- Providing a user interface so that the user need not be concerned about the underlying hardware details

Based on the capabilities, operating systems are divided into different categories:

Single-tasking OS versus Multi-tasking OS: In a single tasking OS, only one task is carried out at a time. For instance, if you are using a word processor, you have to quit this application before invoking another application, say a game. In a multitasking OS, multiple tasks can be run simultaneously. For example, you can play a game while getting connected to the Internet and downloading a file. In a multitasking system, there may be only one CPU, but the CPU is shared by all the tasks. MS DOS is a single tasking operating system. Windows and Unix are multitasking operating systems.

Single-user OS versus Multi-user OS: In a single-user OS, only one user can use the system at a time. In a multi-user system, multiple users can share the system simultaneously. In a multi-tasking system, the application run by each user is given a small slice of time, say 10 msec. However, each user feels as though he is alone using the system. This is known as time-sharing. MS DOS and Windows are single-user operating systems. UNIX is a multi-user operating system.

Command-driven OS versus GUI-based OS: An important function of the OS is to provide an interface to the user to access the computer's resources. The user has to give instructions to the computer to carry out various tasks. One method of giving these instructions is to give commands such as "copy x.c y.c" through the keyboard. Operating system working on commands are said to be command-driven. MS DOS is a command-driven OS. On the other hand, the OS can provide a GUI such as in Windows operating systems and give instructions through mouse clicks. This is a GUI-driven OS.

In embedded systems, the OS provides the same services as in desktop computers. However, as compared to desktops, embedded systems have special requirements as described below:

- **Reliability:** The OS in an embedded system has to be very reliable. If the system has to have an availability of 99.999% of the time, the downtime per year is just about 5 minutes. Is your desktop operating system that reliable?
- **Multi-tasking with time constraints:** Embedded systems need to support multi-tasking. All operating systems used in embedded systems support this feature. But then, the task management has to be done efficiently to meet the real-time performance requirements. Desktop operating systems do not support real-time requirements whereas embedded systems must meet definite deadlines for some tasks.
- **Small footprint:** As the memory devices have limited capacity in embedded systems, they have little memory for the OS. Many frills provided by operating systems such as Windows (the jazzy GUI, for example) are not provided in embedded operating systems. The memory occupied by the operating system is known as the 'footprint'. The footprint should be very small for an embedded OS.
- **Support diskless systems:** Unlike the desktop computers, embedded systems may not have secondary storage such as hard disk or CDROM. The embedded OS along with application software will reside on a memory chip. File system management is not mandatory in embedded systems. However, if the application demands a file system, you can create a small file system on the Flash memory.
- **Portability:** A variety of processors are available for developing embedded systems unlike desktop computers whose processors are predominantly the Intel family processors. So, an important requirement of embedded operating systems is portability.
- **Scalability:** The embedded operating systems may be used on an 8-bit micro-controller or a powerful 64-bit microprocessor. So, scalability is very important for embedded operating systems.
- **Support for standard API:** Application software is developed using the Application Programming Interface (API) of the operating system. API is a set of function calls. An application developed for one OS may not be portable to another OS. To achieve portability, IEEE standardized the API called Portable Operating System Interface (POSIX). Operating systems used in embedded systems must comply with this standard.

Hence, for embedded systems, we need to use operating systems which meet the above requirements. We will study such operating systems in detail in the next section.

In Brief...

The important requirements of embedded operating systems are: reliability, faster performance and meeting real-time requirements, small footprint, support for diskless systems, portability, scalability and support for standard API.

2.2.2 Architecture of Embedded Operating Systems

To meet the special requirements mentioned above, the embedded operating systems need to have mechanisms to manage the tasks and to make the tasks communicate with one another.

The functionality of an embedded operating system can be illustrated through a real-life example. Assume that on a fine day, you have decided to complete the following works:

1. Meet your professor and submit the assignment. You must complete this work, otherwise your cranky professor will put you in deep trouble.
2. You have to discuss a few issues with your boy/girl friend.
3. You have to return a library book as your friend would like to get it issued. If you do not return the book that day, you need to pay fine.
4. You have to discuss with your friend about a forthcoming cultural program.

The work to be done is divided into 'tasks'. In this case, the first task is of the highest priority and it is 'time-critical'—if the deadline is not met, it may result in a catastrophe. It is a 'hard real-time task'. There is another restriction—the professor will meet only one student at a time and a number of students have to meet him that day. So, the professor is a 'shared resource'. When you go to meet him, if the door is closed, it is an indication that someone else is inside, and you need to wait in a queue. The status of the shared resource is known from the position of the door—the shared resource availability for you is known through a 'mutex' or a 'semaphore'. To do the second task, hopefully, your boy/girl friend is not a shared resource. If you give an 'interrupt', immediately (s)he will come out to meet you. It is a task to be completed, but no deadlines are imposed. The third task has a deadline, but the deadline is not very strict. You may have to just pay some fine if you delay the task. So, it is a soft real-time task. But then, there is an additional work to be done—you need to return the book and then inform your friend that the book has been returned so that he can get it issued. So, you need to pass a 'message' to your friend that you have completed the task. The fourth task again does not involve any deadline, but you need to check the availability of your friend. Therefore, you and your friend need to synchronize your timings. So, you need to plan your work in such a way that all the tasks are completed.

While discharging your tasks, you may encounter some problems: if you go to meet your professor, and if there is a long queue, how long do you wait? How do you pass a message to your friend that you have returned the library book? Your boy/girl friend will not wait for you indefinitely, if you are held up with your professor. What do you do? You need to sort out lot of issues. In the process, what you are doing is scheduling the tasks, working out mechanisms for communicating the messages, trying to avoid deadlocks, trying to meet the deadlines, and so on.

While you are developing embedded software, you need to do precisely the same things. These are:

- Identifying the tasks and assigning priorities to each task
- Identifying the time-critical tasks
- Scheduling the tasks in such a way that all the tasks are completed and the tasks which are time-critical meet the deadlines
- Working out when to send interrupts to the processor
- Identifying the shared resources and working out mechanisms for sharing the resource by multiple tasks
- Working out the strategies for inter-task communication
- Keeping track of the time

An embedded operating system does all these activities. Let us discuss these activities in a bit more detail:

Tasks: The work to be done by an embedded system is divided into a number of tasks. Each task competes for the CPU time independently. Each task will have its own stack area. Each task runs forever and hence it is implemented as an infinite loop as in the code segment given below:

```
for ( ; ; )
{
     statements;
}
```

In Brief...

In embedded software, the work to be done is divided into a number of tasks. Tasks compete for CPU time. Each task will have a separate stack. Each task is implemented as an infinite loop.

Alternatively, you can use while loop as in

```
while ( )
{
     statements;
}
```

Each task is assigned a priority. Generally, an operating system can support 256 priority levels.

Notes...

Tasks are similar to processes in the sense that both compete independently for CPU time. However, the difference is that processes have better memory protection features. A task/process is further divided into threads. Each thread runs independently, but multiple threads in a task can share variables.

Task scheduling: Since only one CPU has to handle multiple tasks, the tasks have to share the CPU time in a disciplined way so that one task does not get lot of time while others wait for unduly long time. Important time-critical tasks have to be given high priority; and a mechanism for deciding which task will get the CPU time next has to be worked out. This is known as task scheduling.

If the embedded system has to meet real-time requirements, the task scheduling has to be done in such a way that the time deadlines are met. An operating system in which the time that is required to execute a task can be estimated is called a 'deterministic' operating system—you should be able to determine the worst-case timings for completing a task.

A number of tasks scheduling algorithms are available. In all embedded/real-time operating systems, a scheduling algorithm known as priority-based pre-emptive scheduling algorithm is used. In this algorithm, each task is given a priority. The highest priority task will always be given the CPU time first.

Context switching: Suppose, a low-priority task is presently being executed by the processor but a high-priority task has to run. In this case, CPU will be interrupted through an interrupt signal. The CPU will save the current task's information in a stack and execute the high priority task. The mechanism of storing the current CPU registers in a stack to run the other task is known as context switching.

Mutual exclusion: Different tasks may have to share same resources. For example, two tasks may have to receive data from a serial port. Two tasks may have to share a printer. Resources shared by two or more tasks are called shared resources (serial port or printer in the above examples). You can imagine what would happen if two tasks send data simultaneously to a printer. It will result in a garbled printout. Tasks should maintain discipline to share the resources. Ensuring that two or more tasks access a shared resource without corrupting the data is called mutual exclusion. Embedded systems provide disciplined access to shared resources through special objects such as mutexes and semaphores. Mutex and semaphore are like 'keys'. To access a resource, a task will obtain the key, use the resource and release the key.

Inter-task communication: Tasks may need to exchange data amongst themselves. For instance, a task may write some data to a file and another task has to read that data. This mechanism is known as inter-task communication. The task which has to read the data has to obtain information that data is written by the other task. So, the two tasks have to synchronize their activities. Special OS objects such as mailboxes, message queues, pipes, status registers and event flags are used to achieve inter-task communication and inter-task synchronization.

Memory management: The memory of an embedded system is to be shared by a number of tasks. So, memory management is another service provided by the OS.

Timer services: The operating system needs to keep track of the time for activities such as the time for which a particular task is running, the time for which a task can wait for a shared resource, etc. The OS also provides the timer service.

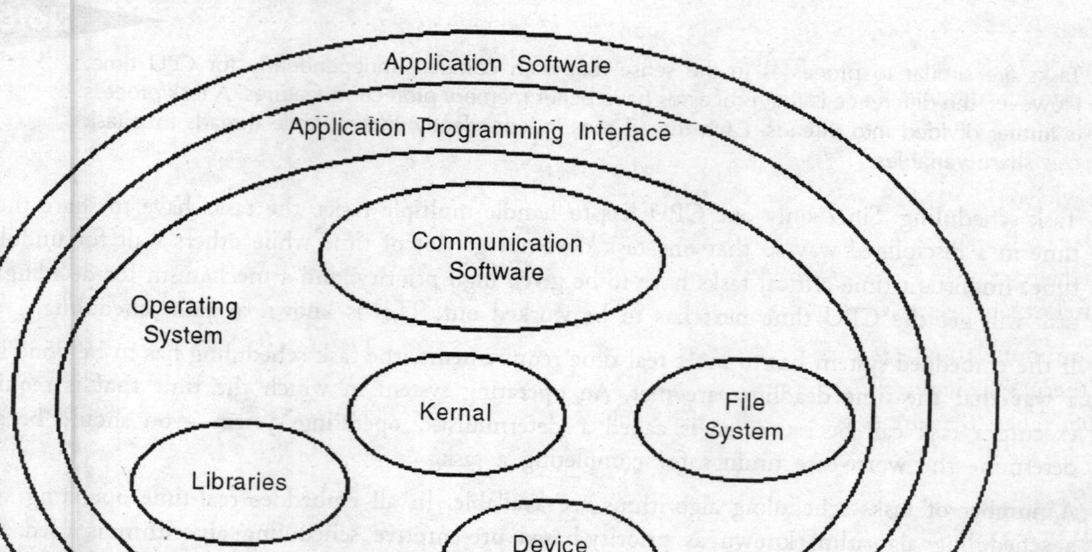

Fig. 2.13: Software Architecture of an Embedded System

Notes...

In addition to the application tasks, the kernel has it own system tasks with its own priorities. One important system task is the idle task. If no other task is running, the idle task is executed.

All the above-mentioned functions are carried out by the operating system kernel. The kernel is the heart of the operating system. As shown in Fig. 2.13, the software in an embedded system can be divided into the operating system and the application software. The in-between layer, the Application Programming Interface (API), is used by the developers to write the application software. API provides the function calls to access the operating system services.

The operating system consists of

- Kernel
- Device manager
- Networking protocol software
- Libraries
- File system (optional)

Kernel: Kernel manages the tasks to achieve the desired performance of the embedded system. To manage the tasks, the important requirements are to schedule the tasks and to provide inter-task communication facilities. To achieve these two requirements, kernel objects are defined such as tasks, mutexes, ISRs, events, message boxes, mailboxes, pipes and timers. Kernel provides the memory management services, time management services, interrupt handling services and device management services.

Device manager: The I/O devices are used to send/receive data from the embedded system. The OS manages the I/O devices through interrupts and device drivers. Device drivers provide the necessary interface between the application and the hardware.

Communication protocol software: If the embedded system has communication interfaces such as Ethernet, USB etc., the upper layer protocols such as TCP/IP stack need to be integrated with the OS. Then the embedded system can be network-enabled.

Libraries: The operating system may have some C/C++ library files in object code, which can be used through the API calls.

File system: Most of the embedded systems do not have a secondary storage. In such cases, the ROM is used to store the program. In case a file system is required, a small file system can be developed on Flash memory. Some embedded systems may use a secondary storage just for booting. For example, an Internet kiosk (which is an embedded system built around, say Pentium-based hardware) may use a CDROM for initial bootup.

In Brief...

The kernel is the heart of the operating system. Its main function is to manage the tasks. A task scheduling algorithm decides which task has to run next.

2.2.3 Categories of Embedded Operating Systems

Operating systems used in embedded systems can be broadly divided into the following categories:

Non-real-time Embedded Operating Systems: These operating systems have a small footprint but they are not suitable for hard real-time applications. Examples are Embedded Linux, Embedded NT and Windows XP Embedded. These operating systems are used in consumer appliances such as DVD players, Set Top Boxes etc. which are soft real-time embedded systems.

Real-time Operating Systems: These operating systems are suitable for hard real-time embedded applications. Examples are QNX Neutrino, VxWorks, RTLinux, MicroC/OS-II and OS/9.

Mobile/Handheld Operating Systems: The operating systems used in mobile devices such as palmtops, PDAs, smart phones are known as mobile/handheld operating systems. Palm OS, Symbian OS, Windows CE are the major OSs in this category. Embedded Linux, VxWorks, OS/9 are also now being used in handheld computers.

Notes...

A number of embedded/real-time operating systems are now being used as handheld/mobile operating systems. These include Embedded Linux, OS/9 etc.

2.3 Application Software

Application-specific software has to be developed above the operating system. Once you decide which operating system to use, you need to obtain the development tools for that operating system. These development tools provide function calls to access the operating system services. For example, if you have to create a task to read data from a serial port, you make a function call to create a new task with the required priority, write the code to read the data and write to a memory location. The various function calls provided by an operating system are:

- To create, suspend and delete tasks
- To do task scheduling for meeting real-time requirements
- To facilitate inter-task communication and synchronization between tasks
- To initialize, increment and reset counters to keep track of time
- To allocate and free memory
- To access the I/O devices
- To access the communication protocol stack

In Brief...

In embedded systems, the application software is integrated with the operating system software and networking software, and then transferred to the memory of the embedded system.

Using these function calls, you can write your application software. Then the operating system, the communication software and the application software together are converted into a relocatable binary file and ported onto the program memory. Generally, the executable file will be residing in the EPROM or EEPROM or Flash memory. On power- on, the program is transferred to the RAM and then the processor executes the program. Sometimes, the program may be executed directly from the program memory device. Such programs are called Execute In Place (XIP) programs.

2.4 Communication Software

Most of the embedded systems need a communication interface to interact with the external world. To communicate with another device, the embedded system will have the hardware interfaces. In addition, communication software needs to be integrated with the firmware. For instance, to make an embedded system network-enabled, in addition to say, Ethernet interface, TCP/IP protocol stack has to run on it. The advantage of these interfaces is that the embedded system can be accessed over a network such as a Local Area network, corporate Intranet or even the public Internet.

In Brief...

To network-enable an embedded system, the embedded system should have the complete TCP/IP protocol stack integrated along with the operating system.

As TCP/IP protocol stack is now being ported onto many embedded systems, we will briefly review the TCP/IP protocol architecture. Note that the software that implements this architecture will need just a few kilobytes of memory and hence integrating the software into an embedded system is pretty easy.

2.4.1 TCP/IP Protocol Suite

The TCP/IP protocol suite was developed during the initial days of research on the Internet. This research led to the most important concept of packet switching. In packet switching, the data to be transmitted (say a file) is divided into small packets and each packet is transmitted from the source to the destination. Each packet may take a different route, but at the destination, all the packets are put together in sequence and given to the application software. Note that during transmission some packets may be lost and packets may not be received in sequence. Using TCP/IP protocols, the problems encountered due to loss of packets and packets arriving out of sequence are taken care of. The user just gives a command for a file transfer and the person at the other end receives the file.

The TCP/IP protocol suite is now an integral part of desktop operating systems such as Window and Unix. Even tiny embedded systems are being provided with TCP/IP support to make them network-enabled. These systems include web cameras, web TVs etc. TCP/IP stack is also being embedded into systems running real-time operating systems and handheld operating systems.

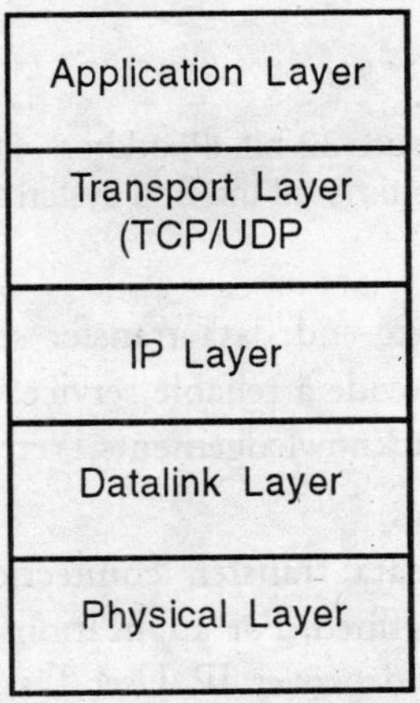

Fig. 2.14: TCP/IP Protocol Suite

The TCP/IP protocol suite is depicted in Fig. 2.14. It consists of 5 layers viz.,

- Physical layer
- Data link layer (referred also as Network layer)
- Internet Protocol (IP) layer
- Transport layer (TCP layer and UDP layer)
- Application layer

Physical layer: This layer defines the characteristics of the transmission such as data rate and signal-encoding scheme.

Data Link layer: This layer defines the protocols to manage the links—establishing a link, transferring the data received from the upper layers, and disconnecting the link. In Local Area Networks, the data link layer is divided into two sub-layers: Medium Access Control (MAC) sub-layer and Logical Link Control (LLC) sub-layer.

Notes...

The IEEE 802.3 Ethernet, IEEE 802.11 Wireless LAN standards specify the first two layers functionality. These two layers are implemented through a combination of hardware and firmware. Above this interface, the software that implements the higher layer protocols has to run.

Internet Protocol (IP) layer: The two important functions of this layer are addressing and routing. IP layer functionality is implemented in software. IP layer software runs on every end system and router connected to the Internet. The presently running IP layer software is called IP version 4. This version will be slowly replaced by IP version 6.

Each system connected to the Internet is given a unique address known as IP address. In IP version 4, the IP address length is 32 bits and in IP version 6, it is 128 bits. Most of the embedded systems use 32-bit IP address.

IP layer also takes care of routing of packets from the source to the destination. Based on the IP address, the router forwards the packet towards the destination. IP provides an unreliable service, i.e. the packets may be lost, arrive out of order or with variable delay.

Notes...

Embedded operating systems presently support 32-bit IP address. It is not a major concern because it is likely to take many years by the time all the end systems and routers support 128-bit addressing.

Transport layer: This layer provides end-to-end data transfer service between two systems connected to the Internet. Since IP layer does not provide a reliable service, it is the responsibility of the transport layer to incorporate reliability through acknowledgements, retransmissions, etc. The transport layer software runs on every end system.

For applications which require reliable data transfer, connection-oriented transport protocol called Transmission Control Protocol (TCP) is defined. For applications which require less protocol overhead, such as network management and voice/video over IP, User Datagram Protocol (UDP) is used as the transport layer.

Transmission Control Protocol (TCP): It is the job of TCP layer to ensure that the data is delivered to the application layer without any errors. So, the functions of TCP are:

- To check whether the packets are received in sequence or not. If they are not in sequence, they have to be arranged in sequence.
- To check whether each packet is received without errors using the checksum. If packets are received in error, TCP layer has to ask for retransmissions.
- To check whether all packets are received or whether some packets are lost. It may so happen that one of the routers may drop a packet (discard it) as its buffer is full or the router itself may go faulty. If packets are lost, the TCP layer has to inform the other end system to retransmit the packet. Dropping a packet is generally due to congestion on the network.
- Sometimes, one system may send the packets very fast and the router or end system may not be able to receive the packets at that speed. The mismatch in speeds is taken care of by flow control mechanism. In flow control, one system informs the other system not to send any more packets till further information.

In Brief...

Transmission Control Protocol (TCP) provides a reliable end-to-end data transfer, i.e. it ensures that all the packets are received without errors, puts all the packets in sequence and gives the packets to the application layer.

User Datagram Protocol (UDP): TCP provides a reliable service by taking care of error control and flow control. However, the processing required for the TCP layer is very high. Hence, it is called a 'heavy-weight' protocol. In some applications such as real-time voice/video communication and network management, such high processing requirements create problems. So, another transport protocol is used for such applications. It is User Datagram Protocol (UDP). UDP provides a connectionless service. It sends the packets to the destination one after the other, without bothering whether they are being received correctly or not. It is the job of the application layer to take care of the problems associated with lack of acknowledgements and error control. Simple Network Management Protocol (SNMP) which is used for network management runs above the UDP.

In Brief...

User Datagram Protocol (UDP) provides a connectionless service, i.e. there is no need for the receiver to transmit acknowledgements to the sender after receiving the packets. Hence, UDP does not provide a reliable service.

Notes...

As the processing power required to process UDP datagrams is less, UDP is used for real-time transmission of voice and video over IP networks.

Application layer: This layer differs from application to application. Two processes on two end systems communicate with application layer as the interface.

The application process (say for transferring a file) generates an application byte stream which is divided into TCP segments and sent to the IP layer. The TCP segment is encapsulated in the IP datagram and sent to the data link layer. The IP datagram is encapsulated in the data link layer frame. The data link layer frame is sent to the physical layer interface and then the bit stream is sent over the transmission medium. At the destination, each layer strips off the header, does the necessary processing based on the information in the header and passes the remaining portion of the data to the higher layer.

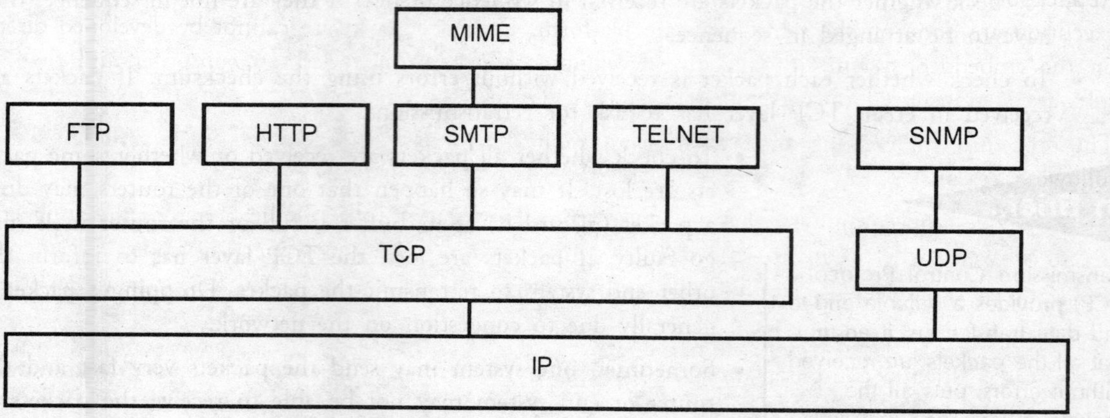

Fig. 2.15: Application Layer Protocols in TCP/IP Protocol Stack

The application layer protocols in the TCP/IP protocol stack are shown in Fig. 2.15. The various application layer protocols are:

- Simple Mail Transfer Protocol (SMTP), for electronic mail containing ASCII text.
- Multimedia Internet Mail Extension (MIME), for electronic mail with multi-media content.
- File Transfer Protocol (FTP) for file transfer.
- TELNET for remote login.
- Hyper Text Transfer Protocol (HTTP) for World Wide Web service
- Simple Network Management Protocol (SNMP) for network management. Note that SNMP runs above the UDP layer and not the TCP layer.

To make an embedded system network-enabled, the TCP/IP protocol stack is integrated with the operating system software and the application software. The entire software is then transferred to the memory of the embedded system.

Notes...

Though we talk about TCP 'connection', it needs to be noted that there is no real connection between the end systems. It is a virtual connection. In other words, TCP connection is only an abstraction.

2.5 Process of Generating Executable Image

On a desktop computer, the procedure for creating and executing the application software is as follows:

- Create the source file
- Create the executable file
- Give the command for execution

- The process is loaded into the RAM by the loader
- Loader transfers the control to the process and the process executes.

Application development on desktop computers is called native development as the development and execution are done on the same hardware platform. Embedded software cannot be developed directly on the embedded system. Initially, the development is done on a desktop computer and then the software is transferred to the embedded system. This is known as cross-platform development.

The procedure for creating and executing an application in an embedded system is different for the following reasons:

- On desktop computers, there is a distinction between the operating system and the application software, whereas in an embedded system everything is a single piece of code.
- In an embedded system, there is only one application that needs to run continuously. Multiple applications need not be loaded on to the embedded system.
- On a desktop computer, in which part of the memory the application is loaded is immaterial; but in embedded systems you need to decide where the code will reside so that the processor executes the instructions from that memory location.
- Desktop computers use virtual memory. In a multi-tasking system, when a new process has to be executed, the presently running process is transferred to the virtual memory (which can be on the hard disk). In embedded systems, the secondary storage is not available.

The operating system, communication software and application software have to be converted into a single executable image and transferred to the memory of the embedded system. This process of creating an executable image is illustrated in Fig. 2.16.

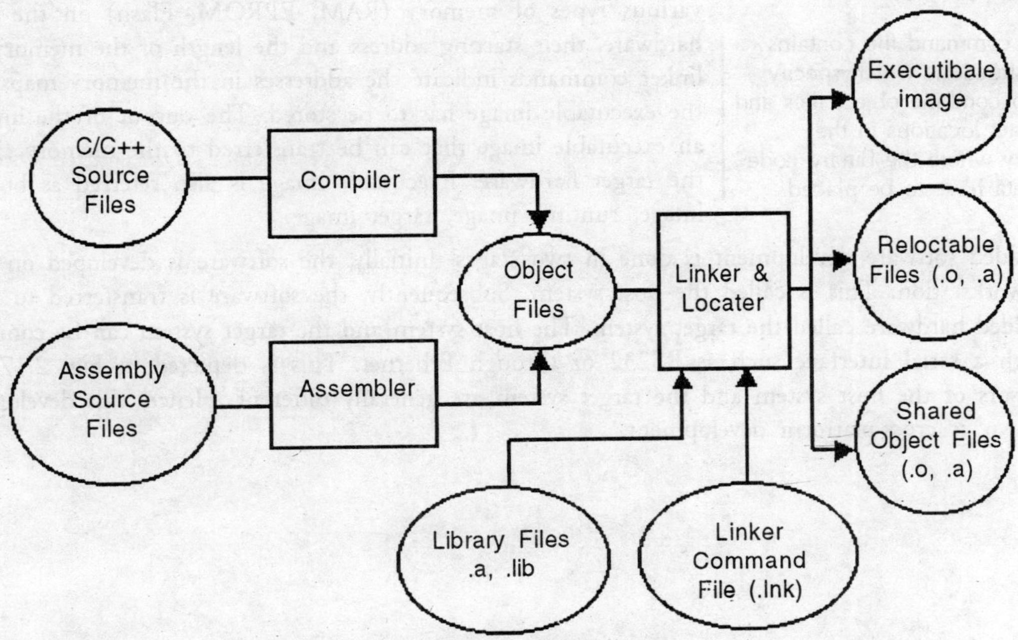

Fig. 2.16: Process of Creating an Executable Image

The source files, written in C or C++ are converted into object files using the compiler. The source files written in the assembly language of the target processor are converted into object files using the assembler. Each object file contains the binary code (instructions) and program data.

Each object file created in the above process will have the following information:

- Name of the source file
- Size of the file, size of the binary instructions and size of the data
- Processor-specific binary instructions and data
- Symbol table that contains details of variables, their data types and addresses
- Debugging information if the compilation is done with the debug option

The format of this object file is called the Object File Format. This format has been standardized. The two standards are: (i) Common Object File Format (COFF) and (ii) Executable and Linking Format (ELF). The format of the object files has been standardized to ensure that the object files generated by different compilers can be combined together. The most widely used format is ELF format. In ELF format, the object file is divided into various "sections".

The linker combines the various object files including the library files used in the program and creates an executable image or a single relocatable object file or a shared library file.

The linker command file contains a number of instructions called linker commands or linker directives. These commands tell the linker how to combine the object files and the exact locations in the memory where the binary code and data have to be placed on the target embedded system. Linker commands also describe the "memory map" of the embedded system. The memory map describes the various types of memory (RAM, EPROM, Flash) on the target hardware, their starting address and the length of the memory. The linker commands indicate the addresses in the memory map where the executable image has to be stored. The output of the linker is an executable image that can be transferred to the memory chip of the target hardware. Executable image is also referred as bootable image, runtime image, target image.

In Brief...

Linker command file contains the instructions which specify how to combine object files and the exact locations in the memory where the binary code and data have to be placed.

Embedded software development is done in two stages. Initially, the software is developed on a PC or a workstation. This is called the host system. Subsequently, the software is transferred to actual embedded hardware called the target system. The host system and the target system can be connected through a serial interface such as RS232 or through Ethernet. This is depicted in Fig. 2.17. The processors of the host system and the target system are generally different. Hence, this development is known as cross-platform development.

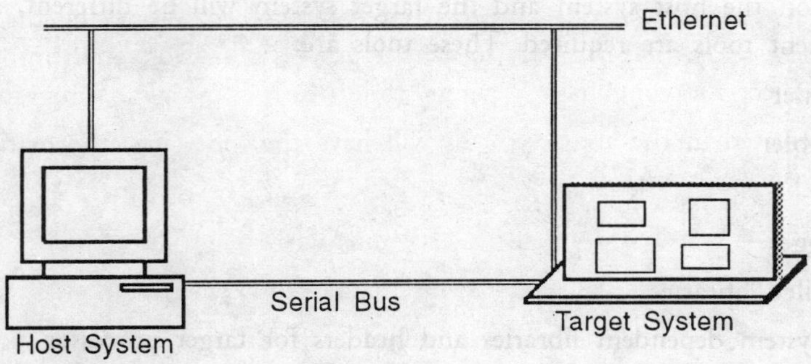

Fig. 2.17: Cross-platform Development using Host System and Target System

2.5.1 Cross-Platform Development

The process of cross-platform development is shown as a flowchart in Fig. 2.18. The source code is written on the host system, compiled and linked using cross-platform development tools and then downloaded onto the target and tested. If the software is not working as per requirements, it can be debugged on the target itself. After ensuring that everything is OK, the executable image is transferred to ROM or Flash memory. Then, the embedded system can run on its own.

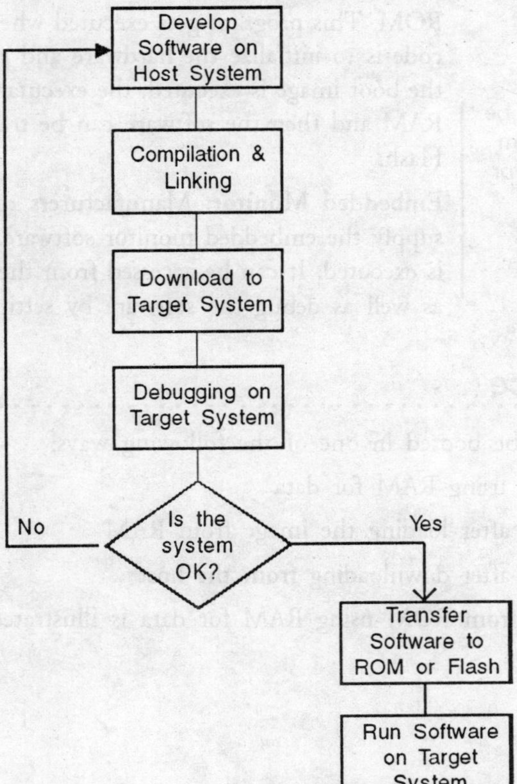

Fig. 2.18: Process of Cross-platform Development

As the processors on the host system and the target system will be different, a number of cross-platform development tools are required. These tools are:

- Cross-compiler
- Cross-assembler
- Cross-linker
- Cross-debugger
- Cross-compiled libraries
- Operating system dependent libraries and headers for target processor

The executable image can be transferred to the target hardware by one of the following mechanisms:

- Programming the EEPROM or Flash
- Downloading the image through a communication interface which requires a file transfer utility and an embedded loader or an embedded monitor on the embedded system
- Downloading through JTAG port

An embedded loader or an embedded monitor is used to do the hardware initialization and run the initial bootup code.

In Brief...

The embedded software can be transferred to the target system by programming a EEPROM or Flash memory using a programmer, or downloading through a communication interface or JTAG port.

Embedded Loader: Embedded loader is a program that resides in the ROM. This program gets executed when power is switched on. This code is to initialize the hardware and execute the boot image. After the boot image is executed, the executable image is transferred to the RAM and then the software can be transferred to the EEPROM or Flash.

Embedded Monitor: Manufacturers of processor evaluation board supply the embedded monitor software. On power-on, this software is executed. It can be accessed from the host to download the image as well as debug the software by setting breakpoints.

2.5.2 Boot Sequence

An embedded system can be booted in one of the following ways:

- Execute from ROM using RAM for data
- Execute from RAM after loading the image from RAM
- Execute from RAM after downloading from the host

The process for executing from ROM using RAM for data is illustrated in Fig. 2.19.

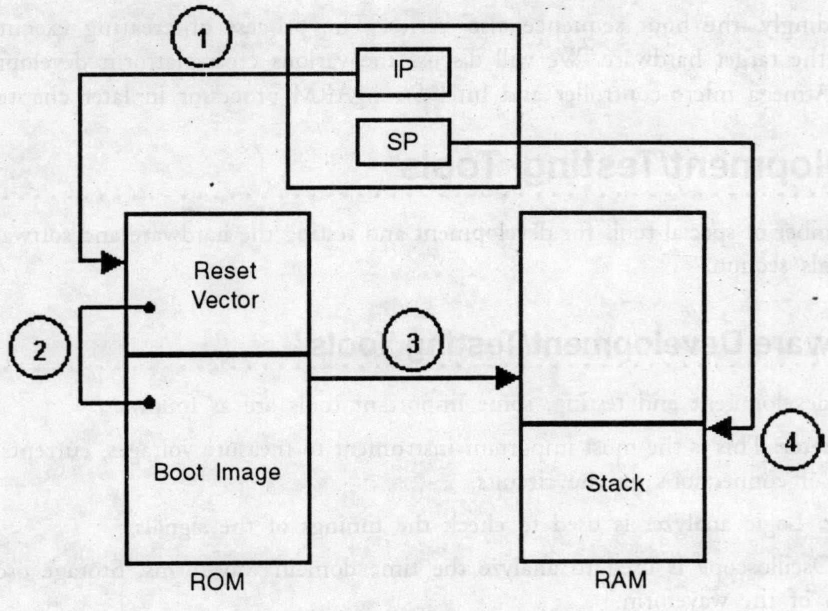

Fig. 2.19 Boot Sequence

1. On power-on, the CPU always executes the code contained at a specific address in ROM. This code is called Reset Vector.
2. The Reset Vector is a jump instruction to jump to another portion of the memory where the code that resides to boot the system is stored. This is called bootstrap code. This code initializes memory including RAM.
3. The executable image contains the data sections. Data sections are both readable and writable, and hence they are copied to RAM. Stack space is reserved in RAM.
4. CPU's Stack Pointer is set to point to the beginning of the stack.

Once the boot sequence is completed, the target software will start running. This software does the following:

- Initialization of the hardware: CPU, memory, bus interfaces and devices are initialized.
- Initialization of the operating system: operating system kernel objects such as tasks, semaphores, memory management services are initialized and stacks for each task are created.
- Initialization of the application code.

In Brief...

On power-on, the CPU executes the code contained at a specific address in the ROM. This code is called Reset Vector. Reset Vector is a jump instruction to another portion of the memory where the code that resides to boot the system is stored.

Up to this point, we studied the architecture and the process of developing the software for embedded systems without reference to any specific processor. Now, you need to appreciate that the development tools required are different for each processor used in the embedded system. The cross-platform development tools are specific to the processor. The format of the linker command file depends on the types of memory devices used in the embedded system. Accordingly, the boot sequence also varies. The process of creating executable image is dependent on the target hardware. We will discuss the various cross-platform development tools for 89C51, AVR Atmega micro-controller and Intel StrongARM processor in later chapters.

2.6 Development/Testing Tools

You need a number of special tools for development and testing the hardware and software. These tools are listed in this section.

2.6.1 Hardware Development/Testing Tools

For hardware development and testing, some important tools are as follows:

Digital Multimeter: This is the most important instrument to measure voltages, currents, and to check the continuity of connections on the circuits.

Logic Analyzer: Logic analyzer is used to check the timings of the signals.

Oscilloscope: Oscilloscope is used to analyze the time domain waveforms. Storage oscilloscopes can store a portion of the waveform.

Spectrum analyzer: Spectrum analyzer is used to analyze the signals in frequency domain.

2.6.2 Software Development/Testing Tools

For software development, the important development tools are listed below.

Operating System Development Suite: If you have to use an off-the-shelf operating system, you need to obtain the development suite from the operating system vendor. This development suite contains the API calls to access the OS services. The development suite may run either on a Windows system or a Unix/Linux system. You can use either an open source OS such as Embedded Linux or a commercial OS.

Cross-platform development tools: For the processor of your choice, you need to have cross-platform development tools such as the cross-compiler, cross-assembler, cross-debugger etc. as discussed in the previous section. Cross-compiler generates the object code of the given processor for the source code developed in a high level language such as C or C++. A number of GNU tools are available which can be downloaded from www.gnu.org for a number of processors. These cross-compilers provide an Integrated Development Environment (IDE) with editor, compiler, debugger etc. all bundled together.

ROM Emulator: ROM emulator emulates ROM in the RAM. It can be used to debug the software by setting the breakpoints in the memory.

EPROM Programmer: If your hardware board does not support in-circuit programming or if you have only EPROM for program memory, you need an EPROM programmer. Along with it, you also need an EPROM eraser.

Instruction Set Simulator (ISS): ISS is a software utility that creates a virtual version of the processor on the PC.

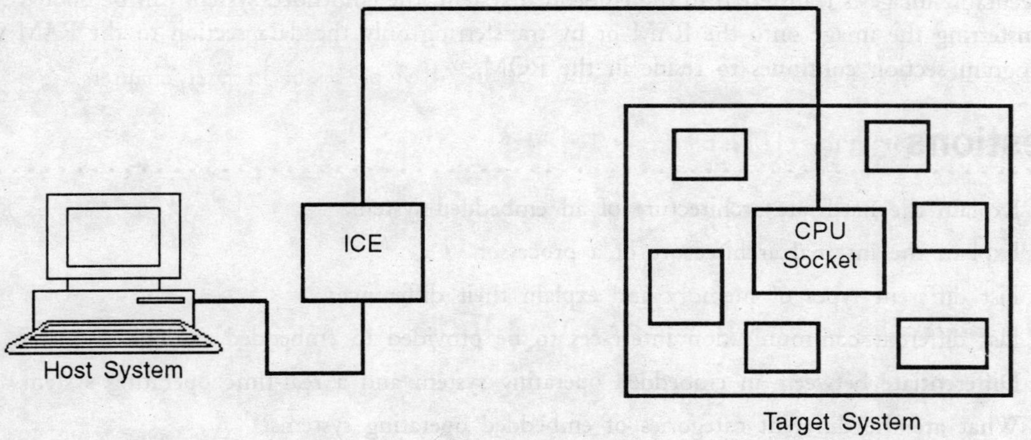

Fig. 2.20: In-Circuit Emulator

In Brief...

Operating system development suite, cross-platform development tools, EPROM programmer, ROM Emulator, Instruction Set Simulator and In-Circuit Emulator are some of the important tools for embedded software development.

In-Circuit Emulator (ICE): ICE is a device that emulates the CPU. You can plug-in this device in the place of CPU on the target hardware board as shown in Fig. 2.20. This device fits into the CPU socket of the target board on one side, and on the other side it is connected to the host through RS232 or USB port. You can run a debugger on the host to debug the code while it is running on the target hardware. ICE is processor-specific and costly, but an excellent tool for debugging.

Summary

In this chapter, the architecture of an embedded system is reviewed. The embedded system consists of three elements: hardware, operating system and application software. The building blocks of the hardware are the processor, Random Access Memory, Read Only Memory, clock circuitry to generate clock signal, input/output devices such as the function keypad, LEDs, LCD, sensors and transducers that convert real-life information into electrical signals, ADC and DAC, DMA controller, watchdog timer and reset circuitry, and power supply unit. The important functionality of each of these blocks is presented. The operating system, which is optional, takes care of task management, memory management, input/output management and provides the user interface. If an operating system is not used in embedded systems, software to provide these services has to be written. The Application Programming Interface of the operating system provides the function calls to access these services for writing application software. To make the embedded system communicate with the external world, the communication software is required. The TCP/IP protocol architecture is briefly discussed in this chapter. The operating system, communication software and the application software are integrated and an executable image is created. The executable image is transferred to the memory of the embedded system. Embedded software development involves cross-platform development as the software is initially developed on a host system and then the executable image is transferred to the target system. After the executable image is transferred to the embedded system, the embedded system can be booted either by transferring the image onto the RAM or by transferring only the data section to the RAM while the program section continues to reside in the ROM.

Questions

1. Explain the hardware architecture of an embedded system.
2. Explain the internal architecture of a processor.
3. List different types of memory and explain their differences.
4. List different communication interfaces to be provided to embedded systems.
5. Differentiate between an embedded operating system and a real-time operating system.
6. What are the different categories of embedded operating systems?
7. Explain the TCP/IP protocol suite.
8. What is cross-platform development? List the tools required for cross-platform development.
9. Explain the process of generating an executable image for embedded software.
10. Explain the boot sequence of an embedded system.

Exercises

1. You need to measure the temperatures in the range –20 degrees to +60 degrees with a resolution of 0.1 degree. What is the resolution of the ADC required?
2. You need to process music signals using a microprocessor. What are the specifications of the ADC you have to choose?
3. Explain why Windows 95/98/2000/NT based systems cannot be used for real-time operations.
4. Is Unix a real-time operating system? Justify your answer.
5. Why desktop computers do not use real-time operating systems?
6. What are the different criteria based on which you can compare different embedded/real-time operating systems.
7. List the important mobile/handheld operating systems.
8. List some embedded systems which can be classified as hard real-time systems.
9. ROM is read-only memory. RAM is read-write memory. Why write-only memory chips are not manufactured?

Chapter 3

Programming for Embedded Systems

CHAPTER OBJECTIVES

After reading this chapter, you will be able to:

- Understand the important features of ANSI standard for C language
- Learn the intricacies of C programming for embedded systems through examples in bit manipulation
- Learn function calls for file I/O and memory management
- Understand the importance of code optimization
- Gain knowledge of coding guidelines
- Appreciate the importance of C++ and Java programming languages for embedded software development.

As compared to writing application software, writing embedded software is a different ball game. You need to manipulate at bit-level and use operating system calls to carry out functionalities such as accessing the hardware. In this chapter, we will discuss the intricacies in C programming through illustrative examples. We will study the issues involved in code optimization. How to write readable and maintainable code is explained by listing the important coding guidelines. We will also study how to optimize the programs to reduce execution speed. We will discuss the importance of C++ and Java programming languages for embedded software development.

Note that all the programs given in this chapter are tested in Linux environment. The code explanation is given in the comments of the code listings. The "$" symbol that precedes the commands is the Linux system prompt.

3.1 Overview of ANSI C

Since 1981 when Unix operating system was commercialized, C became a very popular language. However, the software developed in C using compilers of different vendors led to portability problems.

To achieve portability, American National Standards Institute (ANSI) released the ANSI C specifications in 1989. This standard is specified in ANSI X3 159-1989. International Organization for Standardization (ISO) adapted this standard in 1990, which is ISO/IEC 9899-1990. The latest revision of this standard, released in 1999, is ISO/IEC-1999, also referred to as C99. Majority of the compilers available in the market conform to C99. Conformity is important for portability. Some important features of this standard are listed below:

- **Function prototyping:** Function prototyping is not mandatory, but improves error checking.
- **Parameter passing:** Floats are passed as floats only, not converted to double as in Kirnighan and Ritchie C. Arguments are automatically cast into the right form from the called function.
- **Standard include files:** Assert, ctype, errno, float, limits, locale, math, setjmp, signal, stdarg, stddef, stdio, stdlib, string, time are the standard include files.

In Brief...

American National Standards Institute (ANSI) defined standards for C programming language to ensure that the code is portable across different compilers.

International Organization for Standardization (ISO) developed extensions to the C99 standard specifically for embedded software development. This standard is called "Extensions for the Programming Language C to support embedded processors" and the details of the extension are given in the document ISO/IEC WDTR 18037. These extensions pertain to three important aspects:

- **New data types:** New data types for fixed-point arithmetic have been introduced as most of the embedded software involves only fixed-point arithmetic. These data types are "fract" and "accum". "fract" can take the values between –1.0 and +1.0. "accum" will have both integer and fractional part. Six types of data type modifiers can be used on these basic data types. <stdfix.h> defines the macros that specify the precision of the fixed point types and declares functions that support fixed-point arithmetic.
- **Address space definition:** As embedded systems will have different memory chips (RAM, ROM, Flash), function calls are provided to handle multiple address spaces. OS and compiler will hide these differences through these function calls. The function calls provide a uniform mechanism for defining an address space as well as variables within a specified address space. You can specify which address space is used.
- **I/O hardware addressing:** Generally, the software to address I/O devices is not portable. The file <iohw.h> contains the access functions to promote portability of I/O hardware driver source code across different platforms. iohw access functions create platform independent interfaces between I/O driver source code and underlying access method used when addressing the I/O registers in a given platform.

Notes...

ISO developed extensions to the C99 standard specifically for embedded software development. This standard is called "Extensions for the Programming Language C to support embedded processors". Compilers that conform to this standard will be available soon.

3.2 GNU Development Tools

Under GNU GPL, a number of development tools are available. These tools can be obtained free of cost and also can be distributed. In this chapter, we will use these tools for testing the programs. You need to become familiar with the following tools:

GCC	C compiler
G++	C++ compiler
GDB	Source code level debugger
GNU make	Make utility

If you have a C file with the filename hello.c, to invoke the GCC compiler in Linux environment, give the following command:

```
$gcc hello.c
```

The executable file with the name a.out is created. You can execute the file by giving the command:

```
$./a.out
```

Alternatively, you can create an executable file with the name hello, using the command:

```
$gcc -ohello hello.c
```

You can now execute the file by giving the command:

```
$./hello
```

If your program uses mathematical library, give the command:

```
$gcc hello.c -lm
```

gcc provides a number of options which can be obtained from the online manual.

3.3 Bit Manipulation using C

In this section, we will illustrate the various bit manipulation operators of C. Listing 3.1 gives a simple program (bitwise.c) which illustrates the use of these operators.

Listing 3.1: bitwise.c

```
/*
   This program is the demo of Bitwise operators in 'C'.
*/

#include<stdio.h>

int main()
{
    int a = 16;
    int b = 7;
    printf("\n The value of a & b (a AND b)  : %d",a & b);
    printf("\n The value of a | b (a OR b)   : %d",a | b);
```

```
    printf("\n The value of a ^ b (a XOR b) : %d",a ^ b);
    printf("\n The value of ~b (1's Complement) : %d",~b);
    printf("\n The value of a >> 1 : %d",a >> 1);
    printf("\n The value of a >> 2 : %d",a >> 2);
    printf("\n The value of b << 1 : %d",b << 1);
    printf("\n The value of b << 2 : %d\n",b << 2);
} // end of main
```

The use of bitwise operations (AND, OR, XOR, NOT, left shift and right shift) is illustrated here. You can compile and execute the program using the command format given above to study these operators in action.

Notes...

Bit-shift operators can be used for multiplication and division by 2. Bit-shifting is much more computationally efficient as compared to multiplication and division operations.

Listing 3.2 gives the program checkbit1.c that shows how to check whether a particular bit is set to 1 or not.

Listing 3.2: checkbit1.c

```
#include <stdio.h>
int main(int argc,int argv[])
{
   int value;
   if(argc > 1){
      value = atoi(argv[1]);
      if((value & 0x40) != 0)
      {
         printf("Seventh bit is set \n");
      }
      else
      {
         printf("Seventh bit is not set\n");
      }
   }
   else
   {
      printf("Usage: ./a.out 20\n");
   }
   return 0;
}
```

In many embedded systems, you need to test whether a bit is set to 1 or not. This program is used in such instances. An alternative way of checking whether a bit is set to 1 or not, is given in Listing 3.3.

Listing 3.3: checkbit2.c

```
#include <stdio.h>
int main(int argc,int argv[])
{
   int value;
   if(argc > 1){
      value = atoi(argv[1]);
      if((value & (1 << 6)) != 0)
      {
         printf("Seventh bit is set \n");
      }
      else
      {
         printf("Seventh bit is not set\n");
      }
   }
   else
   {
      printf("Usage: ./a.out 20\n");
   }
   return 0;
}
```

Two other functions that you generally carry out are to set a bit to 1 or to clear a bit, i.e. to set the bit to 0. Listing 3.4 gives the program setbit1.c that demonstrates how to set a particular bit to 1.

Notes...

In communication protocol development, bit setting and bit clearing operations are required.

Listing 3.4: setbit1.c

```
#include <stdio.h>
int main(int argc,int argv[])
{
   int value;
   if(argc > 1)
   {
      value = atoi(argv[1]);
      value |= (1<<5);
      printf("Result: %d\n",value);
   }
   return 0;
}
```

An alternative way of setting a bit to 1 is shown in Listing 3.5.

Listing 3.5: setbit2.c

```
#include <stdio.h>
int main(int argc,int argv[])
{
   int value;
   if(argc > 1)
   {
      value = atoi(argv[1]);
      value = value | (1<<5);
      printf("Result: %d\n",value);
   }
   return 0;
}
```

The program clearbit.c in Listing 3.6 shows how to clear a bit, i.e. to set the bit to 0.

Listing 3.6: clearbit.c

```
#include <stdio.h>
int main(int argc,int argv[])
{
   int value;
   if(argc > 1)
   {
      value = atoi(argv[1]);
      value &= ~(1<<5);
      printf("Result: %d\n",value);
   }
   else
      printf("Usage: ./a.out 38\n");
   return 0;
}
```

3.3.1 Calculation of CRC

Cyclic Redundancy Check (CRC) calculations are required in data communication software as well as for checking the memory of embedded systems. In data communication, when you have to transmit a bit stream, say of 1000 bits, additional 16 or 32 bits are added to provide error detection capability. The bit stream is divided with a polynomial and the result of the division is the CRC. When you transmit the data, CRC is appended to the original data and the data is sent over the medium. At the receiving end, the CRC is again calculated and the calculated CRC is matched with the received CRC. If they match, it can be assumed that the data is received correctly. Otherwise, retransmission of the data is requested. Same technique is used for checking the memory devices such as the RAM.

To calculate CRC, three standard algorithms are available. These are: CRC-16, CRC-32 and CRC-CCITT. The data is divided by a polynomial, and the CRC is calculated. The polynomial used is different for the three standards. Table 3.1 gives the polynomials used for CRC calculations for the three algorithms.

Parameter	CRC-16	CRC-32	CRC-CCITT
CRC bits	16	32	16
Generator polynomial	$x^{16} + x^{15} + x^2 + 1$	$x^{32} + x^{26} + x^{23} + x^{22} + x^{16} + x^{12} + x^{11} + x^{10} + x^8 + x^7 + x^5 + x^4 + x^2 + x + 1$	$x^{16} + x^{12} + x^5 + 1$
Divisor (hexade cimal value)	0x8005	0x04C11DB7	0x1021

Table 3.1: Standards for Calculation of CRC

Listing 3.7 shows the calculation of CRC using CRC-16 algorithm.

Listing 3.7: crc16.c

```
#include <stdlib.h>
#include <stdio.h>
unsigned int CRCfor16(int initialCRC, char *String, int length);

unsigned int CRCLookupTable[16] = {
   0x0000, 0xCC01, 0xD801, 0x1400, 0xF001, 0x3C00, 0x2800, 0xE401,
   0xA001, 0x6C00, 0x7800, 0xB401, 0x5000, 0x9C01, 0x8801, 0x4400 };
int main()
{
   unsigned int FinalCRC;
   int initialCRC = 0x00;
   char *String = "123456789";
   FinalCRC = CRCfor16(initialCRC,String,9);
   printf("CRC: 0x%x",FinalCRC);
         return 0;
}
unsigned int CRCfor16(int initialCRC, char *String, int length)
  {
   unsigned int CRCVALUE =initialCRC ;
   int temp;
   int i;
   for(i=0;i<length;i++)
   {
      //checksum for lower 4 bits
```

```
    temp = CRCLookupTable[CRCVALUE & 0xF];
    CRCVALUE = (CRCVALUE >> 4) & 0x0FFF;
    CRCVALUE = CRCVALUE ^ temp ^ CRCLookupTable[*String & 0xF];

    //checksum for upper 4 bits
    temp = CRCLookupTable[CRCVALUE & 0xF];
    CRCVALUE = (CRCVALUE >> 4) & 0x0FFF;
   CRCVALUE = CRCVALUE ^ temp ^ CRCLookupTable[(*String >> 4) & 0xF];
    String++;
  }

  return(CRCVALUE);
}
```

Listing 3.8 shows the implementation of CRC-32 algorithm.

Listing 3.8 crc32.c

```
#include <stdio.h>
#include <string.h>
unsigned long CRCTable[256];

unsigned long Update(unsigned long ref, char ch)
{
  unsigned long value=0;
          int i;
  // Swap bit 0 for bit 7, bit 1 for bit 6, etc.
  for(i = 1; i < (ch + 1); i++)
  {
    if ref & 1)
       value |= 1 << (ch - i);
    ref >>= 1;
  }
  return value;
}

void CRC32LookupTable()
{
  unsigned long Polynomial = 0x04c11db7;
          int i,j;
  // 256 values representing ASCII character codes.
  for(i = 0; i <= 255; i++)
```

```
    {
        CRCTable[i]=Update(i, 8) << 24;
        for (j = 0; j < 8; j++)
        CRCTable[i] = (CRCTable[i] << 1) ^ (CRCTable[i] & (1 << 31) ?
Polynomial : 0);
        CRCTable[i] = Update(CRCTable[i], 32);
    }
}

int Calculate_CRC(char *Data, int length)
{
    unsigned long  CRC=0xffffffff;  // Initial remainder(CRC Value)
    while(length—)
        CRC = (CRC >> 8) ^ CRCTable[(CRC & 0xFF) ^ *Data++];
    // Exclusive OR the result with the initial remainder value.
    return CRC^0xffffffff;      // Final XOR Value
}

int  main()
{
    int CRCFinal;
    char *String="123456789";
    CRC32LookupTable();
    CRCFinal=Calculate_CRC(String,9);
    printf("0x%x",CRCFinal);
        return 0;
}
```

In Brief...

Cyclic Redundancy Check (CRC) calculations are used in data communication as well as for memory checking. CRC-16, CRC-32 and CRC-CCITT are the three standard algorithms for calculating the CRC.

Note that there are two ways of implementing the CRC. You can use a lookup table for the CRC values or you can calculate in the program itself. To save computation time, you can use the lookup table approach. To save memory, you can use the calculation method.

3.4 Memory Management

In embedded system software development, you may need to allocate memory. The memory allocation programming is a must if you are writing your own operating system kernel. However, you need to use the memory management functions with care.

The function calls **malloc()** and **free()** are used to allocate memory and free the memory. Listing 3.9 shows the use of these function calls.

Listing 3.9: memalloc.c

```
#include <stdio.h>
int main(){
   char *buffer;
   buffer = (char *) malloc(1024);
   if(buffer != NULL)
      sprintf(buffer,"Hello World \n");
   printf("%s",buffer);
   free(buffer);
}
```

In this program, you are allocating a memory block of 1024 bytes and writing a string into the memory.

You need to be very careful while allocating memory. Memory allocated and not freed is bad programming. Writing beyond the allocated size creates major problems.

3.5 Timing of Programs

To measure the time taken to execute a portion of a program is important for embedded software development. This is useful while carrying out simulation studies of algorithms to be implemented on the embedded system. In addition, the timing analysis gives valuable information as to which portions of the code are taking longer time, so that those portions can be written in assembly language, if required, to improve the speed.

In C language, the functions time() and clock() are used to measure the time taken by the program segments. We will illustrate the use of these functions through two examples. Listing 3.10 shows the use of time() function.

Listing 3.10: ttiming.c

```
#include <stdio.h>
#include <stdlib.h>
#include <time.h>
#include <math.h>
int main()
{
  int i;
  double j,l;
  time_t t0,t1;
  t0=time(NULL);
  printf("Time at Start %ld \n",t0);
```

```
   printf("Calculations......\n");
   for(i=0;i<100000000;i++){
   j=sqrt(2.0*i);
   l=1.0/j;
   l=l+j;
   }
   t1=time(NULL);
   printf("Time  at  the  End  %ld  \n",t1);
   printf("Elapsed  time  %ld\n",(t1-t0));
   return  0;
}
```

Here are the important aspects of this program:

- You need to include the file time.h
- Time_t is a structure which stores the time in number of seconds that elapsed since 00:00:00 hours of GMT on 1st January 1970. The significance of this time and date is that Unix was born at time.
- Just before doing some heavy computation, you need to call the time() function which returns the time in seconds since the birth of Unix.
- Then do some computation—here we did square root calculation and took the inverse of it in a loop.
- After the computation, again call the time function—it returns the seconds elapsed since the birth of Unix.
- Now calculate the difference in the times, that is the time taken for the computation.

You can compile the program using the command:

```
$gcc  -ottiming  ttiming.c  -lm
```

You can execute the program using the command:

```
$time  ./ttiming
```

The output will be as shown below:

Time at Start 1061968846

Calculations.....

Time at the End 1061968898

Elapsed time 52

real 0m52.3565

user 0m52.3505

sys 0m0.005

You can compare the CPU time obtained through the time function and the time command of the shell. They will be approximately same.

The program, given in Listing 3.11, illustrates the clock() function call. Note that clock does not give the time in seconds, but in clock ticks. The number of ticks in a second is obtained using the parameter CLOCKS_PER_SEC.

Listing 3.11 ctiming.c

```
#include <stdio.h>
#include <stdlib.h>
#include <time.h>
#include <math.h>
int main()
{
   int i;
   double j,l;
   clock_t t0,t1;
   t0=clock();
   printf("Time at Start %ld \n",t0);
   printf("Calculations.......\n");
   for(i=0;i<100000000;i++){
   j=sqrt(2.0*i);
   l=1.0/j;
   l=l+j;
   }
   t1=clock();
   printf("Time at the End %ld \n",t1);
   printf("No of clocks %ld\n",(t1 - t0));
   printf("Elapsed time %ld\n",(t1-t0)/CLOCKS_PER_SEC);
   return 0;
}
```

Important aspects of this program:

- The clock_t returns the value in integer, not long int.
- Call the clock() function just before the computation
- Call the clock() function after the computation
- Calculate the difference in the return values and then divide by CLOCKS_PER_SEC to obtain the number of seconds for doing the computation.

You can compile the program using the command:

```
$gcc -octiming ctiming.c -lm
```

And then, execute the program using the command:

```
$time ./ctiming
```

The output will be as follows:

Time at Start 0

Calculations.....

In Brief...

To find out the time required to execute segments of program is very important in embedded software development. The function calls time() and clock() can be used to find the execution time of segments of code.

Time at the End 64880000

No. of clocks 64880000

Elapsed time 64

real 1m4.8855

user 1m4.8805

sys 0m0.0005

The timings obtained from the clock function and the shell command time will be approximately the same.

3.6 Device Drivers

In Unix/Linux, each device is considered a file. The directory /dev contains one entry for each file. When you do serial communication programming, you need to find out the corresponding entry. Two special files are:

- /dev/console for system console on which all error/log messages will be displayed.
- /dev/null which is a null device—output written to this device is discarded. It is like a dustbin for the Unix.

Device drivers are low-level interfaces to control the system hardware. The system calls open, read, write, close are used to access the device drivers. Each file will have a file descriptor in Unix. The standard file descriptors are:

0 for stdin (the keyboard)

1 for stdout (the monitor)

2 for stderr (the monitor)

The program given in Listing 3.12 illustrates the use of reading from stdin and writing to stdout using system calls.

Listing 3.12: syscall.c

```
#include <unistd.h>
#include <stdlib.h>

int main(){
   char letters[50];
   int input;
   input = read(0, letters, 50);
   write(1, letters, input);
   exit(0);
}
```

This program uses two system calls `read()` and `write()`. The system call read() will read from the stdin which has a file descriptor of 0. The system call write() will write to the stdout which has a file descriptor of 1.

Instead of reading from and writing to stdin and stdout, you can read data from a file or write data to a file as illustrated in Listing 3.13.

Listing 3.13: fileops.c

```
#include <unistd.h>
#include <fcntl.h>
#include <stdlib.h>
int main(){
    char c;
    int fin,fout;
    fin = open("inputfile",O_RDONLY);
    fout = open("outfile",O_WRONLY);
    while(read(fin,&c,1) == 1)
        write(fout,&c,1);
    exit(0);
}
```

The standard I/O library provided by Unix/Linux consists of a number of function calls such as fopen, fclose, fread, fwrite, fseek, fgetc, getc, getchar, fputc, putc, putchar, fgets, gets, printf, fprintf, sprintf, scanf, fscanf, sscanf. These functions facilitate input/output operations for different data types using formatted and unformatted input/output.

The program given in Listing 3.14 illustrates the use of reading from a file and writing to a file. Note that code related to error checking is not included here. If the file from which you have to read the data is not available, you need to write additional code to print an error message.

Listing 3.14: readwrite.c

```
#include <stdio.h>
#include <stdlib.h>

int main(){
    int c;
    FILE *fpin, *fpout;
    fpin = fopen("inputfile","r");
    fpout = fopen("outputfile","w");
    while((c=fgetc(fpin)) != EOF)
        fputc(c,fpout);
    fclose(fpin);
    fclose(fpout);
}
```

In Brief...

In Unix/Linux, each device is considered as a file, with an entry in /dev directory.

Notes...

Devices are categorized as character devices and block devices. Serial port is a character device. Hard disk is a block device. The category of a device is decided by the way it transfers the data-whether character by character or block by block.

3.6.1 Tools for Device Driver Development

Writing device drivers used to be a Herculean task due to the complexity involved in accessing the hardware. Here are the reasons:

- Device driver software is not portable. You need to write device drivers for each operating system separately.
- You need to know the system calls of each operating system to write the device driver.
- You need to learn the details of the hardware for writing the device driver.

Things have changed recently. With the introduction of embedded C extensions to ANSI C, this will become much more easier in future resulting in portability of device driver software.

Device driver wizards are available using which you can easily build the device drivers. Most of the operating system vendors also provide the Device Driver Kits (DDKs) to facilitate easy development. These kits consist of header files, library routines, and sample code using which you can write the code for your specific requirement. DDKs are available for Windows NT, Solaris, Linux as well as most of the embedded/real-time operating systems.

In Brief...

Device Driver wizards help in fast development of device drivers. The device driver kits of commercial operating systems also facilitate easy development of device drivers.

Some of the device driver wizards which help in fast device driver development are:

- QNX's DDK for graphics, input, printer, networking cards and USB is available from http:qdn.qnx.com/ddks.
- Bsquare's WinDK provides the drivers for Windows 98/ME/CE/2000/NT, Linux, Solaris, VxWorks etc.
- Jungo's WinDriver provides a 30-day trial version for device driver development. It can be downloaded from www.jungo.com/dnload.html.

3.7 Productivity Tools

Unix/Linux provides a number of tools that increase your productivity. These tools are very important for developing software systematically. In this section, we will discuss the most important tools.

3.7.1 Makefile

When a number of people are working on a project, each person will work on a module and then all the modules are combined into a single software package. Even if you are working alone on a project, you may like to write the code by splitting into different files. Makefile is an excellent utility to combine different project files and create the executable file. We will illustrate the use of makefile through an example. To start with, create a number of files as given below:

Listing 3.15: makefile

```
helloworld: main.o hello.o world.o
    gcc -o helloworld main.o hello.o world.o

main.o: main.c
    gcc -c main.c

hello.o: hello.c hello.h
    gcc -c hello.c

world.o: world.c world.h
    gcc -c world.c
```

Listing 3.16: hello.h

```
char str1[] = { 'H','e','l','l','o','\0'};
```

Listing 3.17: hello.c

```
#include"hello.h"
char* fun1()
{
    return &str1[0];
}
/*int main()
{
    printf("%s",fun1());
    return 0;
}*/
```

Listing 3.18 world.h

```
char str2[] = { 'w','o','r','l','d','\0'};
```

Listing 3.19: world.c

```
#include "world.h"
char* fun2()
{
    return &str2[0];
}

char str2[] = { 'w','o','r','l','d','\0'};
/*char* fun2()
```

```
{
   return &str2[0];
}*/
```

Listing 3.20: main.c

```
extern char* fun1();
extern char* fun2();
int main()
{
   printf("%s %s",fun1(),fun2());
   return 0;
}
```

There is one file containing the main() function, two files containing two functions—fun1() and fun2(), and two header files. The makefile is a file that describes the rules for creating the object files and the interdependencies of these files. You can execute the makefile by giving the command:

```
$make
```

The system will display the following lines:

```
gcc -c main.c
gcc -c hello.c
gcc -c world.c
gcc -o helloworld main.o hello.o world.o
```

If you modify a file, say main.c, you can give the command:

```
$touch hello.h
```

Next time when you invoke the make command, the compilation will be done using the latest main.c.

If you create a file with a name different from 'makefile', you need to give the command:

```
$make -f filename
```

makefile has a large number of options which can be obtained from the online manual pages.

3.7.2 Debugger

The utility "gdb" is the most widely used debugger for embedded systems. You need to write a program which has some bugs and then you can try to debug using the gdb (How difficult it is to write a program which has bugs!). To use the debugger, you need to give the compilation command with the following options:

```
$gcc -g -o lousyprog lousyprog.c
```

You can invoke gdb using the command

```
$gdb lousyprog
```

The promp (gdb) will be displayed. You can give a number of debugger commands as listed below:

(gdb) help	(to obtain help)
(gdb) run	(to run the program)
(gdb) print i	(to print contents of variable i)
(gdb)list	(to see program listing)
(gdb) break 20	(to set breakpoint at line 20)
(gdb) cont	(to continue)

gdb is used extensively in embedded systems. You can connect the target system to the host system using an RS232 link. If the RS232 port on the host system is specified by /dev/tty01, the command for debugging a program "myprogram" is

```
$gdbserver  /dev/tty01  /usr/prasad/myporgram
(gdb)  target  remote  /dev/tty001
```

3.7.3 Profiler

While developing embedded software on the host system, you need to check how much time it takes to execute some of the functions/modules. This information is required to find out the time-consuming functions so that either you can optimize the code or you can write computationally intensive portions of the code in assembly language for faster execution.

The command "gprof" gives the timing of different functions. To obtain the timings, you need to compile the program with profiling option as below:

```
$gcc  -pg  -oprogram  program.c
```

Now you can run the program using the command:

```
$./program
```

A file with the name gmon.out is created.

The output will display the time taken by various functions. You can analyze the timings to find out which portions of the code are taking longer time.

In Brief...

In Unix operating system, the profiler command "gprof" is used to find the execution time taken by different functions.

3.7.4 Indenting

When you write lengthy programs, indenting the code increases the readability and hence maintainability of the code. The shell command "indent" provides the automatic indenting feature:

To indent a C program, say hello.c, the shell command is

```
$indent hello.c
```

The following options are available:

-bad	blank lines after indentation
-bap	blank line after each function/procedure body
-bbb	blank line before boxed comments

-sob	remove unnecessary blank lines in the source code
-bl	braces after if line
-bli	brace indent
-bls	braces after structure declaration line
-br	braces on if line
-nbbo	break after Boolean operator
-bbo	break before Boolean operator
-clin	case indentation
-cn	comment indentation
-nsc	do not star comments

In Brief...

Indenting of programs increases the readability and hence maintainability of the code.

3.7.5 Revision Control

Software engineers develop different versions of a program. Every time a program is revised, it is a good practice to record what changes have been made. Also, when many persons are working on a project, only one person should be able to modify the file at a time. To control the revisions to the source files (they can be C/C++ programs or text documents), Source Code Control System (SCCS) and Revision Control System (RCS) are used extensively in Unix/Linux. We will illustrate the use of RCS using a simple example.

Suppose you created a text file called "schedule" with the following lines:

```
10 am   meeting
11 am   lecture
12 noon lunch
2 pm    sleep
```

You need to give control of this file to RCS so that whenever you make changes, the system will force you to add the necessary comments.

When you give the following command, RCS will take control over the file:

$rcs –i schedule

The following message will be displayed, giving a prompt to enter description. You can enter the description as "My schedule for the day" as shown below:

```
RCS file: schedule,v
Enter description, terminated with single '.' Or end of file:
NOTE: This is NOT the log message!
>My schedule for the day
>.
done
```

$

When you see the directory listing, you will find that a new file with ,v (comma v) will be created:

$ls –l

You need to "check-in" the file to give a version number to your file, using the command (note that the message displayed by the system is also shown below):

$ci schedule

schedule,v ← schedule

initial version: 1.1

done

$

Now you can verify that the original file 'schedule' is removed by using the command

$ls –l

To change the file, we must check-out using the command:

$co –l schedule

schedule,v — schedule

revision 1.1 (locked)

done

$

The file is locked so that others cannot modify it.

Now, you can see that the file "schedule" reappears by giving the command:

$ls –l

Now you can make modifications to the file 'schedule'. You replace 'sleep' by 'seminar on Linux'

Now, you need to check-in the file using the command:

$ci schedule

The system will prompt you to add a log message. You can type "changed the schedule at 2 pm" and enter dot on the next line as shown below:

Enter log message

>>changed the schedule at 2 pm

>>.

done

$

Now, again the file disappears, as you can see by giving the command:

$ls –l

To see the summary of the changes, you can give the command:

$rlog schedule

The complete log information will be displayed including the summary of changes made.

To obtain the first revision of the file back, give the command:

$co –r1.1 schedule

To specify the version number as version 2.1, while checking-in, you can give the command:

$ci –r2 schedule

You can find out the difference between two versions of the file by giving the command:

```
$rcsdiff –r1.1 –r1.2 schedule
RCS file: schedule,v
Retrieving version 1.1
Retrieving version 1.2
Diff –r1.1 –r1.2
4c4
< 2 pm sleep
> 2 pm Seminar on Linux
```

In Brief...

For software engineers, it is very important to keep track of the various revisions/versions of the code. Revision Control System (RCS) is an excellent tool for revision/version control of the code.

3.8 Code Optimization

In embedded software development, the two important considerations are speed of execution and memory requirement for the software. Writing the code in assembly language increases speed of execution and also results in optimal code. However, maintaining the code written in assembly language is difficult. Hence, the code is generally written in a high level language such as C or C++ and then some portions of the code, which take lot of execution time, are written in assembly. Even while writing the code in a high-level language, code optimization can be done to make the execution faster. Some important code optimization guidelines are given below:

- **Eliminate dead code:** Dead code is that portion of the code which will not be executed at all. Novice programmers include such code. Examples of dead code are: declaration and initialization of variable that will not be used at all, use of functions that will not be called at all etc. Profilers help in elimination of dead code.
- **Remove unnecessary debugging code:** Lot of code is written during development time for debugging purposes. Unnecessary debugging code needs to be removed. However, note that some debugging code may need to be left out in the final software that helps in debugging the system in the field.
- **Avoid recursion:** Recursive functions require a large stack resulting in higher memory requirement. For example, instead of using recursion for calculating a factorial of a number, a better approach is to use a lookup table that will pick up the factorial.
- **Avoid floating-point operations:** If necessary, floating-point operations can be converted into fixed point operations.

- **Use unsigned integers:** Use unsigned integer variables wherever possible.
- **Avoid large library routines:** To the extent possible, large library routines need to be avoided.
- **Remove loop-invariant code:** The code that has no effect on the loop counter is called the loop-invariant code. Consider the example:

```
for  (i=0;  i  <  10;  ++i)
{
    x=  1.0/b;
    y  =  x  +  i;
}
```

In Brief...

Elimination of dead code, avoiding recursion, avoiding floating-point operations to the possible extent, avoiding large library routines and removal of loop-invariant statements are some of the important guidelines for code optimization.

In this code, the statement x=1.0/b; is loop-invariant because the value of x is not dependent on the value of i. Hence, this statement can appear above the beginning of the for loop. Otherwise, the value of x is calculated every time resulting in unnecessary execution of a statement.

- **Use the correct optimization level of the compiler:** The compiler has an in-built optimizer. Generally the compilers provide different optimization levels—level 0 to level 3. Level 3 offers the highest optimization. Based on the need, the optimization level can be set.

3.9 C Coding Guidelines

Every software engineer has his own idiosyncracies that are reflected in the code developed by him/her. Cryptic filenames, irrelevant variable names, lack of proper commenting etc. make the code difficult to read, understand and maintain. All the project team members need to follow some guidelines while doing the coding. Every organization should have a document called 'coding standards' for each programming language. Every engineer needs to follow these guidelines. The guidelines specify simple rules to be followed by all the engineers. Some important guidelines are given below:

- For every project, a folder should be maintained that contains all the source code files. The folder name should be the name of the project. This folder should have a readme file that gives the list of files and the contents of the file.
- The backup of the project folder should be taken everyday so that at most one day's work only is lost in case there is a major system failure.
- The filenames should reflect the functionality of the source code given in that file.
- Every file should contain a header which gives the copyright information, name of the file, author of the code and revision history.

```
/*  Copyright  Dr.  Prasad,  2003  */
/*  Name  of  the  author:  Dr.  Prasad  */
/*  This  is  a  header  file  containing  global  constants  */
```

```
/* Version 1.0 */
```

- Identifiers such as variables, structure/union members, functions and macros should have meaningful names. ANSI C supports up to 32 characters for these names and hence the identifier name should reflect the functionality. However, temporary variables such as loop counters can be given names such as i, j, k etc. Strings can have a prefix of s, character names can have a prefix of s and pointers can have a prefix of p.
- On-line documentation (comments) should be relevant. A good commenting style is to have the comment in the same line as the code:

```
int max_temperature = 50; /* threshold on temperature is 50 degrees C */
```

- Constants and macros should always be in upper case.

```
#define PI 3.1415
```

- Proper indentation helps readability and understandability of the code. Simple rules that are followed in normal typing need to be followed while coding as well. Comma (,) and semi-colon (;) need to be followed by a single space. There should be no space between the unary operator and the operand. For binary operators, the operator should have a space before and after. The following code snippets demonstrate these indentation guidelines.

```
-b not - b (unary operator)

a = 0    not a=0 or a =0 or a= 0  (binary operator)

if (d > 0) {
        root = sqrt(d);
}



if (d > 0 {
        root1 = -2 * a / d ;
        root2 = 2 * a/d ;
}

else {
printf("No root\n");
}

do {

statements;

} while ( x > 0);
```

You can use the gindent (GNU indent) for indentation.

- Whenever changes are made to a source file, modify the header indicating the date of modification and why the modification has been done

/* Revision history */

/* Date: 17 July 2003 max_temperature initialization value changed to 55 as per client requirement */

In Brief...

In every organization, coding standards need to be developed and all the engineers have to follow these standards. This will help in efficient maintenance of the software.

- It is advisable to use the source code configuration software (sccs or rcs, Clearcase or any other equivalent software) if there are a large number of source code files to be maintained.
- During the course of development, the code written by one engineer should be given to another engineer who has to check whether the coding guidelines are being followed or not.

3.10 Programming in C++

As compared to function-oriented languages such as C, object-oriented languages have many advantages. The main advantage is that the problem can be defined using real-life objects. Secondly, the object-oriented languages facilitate reuse. We can develop software components (just like hardware components) and reuse them in different applications. In embedded systems, the overhead of object-oriented languages is slightly higher—in terms of memory requirements. However, due to reduced cost of memory devices, this is no longer a major issue. Hence, C++ and Java are now becoming very important languages for embedded software development.

Embedded operating systems such as Embedded NT, Windows XP Embedded and Windows CE support Win32 applications. Hence, it is very easy to port software developed on desktop computers onto embedded platforms. Microsoft's eMbedded Visual tools can be used to develop applications for handheld computers. Due to the availability of a large pool of developers in Visual Studio environment, embedded software development using Visual Studio is catching up. In this book, we will develop a few projects using VC++.

3.11 Programming in Java

The main attraction of Java programming language is its platform independence. Presently, Java is the most preferred language for development of Internet applications. Its use for developing mobile applications is catching up. The Java applets can be downloaded from a server on to a mobile device and executed on the mobile device. Java language is likely to play a prominent role even for embedded software development with the development of small footprint Java Virtual Machines.

The application developed in Java is converted into bytecode using a Java compiler. This bytecode is independent of the platform. If a Java Virtual Machine (JVM) is running on a machine, the JVM will interpret the bytecode and produce the output. This platform-independent application development is shown in Fig. 3.1.

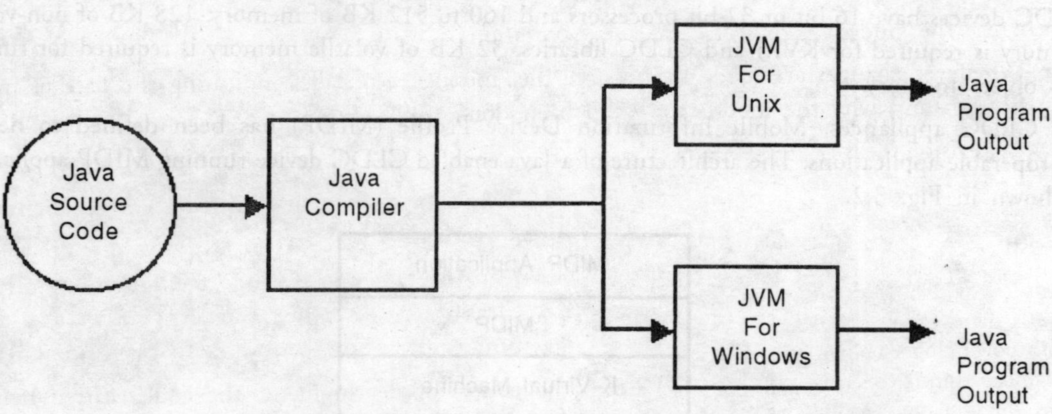

Fig. 3.1: Achieving Platform Independence through Java

To facilitate development of applications for different market segments, Sun Microsystems released three editions of Java. These are:

- Java 2 Enterprise Edition (J2EE) for server market
- Java 2 Standard Edition (J2SE) for desktop market
- Java 2 Micro Edition (J2ME) for consumer appliances and embedded devices market.

3.11.1 Java 2 Micro Edition (J2ME)

J2ME addresses two types of configurations based on the capabilities of the devices:

- Connected Device Configuration (CDC)
- Connected, Limited Device Configuration (CLDC)

Devices such as set top boxes, Internet TVs, Communicators are CDC devices. These devices can be connected to high-speed data networks. They run TCP/IP protocol stack and have high processing power and large memory in the range of 2 to 16 MB. Developing applications for these devices is not much different from developing applications for desktop computers.

Devices such as mobile phones, pagers, Personal Digital Assistants (PDAs) are called CLDC devices. These devices are connected to low-speed networks such as the wireless networks. These devices do not run TCP/IP protocol stack, have low processing power and small memory capacity of the order of 128 KB to 512 KB. Running Java applications for CLDC devices is a challenging task due to the limited capabilities of these devices. To facilitate development of applications that can run on these devices, CLDC devices contain Kilobytes Virtual Machine (KVM) which requires very little memory—just 40 to 80 KB of memory. To run Java applications on CLDC devices, the total memory requirement is about 128 KB for KVM, the class libraries and the application. For large applications, the memory requirement is about 256 KB. Out of which 40 to 80 KB is for KVM and the rest is for class libraries and application.

In Brief...

Connected Device Configuration (CDC) is for devices which have memory up to 16 MB, run TCP/IP protocol stack and get connected to high-speed networks. Devices such as Set Top Boxes and Internet TVs belong to this category.

CLDC devices have 16-bit or 32-bit processors and 160 to 512 KB of memory. 128 KB of non-volatile memory is required for KVM and CLDC libraries. 32 KB of volatile memory is required for runtime and object memory.

For CLDC appliances, Mobile Information Device Profile (MIDP) has been defined to develop interoperable applications. The architecture of a Java-enabled CLDC device running MIDP applications is shown in Fig. 3.2.

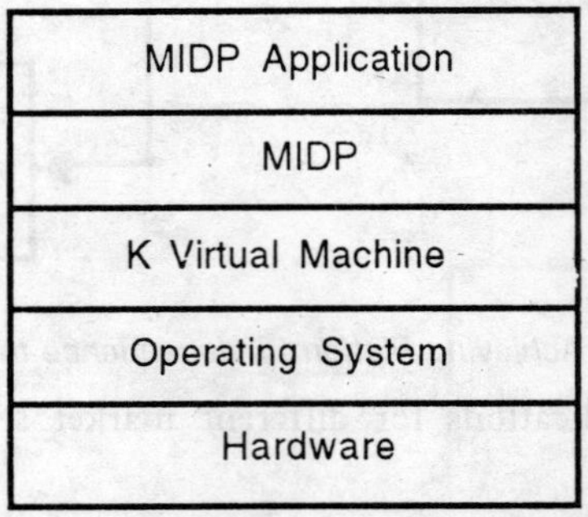

Fig. 3.2: Architecture of Java-enabled CLDC Device

If you know Java, writing CLDC applications is very easy. However, the following restrictions need to be kept in mind:

- There is no floating-point support as the hardware does not support floating-point operations. Hence, floating-point literals, types, values and operations are not allowed.
- Object.finalize() method is not available for finalization of class instances.
- There is limited error handling capability. CLDC libraries support exception handling but their capability is restricted because errors are handled in a hardware-dependent manner. Only java.lang.Error, java.lang.VirtualMachineError and java.lang.OutOfMemoryError classes are supported.
- The following features are removed:
    - o Java Native Interface
    - o User-defined class loaders: Available only as a built-in class loader, which cannot be overridden.
    - o Reflection: Java programs cannot inspect contents of classes, objects, methods, fields, threads, the execution stack, and the runtime status inside the virtual machine.
    - o Thread groups: multithreading is supported but starting and stopping of threads is applied only to individual threads.

In Brief ..

Connected Limited Device Configuration (CLDC) is for devices which have limited memory up to 512 KB and get connected to low-speed networks. Mobile phones and pagers belong to this category.

The process of developing MIDlets (applications for Mobile Information Devices) is shown in Fig. 3.3. The Java source files are compiled into .class files, which are pre-verified and converted into packages to form MIDlet suites. The MIDlet suite is run on the emulator to test its functionality and is subsequently ported to the actual mobile device.

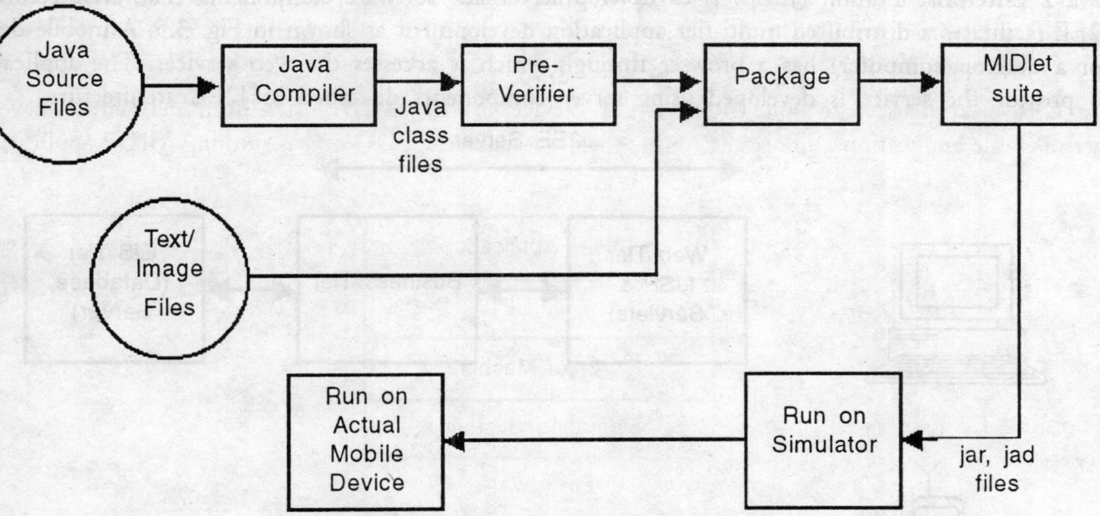

Fig. 3.3 MIDlet Development Process

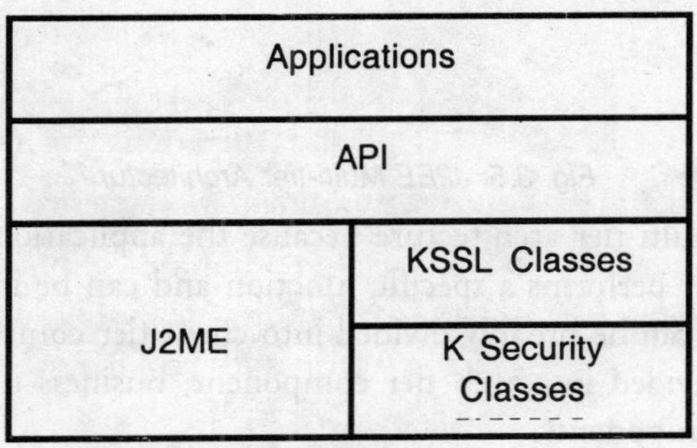

Fig. 3.4: Securing Applications for MIDP in J2ME

In Brief...

To develop applications for devices belonging to CLDC, Mobile Information Device Profile (MIDP) has been standardized.

When a mobile device accesses the application on the Internet, security is an issue. To incorporate security for MIDP in the J2ME environment, the architecture shown in Fig. 3.4 is used. A set of K Security classes and KSSL (K Secure Socket Layer) classes are available for KVM with which the developer can develop secure applications. Note that the Secure Socket Layer (SSL) runs above the TCP in the TCP/IP networks to provide authentication and encryption services.

3.11.2 Server-Side Programming

When you develop applications for mobile devices, the mobile device obtains the information from the Internet server or the Intranet server. The server-side components retrieve the information required by the client and send it in a pre-specified format such as HTML or XHTML code or Java applets.

Java 2 Enterprise Edition (J2EE) is to develop server-side software components. The architecture of J2EE facilitates a distributed multi-tier application development as shown in Fig. 3.5. A mobile device (or a desktop computer) has a browser through which it accesses the web services. The application to provide the service is developed using server components described in J2EE architecture.

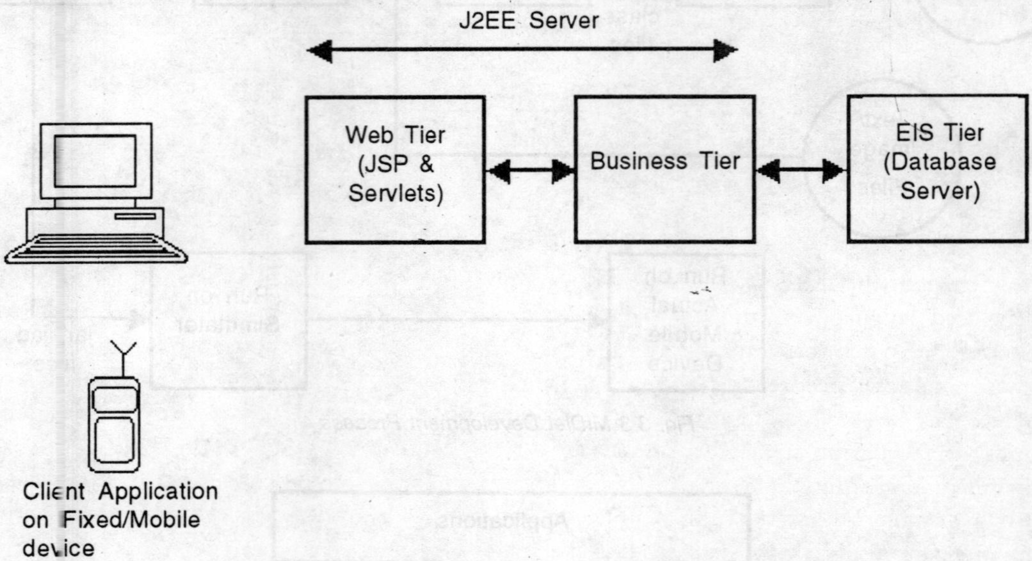

Fig. 3.5: J2EE Multi-tier Architecture

The J2EE architecture is a multi-tier architecture because the application logic is divided into different components. Each component performs a specific function and can be installed on a different machine if desired. These components can be broadly divided into client tier components and seven components. Seven components are sub-divided into web tier component, business tier components and Enterprise information services ties Components.

- Client tier components run on the client machine, such as a desktop computer or a mobile phone.
- Web tier components run on the J2EE server. The web tier consists of components written in JSP (Java Server Pages) or Servlets.
- Business Tier components also run on the J2EE server and consist of Enterprise JavaBeans.
- Enterprise Information Services (EIS) tier components run on the EIS Server. This tier can contain legacy databases from which data has to be retrieved.

In Brief...

Java 2 Enterprise Edition (J2EE) supports multi-tier architecture. Client tier components run on the desktop/mobile device; web tier components and business tier components run on J2EE server; and EIS tier components run on EIS server.

This division into tiers enables a modular design of enterprise applications. Depending on your application requirements, you can also have a three-tier architecture—client, J2EE server and legacy database machines. Alternatively, you need not have an EIS tier, the database can run on the J2EE server itself.

3.11.3 Java Development Tools

In addition to Sun Microsystems' development tools, you can also make use of the following tools:

- GNU Java compiler "gcj". gcj can be obtained from gcc.gnu.org/java. The necessary class libraries and JVM can be obtained from ftp://sourceware.cygnus.com/pub/java.
- Jboss is the open source Java Development products suite. It provides services similar to J2EE. The details can be obtained from www.Jboss.org

We will study the development of mobile applications using J2ME in Chapter 16.

Summary

In this chapter, the intricacies of system programming are discussed. As C continues to be the most widely used language in embedded software development, the important features of ANSI C are presented and system programming using C is demonstrated through illustrative examples. Embedded software engineers need to do programming at bit-level and hence the bit manipulation using C language has been discussed in detail. File input/output operations, device driver development and memory management are also discussed. Important development tools such as debuggers, profilers, code indentation utility and revision control system are discussed. Embedded software developers need to use the profilers to estimate the algorithmic complexity and to optimize the code. Code optimization techniques are also covered. For an effective maintenance of the code, the coding guidelines to be followed are also presented.

A brief overview of Java programming language is given with reference to embedded software development. Java will play a major role in embedded software development due to its platform independence.

Questions

1. What are the special features of ANSI C?
2. What extensions are provided in C language for embedded software development?
3. What is code optimization?
4. Discuss the need and disadvantage of using malloc() function in embedded software development.
5. What is the most attractive feature of Java?
6. Explain the process of creating a MIDlet.

Exercises

1. Write a program that will take the filename as input and calculate the CRC using the CRC-16 for the data in the file. When a file is transferred to an embedded system, this program can be used to check whether the file is transferred correctly.
2. Write a program to calculate the CRC using CRC-CCITT algorithm.

3. Write a C program to transfer a file from one PC to another PC using RS 232 link.
4. Write a C program to count the number of characters in a file.
5. An embedded system sends data (one character) every 20 seconds to a PC through an RS 232 link. Write a C program on the PC that receives the data and transfers it to a file. After every 3 minutes, the data has to be logged into a new file.
6. Write a C program in Linux that displays a character every 10 seconds. Check whether the timing is correctly maintained using a time function.
7. Write a C program which generates packets of 32 bits. The first bit of the packet indicates whether the packet is a control packet or a data packet. You need to set the first bit to 0 to indicate that it is control packet and to 1 to indicate that it is data packet.
8. Write a C program that takes a filename as input and generates packets of 100 bytes. Develop a simple packet format of your own.

Chapter 4

The Process of Embedded System Development

CHAPTER OBJECTIVES

After reading this chapter, you will be able to:

- Appreciate the need for a systematic approach to embedded system development
- Understand the complete process of embedded system development
- Learn about the activities to be performed during each stage of the development
- Appreciate the issues involved in project management
- Know about the major fiascos in embedded system projects, which provide important lessons for developers

Embedded system development is much more challenging than application software development. It involves both hardware development and software development. Integrating the hardware and software, and then testing the embedded system are much more complex than testing an application software package. Due to these reasons, a very systematic approach to embedded system development is a must. In this chapter, we will discuss the process of embedded system development in detail. We will also study the issues related to managing embedded system projects. We will analyze some major embedded system projects that failed so that we can learn from history and do not make similar mistakes.

4.1 The Development Process

The goal of every designer should be to develop a quality product. In descriptive terms, the quality of a product is reflected in its meeting all the customer requirements—functional requirements, performance requirements and reliability requirements. To deliver quality product, a systematic approach to the development is a must. This systematic approach is reflected in defining a "process" for the development. Process is essentially a detailed step-by-step procedure.

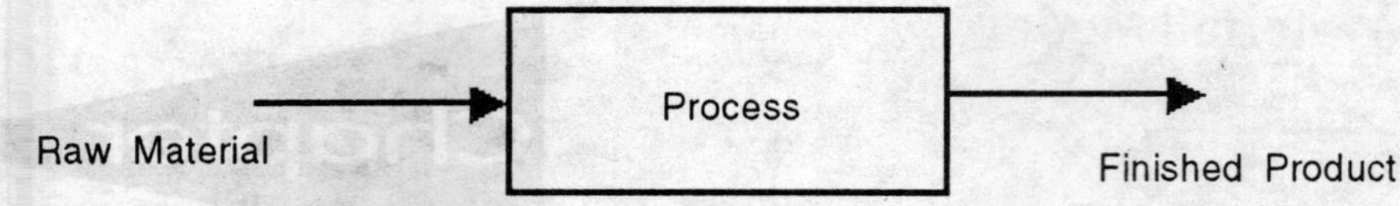

Fig. 4.1: The Process

As shown in Fig. 4.1, 'process' takes the raw material as input and produces the finished product. For example, if a car has to be manufactured, the raw material is the various parts such as the chassis, engine, etc. The finished product is the car. The process is the step-by-step procedure to assemble the various parts and then test the assembled car to check whether it meets all the requirements.

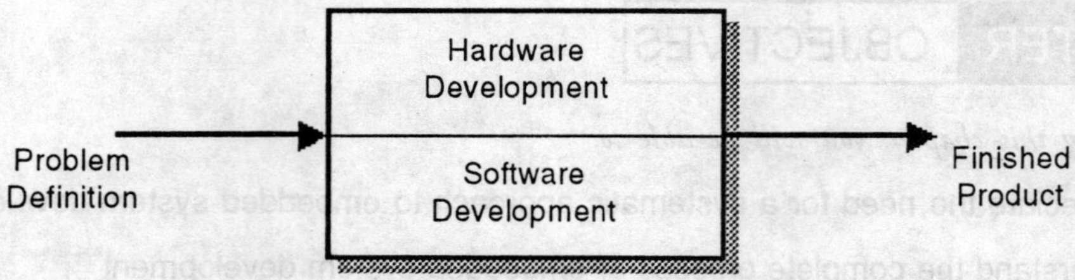

Fig. 4.2: The Embedded System Development Process

As shown in Fig. 4.2, for embedded system development, the development process defines the step-by-step procedure to convert the vague problem definition into a working product. In embedded systems, there are two components—hardware and software. We need to define detailed processes for both hardware and software development.

4.1.1 The Waterfall Model

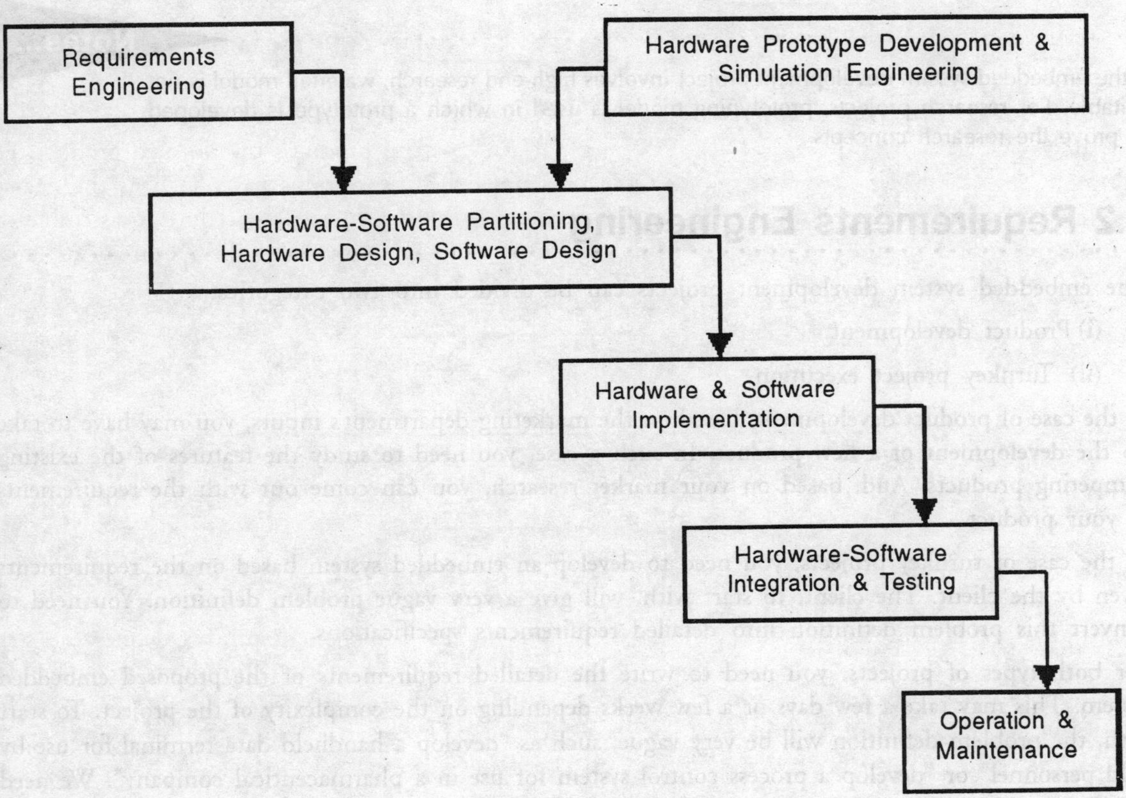

Fig. 4.3: Waterfall Model

In commercial embedded system projects that do not involve very high-end research, the waterfall model is used. In waterfall model, the development process is divided into the following five stages:

- Requirements engineering
- Design which involves hardware-software partitioning, hardware design and software design
- Hardware implementation and software implementation
- Hardware/software integration and testing
- Operation and maintenance

In addition to these stages, as shown in Fig. 4.3, a hardware prototype is developed to prove that the design concepts are OK; and software simulation studies are carried out to test the algorithms used in embedded software. These two activities provide important inputs to the design of the embedded system.

In Brief...

In waterfall model, the development process is divided into five stages viz., requirements engineering, design, implementation, integration and testing, and operation and maintenance. To aid the design phase, a prototype is developed and software simulation is also carried out, if necessary.

The details of each of the five stages of embedded system development process are discussed in the following sections.

Notes...

If the embedded system development project involves high-end research, waterfall model is not suitable. For research projects, prototyping model is used in which a prototype is developed to prove the research concepts.

4.2 Requirements Engineering

The embedded system development projects can be divided into two categories:

(i) Product development

(ii) Turnkey project execution

In the case of product development, based on the marketing department's inputs, you may have to take up the development of a new product. In such a case, you need to study the features of the existing competing products. And, based on your market research, you can come out with the requirements of your product.

In the case of turnkey projects, you need to develop an embedded system based on the requirements given by the client. The client, to start with, will give a very vague problem definition. You need to convert this problem definition into detailed requirements specifications.

For both types of projects, you need to write the detailed requirements of the proposed embedded system. This may take a few days or a few weeks depending on the complexity of the project. To start with, the problem definition will be very vague, such as "develop a handheld data terminal for use by field personnel" or "develop a process control system for use in a pharmaceutical company". We need to convert this problem definition into a detailed requirements document. This process is known as requirements engineering process.

As shown in Fig. 4.4, the requirements engineering process can be divided into three phases: requirements analysis, requirements specifications and requirements validation.

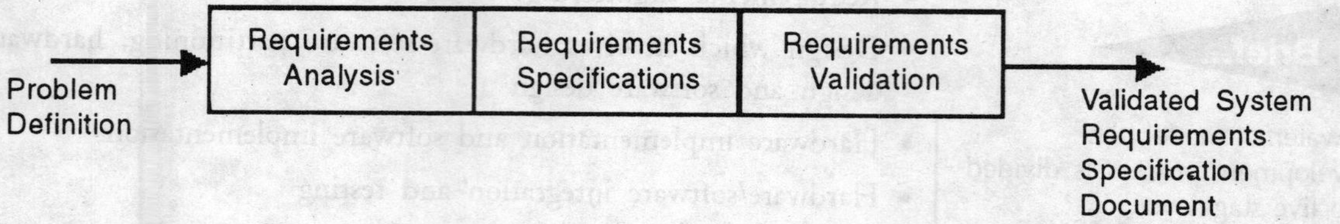

Fig. 4.4: Requirements Engineering Process

In requirements analysis phase, you need to have a series of discussions with the client to obtain the requirements such as

- The inputs to the system
- The outputs of the system

- The processing to be done by the system along with timing restrictions, if any
- Input supply voltage
- The communication interfaces to be provided
- The size of the embedded system (if there are any limitations on the size)
- Operating environment (such as temperature and humidity)
- Standards to be followed. Every industry segment specifies standards. These statutory standards need to be obtained from the client.

It may not be possible to obtain all the requirements in one round of discussion with the client. While carrying out the requirements analysis, you need to obtain enough details so that later on, you will be in a position to do the hardware design and software design. At the end of every round of discussion, the development team has to identify whether more information is required, and if so, go back to the client and discuss further. After a few rounds of discussion, you may be in a position to say that all the requirements of the client are clearly understood.

Once these requirements are obtained, they need to be documented and a document called "System Requirements Specifications" has to be prepared. This document clearly spells out all the information obtained from the client. As this document will be the reference for carrying out the design and subsequently the testing, each and every specification needs to be documented. This document needs to be divided into two parts—one part covering all the functional requirements, i.e. what the system is supposed to do; and the second part covering all the non-functional requirements. The details of non-functional requirements are given below:

Reliability: Always, the goal is to develop a reliable embedded system. However, you need to specify the reliability in quantitative terms. For instance, Mean Time Between Failures (MTBF) is a measure of reliability of a system. MTBF is specified in number of hours, say 49,000 hours. If the system failed 10 times during 1,000 hours of operation, the MTBF value is 100 hours.

Delivery time: The client/marketing department may insist on delivering the product in a specific time. Particularly, in product development, the "Time to Market" is of importance. Many design decisions such as choice of processor, use of an operating system are influenced by the delivery time. You may like to use a new processor that is released into the market, but if it takes a few months to obtain the development tools of that processor, you may decide against using it for your project.

Implementation requirements: The client may indicate the broad requirements for the development environment such as the processor to be used or the embedded/real-time operating system to be used. In such a case, you do not have a choice; you need to stick to that specific processor or operating system.

Standards: To develop the embedded system, you may have to follow national/international standards. For instance, if you are developing a system for data communication, you may have to follow the standards specified by IETF (Internet Engineering Task Force) to implement the protocol stack. If you are developing a wireless LAN system, you need to follow the IEEE standards. To the extent possible, you need to stick to international standards rather than developing proprietary protocols. Similarly, standards such as USB, Ethernet, RS232 need to be followed for communication interfaces.

Debugging of embedded systems is an important issue. The processor manufacturers used to give proprietary interfaces (some pins on the processor) for carrying out debugging. Joint Test Action Group (JTAG) evolved a standard protocol known as JTAG protocol or IEEE 1149.1 protocol for debugging. Nowadays, clients insist on having JTAG support for your embedded system. The Integrated Circuits used in the circuit must be JTAG-compliant, in such a case. JTAG is very useful for testing the embedded systems installed in the field.

The client may also insist on following standards for documentation and coding. In such a case, you need to obtain the relevant standards and follow them during the development life cycle.

Safety requirements: If the embedded system is used in nuclear plants, aircraft, hospitals, military equipment etc., safety regulations have to be met. You need to study the relevant safety standards and incorporate the safety features. The safety regulations include FCC regulations for radio power emission, Electro Magnetic Interference (EMI) regulation, etc.

Security: As the embedded systems are now being networked, providing security features to these systems have become essential. There may be a need to encrypt the data being transmitted by the embedded system. Also, access to an embedded system for remote control needs to be restricted through the use of a username and password. Such security measures need to be built into the system. The development team needs to obtain the security requirements from the client. For example, stringent security measures need to be implemented for financial transactions using smart cards.

The System Requirements Specifications document needs to address all these issues. Though the requirements are documented using data flow diagrams, state transition diagrams etc., the document should explain the requirements in simple and unambiguous English as the client may not be conversant with high-tech representations.

The next phase is requirements validation. This phase is to ensure that the requirements specifications document captures all the requirements of the user and also to ensure that the required embedded system can be designed and developed. You need to discuss with hardware engineers and software engineers to ascertain whether all the specifications could be met. Then you need to submit the document to the client, resolve any differences and obtain the client's approval. Validation ensures that there is no communication gap between the client and the development team.

Note that in many embedded projects, the performance requirements are not clearly defined by the client. For instance, the initial specification may be that a particular task has to be completed within 10 msec., but later on it may be changed to 5 msec. This leads to lot of problems—sometimes the hardware has to be thrown out and the new hardware is designed, just because one performance parameter cannot be met by the previously designed hardware. To avoid such problems, the development team has to focus on the performance parameters and the timing requirements while carrying out requirements engineering. If you are not sure whether a particular specification can be met, the hardware engineers need to study the relevant data sheets of the Integrated Circuits (ICs) to ascertain the timings, the software engineers may have to do simulation studies to study the algorithmic complexity, and the project manager may have to take the opinion of an expert before committing on the performance parameters to the client.

In Brief...

Requirements engineering phase involves: (a) requirements analysis, i.e. obtaining the requirements from the user; (b) requirements specifications, i.e. documenting the requirements; and (c) requirements validation, i.e. ensuring that the document reflects all the requirements specified by the user.

Notes...

System Requirements Specifications are divided into (a) functional requirements; and (b) non-functional requirements. Non-functional requirements include reliability, delivery time, hardware and software platforms to be used, standards to be followed, safety and security requirements.

4.3 Design

The validated system specifications document has to be converted into design. In this phase, the engineers need to carry out a paper design of both hardware and software. To start with, you need to separate out the hardware functionality and the software functionality. This is a complex activity because sometimes, it is difficult to decide whether a particular functionality has to be implemented in hardware or software.

4.3.1 Design Tradeoffs

During designing stage, the design engineers have many options for selection of a processor, an operating system etc. You need to study the various design alternatives keeping in view the design goals. The design goals are:

- To meet all the functional and performance requirements
- To reduce the size and cost of the system to the extent possible
- To reduce the power consumption of the system
- To reduce the development time and effort
- To reduce the maintenance effort and time
- To increase the reliability

While carrying out the design, many a time, you will be in a dilemma. Here are some design tradeoffs that you put you in a dilemma:

- Which processor to use? An 8-bit micro-controller with on-chip memory and peripherals is sufficient to meet all the functional requirements, but you are not sure whether the performance requirements will be met. A 16-bit processor will certainly meet the performance requirements, but the cost and size will go up. Will you take a small 'risk' and go ahead with a micro-controller?
- Is an FPGA required? You can reduce the size of the system by designing an FPGA. In addition to reduction in size, it improves the reliability and reduces the power consumption. However, the cost and time required to do the FPGA design are high, and taking the FPGA path may cause a delay in the project.
- Is it necessary to port an embedded/real-time operating system on the target system? You can write your own kernel if the application is very small. If the application is complex, an operating system is worth it. But if you have to pay royalty for each copy of the OS, your per-system cost will go up.

In Brief...

In addition to meeting the functional and performance requirements, the design goals are: to reduce the cost, size and power consumption; to reduce the development time and effort; to reduce maintenance effort and time as well as to increase the reliability.

There are no simple answers to such questions. Keeping in view the cost and size of the system and the development time, the project manager, in association with the engineers, needs to take a conscious decision. The design process can be divided into hardware-software partitioning or co-design, hardware design and software design.

4.3.2 Co-design

Co-design involves partitioning the design into hardware and software. Sometimes, it is difficult to decide whether functionality has to be implemented in hardware or software. Consider an example: you need to implement Cyclic Redundancy Check (CRC) calculation algorithm. Which is a better choice: hardware or software? Note that CRC calculation involves taking a bit stream, say 1000 bits and calculation of 16 bits or 32 bits based on an algorithm. Hardware implementation results in a fast calculation of CRC as compared to software implementation. However, hardware implementation means an additional IC and hence more space on the board, more power consumption and also inflexibility because a change in the algorithm calls for a change in the entire hardware board. On the other hand, software implementation results in flexibility in changing the algorithm, but it may cause processing delay. Based on your timing requirements and cost/size requirements, you need to take a decision. Hence, decision on implementation in software or hardware needs to be taken keeping in view the following issues:

- **Speed of execution:** If execution time is the most important issue, hardware implementation may be a better choice.
- **Flexibility for making changes:** If flexibility is required then software implementation is a better choice, as it is easier to make changes in the software rather than in the hardware.
- **Size:** If size has to be reduced then software implementation is the choice.
- **Power consumption:** Software implementation does not involve additional components. On the contrary, hardware implementation requires additional ICs and hence more power consumption.
- **Memory:** If the embedded system is constrained for memory, hardware is a better choice.
- **Cost:** Reproduction of hardware is costlier as you need to keep stock of the components. Assembly of the components and testing of every board take time. Software reproduction is just copying the software onto a memory chip.

In Brief...

Partitioning the system into hardware and software is known as co-design. While carrying out the hardware-software partitioning, issues such as size, cost, power consumption, memory requirements, speed of execution, and ease reproduction need to be considered.

Intel's 80386 is an integer-only processor. The computers built on this processor initially used to do the floating-point operations through software and hence the floating-point calculations were very slow. Subsequently Intel introduced the 80387 floating-point processor that made the floating-point operations much faster (almost 10 times faster). Certainly, the 80387 processor increased the cost but gave much higher performance.

Another example is that of graphics accelerators used in video game systems. If there is no graphics accelerator hardware, the graphics rendering is done through the software, but it results in poor performance. When graphics rendering is transferred to the hardware then the rendering effects are more attractive and fast.

Using Programmable Logic Devices (PLDs), Field Programmable Gate Arrays (FPGAs) and System-on-Chip (SoC) solutions, we can build re-configurable hardware and hence we need to study using PLDs, FPGAs and SoC in the hardware to reduce the size, cost and power consumption to the extent possible.

Notes...

During hardware-software partitioning, the hardware engineers need to study the pros and cons of using programmable hardware such as Field Programmable Gate Arrays (FPGAs) and System-on-Chip (SoC). FPGA and SoC are cost-effective only if the embedded systems are to be produced in large quantities or when the size and weight are major issues.

4.3.3 Hardware Design

After the hardware-software partitioning is done, the hardware design and software design need to be carried out. The hardware design involves:

- Selection of the processor
- Calculation of the memory requirements and the types of memory such as RAM (SRAM and DRAM), EPROM, Flash memory
- Identification of input devices such as sensors, keyboard or keypad
- Identification of output devices such as LEDs and LCD
- Identification of communication interfaces such as RS232, Ethernet, USB
- Identification of test points. To debug the hardware, you need test points and they have to be identified during design stage itself. If the processor supports JTAG (Joint Test Access Group) protocols for debugging, you need to design your board keeping in view these debug pins.
- Identification of supply voltages and current requirements for designing the power supply unit.

To start with, you develop a block diagram and then convert each block into a circuit with necessary interconnections. Once the various modules are identified, the circuit has to be designed and the Printed Circuit Board (PCB) has to be obtained.

Since obtaining the final target hardware takes time (a few weeks to a few months), a readily available evaluation board of the required processor can be obtained from the vendor to start the development activity.

In many cases, it is not possible to freeze the hardware design. Generally, hardware prototyping is done on a breadboard to prove the design concept. Note that hardware design is not done in isolation; interaction with the software engineers is required to finalize the processor and memory requirements.

Selection of the Processor

The processor (CPU) selection is the most crucial in hardware design. The processor can be

a. Micro-controller

b. Microprocessor

c. Digital Signal Processor

If your application involves lot of signal processing such as for voice and video applications, modulation/demodulation development etc., a DSP is the best choice. If the application does not require high processing power, has small memory requirement and the on-chip peripherals are sufficient to meet your requirement, then a micro-controller is the best choice. The main attractions of a micro-controller are: small size, low-cost, small-sized system and high reliability due to less number of components. For small applications, a micro-controller gives better performance due to little external circuitry.

If a micro-controller is not sufficient for the application, the selection of the processor is based on the following criteria:

- **Performance requirements:** The speed of the processor is the main parameter. However, it needs to be remembered that the MIPS (Millions of Instructions Per Second) does not reflect the true speed. The clock frequency, number of registers and internal memory are the parameters on which the performance is dependent. EEMBC (EDN Embedded Benchmark Consortium) developed a benchmark that consists of 46 applications for different application suites (automotive/industrial suite, consumer suite, networking suite, office automation suite and telecommunications suite). These tests use standard algorithms to compare the performance of processors. You can ask the manufacturer for the test results for the suite of your requirement to make a comparison.
- **Cost of the processor:** The cost of the processor is of paramount importance if a large number of embedded systems have to be shipped. For a vacuum cleaner or a coffee machine, a 4-bit micro-controller will suffice; you will not use a 32-bit processor or a DSP. For the required performance, the lowest cost processor needs to be chosen.
- **Development tools:** The two important tools required for writing embedded software are the cross-compiler and the debugger. The processor manufacturer's tools need to be evaluated to ensure that they meet your required application needs. GNU development tools such as cross-compilers and debuggers are available for many processors. Use of these tools will reduce your development infrastructure costs.
- **Special requirements:** If you are developing an embedded system for military applications, military version of the processor (MIL grade component) availability needs to be ensured.
- **Support for RTOS:** The processor vendor will indicate the RTOS that will be supported by the processor. Generally, the RTOS kernel will be optimized for each processor. The hardware engineers and the software engineers together need to decide on the RTOS and then check the support for that RTOS.
- **Technical support from the vendor:** The original manufacturer's support centers may not be available in your country. An authorized representative/distributor will handle the technical support staff. Many such distributors are notorious for not providing the necessary technical support. Embedded system development will run into trouble without the necessary technical help.

In Brief...

Selection of a processor needs to be done keeping in view the processing power required, the memory capability, cost of the processor, support for embedded/real-time operating systems, development tools, support from the vendor and availability of people with experience on the processor's tools.

- Availability of people with the expertise on a specific processor: Today, many vendors supply the processors with similar and almost the same performance and cost. So, choosing a processor is certainly a tough task. One criterion used is the availability of human resources with exposure or expertise in a particular family. If your organization has already executed a few projects using, say Intel 8051 family micro-controllers, your choice will be to use the same family due to the following reasons:
  - o There is no need to buy additional development tools.
  - o Portions of the code developed earlier can be reused, if possible.
  - o There will be no additional training costs.
  - o Development time can be reduced considerably.

4.3.4 Software Design

For small embedded systems, there will be no need for an operating system and hence you can write your own software routines for task management, input/output management and memory management; and integrate your application software with these routines. For a complex embedded system, an embedded/real-time operating system will make the development faster. The entire design process is dependent on this important decision: to use an operating system or not.

Software design involves

- Working out the details of the processing to be done by the embedded system
- Decomposition of the processing into different tasks
- Calculation of the processing time and the resources required for each task
- Deciding on the use of an embedded operating system. If the embedded system has strict deadlines to be met then a real-time operating system has to be chosen.
- Studying the need for support for communication protocols stack. If the system has to be network-enabled, the TCP/IP protocol stack has to be ported onto the system. In addition, application layer protocols such as Hyper Text Transfer Protocol (HTTP), Trivial File Transfer Protocol (TFTP) etc. may need to be ported.

In Brief...

While carrying out the software design, the important issues are: whether there is a need for an operating system to be ported on to the system, whether the networking protocol stack needs to be ported and whether the performance parameters can be achieved.

- Study the need for embedding the HTTP server software. If the embedded system has to be Internet-enabled and if you want to access the system over the Internet, the HTTP server software needs to be ported onto the system.
- Study the need for field upgradation of the software. For some embedded systems, you may need to upgrade the software in the field. In such a case, the system needs to have a communication port (such as RS232, USB, Ethernet) and a file transfer protocol

(such as FTP or TFTP), or a JTAG port so that the upgraded software can be downloaded into the program memory. For such a requirement, it will be a good idea if you can develop a Flash file system. A Flash file system is similar to the file system on hard disk of your desktop. It enables you access the program memory using file names instead of memory addresses. The Flash memory, in effect, acts as the 'hard disk' of your embedded system. Such Flash device is called 'disk on a chip'.

Note that the software design and hardware design need to be done iteratively as the hardware design is influenced by the software design. For example, if it is decided that an operating system has to be embedded in the system, the memory requirements will be slightly higher.

Selection of an Operating System

The embedded operating system needs to be chosen keeping in view the following criteria:

- **Optimized kernel for the chosen processor:** If you have already decided which processor to use, you need to check which operating systems have optimized kernel for that processor. An optimized kernel gives excellent performance.
- **Support for languages:** You need to find out which high level languages are supported. C and C++ are generally supported. Support for ANSI C standard, the latest being 1999 version, called C99, has to be ensured. If your application demands development in Java, ensure that Java support is there. If you are developing an application for defence and ADA needs to be used as the programming language, the OS should have the support for ADA language.
- **Support for POSIX function calls:** IEEE POSIX 1003.1c standard specifies the function calls for embedded/real-time systems. Conforming to this standard will ensure that your application software is portable.
- **Footprint:** The footprint or the memory occupied by the OS needs to be found out. A few kilobytes is all that is required for the kernel, but you may need to include a number of device drivers, virtual machines, protocol stacks etc. The OS, software components and the application software together decide the total memory requirement of your embedded system.
- **Software components:** The software components provided by the vendor also need to be checked up. These software components include protocol stack, graphics libraries, device drivers, debugging tools, virtual machines, web server, etc.
- **Source code/object code:** When you buy a commercial OS development system, you may get only the object code along with the function call library. For additional price, you may get the source code as well. You can download open source operating systems (such as Embedded Linux, RTLinux etc.) which have complete source code listings.
- **Licensing fee:** If you use a commercial operating system, you need to pay royalty for run-time license i.e., for each embedded system you sell, you need to pay royalty to the OS vendor. For some commercial operating systems, you need to pay only one-time fee, there will be no royalty. If you use the GNU Public License (GPL) software, there will be no royalty.

In Brief ..

Selection of an operating system is based on the following criteria: whether the processor chosen supports the operating system, the footprint of the operating system, languages supported, availability of the required software components, availability of source code and the licensing fee.

Keeping in view, these considerations, you need to choose an embedded/real-time operating system. Though open source operating systems are an attractive choice, note that you will not get any support and hence maintenance is your headache. However, in the next few years, open source software will gain much more popularity and hence you need to consider this option and also develop in-house expertise in developing applications over open source software.

4.4 Implementation

The hardware implementation and the software implementation go in parallel. The hardware implementation involves:

- Developing the circuit schematics
- Obtaining the PCBs
- Procuring the components
- Assembling the components and testing the individual modules on the populated PCB
- Testing the complete hardware

In Brief...

For both hardware implementation and software implementation, a detailed process needs to be worked out so that later on, integration and testing effort is minimized.

Ask any hardware engineer how complex the whole process is! A very rigorous quality management is required in every phase of hardware development—the bare PCB has to be tested; the procured components need to be tested separately before mounting on the PCB; and, the assembling of the components on the PCB has to be done incrementally: mount components of one module, test that module and then add the components for the next module.

Software implementation involves converting the design into code. Implementation of the software is generally done on a host system and then the executable code is transferred to the target hardware. When many engineers work on a project, the software is divided into different modules and each module is tested separately and then all the modules are integrated and tested. While coding, the engineers need to optimize the code to the extent possible. Generally, the engineers postpone code optimization to a later date and as a result, project deadlines cannot be met. You will be debating how to reduce the executable file size by 100 bytes on the day the system has to be delivered to the client!

Though assembly language is still used in embedded system development, it is always good to write the code in a high level language such as C or C++ as maintenance of the software is easier. However, to improve performance, some portions of the code may need to be written in assembly language later on. You can use the profilers to study which portions of the code are taking long time to execute and then convert those portions to assembly language if timing considerations become important.

Every engineer needs to appreciate that it is very difficult for anyone to understand the code written by someone else, unless proper online documentation is included. If you use strange variable names (your boy/girl friend's name) or give some strange constants which cannot be understood (temp = 76; what is the significance of 76? Such numbers are called magic numbers), then it is difficult for anyone else to maintain your software. Every organization involved in embedded software development has to frame a set of coding guidelines to be followed by all the engineers so that the code can be easily tested and maintained.

4.5 Integration and Testing

Testing is the most difficult and time-consuming process. The project team needs to assign sufficient time for testing the embedded system not only for its performance characteristics but also for checking its reliability. Now, the fundamental question—what is testing? Consider the following definition:

"Testing is the process to prove that the system works correctly"

At the outset, this definition appears correct. And, this is the definition you use when you have to demonstrate your program to your Professor during the lab exam. You give only those inputs for which the program works correctly, because you know for which inputs the system will hang! So, this definition is not correct; if you use this definition, you will not be able to bring out the defects in the system. Now consider the following definition:

"Testing is the process to prove that the software does not work correctly"

This sounds a crazy definition, but if you use this definition while testing your system, you will try your best to bring out as many defects as possible. A good test engineer will follow this definition for testing any system. But how long you keep on testing the system to say that it is bug-free? It is difficult to answer this question, because testing can never be completed. So, a practical definition of testing is as follows:

"Testing is the process to reduce the risk associated with the residual defects"

If you follow this definition, you will uncover many bugs; and even if some bugs are still present in the software but their impact is minimal, you can release the software to the client.

While testing the software, the test engineers have to keep a record of all the defects or bugs found in it. Each bug has to be classified as minor, major and critical. A minor defect does not affect the functionality of the product. An example of a minor defect is a spelling mistake in a user prompt. A major defect affects the performance of the system, but the system will continue to work. A critical defect halts the system. In embedded systems, it needs to be ensured that there are no critical or major defects. To declare that the testing is complete, a graph can be drawn which shows the number of defects found, say per day, as shown in Fig. 4.5. You need to fix a threshold on the number of defects, and if the number of defects found per day is less than the threshold continuously for, say three days, you can declare that the testing is complete.

In Brief...

The objective of testing should be to uncover as many defects as possible. The risk associated with the residual defects should be minimized before delivering the product to the customer.

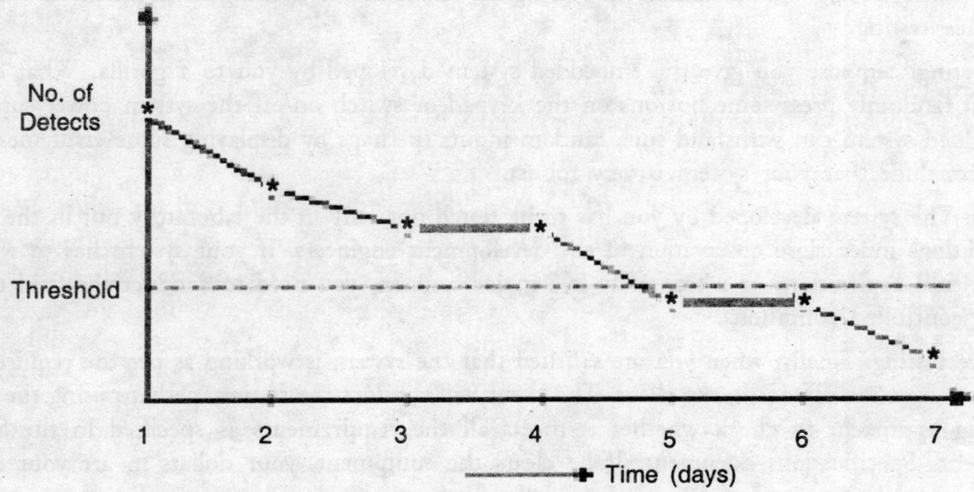

Fig. 4.5: Criterion for Completion of Testing

4.5.1 Types of Testing

While carrying out the testing of the embedded system, different types of testing, as explained below, needs to be done.

Black-box testing: In black-box testing, the functionality of the product is tested. The system is considered as a black box, i.e. the implementation details are not considered at all. Inputs are given and it is checked whether the desired outputs are available or not. Generally, the end user of the product is concerned only about the functionality, hence this type of testing is useful for user acceptance.

White-box testing: In white-box testing, the implementation details are considered while testing the system—you give the test inputs in such a way that each and every line of code is tested. For example, consider the following code segment:

```
if (i < 5 && j < 6) {
   statements;
}
else {
   statements;
}
```

If you give the input i = 4 and j = 3, only the statements in the 'then' clause are executed, but not the statement in the 'else' clause. To test the statements in the 'else' clause, you need to give input such as i = 6 and j = 7.

Performance testing: Performance testing is to check whether the system is meeting the time constraints as per the requirements. Particularly for hard real-time systems, a rigorous testing has to be done to ensure that deadlines are not missed at all. This is a very challenging task: how do you test the embedded system used in a missile or a spacecraft or a nuclear plant? You may need to develop special hardware (called test jig) that simulates the real signals of the actual working environment to carry out performance testing.

Gorilla testing: Suppose you give the embedded system developed by you to a gorilla. What does it do? It will randomly press some buttons on the keypad or switch on/off the system power supply. If the embedded system can withstand such random inputs (perhaps by displaying some error messages), you can conclude that your system is very robust.

Field trial: The system developed by you has to be tested not only in the laboratory but in the actual field conditions inder close observation of the development engineers. If your system has to work in mission-critical applications or when safety is a major concern, you need to conduct the field trial in extremely controlled conditions.

Acceptance testing: Finally, when you are satisfied that the system is working as per the requirements of the client you can offer it to the client. The client will conduct the testing, perhaps using the black-box testing approach, to check whether it meets all the requirements as specified in the System Requirements Specifications document. If he clears the equipment, your dollars in are your hands.

Regression testing: After testing the system for a considerable amount of time (say, a few weeks), you find suddenly one bug. You will now modify the software to remove the bug. What is the guarantee that this modification has not affected other parts of the program? There is no guarantee. To ensure that modification in one portion of the code has no ill effect on other portions of the code, you need to carry out once again the testing of the total system. This is known as regression testing. Generally, you use a set of test cases for regression testing to test the software whenever it is modified.

In Brief...

The various types of testing to be carried out are: black box testing, white box testing, performance testing, Gorilla testing, field trial, acceptance testing and regression testing.

Notes...

Regression testing is done to ensure that modifications to one portion of the code have no ill effects on other parts of the code. Using a set of test cases, regression testing has to be done every time changes are made to the source code.

When is testing complete?

This is a very difficult question to answer. As you keep testing the system, you uncover some bugs and then you rectify the bugs. Certainly, the number of bugs found per week keeps reducing, but once in a while you will still find a bug. You can keep track of the number of bugs or defects found per day (or week) and draw a graph as shown in Fig. 4.5 and then using a reasonable threshold on the number of defects per day/week, you can declare that the testing is complete.

As reliability is the most important requirement for embedded systems, you need to by keep track of the number of failures and time to repair the system. You need to analyze these times to calculate the values of Mean Time Between Failures (MTBF), Mean Time To Repair (MTTR) and Mean Time to Fail (MTTF). The relation among these values is shown in Fig. 4.6.

In Brief...

To declare that the testing of the embedded system is complete, the test engineers need to carry out a sstatistical analysis of the number of defects found per unit time (say, one day). The values of MTBF, MTTR and MTTF need to be measured.

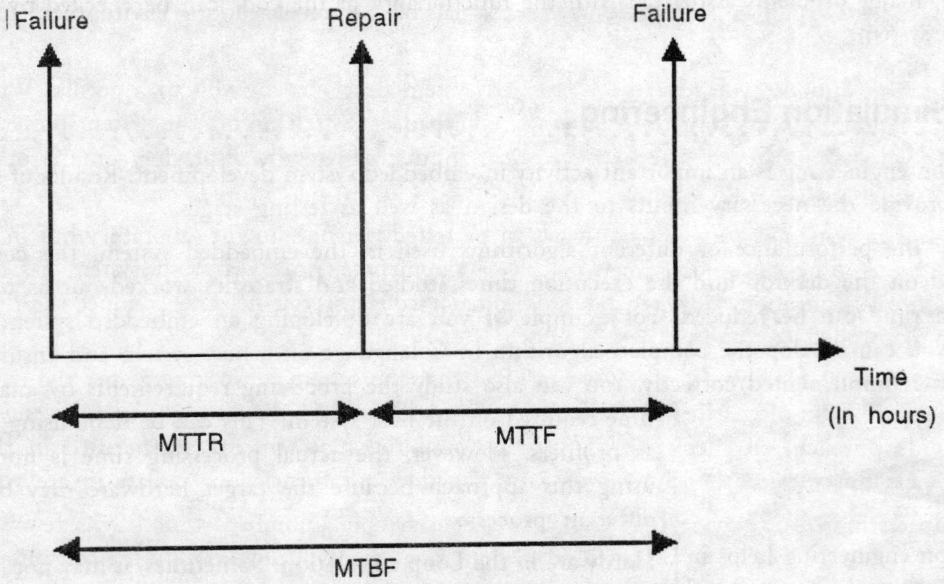

Fig. 4.6: Relation between MTBF, MTTR and MTTF

Notes...

The ratio of number of development engineers to number of test engineers in NASA Goddard Space Flight Center is 1:7, i.e. for every development engineer, there are seven test engineers. This reflects the importance given to testing in mission-critical applications.

4.5.2 Testing on the Host System

Testing the embedded system involves two steps:

- Testing on the host system
- Testing on the target system

Testing on the host system is done to validate the software. Using the tools such as ROM emulator, code simulator, In-Circuit Emulator, etc. you need to test your code. The following points need to be kept in mind while testing the software on the host system.

a. The word lengths of the host system and the target processor may be different. For example, the host system may have a word length of 32 bits whereas the target processor word length may be 16 bits only.

b. The byte order of the host and target processor may be different: one may be using the big-endian format and the other may be using the little-endian format.

In Brief...

Testing on the host system involves testing the hardware functionality partially. The performance characteristics cannot be tested on the host system.

Testing on the host system has the following limitations:

- The complete functionality is not tested as the target hardware is not used.
- The performance characteristics cannot be checked.

However, major problems associated with the functionality of the code can be checked by testing on the host system.

4.5.3 Simulation Engineering

Simulation engineering is an important activity in embedded system development. Results of simulation studies provide the necessary inputs to the design as well as testing stages.

To study the performance of different algorithms used in the embedded system, the code can be developed on the desktop and the execution times studied and strategies worked out as to how the execution time can be reduced. For example, if you are developing an embedded system for voice coding, you can develop the complete algorithm in C language on a host system and ensure that the algorithm is implemented correctly. You can also study the processing requirements by analyzing the time required on the host system. This can be done using tools such as profilers. However, the actual processing time is not obtained using this approach because the target hardware may be using a different processor.

In Brief...

Simulation engineering helps in testing the system in simulated environment. Using Hardware in the Loop simulation, the field conditions are simulated and the hardware is tested.

Hardware in the Loop simulation: Sometimes, it may not be possible to test the complete embedded system in actual working environment. For example, we cannot test the embedded systems used in the missiles in laboratory conditions. In such cases, a simulated environment is created and the software is tested along with the hardware. This is known as Hardware in the Loop testing.

4.5.4 Testing on the Target System

The software is transferred to the target system after ensuring that the hardware is thoroughly tested. Then the complete testing has to be done for

- Functional requirements
- Performance requirements
- Environmental requirements

In Brief...

Co-verification involves integrating the hardware and software and then carrying out the testing. A modular and step-by-step approach is required as it is difficult to identify whether the problem is in the hardware or in the software.

If the software is ported on to the target hardware and if everything works, it is a miracle! If it does not work, it may be due to a hardware problem or a software problem. Testing the embedded system by integrating the hardware and software is called co-verification. Co-verification is an extremely difficult task because it is difficult to pinpoint where the problem is. To solve this issue, it is better to build the system incrementally. To start with, only the software that does a specific task (say initializing the hardware and making a LED glow) has to be ported and checked. If it works then add another software module and then carry out the testing. This incremental approach will make debugging easier.

4.5.5 Environmental Testing

Many embedded systems have to work in hazardous environments. In industrial control applications, the systems have to work in a temperature range of – 40 to +70^0 C. In airborne equipment, the systems have to withstand bump, vibration etc. Such systems also need to be tested testing for these environmental specifications. The following environmental specifications are generally applicable to the military equipment and mobile devices:

Operating temperature:	-20 to + 55^0 C
Storage temperature:	-20 to +70^0 C
Altitude:	4000 meters
Humidity:	95% at 40^0 C
Vibration:	± 20 m/sec^2 constant acceleration
Rapid temperature cycling:	4 cycles (1 hour 26 minutes cycle)
Drop test:	6 drops on each face
Toppling:	4 topplings on wooden platform
Bump:	500 bumps, at the rate of 2 to 4 bumps per second.

Special testing laboratories carry out these tests. The system under test is kept in a special environmental chamber to simulate the necessary test conditions and the testing is carried out. For example, for toppling test, the equipment under test is subjected to toppling four times on a wooden platform and then it is checked whether the system is still functional. In rapid temperature cycling test, the temperature inside the environmental chamber is changed rapidly from -20^0 C to 55^0 C in 1 hour 26 minutes to check whether the system can withstand the rapid changes in the temperature.

In Brief...

As many embedded systems have to work in extreme environmental conditions, they to be tested against various specifications such as temperature, humidity, bump, vibration, altitude, rapid temperature changes, etc.

Electromagnetic Interference (EMI) is a major issue in embedded systems. EMI is the noise generated by sources external to the embedded system. For instance, motors, RF transmitters, generators, etc. may affect an embedded system's operation. Proper EMI shielding is to be done to overcome the effect of EMI.

While designing the system itself, these environmental specifications need to be kept in mind. The choice of the Integrated Circuits, the connectors to be used, the mechanical packaging, etc. are influenced by these environmental specifications.

4.6 Packaging

After the complete system is tested and ensured that the hardware and software together are meeting all the requirements, the embedded system has to be packaged in the desired cabinet. For military equipment, special packaging requirements are specified to meet the environmental specifications. For consumer items, an attractive packaging is a must. Mechanical engineers' advice needs to be taken for packaging the product. Packaging issues need to be considered from requirements engineering stage itself.

4.7 Configuration Management

During the course of development of an embedded system, a number of documents, called work products, are generated. These work products are:

- System requirements specifications
- Project plan
- Hardware design document
- Software design document
- Circuit diagrams
- Source code
- Acceptance test procedure
- Test plans
- User manual

To start with, the system requirements specifications document will be prepared. While carrying out the design, you may feel the need to modify the specifications document because a particular requirement needs to be changed—your development team or the client may initiate this change. So, initially you have version 1.0 of the specifications document and you will later modify the document and release version 1.1. Similarly, you may need to make changes to any of the above-mentioned work products. The process of making changes to the work products in a systematic manner is called configuration management. As shown in Fig. 4.7, configuration management process involves the following procedure:

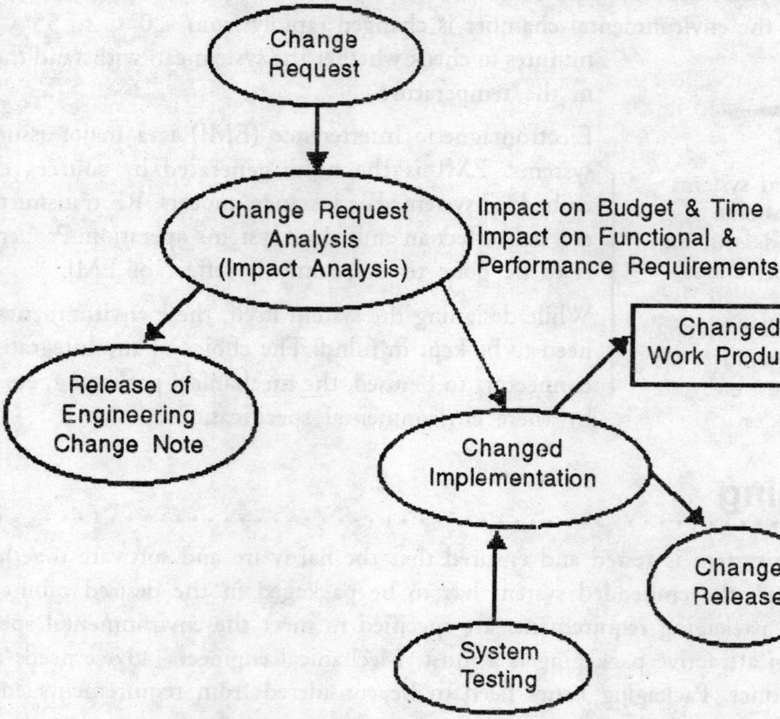

Fig. 4.7: Configuration Management Process

- Whenever a change is proposed (either by the client or an engineer in the development team), a change request has to be sent to the project manager in a specific format giving the details of the proposed change: what is the change and why the change is required.
- The project manager and the team members have to analyze the proposed change to study its impact on the functional requirements, performance requirements, budget and time.
- If the change is acceptable then an Engineering Change Note (ECN) has to be prepared and the corresponding work product has to be modified. The accepted change has to be communicated to all the employees concerned.
- In many projects, the number of ECNs will be in hundreds. So, the project manager has to keep track of these ECNs and ensure that each and every accepted change is actually implemented.
- Tools such as SCCS (Source Code Control System) and RCS (Revision Control System) of Unix/Linux, Visual SourceSafe of Windows can be used to keep track of the changes to the work products.

In Brief...

The configuration management process involves making the changes to the work products in a systematic way. Every proposed change has to be analyzed for its impact on the design and time frame; every accepted change has to be communicated to all the team members, and it has to be ensured that all the accepted changes are incorporated in the implementation.

Note that many embedded system projects get delayed because of lack of a configuration management process. In large projects, some team members are not even aware that a specification has been changed. The object of a configuration management process is to ensure that every change is analyzed in a systematic way and every change is communicated to all the team members. Even after the development is completed and the system is delivered to the client, the configuration management process needs to be followed for maintaining the various versions of the source code. Each version of the source code needs to be maintained along with the corresponding documentation on the changes incorporated.

Notes...

The work products produced during the development life cycle are: specifications document, design document, source code, circuit diagrams, test plans, acceptance test procedure, project plan document and user manual.

4.8 Managing Embedded System Development Projects

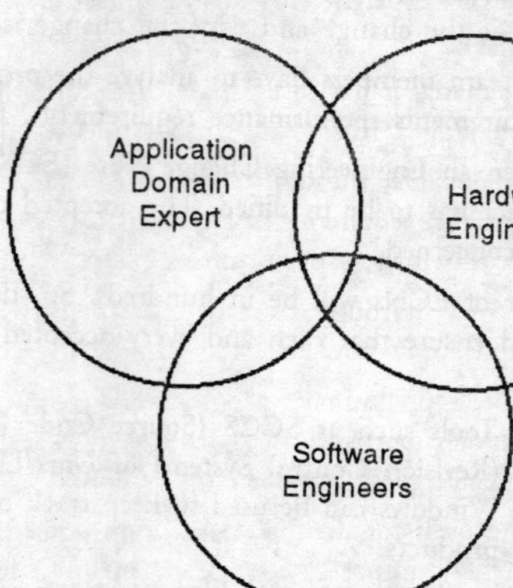

Fig. 4.8: Synergy of Expertise for Embedded System Development

Managing embedded systems projects is a very challenging task because it involves bringing a synergy among the hardware engineers, software engineers and application domain experts, as shown in Fig. 4.8. The software engineers do not understand the intricacies of the hardware, the hardware engineers do not understand the intricacies of the software and both hardware and software engineers do not understand the jargon of the application domain experts. The project manager has to bring in the synergy to ensure that the project is success by delivering a quality product within the budget and within the time frame. The various challenges faced by the project manager are discussed in this section.

4.8.1 Project Proposal Preparation

When the marketing department gets an inquiry or when your organization decides to develop a product then as the project manager, you need to prepare a project proposal giving an estimate of the time and budget. It is suicidal to give a proposal (indicating that, say, it will take six months for development and the estimated cost is US$ 100,000) without a clear understanding of the project requirements. Project proposal preparation giving an estimate of effort, time and money required to develop an embedded system is a difficult task due to the following reasons:

- The requirements may not be very clear and you need to do the estimation with limited information.
- The risks associated with the project are very high mainly because you will not be able to know whether the performance requirements can be met or not, without carrying out a detailed design. Your top management will not allow you to do a detailed design unless the project is on hand!

- To get people with the required skill sets is not an easy task. Even if you have the people in your organization with the necessary expertise, it remains doubtful whether these people will continue till the end of the project.

In spite of these risk factors, the project manager has to estimate the effort, time and money required. The following process would help in making a reasonably good estimate:

- Obtain, to the maximum extent possible, the clear requirements from the user. Focus on the performance requirements. Document all the assumptions made during the requirements specifications phase.
- Do a thorough risk analysis. Identify the possible risk factors and study how the risks can be overcome.
- Do a preliminary design and if required carry out simulation studies to ensure that the system is realizable. Take the opinion of an expert consultant if required.
- Account for manpower attrition and keep some backup personnel for important activities. Include the cost of the additional personnel in the project cost estimation.

In Brief...

To estimate the effort, time and budget required for an embedded system development project is a challenging task due to the many uncertainties involved. A process-oriented approach coupled with expert advice is required for making realistic estimates.

4.8.2 Project Planning

It is naïve to assume that everything will go smoothly during the development phase. The design team would have worked out a design and developed a prototype only to realize that a particular performance parameter cannot be met. This may call for a major change in the design. The project manager has to avoid such unpleasant news by taking the necessary precautions during the project planning stage. The manager has to plan the necessary simulation studies and prototype development during the requirements analysis stage itself. Another major problem in the project execution is the attrition of the employees. If the development engineers leave in the middle of the project, the timeframe is badly affected. Though this is true for any project, the impact of people leaving in the middle of the project is much more for embedded systems because it is difficult to ensure continuity in hardware design and firmware development. The project manager needs to have enough backup personnel from the start of the project itself. During project planning stage, the project manager needs to take into consideration all these aspects.

The project manager has to prepare a project plan document that clearly indicates the various activities along with time frames, responsibilities of each person working on the project, development environment and tools required, test equipment required, risk items and risk management procedure, configuration management process, reviews to be carried out etc. The project plan document has to be periodically reviewed to ensure that everything is going as per the plan. It a certain aspect of planning fails, corrective action needs to be taken.

In Brief...

The project manager has to develop a project plan that clearly indicates the total plan for the entire project duration. The project reviews need to be conducted using the project plan document as the reference.

4.8.3 Providing the Development Infrastructure

Many embedded system designers are handicapped due to lack of the necessary infrastructure. The hardware engineers need test instruments such as oscilloscopes, logic analyzers, spectrum analyzers, etc. The software engineers need development tools such as cross-compilers, debuggers, In-Circuit Emulators, ROM emulators etc. The project manager has to identify the test instruments and the development tools necessary for the project and provide these facilities.

4.8.4 Co-design and Co-verification

During the design stage, it is difficult to partition the hardware and software functionality (the co-design problem). Similarly, while testing the system after the hardware and software are integrated, it is difficult to find out whether the problem is in the hardware or software (co-verification problem). In many embedded system projects, the hardware engineers and software engineers could be found blaming each other for an unresolved problem. The project manager has to work out a detailed process for separate testing of the hardware and the software; and then the hardware and software are integrated. The integration testing has to be done step-by-step so that debugging is easy.

4.8.5 Risk Management

In Brief...

Risk management is one of the most important activities of the project manager. The manager has to identify the possible risk items and periodically review the project to overcome the risks.

Many embedded system development projects have a high element of risk. The major risk items are: the personnel leaving in the middle of the project, interfacing the embedded system with other systems such as external hardware, meeting the real-time performance requirements, etc. The project manager has to periodically review the project for the possible risk factors and take corrective action. A major risk factor in most of the projects is the continuous stream of requirements changes. The client keeps telling you that a particular specification needs a 'small' change without realizing that the 'small' change may call for a major design change in the hardware or the software. As the project manager, you need to work out a mechanism wherein the impact of a proposed change is studied. If the impact is very high, you need to inform the client regarding its effect on budget or timeframe or both.

4.8.6 Quality Management

To bring out a quality product, quality has to be ensured in every phase of development. As discussed in the previous sections of this chapter, the development process is divided into different stages, and the project manager has to ensure that the process is followed strictly in every stage. For an effective project management, the project manager has to quantify the quality parameters. For example, instead of saying that the requirements engineering was done 'badly' there should be a measure to indicate how bad it was. These measures are known as "metrics". The project manager has to obtain the following metrics to quantify the process quality and product quality:

- Number of changes proposed and accepted after the specifications document has been finalized.
- Number of changes proposed and accepted after the design document has been finalized.
- The estimated and actual values of time, effort and money for the various stages viz., requirements engineering, prototype development, design, implementation, integration and testing, and maintenance.
- The number of defects found per week/day after the system is integrated and commencement of the testing phase. Keeping track of this number is very important to decide when the product is mature enough to be released into to the market/to the client.
- The reliability metrics such as the Mean Time Between Failures (MTBF), Mean Time to Repair (MTTR) and Mean Time to Fail (MTTF). Once the embedded system has reached a mature stage after enough testing, it has to be continuously tested in the field conditions and the values of MTBF, MTTR and MTTF have to be obtained for a reasonably large testing time.

4.9 Embedded System Fiascos

As you keep working on embedded systems, you will improve the development process analyzing the mistakes committed earlier, and ensuring that the same mistakes do not recur. In addition, we can also learn a lot from others' mistakes. This section gives some of the major fiascos in embedded system development, which emphasize the importance of a process-oriented embedded system development.

4.9.1 Patriot Missile

During the 1991 Gulf war, an Iraqi Scud missile hit an American army barrack killing many soldiers. An American Patriot missile could not track and intercept the Scud missile. The reason: a software bug in the Patriot missile. Whenever the tracking system of the Patriot was switched on, it measured the elapsed time from an internal clock in tenths of a second. This value was multiplied by 10 to get the time in seconds. The calculation was performed using 24-bit fixed-point registers. Hence, the value of 1/10 stored in a register was truncated to 24 bits whereas the exact value is 0.000110011001100110011001100….. When the value is truncated, an error is introduced and this error accumulates over a period of time. The Patriot missile was switched on for about 100 hours and so the accumulated error was 0.34 second. Scud travels with a speed of 1,676 meters per second, i.e. more than half a kilometer in 0.34 seconds. As a result, the Patriot could not intercept the Scud.

In Brief...

The Patriot Missile example demonstrates the importance of meeting the real-time performance requirements and how a small software bug, accumulation of error due to rounding off a number, can lead to a catastrophe.

4.9.2 Ariane 5

On June 4, 1996, European Space Agency launched the Ariane 5 satellite launch vehicle. Exactly 40 seconds after the lift-off at an altitude of 3700 meters, the launcher exploded and became a ball of fire. The project, which was uninsured, cost US$ 500 million. What went wrong? In one of the embedded systems, a software exception caused the problem. A 64-bit floating-point number was to be converted into a 16-bit signed integer value. During one calculation, the converted integer value was more than the value that can be represented by a 16-bit signed integer. This caused an operand error. Yes, the software exception was handled, but badly. The specification of the exception handling routine was: to indicate the failure on the data bus, to store the context in the EPROM and to shut down the processor. The processor was shut down, and it created the chaos. The mishap can be attributed to lack of enough testing as well as the flaw in the software design, particularly in exception handling. This error is known as '500 million dollar software error' in the software literature. Interestingly, the software used in Ariane 4 was reused in Ariane 5, and Ariane 4 was a successful launch. The only difference is that in Ariane 5, this calculation was not at all required!

In Brief...

Ariane 5 project illustrates the possible dangers associated with reuse of software as well as the importance of specifying the exception handling routines.

The failure of this project is a lesson for every software engineer—one line of code can cause irreparable damage.

4.9.3 Mars Pathfinder

In Brief...

Mars Pathfinder is an excellent example to understand the real-time systems. The bad things are the bad design and the approach taken by some engineers when a problem was encountered while testing the software in the laboratory. The marvel is that the problem could be solved without someone flying to the Mars to upgrade the software in the field!

The NASA mission Pathfinder landed on the Mars on 4 July, 1997. The mission was successful—a perfect launch, a perfect landing on the Mars and lot of important data was sent to the earth. After a few days, the computing system started resetting intermittently and important data was not being received on the earth. The on-board computer used a real-time operating system. Using an exact replica of the computer on the earth, the debugging was done to find the fault.

Three tasks were running on the system—one with high priority, one with low priority and one with medium priority. Intermittently, the task with medium priority was running for a long time, while the task with high priority was waiting for the task with low priority to complete. The task with low priority was not getting the CPU time because a higher priority task was running. Meanwhile, the watchdog timer, suspecting a deadlock, used to reset the processor. This problem was due to a bug in the initialization of a mutex used for inter-task communication. Of course, the story ended on a positive note as the engineers were able to upload a file onto the Pathfinder which rectified the software bug.

The story of Pathfinder teaches us many lessons in embedded software development. While doing the simulation studies, the engineers noticed such a problem before the launch of the Pathfinder, but they thought that the problem was due to a hardware glitch as it was observed only a very few times—we should not set aside the problems encountered even occasionally. The engineers on the Earth could analyze and rectify the bug only because the debug code was also running on the computer of Pathfinder. Sometimes the debug code is very important. We should not think that the debug code is only for development, it is very useful for maintenance as well.

Summary

In this chapter, we discussed the detailed process of embedded system development. The development process is divided into five stages viz., requirements engineering, design, implementation, integration and testing, and maintenance. To deliver a quality product, we need to ensure that quality is maintained at each stage by following a systematic procedure. Requirements engineering phase involves requirements analysis, requirements specifications and requirements validation. During design phase, the hardware-software partitioning is done, and the designing of hardware and software is carried out. To aid the design process, a prototype is developed. Implementation phase involves converting the hardware design into a Printed Circuit Board with all components assembled, and converting the software design into code in the given programming language. During the integration and testing phase, the hardware and software are integrated and the system is tested for functionality, performance and reliability. During development and maintenance of the system, the configuration management process needs to be followed which involves making changes to the work products systematically.

The art of embedded system project management is also discussed briefly. Managing embedded system development is a challenging task due to many risks associated with such projects. The project manager needs to work out detailed processes of project estimation, project planning and risk management to make the projects successful.

Three often-quoted important embedded systems fiascos viz., Patriot missile, Ariane 5 and Mars Pathfinder, are briefly discussed. The problems encountered with these systems teach us very important lessons in developing embedded systems.

Questions

1. What is a process? What is development process?
2. Explain the waterfall model as applied to embedded system development.
3. Describe the activities to be performed in each phase of embedded system development.
4. Define testing process. When is testing complete?
5. List the important issues in managing embedded system development.

Exercises

1. List the input/output requirements of a hand-held data terminal that can be used to collect field data.
2. You need to develop an embedded system that can be attached to a telephone. This embedded system has to record the telephone conversations. List the requirements and carry out a preliminary design. Estimate the effort, time and budget to do this project.
3. You need to develop a navigation system that can be used in the cars to provide navigation information. Discuss the pros and cons of using an operating system for this product. Do you need a real-time operating system for this product? Justify your answer.

4. You have to develop a Software-Defined Radio to generate various types of modulations (Amplitude Modulation, Frequency Modulation, Amplitude Shift Keying, Frequency Shift Keying and Phase Shift Keying). Which processor would you choose: a Digital Signal Processor or a General Purpose Processor? Why?
5. You have to develop an embedded system that tracks a person's movement. The person to be tracked will be given this system consisting a GPS receiver and a small radio transmitter. The radio transmitter keeps sending the location information to a centralized place where you have to observe the person's movement on a digitized map. List the important requirements of this embedded system and prepare a project proposal indicating the effort, time and budget required to do the development.
6. List the features of a software product that reflect its quality.

Chapter 5

Hardware Platforms

CHAPTER OBJECTIVES

After reading this chapter, you will be able to:

- Gain knowledge of different types of hardware platforms
- Learn the design details of a simple 89C51-based development board
- Learn the design details of AVR ATmega128 micro-controller based development board

Embedded systems are developed on different hardware platforms such as single board computers, PC add-on cards and stand-alone development boards. In this chapter, we will take a quick look at these platforms. We will also study the hardware details of two development boards built around ATMEL 89C51 micro-controller and AVR ATmega128 micro-controller.

5.1 Types of Hardware Platforms

In Brief...

The hardware platforms for embedded systems can be (a) single board computer; (b) PC add-on card; or (c) custom-built hardware.

Embedded systems come in different types and shapes. We can divide the embedded systems into the following categories:

- Embedded systems built around Single Board Computers
- PC add-on cards
- Custom-built hardware platforms

5.1.1 Single Board Computers

Single Board Computer (SBC) is one of the widely used hardware platforms for embedded systems. If the embedded system requires high processing power, it is built around an SBC. The SBC is no different from a desktop computer hardware platform except that the entire hardware is built on a single board. In many industrial applications, the SBC is housed in a cabinet of 19-inch rack. Hence, it looks different from the desktop tower model.

In Brief...

Single Board Computer (SBC) is built around a 32-bit or 64-bit processor with all the peripherals integrated into a single Printed Circuit Board (PCB). For industrial use, the SBC is housed in a 19-inch rack mountable cabinet.

The embedded system can be built around the SBC by integrating other application specific hardware. The SBC will generally have a 32-bit/64-bit processor along with the necessary peripherals such as the memory, communication interfaces, input/output devices and if required even secondary storage such as the CDROM. The SBC can be built around processors such as x86/Pentium, PowerPC and ARM. Internet Kiosks, Automatic Teller Machines etc. use this platform.

5.1.2 PC Add-on Cards

PC add-on cards are plugged into the motherboard of a PC. In many process control applications, these PC add-on cards are used for data acquisition. These cards use different types of buses for communication with the processor board. These buses are:

- ISA bus
- PCI bus
- Compact PCI bus
- PCMCIA bus

Table 5.1 summarizes the features of various buses.

Bus	Bus Clock Frequency	Bus Width	Max. Data Transfer Rate	Special Features
ISA	8 MHz	16 bit	8 MB/sec	Low cost, Low speed; becoming obsolete
PCI	133 MHz	64 bit	1 GB/sec	Plug and Play, costlier than ISA
Compact PCI	33 MHz	64 bit	13 MB/sec	Plug and Play, hot swapping, suitable for embedded systems
PCMCIA	10 MHz	16 bit	20 MB/sec	Plug and Play, hot swappable, suitable for portable systems

Table 5.1: Features of Various Standard Buses

In Brief...

The PC add-on cards will have a PCI interface. The earlier versions of PCI used 66 MHz clock frequency and 32-bit bus. The latest version uses 133 MHz clock frequency and 64-bit bus.

Notes...

PCMCIA bus is well suited for mobile/handheld devices. Compact PCI is suitable for embedded systems.

The PC add-on card will have application-specific hardware that includes a processor (micro-controller, microprocessor or a digital signal processor) for real-time data acquisition. The acquired data is transferred to the PC's processor for further analysis and presentation to the user. A few such applications are given below:

- Virtual Instrumentation in which the PC add-on card is used to acquire the signals in real-time. The PC's resources (hard disk, monitor) are used for signal analysis and display.
- Interactive Voice Response (IVR) systems in which the PC add-on card is used to interface with the telephone network. Any person who calls the IVR system can retrieve the information stored in the PC's database.
- Software-Defined Radio (SDR) in which the radio signals are acquired in real-time. These analog signals are converted to digital format and processed through the DSP on the PC add-on card.
- Telephone tapping system in which the PC add-on card captures the telephone conversation and the PC's hard disk is used to store the conversation for later analysis.
- In process control systems, the PC add-on card will have multi-channel ADC chips that acquire the data from multiple sensors and transducers, and send the data to PC for analysis.

Note that these systems can also be developed using custom-built hardware. However, based on the application needs, a PC add-on card may be a preferred choice due to faster development and higher processing capability required to do off-line analysis. To meet the performance requirements, the PC add-on card can have multiple processors. An embedded/real-time operating system can also be ported onto the PC add-on card hardware.

5.1.3 Custom-built Hardware Platforms

Custom-built hardware platforms are used when the application demands design of a processor-based system as per the customer requirements. In the following sections, we will study two custom-built hardware platforms built around ATMEL 89C51 and AVR ATmega 128 micro-controllers. The details will give you an insight into the design of custom-built hardware platforms.

5.2 89C51 Micro-controller Development Board

Intel 8051 family processors are widely used in small embedded systems. In this section, we will study the hardware details of a development board based on a micro-controller that belongs to this family, i.e. ATMEL 89C51 Flash micro-controller. A detailed circuit-level description of the hardware of this board is given. If you would like to brand yourself as a hardware engineer, you can develop the board on your own very easily.

5.2.1 Development Board Features

The important features of this development board are listed below:

- On-board 64 MB code flash and 32 KB Data RAM
- RS-232 Interface
- Regulated Power Supply
- 8 Push Buttons
- 8 LEDs

- All I/O Ports easily accessible through Pin Header Connectors
- 11.059 MHz crystal
- The micro-controller can be any of the MCS-51 compatible 40 Pin DIP micro-controllers.

5.2.2 Hardware Description

The block diagram of ATMEL 89C51 development board is given in Fig. 5.1.

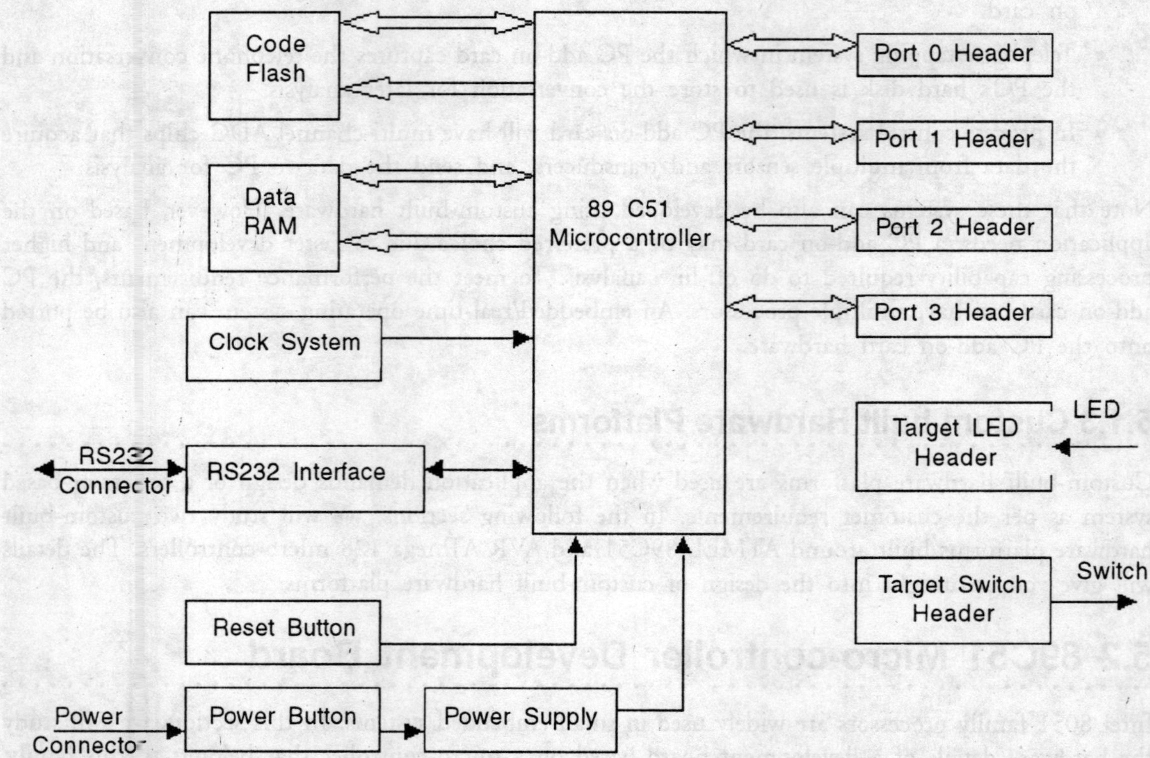

Fig. 5.1: Block Diagram of ATMEL 89C51 Development Board

The important components used in the development board are listed below. The component reference on the PCB is given in brackets.

- 89C51 Micro-controller (U2)
- Data Memory (U4)
- Code Flash (U5)
- LED Header (LED JP1)
- Switch Header (SW JP4)
- Port-0 (P0 JP2), Port-1 (P1 JP3), Port-2 (A(h) JP5), Port-3 (P3 JP6) and Address Line Header (A(l) JP7)
- RS232 interface (U3)

The component layout diagram is given below in Fig. 5.2.

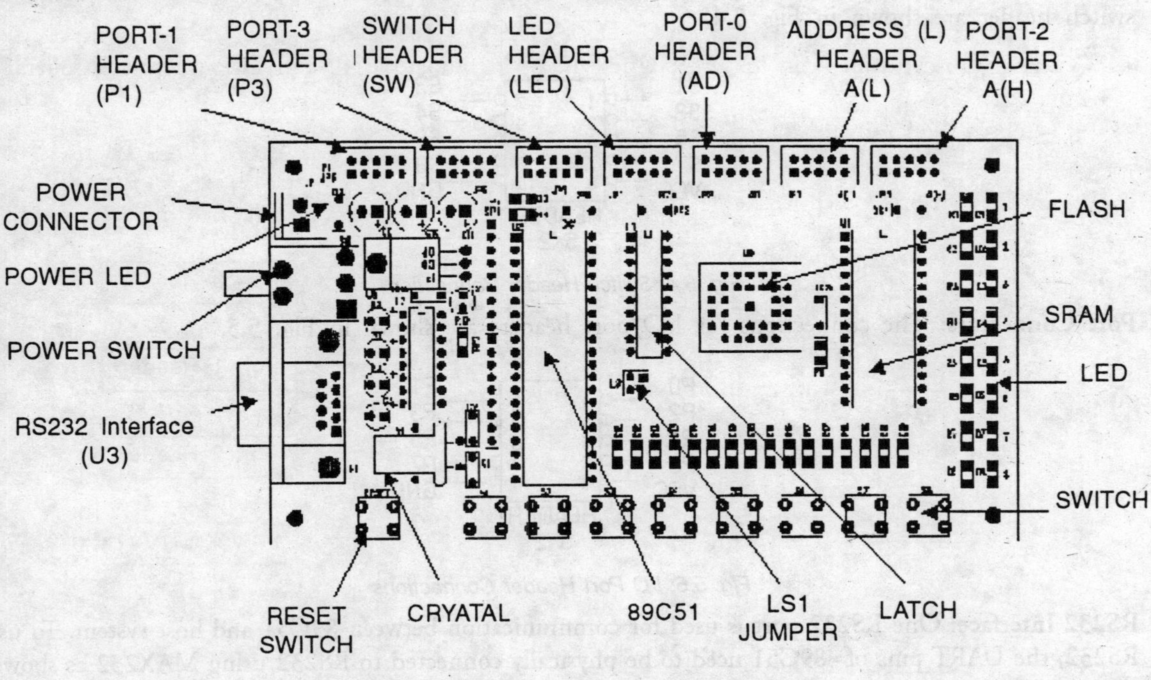

Fig. 5.2: Component Layout Diagram on the PCB

89C51: It is a 40-pin DIP IC (600 mils). You can use any 40-pin DIP micro-controller of Intel 8051 family here.

Data RAM: It is a 28-pin DIP IC (600 mils). The size of the Data RAM is 32 KB. The access time is 70 ns.

Code Flash: It is a 32-pin PLCC IC. Its size is 64 KB. When you set the jumper (LS1) for the external code memory, the 89C51 fetches the code from external code Flash. For programming the Flash, remove the Flash with the help of a plucker and program with any standard Flash programmer.

LEDs: The development board has 8 Green LEDs and 8 push-button switches. The LEDs and switches are connected to debug headers (JP1 and JP4) that are separated from the rest of the board. They can be connected with a 10-wire cable to the pin header of 89C51 I/O ports. The cables should be connected directly from the port header to the LEDs or switches. The cable should not be twisted. Fig. 5.3 shows the connections.

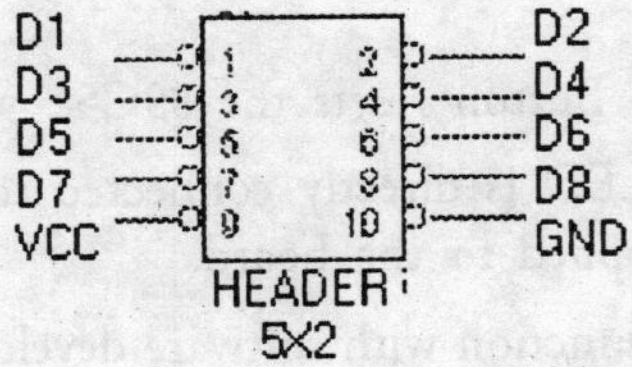

Fig. 5.3: LED Header Connections

Switches: Pushing a switch causes the corresponding signal to be pulled low. The pin connections for switch header are shown in Fig. 5.4.

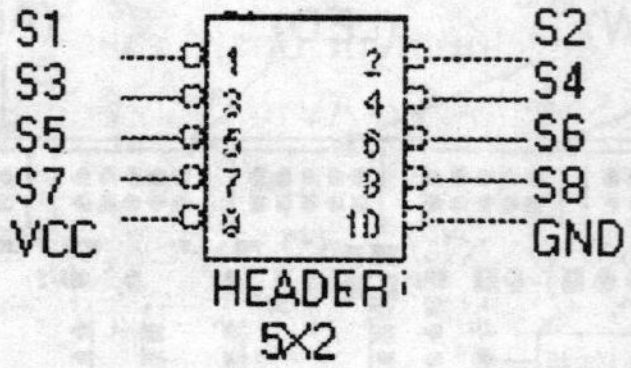

Fig. 5.4: Switch Header Connections

Port Connectors: The connections for I/O port headers are shown in Fig. 5.5.

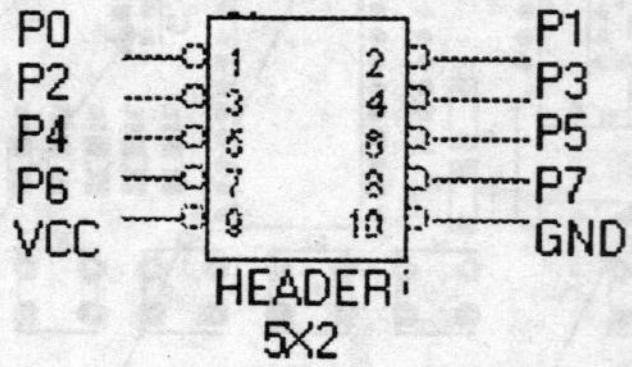

Fig. 5.5: I/O Port Header Connections

RS232 Interface: One RS232 port is used for communication between 89C51 and host system. To use RS232, the UART pins of 89C51 need to be physically connected to RS232 using MAX232 as shown in Fig. 5.6.

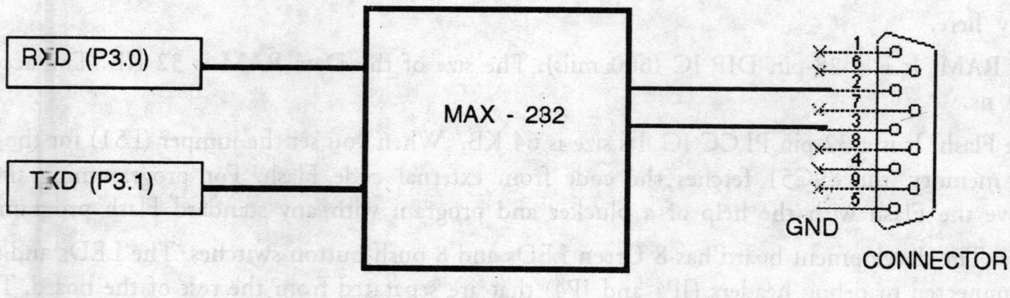

Fig. 5.6: RS232 Interface Connections

Jumper Connection LS1: It must be strapped to Position-1 in order to enable the device to fetch code from external program memory location. Connect to Position-2 for internal program execution.

Reset Push Button: The Reset Push Button resets the 89C51 when pushed.

Main Power LED: The red power LED is directly connected to the main power supply. The Power LED is always lit when power is applied to the board.

Using this development board in conjunction with software development tools, you can get started with embedded system development. We will discuss the software tools that need to be used in conjunction with this board in Chapter 17.

5.3 AVR Micro-controller Development Board

In this section, we will study the hardware details of a development board based on AVR ATmega128 micro-controller. It is a very powerful development board that can be used to develop prototype of your system and test the software. The AVRStudio and AVR-GNU development tools provide the environment for embedded system development. The board can be used for a variety of applications to develop prototypes to prove your design concepts. You can also port an operating system on this board.

Notes...

AVR micro-controllers are available with different capabilities to suit your application needs. This family of micro-controllers can be used for tiny applications as well as large applications. You need to choose the right controller based on the peripherals and memory requirements.

5.3.1 Development Board Features

The important features of AVR micro-controller development board are listed below:

- Board is built around ATMEL AVR ATmega128-16AI micro-controller, that has RISC architecture, with maximum 16 MIPS at 16 MHz clock
- Microphone input through 3.5mm Stereo Jack.
- Tape / CD Input through 3.5mm Stereo Jack.
- Speaker Output through 3.5mm Stereo Jack
- On board Data Memory 32 K x 8
- Interface Connectors
    - o All I/O Ports easily accessible through Pin Header Connectors
    - o 4 * 4 Keypad Connector
    - o 12 * 2 LCD Connector
    - o RS232 Connector
    - o USB Connector
    - o Interrupt Connector
    - o SPI Connector
    - o In-System Programming (ISP) Port
- General Purpose I/O
    - o 8 Push Button Inputs
    - o 8 LED Outputs
- LM7805, LP3965 and LM1085 Voltage Regulators

The AVR ATmega128 board has the feature of In-System Programming (ISP). For ISP, you have to connect the ISP port to the Parallel Port of the PC to program the internal 128 K byte Flash of

ATmega128 Microphone, Tape/CD and speaker interface are used for voice processing applications. User can easily access all the Ports (Port A to Port G) through 10-pin Headers. Keypad and LCD interfaces are also provided. The RS232 and USB connector are provided for serial communication applications The general purpose LED and Switch port are also provided. The input power supply is 12 V DC, 500 mA minimum.

5.3.2 Hardware Description

The block diagram of AVR ATmega 128 development board is shown in Fig. 5.7.

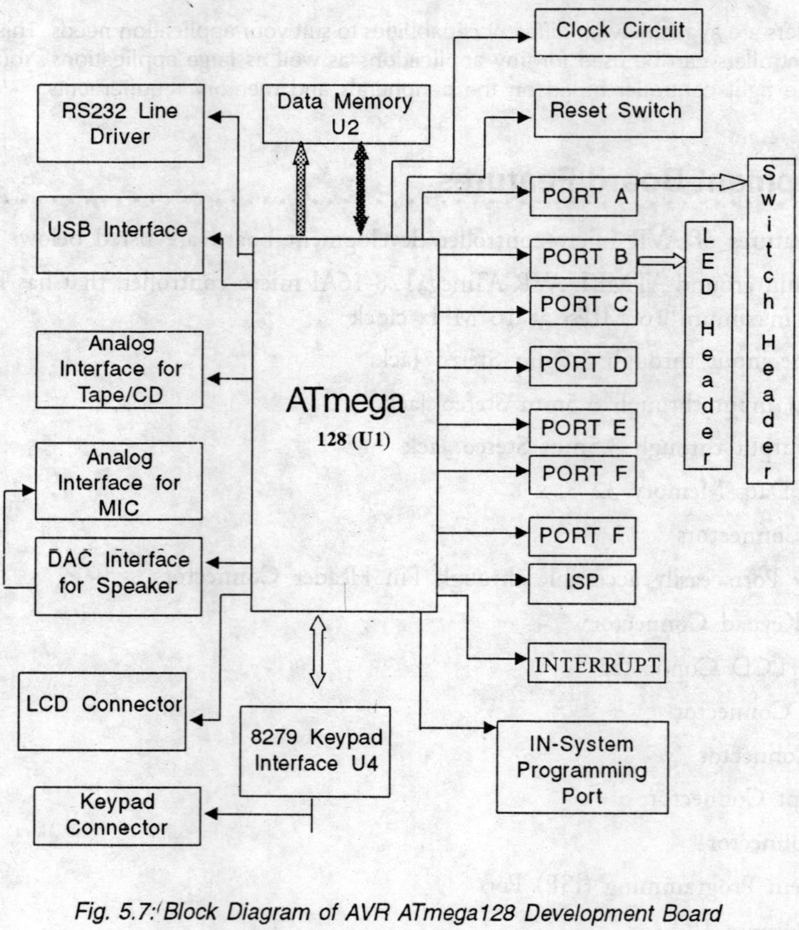

Fig. 5.7: Block Diagram of AVR ATmega128 Development Board

Fig. 5.8 shows the component layout diagram.

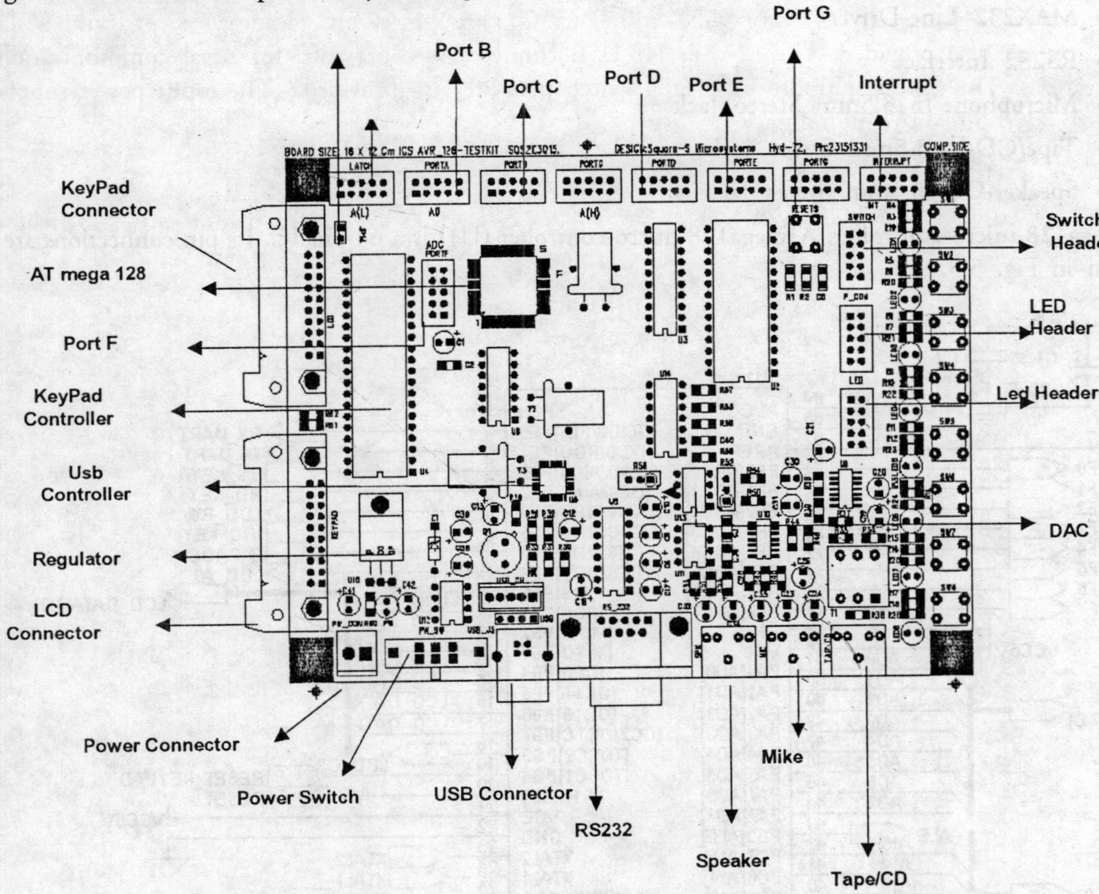

Fig.5.8: Component Layout of AVR ATmega128 Development Board

The important components of this development board are as follows:

- ATmega128 micro-controller (U1)
- Data Memory (U2)
- 8279 Keypad controller (U4)
- 20 Pin FRC connector for LCD Interface
- 20 Pin FRC connector for Keypad Interface
- USB Controller (U8)
- USB connector
- DAC (U13)
- LEDs Header (LED)
- Switch Header (SWITCH)
- Port A, Port B, Port C(A(H)), Port D, Port E, Port F(ADC),

- Port G, Address Line Header (LATCH A (L)), INTERRUPT Header
- MAX232 Line-Driver
- RS232 Interface
- Microphone-In 3.5mm Stereo Jack
- Tape/CD-In 3.5mm Stereo Jack
- Speaker-Out 3.5mm Stereo Jack

ATmega128 micro-controller: ATmega128 micro-controller (U1) is a 64-pin IC. Its pin connections are shown in Fig. 5.9.

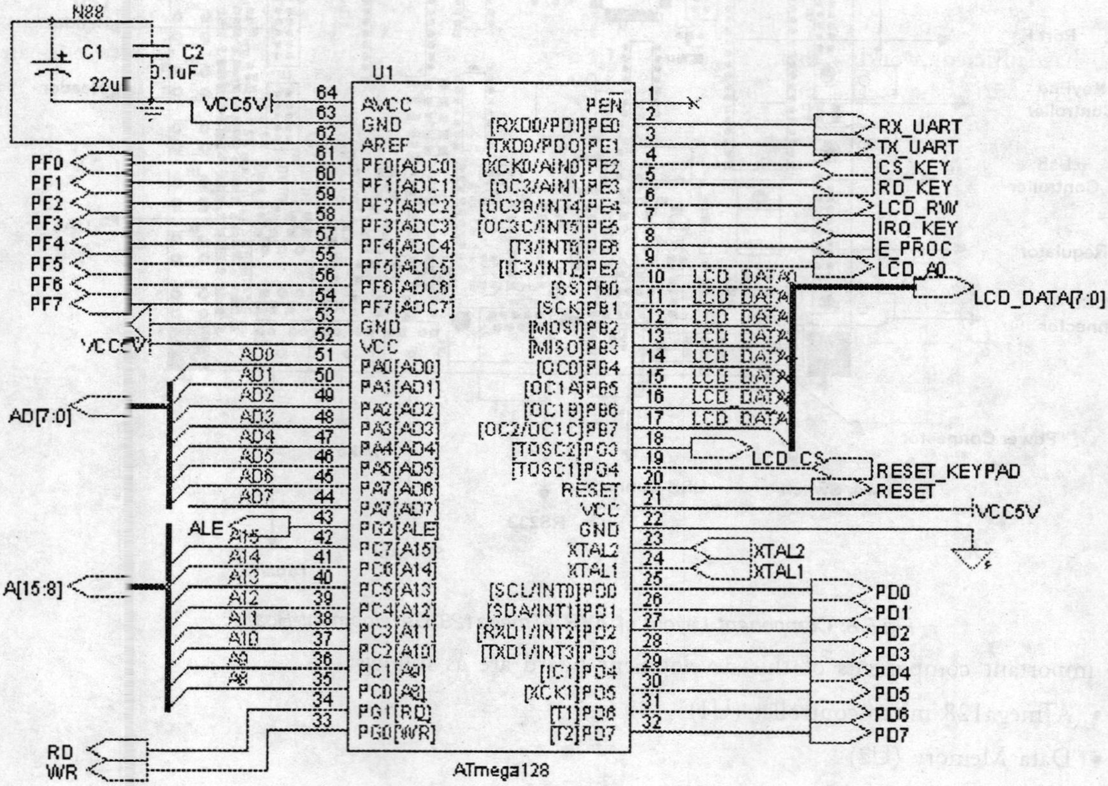

Fig. 5.9: ATmega128 Connections

ATmega128 is a low-power CMOS 8-bit micro-controller based on AVR enhanced RISC architecture. By executing powerful instructions in a single clock cycle, this micro-controller achieves a throughput of 16 MIPS @ 16 MHz. This micro-controller has the following features:

- On-chip 128 K byte of In-system Programmable Flash with Read/Write capability
- On-chip 4 K byte EEPROM
- On-chip 4 K byte SRAM
- 53 General Purpose I/O lines

- 32 General Purpose Registers
- Real Time Clock
- Four Flexible Timers
- Two-Wire Interface
- 8 channel ADC
- Programmable Watch-dog timer
- SPI Port
- 8 Programmable Interrupts

SRAM : It is a 28-pin DIP IC. The size of the Data RAM is 32 KB. The access time is 70 ns. The board has sufficient working memory (SRAM) to develop large application and you can also port an RTOS. Fig. 5.10 shows the pin connections.

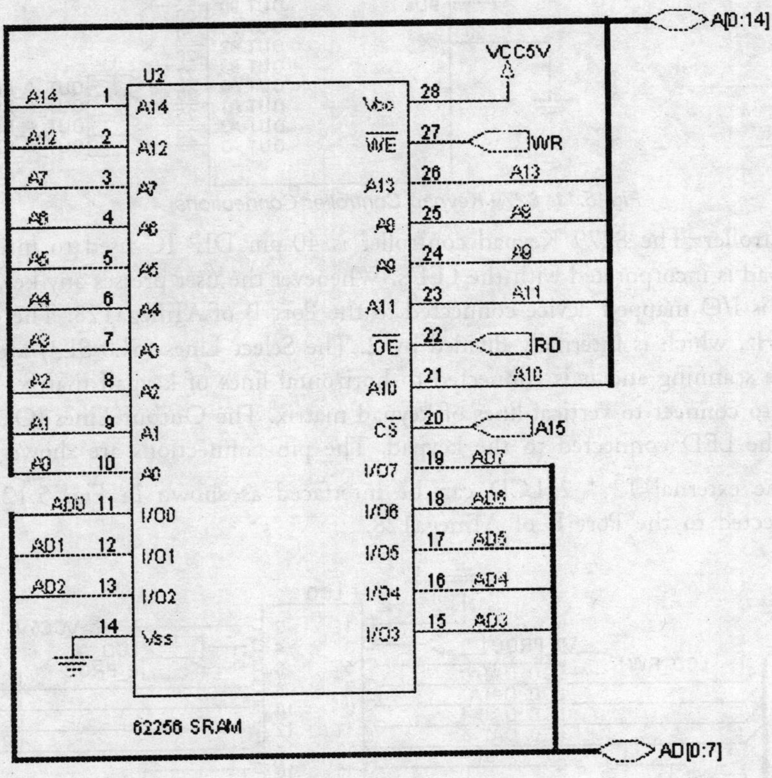

Fig. 5.10: SRAM Connections

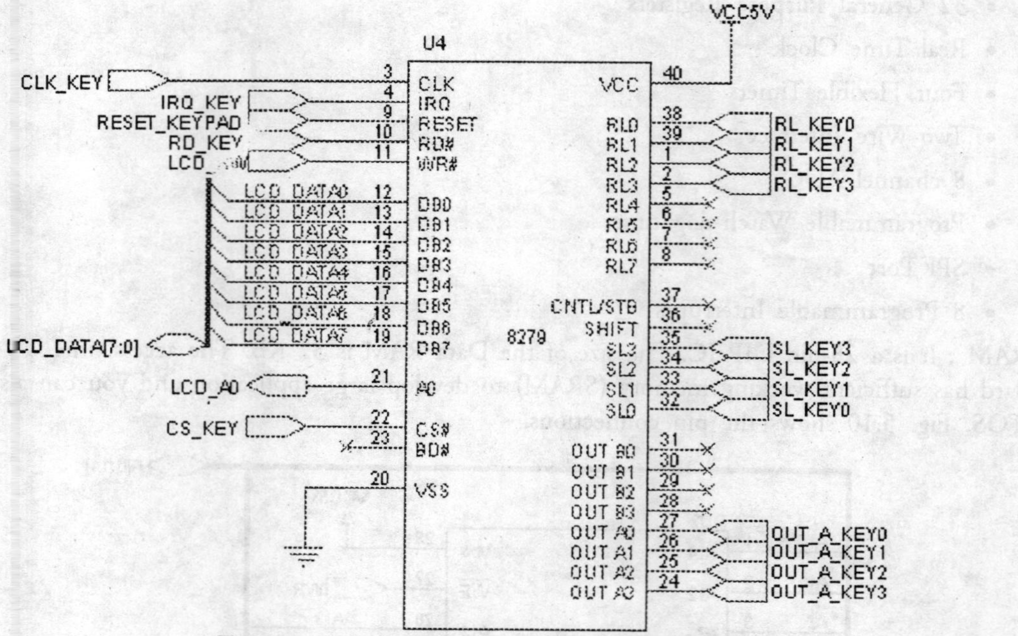

Fig. 5.11: 8279 Keypad Controller Connections

8279 Keypad Controller: The 8279 Keypad controller is 40-pin DIP IC used to interface with 4 * 4 keypad. The keypad is incorporated with the LEDs. Whenever the user presses any key, corresponding LED will glow. It is I/O mapped device connected to the Port B of ATmega128. The clock input for 8279 is 1.8432 MHz, which is internally divided by 2. The Select Lines (SL0-SL3) are used to select the Line during the scanning and it is connected to horizontal lines of keypad matrix. The Read Line (RL0-RL7) is used to connect to vertical lines of keypad matrix. The Output Lines (OUTA0-OUTA3) are used to glow the LED connected to the keypad. The pin connections are shown in Fig. 5.11.

LCD Interface: The external 12 * 2 LCD can be interfaced as shown in Fig. 5.12. The LCD is I/O mapped, connected to the Port B of ATmega128.

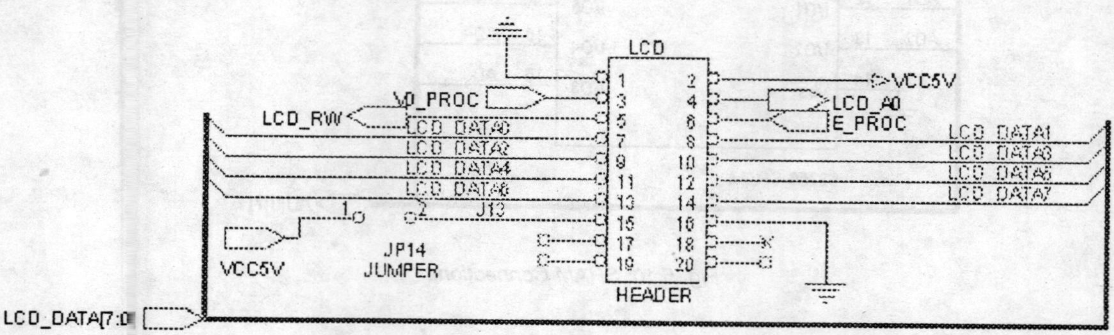

Fig. 5.12: LCD Interface

Keypad interface: 20-Pin FRC (Free Ribbon Cable) connector is used to interface the keypad. The Free Ribbon Cable can be connected as shown in Fig. 5.13.

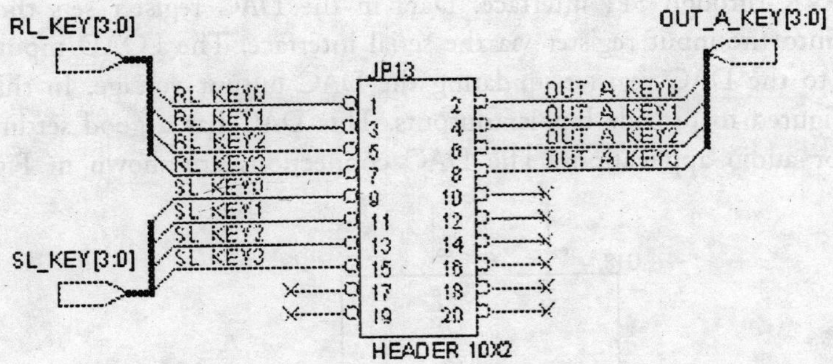

Fig. 5.13: Keyboard Interface Connections

USB Controller: The FTDI232 chip is connected for USB interface. It supports USB1.1 version. Fig. 5.14 shows the USB connections.

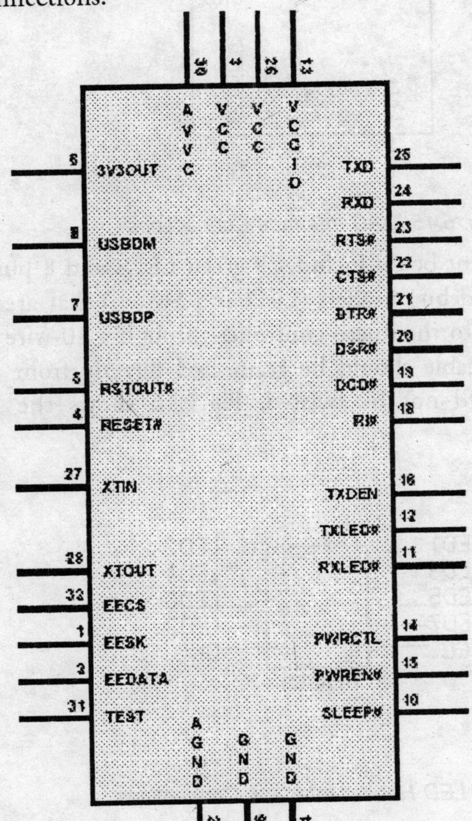

Fig. 5.14: USB Interface Connections

DAC: The MAX551 from Maxim is 12-bit, current-output, and 4-quadrant multiplying digital-to-analog converter (DAC). This device is capable of providing unipolar or bipolar outputs. The DAC is interfaced with the AVR through SPI interface. Data in the DAC register sets the DAC output voltage. Data is loaded into the input register via the serial interface. The LOAD input transfers data from the input register to the DAC register, updating the DAC output voltage. In this development board, the DAC is configured to provide bipolar outputs. This DAC has a good settling time of one microsecond suitable for audio applications. The DAC connections are shown in Fig. 5.15.

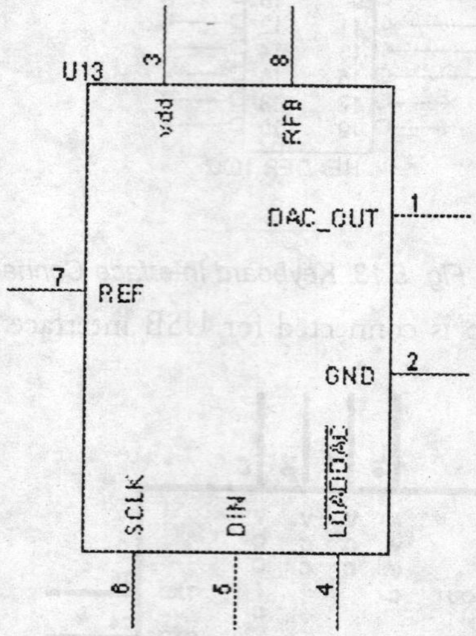

Fig. 5.15: DAC Interface Connections

LEDs Header (LED): The development board includes 8 green LEDs and 8 push-button switches. The LEDs and switches are connected to debug headers (LED and Switch) that are separated from the rest of the board. They can be connected to the micro-controller through a 10-wire cable to the pin header of micro-controller I/O ports. The cable should be connected directly from the port header to the LEDs or switches. The cable should not be twisted. Fig.5.16 shows the LED Header interface connections.

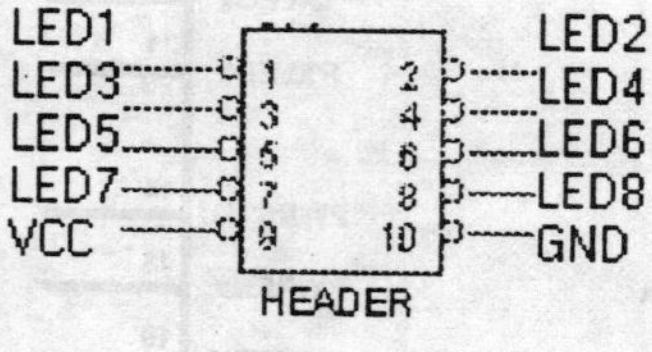

5.16: LED Header Interface Connections

Switch Header (SWITCH): Pushing a switch causes the corresponding signal to be pulled low, while releasing it will result in voltage on the appropriate switch header connector. The interfacing details are shown in Fig. 5.17.

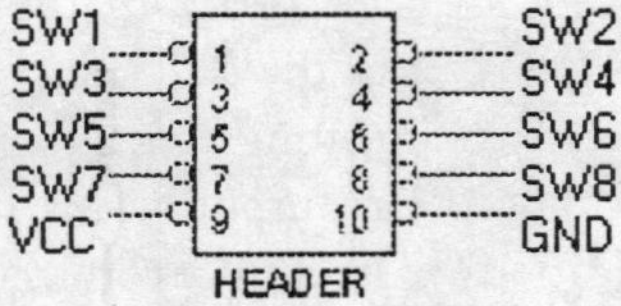

Fig. 5.17: Switch Header Interface Connections

Port A, Port B, Port C(A(H)), Port D, Port E, Port F(ADC), Port G, Address Line Header (LATCH A (L)), INTERRUPT Header: The connections for I/O port headers are shown in Fig. 5.18.

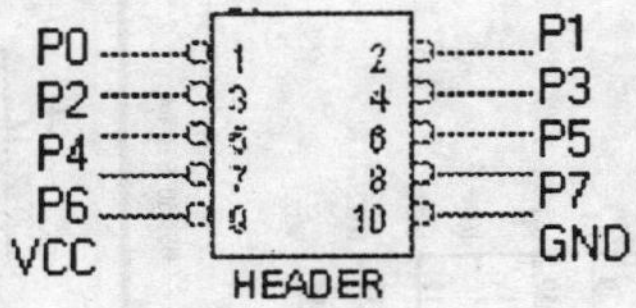

Fig. 5.18: Port Header Connections

RS232 connector: ATmega128 has an in-built UART controller, which is connected to the RS232 line driver chip whose Tx and Rx I/O's are extended to the 9-pin D-type connector. To use RS232, the UART pins of micro-controller need be to physically connected to RS232 connector through MAX232 as shown in Fig. 5.19.

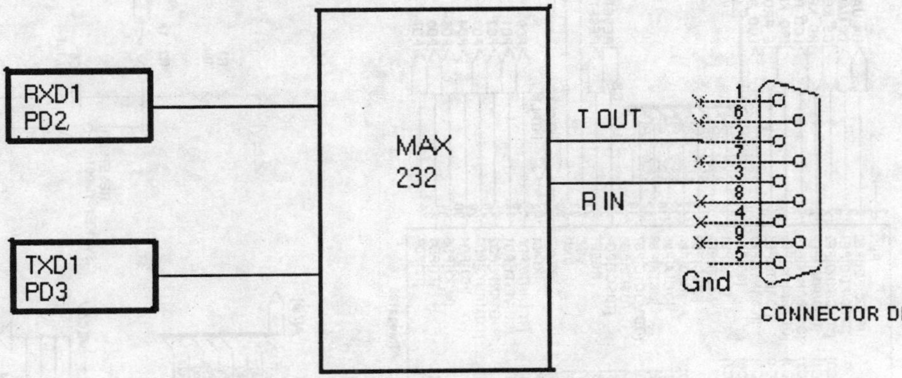

Fig. 5.19: RS232 Interface Connections

Reset Push Button: The Reset Push Button resets the micro-controller when pushed.

Main Power LED: The red LED is directly connected to the main power supply. This LED is always lit when power is applied to the board.

5.3.3 Circuit Schematics of the Development Board

You can develop the board using the circuit schematics given in this section. The circuit schematics of ATmega128, SRAM and Latch are shown in Fig. 5.20.

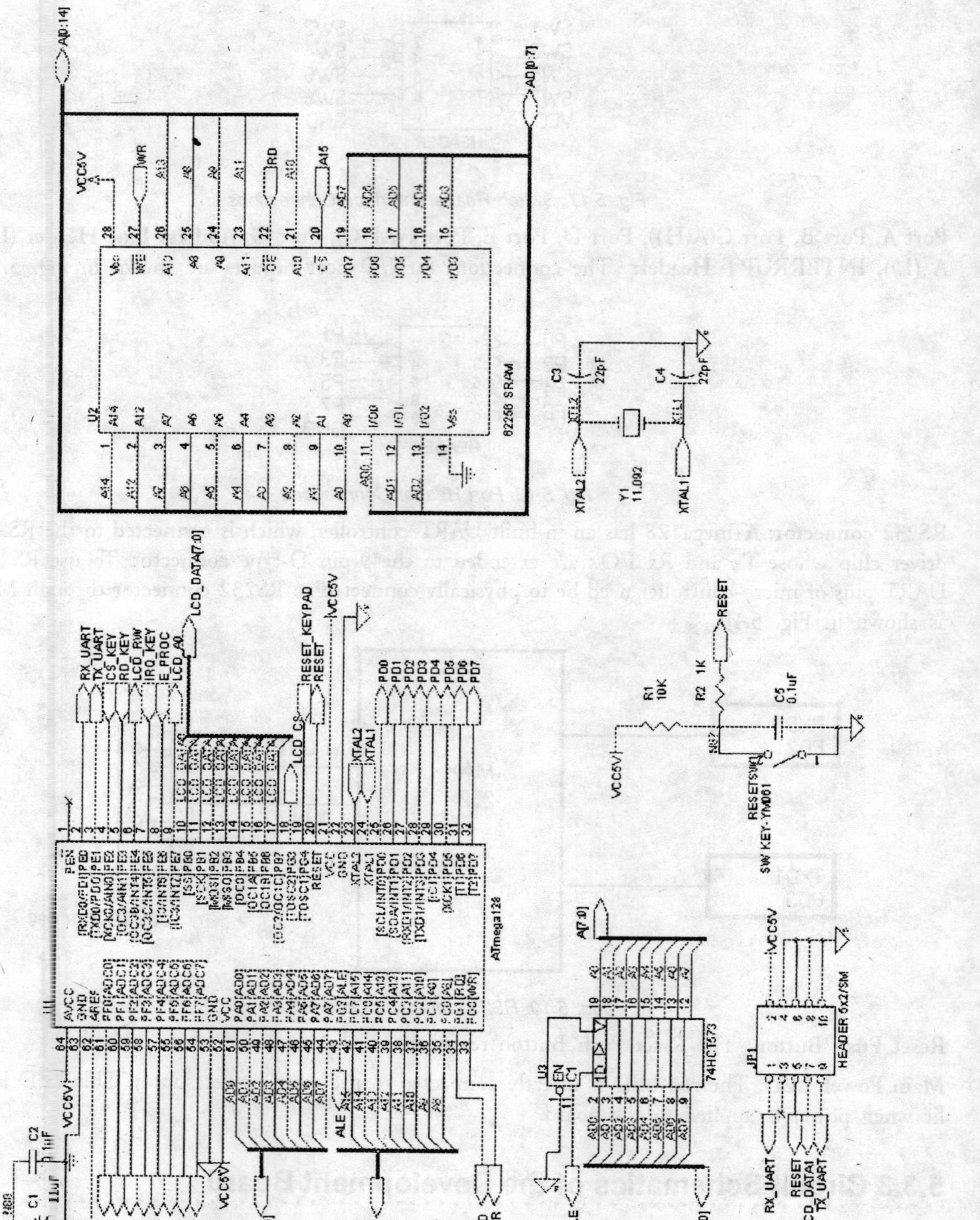

Fig. 5.20: Circuit Schematics of ATmega128, SRAM and Latch

The circuit schematics of headers are shown in Fig. 5.21.

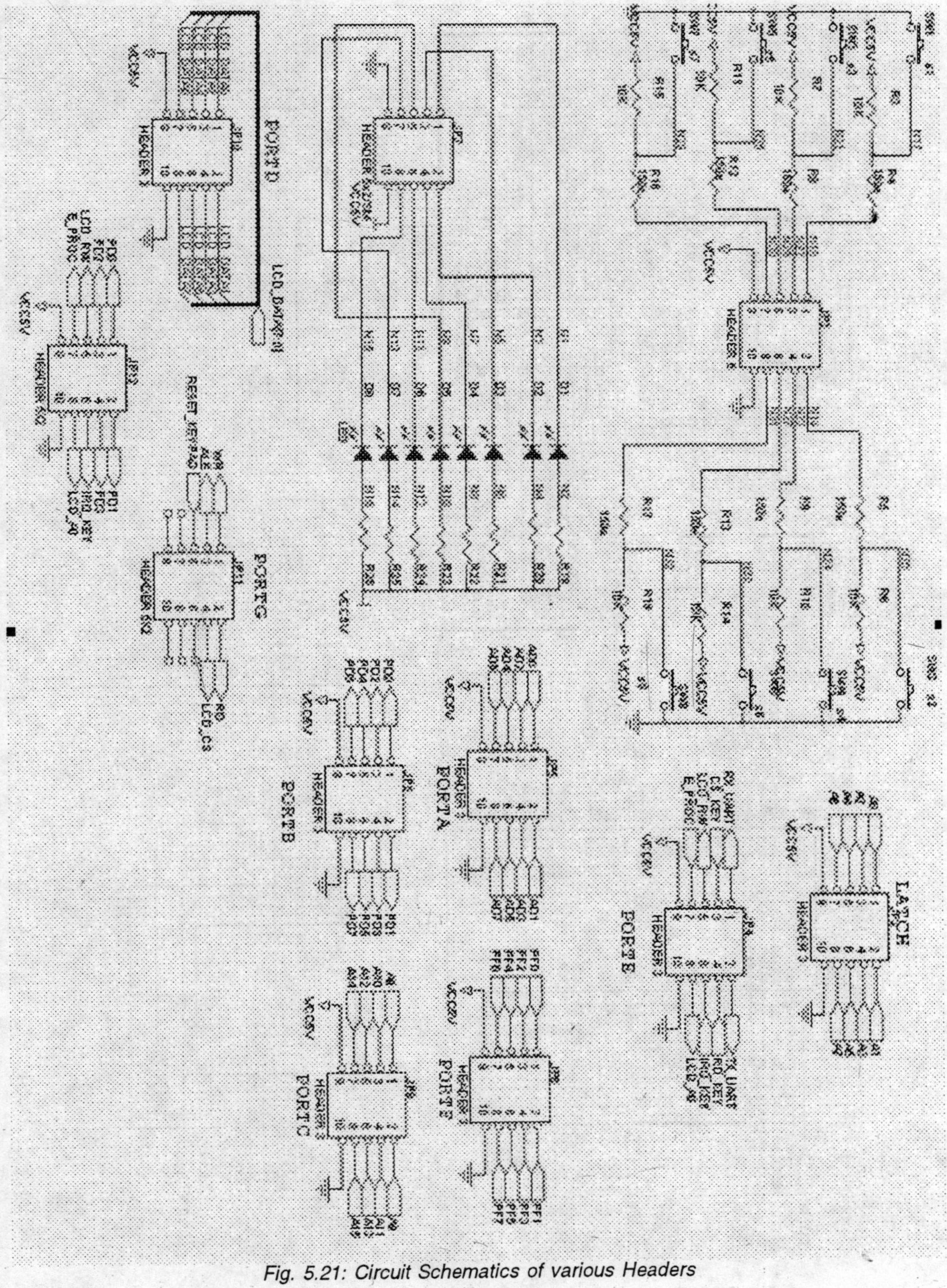

Fig. 5.21: Circuit Schematics of various Headers

The circuit schematics of LCD and Keypad interface and RS232 interface are shown in Fig. 5.22.

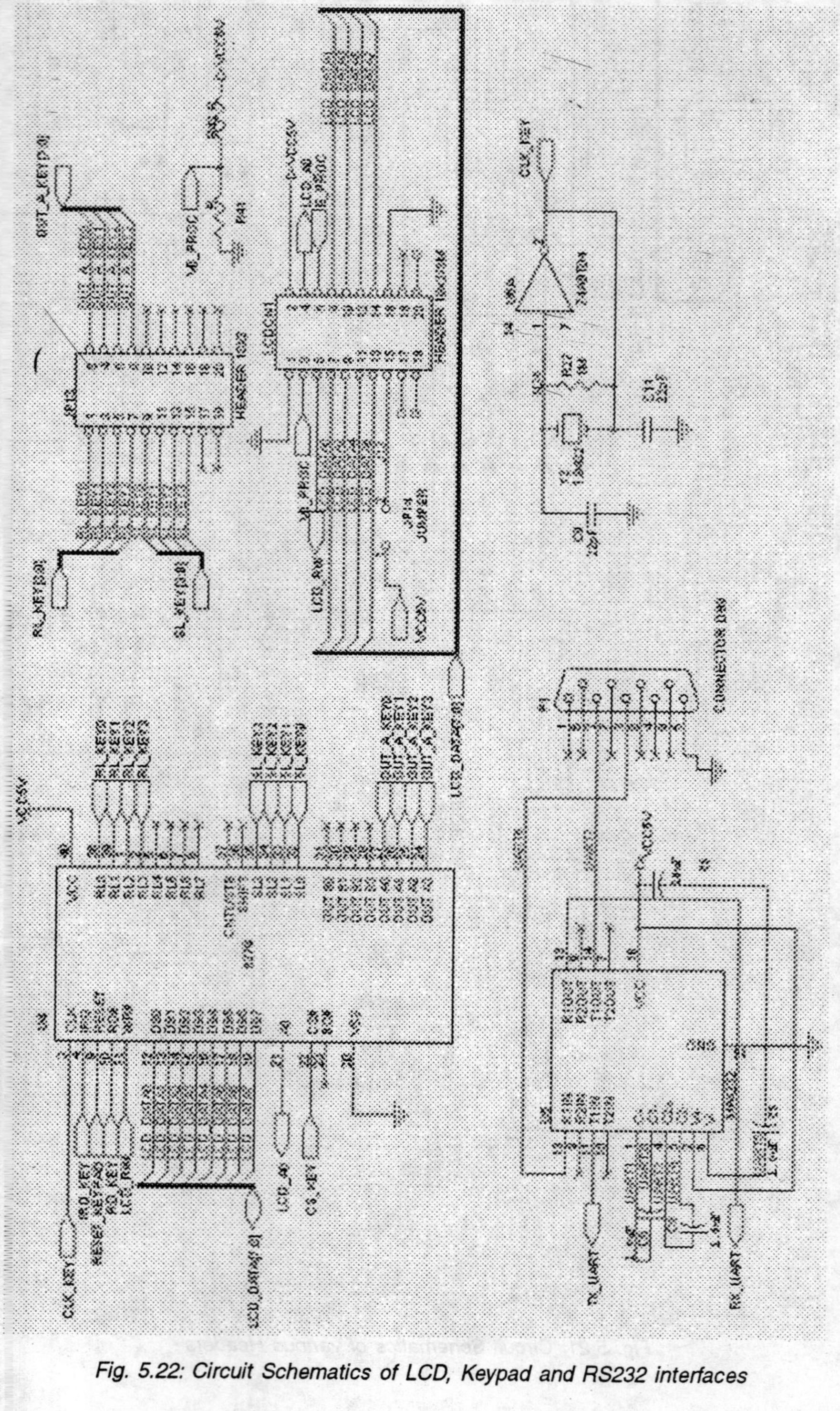

Fig. 5.22: Circuit Schematics of LCD, Keypad and RS232 interfaces

The circuit schematics of USB interface are shown in Fig. 5.23.

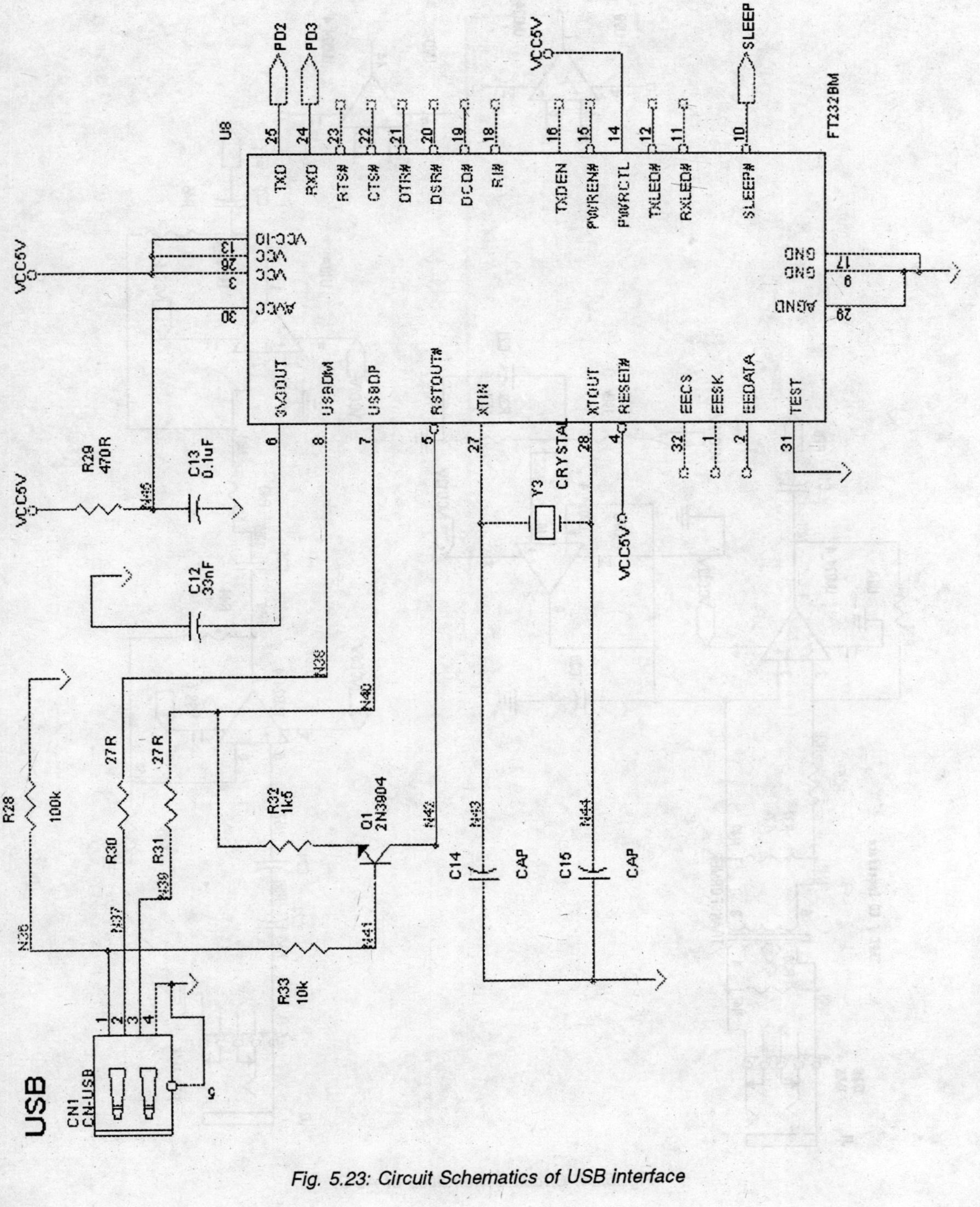

Fig. 5.23: Circuit Schematics of USB interface

The circui schematics of ADC are shown in Fig. 5.24.

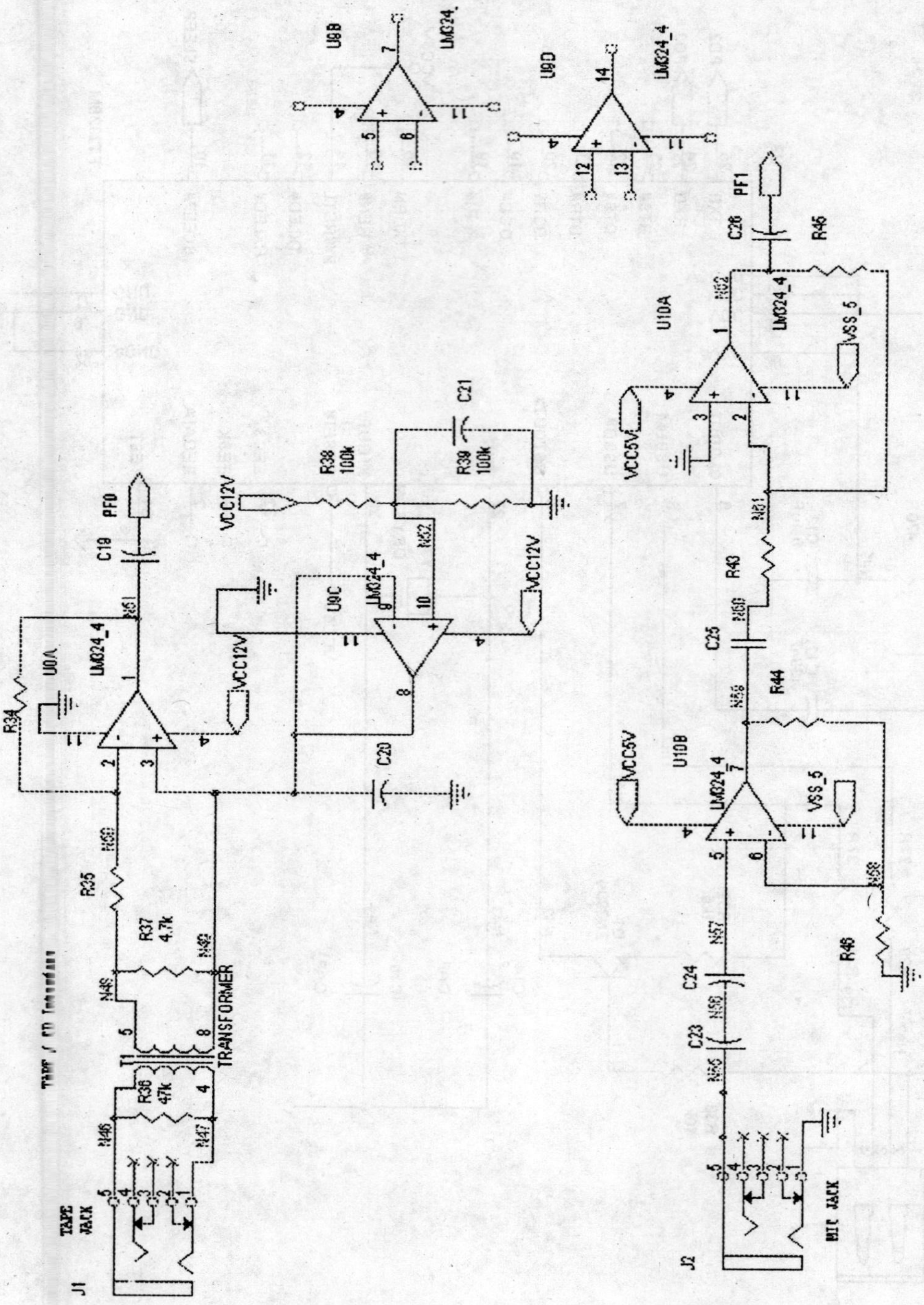

Fig. 5.24: Circuit Schematics of ADC

The circuit schematics of DAC and Regulators are shown in Fig. 5.25.

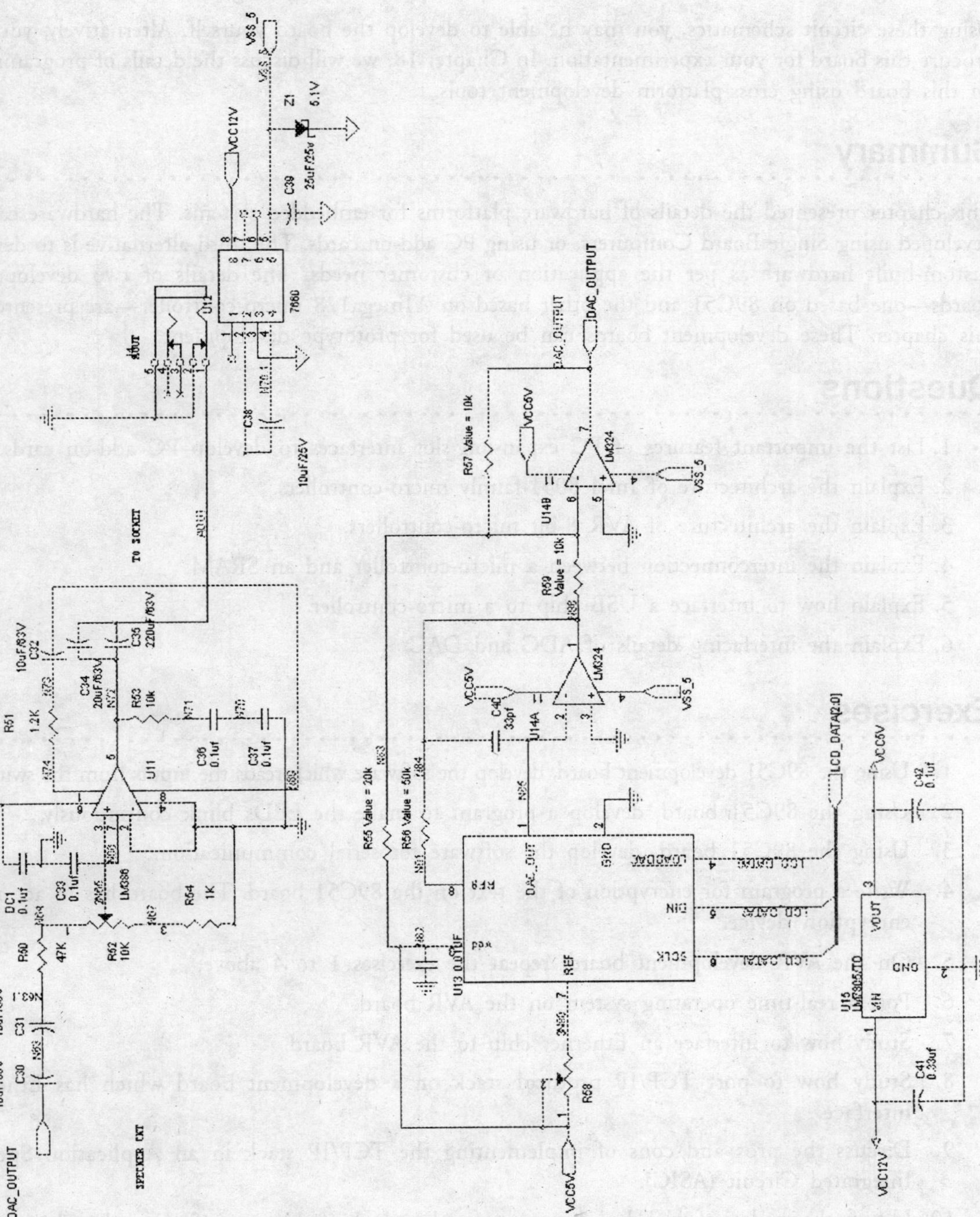

Fig. 5.25: Circuit Schematics of DAC and Regulators

You can connect a microphone in the 3.5mm Stereo Jack, tape/CD and speaker to the development board using 3.5mm stereo jacks as shown in the component layout diagram.

Using these circuit schematics, you may be able to develop the board yourself. Alternatively, you can procure this board for your experimentation. In Chapter 18, we will discuss the details of programming on this board using cross-platform development tools.

Summary

This chapter presented the details of hardware platforms for embedded systems. The hardware can be developed using Single Board Computers, or using PC add-on cards. The third alternative is to develop custom-built hardware as per the application or customer needs. The details of two development boards—one based on 89C51 and the other based on ATmega128 micro-controller—are presented in this chapter. These development boards can be used for prototype development.

Questions

1. List the important features of PC expansion slot interfaces to develop PC add-on cards.
2. Explain the architecture of Intel 8051-family micro-controllers.
3. Explain the architecture of AVR 8-bit micro-controllers.
4. Explain the interconnection between a micro-controller and an SRAM.
5. Explain how to interface a USB chip to a micro-controller.
6. Explain the interfacing details of ADC and DAC.

Exercises

1. Using the 89C51 development board, develop the software which reads the inputs from the switches.
2. Using the 89C51 board, develop a program to make the LEDs blink continuously.
3. Using the 89C51 board, develop the software for serial communication.
4. Write a program for encryption of the text on the 89C51 board. The board has to act as an encryption device.
5. On the AVR development board, repeat the exercises 1 to 4 above.
6. Port a real-time operating system on the AVR board.
7. Study how to interface an Ethernet chip to the AVR board.
8. Study how to port TCP/IP protocol stack on a development board which has Ethernet interface.
9. Discuss the pros and cons of implementing the TCP/IP stack in an Application Specific Integrated Circuit (ASIC).
10. Identify the vendors of single board computers and study the architecture of a single board computer.
11. You need to design a PC add-on card with PCI interface. Identify a suitable chip for providing the PCI interface.

Chapter 6

Communication Interfaces

CHAPTER OBJECTIVES

After reading this chapter, you will be able to:

- Appreciate the need for communication interfaces
- Learn the details of various serial communication interfaces
- Understand the Ethernet and wireless LAN interfaces
- Grasp the details of IEEE 1394 interface
- Gain knowledge of infrared and Bluetooth wireless interfaces

Most of the embedded systems have to interface with the external world. This requirement may be to transmit the data to a PC or workstation, or to interact with another system for sharing the data. To meet this requirement, the embedded systems need to be provided with communication interfaces. In this chapter, we will study the various standard communication interfaces that can be provided to the embedded systems. We will discuss the details of RS232/UART, RS422/RS485, IEEE 1394, Universal Serial Bus (USB), Ethernet as well as wireless interfaces such as IrDA, IEEE 802.11 and Bluetooth.

6.1 Need for Communication Interfaces

The need for providing communication interfaces arises due to the following reasons:

- The embedded system needs to send data to a host (a PC or a workstation). The host will analyse of data and present the data through a Graphical User Interface.
- The embedded system may need to communicate with another embedded system to transmit/receive data. Providing a standard communication interface is preferable rather than providing a proprietary interface.
- A number of embedded systems may need to be networked to share data. Network interfaces need to be provided in such a case.

- An embedded system may need to be connected to the Internet so that anyone can access the embedded system. An example is a real-time weather monitoring system. The weather monitoring system can be Internet-enabled using TCP/IP protocol stack and HTTP server.
- Mobile devices such as cell phones and palmtops need to interact with other devices such as PCs and laptops for data synchronization. For instance, you need to ensure that the address book on your palmtop is the same as that on your laptop. When the palmtop comes near the laptop, automatically the two can form a network to exchange data.
- For some embedded systems, the software may need upgradation after it is installed in the field. The software can be upgraded through communication interfaces.

Due to these reasons, providing communication interfaces based on standard protocols is a must. Not surprisingly, many micro-controllers have on-chip communication interfaces such as a serial interface to meet these requirements. Now, we will discuss the following communication interfaces.

In Brief...

Embedded systems are provided with communication interfaces for monitoring and control by a host system or a node on a network. Through these interfaces, an embedded system can also be accessed over the Internet.

- RS 232/UART
- RS 422, RS 485
- Universal Serial Bus
- Infrared
- IEEE 1394 Firewire
- Ethernet
- IEEE 802.11 wireless interface
- Bluetooth

For each of these interfaces, we will discuss the hardware details and the protocol stack that needs to be implemented in software.

6.2 RS232/UART

RS232 is a standard developed by Electronic Industry Association (EIA). This is one of the oldest and most widely used communication interfaces. The PC will have two RS232 ports designated as COM1 and COM2 Most of the micro-controllers have an on-chip serial interface. The evaluation boards of the processors are also connected to the host system using RS232.

RS232 is used to connect a DTE (Data Terminal Equipment) to a Data Circuit Terminating Equipment (DCE). A DTE can be a PC, serial printer or a plotter. DCE can be a modem, mouse, digitizer or a scanner. RS232 interface specifies the physical layer interface only. The specifications describe the physical, mechanical, electrical, and procedural characteristics for serial communication.

In Brief..

RS232 standard is used for serial communication between two devices for speeds up to 115.2 Kbps over distances up to 100 meters.

RS 232 is a standard for serial communication, i.e. the bits are transmitted serially. The communication between two devices is in full duplex, i.e. the data transfer can take place in both directions.

6.2.1 RS232 Communication Parameters

When two devices have to communicate through RS232, the sending device sends the data character by character. The bits corresponding to the character are called data bits. The data bits are prefixed with a bit called start bit, and suffixed with one or two bits called stop bits. The receiving device decodes the data bits using the start bit and stop bits. This mode of communication is called asynchronous communication because no clock signal is transmitted. In addition to start bit and stop bits, an additional bit called parity bit is also sent. Parity bit is used for error detection at the receiving end.

For two devices to communicate with each other using RS232, the communication parameters have to be set on both the systems. And, for a meaninginful communication, these parameters have to be the same. The various communication parameters are listed below:

Data rate: The rate at which data communication takes place. The PC supports various data rates such as 50, 150, 300, 600, 1200, 2400, 4800, 9600, 19200, 38400, 57600 and 115200 bps. The oscillator in the RS232 circuitry operates at 1.8432 MHz and it is divided by 1600 to obtain the 115200 data rate.

Data bits: Number of bits transmitted for each character. The character can have 5 or 6 or 7 or 8 bits. If you send ASCII characters, the number of bits is 7.

Start bit: The bit that is prefixed to the data bits to identify the beginning of the character.

Stop bits: These bits are appended to the data bits to identify the end of character. If the data bits are 7 or 8, one stop bit is appended. If the data bits are 5 or 6, two stop bits are appended.

Parity: The bit appended to the character for error checking. The parity can be even or odd. For even parity, the parity bit (1 or 0) will be added in such a way that the total number of bits will be even. For odd parity, the parity bit will make the total number of bits odd. If the parity is set to 'none', the parity bit is ignored. For example, if the data bits are 1010110, the parity bit is 0 if even parity is used; and the parity bit is 1 if odd parity is used. At the receiving end, the device will calculate the parity bit and if the received parity bit matches with the calculated parity bit, it can be assumed that the data is without errors. But this is not the reality. If two bits are in error, the receiver cannot detect that there is an error!

Flow Control: If one of the devices sends data at a very fast rate and the other device cannot absorb the data at that rate, flow control is used. Flow control is a protocol to stop/resume data transmission. This protocol is also known as handshaking. If you are sure that there will be no flow control problem, there is no need for handshaking. You can do hardware handshaking in RS232 using two signals: Request to Send (RTS) and Clear to Send (CTS). When a device has data to send, it asserts RTS and the receiving device asserts CTS. You can also do software handshaking — a device can send a request to suspend data transmission by sending the character Control S (0x13). The signal to resume data transmission is sent using the character Control Q (0x11). This software handshaking is also known as XON/XOFF.

In Brief...

The communication parameters to be set for serial communication are: data rate, number of data bits, number of stop bits, parity and flow control.

Notes...

Communication using RS232 involves lot of overhead due to the additional bits to be transmitted—for 7-bit data, the additional bits to be transmitted are 1 start bit, 1 stop bit and 1 parity bit.

6.2.2 RS 232 Connector Configurations

RS232 standard specifies two types of connectors: 25-pin connector and 9-pin connector. In the 25-pin configuration, only a few pins are used. The description of these pins is given in Table 6.1.

Pin number	Function (abbreviation)
1	Chassis ground
2	Transmit data (TXD)
3	Receive data (RXD)
4	Request To Send (RTS)
5	Clear To Send (CTS)
6	Data Set Ready (DSR)
7	Signal Ground (GND)
8	Carrier Detect (CD)
20	Data Terminal Ready (DTR)
22	Ring Indicator (RI)

Table 6.1: 25-pin Connector Pin Details

For the 9-pin connector, the pin details are given in Table 6.2.

Pin number	Function (abbreviation)
1	Carrier Detect (CD)
2	Receive Data (RXD)
3	Transmit Data (TXD)
4	Data Terminal Ready (DTR)
5	Signal Ground (GND)
6	Data Set Ready (DSR)
7	Request to Send (RTS)
8	Clear to Send (CTS)
9	Ring Indicator (RI)

Table 6.2: 9-pin Connector Pin Details

For transmission of 1's and 0's, the voltage levels are defined in the standard. The voltage levels are different for control signals and data signals. These voltage levels are given in Table 6.3. The voltage level is with reference to the local ground and hence RS232 uses unbalanced transmission.

Signal	Voltage Level
Data input	+3 volts and above for 0-3 volts and below for 1
Data output	+5 volts and above for 0-5 volts and below for 1
Control input	+3 volts and above for 1 (ON)-3 volts and below for 0 (OFF)
Control output	+5 volts and above for 1(ON)-5 volts and below for 0 (OFF)

Table 6.3: Voltage Levels for Data and Control Signals

In Brief...

Two types of connectors are used in RS232—25-pin connector and 9-pin connector. The three important pins are—2 for transmit, 3 for receive and 7 for signal ground in a 25-pin connector.

Note that the voltage levels used in RS232 are different from voltage levels used in embedded systems (as most chips use 5 volts and below only). Another problem is that the processor gives out the data in parallel format, not in serial format. These problems are overcome through the use of UART (Universal Asynchronous Receive Transmit) chips.

Notes...

RS232 uses unbalanced transmission i.e., the voltage levels are measured with reference to the local ground. Hence, this transmission is susceptible to noise.

6.2.3 UART

In Brief...

Universal Asynchronous Receive Transmit (UART) chip converts the parallel data received from the processor into serial format and sends it to RS232 level shifter. It also takes the serial data from the RS232 level shifter and converts into parallel format.

The processors process the data in parallel format, not in serial format. To bridge the processor and the RS232 port, Universal Asynchronous Receive Transmit (UART) chip is used. UART has two sections: receive section and transmit section. Receive section receives the data in serial format, converts it into parallel format and gives it to the processor. The transmit section takes the data in parallel format from the processor and converts it into serial format. The UART chip also adds the start bit, stop bits and parity bit. Many micro-controllers have on-chip UART. However, the necessary voltage level conversion has to be done to meet the voltage levels of RS232. This is achieved using a level shifter as shown in Fig. 6.1.

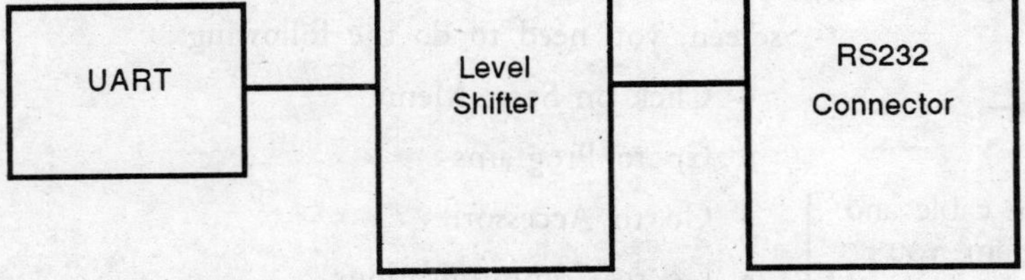

Fig. 6.1: Hardware for RS 232 Interface

UART chip operates at 5 Volts. The level conversion to the desired voltages is done by the level shifter, and then the signals are passed on to the RS232 connector.

RS232 standard specifies a distance of 19.2 meters. However, you can achieve distances up to 100 meters using RS232 cables. The data rates supported will be dependent on the UART chip and the clock used.

Most of the processors including Digital Signal Processors have on-chip UART. ICs such as MAX 3222, MAX 3241 of Maxim can be used as level shifters.

6.2.4 Null Modem Cable Connection

If you want to connect two DTEs such as two PCs, you need to interconnect the two RS232 ports using a null modem cable. The null modem cable connections are shown in Fig. 6.2. Fig. 6.2(a) shows the connections for 25-pin connectors and Fig. 6.2(b) shows the connections for 9-pin connectors. However, the minimal connections required are for TD, RD and GND. If you are using 25-pin connector, it is sufficient if you connect pin 2 to pin 3, pin 3 to pin 2 and pin 7 to pin 7. This is the minimal configuration.

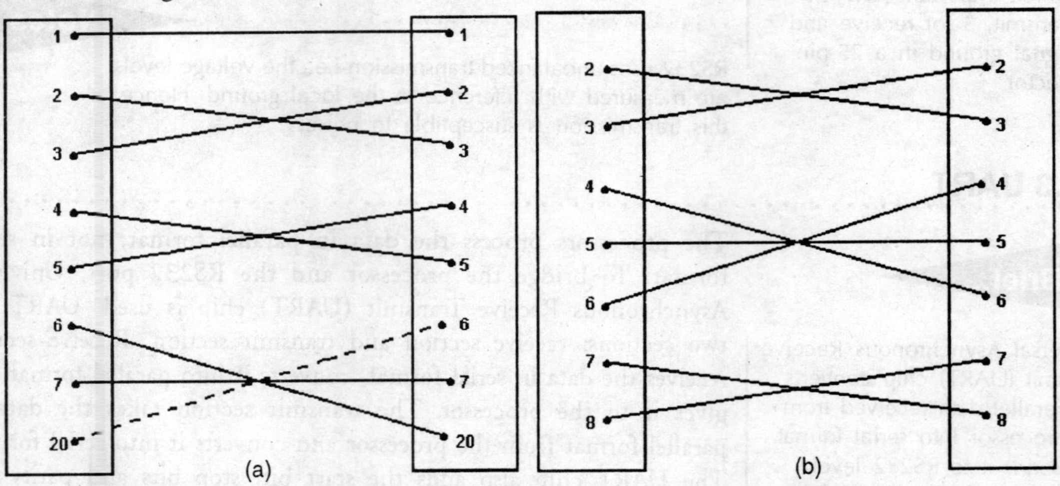

Fig. 6.2 Null Modem Cable Connections: (a) 25-pin Connectors (b) 9-pin Connectors

To make two devices communicate with each other using RS232 interface, you need to connect the two PCs using a null modem cable and set the communication parameters on both the devices. You can experiment with various parameters for serial communication using the HyperTerminal program on Windows. Fig. 6.3 shows the screenshot to set the serial communication parameters. To obtain this screen, you need to do the following:

In Brief...

Using a null modem cable and HyperTerminal program, you can establish serial communication between two machines running the Windows operating system.

- Click on Start Menu
- Go to Programs
- Go to Accessories
- Go to Communications
- Go to HyperTerminal
- Double click on HYPERTRM.EXE

- Enter a name for New Connection "xxxx" and Click OK
- You will get a screen with the title "Connect To". Select COM1 or COM2 from the "Connect Using" list box and click OK.

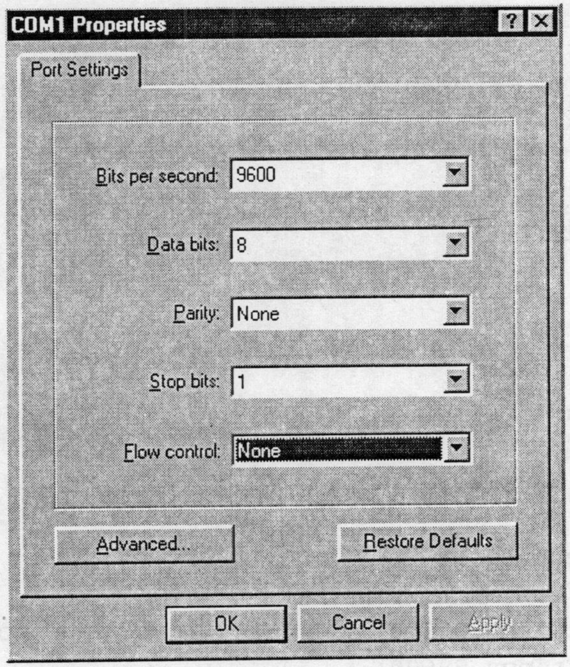

Fig. 6.3: Screenshot to set the Serial Communication Parameters

6.2.5 Serial Communication Programming

In this section, we will study how to establish communication between two PCs, one PC running the Windows operating system and another running the Linux operating system. On the Windows system, we will use the HyperTerminal program and on the Linux system we will write a C program to send and receive data from the Windows system. You need to interconnect the two PCs through a null modem cable to test this program.

On the Windows system, you need to run the HyperTerminal as described earlier. On the Linux system you need to compile and execute the code given in Listing 6.1.

Listing 6.1 serialcom.c

```
#include <stdio.h>
#include <string.h>
#include <unistd.h>
#include <fcntl.h>
#include <errno.h>
#include <termios.h>
```

```
int port_open(void)
{
   int fd;
   fd = open("/dev/ttyS0",O_RDWR | O_NOCTTY | O_NDELAY);
   if(fd == -1)
   {
      perror("Unable to open the port: /dev/ttyS0");
   }
   else
   {
      fcntl(fd,F_SETFL,0);
   }
   return(fd);
}

void port_config(int fd)
{
   struct termios settings;

   tcgetattr(fd,&settings);

   cfsetispeed(&settings,B9600); // Set baud rate to 9600
   cfsetospeed(&settings,B9600);

   settings.c_cflag |= (CLOCAL | CREAD);// set to local mode

   settings.c_cflag &= ~PARENB; //no parity bit
   settings.c_cflag &= ~CSTOPB; // two stop bits
   settings.c_cflag &= ~CSIZE;  //bit mask for data bits
   settings.c_cflag |= CS8;          //8 data bits

   tcsetattr(fd,TCSANOW,&settings);
}

void write_data(int fd,char *c)
{
   int n;
   n = write(fd, c, strlen(c));
   if(n<0)
   {
      fputs("write() of data failed! \n",stderr);
```

```
    }
}

void read_data(int fd)
{
    char array[255];
    char *ptr;
    int nbytes;

    ptr = array;
    while((nbytes = read(fd, ptr, array + sizeof(array)-ptr-1)) > 0)
    {
        ptr += nbytes;
        if((ptr[-1] == '\n') || (ptr[-1] == '\r'))
            break;
    }
    *ptr = '\0';
    printf("Received String: %s",array);
}

void port_close(int fd)
{
    close(fd);
}

int main(void)
{
    int fd;
    fd = port_open();
    port_config(fd);
    write_data(fd,"Hello World");
    read_data(fd);
    port_close(fd);
    return 0;
}
```

The function **`port_open(void)`** opens the serial port. **`/dev/ttyS0`** is the device file. You can find out the device file of your Linux installation in the /dev directory and use that file name instead of **`/dev/ttyS0`**.

The function **`port_config(int fd)`** is to configure the port parameters.

The function **`write_data (int fd,`** char *c) is to write data onto the port. The pointer to a character array is passed from this function.

The function `read_data(int fd)` is to read the data from the port.

The function `port_close(int fd)` closes the port.

The main(void) function calls the functions to open the port, configure the port parameters, write the data, read the data and then close the port.

In Brief..

Serial communication programming involves opening the device file, configuring the port by setting the communication parameters, reading/writing data and then closing the port.

You can compile this program using the following shell command. Note that the $ sign is the system prompt.

```
$gcc serialcom.c
```

The file a.out will be created. You can execute this file by giving the command

```
$./a.out
```

The message "Hello World" will be displayed on the Windows system. You can type some text on the Windows system and it will be displayed on the Linux system.

6.3 RS422/RS485

RS422 standard for serial communication is used in noisy environments. Using this standard interface, the distance between two devices can be up to 1200 meters. Twisted copper cable is used as the transmission medium. Unlike RS232 in which the voltage levels are measured with reference to local ground, in RS422, voltage difference between the two copper wires represents the logic levels. Hence, RS422 uses balanced transmission. Two channels are used for transmit and receive paths. As compared to RS232, RS422 is better suited to work in noisy environments over longer distances because of balanced transmission.

In Brief...

In RS422 and RS485, twisted copper pair is used as transmission medium. The voltage difference between the two wires represents logic levels, i.e. balanced transmission is used and hence this transmission is immune to noise.

RS485 is a variation of RS422 to connect a number of devices in a network. An RS485 controller chip is used on each device. A network using RS485 protocols operates in a Master/Slave configuration. Up to 512 devices can be networked. Using one twisted pair, half-duplex communication can be achieved and using two twisted pairs, full-duplex communication can be achieved.

Chips such as MAX3488 are used for RS422. MAX 3483 is an RS 485 controller for half-duplex communication and MAX 3491 is for full-duplex communication.

6.4 USB

Universal Serial Bus has gained immense popularity in recent years. Desktops, laptops, printers, display devices, video cameras, hard disk drives, CDROM drives, audio equipment etc. are now available with USB interface. Using USB, a number of devices can be networked using Master/Slave architecture. A host, such as the PC, is designated as a master. As shown in Fig. 6.4, a number of devices, up to a maximum of 127, can be connected in the form of an inverted tree. On the host, such as a PC,

In Brief...

Universal Serial Bus (USB) is a serial communication protocol to connect up to 127 devices to a host. A USB device can be self-powered, or it can be powered by the bus.

there will be a host controller — a combination of hardware and software — to control all the USB devices. Devices can be connected to the host controller either directly or through a hub. A hub is also a USB device that extends the number of ports — from 2 to 8 — to connect other USB devices. A USB device can be self-powered, or powered by the bus. USB can supply 500 mA current to the devices.

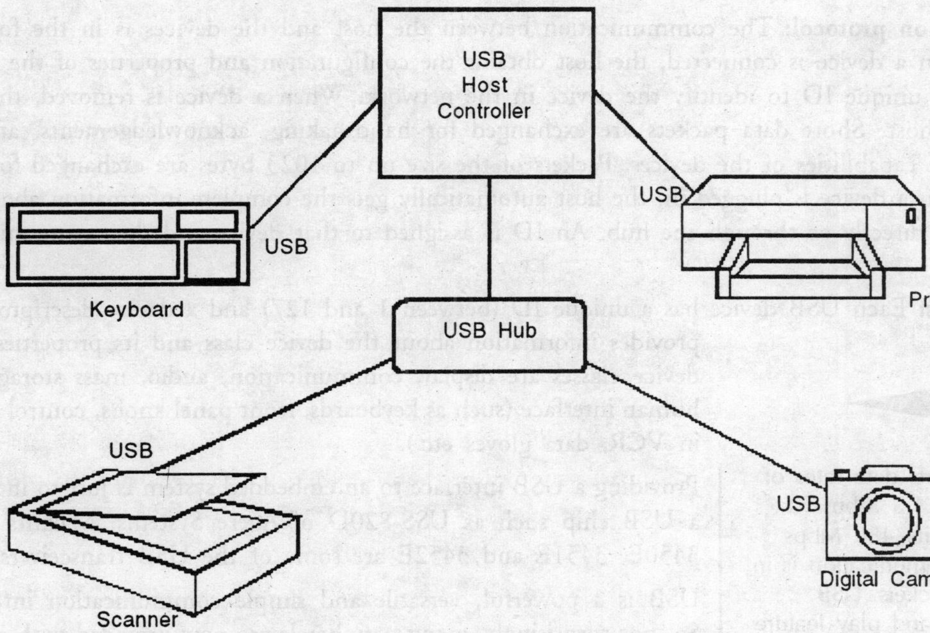

Fig. 6.4: USB Device Connection Hierarchy

6.4.1 USB Physical Interface

In Brief...

USB uses a twisted pair of wires as the medium. Data is transmitted over the twisted pair using differential data lines and hence balanced communication is used.

A shielded 4-wire twisted copper cable is used with the pin connections as shown in Table 6.4. Data is transmitted over a differential twisted pair of wires labeled D+ and D-.

Pin number	Function (abbreviation)
1	+5 V Power (VBUS)
2	Differential data line (D+)
3	Differential data line (D-)
4	Power and Signal ground (GND)

Table 6.4: Pin Connections for USB Interface

6.4.2 Features of USB

Data rates: USB 1.1 standard supports 12 Mbps data rate, and 1.5 Mbps for slower peripherals. USB2.0 supports data rates up to 480 Mbps.

Special features: USB supports plug and play, i.e. you can connect USB devices to the hub or the host without any need for configuration settings. The host will detect and identify the device by exchanging a set of packets. This is known as "Bus Enumeration". The devices are hot-pluggable, i.e. there is no need to switch off the power to connect the device.

Communication protocol: The communication between the host and the devices is in the form of packets. When a device is connected, the host obtains the configuration and properties of the device and assigns a unique ID to identify the device in the network. When a device is removed, the hub informs the host. Short data packets are exchanged for handshaking, acknowledgements, and for informing the capabilities of the devices. Packets of the size up to 1023 bytes are exchanged for data transfer. When a device is plugged in, the host automatically gets the complete information about the device, either directly or through the hub. An ID is assigned to that device and the communication can start.

Device classes: Each USB device has a unique ID (between 1 and 127) and a device descriptor that provides information about the device class and its properties. The device classes are display, communication, audio, mass storage and human interface (such as keyboards, front panel knobs, control panels in VCR, data gloves etc.).

In Brief...

USB1.1 supports data rates of 12 Mbps and 1.5 Mbps. USB2.0 supports 480 Mbps data rate. Communication is in the form of packets. USB supports plug and play feature as well as hot insertion.

Providing a USB interface to an embedded system is just to integrate a USB chip such as USS-820D of Agere Systems. Maxim's MAX 3450E, 3451E and 3452E are some of the USB transceivers.

USB is a powerful, versatile and simple communication interface. So, not surprisingly, many peripherals are now provided with a USB interface. RS232 will be confined to the technology museums.

6.5 Infrared

Infrared interfaces are used in remote control units of TV, VCR, air-conditioner, etc. However, these interfaces are all based on proprietary protocols. Infrared Data Association (IrDA), a non-profit industry association (www.irda.org) founded in 1993, released the specifications for low-cost infrared communication between devices. Infrared interfaces are now commonplace for a number of devices such as palmtops, cell phones, digital cameras, printers, keyboards, mice, LCD projectors, ATMs, smart cards etc. Infrared interface provides a low-cost, short range, point-to-point communication between two devices. The only drawback with infrared is that it operates in line of sight communication mode and it cannot penetrate through walls. It supports only data.

In Brief..

Infrared is a low-cost, point-to-point communication mechanism for short ranges.

The block diagram of IrDA module is shown in Fig. 6.5(a) and the protocol architecture is shown in Fig. 6.5(b). As shown in Fig. 6.5(a), the device will have an infrared transceiver. The transmitter is a LED and the receiver is a photodiode. Agilent's HSDL-1001 can be used as a transceiver. For low data rates, the processor of the embedded system itself can be used whereas for high data rates, a different processor may be needed.

The data to be sent on the infrared link is packetized and encoded as per the IrDA protocols and sent over the air to the other device. The receiving device will detect the signal, decode and depacketize the data.

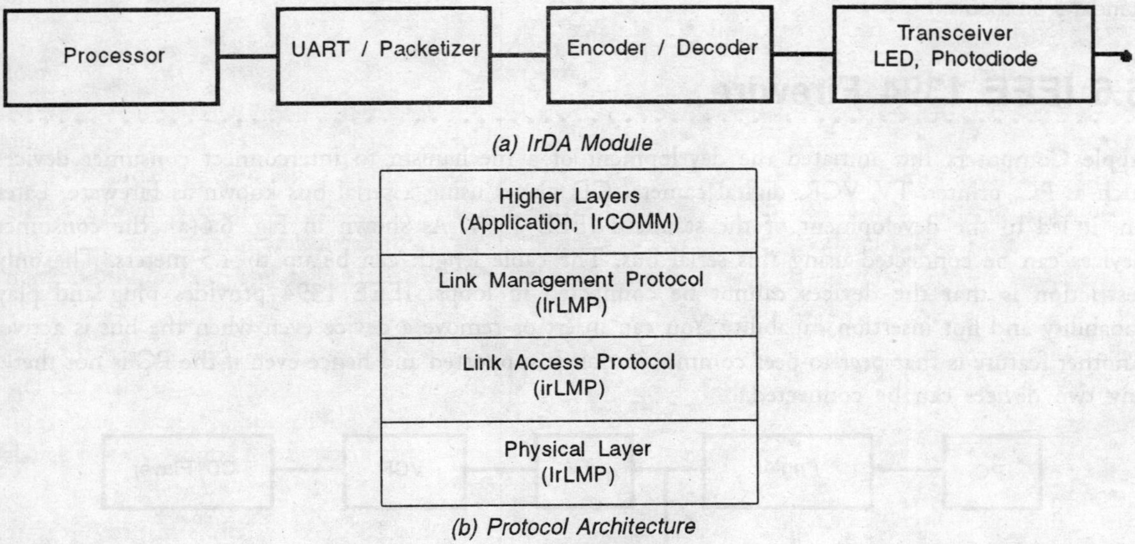

Fig. 6.5: Infrared Interface

As shown in Fig. 6.5(b), for communication through infrared interface, the physical layer (IrPHY) and data link layer (IrLAP) are specified in the standards. Link Management is done through IrLMP, above which the application layer protocols will be running.

Physical layer: IrPHY specifies the data rates and the mode of communication. IrDA has two specifications viz., IrDA Data and IrDA control. IrDA Data has a range of 1 meter with bi-directional communication. Serial IR (SIR) supports data rate up to 115 Kbps and Fast IR (FIR) supports data rates up to 4 Mbps. IrDA Control has a range of 5 meters with bi-directional communication speed up to 75 Kbps. A host such as PC can communicate with 8 peripherals using IrDA protocols.

Data link layer: The data link layer is called the IrLAP. IrLAP is based on HDLC protocol. Master/Slave protocol is used for communication between two devices. The device that starts the communication is the master. The master sends the command and the slave sends a response.

Link management layer: This layer facilitates a device to query the capabilities of other devices. It also provides the software capability to share IrLAP between multiple tasks.

Higher layers: The higher layer protocols are application specific. IrCOMM protocol emulates the standard serial port. When two devices such as palmtop and mobile phone both fitted with infrared interface come face to face, they can exchange the data (say, the address book) using the application layer protocols.

In spite of its limitations such as short range, low data rates and point-to-point communication, infrared is a very popular communication interface for consumer items and office automation equipment because of its low cost.

Notes...

Infrared communication using IrDA standards provides interoperability between IR ports supplied by different manufacturers. The present IR ports of TVs, air-conditioners etc. do not support these standard protocols.

6.6 IEEE 1394 Firewire

Apple Computers Inc. initiated the development of a mechanism to interconnect consumer devices such as PC printer, TV, VCR, digital camera, CD player using a serial bus known as Fireware. Later on, it led to the development of the standard IEEE 1394. As shown in Fig. 6.6(a), the consumer devices can be connected using this serial bus. The cable length can be up to 4.5 meters. The only restriction is that the devices cannot be connected in loops. IEEE 1394 provides plug and play capability and hot insertion capability. You can insert or remove a device even when the bus is active. Another feature is that peer-to-peer communication is supported and hence even if the PC is not there, any two devices can be connected.

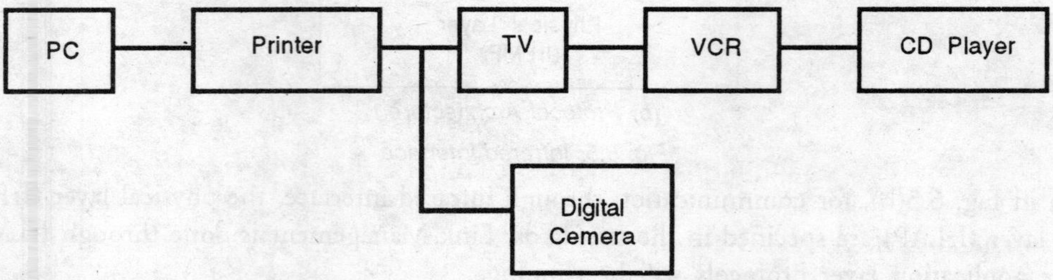

(a) Cosnnecting Devices through IEEE 1394 Bus

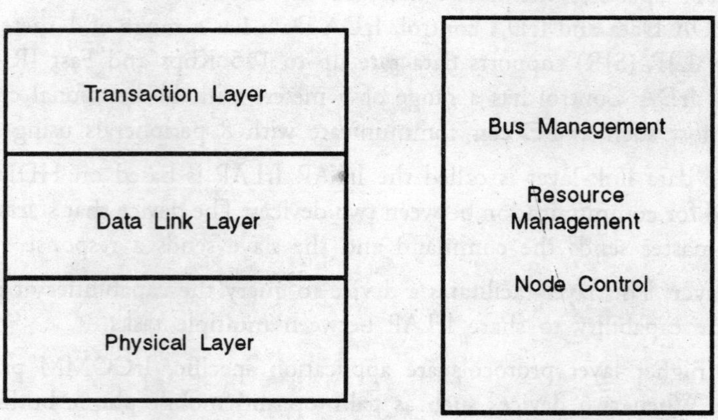

(b) Protocol Architecture

Fig. 6.6: IEEE 1394

In Brief...

IEEE 1394 Firewire is a standard for interconnecting consumer electronic devices using a serial bus. Each bus can support 63 devices.

Each device is given a 6-bit identification number and hence a maximum of 63 devices can be interconnected on a single bus. Using bridges, multiple buses can be connected. Each bus is given a 10-bit identification number and hence 1023 buses can be interconnected. The standard specifies copper wire or optical fiber as the transmission medium with data rates 100, 200, 400, 800, 1600 and 3200 Mbps.

The protocol architecture for the communication between devices is shown in Fig. 6.6(b). The functionality of various layers is as follows:

Physical layer: This layer specifies the electrical and mechanical connections. Bus initialization and arbitration are the functions of this layer. These functions ensure that only one device transmits data at a time.

Data link layer: The layer takes care of packet delivery, acknowledgements and addressing of the devices.

Transaction layer: This layer handles the writing and reading of the data from the devices.

Management protocols: These protocols are used to manage the bus and they run on each of the devices. These protocols do the necessary resource management and control the nodes.

Many consumer appliances are being provided with IEEE 1394 interface. Note that this interface itself is an embedded system.

6.7 Ethernet

Ethernet interface is now ubiquitous. It is available on every desktop and laptop. With the availability of low-cost Ethernet chips and the associated protocol stack, providing an Ethernet interface is very easy and useful to the embedded system. Through the Ethernet interface, the embedded system can be connected to the LAN. So, a number of embedded systems in a manufacturing unit can be connected as a LAN; and, another node on the LAN, a desktop computer, can monitor all these embedded systems. The data collected by an embedded system can be transferred to a database on the LAN.

The Ethernet interface provides the physical layer and data link layer functionality. Above the data link layer, the TCP/IP protocol stack and the application layer protocols will run. This protocol architecture is shown in Fig. 6.7.

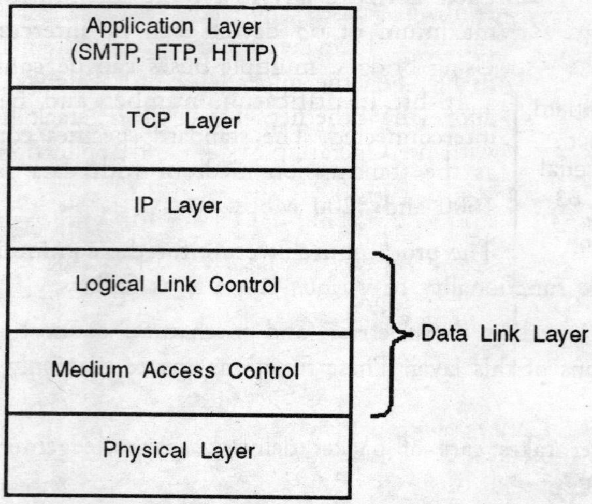

Fig. 6.7: Ethernet LAN Protocol Architecture

Physical layer: The Ethernet physical layer specifies a RJ 45 jack using which the device is connected to the Local Area Network. Unshielded twisted pair or coaxial cable can be used as the medium. Two pairs of wires are used for transmission, one for transmit path and one for receive path. Ethernet transmits balanced differential signals. In each pair, one wire carries signal voltage between 0 to +2.5 volts and the second wire carries signals with voltage between –2.5 volts and 0 volts, and hence the signal difference is 5 volts. The various pin connection details of RJ 45 connector are given in Table 6.5. Speeds of 10 Mbps and 100 Mbps are supported.

Pin number	Function (abbreviation)
1	Transmit Data (TD+)
2	Transmit Data (TD-)
3	Receive Data (RD+)
4	No connection (NC)
5	No connection (NC)
6	Receive Data (RD-)
7	No Connection (NC)
8	No Connection (NC)

Table 6.5: Pin Connections for Ethernet Interface

Data link layer: The data link layer is divided into Medium Access Control (MAC) layer and Logical Link Control (LLC) layer. The MAC layer uses the Carrier Sense Multiple Access/Collision Detection (CSMA/CD) protocol to access the shared medium. The LLC layer specifies the protocol for logical connection establishment, flow control, error control and acknowledgements. Each Ethernet interface will have a unique Ethernet address of 48 bits.

Due to the availability of low-cost Ethernet chips (such as CS 8900A of Cirrus Logic), with little additional cost, an embedded system can be provided with Ethernet connectivity. Even 8-bit micro-

In Brief...

Ethernet standard specifies the physical layer and data link layer standards to connect devices in a Local Area Network. Above the Ethernet protocols, TCP/IP protocol has to be run to make the embedded system Internet-enabled.

controller based embedded systems can be provided the Ethernet interface. To make the embedded system network-enabled, as shown in Fig. 6.7, the upper layer protocols viz., TCP/IP stack has to run above the Ethernet. The TCP/IP stack has to be embedded along with the Operating System and application software in the firmware. If the embedded system has to send mails, Simple Mail Transfer Protocol (SMTP) has to run. To support file transfer application, File Transfer Protocol (FTP) software has to be ported. If the embedded system has to work as a web server, the HTTP server software has to run on the system.

Notes...

In Ethernet, the data link layer is divided into two sub-layers—Medium Access Control (MAC) sub-layer and Logical Link Control (LLC) sub-layer. MAC sub-layer facilitates multiple nodes to access the medium using CSMA/CD protocol. LLC sub-layer defines the protocols for link establishment, flow control and error control.

6.8 IEEE 802.11

IEEE 802.11 family of standards is for Wireless Local Area Networks and Personal Area Networks. These standards cover the physical and MAC layers of Wireless LANs. The LLC layer is same as for the Ethernet LAN. The architecture of IEEE 802.11 standard for Wireless LAN is shown in Fig. 6.8. Each wireless LAN node has a radio and an antenna. All the nodes running the same MAC protocol and competing to access the same medium will form a Basic Service Set (BSS). This BSS can interface to a backbone LAN through Access Point (AP). The backbone LAN can be a wired LAN such as Ethernet LAN. Two or more BSSs can be interconnected through the backbone LAN. In trade magazines, the Access Points are referred as "Hotspots".

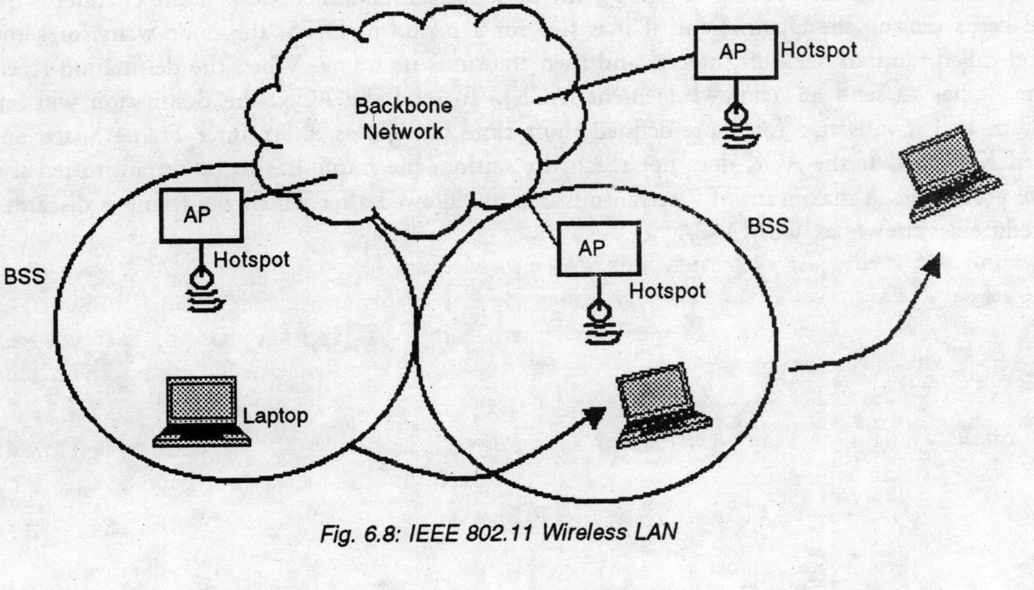

Fig. 6.8: IEEE 802.11 Wireless LAN

The physical medium specifications for 802.11 WLANs are:

- Diffused Infrared with anto operating wavelength between 850 and 950 nm. The data rate supported using this medium is 1 Mbps. 2 Mbps data rate is optional.
- Direct Sequence Spread Spectrum operating in 2.4 GHz ISM band. Up to 7 channels each with a data rate of 1 Mbps or 2 Mbps can be used.
- Frequency hopping spread spectrum operating in 2.4 GHz ISM band with 1 Mbps data rate. 2 Mbps data rate is optional.

ISM (Industrial, Scientific and Medical) band is a 'free' band and hence no government approvals are required to operate radio systems in this band. ISM band frequency range is 2400 – 2483.5 MHz.

Extensions to IEEE 802.11 have been developed to support higher data rates. 802.11b standard has been developed which supports data rates up to 22 Mbps at 2.4 GHz, with a range of 100 meters. Another extension, 802.11a, operates in the 5 GHz frequency band and can support data rates up to 54 Mbps, with a range of 100 meters. 802.11g supports 54 Mbps data rates in the 2.4 GHz band.

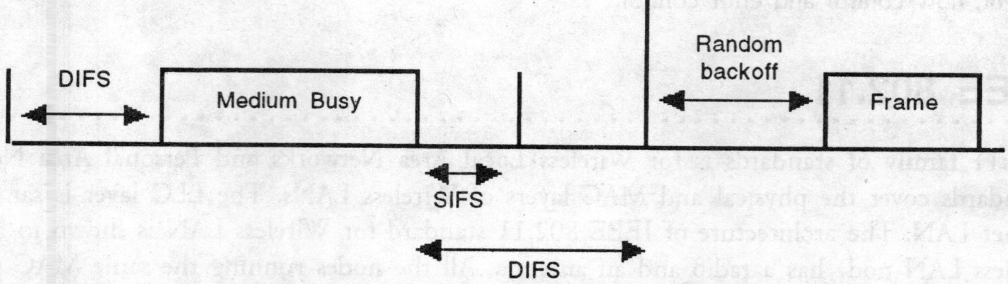

Fig. 6.9: CSMA/CA protocol

The MAC protocol used in 802.11 is called CSMA/CA (Carrier Sense Multiple Access with Collision Avoidance). The CSMA/CA operation is shown in Fig. 6.9. Before transmitting, a node senses the radio medium and if the channel is free for a period longer than a pre-defined value (known as Distributed Inter Frame Spacing or DIFS), the node transmits immediately. If the channel is busy, the node keeps sensing the channel and if it is free for a period of DIFS, the node waits for some more period called random back-off interval and then transmits its frame. When the destination receives the frame, it has to send an acknowledgement (ACK). To send the ACK, the destination will sense the medium and if it is free for a pre-defined short time (known as Short Inter Frame Space or SIFS), the ACK is sent. If the ACK does not reach the station, the frame has to be retransmitted using the above procedure. A maximum of 7 retransmissions are allowed after which the frame is discarded. This procedure is known as CSMA/CA.

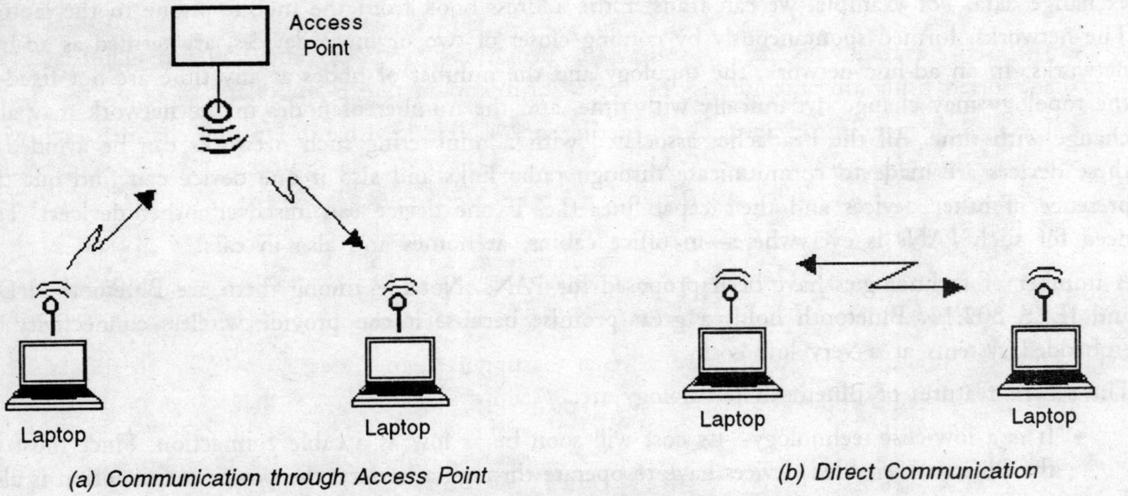

Fig. 6.10: Communication between nodes in Wireless LAN

An important feature of IEEE 802.11 wireless LAN is that two or more nodes can communicate directly also without the need for a centralized control. The two configurations in which the wireless LAN can operate are shown in Fig. 6.10. In Fig. 6.10(a), the configuration uses the Access Point as described earlier. In Fig. 6.10(b), direct communication between two devices is shown. When two or more devices form a network without the need for centralized control, they are called ad hoc networks. For instance, a mobile phone can form a network with a laptop and synchronize data automatically.

In Brief...

IEEE 802.11 family standards specify the physical and data link layer protocols for providing wireless connectivity to devices. Infrared and ISM bands are used for transmission.

Embedded systems are now being provided with wireless LAN connectivity to exchange data. The main attraction of wireless connectivity is that it can be used in environments where running a cable is difficult such as in shop floors of manufacturing units.

Notes...

IEEE 802.11b is popularly known as WiFi or Wireless Fidelity. If WiFi Access Points are installed, say all over the city, wireless Internet access can be provided to people on the move.

To provide wireless Internet access to mobile devices, a special protocol called Mobile IP has to run on the mobile devices.

6.9 Bluetooth

A typical office cabin or a home or even a car is equipped with a number of electronic gadgets such as desktop, laptop, printer, modem, mobile phone, etc. These devices are interconnected through wires for using a service (e.g. a print service) or for sharing information (e.g. transferring a file from desktop to laptop). These devices form a Personal Area Network (PAN). When we bring two devices, say a laptop and a mobile phone, close to each other, these two can automatically form a network and exchange data. For example, we can transfer the address book from the mobile phone to the laptop. The networks, formed spontaneously by coming closer of two or more devices, are termed as ad-hoc networks. In an ad-hoc network, the topology and the number of nodes at any time are not fixed—the topology may change dynamically with time, and the number of nodes in the network may also change with time. All the headaches associated with administering such networks can be avoided if these devices are made to communicate through radio links and also if one device can find out the presence of other devices and their capabilities (i.e. if one device can 'discover' other devices). The need for such PANs is everywhere—in office cabins, at homes and also in cars.

A number of technologies have been proposed for PANs. Notable among them are Bluetooth, IrDA and IEEE 802.11. Bluetooth holds a great promise because it can provide wireless connectivity to embedded systems at a very low cost.

The salient features of Bluetooth technology are:

- It is a low-cost technology—its cost will soon be as low as a cable connection. Since most of the Bluetooth-enabled devices have to operate through a battery, the power consumption is also very low.
- It is based on radio transmission in the ISM band. ISM band is not controlled by any government authority and hence no special approval is required to use Bluetooth radio systems.
- It caters to short ranges. The range of a Bluetooth device is typically 10 meters, though with higher power, the range can be increased to 100 meters.
- It is based on open standards formulated by a consortium of industries and a large number of equipment vendors are committed to this technology.

Bluetooth Special Interest Group (SIG) founded in February 1998 by Ericsson, Intel, IBM, Toshiba and Nokia released version 1.0 of Bluetooth specifications in July 1999. Version 1.1 of Bluetooth specifications was released in February 2001.

Most of electronic devices can be Bluetooth-enabled. These include a PC, laptop, PDA, digital camera, mobile phone, pager, MP3 player, headset, printer, keyboard, mouse, LCD projector, domestic appliances such as TV, microwave oven, music players etc. To make a device Bluetooth-enabled, a module containing the Bluetooth hardware and firmware is attacked to the device. And, a piece of software is run on the device. A Bluetooth-enabled device communicates with another Bluetooth-enabled device over the radio medium to exchange information or transfer data.

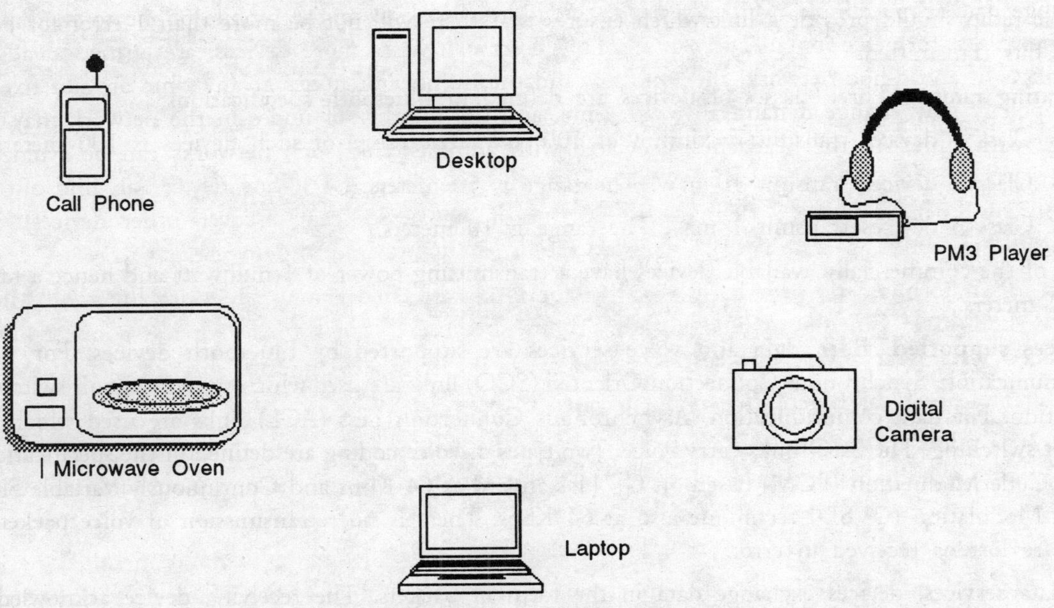

Fig. 6.11: Wireless Personal Area Network

As shown in Fig. 6.11, a set of devices can form a Personal Area Network if they are in the radio vicinity of each other (typically 10 meters radius). When a device comes in the vicinity of another device, Bluetooth protocols facilitate their forming a network. A device can find out what services are offered by the other device and then obtain that service. For example, a laptop can discover the printer automatically and then obtain the print service. Such networks are called ad-hoc networks as the network is formed on the fly and once the device gets out of sight, the network is no longer there. Such networks can be formed in office, at home, in cars and also in public places such as shopping malls, airports etc.

In Brief...

Bluetooth is a low-cost wireless technology to develop Personal Area Networks. Various devices within a vicinity of about 10 meters can form a network using Bluetooth wireless link.

6.9.1 Bluetooth System Specifications

The specifications of the Bluetooth system are as follows:

Frequency of operation: Bluetooth devices operate in the ISM band in the frequency range 2400 – 2483.5 MHz. This band consists of 79 channels each of 1 MHz bandwidth, with a lower guard band of 2 MHz and upper guard band of 3.5 MHz. When a device transmits its data, it uses frequency hopping, i.e. the device transmits each packet in a different channel. The receiving device has to switch to that channel to receive that packet. Though the radio design becomes complex when frequency hopping is used, the advantage is that it provides secure communication. Nominal frequency hop rate is 1600 hops per second.

Modulation: Gaussian Frequency Shift Keying (GFSK) is used as the modulation technique. Binary 1 is represented by a positive frequency deviation and 0 by negative frequency deviation. The radio receiver has to be designed in such a way that the Bit Error Rate (BER) of minimum 0.1% is ensured, i.e. the radio should provide a link which ensures that there will not be more than 1 error for every 1000 bits transmitted.

Operating range: Three classes of devices are defined in Bluetooth specifications:

- Class 1 devices transmit maximum of 100 mW. The range of such devices is 100 meters.
- Class 2 devices transmit 10 mW. The range is 50 meters.
- Class 3 devices transmit 1 mW. The range is 10 meters.

Most of the commercially available devices have a transmitting power of 1 milliwatt and hence a range of 10 meters.

Services supported: Both data and voice services are supported by Bluetooth devices. For voice communication, Synchronous Connection Oriented (SCO) links are used which support circuit switching operation. For data communication, Asynchronous Connection Less (ACL) links are used which use packet switching. The SCO links carry voice. Two types of voice coding are defined in the specifications: Pulse Code Modulation (PCM) based on G.711 standard at 64 Kbps and Continuously Variable Slope Delta Modulation (CVSD) technique also at 64 Kbps. There is no retransmission of voice packets if they are lost or received in error.

For data services, devices exchange data in the form of packets. The receiving device acknowledges the packet or reports that the packet is received in error. If a packet is received with errors, the packet is retransmitted. It is also possible to broadcast packets by one device to all the other devices in the network. However, in broadcast mode there is no acknowledgement or indication that the packet is received with errors. The broadcasting device informs the receiving devices how many times a broadcast packet will be transmitted so that at least once every device will receive the packet without errors.

Data rates: A Bluetooth device can support three synchronous voice channels and one asynchronous data channel. For voice communication, 64 Kbps data rate is used in both directions. For asynchronous links, two types of channels are defined with different data rates. In asymmetric channel, data rates are 723.2 Kbps in one direction and 57.6 Kbps in the other direction. In symmetric channel, data rate is 433.9 Kbps in both directions.

Network topology: In a PAN, a set of devices form a small network called piconet. In a piconet, there will be one Master and one or more Slaves. All the Slaves tune to the Master. The Master decides the hop frequency sequence and all the Slaves tune to these frequencies to establish communication links. Any device (desktop, mobile phone etc.) can be a Master or Slave. The Master/Slave terminology is only for the protocols, the device capabilities are not defined by this terminology. It is also possible for a Master and Slave to switch roles—a Slave can become a Master. A piconet can have maximum number of seven slaves which can actively communicate with the Master. In addition to these active slaves, a piconet can contain many Slaves that are in parked mode. These parked devices are synchronized with the Master, but they are not active on the channel. The communication between the Master and the Slave uses Time Division Duplex (TDD).

Fig. 6.12 shows the various topologies of a Bluetooth piconet. In Fig. 6.12(a), a piconet is shown with one Master and one Slave. It is a point-to-point communication mode. In Fig. 6.12(b), the piconet consists of a Master and a number of Slaves. It is a point-to-multipoint communication mode. Fig. 6.12(c) shows a scatternet which is formed by a number of piconets. In this scatternet, each piconet will have a Master and a number of Slaves. The Master of a piconet can be a Slave in another piconet.

Each piconet in the scatternet will have its own frequency hopping sequence and hence there will be no interference between two piconets. In a scatternet, even if the coverage areas of two piconets overlap, there will be no interference.

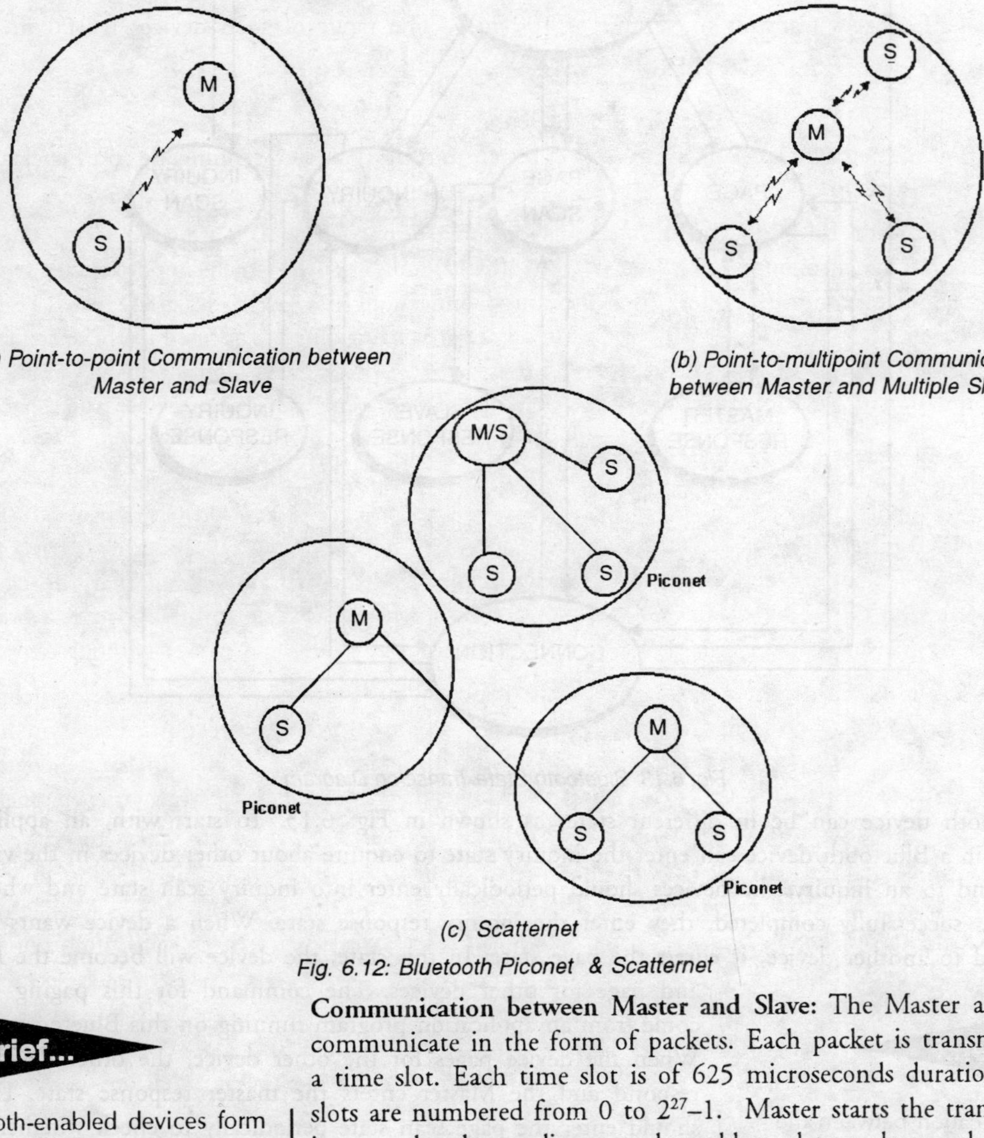

(a) Point-to-point Communication between Master and Slave

(b) Point-to-multipoint Communication between Master and Multiple Slaves.

(c) Scatternet

Fig. 6.12: Bluetooth Piconet & Scatternet

In Brief...

Bluetooth-enabled devices form a network known as piconet. In a piconet, there will be one master and up to seven active slaves. Communication between the master and slaves can be point-to-point or point-to-multipoint.

Communication between Master and Slave: The Master and Slave communicate in the form of packets. Each packet is transmitted in a time slot. Each time slot is of 625 microseconds duration. These slots are numbered from 0 to $2^{27}-1$. Master starts the transmission in even slots by sending a packet addressed to a slave and the slave sends the packets in odd numbered slots. A packet generally occupies one time slot, but can extend up to five slots. If a packet extends more than one slot, the hop frequency will be the same for the entire packet. If the Master starts the transmission in slot 0 using frequency f1, the slave transmits in slot 1 using frequency f2, master transmits in slot 2 using frequency f3, and so on.

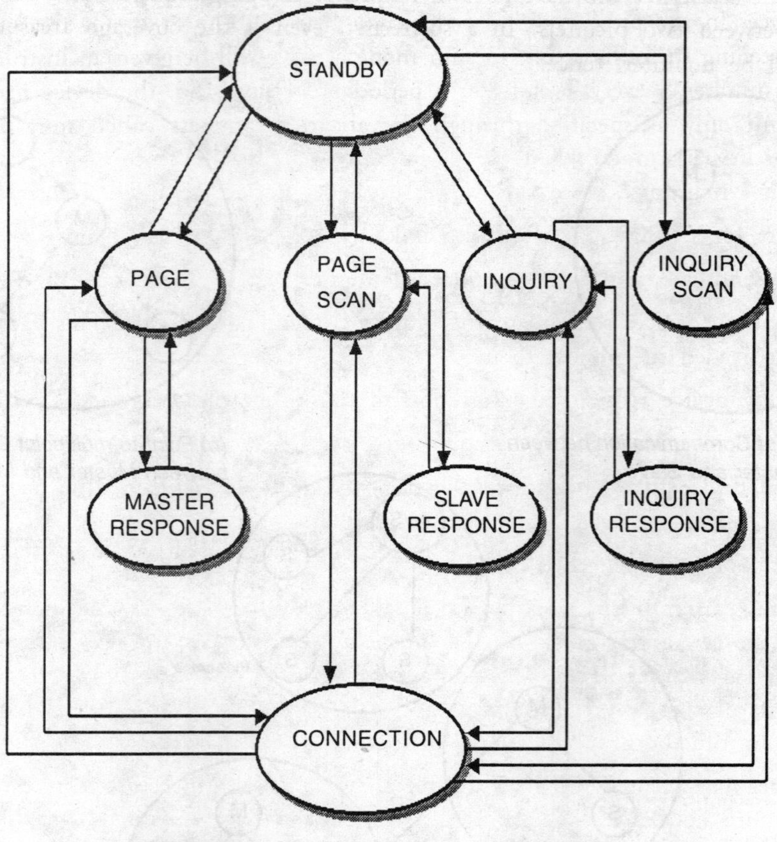

Fig. 6.13: Bluetooth State Transition Diagram

A Bluetooth device can be in different states as shown in Fig. 6.13. To start with, an application program in a Bluetooth device can enter the inquiry state to enquire about other devices in the vicinity. To respond to an inquiry, the devices should periodically enter into inquiry scan state and when the inquiry is successfully completed, they enter the inquiry response state. When a device wants to get connected to another device, it enters the page state. In this state, the device will become the Master and page for other devices. The command for this paging has to come from an application program running on this Bluetooth device. When the device pages for the other device, the other device may respond and the Master enters the master response state. Devices should enter the page scan state periodically to check whether other devices are paging for them. When device receives the page scan packet, it enters the slave response state.

In Brief...

Communication between the master and slaves is achieved using packet transmission. Each device sends its packets using frequency hopping. Master sends the packets in even numbered slots and the slaves send the packets in odd numbered slots.

Once paging of devices is completed, the Master and the Slave establish a connection. Thereafter, the connection is in active state, during which the packet transmission takes place. The connection can also be put in one of the three modes: 'hold' or 'sniff' or 'park' modes. In hold mode, the device will stop receiving the data traffic for a specific amount of time so that other devices in the piconet can use the channel. After the expiry of the specific time, the device will start listening to traffic again. In sniff mode, a slave will be given an instruction like 'listen starting with slot number S every T slots for a period of N slots'. So, the device need not listen to all the packets, but only as specified through the above parameters called sniff parameters. The connection can be in park mode when the device only listens to a beacon signal from the Master occasionally, and it synchronizes with the Master but does not do any data transmission.

A typical procedure for setting up a Bluetooth link can be:

- The device sends an inquiry using a special inquiry hopping sequence.
- Inquiry scanning devices respond to the inquiry by sending a packet. This packet contains the information needed to connect to it.
- The inquiring device requests a connection to the device that responded to the inquiry.
- Paging is used to initiate the connection with the selected device.
- The selected device that has entered the page scan state responds to the page.
- If the responding device accesses the connection, it synchronizes with the Master's timing and frequency hopping sequence.

Bluetooth Addressing: Each Bluetooth module (the radio transceiver) is given a 48-bit address containing three fields: LAP (Lower Address Part) with 24 bits, Upper address part (UAP) with 8 bits and Non-Significant Address Part with 16 bits. This address is assigned by the manufacturer of the Bluetooth module and consists of company ID and company assigned number. This address is unique to every Bluetooth device. In Bluetooth specifications, this address is referred to as BD_ADDR.

Each active member in a piconet will have a 3-bit address. In addition to the maximum of 7 active members, many more devices can be in 'parked' mode. The parked members also need to have addresses so that the master can make them active for exchange of packets. Parked member address is either the BD_ADDR of 48 bits or an 8-bit parked member address denoted by PM_ADDR.

Bluetooth profiles: To ensure interoperability between devices manufactured by different vendors, Bluetooth SIG released the Bluetooth 'profiles' which define the precise characteristics and protocols supported by these devices. The Blueooth profiles are defined for headset, cordless phone, fax machine, LAN Access Point, serial communication, dial-up networking, file transfer, synchronization of data between two devices, etc.

Notes...

To achieve interoperability of Bluetooth modules of different manufacturers, Bluetooth profiles are defined for different devices and services.

6.9.2 Bluetooth Protocol Architecture

The complete protocol stack of Bluetooth system is given in Fig. 6.14.

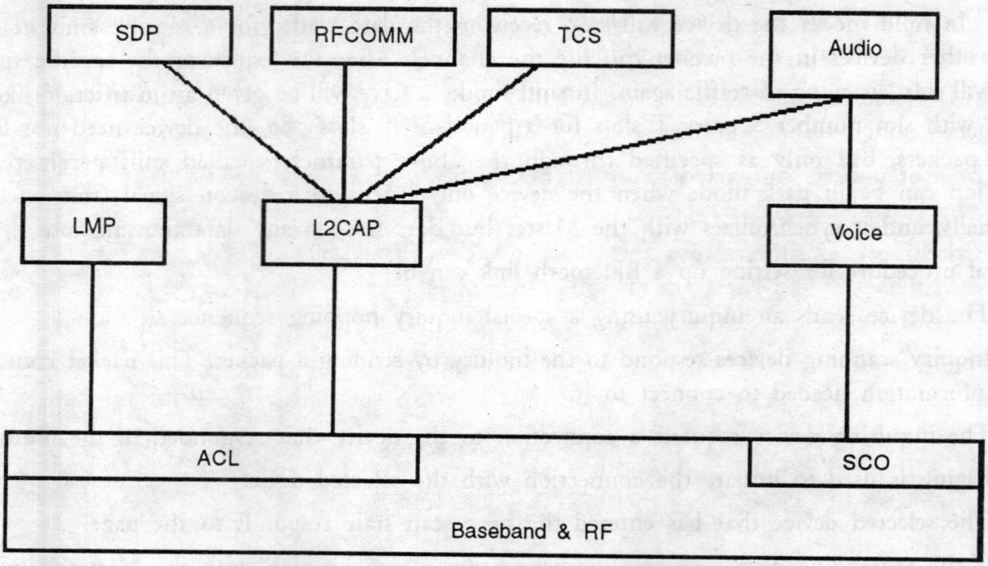

Fig. 6.14: Bluetooth Protocol Architecture

Baseband and RF

The baseband layer is for establishing the links between devices based on the type of service required—ACL for data services and SCO for voice services. This layer also takes care of addressing and managing the different states of the Bluetooth device. The RF portion provides the radio interface.

Link Manager Protocol (LMP)

The Link Manager Protocol (LMP) is used to set up and control links. The three layers—RF, Link controller and the Link manager—will be on the Bluetooth module attached to the device. The link manager on one device exchanges messages with the link manager on the other device. These messages, known as LMP messages, are not sent to higher layers. Link messages have higher priority compared to data. LMP messages are sent as single slot packets, with a header of 1 byte. The functions of the LMP are as follows:

- **Authentication:** When two devices have to communicate with each other, one has to verify the other device. So, one device is called verifier and the other is called claimant. The verifier sends a message, a packet containing a random number, which is called a challenge. The claimant calculates the response which is a function of challenge and sends the response along with its Bluetooth address (48-bit address) and secret key. This is known as Challenge-Response scheme—you throw a challenge and check whether the other device can correctly respond to that challenge.
- **Encryption:** To maintain confidentiality of data over the radio link, the data is encrypted. The Master sends a key with which the data is encrypted to all the slaves, through an LMP message.
- **Clock offset request:** Synchronizing the clocks between the Master and the Slaves is a must for proper exchange of data. If the clock has to be offset, the LMP exchanges messages to ensure clock synchronization.

- **Timing accuracy information request:** To ensure synchronization, the master can request the slaves for timing accuracy information.
- **LMP version:** It needs to be ensured that both the devices use the same version of LMP. To achieve this, version number of the LMP protocol is exchanged.
- **Type of packets supported:** As different Bluetooth-enabled devices may support different features, LMP features request and response are exchanged between the devices.
- **Switching Master/Slave role:** In a piconet, a device will act as a Master and other devices will act as Slaves. The Master and the Slave in a piconet can switch roles using the LMP messages. The Master or the Slave can initiate the switching operation.
- **Name request:** Each device can be given a user-friendly name having a maximum of 248 bits in ASCII format. A device can request for the name through an LMP message and obtain the response.
- **Detach:** Messages exchanged to close a connection.
- **Hold mode:** To place ACL link in hold for a specified time when there is no data to send. This feature is mainly to save power.
- **Park mode:** To be in synchronization with the Master but not participate in data exchange.
- **Power control:** To request for transmitting less power. This is useful particularly for class 1 devices which are capable of transmitting 100 mW power.
- **Quality of Service (QoS) parameters exchange:** In applications that require good quality transmission link, quality of service parameters can be specified. These parameters include number of repetitions for broadcast packets, delay and bandwidth allocation.
- **Request SCO link:** To request for an SCO link after the ACL link is established.
- **Multi-slot packet control:** To control the procedure when data is sent in consecutive packets.
- **Link supervision:** To monitor link when device goes out of range (through a time-out mechanism).
- **Connection establishment:** After paging is successfully completed, to establish the connection.

In Brief...

The important functions of Link Management Protocol are: link establishment and disconnection, switching between master and slave roles, authentication, encryption and controlling quality of service parameters.

A Bluetooth device will implement the base band, RF and LMP/ layers in a hardware/firmware combination. A 16-bit processor based system is used to implement these three layers of protocols. However, to reduce the cost, single chip solutions are now available which will reduce the cost to make a device Bluetooth-enabled.

These three layers ensure establishment of a connection and managing the connection for transfer of voice or data. But to ensure that the whole application runs as per user requirements, we need lot of other protocols.

In Brief...

To Bluetooth-enable a device, a Bluetooth module is attached to the device. This module contains the hardware and firmware that implements the baseband, RF and link management protocols.

Logical Link Control and Adaptation Protocol (L2CAP)

L2CAP runs above the baseband and carries out the data link layer functionality. L2CAP layer is only for ACL links. L2CAP data packets can be up to 64 Kilobytes long. L2CAP protocol runs on hosts such as laptop, cellular phone or other wireless devices.

When L2CAP messages are exchanged between two devices, it assumes that an ACL link is already established between two devices. It also assumes that packets are delivered in sequence. L2CAP does not do any checksum calculation. Note that L2CAP does not support SCO links for voice communication. L2CAP does not support multicasting.

The functions of L2CAP layer are:

- **Protocol multiplexing:** In the protocol stack given in Fig. 6.14, above L2CAP, a number of other protocols can be running. A packet received by L2CAP has to be passed onto the correct higher layer. This is protocol multiplexing.
- **Segmentation and reassembly:** Baseband packets are limited in size. Large L2CAP packets are segmented into small baseband packets and sent to the baseband layer. Similarly, the small packets received from the baseband layer are reassembled and sent to higher layers.
- **Quality of Service:** Quality of Service (QoS) parameters such as delay can be specified, and this layer ensures that the QoS constraints are honored.

In Brief...

The functions of Logical Link Control and Adaptation Protocol (L2CAP) are protocol multiplexing, segmentation and reassembly and ensuring that the quality of service parameters are honored.

L2CAP layer sends connection request and QoS request messages from the application programs through the higher layers. It receives from the lower layers the responses for these requests. The responses can be: connection indication, connection confirmation, connect confirmation negative, connect confirmation pending, disconnection indication (from remote), disconnect confirmation, timeout indication and quality of service violation indication.

Service Discovery Protocol (SDP)

The Service Discovery Protocol (SDP) provides the Bluetooth environment the capability to create ad-hoc networks. This protocol is used for discovering the services offered by a device. SDP offers the following services:

- A device can search for the service needed by it in the piconet.
- A device can discover a service based on a class of services (e.g. A laptop wants a print service, and it can find out the different printers available in the piconet—dot matrix printer, laser printer etc., and subsequently select the desired print service).
- Browsing of services.
- Discovery of new services when devices enter in the radio range of other devices.
- Mechanism to find out when a service becomes unavailable when the device goes out of radio range.
- The details of services such as classes of services and the attributes of services.
- To discover services on another device without consulting the third device.

When a device wants to discover a service, the application software initiates the request (which is the client) and the SDP client sends SDP request to the server (the device which can provide the required service). SDP client and server exchange SDP messages. Note that the server and client can be any two devices—the server is the device that can provide the service being requested by the client.

The server maintains list of service records. Each record is identified by a unique 32-bit number. Service record will have a number of attributes. The attributes can be service class ID list (type of service), service ID, protocol description list (protocol used for using the service), provider name, Icon URL (an iconic representation of the service), service name and service description. Each attribute will have two components: attribute ID and attribute value.

For instance, consider a device (a laptop) that requires a print service. The laptop is a client looking for a print service in a Bluetooth environment. The procedure for obtaining this service is as follows:

- Client sends a service search request specifying the print service class ID to the Server.
- Server sends a service search response to the client indicating that two print services are provided.
- Client sends a service attribute request, protocol descriptor list to the server, asking for the details of the service.
- Server sends the response to the client indicating that PostScript print service is provided.
- If the client wants to use the service, it sends a command to print the desired document.

The SDP is the heart of the Bluetooth system as it provides the capability to discover availability of services and the details of the services along with the necessary information such as protocols to access the service.

In Brief...

Service Discovery Protocol (SDP) provides the capability to discover the availability of services in a Bluetooth network and to access these services.

Notes...

Service Discovery Protocol (SDP) is the heart of any network that supports ad-hoc networking of computers/devices. Sun Microsystems' Jini technology also has SDP that facilitates development of 'administration-free' networking of devices.

RFCOMM

RFCOMM is a transport protocol to emulate serial communication (RS232 serial port) over L2CAP. Through RFCOMM, two devices can communicate using serial communication protocols over Bluetooth radio. To achieve this, RFCOMM emulates the 9 signals of RS 232. These signals are:

102 Signal Ground (GND)

103 Transmit Data (TD)

104 Received Data (RD)

105 Request to Send (RTS)

106 Clear to Send (CTS)

107 Data Set Ready (DSR)

108 Data Terminal Ready (DTR)

109 Data Carrier Detect (DTR)

125 Ring Indicator (RI)

In Brief...

RFCOMM emulates serial communication protocol, i.e. using radio as the transmission medium, data can be transmitted using the serial communication protocol such as RS232 standard.

RFCOMM is derived from the GSM (Global System for Mobile Communications) specifications TS 07.10 for serial emulation. It supports two types of devices. Type 1 devices are communication end-points such as computers and printers. Type 2 devices are part of communication segment such as modems.

Telephony Control Protocol Specifications (TCS)

To establish voice communication between two Bluetooth devices, we need the SCO links. SCO links are not handled by L2CAP protocol. However, L2CAP handles the signaling required for establishing voice connections through Telephony Control Protocol Specification abbreviated TCS. Note that it is not abbreviated as TCP: TCP stands for Transmission Control Protocol used in the Internet protocol architecture. TCS defines call control signaling for establishing speech and data calls between Bluetooth devices and mobility management procedures. This protocol is based on the International Telecommunications Union (ITU) standard Q.931, which is the standard for signaling in Integrated Services Digital Network (ISDN). TCS messages are exchanged between devices to establish and release connections and to provide supplementary services such as calling line identification (to identify the telephone number of the calling subscriber).

In Brief ..

Telephony Control Protocol Specification (TCS) handles signaling information to establish voice and data calls between Bluetooth devices. This protocol is based on Q.931 standard using in ISDN.

Host Control Interface

If we have to Bluetooth-enable a laptop computer, we can connect a small Bluetooth module to the USB port of the laptop and run the protocol stack on the laptop (called the host). Bluetooth device will have two parts: a module implementing the lower layers (LMP and below) and a software module implementing higher layers stack (L2CAP and above). The software module runs on the laptop (the host). The Host Controller Interface (HCI) provides a standard interface between the Bluetooth module and the host software, so that we can buy the hardware module from one vendor and software module from another vendor. HCI uses three types of packets:

- Commands which are sent from the host to the module,
- Events which are sent from the module to the host, and
- Data packets which are exchanged between the host and the module.

The functions of HCI are

- Setting up and disconnection of the links and configuring the links.
- Control of baseband features such as timeouts.

- Retrieving of status information of the module.
- Invoking the test modes to test the module for local testing of Bluetooth devices.

HCI provides command interface to the baseband controller and link manager as well as access to hardware status and control registers. HCI has to reside in the Bluetooth module connected to the laptop as well as the host. In the Bluetooth module firmware, HCI commands are implemented so that the host can access the baseband commands, link manager commands, hardware status registers, control registers and event registers. The Bluetooth module is connected to the USB port (say, of the laptop). Three interfaces are defined to get HCI packets from host to the Bluetooth module: (a) USB; (b) RS232; and (c) UART.

In the host, the bus driver is implemented as software above which the HCI driver software and other higher layer protocol softwares are implemented. The HCI commands can be categorized as

- Link control commands to establish piconets and scatternets
- Link policy commands to put devices in hold mode or sniff mode
- Commands to get information about the local hardware
- Commands to get the status parameters
- Commands to test the local Bluetooth module.

Each Bluetooth module is itself an embedded system built around a 16-bit processor. To make low-cost Bluetooth module, single-chip solutions are now becoming available. Bluetooth-enabling consumer electronic items as well as embedded systems will facilitate low-cost networking.

In Brief...

Host Control Interface (HCI) provides a standard interface between the Bluetoth module attached to a device and the software running on the device. Through the HCI, the Bluetooth device obtains the commands to establish piconets and scatternets, to obtain status information and test the Bluetooth module.

Summary

In this chapter, the important communication interfaces for embedded systems are presented. RS232 interface provides a serial communication interface for data rates up to 115.2 Kbps and distances up to about 100 meters. It is one of the most widely used interfaces. For longer distances and for noisy environments, RS422 and RS485 interfaces are used. These serial interfaces are now being replaced by Universal Serial Bus which provides very high data rates. USB 1.1 supports up to 12 Mbps and USB 2.0 up to 480 Mbps. Up to 127 devices can be connected in hierarchical fashion using USB. Infrared interface provides low-cost point-to-point communication between devices. With the availability of low-cost Ethernet chips, Ethernet interfaces can be provided to embedded systems to make them network-enabled. By incorporating Ethernet interface and running the TCP/IP protocol stack in the embedded software, the embedded system can be Internet-enabled and can be accessed over a LAN or over the public Internet. Wireless LAN interfaces based on IEEE 802.11 family standards provide wireless communication interface to the embedded systems. Bluetooth is another communication interface that uses wireless technology. Using Bluetooth, two or more devices can form an ad hoc network and share data. In fact, Ethernet, IEEE 802.11 and Bluetooth interfaces are embedded systems and when these embedded systems are integrated into the embedded devices, they become powerful communicating devices.

Questions

1. Explain the RS 232 interface specifications.
2. What are the advantages of USB over RS 232?
3. Where is IEEE 1394 interface used? Explain the protocol architecture of IEEE 1394.
4. Explain the protocol architecture of Ethernet LAN.
5. Give the broad specifications of Bluetooth standard.
6. What is IrDA interface? What are its advantages and limitations?

Exercises

1. If you want to network-enable an embedded system, study the additional memory required to port the protocol stack.
2. Study a commercially available Bluetooth development kit architecture. Study the processing power requirement of a Blueooth device. Explain how the cost of a Bluetooth module can be reduced.
3. What is data synchronization? Study how data can be synchronized between a palmtop computer and a desktop computer.
4. An exhibition ground is of the size of 5 square kilometers. You need to design a wireless system that provides location information on the palmtops. If you select a particular stall number, its location should be displayed. If you select a particular item (say TV), the stalls that have TVs should be displayed. Design the wireless system using Bluetooth.
5. An embedded system has to obtain data from 20 sensors, convert the signals into digital format using ADCs, multiplex the digital data and transmit the data to a PC. If each signal is sampled at 10 KHz and the resolution of each ADC is 16 bits, suggest a suitable communication link between the embedded system and the PC.
6. An embedded system has to record the telephone conversations of 2 channels. The recorded messages have to be transferred on to a PC. Calculate the memory capacity required in the embedded system and the periodicity with which the recorded messages have to be transferred to the PC.

Chapter 7

Embedded/Real-Time Operating System Concepts

CHAPTER OBJECTIVES

After reading this chapter, you will be able to:

- Understand the architecture of the kernel of an operating system
- Learn the details of task scheduling algorithms
- Gain knowledge of inter-task communication
- Understand the details of kernel objects such as tasks, task scheduler, Interrupt Service Routines, semaphores, mutexes, mailboxes, message queues, event registers, pipes, signals and timers.

This chapter gives the important concepts of embedded/real-time operating systems. We will discuss the details of operating system kernel. The various kernel objects and the operations on these objects are presented. The task scheduling algorithms are explained. Though the implementation details vary from operating system to operating system, in this chapter we will focus on the concepts. A thorough conceptual understanding will enable you to work on any operating system with ease.

7.1 Architecture of the Kernel

In Chapter 2, the software architecture of an embedded system is presented. The embedded software consists of the operating system and the application software. The services provided by the operating system are accessed through the Application Programming Interface (API) to develop application software. The API is a set of function calls using which you can access the various kernel objects and the services provided by the kernel.

Let us now dissect the kernel and look into its details.

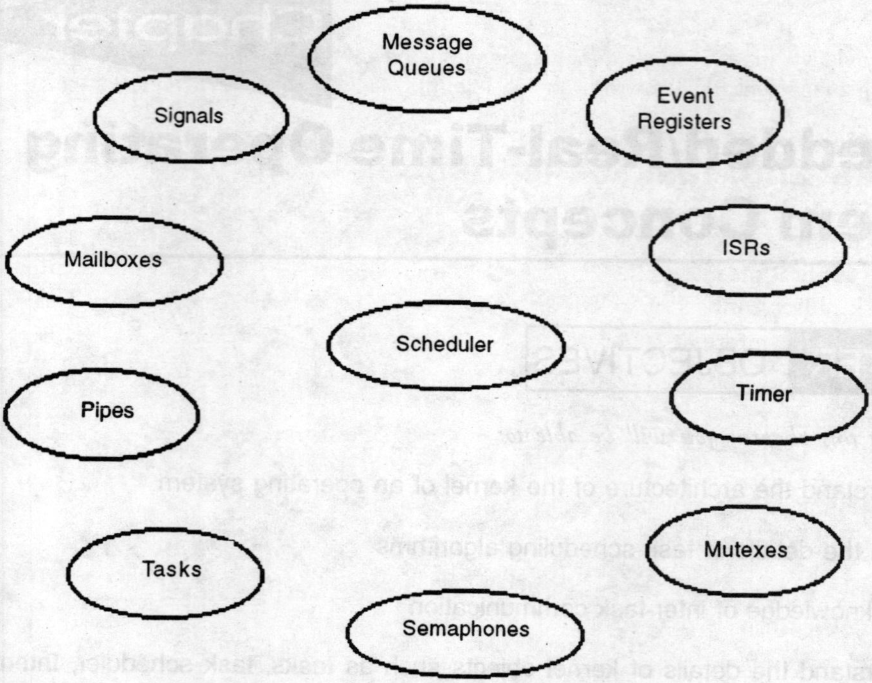

Fig. 7.1: Kernel Objects

The various kernel objects, as shown in Fig. 7.1, are:

- Tasks
- Task scheduler
- Interrupt Service Routines
- Semaphores
- Mutexes
- Mailboxes
- Message queues
- Pipes
- Event Registers
- Signals
- Timers

In Brief...

The various kernel objects are: tasks, task scheduler, Interrupt Service Routines, semaphores, mutexes, mailboxes, message queues, event registers, pipes, signals and timers.

We will discuss the details of these objects in the following sections. The API of the operating system gives the function calls to manage these objects. While discussing the kernel objects, the function calls for managing the objects are also given. The exact syntax of each function call may differ from operating system to operating system. The programming aspects using the API are discussed in Chapters 11 and 12.

Notes...

The kernel provides various services through operations on the kernel objects. These services are: memory management, device management, interrupt handling and time management.

7.2 Tasks and Task Scheduler

The embedded software consists of a number of tasks. These tasks include the operating system tasks as well as the application-specific tasks. Each task in an embedded system is implemented as an infinite loop. The task object consists of its name, a unique ID, a priority, a stack and a Task Control Block that contains all the information related to the task.

In addition to the tasks required for the application software, the kernel has its own system tasks with priorities. These tasks are:

- Startup task, which is executed when the operating system starts
- Exception handling task to handle the exceptions
- Logging task to log the various system messages
- Idle task, which will have the lowest priority and will run when there is no other task to run. This task ensures that the CPU is not idle.

Since only one CPU has to handle multiple tasks, the tasks have to share the CPU time in a disciplined manner so that one task does not get lot of time while others are waiting forever. Therefore, each task has to be assigned a priority; and a mechanism for deciding which task will get CPU time next has to be worked out. This is known as task scheduling. The object that does task scheduling is the task scheduler. In addition to the CPU time, the tasks have to share the system resources such as CPU registers, external memory and input/output devices. Another important requirement is that one task should not corrupt the data of another task. While scheduling the tasks, a number of issues, as described below, need to be kept in mind:

- Many tasks may make calls to a function. A function that can be used by more than one task without data corruption is called reentrant function. If data is corrupted when more than one task calls the function, such a function is called non-reentrant function. If you use global variables, then the function is non-reentrant. Consider the following code segment:

```
int x;
void findsq( int x)
{
return (x * x);
}
```

This function is non-reentrant because x is a global variable. It can be made reentrant by declaring the variable as local.

When you are running a task, some portion of the code should not be interrupted. Such code is called critical section of the code. Interrupts are disabled before the start of the execution of the code's critical section and enabled after the execution is completed. In the code snippet given above, the global variable x can be protected by first disabling the interrupts, then calling the function, and then enabling the interrupts. Kernel objects such as semaphores are used to protect the data.

- Every task requires resources such as serial port, keyboard, display or memory locations. These resources may need to be shared. For example, two tasks may like to send data to the display. Resources shared by two or more tasks are called shared resources. Tasks should maintain discipline to access shared resources. Semaphore and mutexes are used to share resources with discipline.

In Brief...

A resource which has to be shared by two or more tasks is called a shared resource. To avoid data corruption, kernel objects such as semaphores and mutexes are used for accessing shared resources in a disciplined way.

- Tasks may need to communicate data amongst themselves. For instance, a task writes data into an array and another task has to read the data from that array. Inter-task communication needs to be achieved through special mechanisms such as mailboxes, message queues, pipes, event registers, and signals.

The kernel of the operating system manages the tasks keeping in view the restrictions imposed mentioned above.

7.2.1 Task States

In an embedded system, each task has to do a specific job. For instance, consider an embedded system that obtains data from a serial port and converts the data into Ethernet packets. One task (task1) reads the data from a serial port, another task (task2) keeps converting the serial data (characters) into packets and puts them in a buffer. Another task (task3) reads the buffer and sends it over an Ethernet interface. Tasks2 has to wait for task1 to complete its work, and then inform task3 that it can do its work. So, at any instant, only one task is being executed by the CPU whereas other tasks are either waiting for some external event to occur or waiting for the CPU time.

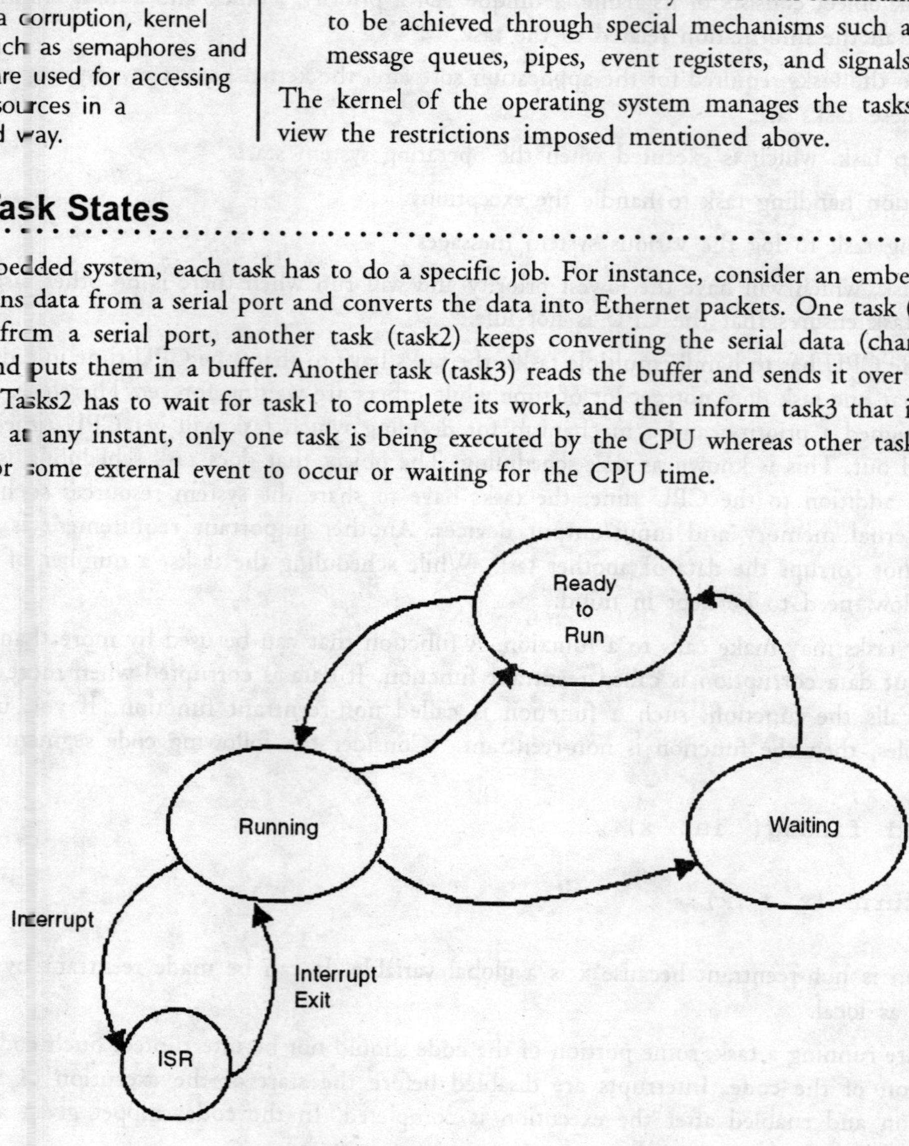

Fig. 7.2: States of a Task

As shown in Fig. 7.2, a task can be in one of the following states:

- Running
- Waiting
- Ready-to-Run

Running state: A task is said to be in running state if it is being executed by the CPU.

Waiting state: A task is said to be in waiting state if it is waiting for another event to occur. For instance, a task may be waiting to get some data from serial port. Even if the CPU is free, the task which is in waiting state cannot be executed till the external event occurs.

Ready-to-Run state: A task is said to be in Ready-to-Run state if it is waiting in a queue for the CPU time.

The arrows in Fig. 7.2 depict how a task can move from one state to another. A task which is in waiting state can move to the Ready-to-Run state after the external event occurs. Note that it cannot move directly to the Running state. A task which is in Ready-to-Run state can move to the Running state. A task in the Running state can move to the Waiting state if it has to wait for an external event to occur; or it can move to the Ready-to-run state if its job is not completed, but the CPU has to run another task.

A task which is presently running may be interrupted to run an Interrupt Service Routine (ISR) for a short time. After the ISR is executed, the CPU continues to execute the task which was interrupted or the highest priority task which is Ready-to-Run. The ISR can do the job of changing the state of a task. For instance, a high priority task which was in waiting state has to move to Ready-to-Run state. This operation can be handled by the ISR.

In Brief...

A task can be in one of the three states: (a) Running; (b) Ready-to-Run; and (c) Waiting.

Task stack: Every task will have a stack that stores the local variables, function parameters, return addresses and CPU registers during an interrupt. At the time of creating a task, the size of the stack has to be specified or a default stack size has to be used.

7.2.2 Context Switching

The CPU has to execute one task for some time and then execute another task which is in the queue. Consider a situation when the CPU is executing a low priority task, during which time the CPU registers contain the data corresponding to this task. The CPU now has to take out the low priority task (in other words, "preempt the low priority task") and execute the high priority task. In this case, the contents of the CPU registers have to be saved before executing the high priority task. The state of the CPU registers when a task is to be pre-empted is called the context. Saving the contents of the CPU registers and then loading the new task is called context switching.

In Brief...

The state of the CPU registers when a task has to be preempted is called the context. Saving the contents of the CPU registers and loading the new task parameters is called context switching.

7.2.3 Scheduling Algorithms

How does the kernel decide which task has to run? Various scheduling algorithms have been developed to tackle this problem. Depending on the requirement of the embedded system, the scheduling algorithm needs to be chosen. In this section, we will review the following scheduling algorithms:

- First In First Out
- Round-robin algorithm
- Round-robin with priority
- Shortest job first
- Non-preemptive multitasking
- Preemptive multitasking

First In First Out (FIFO)

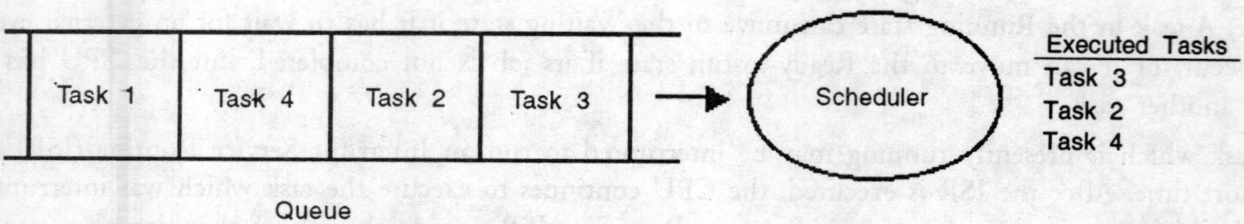

Fig. 7.3 Scheduling Algorithm: FIFO

In First In First Out scheduling algorithm, the tasks which are Ready-to-Run are kept in a queue and the CPU serves the tasks on first-come-first served basis. This scheduling algorithm, shown in Fig. 7.3, is very simple to implement, but not well suited for most applications because it is difficult to estimate the amount of time a task has to wait for being executed. However, this is a good algorithm for an embedded system has to perform few small tasks all with small execution times. If there is no time criticality and the number of tasks is small, this algorithm can be implemented.

Round-robin Algorithm

In the round-robin algorithm, the kernel allocates a certain amount of time for each task waiting in the queue. The time slice allocated to each task is called quantum. As shown in Fig. 7.4, if three tasks 1, 2 and 3 are waiting in the queue, the CPU first executes task1 then task2 then task3 and then again task1.

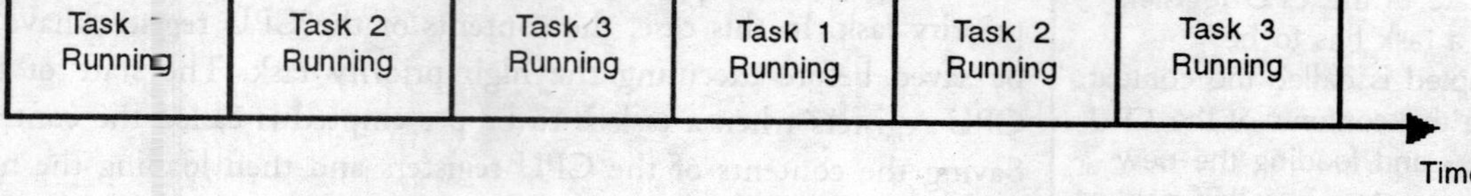

Fig. 7.4 Round-robin Scheduling Algorithm

> **In Brief...**
>
> In round-robin algorithm, each task waiting in the queue is given a fixed time slice. The kernel gives control to the next task if the current task has completed its work within the time slice or if the current task has completed its allocated time.

The kernel gives control to the next task if

(a) The current task has completed its work within the time slice

(b) The current task has no work to do

(c) The current task has completed its allocated time slice

This algorithm is very simple to implement, but note that there are no priorities for any task. All tasks are considered of equal importance. If time-critical operations are not involved then this algorithm will be sufficient. Digital multimeters and microwave ovens use this scheduling algorithm.

Round-robin with Priority

The round-robin algorithm can be slightly modified by assigning priority levels to some or all the tasks. A high priority task can interrupt the CPU so that it can be executed. This scheduling algorithm can meet the desired response time for a high priority task. For example, in a bar code scanner, high priority is assigned to the scanning operation. The CPU can execute this task by suspending the task that displays the item/price value. Soft real-time systems can use this algorithm.

Shortest-Job First

> **In Brief...**
>
> In shortest-job first task scheduling algorithm, the task that will take minimum time to be executed will be given priority. This approach satisfies the maximum number of tasks, but some tasks may have to wait forever.

If the time for each task can be estimated beforehand, the CPU can execute the task which takes the least amount of time. Effectively, this is like a priority assignment, the priority being decided by the amount of time—the higher the execution time, the lesser the priority. The advantage of this scheduling algorithm is that a high number of tasks will be executed, but the task with the highest amount of time will have to wait, perhaps forever!

The task scheduler is the heart of the operating system. It is the task scheduling algorithm which decides whether the necessary time constraints can be met or not. If the embedded system is a hard-real time system, none of the above scheduling algorithms can be used at all.

The kernels used in embedded systems can implement priority-based multi-tasking scheduling algorithms of two types:

- Non-preemptive multi-tasking
- Preemptive multitasking

Non-preemptive Multi-tasking

Assume that you are making a telephone call at a public call office. You need to make many calls, but you see another person waiting. You may make one call, ask the other person to finish his call, and then you can make your next call. This is non-preemptive multitasking, also known as cooperative multitasking—you are cooperating with the others in the queue.

In non-preemptive multitasking, the tasks cooperate with each other to get their share of the CPU time. Hence, each task has to release the CPU and give control to another task on its own. Each task is given a priority, but the priority has to be respected by the other tasks. If interrupts are enabled, a high priority task can interrupt the running task and make the high priority task Ready-to-Run. After the ISR is executed, the CPU will continue to execute the low priority task only. And, when the low priority task releases the CPU, the high priority task is executed.

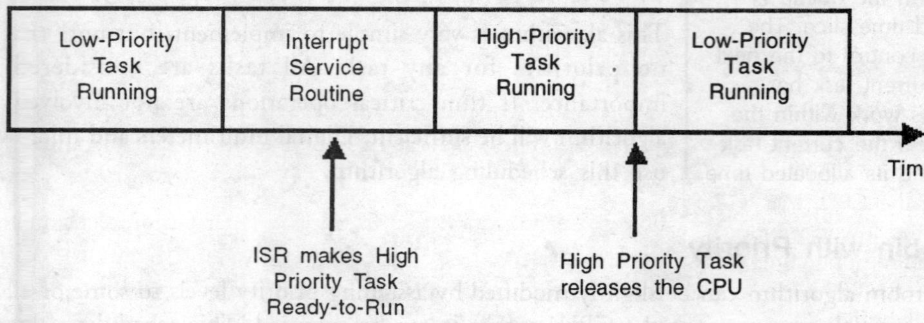

Fig. 7.5 Non-preemptive Multitasking

Fig. 7.5 shows the non-preemptive kernel operation. Assume that there are two tasks to be executed—one high priority task and one low priority task. To start with, the high priority task is in Waiting state, waiting for an external event to happen, and the low priority task is Running. After some time, the high priority task is ready. Using an ISR, the high priority task is moved to Ready-to-Run state. After the ISR is executed, the low priority task will continue to be executed. After some time, the low priority task releases the CPU and then the high priority task gets executed.

In Brief...

Non-preemptive multitasking is also called cooperative multitasking as the tasks have to cooperate with one another to share the CPU time.

The main disadvantage of non-preemptive multitasking is that a high priority task may have to wait for a long time. Also, it is not possible to determine the exact response times for each of the tasks. So, this type of multitasking is not suitable for embedded real-time systems.

Preemptive Multi-tasking

In preemptive multitasking, the highest priority task is always given the CPU time. If a lower priority task is presently running and a higher priority task is in Ready-ro-Run state, the running task is "preempted" and the higher priority task is executed. This mechanism is shown in Fig. 7.6.

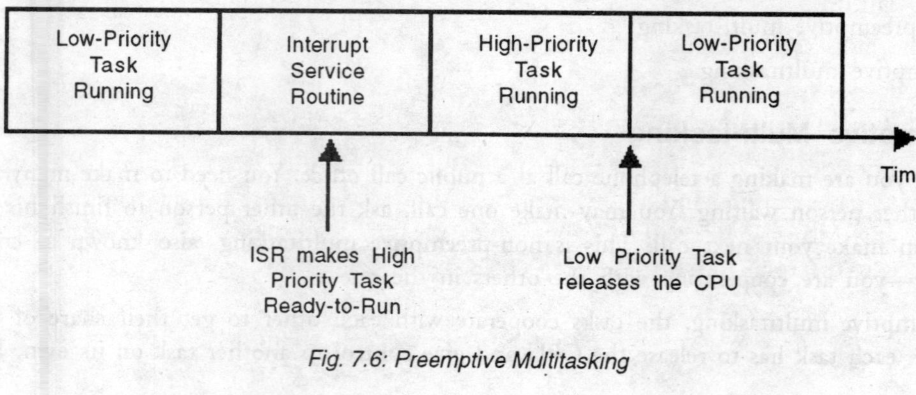

Fig. 7.6: Preemptive Multitasking

Consider two tasks—one low priority task and one high priority task. To start with, the low priority task is running as the high priority task is in waiting state, waiting for an external event to occur. After some time, the external event occurrs and the high priority task now move to Ready-to-Run state. Through an interrupt, the ISR is executed to move the high priority task from Waiting state to Ready-to-Run state. Then another the ISR is executed to put the high priority task in the Running state. Again after some time, the high priority task may release the CPU and then the low priority task is executed.

In Brief...

In preemptive multitasking, the highest priority task is always executed by the CPU, by preempting the lower priority task. All real-time operating systems implement this scheduling algorithm.

If there are a number of tasks in the Ready-to-Run state, the task with the highest priority is always given the first chance by the task scheduler.

The main attraction of this scheme is that the execution time of the highest priority task can be calculated and hence the kernel is said to be deterministic. Most of the commercial embedded operating systems use preemptive multitasking to meet real time requirements.

Notes...

The module within the scheduler that performs context switching is called dispatcher. If ISR makes a system call, the dispatcher is bypassed.

7.2.4 Rate Monotonic Analysis

Priority assignment to a task can be static or dynamic. In static priority assignment, a task will be assigned a priority at the time of creating the task and it remains the same. In dynamic priority assignment, the priority of the task can be changed during execution time. While designing your application, it is not very easy to assign priorities to tasks. A good starting point is the Rate Monotonic Analysis used for assigning priorities.

While designing an embedded system, you need to make a list of all the tasks. And, then you need to assign priority to each task. Subjectively, we know that some tasks should have high priority, but nothing beyond! Rate Monotonic Analysis (RMA) provides an answer. It may not be accurate for any application, but it is a good starting point.

RMA makes the following assumptions:

(a) Highest priority task will run first, i.e. the priority-based preemptive multitasking is the scheduling algorithm.

(b) All the tasks run at regular intervals i.e. the tasks are periodic.

(c) Tasks do not synchronize with each other, i.e. they do not share resources or share data (which is not a valid assumption).

In RMA, the priority is proportional to the frequency of execution. If (i)th task has an execution period of Ti, and Ei is its execution time, Ei/Ti gives the percentage of the CPU time required for execution of (i)th task. In RMA, the "schedulability test" indicates how much CPU time is actually utilized by the tasks. If n is the total number of tasks, the equation for schedulabiity test is given by

$$\Sigma \ (Ei/Ti) \le U(n) = n(2^{1/n} - 1)$$

U(n) is called the utilization factor. The value of number of tasks (n) and the utilization factor for different values of n is given in Table 7.1. If the number of tasks is infinity, then about 70% of the CPU time is utilized.

n	U(n)
1	1.000
2	0.828
3	0.779
4	0.756
Infinity	0.693

Table 7.1: Rate Monotonic Scheduling: Percentage of CPU time utilized

In Brief...

Rate Monotonic Analysis is used to calculate the percentage of CPU time utilized by the tasks and to assign priorities to tasks. Priorities are proportional to the frequency of execution. Note that the assumptions made in RMA are not always valid.

When you are designing an embedded system, it will be a good idea to start with RMA. List all the tasks, estimate the execution period and execution time, and then calculate the value of U(n). As a thumb rule, ensure that the CPU utilization is not above 70%. Assign priorities based on execution frequency.

7.2.5 Task Management Function Calls

The various function calls provided by the operating system API for task management are:

- Create a task
- Delete a task
- Suspend a task
- Resume a task
- Change priority of a task
- Query a task

7.3 Interrupt Service Routines

Interrupt is a hardware signal that informs the CPU that an important event has occurred. When interrupt occurs, CPU saves its context (contents of the registers) and jumps to the ISR. After ISR processes the event, the CPU returns to the interrupted task in a non-preemptive kernel. In the case of preemptive kernel, highest priority task gets executed.

In real-time operating systems, the interrupt latency, interrupt response time and the interrupt recovery time are very important.

Interrupt Latency: The maximum time for which interrupts are disabled + time to start the execution of the first instruction in the ISR is called interrupt latency.

Interrupt Response Time: Time between receipt of interrupt signal and starting the code that handles the interrupt is called interrupt response time.

In a preemptive kernel, response time = interrupt latency + time to save CPU registers context.

Notes...

System's worst-case interrupt response time has to be considered while evaluating the performance of an operating system/embedded software.

Interrupt Recovery Time: Time required for CPU to return to the interrupted code/highest priority task is called interrupt recovery time.

In non-preemptive kernel, interrupt recovery time = time to restore the CPU context + time to execute the return instruction from the interrupted instruction.

In preemptive kernel, interrupt recovery time = time to check whether a high priority task is ready + time to restore CPU context of the highest priority task + time to execute the return instruction from the interrupt instruction.

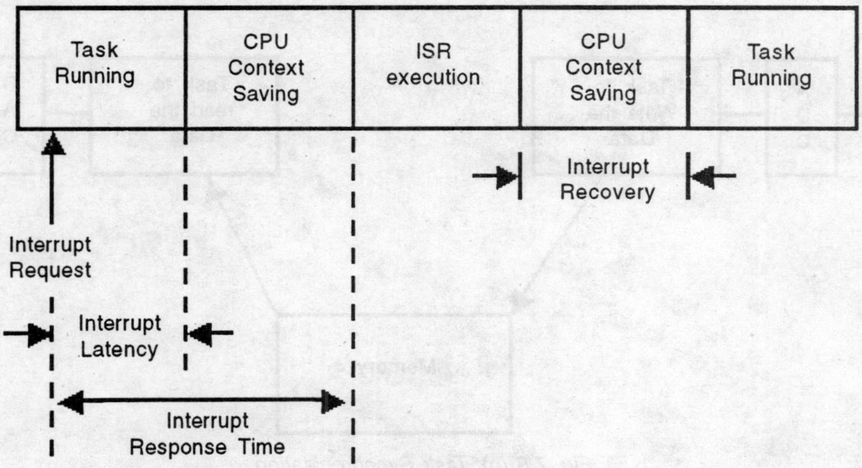

Fig. 7.7 Interrupt Latency, Interrupt Response Time and Interrupt Recovery Time

The interrupt latency, interrupt response time and interrupt recovery time are shown in Fig. 7.7.

7.4 Semaphores

When multiple tasks are running, two or more tasks may need to share the same resource. As shown in Fig. 7.8(a), consider a case where two tasks want to write to a display. Assume that task1 wants to display the message "temperature is 50" and task2 has to display the message "humidity is 40%". The display is a shared resource and if there is no synchronization between the tasks, then a garbled message is displayed such as "temphumieratiditurey is is 50 40%". To access a shared resource, there should be a mechanism so that there is discipline. This is known as resource synchronization.

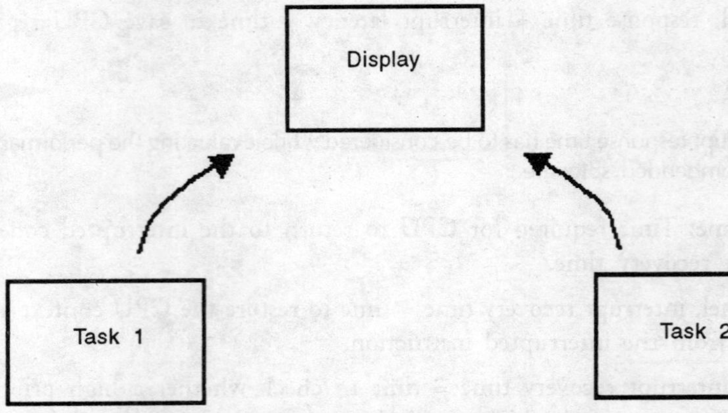

Fig. 7.8 (a): Resource Synchronization

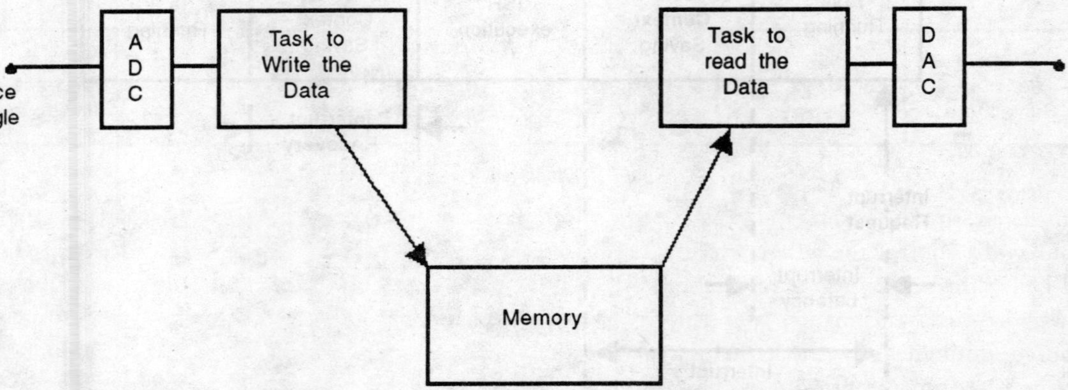

Fig. 7.8 (b): Task Synchronization

Now consider another situation shown in Fig. 7.8(b). In this case, one task reads the data from an ADC and writes it to memory. Another task reads that data and sends it to a DAC. The read operation takes place only after write operation and it has to be done very fast with minimal time delay. In this case, there should be a mechanism for task1 to inform task2 that it has done its job. This has to be done through a well-defined procedure. This is known as task synchronization.

Semaphore is a kernel object that is used for both resource synchronization and task synchronization.

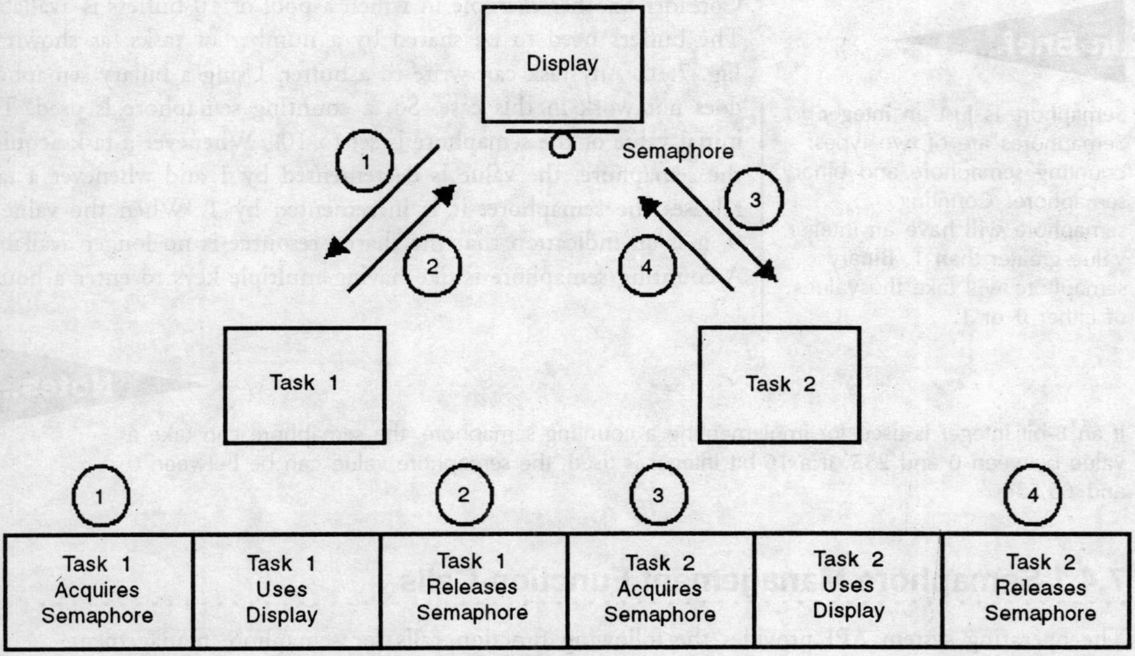

Fig. 7.9: Display Semaphore

Consider a situation shown in Fig. 7.9. Two tasks want to access a display. Display is a shared resource. To control the access, a semaphore is created. The semaphore is like a key to enter a house, and hence the semaphore is represented as a 'key'. If task1 wants to access the printer, it acquires the semaphore, uses the printer and then releases the semaphore. If both the tasks want to access a resource simultaneously, the kernel has to give the semaphore only to one of the tasks. This allocation may be based on the priority of the task or on first-come-first-served basis. If a number of tasks have to access the same resource then the tasks are kept in a queue and each task can acquire the semaphore one by one.

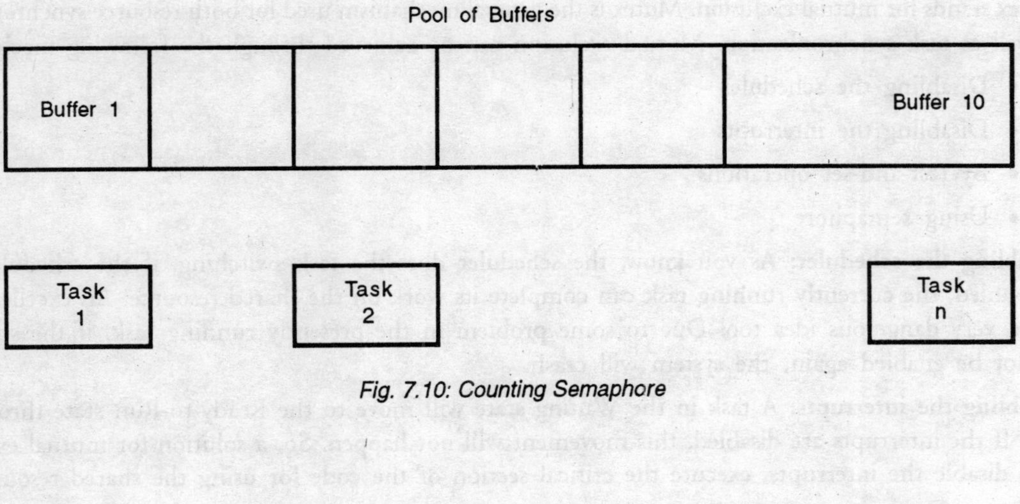

Fig. 7.10: Counting Semaphore

In Brief...

Semaphore is just an integer. Semaphores are of two types: counting semaphore and binary semaphore. Counting semaphore will have an integer value greater than 1. Binary semaphore will take the values of either 0 or 1.

Consider another example in which a pool of 10 buffers is available. The buffers need to be shared by a number of tasks, as shown in Fig. 7.10. Any task can write to a buffer. Using a binary semaphore does not work in this case. So, a counting semaphore is used. The initial value of the semaphore is set to 10. Whenever a task acquires the semaphore, the value is decremented by 1 and whenever a task releases the semaphore, it is incremented by 1. When the value is 0, it is an indication that the shared resource is no longer available. A counting semaphore is like having multiple keys to enter a house.

Notes...

If an 8-bit integer is used for implementing a counting semaphore, the semaphore can take a value between 0 and 255. If a 16-bit integer is used, the semaphore value can be between 0 and 65,535.

7.4.1 Semaphore Management Function Calls

The operating system API provides the following function calls for semaphore management:

- Create a semaphore
- Delete a semaphore
- Acquire a semaphore
- Release a semaphore
- Query a semaphore

7.5 Mutex

Mutex stands for mutual exclusion. Mutex is the general mechanism used for both resource synchronization as well as task synchronization. Mutual exclusion can be achieved through the following mechanisms:

- Disabling the scheduler
- Disabling the interrupts
- By test-and-set operations
- Using semaphore

Disabling the scheduler: As you know, the scheduler does the task switching, if the scheduler itself is disabled, the currently running task can complete its work on the shared resource. An excellent idea, but a very dangerous idea too! Due to some problem in the presently running task, if the scheduler cannot be enabled again, the system will crash.

Disabling the interrupts: A task in the Waiting state will move to the Ready-to-Run state through an ISR. If the interrupts are disabled, this movement will not happen. So, a solution for mutual exclusion is to disable the interrupts, execute the critical section of the code for using the shared resource and then enable the interrupts. This is certainly a good solution, but the interrupt latency will be more. Certainly, this method can be used, but with caution.

Test-and-set operations: When two tasks have to share a resource, the functions in each of the tasks can check the value of a global variable to obtain the status of the shared resource. For instance, a global variable 'x' can be set to 0 if the resource can be used and it can be set to '1' if it cannot be used. The task has to first check the value of 'x'. If it is 0, it is set to 1—the resource is used, and then it is set back to 0. Meanwhile, if the second task wants to use the resource, it will find that the value is 1 and so it waits for some more time and checks again. Note that while the test-and-set operation is in progress, the interrupts have to be disabled. So, the procedure is

- Disable the interrupts
- Set the variable
- Access the shared resource
- Set the variable
- Enable the interrupts

Note that mutex is a special binary semaphore. A mutex can be either in locked state or unlocked state. A task acquires (locks) a mutex and after using resource, releases (unlocks) it. It is much more powerful than semaphore because of its special features listed below:

- It will have an owner. Initially, the mutex is in unlocked state. The task which acquires it is the owner. Only the task that is the owner can release the mutex, not any other task. Binary semaphore can be released by any task that did not originally acquire it.
- Owner can acquire a mutex multiple times in the locked state. If the owner locks it 'n' times, the owner has to release it 'n' times.
- A task owning a mutex, cannot be deleted.
- The mutex supports priority inheritance protocol to avoid priority inversion problem, which will be discussed later.

7.5.1 Mutex Management Function Calls

The operating system function calls provided for mutex management are:

- Create a mutex
- Delete a mutex
- Acquire a mutex
- Release a mutex
- Query a mutex
- Wait on a mutex

In Brief...

Mutex stands for mutual exclusion. Mutual exclusion can be achieved by (a) disabling the scheduler; (b) disabling the interrupts; (c) by test-and-set operations; or (d) semaphores.

Notes...

Mutex and semaphore can be used for a number of activities such as: (a) to control access to a shared resource; (b) to indicate (signal) the occurrence of an event; and, (c) to synchronize the activities of tasks.

In Brief...

Deadlock occurs when two or more tasks wait for a resource being held by another task. If the resource is not released for a long time due to some problem in that task then the system may be reset by the watchdog timer.

Deadlock

Deadlock occurs when two or more tasks wait for resource being held by another task. To avoid deadlock, a time limit can be set. When a task is waiting for a semaphore or mutex, it can wait for a fixed time; if even after this wait, the resource is not available, the queue can be emptied.

7.6 Mailboxes

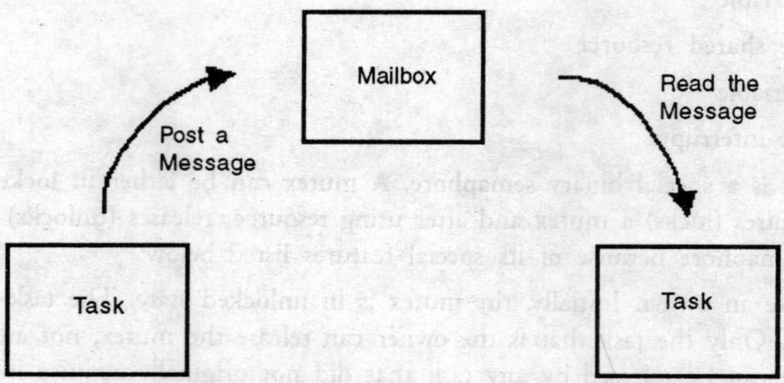

Fig. 7.11 Inter-task Synchronization through Mailbox

A mailbox object is just like your postal mailbox. Someone posts a message in your mailbox and you take out the message. A task can have a mailbox into which others can post a mail. A task or ISR sends the message to the mailbox.

7.6.1 Mailbox Management Function Calls

To manage the mailbox object, the following function calls are provided in the operating system API:

- Create a mailbox
- Delete a mailbox
- Query a mailbox
- Post a message in a mailbox
- Read a message from a mailbox

In Brief...

Mailbox is a kernel object for inter-task communication. A task posts a message in the mailbox and another task will read the message.

7.7 Message Queues

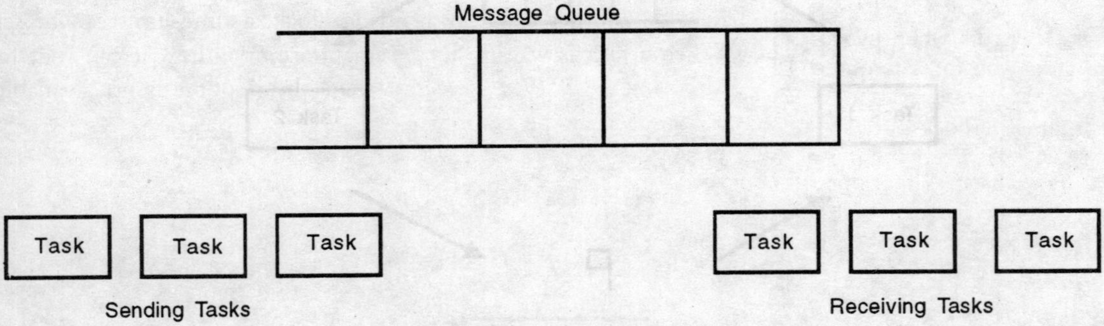

Fig. 7.12: Message Queue

Message queue can be considered as an array of mailboxes. Some of the applications of message queue are:

- Taking the input from a keyboard
- To display output
- Reading voltages from sensors or transducers
- Data packet transmission in a network

In each of these applications, a task or an ISR deposits the message in the message queue. Other tasks can take the messages. Based on your application, the highest priority task or the first task waiting in the queue can take the message.

At the time of creating a queue, the queue is given a name or ID, queue length, sending task waiting list and receiving task waiting list.

7.7.1 Message Queue Management Function Calls

The following function calls are provided to manage message queues:

- Create a queue
- Delete a queue
- Flush a queue
- Post a message in queue
- Post a message in front of queue
- Read message from queue
- Broadcast a message
- Show queue information
- Show queue waiting list

Message queues have a number of applications as shown in Fig. 7.13.

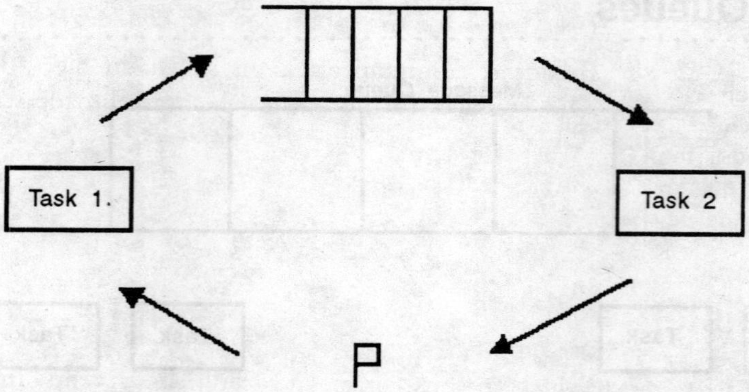

(a) One-way Communication with ACK

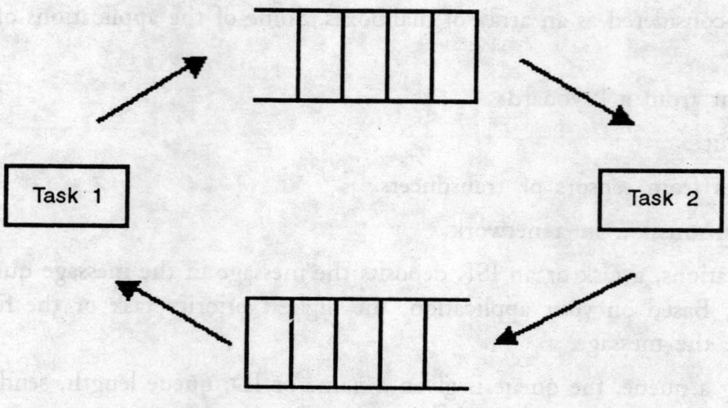

(b) Two-way Communication

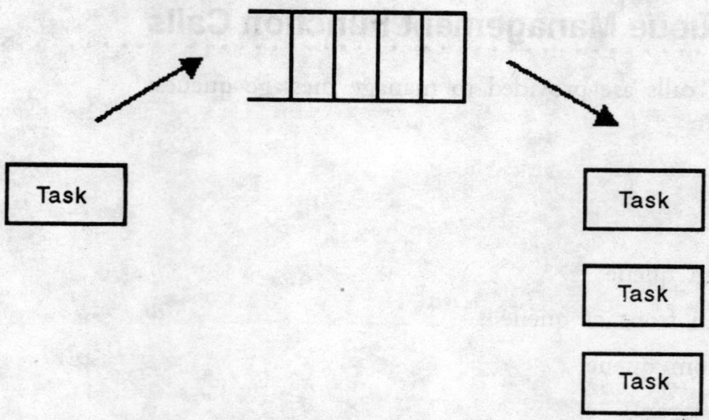

(c) Broadcasting

Fig. 7.13: Applications of Message Queues

One-way data communication: As shown in Fig. 7.13(a), a task can send messages to the queue which are read by the other task. For each message received, the second task uses a semaphore to indicate an acknowledgement.

In Brief...

Message queue is a kernel object used for inter-task communication. A task posts the messages in the message queue and other tasks will read the messages.

Two-way data communication: As shown in Fig. 7.13(b), two tasks can have two queues to send messages in both directions.

Broadcast communication: As shown in Fig. 7.13(c), a task can send messages to the queue which are broadcast to a number of tasks.

7.8 Event Registers

A task can have an event register in which the bits correspond to different events. In Fig. 7.14, a 16-bit event register is shown. These 16 bits are divided into four portions corresponding to the events of three tasks and one ISR. For example, task2 can set the first four bits to 1 or 0. Using a predetermined protocol, the meaning for each of these bits is decided. Task1 comes to know the status of events from these bits. Each of the bits in the event register is an event flag.

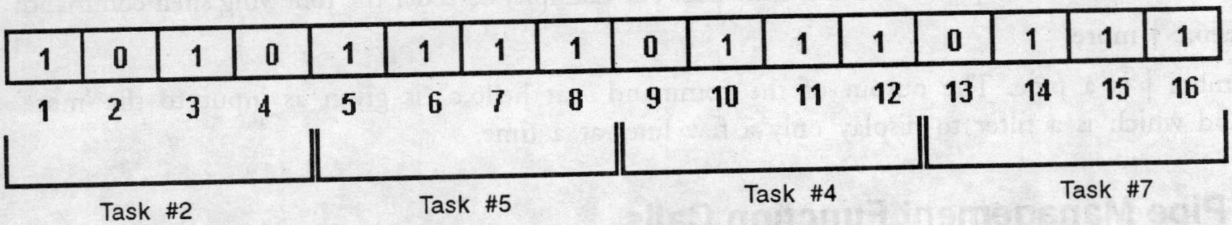

Fig. 7.14: 16-bit Event Register

7.8.1 Event Register Management Function Calls

For managing the event registers, the following function calls are provided:

- Create an event register
- Delete an event register
- Query an event register
- Set an event flag
- Clear an event flag

In Brief...

Each bit in an event register can be used to obtain the status of an event. A task can have an event register and other tasks can set/clear the bits in the event register to inform the status of an event. The meaning of 1 or 0 for a particular bit has to be decided beforehand.

7.9 Pipes

Fig. 7.15: Pipe

As shown in Fig. 7.15, a task can write into a pipe and the other task reads the data that comes out of the pipe. In other words, the output of one task is passed on as input to the other task. Task-to -task or ISR-to-task data transfer can take place using pipes.

Fig. 7.16 Pipes for Inter-task Communication

Pipes can be used for inter-task communication as shown in Fig. 7.16. One task may send the data packets through one pipe and the other task may send acknowledgements through the other pipe.

In Unix/Linux, we use the pipes as shell commands. For example, consider the following shell command:

$cat hello.c | more

The symbol | is a pipe. The output of the command "cat hello.c" is given as input to the 'more' command which is a filter to display only a few lines at a time.

7.9.1 Pipe Management Function Calls

The function calls in the operating system API to manage the pipes are:

- Create a pipe
- Open a pipe
- Close a pipe
- Read from the pipe
- Write to the pipe

In Brief...

Pipe is a kernel object for inter-task communication. Pipe is used to send the output of one task as input to another task for further processing.

7.10 Signals

Signals can be passed to indicate an event. However, many RTOS do not support it then and their use is discouraged. Again, in shell commands, the signals are sent to kill a process. Consider the following command:

$kill –9 879

This is a command to send a signal (Signal Number 9) to a process with a process ID of 879. When the signal is received, the process is terminated.

7.10.1 Signal Management Function Calls

The function calls to manage a signal are:

- Install a signal handler
- Remove an installed signal handler
- Send a signal to another task
- Block a signal from being delivered
- Unblock a blocked signal
- Ignore a signal

In Brief...

Signal is a kernel object to indicate the occurrence of an event to a task. The use of signals is generally discouraged.

7.11 Timers

Timers are used to measure the elapsed time of events. For instance, the kernel has to keep track of different times:

- A particular task may need to be executed periodically, say, every 10 msec. A timer is used to keep track of this periodicity.
- A task may be waiting in a queue for an event to occur. If the event does not occur for a specified time, it has to take appropriate action.
- A task may be waiting in a queue for a shared resource. If the resource is not available for a specified time, an appropriate action has to be taken.

7.11.1 Timer Management Function Calls

The following function calls are provided to manage the timer:

- Get time
- Set time
- Time Delay (in system clock ticks)
- Time delay (in seconds)
- Reset timer

7.12 Memory Management

In addition to the kernel objects discussed above, memory management is an important service provided by the kernel. The API provides the following function calls to manage memory:

- Create a memory block
- Get data from memory
- Post data in the memory
- Query a memory block
- Free the memory block

7.13 Priority Inversion Problem

When tasks share a resource, there is a possibility of getting into a problem, known as priority inversion problem. Mars Pathfinder software bug (mentioned in Chapter 4) got into this problem. Let us study this problem with just three tasks—Low Priority (LP) task, Medium Priority (MP) task and High Priority (HP) task.

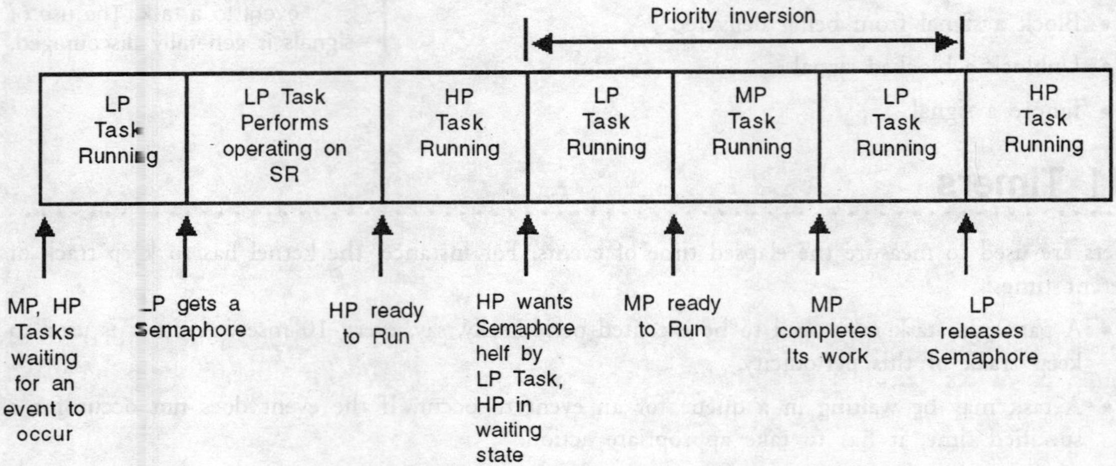

Fig. 7.17: Priority Inversion Problems

As shown in Fig. 7.17, to start with, the MP task and HP task are in the Waiting state and the LP task is Running. After some time, LP gets a mutex for a shared resource (SR) and performs some operations on the shared resource, but it still has not completed its operations. Meanwhile, the HP is Ready-to-Run and hence the HP task is executed by the CPU. Now the HP wants the mutex of the shared resource being held by LP task. So, HP task is moved to the Waiting state and the LP task is executed. After some time, the MP task is Ready-to-Run and hence the LP task is preempted and the MP task is Running. The MP task completes its job and now the LP task is Running. When LP task releases the mutex, HP task acquires it and now this task gets executed. In this process, the high priority task has to wait for a very long time, in spite of its high priority due to the semaphore held by the LP task. This problem is called the priority inversion problem because the priorities of LP task and HP task are effectively inversed!

In Brief...

Priority inversion problem arises when a high priority task has to wait while a lower priority task executes. To overcome this problem, priority inheritance protocol is used.

7.13.1 Priority Inheritance

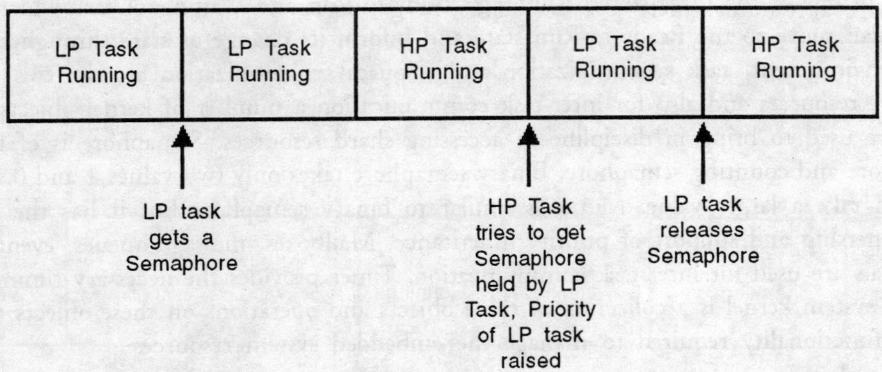

Fig. 7.18 Priority Inheritance

Priority Inheritance provides a solution to the problem of priority inversion. When the LP task acquires the mutex, its priority can be increased to a value more than the priority of the HP task. Kernel has to automatically change this priority. In such a case, the LP task will complete its work very fast and release the mutex which can be acquired by the HP task. Generally, in Priority Inheritance, the priority of the task which acquired the mutex will be increased to a value higher than the priority of the task competing for that resource.

7.13.2 Pathfinder Problem Revisited

In the Mars Pathfinder, priority-based preemptive multitasking operating system was used. Information bus management task was of high priority, communication management task was of medium priority and meteorological data collection task was of low priority. The high priority task and the low priority tasks shared a resource—shared memory. Whenever the low priority task has to access the shared medium, it would acquire a mutex, write the data to the shared memory and release the mutex. Occasionally, the medium priority task was running, while the high priority task was waiting for the low priority task to release the mutex. If the medium priority task was running for a longer time, the watchdog timer used to suspect that something was wrong, and it used to reset the processor. The problem was solved using priority inheritance. The low priority task would become high priority task while holding the mutex. To make this change, while initializing the mutex, the parameter to set the priority inheritance was to be changed from FALSE to TRUE. This is just a change in the file that declares global variables. So, this change was made in the file and the file uploaded to the Pathfinder embedded system. And, no longer the system was reset due to the priority inversion problem.

Summary

This chapter presented a conceptual overview of the embedded/real-time operating system kernel objects and services. The kernel objects are: task scheduler, tasks, semaphores, mutexes, Interrupt Service Routines, mailboxes, message queues, event registers, pipes, signals and timers. The task scheduler is the heart of the operating system. It decides which task has to run next based on a scheduling algorithm. Preemptive multitasking scheduling algorithm is used in embedded/real-time operating systems. In this algorithm, the highest priority task which is Ready-to-Run will be executed. A task can be in one of the three states: Running, Ready-to-Run and Waiting. A task which is in the Waiting state can move to the Ready-to-Run state and inform its change of state through an ISR. In multitasking environment, task synchronization and resource synchronization are the two important issues. To share resources and also for inter-task communication a number of kernel objects are used. Semaphores are used to bring in discipline in accessing shard resources. Semaphore is of two types: binary semaphore and counting semaphore. Binary semaphore takes only two values 1 and 0. Counting semaphore can take a larger value. Mutex is similar to binary semaphore but it has the additional features of ownership and support of priority inheritance. Mailboxes, message queues, event registers, pipes and signals are used for inter-task communication. Timer provides the necessary timing services. The operating system kernel is a collection of these objects and operations on these objects to provide the necessary functionality required to manage the embedded system resources.

Questions

1. What are the objects of an operating system kernel?
2. What is task scheduling? Explain the various scheduling algorithms.
3. What is interrupt latency?
4. Explain how a semaphore can be used for inter-task synchronization.
5. What is the difference between semaphore and mutex?
6. Explain the use of message queues, mailboxes and pipes.
7. Differentiate between preemptive and non-preemptive operating systems.

Exercises

1. You need to develop an embedded system that takes analog voice signal as input, converts it into digital format using an ADC, converts the digital data into packets and sends the packets over a data network. List the various tasks in the embedded software. How do you assign priorities to the tasks? Do you need an embedded operating system? If so, of what type of operating system?
2. Is priority inheritance an important feature? Discuss.
3. List some real-time applications for which you cannot use the desktop computer.
4. Semaphores can be used for data communication. List such applications.
5. Run the following program on a Linux machine and analyze the output:

```
int main(void)
{
        printf("Hello\n");
        if(fork() = = 0)
           printf("World\n");
}
```

6. Run the above program and redirect the output to a file. Analyze the output.

Chapter 8

Overview of Embedded/Real-Time Operating Systems

CHAPTER OBJECTIVES

After reading this chapter, you will be able to:

- Understand the commonalities and differences in the operating systems available off-the-shelf
- Get a good understanding of commercial and open source operating systems used in embedded/real-time systems as well as handheld/mobile devices.

To develop embedded software, a number of commercial and open source operating systems are available. In this chapter, we will study the features that are common to all the operating systems and also the features that differ. We will also study the salient features of some of the widely used operating systems.

8.1 Off-the-Shelf Operating Systems

To reduce development time and effort, it is preferable to use an off-the-shelf operating system that suits your application needs. Depending on the application, you need to choose one of the following categories of operating systems:

- **Non-real-time embedded operating systems:** These operating systems are suitable for non-real-time applications. They use a preemptive kernel, but strict deadlines cannot be met.

In Brief...

The operating systems used in embedded systems can be classified as (a) embedded operating systems that do not meet real-time requirements; (b) real-time operating systems; and (c) handheld/mobile operating systems.

- **Real-time operating systems:** These operating systems provide the necessary functionality for achieving real-time performance through very low interrupt latency. These are 'deterministic' operating systems, i.e. the worst-case response time can be predicted.
- **Handheld/mobile operating systems:** These operating systems are meant for handheld computers and mobile devices such as smart phones. Operating systems such as Palm OS, Symbian OS and Windows CE have been develo .d to address this

market. But in recent years, many other embedded/real-time operating systems are being ported onto the handheld/mobile devices.

8.1.1 Commonalities of the Operating Systems

Because of the immense competition in the embedded/real-time operating system market, the features supported by operating systems of different vendors appear almost the same. Of course, every vendor claims that his operating system is the best. The features listed below are common to most of these operating systems:

- **Integrated Development Environment** (IDE): To facilitate easy and fast development, vendors supply an IDE that includes editor, compiler, debugger and also the necessary cross-platform development tools.
- **POSIX compatibility:** POSIX1003.1-2001 standard specifies the Application Programming Interface to achieve portability of applications. Many off-the-shelf operating systems provide compliance to POSIX.
- **TCP/IP support:** TCP/IP protocol stack, including application layer protocols such as FTP, SMTP, HTTP, is integrated along with the operating system software. Function calls will be provided to access the network-related services.
- **Device drivers:** A number of device drivers are provided for commonly used devices such as serial port, parallel port, USB etc. A Device Driver Kit (DDK) is also generally included that facilitates fast development of device drivers.

In Brief...

An Integrated Development Environment, POSIX compatibility, TCP/IP support and device driver kit are some of the important features offered by all the embedded operating system vendors.

8.1.2 Portable Operating System Interface (POSIX)

POSIX is a standard developed by IEEE. Before POSIX was standardized, every OS vendor used to give his proprietary Application Programming Interface (API) for application development. This interface is a set of function calls to access the operating system objects and services. If you developed the application using the API supplied by one vendor, it was not possible to port the application to another operating system. POSIX standard addressed this problem and the API was standardized. IEEE POSIX 1003.1c-2001 standard specifies the API for portable operating system interface. IEEE POSIX 1003.13 "Standardized Application Environment Profile—POSIX Real-time Application Support" addresses the API for real-time embedded systems. This standard gives the various C language function calls and library functions that need to be implemented by the Operating System (OS) vendors. The concept of threads became popular only because of this standard in fact, threads are referred as POSIX threads. As operating systems can be used for wide range of applications from tiny systems to very large multi-processor based systems, different profiles are defined in the POSIX standard. Small System POSIX Profile is for small embedded systems that have a single process with multiple threads.

In Brief...

Portable Operating System Interface (POSIX) standard facilitates portability of applications across different operating systems.

Notes...

POSIX standards are also available for other programming languages such as ADA and FORTRAN.

8.1.3 Differences in Operating Systems

Off-the-shelf operating systems differ in the following aspects:

- **Support for processors:** The operating system code consists of (a) processor-independent code; and (b) processor-dependent code. Operations such as context switching, in which the contents of the CPU registers have to be stored in the memory, have to be done through assembly language programming. Hence, a small portion of the operating system software is processor-dependent. As a result, every operating system may not support all the processors. Commercial operating systems support the popular processors such as Intel x86/Pentium, MIPS, PowerPC, Intel StrongARM etc. For the specific processor of your choice, you need to check whether the operating system 'port' is available.
- **Footprint:** The footprint or the memory occupied by the kernel differs from OS to OS. Real-time operating system kernels require only a few Kilobytes of memory. The operating system vendor specifies the minimum amount of RAM and ROM required for the kernel. Of course, you need to calculate the total memory requirement for your embedded system keeping in view the size of the application software and the communication software.
- **Java environment:** In tune with the recent trends in using Java for embedded systems, some vendors provide a Java Virtual Machine (JVM) support on their OS. If you want to develop applications in Java, you need to check on the availability of the JVM.
- **Board Support Packages (BSPs):** Some vendors supply hardware boards built around different processors with OS ported onto the hardware. These are called BSPs. BSPs speed up software development.
- **Scheduling algorithms:** Some operating systems provide a number of scheduling algorithms such as round-robin, first-in-first-out etc. whereas some operating systems support only priority-based preemptive scheduling. If you want flexibility in scheduling algorithms, your choice may be comparatively limited.
- **Priority inheritance:** Whether priority inheritance is a good feature or not, it is a debatable issue. Some operating systems do not support this feature, as their developers dislike it. Some operating systems do support it as their developers feel that the designer should be given flexibility in application development.
- **Maximum number of tasks:** The maximum number of tasks supported differs from OS to OS. Some OSs support only 64 tasks, some OSs claim 'unlimited' number though there certainly will be a limit. For example, if a 32-bit integer is used for task ID, the number of tasks is limited to 2^{32}.
- **Assigning task priorities:** In some OSs, each task should have a unique priority and the priority is fixed. In some other OSs, the priority can be changed dynamically during execution time.

- **POSIX support:** In the section on commonalities of operating systems, we discussed POSIX support. Why is it appearing here again?! Though many vendors claim POSIX support, you need to check the details. Small System POSIX profile is for minimal real-time environment. Multi-threaded single POSIX process is supported in such environments. Support for this profile does not mean full-fledged POSIX support. If you are gullible, the vendor may take you for a ride!

In Brief..

Embedded operating systems differ in many aspects: the processors supported, footprint, support for Java environment, Board Support Packages availability, scheduling algorithms, number of tasks and methodology for assigning priorities, support for priority inheritance and licensing terms.

- **Licensing terms:** The prices of the operating systems differ. Some are free under the GPL licence. For some operating systems, one-time payment will entitle you to the entire source code and you need not pay any royalty for each copy of runtime licence. Some vendors ask for a small amount for the development system without source code, and exorbitant amount for the source code. Check on these cost aspects and then do a hard bargain to get the best deal.

In the following sections, we will briefly review the various off-the-shelf operating systems available from commercial vendors as well as under the GPL licence.

Notes...

Though operating system vendor claim POSIX support, this support, in fact, may be only for "small system POSIX profile" which is for small real-time systems. Support for this profile does not mean a full-fledged POSIX support.

8.2 Embedded Operating Systems

In Brief...

Embedded operating systems that do not meet real-time requirements use a preemptive priority based kernel, but they cannot meet strict deadlines. Stripped-down versions of desktop operating systems can be used as embedded operating systems.

Embedded operating systems use a preemptive priority based kernel, but they do not meet strict deadlines. The stripped-down versions of the desktop operating systems can be used as embedded operating systems i.e., in the operating system software, remove all the unnecessary features and make the kernel occupy a small memory and you have the embedded operating system. This strategy is used in developing the following three embedded operating systems:

- Embedded NT
- Windows XP Embedded
- Embedded Linux

8.2.1 Embedded NT

Many embedded systems use the Single Board Computer (SBC) hardware. This hardware is essentially same as the desktop computer's hardware. The embedded system, however, does a focused job; hence the application and the operating system together need to be bundled and transferred to the target hardware. Typical applications include Internet Kiosk, ATM etc. For such applications, Microsoft's Embedded NT is an excellent choice. Embedded NT is based on Windows NT4.0. Embedded NT works on 80x86 and Pentium processors only.

The requirement of Embedded NT for minimal operating system functionality without any network support is 9 MB of RAM and 8 MB of program such as Flash. The exact memory requirement of the target hardware depends on the application. If the application is a single Win32 application with networking capability, minimum RAM requirement is 16 MB. With network components and device drivers, the requirement is about 16 MB of RAM and 16 MB of program memory.

Application development using Embedded NT is very easy. You can develop the applications in Visual Studio environment (Visual Basic or Visual C++) and the application can be ported onto the target system. IIS 3.0 is included in Embedded NT.

To develop applications using Embedded NT, the development system has to be installed on a system with the following configurations:

- Windows NT 4.0
- Service Pack 4.0 or later
- Internet Explorer 5.0 or later
- Visual Studio 6.0 development environment
- Windows NT 4.0 Service Resource Kit

Development tools called the Component Designer and the Target Designer are provided in Embedded NT. The Component Designer facilitates defining and adding components to the Target Designer. The Target Designer is used to create a bootable NT target system. It generates a target image, which consists of a number of directories. All these directories and files need to be copied onto the target machine's file system. Target system can be created in any of the following ways:

- **Create a headless system:** Embedded systems that do not have a monitor, keyboard or mouse are called headless systems. To create a headless system, the following components need to be added:
  - Null VGA
  - Null Keyboard Drive
  - Null Mouse

  Debugging a headless system is a problem because of lack of input/output devices. To overcome this problem, "Console Administration Component" is provided. This component allows monitoring the embedded system through a serial interface.
- **Create a target system that boots from a CDROM:** The target image generated by the Target Designer is transferred to a CDROM and the embedded system boots from the CDROM.
- **Create a bootable partition on the hard disk:** In this case, a partition can be created on the hard disk from which the Embedded NT target image can boot.

In Brief...

Embedded NT is only for x86/Pentium processors. It is suitable for embedded systems built around single board computers for applications such as Internet kiosks and Automatic Teller Machines. 9 MB of RAM and 8 MB of ROM are the minimum requirements.

- **Create the target image on an empty hard disk:** Target image can be transferred to an empty hard disk and the hard disk can be connected to the embedded system. This approach is the best while testing the embedded software in the lab environment.

8.2.2 Windows XP Embedded

Microsoft's Windows XP Embedded (abbreviated Embedded XP in this section), is the successor to Embedded NT. Like Windows NT, it is also a preemptive multitasking operating system and uses Win32 applications and drivers. Hence, the main attraction of this operating system is that applications developed on desktop using Visual Studio can be ported onto the embedded system. However, as compared to many other embedded operating systems, it requires huge resources particularly the RAM and the Flash memory.

In Brief...

Windows XP Embedded is a good choice for single board computer-based embedded systems that do not have real-time requirements. Support for IEEE 802.11 and infrared interfaces, and IP version 6 are its attractions.

Embedded XP is now being used in a number of embedded systems such as set top boxes, point of sale terminals, Internet Kiosks, etc. Embedded XP has many attractive features such as support for IP version 6, IrDA compliance, 802.11 LAN connectivity, Universal Plug and Play feature, etc. It also has support for Telephony APIs (TAPI) and NetMeeting to provide multimedia applications.

The application software to be embedded can be created using Embedded Visual Studio which provides the following utilities to create the target image:

- Target Designer, which is used to create bootable runtime image of the application you have developed. You can transfer the runtime image to the target system, and the system will boot with Embedded XP and the application will run from this image.
- Component Designer, which is used to create components required for the embedded application.
- Deployment tools, which are used to prepare the target device for the runtime image.

The bootable image is created using the Target Designer and transferred to a CDROM or a Flash (disk on a chip). The memory requirement of the embedded system depends on the application, but minimum of 9 MB RAM and 8 MB of ROM are required.

Notes...

The attractive feature of Windows-based embedded operating systems is that applications developed using Visual Studio can be easily ported onto the embedded system.

8.2.3 Embedded Linux

Open source software revolution started with the development of Linux. Like Linux kernel, Embedded Linux kernel is covered by the GNU General Public License (GPL) and hence the complete source code is available free of cost. GPL also permits redistribution of the source code even if it is modified as per the requirements of your application. However, modified source code should be made available, usually for a nominal cost which is not more than the cost of reproducing the software. You can get the details of open source and its implications at www.gnu.org/copyleft/gpl.html. It is expected that open source software will have profound impact on the industry in the coming years and Embedded Linux is likely to be used extensively in embedded applications. It is now being used on a number of devices such as PDAs, Set Top Boxes, cellular phones, Internet appliances and also in major mission critical equipment such as telecommunication switches and routers.

Embedded Linux (www.embedded-linux.org) is available freely and openly in source code form and is gaining popularity. The vendors who offer embedded Linux solutions and support for both real-time and non real-time applications include Coventive, FSM Labs, Lineo, LynuxWorks, Mizi, MontaVista, PalmPalm, RedHat, ridgeRun, TimeSys etc.

The main attractions of embedded Linux are:

- Open source software
- Availability of a large number of software resources in source code form (device drivers, application software, networking software, protocol software, speech/image processing software, etc.)
- Support for POSIX
- No royalty
- Availability of many people with expertise in Unix/Linux programming.

In Brief...

The attractive features of embedded Linux are: open source software, POSIX support, availability of many software resources in source code form and availability of a large pool of experts for programming.

As many non-standard variations of embedded Linux are available (mainly due to the fact that the source code is available to everyone and anyone can make the changes), it may lead to non-portable applications.

Embedded Linux Consortium Platform Specifications

Embedded Linux Consortium (ELC) released the Embedded Linux Consortium Platform Specifications (ELCPS) to bring in standardization for using Linux in embedded systems. ELCPS Version 1.0 was released in December 2002. It is compatible with POSIX 1003.1-2001 as well as POSIX1003.13.

ELCPS defines three environments to cater to different embedded system requirements. These are

- Minimal system environment
- Intermediate system environment
- Full system environment

For each of these environments, the APIs to be supported are defined in ELCPS. Operating system vendors can ensure conformance to these specifications so that the applications can be made portable. If you are modifying the Linux kernel to suit your embedded system requirements, you need to ensure ELCPS conformance.

Minimal system environment: This configuration is applicable for embedded systems with one processor and associated memory. These embedded systems work in isolated mode without any user interaction and have no secondary storage or file system. Only one process with one or more Linux tasks or POSIX threads will be running. Hence, the set of APIs required for this type of embedded software development will be minimal and also the OS footprint will be very small.

Intermediate system environment: Embedded systems of this category will have one or more processors, but need not have any secondary storage. A file system can be built, say, in a Flash memory device. There will be multiple processes, asynchronous input/output operations and support for dynamic linking of objects (libraries). Support for secondary storage is also provided.

Full system environment: The embedded systems of this category will have one or more processors, secondary storage, network support, and user interfaces. This environment supports full multi-purpose Linux.

In Brief...

Embedded Linux Consortium Platform Specifications (ELCPS), finalized in December 2002, will ensure portability of applications.

The vendor can obtain conformance for any of the three environments. For each environment, the various API calls to be supported such as for task management, inter-process communication, file management, thread-safe general ISO C library interface, mathematical function library calls, header file definitions for symbolic constants etc. are specified.

Notes...

Embedded Linux Consortium Platform Specifications address three types of embedded systems: (a) minimal system environment for systems with one processor and memory; (b) intermediate system environment for systems with one or more processors and secondary storage; and, (c) full system environment which requires one or more processors, secondary storage, user interface and network support.

8.3 Real-Time Operating Systems

There are nearly 100 real-time operating systems in the commercial market. So, shopping for a real-time operating system is not an easy task. We will review the following operating systems:

- QNX Neutrino
- VxWorks
- MicroC/OS-II
- RTLinux

8.3.1 QNX Neutrino

In Brief...

QNX Neutrino is a real-time operating system that supports multiple scheduling algorithms and up to 65,535 tasks. MySQL can be integrated with this OS to create embedded database applications.

QNX Neutrino is a popular real-time operating system of QNX Software Systems Limited (www.qnx.com). It supports a number of processors such as ARM, MIPS, Power PC, SH-4, StrongARM, x86 and Pentium. Board Support Packages and Device Driver Kit help in fast development of your prototype. It provides an excellent Integrated Development Environment. It has support for C, C++ and Java languages and TCP/IP protocol stack.

It has support for multiple scheduling algorithms such as round-robin, FIFO etc. and the same application can use different scheduling algorithms for different tasks. Up to 65,535 tasks are supported and each task can have 65,535 threads. Minimum time resolution is one nanosecond. Even small embedded systems can use this OS as it requires 64K kernel ROM and 32K kernel RAM.

8.3.2 VxWorks

Wind River's VxWorks (www.windriver.com) is one of the most popular real-time operating systems. This OS has been used in the Mars Pathfinder. It supports a number of processors including PowerPC, Intel StrongARM, ARM, Hitachi SuperH, Motorola ColdFire, etc.

In Brief...

VxWorks is a real-time operating system that supports multiple scheduling algorithms and also priority inheritance.

It supports both preemptive and round-robin scheduling algorithms. 256 priority levels can be assigned to the tasks. It supports priority inheritance. Those who are against priority inheritance need not use this feature, which is an option provided to the developer.

8.3.3 MicroC/OS-II

Micro-controller Operating System version II developed by Jean J. Labrosse (www.ucos-II.com) is a preemptive real-time operating system which is popular for teaching RTOS concepts. It is also used widely in many commercial applications including mission-critical applications. It is certified for use in commercial aircraft by Federal Aviation Administration. The standard RTCA.DO-178B specifies the requirements.

In Brief...

MicroC/OS-II is a real-time operating system used extensively in academic institutions for teaching operating system concepts. It is available in source code form for non-commercial purposes. The number of tasks can be 64 out of which eight are system tasks. Round-robin scheduling is not supported.

The author of this OS summarizes its features beautifully: "source code availability, ROMable, scalable, preemptive, portable, multitasking, deterministic, reliable, support for different platforms".

This OS supports 64 tasks out of which eight are system tasks. Hence, the application can have up to 56 tasks. Each task is assigned a unique priority. Round-robin scheduling algorithm is not supported by this operating system.

8.3.4 RTLinux

FSM Labs (www.fsmlabs.com) has two editions of RTLinux—RTLinuxPro and RTLinuxFree. RTLinuxPro is a priced-edition and RTLinuxFree is the open source release. RTLinux is a hard real-time operating system with support for many processors such as x86, Pentium, PowerPC, ARM, Fujitsu, MIPS and Alpha. A footprint of 4 MB is required for RTLinux. It does not support priority inheritance.

RTLinux runs underneath the Linux operating system. The Linux OS becomes an idle task for RTLinux. RTLinux tasks are given priority as compared to Linux tasks. Interrupts from Linux are disabled to achieve real-time performance. This interrupt disabling is done using a layer of emulation software between the Linux kernel and the interrupt controller hardware.

In Brief...

RTLinux runs underneath the Linux operating system. The Linux is an idle task for RTLinux. The real-time software running under RTLinux is given priority as compared to non-real-time threads running under Linux. This OS is an excellent choice for 32-bit processor based embedded systems.

The tasks, which do not have any timing constraints, will run in the Linux kernel only. Soft real-time capability is provided by Linux system. Hard real-time tasks run in the real-time kernel. Worst case time is 15 microseconds between giving an interrupt signal and starting of the real-time handler.

MiniRTL, a tiny implementation of RTLinux, runs on 486 machines. This implementation is targeted towards PC/104 boards.

8.4 Handheld Operating Systems

Handheld computers are becoming very popular as their capabilities are increasing day by day. Handheld computers integrated with mobile phones are called smart phones. The smart phones support data, voice and video services. The important requirements for a mobile operating system are:

- To keep the cost of the handheld computer low, small footprint of the operating system is required. A footprint of 64 KB to 2MB for the OS would be attractive. Generally, low-cost handheld computers will have 2 to 4 MB of ROM and 2 to 16 MB of RAM.
- The operating system should have support for soft real-time performance. For audio and video applications, timing constraints are imposed though the deadlines are not critical.
- TCP/IP stack needs to be integrated along with the operating system.
- Communication protocol stacks for Infrared, Bluetooth, IEEE 802.11 interfaces need to be integrated.
- There should be support for data synchronization. A special utility is required using which the data, in say, the desktop computer and the handheld computer can be synchronized. For instance, when you connect your handheld computer to your desktop computer and run the data synchronization software, the address book information in both the computers should be made to contain the same addresses. Each handheld operating system vendor presently gives proprietary software for data synchronization.

The popular handheld/mobile operating systems are:

- Palm OS
- Symbian OS
- Windows CE
- Windows CE.NET

An overview of these operating systems is given below.

Notes...

Data synchronization between two devices is presently done through proprietary protocols. SyncML, a markup language, has been standardized that uses standard protocols and a standard markup for data synchronization.

8.4.1 Palm OS

Palm OS (www.palmos.com) is perhaps the most popular handheld operating system. In addition to Palm Computing Inc.'s palmtops, many other vendors such as Sony, Hndspring use this OS in their handheld computer hardware. The OS will run on even low-end processors of 16 MHz to 33 MHz clock speed with 512 KB ROM, and 32 KB RAM. Bluetooth and IrDA protocol stacks are integrated into the OS to provide wireless interfaces to the handheld computer.

Using Palm OS SDK, application software can be developed for these devices. The applications can be developed in C or C++ or Java. The data between a handheld and a desktop computer can be synchronized using a utility called HotSync. The Palm Conduit Development Kit (CDK) is used to develop conduits (plug-ins to HotSync) in VC++ or VB or Java. Palm OS also provides a virtual file system API to develop a file system. Software development can be done on a desktop and tested on an emulator. The emulator can run on Windows, Unix/Linux, and Mac operating systems.

In Brief...

Palm OS is a popular handheld operating system. Application development on this OS can be done in C, C++ or Java. HotSync is used for data synchronization. Conduit Development Kit is used to develop applications for synchronization of data.

Though nearly 37% of the market share of handheld operating systems was held by Palm OS, now there is stiff competition from Symbian OS and Windows CE.

8.4.2 Symbian OS

Symbian OS (www.symbian.com) has a good market share of handheld operating systems. Licensees of Symbian OS include major mobile phone suppliers such as Ericsson, Kenwood, Motorola, Nokia, Panasonic, Psion, Sanyo, Siemens and Sony. Ericsson's R380 smart phone and Nokia's 9210 communicator are based on Symbian OS. The OS architecture supports both voice service and packet data services. Support for Bluetooth and IrDA is provided. The software development kit enables programmers develop applications in C++ or Java. Data synchronization is achieved with Symbian Connect.

In Brief...

Symbian OS is a popular handheld operating system which has been licensed to a number of mobile device manufacturers. Data synchronization is done through Symbian Connect.

8.4.3 Windows CE

Micorosft's Pocket PC hardware runs the Windows CE operating system. This OS runs on Intel x86 family processors as well as Alpha, NEC, Toshiba, PowerPC and Hitachi's Super H. The handheld computers of Casio, HP, NEC, Philips, Sharp etc. run this operating system. It requires 2 MB ROM.

Embedded Visual Tools are used to develop applications above Windows CE. The main attraction of these tools is that a subset of Win32 API is used to develop applications. Application software

In Brief...

Windows CE is a handheld operating system for Pocket PCs. As it uses a subset of Win32 APIs, application software can be developed in VB or VC++ using embedded visual tools.

developers well versed in VB or VC++ can develop applications for Windows CE without much effort or training and this is the main attraction of using this operating system. "Pocket" versions of Microsoft Office applications (Outlook, Excel, Word etc.) are available. For end users, this is a blessing as they need not learn a new user interface for running a word processor or a spreadsheet. ActiveSync is used to synchronize the data between the desktop and the handheld computer.

8.4.4 Windows CE.NET

Microsoft's Windows CE.NET is successor to Windows CE. It is a real-time embedded operating system and is now becoming a popular operating system for smart phones, PDAs, set top boxes, IP Phones, CD players, digital cameras, DVD players, etc. In tune with the other operating systems of Microsoft, this OS facilitates development of applications either using Microsoft Visual Studio.NET or using embedded Visual C++. Hence, developing new applications or porting existing applications is very easy. With support for TCP/IP, IP version 6, Bluetooth, 802.11 and Ethernet and Infrared interfaces as well as Pocket Internet Explorer, handheld computers and smart phones will look like desktop computers in your palm. The minimal kernel functionality requires just 200 KB. Average ISR latency is 2.8 microseconds on a 166 MHz Pentium processor.

Windows CE.NET 4.2 Emulation Edition and Evaluation Kit are freely downloadable for non-commercial purposes and evaluation. Without the target hardware, the application software can be tested using the emulators. Applications can be developed and tested on a desktop computer running Windows XP.

Microsoft provides nearly 2 million lines of source code under the Shared Source Program that enables modification to the source code to suit your application requirements.

In Brief...

Windows CE.NET is a hard real-time operating system that is being used in a number of consumer devices. Applications can be developed using Microsoft Visual Studio.NET.

Summary

In this chapter, selected commercial and open source operating systems are reviewed. These operating systems have the following commonalities: an Integrated Development Environment which contains all the development tools, POSIX compatibility, support for TCP/IP protocol stack and provision of Device Driver Kits. However, these operating systems differ in a number of aspects which include: processors supported, footprint, support for Java or lack of it, availability of Board Support Packages, support for different scheduling algorithms, number of tasks supported and assignment of priorities, support for priority inheritance and the licensing fee. An overview of the salient features of selected operating systems is presented. Embedded NT, Windows XP embedded and Embedded Linux are reviewed. An overview of some real-time operating systems viz., QNX Neutrino, VxWorks, MicroC/OSII and RTLinux is also given. Palm OS, Symbian OS, Windows CE and Windows CE.NET handheld/mobile operating system features are also discussed briefly.

Questions

1. List the various commercially available embedded operating systems and explain their features.
2. List the various open source embedded operating systems and explain their features.
3. List the various mobile/handheld operating systems and explain their features.
4. What is POSIX compatibility?

Exercises

1. List a few other embedded/real-time operating systems not covered in this chapter.
2. What are the issues involved in synchronization of data between the handheld computer and the desktop computer? Explore the standardization activities for data synchronization.
3. Develop a software package that measures the typing speed. The software has to run on a handheld computer such as the Pocket PC.
4. What type of an operating system you will use for the following applications:
   a. An Internet kiosk installed in a rural area.
   b. A navigation system used in an aircraft
   c. A navigation system used in a car
   d. A DVD player
   e. A desktop computer to be used as a process control system with hard real-time requirements
   f. An electronic toy helicopter

Chapter 9

Target Image Creation

CHAPTER OBJECTIVES

After reading this chapter, you will be able to:

- Appreciate the issues involved in creating the target image
- Understand the process of creating a target image of an application developed in Windows XP Embedded
- Gain knowledge of porting a real-time operating system on a custom-built hardware platform

After the software development is completed on the host system, the executable image is transferred to the target hardware. Based on the requirements, the operating system and the communication software are integrated along with the application software and an executable image is created and transferred to the target hardware. In this chapter, we will discuss the general issues involved in creating the target image. We will also take up two specific case studies.

9.1 Operating System Software

For the specific processor chosen for your embedded system, the operating system software can be divided into:

- Processor-independent code
- Processor-dependent code

The processor-independent code is written in a high-level language such as C. The processor-dependent code consists of both C and assembly or only assembly language. The processor-dependent code is required because operations such as context switching have to be implemented in assembly language only. Recall that context switching involves storing the CPU register contents of the currently running process and loading the new task parameters in the CPU registers. Handling the CPU registers is done using assembly language code.

Hence, while choosing an operating system, you need to first check up whether the operating system being considered by you has the support for the processor chosen for your embedded system. When you obtain the operating system, you need to obtain the processor-dependent code as well as the code for the processor of your choice.

Operating system vendors give Board Support Packages (BSPs) wherein the operating system will be ported on to a processor-based board. The OS is already ported on to the hardware and hence you need not get into the details of porting. You can focus only on your application development.

Porting the operating system is not a difficult task due to the GUI provided by the OS vendor to facilitate easy creation of the target image. For x86/Pentium systems, the OS suppliers give readily built 'port' and hence you can get started very easily.

In Brief...

The operating system software consists of processor-independent code as well as processor-dependent code. Processor-dependent code is used to manipulate the CPU registers.

You can experiment with porting on RTOS on your desktop computer, by downloading an evaluation copy of the QNX Neutrino RTOS. When you install the OS on your desktop, every time you boot your system, you have an option to boot either Windows or QNX. If you opt for QNX, you will be running the QNX on your Pentium hardware.

As the procedure for creating the target image varies from OS to OS, we will discuss how to create the target image for two representative operating systems in the following sections.

Notes...

Executable image that is transferred to the program memory is also referred as target image, bootable image and runtime image.

9.2 Target Image Creation for Windows XP Embedded

For embedded systems which use Windows XP Embedded operating system, the application software can be written using Visual Studio. To start with, you create the executable file of the application software and then use the following steps to create a target image. Assume that the application software executable filename is ACRemote.EXE.

For creating the target image, Windows XP Embedded Development Studio provides component designer and target designer as discussed in Chapter 8. We will use these designers to create the target image.

- Collect all the files required to run the application in the target system. In addition to the application software executable file, you need additional DLLs. Assume that your application needs the following DLLs for running the application on the target system:

  MFC42D.DLL

  MFCO42D.DLL

  MSVCRTD.DLL

- Create a component using the Component Designer as per the procedure given below:

Open the Component Designer (on the Start menu, point to Programs and Microsoft Windows Embedded Studio, and then click Component Designer).

Save the component as ExampleComponent.

In the navigation pane, right click **components** which is under **Windows XP Embedded Client (x86)** and then click add component.

In the component properties box, type **Name** as **ACRemoteComponent.**

In the navigation pane right click on **files** which is under **Components/ACRemoteComponent** and click **add - file.** Type the following information:

Target Name: ACRemote.EXE

Source Name: ACRemote.EXE

Destination Path: %24%\Documents and Settings\Administrator\Desktop\Examples.

Click **Advanced...** button. The window will be as shown in Fig. 9.1.

Similarly add the remaining three files which are listed above.

Finally, the window appears as shown in Fig. 9.2.

Save the component and Exit.

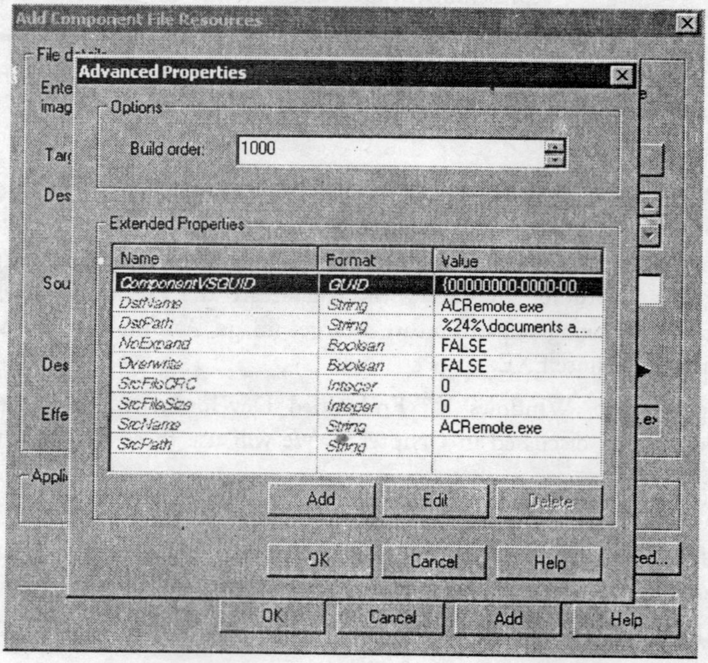

Fig. 9.1: Advanced Properties for Adding Components

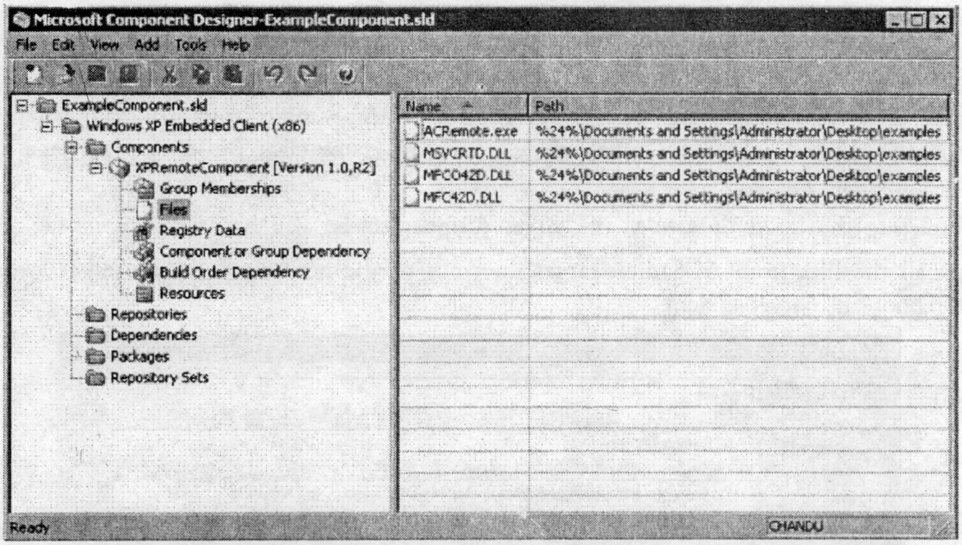

Fig. 9.2: Component Designer

- Create the target image using the Target Designer.

Run the **tap.exe,** which is given with the Embedded XP software at the DOS prompt of the **Target** system. This file creates **devices.pmq** file which contains information about the target system hardware.

Run the Target Designer (on the Start menu, point to Programs and Microsoft Windows Embedded Studio, and then click Target Designer).

Create a new configuration by clicking **New** on the **File** menu and type the configuration name as **TargetConfiguration.** Save it as **XPTarget.**

Now import the **devices.pmq** file from the File menu and then click Start.

After completion of the import operation, add the following components from the component navigation pane:

FAT component, which is under **Software/System/Storage and File System/ Infrastructure/File System.**

English Language Support component, which is under **Software/System/International/ Infrastructure.**

Windows Logon component, which is under **Software/System/Security/Infrastructure.**

NT Loader component, which is under **Software/System/System Services/Base.**

FAT Format component, which is under **Software/System/Storage and File**

System/ Applications.

Explorer Shell component, which is under **Software/System/User Interface/Shells.**

Import the custom component (**ExampleComponent**) by clicking **Component Database Manager** under **Tools** menu.

After importing the custom component, save and restart the Target Designer and open **XPTarget** to load the custom component.

Right click on **ACRemoteComponent** in the component navigation pane and click **add.**

Click the **Check Dependencies** option under **Configuration** menu. If any error occurs, add the corresponding components depending on the target system configuration. After clearing all the errors, click **Build Target Image** which is under **Configuration** menu. In the **Build Target Image** window, select **Build Type** as **Release** and type **Destination** as **F:\ACSampleTarget** (ACSampleTarget is the directory in the F drive, where the target image is stored). Now click **Build.** At this stage the screen will be as shown in Fig. 9.3.

After completing the build operation, the target designer screen will be as shown in Fig. 9.4.

Now copy all the files from **ACSampleTarget** directory to the boot drive of the target system's hard disk and reboot the target system.

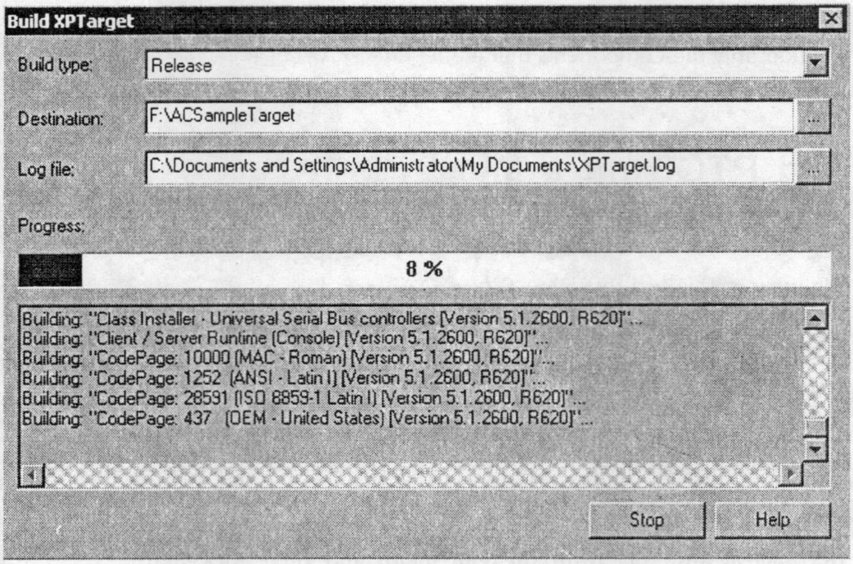

Fig. 9.3: Building XP Target

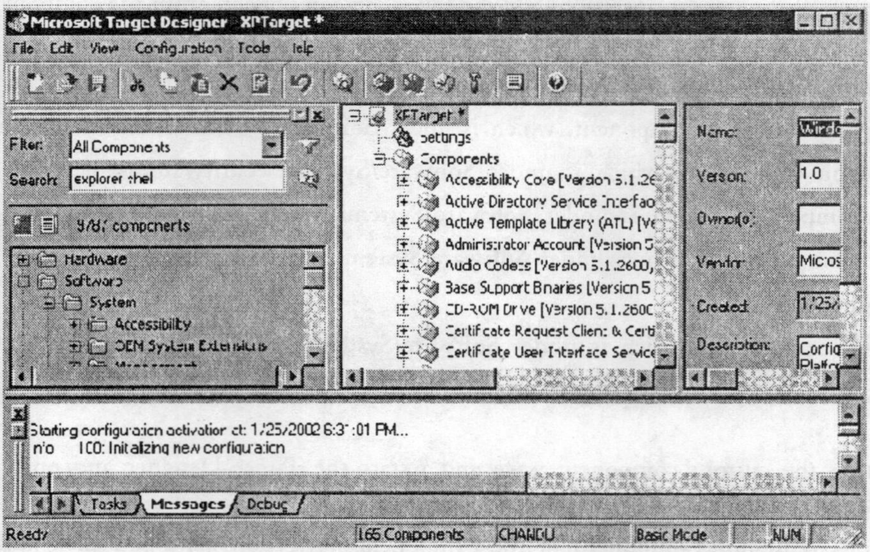

Fig. 9.4: Target Designer

In Brief...

You can create the target image and transfer it to a memory chip such as Flash or you can create a bootable CDROM.

Note that you can build the target image in a number of ways: If you have the target hardware with enough Flash memory, you can transfer the image to the memory device. Otherwise, you can create a CDROM which contains the target image and boot the embedded system using the CDROM. Alternatively, you can take an empty hard disk and transfer the image on to it and then boot the embedded system using the hard disk. This is a good approach for testing in the laboratory.

Notes...

The various options provided by Windows XP Embedded Studio in the component designer are mainly to include only the components that are required for your application. For example, if network support is not required, you need not include the TCP/IP protocol stack.

9.3 Porting RTOS on a Micro-controller based Development Board

To appreciate the issues involved in porting an operating system onto a custom-built hardware platform, you can try out porting MicroC/OS-II on ATmega128-based development board whose hardware architecture is given in Chapter 5. You can obtain this RTOS from the site www.uCOS-II.com. This operating system software is not free, but you can download it for research purposes. The procedure for porting the RTOS is as follows:

- For the processor of your choice, you need to download the processor-specific code, in addition to the processor-independent code from the above site. The processor-independent code contains the C programs related to the core operating system, tasks, semaphores, mailboxes, mutexes, queues, timers, flags etc. The processor-dependent code contains both assembly and C code specific to the processor for accessing processor resources.

In Brief...

The target image can be created on the host system using cross-platform development tools. The image is then transferred to the memory device using the device programmer tool.

- Compile the code using AVRGCC and AVR Studio cross-platform development tools.
- To program the Flash memory, the procedure is as follows:

Run the Serial Device Programmer (Pony-Prog2000) on AVR Studio and select the Target device as ATmega128, as shown in Fig. 9.5.

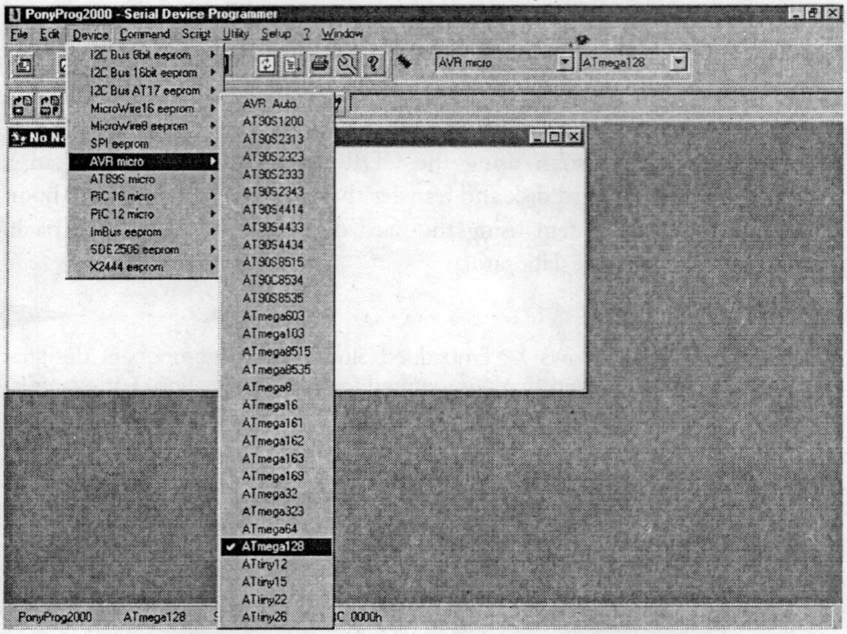

Fig. 9.5: Running the Serial Device Programmer

Set the I/O parameters as Parallel Port with AVRISP API, as shown in Fig. 9.6.

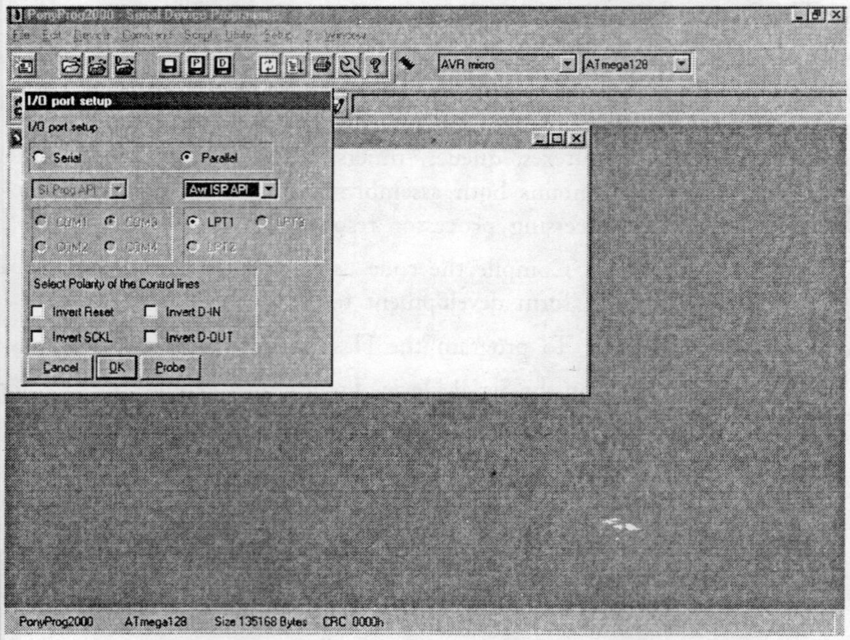

Fig. 9.6: I/O Port Setup

Click on the Open button of main Menu to select the Hex file as shown in Fig. 9.7

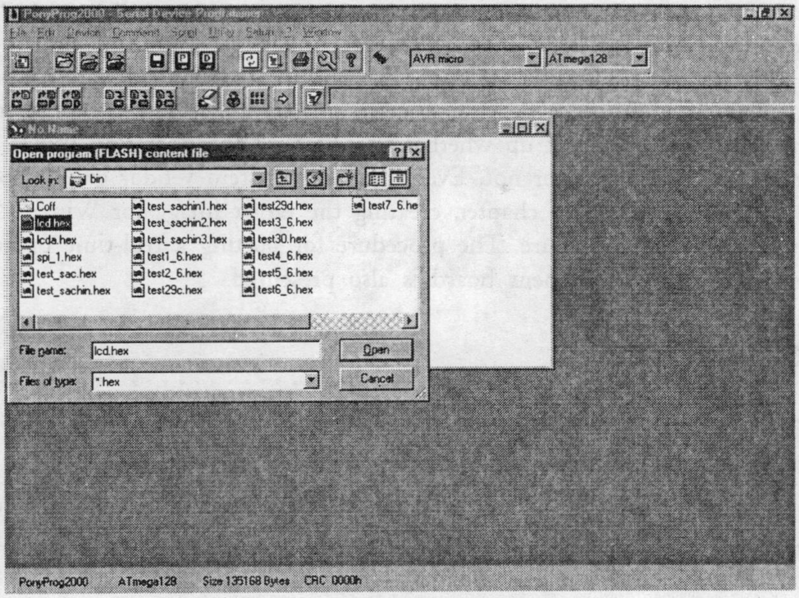

Fig. 9.7: Flash Content File Selection

Using the Erase option, erase the Internal Flash of ATmega128. After erasing, select the Program option to program the device, as shown in Fig. 9.8.

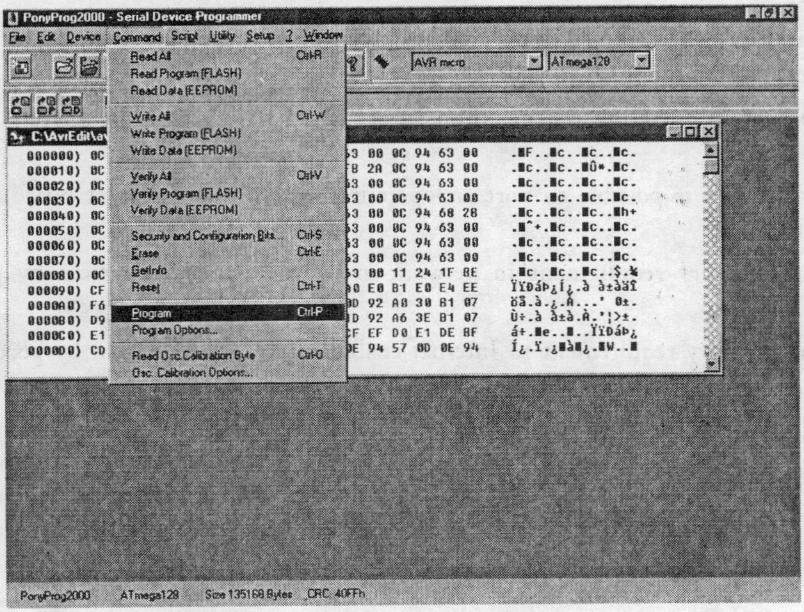

Fig.9.8: Programming the Flash

Summary

This chapter addressed the issues of creating target image by bundling the operating system, communication software and application software. The operating system software consists of processor-independent code as well as processor-dependent code. Hence, an operating system may not support all the processors. You need to check up whether the 'port' of the operating system for the specific processor chosen by you is available or not. Every operating system vendor gives a specific procedure for creating the target image. In this chapter, creating the target image for Windows XP Embedded is presented as a step-by-step procedure. The procedure for porting a real-time operating system on to a micro-controller based development board is also presented.

Questions

1. Why the OS software is not independent of the processor?
2. Study the process of porting QNX Neutrino OS on your desktop.
3. Study the process of creating a target image for Windows XP Embedded platform.
4. Explain the process of porting an RTOS on a custom-built development board.

Exercises

1. Explain the pros and cons of leaving the debugging software in the final embedded system's firmware.
2. Download QNX Neutrino software evaluation version and experiment with porting the software on to an evaluation board of your choice.
3. Can you port an operating system onto a target board having an 8-bit micro-controller? If not, why?
4. Study whether it is possible to port an operating system onto a target board having a digital signal processor.
5. Study the memory requirement to network-enable an embedded system by porting TCP/IP stack.
6. Study the memory requirement to Internet-enable an embedded system by porting the TCP/IP stack and the HTTP server.

Chapter 10

Representative Embedded Systems

CHAPTER OBJECTIVES

After reading this chapter, you will be able to:

- Understand the architecture of representative embedded systems viz., digital thermometer, handheld computer, navigation system, IP Phone and Software-defined Radio.
- Gain knowledge of tiny embedded systems such as smart cards and RF tags.
- Learn how to integrate DSP and GPP in an embedded system.

Every embedded system project will be a new experience for the developers. The inputs, outputs, processing requirements, and hardware and software architecture will be different. In this chapter, we will study some representative embedded systems to gain a deeper understanding of the architectures as well as to appreciate the intricacies in embedded system design.

10.1 Digital Thermometer

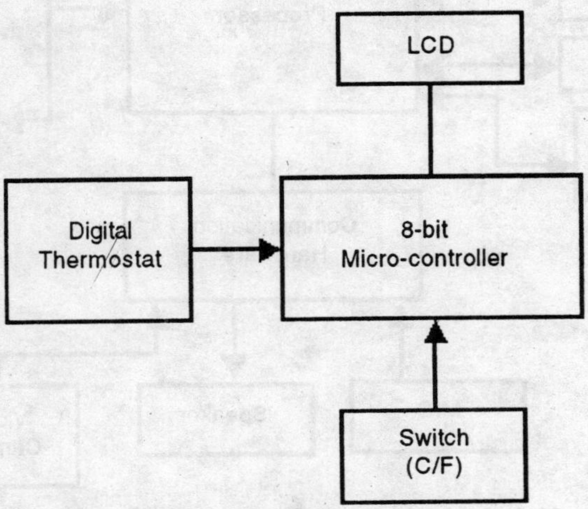

Fig. 10.1: Digital Thermometer

A very small embedded system is the digital thermometer shown in Fig. 10.1. It measures the temperature inside and outside the room and displays the values in Centigrade or Fahrenheit. The sensor required is a digital thermostat such as Dallas Semiconductors' DS1620. An LCD with 2 lines x 8 characters can be used for displaying the temperature. A small switch is required using which the user can make a selection for Centigrade or Fahrenheit. You can use an 8-bit micro-controller that processes the sensor data, does the conversion from Centigrade to Fahrenheit and sends the output to display. No external memory is required, the internal program memory and data memory are sufficient for the little processing to be done. It can operate from a 1.5 volt battery and hence a DC-DC converter is used to derive the necessary voltages.

In Brief...

Digital Thermometer is a simple embedded system built around a micro-controller with a sensor and an LCD. No external memory is required.

10.2 Handheld Computer

Handheld computers are now becoming very popular. You can use the handheld computer as a digital diary and also for applications such as composing mails, preparation of small text documents, playing MP3 music files or video clippings. The processing power of these handheld computers is increasing day by day and hence applications that are supported are also increasing. A handheld computer integrated with a mobile phone is called a smart phone. The hardware architecture of a handheld computer is shown in Fig. 10.2.

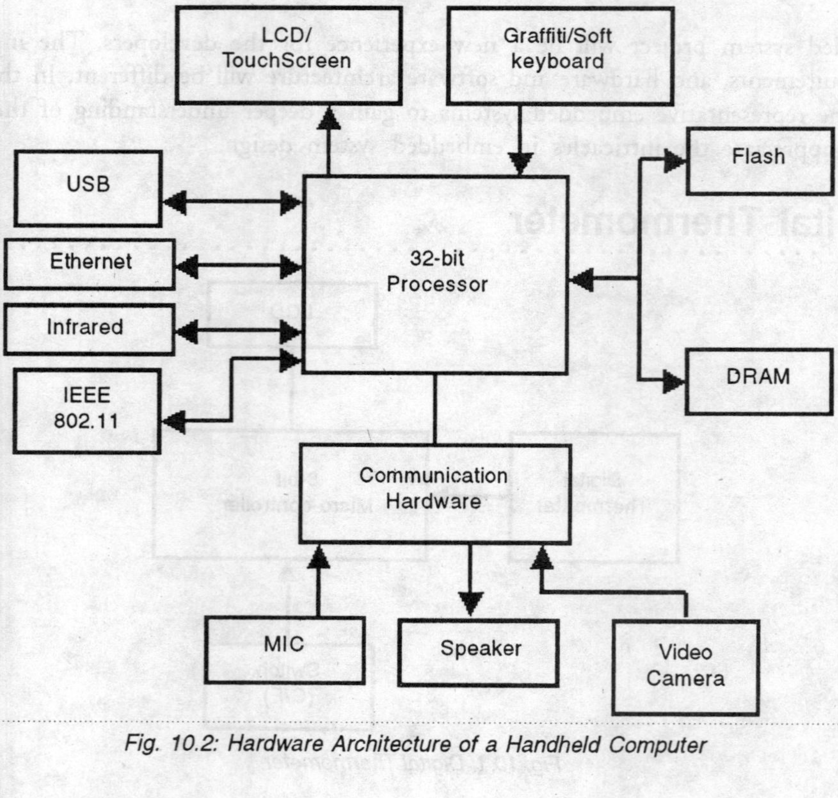

Fig. 10.2: Hardware Architecture of a Handheld Computer

The handheld computer is built around a 32-bit processor such as ARM, Intel StrongARM, Motorola PowerPC etc. As it is a consumer item, the cost has to be kept low. Hence, DRAM (16 MB/32 MB), which is of low cost as compared to SRAM, is used. Flash memory is used for program memory. The memory capacity can be enhanced using memory sticks. Typically, the following communication interfaces are provided: USB, Ethernet, Infrared and IEEE 802.11/Bluetooth. An LCD/Touch Screen display is provided for output. Inputting text is a problem because of the small size of the computer. It is possible to develop a very small keyboard with 108 keys, but human fingers cannot be miniaturized! Inputting of data is done in one of the following ways:

(a) **Graffiti**: You need to learn how to write letters and digits using a stylus to input text. A character recognition software will identify the characters written.

(b) **Soft keyboard**: The keyboard is displayed on the LCD screen and the required key is pressed using a stylus.

If the handheld computer is integrated with a mobile phone, the communication hardware is also integrated with the processor. Necessary audio/video interfaces such as microphone, speakers and video camera are provided. The communication hardware is dependent on the type of wireless network. The hardware is different for GSM networks and CDMA networks.

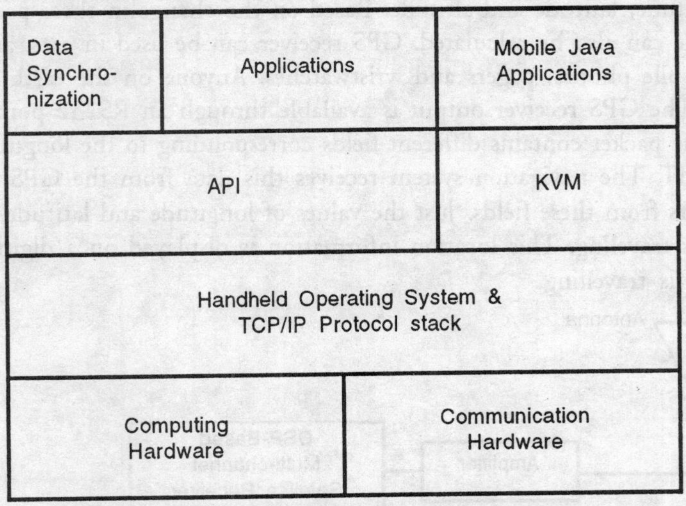

Fig. 10.3: Software Architecture of Handheld Computer

In Brief...

Handheld computer is built around a 32-bit processor. Communication interfaces such as Ethernet, USB, Bluetooth, Infrared, IEEE 802.11 are provided. A handheld operating system along with TCP/IP protocol stack will be ported onto the system.

The software architecture of a handheld computer is shown in Fig. 10.3. An operating system such as Palm OS, Symbian OS, Windows CE, Embedded Linux is ported on the handheld device along with TCP/IP protocol stack. Operating system-specific Application Programming Interface (API) is used to develop applications that run on the handheld computer. Software development kits are available for Palm OS, Symbian OS, Windows CE etc. In addition, a small footprint virtual machine, called Kilobytes Virtual Machine (KVM), can be ported onto the device to make the device Java-enabled. A number of applications can be ported onto it such as:

- Address book
- Calculator
- Memopad
- World clock
- Office automation software packages such as word processor, spreadsheet software and presentation software.
- Data synchronization software such as HotSync for Palm OS, Symbian Connect for Symbian OS and ActiveSync for Windows CE.

10.3 Navigation System

A navigation system is used to find out the location of a moving vehicle or person. The navigation system consists of a GPS receiver and processor-based hardware to show the location on a digitized map.

Global Positioning System (GPS) has been developed by Department of Defence, USA to provide location information to anyone on the earth. The GPS system consists of a set of 24 NAVSTAR satellites that continuously transmit Radio Frequency (RF) signals. These signals are received by a GPS receiver and using the information in the RF signals, the GPS receiver calculates its own location parameters, i.e. longitude, latitude and altitude. Based on the change in these parameters, the velocity of the moving vehicle can also be calculated. GPS receiver can be used in cars, aircraft, ships and can be even fitted to mobile phones, pagers and wristwatches. Anyone on the earth can receive the GPS signals free of cost. The GPS receiver output is available through an RS232 port or USB port in the form of a packet. The packet contains different fields corresponding to the longitude, latitude, altitude and the time in GMT. The navigation system receives this data from the GPS receiver and decodes the various parameters from these fields. Just the values of longitude and latitude are of not much use to the person who is traveling. This location information is displayed on a digitized map of the area in which the person is travelling.

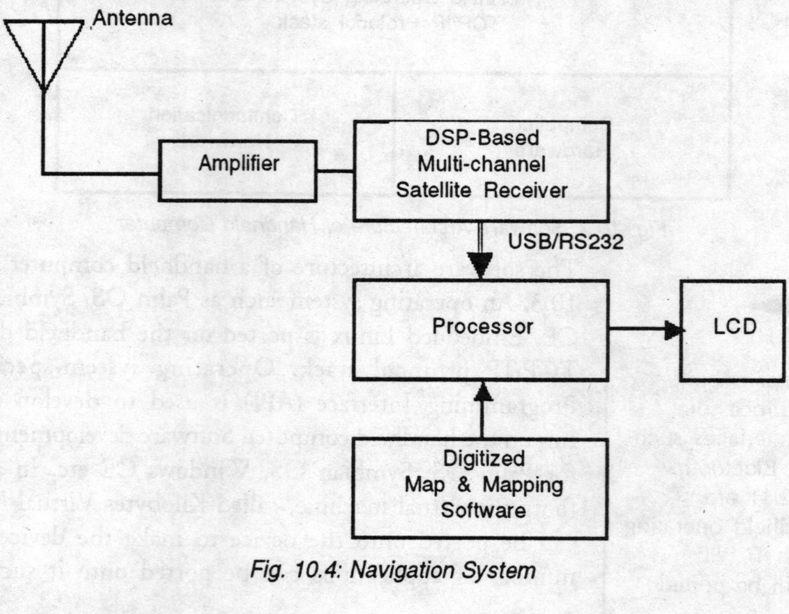

Fig. 10.4: Navigation System

At any time, from any location on the earth, at least five satellites will be visible. The GPS receiver obtains the signals from these five satellites and carries out lot of mathematical operations to calculate the location of the moving vehicle. This is done using a Digital Signal Processor (DSP) in the GPS receiver.

The block diagram of a navigation system is shown in Fig. 10.4. The satellite signals received from the antenna are amplified and then sent to a DSP-based multi-channel satellite receiver. This DSP-based system does the mathematical computations to obtain the location parameters This information is sent in the form of a packet to a processor through RS232/USB interface. The processor decodes the information from the packet and displays the location on a digitized map. The processor also calculates the velocity of the moving vehicle from the changes in longitude/latitude values. The navigation system should have a high-resolution LCD screen (at least 640 x 480 pixels) for displaying the digitized map. The GPS receiver keeps sending a packet every one second and hence the processor has to keep updating the location of the object under observation on the map every one second.

As GPS receivers are now fitted to many consumer devices such as mobile phones, wristwatches, pagers etc., an Application-Specific Integrated Circuit (ASIC) is used which has a DSP-core inside. This is mainly to reduce the cost of the GPS receiver.

Assume that the car in which the navigation system is installed is going with a speed of 120 kilometers per hour. So, in one second, it will travel about 34 meters. The navigation system has to display the information in real-time without any appreciable delay in showing where the vehicle is. Hence, generally a real-time operating system is required. However, note that there is no time-criticality in navigation systems fitted in cars. But, navigation systems fitted in aircraft need to update the position information without delay, otherwise it may result in a catastrophe—the aircraft may hit a mountain and kill all the people on-board. So, a soft real-time operating system is OK for consumer appliances but a hard real-time operating system is required for navigation systems used in aircraft, missiles, etc.

In Brief...

The navigation system consists of a DSP-based GPS receiver and a processor-based system for displaying the location on a digitized map. A real-time operating system is ported to show the position accurately in real-time.

10.4 IP Phone

IP Phone is now being used for Internet telephony i.e. to make voice calls over an IP network such as the LAN, corporate Intranet or the public Internet. You can connect an IP phone to a LAN and make calls to a multimedia PC; or an IP phone can be used to make long distance calls over the Internet. IP Phone is a powerful embedded system that uses a DSP as well as a General Purpose Processor (GPP).

In the normal telephone network, voice signals are coded into digital format using Pulse Code Modulation (PCM). In PCM coding, voice signals are sampled at 8,000 samples per second and each sample is coded using 8 bits. Hence, PCM requires a data rate of 64 Kbps. For Internet telephony, this data rate is very high. So, special coding techniques are used to reduce the data rate to 5.3 Kbps/6.3 Kbps. This is known as low bit rate coding of voice. Low bit rate coding involves lot of digital signal processing.

An IP Phone has to carry out the following functions:

- Take voice input and convert it into digital format using low bit rate coding techniques.
- Convert the low bit rate coded voice into packets and transmit them over the IP network through Ethernet interface.
- Receive the packets from the IP network through Ethernet interface and reconstruct the low bit rate coded voice.
- Convert the low bit rate coded voice back into voice signals.
- The entire processing has to be done in real-time as delay is not acceptable in voice communication.

The IP phone should have an Ethernet interface to get connected to the IP network. It also should have a telephone keypad for entering the digits. A display is provided to display the dialled digits. Also, note that the IP Phone should be assigned an IP address; configuring the IP Phone for assigning the IP address is done through the keypad.

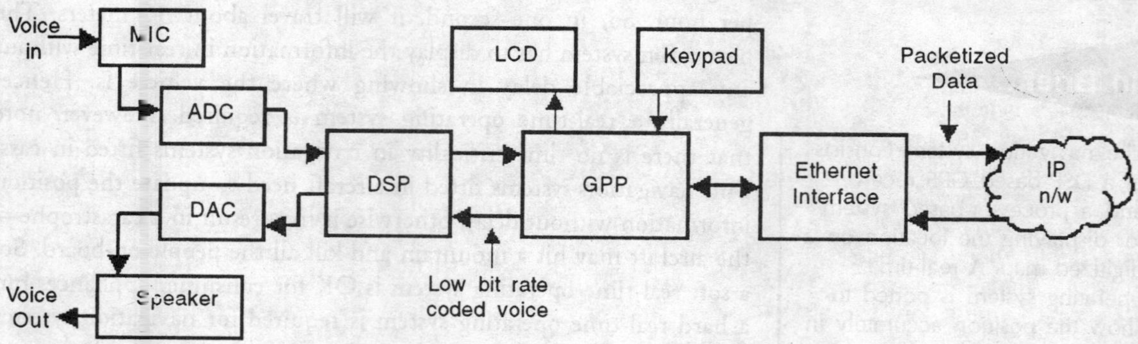

Fig. 10.5: IP Phone Hardware Architecture

To carry out all these functions, the IP Phone has to do lot of signal processing as well as lot of protocol processing. Hence, a DSP and GPP are used. DSP carries out the low bit rate coding and decoding of voice signals. The GPP takes care of converting the voice data into packets and de-packetization in the reverse direction, as well as handling other protocols. The hardware architecture of IP phone is shown in Fig. 10.5. The protocol architecture of the IP Phone is shown in Fig. 10.6.

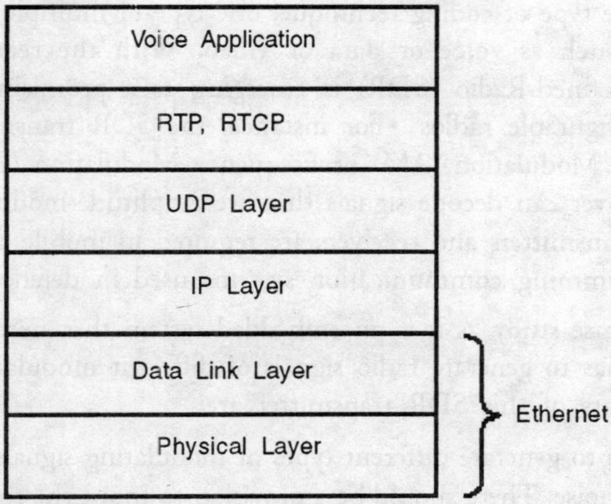

Fig. 10.6: IP Phone Protocol Architecture

In Brief...

IP Phone needs to carry out two distinct functions: (a) voice encoding at low bit rates which involves lot of signal processing, and (b) packetization/de-packetization of the voice data. Hence, the IP Phone will have both Digital Signal Processor and General Purpose Processor.

In Internet telephony, voice has to be transmitted in real-time as delay will be very irritating to the listeners. TCP/IP protocol stack is not suitable for real-time communication because it causes variable delay in receipt of packets. Hence, the protocol architecture shown in Fig. 10.6 is used for voice over IP. Real-time Transport Protocol (RTP) and Real-Time Control Protocol (RTCP) are specially designed to achieve real-time communication. These protocols run above User Datagram Protocol (UDP) because UDP has less protocol overhead as compared to TCP. The software ported onto the GPP handles the RTP, RTCP protocols. 16/32-bit processor is used as the GPP. The GPP will have an Ethernet interface for connecting to an IP network such as the LAN.

As the complexity of the software is high in IP Phone, it is a wise decision to port an operating system as it will reduce the development time considerably. A soft real-time operating system will be sufficient as there is no time criticality in this application. An open source operating system such as Embedded Linux is a good choice for this application.

Notes...

The TCP/IP protocol stack used for data applications is not suitable for real-time transmission of voice over IP networks. Real-time Transport Protocol (RTP) and Real Time Control Protocol (RTCP) are used over UDP for voice over IP communication.

The protocol stack used for voice over IP is also used for video transmission over IP networks. Video is encoded at data rates ranging between 64 Kbps and 384 Kbps for video over IP.

10.5 Software-defined Radio

During the last decade of the 20th century, there have been tremendous improvements in radio technology. Radio-based systems for mobile communications, satellite communications etc. are widely used for data, voice and video communication as well as for broadcasting. However, these radio systems operate for a fixed set of communication parameters i.e., the radio hardware can cater to one type of modulation, one type of coding technique, one type of multiple access technique and one type of modulating signal such as voice or data or video. With the recent advances in digital signal processing, Software-Defined-Radio (SDR) is emerging as a promising technology. SDR facilitates development of "reconfigurable radios". For instance, the SDR transmitter can transmit modulated signals with Amplitude Modulation (AM) or Frequency Modulation (FM) through software control. Similarly, an SDR receiver can decode signals that are amplitude-modulated or frequency-modulated. Such re-configurable transmitters and receivers are required in mobile communication systems as well as jamming and anti-jamming communication systems used in defence.

SDR is an interesting case study as it is an embedded system that needs DSP and GPP. Consider an SDR transmitter that has to generate radio signals of different modulations and different modulating signals. The requirements of this SDR transmitter are:

- It should be able to generate different types of modulating signals viz., single tone, double tone, voice and white noise. There should be a provision to input the tone frequency or the bandwidth of the modulating signal in the case of voice or noise.
- It should be able to generate different types of modulations viz., amplitude modulation and frequency modulation. There should be a provision to input modulation parameters such as modulation index.
- There should be a provision to input the desired radio frequency that has to be generated.

The block diagram of this SDR transmitter is given in Fig. 10.7. The system consists of a GPP and a DSP. The GPP takes the user inputs and sends this data to the DSP. The DSP generates the corresponding modulating signal and the modulated signal and then sends the output to a DAC. The output of the DAC is the desired RF signal. The important issue here is: how does the GPP send the data to the DSP? There are a number of alternatives: using a data bus, using UART or using a Dual Port RAM (DPRAM). Using DPRAM is a simple and efficient mechanism—the GPP writes data into the DPRAM and the DSP reads the data from the DPRAM.

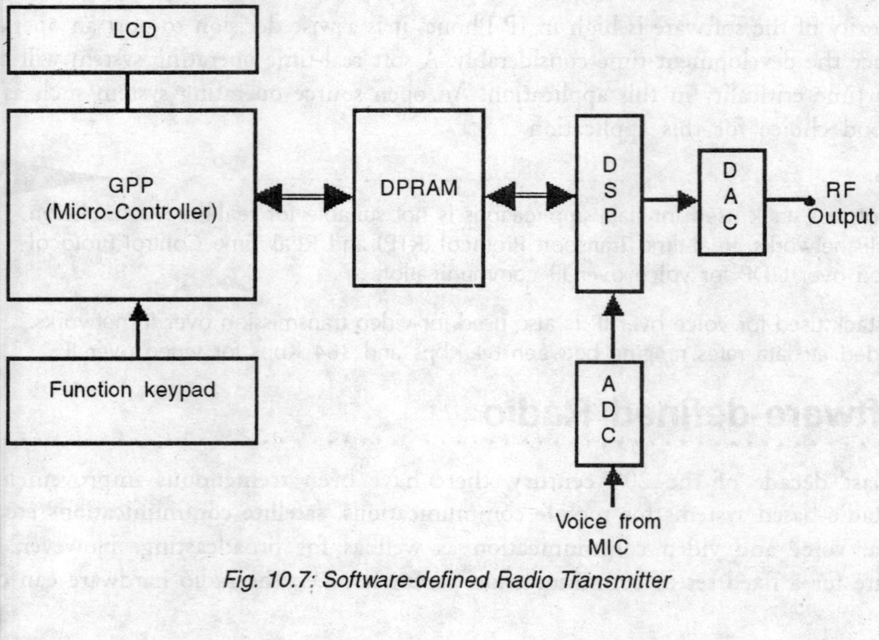

Fig. 10.7: Software-defined Radio Transmitter

The GPP has to do very little processing—just providing the user interface and writing the data into the DPRAM. Hence an 8-bit micro-controller will be sufficient. However, the choice of the DSP has to be done with care. The clock speed and the word length will decide the frequency of the RF signal that can be generated. You need a 32-bit DSP with up to 250 MHz clock speed for generating High Frequency (HF) signals.

Fig. 10.8: Function Keypad for Software-defined Radio

The inputs to be given to the GPP are the various communication parameters such as the type of modulating signal, modulating signal bandwidth in case of voice or noise, tone frequency in case of tones, type of modulation and modulation parameters. The user has to be provided with the various options for selection of these parameters. In addition, there should be a provision for giving numeric values as inputs. Hence, a customized function keypad is required. Such a function keypad is shown in Fig. 10.8.

In Brief...

Software-Defined Radio is a combination of DSP and GPP. SDR is used to develop re-configurable radio systems used in wireless networks.

SDR is used extensively in mobile communication systems. In future, the mobile phones will use SDR to be able to access different mobile networks. In the defence sector, jamming and anti-jamming communication systems also use SDR. In these applications, very strict timing requirements need to be met. The time gap between giving a command to the GPP and the time for the RF signal appearance should be of the order of a few microseconds. To meet the timing requirements, a real-time operating system should be ported.

Notes...

In wireless communication systems, communication parameters such as type of modulation, type of modulating signal, bandwidth of the signal etc. vary. Using SDR, the wireless device can be programmed to transmit/receive communication signals of different parameters.

10.6 Smart Cards

Smart card is of the size of a credit card with silicon chip embedded in it. The smart card is activated through contact with a smart card reader (such as an ATM machine) or through radio link. Smart card reader is also capable of writing into the smart card. Smart cards are now being widely used in mobile phones and prepaid telephone calling cards. Nearly 2 billion smart cards are now being used and in the next 5 years, this number is likely to become 6 billion.

The simplest smart cards used in payment systems only have memory and hence they are called 'memory-only smart cards'. The Subscriber Identity Module (SIM) used in mobile phones is a processor-based card. It has a 10 square mm chip based on 0.35 micron technology. It has a processor, memory, interfaces for sending and receiving data from a smart card reader and security blocks to take care of security of data. An 8-bit micro-controller, 8051 or its equivalent, is used along with 32 KB or 64 KB EEPROM and 1 to 4 KB RAM. The software that runs is a proprietary operating system.

Smart cards for use in financial transactions will be the next major application. However, for secure financial transactions, the cryptographic algorithm implementation cannot be done on 8-bit micro-controllers. Hence, smart cards with 32-bit processors are on the anvil. These smart cards will have 32-bit processor, RAM, ROM and EEPROM. Presently, the operating system that runs on these smart cards is proprietary to the financial organizations. Multos is an operating system that passed all the standards specified for an operating system for banking applications. A standard called EMV (Euro pay, MasterCard, Visa) has been formulated for smart card software. Conforming to this standard will ensure interoperability of smart cards and smart card readers. By 2005, all credit card organizations in Europe will switch over to smart cards. By 2008, smart card technology is likely to be mandatory in North America.

Governments are planning to introduce smart cards for their citizens. The smart card will have the complete citizen information such as fingerprints, retinal prints, passport information, driving licence information etc. A 32-bit processor and at least 1 MB of memory are required for such cards. The card can serve multiple purposes—as identity card, to store the medical history of the person, etc. To reduce silicon size, encryption is done through software and not hardware. It also allows flexibility in changing the security algorithms.

In Brief...

Smart card is built around an 8-bit micro-controller with an EEPROM and RAM. The smart card reader/writer is used to read and write data into the smart card.

To ensure interoperability between smart cards of different manufacturers and the smart card readers of different manufacturers, standardization has been done by ISO. The physical structure and the protocols for communication between the smart card and the smart card reader are specified in ISO 7810, 7816/1 and 7816/2. Smart card consists of three elements:

- Plastic card of size: 85.60 mm x 53.98 mm x 0.80 mm.
- Printed circuit and IC embedded on the card with 5 connections for power and data.
- The IC containing processor, ROM, RAM and EEPROM.

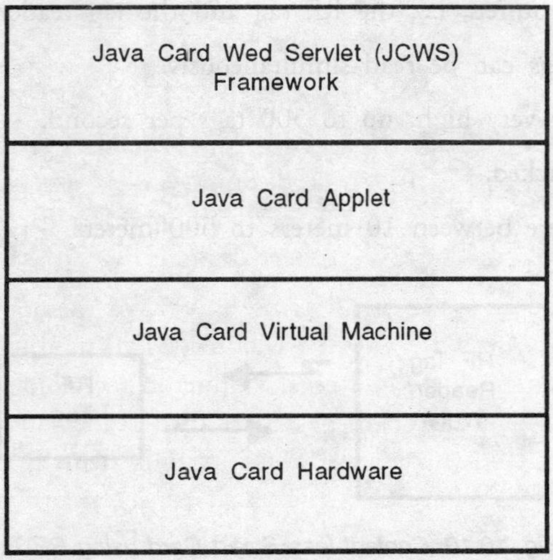

Fig. 10.9: Java-enabled Smart Card

In Brief...

Java Card Web Servlet framework facilitates access to web services by the smart card. Using a small footprint Java Card Virtual Machine, platform independence can be achieved for smart card software.

A wide range of processors are likely to be used in smart cards. Therefore, to achieve platform independence, Sun Microsystems developed the Java Card Web Servlet (JCWS) framework. As shown in Fig. 10.9, a smart card can be Java-enabled. A small footprint Java Virtual Machine—Java Card Virtual Machine—runs above the hardware. HTML pages and Java applets can be interpreted by the smart card. JCWS permits access to the web services. As a result, the smart card will be a powerful computing and communicating device. If each smart card is given an IP address, and TCP/IP protocol stack is ported onto it, it becomes an Internet access device. If the HTTP web server software is also ported, then the smart card can become an Internet information appliance—the data on the smart card can be accessed by any one on the earth. If a patient's medical record is stored in a smart card, a doctor in another country can gain access to the patient's information. It becomes possible when the patient's smartcard is plugged into a smart card reader which is connected to the internet.

10.7 RF Tags

Presently, bar codes are used for a number of applications such as tracking of goods, point of sale terminals, luggage handling at airports, etc. However, this technology has a few drawbacks: the bar code can be spoiled by dirt, the bar code has to come in close contact with the bar code reader and the card reader speed is very low.

Bar code technology can be replaced by Radio Frequency (RF) tag technology. The item to be tracked will have an RF tag attached to it. When this item comes closer to an RF tag reader, data can be exchanged between the tag and the reader. The main advantages of the RF tag are:

- The tag and the tag reader need not come in close contact with each other.

- Line-of-sight is not required, i.e. the RF tag and the tag reader need not be face to face.
- A large number of tags can be read simultaneously.
- Reading speed will be very high, up to 500 tags per second.
- Lost items can be tracked.
- Range can be anywhere between 10 meters to 500 meters.

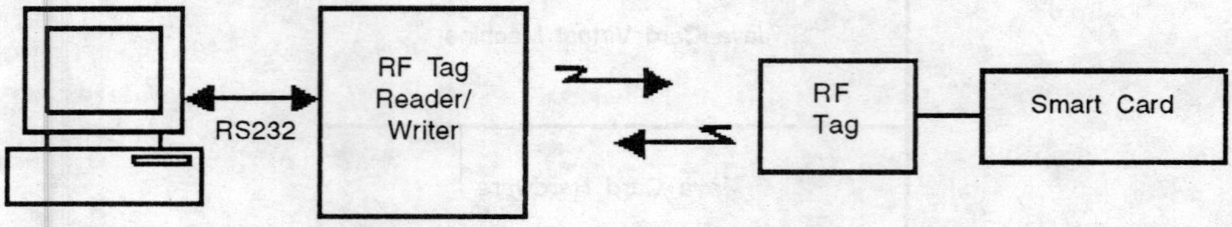

Fig. 10.10: Contact-less Smart Card using RF Tag

RF tag is a relatively new technology. Its use is primarily in shopping malls to check shoplifting. RF tag can be attached to a smart card to make it a powerful gadget for financial transactions. As shown in Fig. 10.10, contact-less smart card is a smart card attached with an RF tag. The tag reader/writer is a micro-controller based embedded system with Flash memory, LEDs for status display, communication ports and antennas. The information collected by the RF tag reader can be logged onto a PC using RS232/RS422 interface. Alternatively, the RF tag writer can write the information obtained from the PC to the RF tag.

RF ID tag consists of a microchip attached to a micro-antenna. The radio frequencies used in this technology are:

- 13.56 MHz for distances up to one meter
- 868 MHz in Europe and 915 MHz in USA for distances up to several meters

RF tags are classified as passive tags and active tags. Passive tags do not have any battery. Power for passive RF tag communication comes from the incident radiation of the RF tag reader/writer. Active RF tags will have a battery. For passive tags, the range is generally limited to 10 meters. Memory size of an RF tag depends on the application—it can be anywhere from 256 bits to a few Megabits.

Atmel's AT88RF001 contact-less chip is a 64 Mbit tag that can be used in conjunction with EEPROM's such as AT24Cxx12C and AT25xx. It is powered by the RF radiation. It uses a radio frequency of 13.56 MHz. The transmit/receive data rate is 106 Kbps and range is 10 meters.

The RF tag technology has applications in many areas. Here are some representative applications:

- In airports, the RF tag technology can be effectively used for baggage handling. An RF tag is attached on each item which will have the information of the owner of the baggage along with details such as the destination, flight number, etc. The RF tag reader located at the conveyer belt will read the information when the item passes by. The information can be logged onto a PC for records and analysis.
- RF tags can be attached to smart cards so that smart cards need not come into contact with a smart card reader such as the ATM, but wirelessly they can communicate with each other.

- Smart cards attached to RF tags can be used for access control. At high-security buildings, the information stored in the smart card is transferred to the smart card reader through the RF tag. Authentication is done by the smart card reader, for example, by comparing the fingerprint information received from the smart card with the database stored in the PC.
- RF tags can be used in point-of-sale terminals.
- RF tags can be used in transportation industry for vehicle movement tracking, toll collection, etc.
- Supply chain management will be a big market for RF tags. Any item whose movement needs to be tracked can be attached with an RF tag.

To achieve interoperability between RF tags and readers manufactured by different vendors, a number of ISO standards have been formulated. These standards for different market segments are as follows:

- Security/access control: ISO 15693, ISO TC204
- Transportation: ISO 14443
- Asset tracking: ISO 18000

It is expected that RF tag technology will be a US $ 3.6 billion industry by 2006.

In Brief...

RF tags are tiny embedded systems which have a small memory chip. The data in the chip is transferred to an RF tag reader when the tag comes near the reader. Passive tags do not have a battery but active tags have a battery.

Notes...

Smart cards can be integrated with RF tags so that the smart card reader can interact with the smart card using radio as the transmission medium. The reader will also have the capability to write into the smart card's memory.

Summary

In this chapter, we studied the architecture of the following embedded systems: digital thermometer, handheld computer, navigation system, IP Phone and Software-defined Radio. The architecture and applications of tiny embedded systems viz., smart card and RF tag are also discussed. The embedded system designers need to appreciate that each embedded system design poses new challenges and new issues to be resolved—inputs are different, outputs are different, processing requirements are different and hence the software and hardware architecture are different. If the application demands, the embedded system may need to have both a Digital Signal Processor and a General Purpose Processor as in the case of a navigation system, IP Phone and Software-defined Radio. Smart cards are tiny embedded systems that can store data which can be read by the smart card reader. Presently, the smart cards have an 8-bit controller; but future applications for financial transactions require 32-bit processors. Smart cards are used as Subscriber Identity Module (SIM) in mobile phones. In the next few years, all credit card organizations will switch over to smart cards from the present magnetic cards. If the smart card is attached with an RF tag, the smart card and the smart card reader can communicate using the radio medium. RF tag technology has a potential to replace the bar code technology used in asset tracking and supply chain management.

Questions

1. Explain the hardware and software architecture of a handheld computer.
2. Explain the building blocks of a navigation system.
3. Explain the architecture of an IP Phone. Why TCP/IP protocol stack cannot be used for real-time voice communication?
4. What is Software-defined Radio? Explain how a re-configurable radio can be developed using a Digital Signal Processor and a General Purpose Processor.
5. What is a smart card? List the various applications of smart cards.
6. What is RF tag? What is the difference between passive RF tag and active RF tag?

Exercises

1. You need to develop a smart-card based system for your college for making all payments such as college fee, hostel fee, library fine, etc. Work out a complete architecture for this system and list the various embedded systems you need to develop for this system.
2. You need to develop a system for your college library that will track all the library books through RF tags. Each book will have an RF tag attached to it. For issue and return of the books, the RF tag will interact with a reader which will record the information about the book. Work out the complete requirements of the embedded systems you need to develop for such an RF tag based system.
3. You need to develop a Calling Line Identification Device (CLID). When the CLID is attached to your telephone, it will display the calling number. Work out the detailed requirements of this embedded system. What processor will you choose? What are the interface requirements?
4. You need to develop a signal generator that generates sine waves of given frequency and white noise of given bandwidth. Work out the architecture of this system giving the details of the processor and the peripherals to be used.
5. Study the details of BREW (Binary Runtime Environment for Wireless) of Qualcomm to develop mobile data applications.
6. Study the details of HP Chai to develop Internet information appliances.

Chapter 11

Programming in Linux

CHAPTER OBJECTIVES

After reading this chapter, you will be able to:

- Master the Linux commands
- Gain knowledge of shell programming
- Understand how processes are managed in Linux
- Understand the system level programming in Linux environment
- Learn the intricacies of inter-process communication through semaphores, shared memory and message queues.

The Unix operating system has been the darling of system-level programmers for the past three decades. However, in recent years, Linux, a Unix-like open source software, has become very popular for both application software and embedded software. The scaled-down version of the Linux kernel can be used as an embedded operating system. In this chapter, we will take a quick voyage into the deep ocean of Linux programming. We will study Linux architecture, various user commands and shell programming. We will also study how Linux manages the processes and the various system calls used for process management. We will discuss the system calls used for inter-process communication. The practical implementation of the operating system concepts discussed in Chapter 7 will be demonstrated in this chapter.

11.1 Overview of Unix/Linux

Unix is not just an operating system, it is a "great programming environment" as described by its authors. Unix was developed by Ken Thomson and Dennis Ritchie beginning 1969. It became the most popular operating system in the academic community during 1970's. It was commercialized in 1981 and since then, its use in both academic and commercial world has grown tremendously. The main attractions of UNIX are:

- Most of the operating system was developed in a high level language i.e. C. This was revolutionary during those days because before the advent of Unix, operating systems were developed in assembly languages.
- As very little code of Unix is written in processor-specific assembly language, porting the operating system is very easy. As a result, Unix can be ported to hardware built around different processors.
- The main attraction of Unix is that it provides a large number of utilities for software development—editors, compilers, debuggers, source code control system, utilities for string processing (awk), utilities for developing new compilers (lex and yacc), and a very powerful user interface, the shell.

But then, a good number of programmers are scared of Unix, due to some popular myths.

In Brief...

Unix operating system is the first operating system to be developed in a high-level language, C. Hence, it is a portable operating system. Only a small portion of the operating system will have processor-dependent code.

"It is a complicated operating system": Any operating system which has many features and utilities will appear complicated. If you want to learn Unix completely and only then want to start working on projects, you may need to spend your whole lifetime learning, without contributing to your organization. So, learn the basics and then focus on problem solving.

"Too many options for each command": Yes, a simple command to list the contents of a directory has nearly 20 options. Do not try to remember every option, it is just a waste of the precious memory of your brain. Look up the manual to see when you require a special option.

"Too many commands and utilities": It is important to know the features supported by Unix, and then learn only those utilities that are required for your project. For example, "awk" programming language is an excellent tool for string processing and non-time- critical database development. If your project does not require such facilities, please ignore awk!

A number of Unix flavors are available such as AT & T Unix, HP UX, Sun Solaris, IBM AIX, DEC Ultrix and Linux. Linux, developed by Linus Trovalds at the University of Helsinki, is a freely distributed implementation of UNIX-like kernel. Even the source code for Linux kernel is freely available. The Linux community supports the concept of free software, promoted by Free Software Foundation. Programming in Linux environment is essentially same as programming in Unix environment. The GNU Compiler Collection provides a number of compilers for various languages. However, as the source code is available free of cost to every one, many variations of Linux are available. In this chapter, we will talk about Linux commands, but remember that all these commands are just as well available on most of the Unix systems.

11.1.1 Features of Linux

The important features of Linux are listed below:

- It is a multi-user operating system. Every user is given a username or login name. The system administrator logs in as 'root'. A number of users can form a 'group' and each of these groups is given a name.

- The file system is organized hierarchically. At the topmost level is the root directory denoted by / under which there will be sub-directories. Under each subdirectory there can be directories or files. Some important directories are
  - /bin contains commonly used commands
  - /usr/bin contains less commonly used commands
  - /etc contains the system administration commands
  - /dev contains device files
  - /usr/spool/mail contains mail files
  - /usr contains users' directories
- A variety of user interfaces are available. The command user interfaces are shell (sh,) kshell (ksh) and C shell (csh). Menu-driven interface is through curses. X-Windows provides the Graphical User Interface.
- All devices are treated as files. In /dev directory, there will be one entry for each file. Writing to a printer or a serial port is no different from writing to a file in the hard disk.
- To provide security for user's files, a user will have a password. Only the encrypted password is stored in the system. The file /etc/passwd contains the list of all authorized users. It also contains the encrypted passwords, default working directory of the users and their default shell.
- Every file is given protections—read, write and execute permissions are given to the owner, group and others. The owner of a file can give permission to the group members and others to read, write or execute the files.

In Brief...

The important features of Unix are: (a) it is a multi-user, multi-tasking operating system; (b) it has a rich set of utilities and productivity tools; (c) all devices are treated as files; (d) it has a very powerful user interface.

Many fresh graduates indicate in their CV that they are proficient in Unix/Linux. Be careful, Unix/Linux being such a huge operating system, writing Unix/Linux is inviting trouble, unless you know the basics very well. In this section, the most commonly used commands are briefly explained. If you do not remember these commands, it is doing injustice to Unix and, of course, to yourself. More than that, it is putting yourself in an embarrassing situation in front of job interview panel members.

11.1.2 Linux Command Summary

When you login to the Unix system using the username and password given by your system administrator, the "$" sign will be displayed. This is the system prompt. The system prompt is an indication that the system is ready to take commands from you. Now you can try out the following commands. After typing the command as given in the example column, you have to press enter key. If you make typing mistakes or give wrong arguments, Linux gives very cryptic error messages. If the command is correct, the system will execute the command and display the "$" prompt again. A command will be in the format

$commandname options arguments

A sample command is as follows:

$nl –d hello.c

In this command, nl is the commandname, -d is the option and hello.c is the argument.

Some general commands are listed in Table 11.1

Command	Function	Example
banner	To display a banner	banner prasad
cal	To display calendar for a month or year	cal 2004 cal 1 2004
date	To display today's date	date
sleep	To make the shell sleep for a few seconds	sleep 10
who am i	To know about your login details (sometimes you forget who you are!)	who am i
who	To display the list of users who are presently logged in	who
clear	To clear the screen	clear
passwd	To change the password	passwd
echo	To echo a string	echo "How are You"

Table 11.1: General Shell Commands

11.1.3 File Manipulation Commands

A number of shell commands are available to display the files in a directory; to see the contents of a file in different formats; to copy, delete and rename files; to count the number of lines, words and characters in a file, etc. The most commonly used file manipulation commands are listed in this section.

You can create a small text file in your directory, using the command:

$cat > hello

After giving this command, type a few lines of text, and then in a new line press ^d (Control and d together). Note that ^d is called the End Of File (EOF) character.

Now you will see the $ prompt again. You have created a text file with the name hello.

Using the same command but using different words in place of hello, create a few more text files. Now you can experiment with the commands listed in Table 11.2.

Command	Function	Example
ls	To see the files in the directory	ls
ls –l	Displays details of the files such as permissions, size, date of last update	ls –l
ls –a	To list hidden files (files with the name starting with or hidden files)	ls –a
cat	To display contents of one or more files	cat hello cat hello.c hello2.c
cp	Copy file1 to file1	cp file1 file2
rm	To delete a file	rm hello
rm -i	To delete a file, ask for confirmation before deletion	rm –i *
mv	To rename a file	mv hello mytextfile
head	To display top 10 lines of the file	head hello
tail	To display bottom 10 lines of the file	tail hello
spell	To check the spelling of words in a file	spell hello
wc	To display number of lines, words and characters in a file	wc hello
wc –w	To display number of words in a file	wc –w hello
wc –l	To display number of lines in a file	wc –l hello
wc –c	To display number of characters in a file	wc –c hello
nl	To display a file with line numbers	nl hello

Table 11.2: File Manipulation Commands

11.1.4 Editors

To create text files or C/C++/Java programs, you need a text editor. The two most commonly used editors are "ed" and "vi". "ed" is a line editor you can edit one line at a time. "vi" is a screen editor—you can freely move around the screen and edit the text wherever you want. vi will appear a bit complicated to start with, but soon you will start liking it for its rich editing features. You need to spend a few hours on "vi" editor with the online manual pages to get a good hang of the screen editor.

11.1.5 Directory Commands

When you login to the Linux system, by default, you will be given a directory. This is your home directory, denoted by HOME. All your files will be stored in this directory. Within your directory, you can create sub-directories—for example, one sub-directory to store C files, one directory to store Java files, etc. You can also move around to other directories—in fact, you can freely move to the root directory. Every directory will have a parent directory to which it is a child. For example, assume that your default directory is /usr/john. /usr is your parent directory. You can move to the parent directory by giving the following command:

$cd ..

Note that cd stands for change directory. This is followed by two dots to move to the parent directory. Alternatively, you can also give the command

$cd /usr

In this command, you are specifying the absolute path, whereas in the earlier command, you are specifying the relative path.

Now let us try out the various commands that are related to directories, listed in Table 11.3.

Command	Function	Example
pwd	To know the present working directory	pwd
cd	To change the directory, you can specify either the relative path or absolute path.	cd /etc cd .. cd ./cprograms
mkdir	To create a new directory	mkdir hello mkdir /usr/prasad/hello
rmdir	To delete a directory (only when it is empty)	rmdir hello
find	To search for a file	find / -name hello –print
du	To know the directory size in number of blocks	du prasad
df	To know the disk space occupied by the total file system	df

Table 11.3: Directory Commands

11.1.6 Input/Output Redirection

Normally, the input is given through the keyboard which is called the standard input, abbreviated stdin. The output is displayed on the monitor which is called the standard output, abbreviated stdout. The error messages are also displayed on the monitor which is called the standard error device, abbreviated stderr. In Linux, all devices are considered as files, hence we have three standard files—stdin, stdout and stderr.

Instead of taking the input from the keyboard, you can take the input from a file. Similarly, the output can be redirected to a file instead of monitor. Hence, you can redirect the output to a file instead of stdout; or you can take the input from a file instead of stdin. Give the following commands one after the other:

$ls –l > filelist

$cat filelist

The first command is to display the contents of the directory. Instead of displaying the contents on the monitor, the output of the command is sent to a file named filelist. Using the second command, you can see the contents of the file, i.e. the result of the command "ls –l". This is output redirection.

The output is redirected using the symbol ">".

You can append a file to another file using output redirection through the following command:

$cat file2 >> file1

Suppose you have two files with the filenames file1 and file2 in your directory. Now, guess what happens when you give the following command:

$cat file2 > file1

You have overwritten file1!

Instead of taking the input from the stdin, input can be taken from a file as in the following command:

$wc < filename

This is called input indirection and the symbol used is "<".

You can combine both input indirection and output redirection in one command as in the following command:

$wc < file1 > file2

This command will read the contents of file1, do a word/line/character count and the counts are put in file2.

In Brief...

The standard input, standard output and standard error files will have file descriptors 0, 1 and 2, respectively. They are abbreviated stdin, stdout and stderr.

11.1.7 Pipes and Filters

You can pass the output of one command to another command using pipes. When you give the shell command:

$cat hello.c

the file hello.c will be displayed in one shot. If it is a large file, you will see only the last few lines. If you want to see few lines at a time, you can give the command:

$cat hello.c | more

Here, the vertical line | is used for the piping operation. The output of the cat command is passed to the more command which displays a few lines at a time. You can press the space bar or the return key to see the next set of lines.

Alternatively, you can give the command:

$more filename

"more" is a filter that processes the input data to display a few lines at a time. In the first command, you are piping the output of cat filename to "more" filter. In the second command, you are invoking the filter directly.

The important filters that can be used directly as commands or that can be used through the pipe operation are:

sort Sorting utility. To sort a file in an order, such as alphabetical order, numerical order etc.

grep Pattern matching utility. To match patterns in strings such as to check whether a pattern exists in a file or not.

tr Translation utility. To translate upper case to lower case, remove punctuation marks, etc.

prep File splitting utility. To split the file so that each word is placed in a separate line.

We will illustrate the use of these filters through examples. The following command sorts the contents of a directory:

$ls | sort

The following command sorts the contents of a directory in reverse alphabetical order:

$ls | sort –r

The following command sorts the numbers in a file:

$sort –n filename

The following command displays all the lines in a file which contain the string "how".

$grep "how" filename

Alternatively, you can give the following command to get the same result:

$ cat filename | grep "how"

The following command takes the input file city1, converts all upper case letters to lower case and produces a file city2.

$ tr "[:upper:]" "[:lower:]" < city1 > city2

[:upper:] and [:lower:] are translation arguments. You can use a number of translation arguments such as alnum, alpha, blank, digit, lower, upper, punct, space and xdigit to represent alphanumeric, alphabetic, blank, digit, lower case, upper case, punctuation marks, space and hexadecimal characters.

In Brief...

A pipe is used when the output of a command has to be given as input to another command.

Now, guess what the following command will do:

$tr –s "[ ]" "[\012]" < temp > temp0

It will read the file temp, replace each space (blank character) by a new line, and the output will be kept in the file temp0. So, if the file "temp" contains a sentence, the file "temp0" will contain one word of that sentence in each line. Now you can write a C program to do the same thing, and you will take half an hour to do that! It is time to appreciate the power of Unix/Linux utilities.

Now you can combine the basic shell commands, filters, pipes and input/output redirection as in the following commands:

$who > log

$who | wc –l

$who | sort

$who | grep prasad

$</etc/passwd | wc –l

The following command illustrates how you can give more than one shell command in the same line:

$date; who | wc –l > log

The following command is a powerful command that uses many of the features of the shell. The tr utility takes file1 as input, and produces one word per line. The output is passed through the grep which matches with only words with four letters (see the pattern which contains ^, three dots and $). The output of grep is sorted. The sorted output will contain multiple entries for the same word, and such repeated words are removed by uniq. Here is this powerful command:

$tr –s "[ ]" "[\012]" < file | grep "^...$" | sort | uniq –c > fours

Now try the following commands:

$tr "[:upper:]" "[:lower:]" < text > temp1

(to translate all upper case letters to lower case)

$tr –s "[ ]" "[\012]" < temp1 > temp2

(to create a file with one word per line)

$sort temp2 > temp3

(to sort in alphabetical order)

$uniq –c temp3 > output

(to find frequency count of words)

The first command translates all upper case letters to lower case letters. The second command creates a file with one word per line. The third command sorts the file in alphabetical order and the fourth command finds the frequency count of words. Each command creates a temporary file which is given as the input to the next command. This set of commands can now take a file "text" and produce the frequency count of words. If you observe the output, you will realize a bug. For example, the word "so" is taken as a word, and "so," is taken as a different word. Here the bug is that we did not remove the punctuation mark. Here is the command to remove punctuation marks from a file:

$tr –d "[:punct:]" < text > temp0

11.1.8 File Protections

Each file will be owned by a user. The owner of the file can assign read, write and execute permissions to a file. To avoid accidental deletion of a file, you can assign read-only permission to your file. You can also assign these permissions to your group members or others. When you give the command:

$ls –l

the first field in the output of each line displays the file permissions in the format:

drwxrwxrwx

If the first field is in the format:

drw-r— r —

This indicates that the file is a directory, owner has read and write permissions, group members have only read permission and others also have only read permission. The read, write and execute bits are set to 1 or 0 depending on whether the permission is granted or not. For example, let us say, you want to assign read and write permissions to yourself, only read permission to group members and others. The command to set the permissions is as follows:

$chmod 644 filename

If you want to give read, write and execute permissions to everyone, the command is

$chmod 777 filename

Alternatively, you can use the command with –r, -w, -x or +r, +w, +x options, – to indicate denial of permission and + to give permission, as below:

$chmod –w filename

$chmod +w filename

To change ownership of a file, the command is

$chown username filename

In Brief...

A file will have read, write and execute permissions. These permissions can be given to the owner, group members and others.

To change group ownership of file, the command is

$chgrp groupname filename

11.1.9 Process Commands

When you login, a process is created which is the shell. When you give a shell command, the shell creates another process. The shell process is the parent and the command process is the child process. Each process is given a process ID denoted by PID. Each PID will have PPID which is the parent process ID. You can see the various processes running on your Linux system by giving the command:
$ps –ef

When you observe the output, you will see the PID, PPID, the time of creating the process and the command given.

Background processing

When you give a command, it will be executed and then the shell prompt will reappear. This is called foreground processing. If you want the command prompt to appear immediately before the command execution is complete, you can give a command as below. This command prints a file in the background. Note that /dev/lp0 is the device file for the printer.

$cat filename > /dev/lp0 &

In Brief...

When a process is run in the background, the shell prompt returns immediately without waiting for the child process to complete.

Using this command, the printing will be done in the 'background' and the prompt will appear so that you can give another command. This is useful for executing time-consuming programs such as executing a C program.

A running process can be terminated by using the kill command. The kill command sends a signal to the process for termination. You can terminate a process running in the background using the kill command.

$kill –9 <pid>

You need to replace the <pid> with the process ID obtained using the ps –ef command. Note that only the system administrator (the super user) can kill any process. You are not authorized to kill others' processes, but only your processes.

You can find out the time taken for a process to execute by giving the command:

$time <command>

$time ls –l

Three times will be displayed—total time, user time and CPU time.

Process Priorities

The process scheduler of Linux assigns CPU time using time slices. Each process will have a priority. A higher priority process gets CPU time more frequently. The following command can be issued by the super user to assign a high priority to his process:

$nice - - 10 ./a.out > filnename

where 10 is priority to the process.

11.1.10 About the Shell

Shell provides a very powerful interface to the user of the operating system. But note that the shell is not a part of the operating system. It is just a C program to provide the interface between the user and the operating system. It interprets each command, and then takes appropriate action. When a command is given by you, shell will search for the command in /bin, and then /usr/bin and then your current working directory. The procedure for command line interpretation is as follows:

- Shell waits for user to enter a command
- When the user enters a command and presses the enter key, shell reads the command, analyzes and checks for syntax. If there are syntax errors, an error message is displayed. Otherwise, the command is broken into words.
- Any special processing to be done is identified: such as input/output redirection, command and variable substitution, filename expansion, etc.
- First word is taken as the command and rest of the words as arguments.
- Shell creates a child process. This operation is known as fork. The child process executes the command and the parent process, the shell, waits for the child to complete.
- The child executes the command using the exec command.
- The parent process issues a new prompt for the next command.
- If the command is placed in background, the parent does not wait for the child to complete. It displays the system prompt immediately, ready to take a command from you.

11.2 Shell Programming

The shell commands given at the $ prompt can be grouped together and executed in batch mode. This is known as shell scripting. The shell allows C-like structures such as if-then-else, while-do-done etc. Shell script or a shell procedure is a group of commands stored in a file. Create a text file "myscript" with the following commands, one per line:

date

who

echo "number of users logged in"

who | wc –l

You can execute the shell script, by giving the command:

$sh myscript

You can check the file permissions of this file using the command:

$ls –l myscript

You can make it an executable file using the command:

$chmod +x myscript

Now, an alternative way of executing the shell script is through the command:

$./myscript

You can use the following shell commands in shell script:

basename: basename gives the leaf name of a directory. The basename of /usr/prasad/progs is progs.

sleep 10: to make the shell sleep for 10 seconds.

true: a command that always returns true. This is useful for implementing infinite loops as in

```
while true
do
echo "infinite loop"
done
```

read: to read input. e.g. read name city

You can substitute the output of a command into a variable as illustrated below. The output of the command "date" is assigned to the variable today. The variable can be echoed by the command echo $today.

Note the $ sign before the variable reference.

today= 'date'

echo $today

In Brief...

Shell programs or shell scripts are used to execute a number of processes in batch mode. Shell scripts can be used for fast prototyping.

The "test" command can be used in shell scripts to check file permissions, to compare strings etc.

test –r file	(true if file exists and has read permission)
test –w file	(true if file exists and has write permission)
test –x file	(true if file exists and executable)
test –d file	(true if file is a directory)

11.2.1 Shell Variables

The following are the important shell variables:

PS1	primary prompt
PS2	secondary prompt
PATH	search path
HOME	login directory
$1, $2,...	command arguments
$#	number of arguments passed to the shell
$*	list of all command arguments
$!	process number of the last process run in the background
$$	process number of current process (to uniquely name a temporary file)

The default system prompt is the $ sign. If you want to change it, you can use the shell variable PS1.

$PS1="Hello"

Now the system prompt is changed to Hello.

You can create a temporary file using the shell variable $$ as shown in the shell script below:

```
temp = /usr/tmp/$$
cat xyz > temp
rm –f temp
```

We will illustrate the use of these shell variables in the following sections.

11.2.2 Shell Programming Constructs

You can create shell scripts or shell programs using the following control structures. The control structures are similar to C control structures, but note the specialties carefully:

```
if  command_list
   then  command_list
fi

case  string  in
  pattern)  command_list;;

   pattern)  command_list;;
easc

while  command_list
do
```

```
    command_list
done

for variable in wordlist
    do
        command_list
    done

break

continue
```

A few shel scripts given below illustrate the use of special shell commands, shell variables and control structures.

The following shell script displays the contents of directories /bin and /usr/bin:

```
for name in /bin /usr/bin
    do
    ls $name
    done
```

The following shell script prints whether each file in a directory is readable or writable:

```
for word in `ls`
do
if test -r $word
then echo "$word is readable"
fi
if test -w $word
then echo "$word is writable"
fi
done
```

Create a shell script "argnum" which just contains one line

```
echo "Number of arguments is $#"
```

When you execute the shell script "argnum" by giving the command:

```
$./argnum one two three four
```

The output will be: "Number of arguments is 4"

You can create temporary files in a shell script using the $$ shell variable as shown in the following shell script:

```
echo "The current process id is $$"
cat abc.c > abc.$$
```

Suppose you have a file "data" which contains the names of a few persons. You can create a shell script which asks for a name and removes that entry from the data file. Create a shell script "askname" as given below:

```
# asks for name to remove and removes
echo "enter name to remove \c"
read name
grep -v "$name" data > data.$$
mv data.$$ data
```

The first line is a comment. The second line gives a prompt to the user, the third line reads the name. The fourth line is to create a temporary file that will have lines excluding the line with the given name. Then the temporary file is moved to the original data file.

Here is a shell script "args" that prints the number of arguments:

```
echo "the arguments to command $0 are $*"
```

Here is a shell script "echo2" that echoes each argument twice:

```
#shell script to echo argument twice
for word
   do echo $word $word
done
```

You can execute the shell script by giving the command:

```
$echo2 sa ri ga ma
```

Output is:
```
sa sa
ri ri
ga ga
ma ma
```

11.3 System Programming

In this section, we will study how to access the various function calls provided by Linux API to do system-level programming. We will illustrate how to create new processes, multithreading, semaphore and mutex usage, shared memory and message queue usage for inter-task communication.

11.3.1 Processes

In Brief...

Every process is given a process ID. When a shell command is given, the shell creates a child process. The shell is the parent. The process IDs of the parent and child can be obtained using the ps –ef command.

In Linux, each instance of a running program is called a process. Each process will have a unique ID called PID. The value of PID will be between 2 and 32768. The process with PID of 1 is the "init" process which manages all other processes. Each process has a stack space of its own in which local variables of the functions and the return values are stored. The following shell command displays the running processes:

$ps –ef

A table will be displayed. This is the process table which gives the details of the PID, the parent process ID, the time the process started, the actual command etc.

As Linux is a multitasking operating system, many processes share the CPU time. Each process is given a priority, higher priority task gets more number of turns. If you give the following shell command, the nice values are displayed which show the priority of the processes:

$ps –l

When you give a shell command, a new process is created. You can create a new shell process through a C program as shown in Listing 11.1.

Listing 11.1: cproc.c

```
#include <stdlib.h>
#include <stdio.h>
int main(){
   system("ls -l"); // running a shell command with system function
   printf("Execution completed\n");
   exit(0);
}
```

Note that when you run the program, a process is created. This in turn creates a new process to run the command "ls –l"

When shell has to create a new process, it calls a function fork(). This function call returns a new PID and the original process continues. When the fork() call returns 0 on success, a new process is created. The new process runs independent of the earlier process or the parent process. The following program illustrates the use of fork() function call.

Listing 11.2: forkdemo.c

```
#include <sys/types.h>
#include <unistd.h>
#include <stdio.h>

int main(){
   pid_t pid;
   char *message;
   int i,l;
   printf(" Calling fork \n");
   pid = fork(); // create a new process by calling fork(), and it
returns PID of child process.
   switch(pid)
   {
     case -1:
         perror("fork failed\n");
         exit(1);
     case 0:
         message = "Child process";
         i = 3;
```

```
         break;
      default:
         message = "Parent process";
         i = 2;
         break;
   }
   for (l=i;l>0;—l){
      puts(message);
      sleep(5);
   }
   exit(0);
}
```

In Brief...

The child process and the parent process run independently of each other. The function call fork() is used to create a new process.

Note that the parent process and child process run independently (just like the younger generation of students who do not like to be dependent on their parents except for pocket money).

A parent can wait till the child finishes by calling wait() function as illustrated in Listing 11.3.

Listing 11.3: forkwait.c

```
#include <sys/types.h>
#include <unistd.h>
#include <stdio.h>
#include <sys/wait.h>

int main(){
   pid_t pid,child_pid;
   char *message;
   int i,l,flag,status;
   printf(" Calling fork \n");
   pid = fork(); /* create a new process by calling fork(), and it
returns PID of the child process */
   switch(pid)
   {
      case -1:
         perror("fork failed\n");
         exit(1);
      case 0:
         message = "Child process";
         i = 3;
         flag = 100;
```

```
        break;
    default:
        message = "Parent process";
        i = 2;
        flag = 1000;
        break;
    }
    for (l=0;l<i;l++){
        puts(message);
        sleep(5);
    }
    if(pid != 0){
        child_pid = wait(&status); /* The wait system call causes a parent
process to pause until one of its child processes is stopped. */
        printf("child process completed PID, %d\n",child_pid);
        if(WIFEXITED(status))  // Non-zero if the child is terminated
normally.
            printf("Child exited with code, %d \n",WEXITSTATUS(status));
        else
            printf("Child terminated abnormally \n");
    }
    exit(0);
}
```

When you execute this program, the parent process will wait for the child process to finish and then it will exit.

11.3.2 Signals

An Event generated by Linux system in response to some condition is called a signal. When you start running a program and press DEL key or ^c, then you are sending a signal to the process to abruptly terminate. The following program illustrates the use of signal function calls.

Listing 11.4: sendsignal.c

```
#include <signal.h>
#include <stdio.h>
#include <unistd.h>

void problem(int signal)
{
    printf("Problem encountered %d \n",signal);
}
```

```
int main()
{
   /*
      sigaction structure, used to define the action to be taken
               on receipt of the signal specified by 1st parameter,
defined in signal.h
           */
   struct sigaction s;
   s.sa_handler = problem; // function, SIG_DFL or SIG_IGN
   sigemptyset(&s.sa_mask); /* initializes a signal set to be empty
        and sa_mask is for signals to block in sa_handler */
   s.sa_flags = 0;            // signal action modifiers, set to 0
   sigaction(SIGINT, &s, 0); // sets the action for the SIGINT
   while(1){
      printf("Hello \n");
      sleep(10);
   }
}
```

11.3.3 Multithreading

Within a process, a number of threads can be running. However, note that all these threads have to still share the CPU time. Listing 11.5 shows a multithreading program.

Listing 11.5: multithreading.c

```
#include<stdio.h>
#include<unistd.h>
#include<stdlib.h>
#include<string.h>
#include<ctype.h>
#include<pthread.h>

#define BUFFER_SIZE 1024

char buffer[BUFFER_SIZE];

void *read_thread(void *arg) {
   while(strncmp("stop",buffer,4) != 0){
      printf("Enter text: ");
      fgets(buffer, BUFFER_SIZE, stdin);
      sleep(2);
   }
```

```
  pthread_exit("read_thread exit successful");
}

void *convert_thread() {
  int i;
  while(strncmp("stop", buffer, 4) != 0) {
    sleep(3);
    printf("Converted text: ");
    for(i=0;i<strlen(buffer);i++)
      printf("%c",toupper(buffer[i]));
  }
  pthread_exit("convert_thread exit successful");
}

int main()
{
  int result;
  pthread_t rthread,cthread;
  void *thread_result;

  printf("Enter text, the program will convert it into upper case, \n
        To stop enter 'stop'\n");

  result = pthread_create(&rthread, NULL, read_thread, NULL);
  if(result != 0){
    printf("read_thread creation failed");
    exit(1);
  }

  result = pthread_create(&cthread, NULL, convert_thread, NULL);
  if(result != 0){
    printf("convert_thread creation failed");
    exit(1);
  }

  result = pthread_join(rthread, &thread_result);
  if(result != 0){
    printf("read_thread join failed");
    exit(1);
```

```
    }
    printf("read_thread joined, %s\n",thread_result);

    result = pthread_join(cthread, &thread_result);
    if(result != 0){
        printf("convert_thread join failed");
        exit(1);
    }
    printf("convert_thread joined, %s\n",thread_result);

    exit(0);
}
```

In this program, one thread reads the input from the keyboard, and another thread converts the input string into upper case letters. This is repeated till you type "stop". You can compile the program with the following command (note the –lpthread option):

$gcc –o multithreading multithreading.c –lpthread

You can execute the program using the command:

$./multithreading

When you observe the output, the lack of coordination between the two threads is evident. Even if you do not give any input from the keyboard, the thread that does the conversion to upper case letters gets invoked! So, we need to use the semaphore or the mutex for communication between the threads.

11.3.4 Semaphores

In Linux, semaphore functions are included in the file <sys/sem.h> and hence you need to include the preprocessor directive

#include <sys/sem.h>

The functions semctl(), semget(), semop() are used as illustrated in the program given in Listing 11.6.

Listing 11.6: sema.c

```
#include<stdio.h>
#include<unistd.h>
#include<stdlib.h>
#include<string.h>
#include<ctype.h>
#include<pthread.h>
#include<semaphore.h>

#define BUFFER_SIZE 1024
```

```
sem_t sem;

char buffer[BUFFER_SIZE];

void *read_thread(void *arg) {
   while(strncmp("stop",buffer,4) != 0){
      printf("Enter text: ");
      fgets(buffer, BUFFER_SIZE, stdin);
      sem_post(&sem);
   }
   pthread_exit("read_thread exit successful");
}

void *convert_thread() {
   int i;
   sem_wait(&sem);
   while(strncmp("stop", buffer, 4) != 0) {
      printf("Converted text: ");
      for(i=0;i<strlen(buffer);i++)
         printf("%c",toupper(buffer[i]));
      sem_wait(&sem);
   }
   pthread_exit("convert_thread exit successfully");
}


int main()
{
   int result;
   pthread_t rthread,cthread;
   void *thread_result;

   result = sem_init(&sem, 0, 0);

   if(result != 0){
      printf("Semaphore initialization failed");
      exit(1);
   }

   printf("Enter text, the program will convert it into upper case,
```

```
        To stop enter 'stop'\n");

    result = pthread_create(&cthread, NULL, convert_thread, NULL);
    if(result != 0){
        printf("convert_thread creation failed");
        exit(1);
    }

    result = pthread_create(&rthread, NULL, read_thread, NULL);
    if(result != 0){
        printf("read_thread creation failed");
        exit(1);
    }

    result = pthread_join(rthread, &thread_result);
    if(result != 0){
        printf("read_thread join failed");
        exit(1);
    }
    printf("read_thread joined, %s\n",thread_result);

    result = pthread_join(cthread, &thread_result);
    if(result != 0){
        printf("convert_thread join failed");
        exit(1);
    }
    printf("convert_thread joined, %s\n",thread_result);
    sem_destroy(&sem);
    exit(0);
}
```

This program has two threads, one for reading the input and one for converting the text into upper case letters. However, the thread for converting the text will wait for a semaphore to be released before it starts the operation.

You can compile the program using the command:

$gcc –osema sema.c –lpthread

Execute the program using the command:

$./sema

If you compare the functionality of the program which does not use the semaphore, and this program, you can appreciate the importance of semaphore.

11.3.5 Mutex

The program given in Listing 11.7 illustrates the use of mutex function calls. The functionality of the program is same as that of the above program used for semaphores. However, instead of semaphore, we will use a mutex here.

Listing 11. 7: mutex.c

```
#include<stdio.h>
#include<unistd.h>
#include<stdlib.h>
#include<string.h>
#include<ctype.h>
#include<pthread.h>

#define BUFFER_SIZE 1024

pthread_mutex_t mutex;

char buffer[BUFFER_SIZE];

void *read_thread(void *arg) {
   while(strncmp("stop",buffer,4) != 0){
      printf("Enter text: ");
      fgets(buffer, BUFFER_SIZE, stdin);
      pthread_mutex_unlock(&mutex);
   }
   pthread_exit("read_thread exit successful");
}

void *convert_thread() {
   int i;
   pthread_mutex_lock(&mutex);
   while(strncmp("stop", buffer, 4) != 0) {
      printf("Converted text: ");
      for(i=0;i<strlen(buffer);i++)
         printf("%c",toupper(buffer[i]));
      pthread_mutex_lock(&mutex);
   }
   pthread_exit("convert_thread exit successful");
}
```

```
int main()
{
   int result;
   pthread_t rthread,cthread;
   void *thread_result;

   result = pthread_mutex_init(&mutex, NULL);

   if(result != 0){
      printf("Mutex initialization failed");
      exit(1);
   }

   printf("Enter text, the program will convert it into upper case,
        To stop enter 'stop'\n");

   pthread_mutex_lock(&mutex);

   result = pthread_create(&cthread, NULL, convert_thread, NULL);
   if(result != 0){
      printf("convert_thread creation failed");
      exit(1);
   }

   result = pthread_create(&rthread, NULL, read_thread, NULL);
   if(result != 0){
      printf("read_thread creation failed");
      exit(1);
   }

   result = pthread_join(rthread, &thread_result);
   if(result != 0){
      printf("read_thread join failed");
      exit(1);
   }
   printf("read_thread joined, %s\n",thread_result);

   result = pthread_join(cthread, &thread_result);
   if(result != 0){
      printf("convert_thread join failed");
```

```
        exit(1);
    }
    printf("convert_thread joined, %s\n",thread_result);

    pthread_mutex_destroy(&mutex);
    exit(0);
}
```

You need to observe the syntax of the function calls to lock and unlock the mutex. You can compile the program using the command:

$gcc –o mutex mutex.c –lpthread

Execute the program using the command:

$./mutex

Functionally semaphore and mutex work in the same fashion as is evident from the output of this program and the previous program.

11.3.6 Shared Memory

In this section, we will illustrate the use of shared memory. You need to create a memory block (say, of size 1024 bytes). One program will read the contents from this memory (prg1.c) and another program (prg2.c) will take input from keyboard and write the data to the memory. A flag something_is_there is used to indicate whether the memory contains some data or not. The program that reads the memory will clear the flag after reading. The program that puts data in the memory will set the flag after putting the data.

Listing 11.8 is a header file for defining the buffer size, and a structure that contains the flag and buffer.

Listing 11.8 common.h

```
#define BUFFER_SIZE 1024

struct common_struct {
    int something_is_there;
    char buffer[BUFFER_SIZE];
};
```

Listing 11.9 gives the program prg1.c that reads the data from the shared memory and converts the text into upper case letters.

Listing 11.9: prg1.c

```
#include <stdio.h>
#include <stdlib.h>
#include <unistd.h>
#include <ctype.h>
#include <string.h>
#include <sys/shm.h>
#include <sys/ipc.h>
#include <sys/types.h>
#include "common.h"

int main()
{
   int flag = 1;
   void *shrd_memory = (void *)0;
   struct common_struct *shm_block;
   int smemid,i,result,len;

   smemid = shmget((key_t)2377, sizeof(struct common_struct), 0666 |
IPC_CREAT);
   if(smemid == -1) {
      printf("An error occurred: shmget failed\n");
      return 1;
   }

   shrd_memory = shmat(smemid, (void *)0, 0);
   if(shrd_memory == (void *) -1) {
      printf("An error occurred: shmat failed\n");
      return 1;
   }
   printf("Shared Memory at %X\n", (int)shrd_memory);

   shm_block = (struct common_struct *)shrd_memory;
   shm_block->something_is_there = 0;
   while(flag == 1) {
      if(shm_block->something_is_there) {
         len = strlen(shm_block->buffer);
         printf("Converted Text: ");
         for(i=0;i < len;i++)
            printf("%c",toupper(shm_block->buffer[i]));
         sleep(1);
```

```
            shm_block->something_is_there = 0;
            if(strncmp(shm_block->buffer, "stop", 4) == 0) {
               flag = 0;
            }
         }
      }

      result = shmdt(shrd_memory);
      if(result == -1) {
         printf("An error occurred: shmdt failed \n");
         return 1;
      }

      result = shmctl(smemid, IPC_RMID, 0);
      if(result == -1) {
         printf("An error occurred: shmctl(IPC_RMID) failed\n");
         return 1;
      }
      return 0;
}
```

Listing 11.10 gives the program prg2.c that takes input from the keyboard and writes the data to the shared memory.

Listing 11.10: prg2.c

```
#include <stdio.h>
#include <stdlib.h>
#include <unistd.h>
#include <string.h>
#include <sys/shm.h>
#include <sys/types.h>
#include <sys/ipc.h>
#include "common.h"

int main()
{
   int flag = 1;
   void *shrd_memory = (void *)0;
   struct common_struct *shm_block;
   char buffer[BUFFER_SIZE];
   int smemid,result;
   smemid = shmget((key_t)2377, sizeof(struct common_struct), 0666 |
```

```
IPC_CREAT);
   if(smemid == -1) {
      printf("An error occurred: shmget failed \n");
      return 1;
   }

   shrd_memory = shmat(smemid, (void *)0, 0);
   if(shrd_memory == (void *) -1) {
      printf("An error occured: shmat failed \n");
      return 1;
   }
   printf("Shared Memory at %X\n", (int) shrd_memory);

   shm_block = (struct common_struct *)shrd_memory;
   printf("Enter text, the other program, prg1 converts it into upper
case,     To stop the execution of these programs enter 'stop'\n");

   while(flag) {
      while(shm_block->something_is_there == 1) {
         sleep(1);
         printf("waiting .... \n");
      }
      printf("Enter text: ");
      fgets(buffer, BUFFER_SIZE, stdin);

      strncpy(shm_block->buffer, buffer, BUFFER_SIZE);
      shm_block->something_is_there = 1;

      if(strncmp(buffer, "stop", 4) == 0) {
         flag = 0;
      }
   }

   result = shmdt(shrd_memory);
   if(result == -1) {
      printf("An error occurred: shmdt failed \n");
      return 1;
   }
   return 0;
}
```

You can compile prg1.c and prg2.c using the commands:

$gcc –o prg1 prg1.c

$gcc –o prg2 prg2.c

Now, you run prg1 in the background, using the command:

$./prg1 &

You can run prg2 in the foreground, using the command:

$./prg2

11.3.7 Message Queue

A message queue is used for inter-process communication. One process can write data into the queue and another process will read that data. The function calls for message queue are illustrated in this section.

Listing 11.11 gives a program converter.c which reads the data from the queue and converts the text into upper case letters.

Listing 11.11: converter.c

```
#include <stdio.h>
#include <stdlib.h>
#include <unistd.h>
#include <string.h>
#include <ctype.h>
#include <sys/msg.h>
#include <sys/ipc.h>
#include <sys/types.h>

#define TEXT_SIZE 1024

struct data_struct {
   char text_to_convert[TEXT_SIZE];
};

int main()
{
   int flag = 1;
   int msgqid;
   int i, result, len;
   struct data_struct convert_data;

   msgqid = msgget((key_t)2377, 0666 | IPC_CREAT);
   if(msgqid == -1){
```

```
        printf("An error occured: msgget failed\n");
        return 1;
    }

    while(flag) {
        if(msgrcv(msgqid,(void *)&convert_data,TEXT_SIZE,0,0) == -1) {
            printf("An error occured: msgrcv failed\n");
            return 1;
        }
        len = strlen(convert_data.text_to_convert);
        printf("Converted text: ");
        for(i = 0;i < len; i++)
            printf("%c",toupper(convert_data.text_to_convert[i]));
        if(strncmp(convert_data.text_to_convert, "stop", 4) == 0 ) {
            flag = 0;
        }
    }
    result = msgctl(msgqid, IPC_RMID, 0);
    if(result == -1) {
        printf("An error occured: msgctl(IPC_RMID) failed \n");
        return 1;
    }
    return 0;
}
```

Listing 11.12 gives the program input.c that reads the text from keyboard and puts it in a message queue.

Listing 11.12: input.c

```
#include <stdio.h>
#include <stdlib.h>
#include <unistd.h>
#include <string.h>
#include <sys/msg.h>
#include <sys/ipc.h>
#include <sys/types.h>

#define TEXT_SIZE 1024

struct data_struct {
    char text_to_convert[TEXT_SIZE];
```

```
};

int main()
{
   int flag = 1;
   int msgqid;
   char buffer[TEXT_SIZE];
   struct data_struct user_data;

   msgqid = msgget((key_t)2377, 0666 | IPC_CREAT);

   if(msgqid == -1){
      printf("An error occurred: msgget failed\n");
      return 1;
   }

   printf("Enter text, to put it in a message queue,
             To exit enter 'stop' \n");

   while(flag) {
      printf("Enter text: ");
      fgets(buffer, TEXT_SIZE, stdin);
      strcpy(user_data.text_to_convert, buffer);
      if(msgsnd(msgqid, (void *)&user_data, TEXT_SIZE, 0) == -1) {
         printf("An error occurred: msgsnd failed\n");
         return 1;
      }

      if(strncmp(buffer, "stop", 4) == 0 ) {
         flag = 0;
      }
   }
   return 0;
}
```

You can compile the two programs using the commands:

$gcc –o converter converter.c

$gcc –oinput input.c

You can now execute the two programs using the commands:

$./input

$./converter

We will illustrate the use of message queue using another example that simulates a process control system. One process generates the values of temperatures using a random number generator. The temperature will be between 50 and 60 degrees. The values are written to a message queue. Another process reads the contents of the message queue and gives an alarm if the temperature is above 57 degrees.

Listing 11.13 gives the program generator.c which is to generate the temperature values and put the data in the message queue.

Listing 11.13: generator.c

```
#include <stdio.h>
#include <time.h>
#include <stdlib.h>
#include <unistd.h>
#include <string.h>
#include <sys/msg.h>
#include <sys/ipc.h>
#include <sys/types.h>

struct temp_struct {
   int temperature;
};

int main()
{
   int msgqid;
   int temp,i=0;
   struct temp_struct temp_data;
   time_t t;

   msgqid = msgget((key_t)2377, 0666 | IPC_CREAT);

   if(msgqid == -1){
     printf("An error occurred: msgget failed\n");
     return 1;
   }

   srand((unsigned) time(&t));   // Sets a random starting point.

   while(i<20) {
     temp = rand() % 60;
```

```
    if((temp >= 50) && (temp<= 60)){
        temp_data.temperature = temp;
        i++;
        if(i==20)
            temp_data.temperature = 1;
        printf("Temperature: %d \n",temp);
        sleep(1);
        if(msgsnd(msgqid,(void *)&temp_data,sizeof(temp_data),0) == -
1){
            printf("An error occurred: msgsnd failed\n");
            return 1;
        }
    }
  }
  return 0;
}
```

Listing 11.14 gives the program monitor.c which reads the data from the message queue and displays the alarm message.

Listing 11.14: monitor.c

```
#include <stdio.h>
#include <stdlib.h>
#include <unistd.h>
#include <string.h>
#include <ctype.h>
#include <sys/msg.h>
#include <sys/ipc.h>
#include <sys/types.h>

struct temp_struct {
  int temperature;
};

int main()
{
  int msgqid;
  int result;
  struct temp_struct temp_data;

  msgqid = msgget((key_t)2377, 0666 | IPC_CREAT);
```

```
    if(msgqid == -1){
      printf("An error occurred: msgget failed\n");
      return 1;
    }

    while(1) {
      if(msgrcv(msgqid,(void *)&temp_data,sizeof(temp_data),0,0) == -
1) {
        printf("An error occurred: msgrcv failed\n");
        return 1;
      }
      if(temp_data.temperature == 1)
        break;
      if(temp_data.temperature > 57)
        printf("Warning: Temperature limit exceeds,
%d\n",temp_data.temperature);
      else
        printf("Temperature: %d\n",temp_data.temperature);
    }
    result = msgctl(msgqid, IPC_RMID, 0);
    if(result == -1) {
      printf("An error occurred: msgctl(IPC_RMID) failed \n");
      return 1;
    }
    return 0;
}
```

In Brief...

Message queues are used for inter-process communication. One process can write data into the message queue and other processes can read the data.

You can compile the two programs using the commands:

$gcc –o generator generator.c

$gcc –o monitor monitor.c

Now, execute the program using the commands:

$./generator

$./monitor

Summary

This chapter focuses on programming in Linux. The commonly used shell commands are reviewed and the shell programming concepts are illustrated with examples. Linux provides an excellent programming environment by providing a number of utilities and a powerful user interface through the shell. The operating system Application Programming Interface (API) function calls are explained. The use of semaphores, mutexes, shared memory and message queues is illustrated with examples.

Questions

1. List the file manipulation commands of Linux.
2. List the directory command of Linux.
3. Explain how the shell processes the commands.
4. What are the function calls for semaphore management in Linux?
5. What are the function calls for mutex management in Linux?
6. List the function calls used for shared memory and message queues.

Exercises

1. Create a shell script "test" which contains the line:

   echo "How are you?"

   Give execute permission to the "test" file and then execute the shell script? What is the output? Explain.
2. Write a shell script to find single letter, two-letter and three-letter words in a text file.
3. Write a shell command to find the number of users logged in.
4. Write a shell command to find all the executable files in your home directory.
5. Write a shell script to obtain the word frequency counts in English text sorted in alphabetical order and numerical order.
6. Write a shell script to count the frequency of of single letter (a,b,c...), two-letter combinetions (aa, ab,...ba, bb..., ...zy, zz) and three-letter combinations (aaa, aab, ...) in an English text file. Assume 26 letter and space character only and remove all punctuation marks before processing the file.
7. Write a shell script that displays the number of readable, writable and executable files in a specified directory.
8. Write a C program that takes input from keyboard, converts the characters to upper case and prints them. The program will exit when you press ^c.
9. Write a C program that takes a string input from keyboard and displays the length of the string. Use multithreading.
10. Write a C program that takes a string input from keyboard and displays the length of the string. Use message queue.
11. Write a C program that takes a string input from keyboard and displays the length of the string. Use shared memory.

Chapter 12

Programming in RTLinux

CHAPTER OBJECTIVES

After reading this chapter, you will be able to:

- Understand the architecture of RTLinux
- Learn how to create RTLinux modules
- Gain knowledge of semaphore and mutex management function calls
- Develop an application to control an appliance through RTLinux

In this chapter, we will study the details of programming in RTLinux environment. Through illustrative examples, we will study the intricacies of developing real-time embedded systems using one of the most popular open source embedded real-time operating systems.

12.1 Overview of RTLinux

Linux operating system is not a hard real-time operating system because the kernel suspends a task once its time slice is over. In a multi-user, multi-tasking environment, this task scheduling algorithm maximizes the throughput; but if a particular task has to meet a strict deadline, it cannot be guaranteed.

To support hard real-time applications, the Linux kernel has been modified by adding a layer of software between the hardware and the Linux kernel. This additional layer is called 'virtual machine'. This new layer, RTLinux layer, has a separate task scheduler. This task scheduler assigns lowest priority to the standard Linux kernel. Any task that has to meet real-time constraints will run under RTLinux.

In Brief...

To achieve real-time performance, the Linux kernel is modified by introducing a layer between the hardware and the standard Linux kernel. This layer has a separate task scheduler that meets real-time constraints.

Programming in RTLinux is not much different from programming in Linux. Any task that has to meet real-time constraints has to run as an RTLinux process and all other non-real-time tasks can run as processes in Linux.

In your RTLinux system, note the following points as regards the location of the various files:

- RTLinux will be installed in the directory /usr/rtlinux-xxx, where xxx is the version number
- /usr/rtlinux/include contains all the include files necessary for development projects
- /usr/rtlinux/examples contains the RTLinux example programs. They illustrate the use of most of the API calls
- /usr/doc/rtlinux/man contains the manual pages for RTLinux
- /usr/rtlinux/modules contains the core RTLinux modules
- /usr/rtlinux/bin contains RTLinux scripts and utilities

While working on the RTLinux system, particularly when you are doing the programming for the first time, the system may crash once in a while. This is because there is no protection against the bugs in the application source code written by you. As the real-time programs are executed in the kernel space, you may be just creating a situation where the processor will go to a state from which it cannot recover leading to the crash. To minimize this risk, use the debugger before the final testing. Note the two important aspects while doing programming in RTLinux:

- By default, the RTLinux tasks do not have access to the computer's floating-point unit. Hence you need to explicitly set the permission for every RTLinux task which requires floating-point unit.
- You cannot pass arguments from the command prompt.

Notes...

In RTLinux, you cannot pass arguments form the command prompt.

12.1.1 RTLinux Modules

RTLinux programs are not created as stand-alone units; they are created as modules, which are loaded into the Linux kernel space. The C source files are compiled into object files using the gcc command with the argument –c flag. In the C file, the main() function gets replaced with the following lines:

```
int  init_module();
void cleanup_module();
```

init_module() is called when the module is first loaded into the kernel. This function returns 0 if the module is successfully loaded; it returns a negative value in case of failure. When the module is to be unloaded, the cleanup_module() is called.

In Brief...

In RTLinux, programs are not created as stand-alone units, they are created as modules. The main() function gets replaced by init_module() and cleanup_module() functions.

Compiling modules in RTLinux

In RTLinux, a program is viewed as a module. To compile the C modules in the RTLinux environment, the presence of a file with the name rtl.mk is a must. It is created during installation of RTLinux and contains the paths to include files and compiler options. This file should be in the directory /usr/include/rtlinux.

You can compile a module using the following command:

make –f rtl.mk filename.o

Executing the RTLinux Modules

You can load (or start) and remove (or stop) user modules using the rtlinux command. Using this command, you can also obtain status information about RTLinux modules. The command syntax is as follows:

$rtlinux start my_program

$rtlinux stop my_program

$rtlinux status my_program

The first command starts the program; the second command stops the program when it is running; and, the third command gives the status of the running program. Note that the character $ is the command prompt.

To determine the status at the beginning of an RTLinux session, type the following command:

$rtlinux status

The output will be as follows:

Scheme : (-) not loaded (+) loaded

(-) mbuff

(-) rtl_fifi

(-)rt;

(-)rt_posixio

(-)rt_sched

(-)rtl_time

To determine the status after running the RTLinux program, type the command:

$rtlinux status

The output will be as follows:

Scheme (-) not loaded (+) loaded

(+) mbuff

(+)rtl_fifo

(+) rt;

(+) rt_posixio

(+)rt_sched

(+)rtl_time

An alternative method of compiling modules is to use the command "modprobe". The syntax of this command is as follows:

$modprobe –a rtl_time rtl_sched rtl_posixio rtl_fifo

If you use this command, the modules must be installed in /lib/modules/kernelversion.

Use the insmod and rmmod commands if you have the object file program.o. If all the other modules corresponding to a project have already been loaded and only one particular module has to be loaded into the kernel, you can issue the following command:

In Brief...

The rtlinux command is used to add a module, remove a module and to find the status of a module.

$insmod program.o

To stop the module, the command is as follows:

$rmmod program

12.1.2 Creating RTLinux POSIX Threads

A real-time program generally consists of a number of threads. Each thread is a light-weight process. The threads share a common address space. pthread_create() function is used to create a new real-time thread. It will be called from the Linux kernel thread by using init_module().

The corresponding header file is

```
#include <pthread.h>
```

To achieve real-time performance, the various POSIX compliant API function calls are used. These function calls are related to create and cancel threads, mutexes and semaphores.

In Brief...

The RTLinux Application Programming Interface (API) is compliant to Portable Operating System Interface (POSIX) standards and hence the application software is portable.

To implement mutex, you have to include the header file <rtl_mutex.h> in the C program.

Semaphore is another utility for synchronization in operating systems. A semaphore is an integer value (positive or negative) manipulated by the kernel. RTLinux provides a number of system calls to handle mutexes and semaphores.

Thread-related System Calls

The following system calls are related to threads which get/set the attributes related to the threads:

```
pthread_attr_init()
pthread_attr_setschedparam()
pthread_attr_getschedparam()
pthread_attr_getcpu_np()
pthread_attr_setcpu_np()
```

To cancel a thread, the system call is pthread_cancel (pthread thread)

For the resources of a thread to be de-allocated, we have to join the thread in cleanup_module using the function call pthread_join().

12.1.3 Timer Management

RTLinux provides a number of system calls for timing related activities. A number of internal clocks are available to manage the timers.

To obtain the current clock reading, we can use clock gettime() function. Clock_id gives the identification of the clock to be read and its structure, which stores the value obtained.

A general timer module will be as follows:

```
#include <rtl_time.h>
int clock_gettime (clockid_t click_id, struct time spec *ts);
hr time_t clock_gethrtime (clockid_t clock);
struct timespec {
time_t      tr_sec;         /*seconds*/
long     tr_nsec;     /*nano seconds*/
}
```

In the next section, the complete list of function calls is given. The subsequent sections demonstrate the usage of these function calls through illustrative examples.

12.2 Core RTLinux API

The important RTLinux API function calls are listed below:

`clock_gethrtime`: To get high resolution time using the specified clock

`clock_gettime`: To get the system clock time

`clock_settime`: To set the system clock time

`gethrtime`: To get high resolution time

`nanosleep`: For high resolution sleep

`pthread_attr_getcpu_np`: To examine and change the CPU pthread attribute

`pthread_attr_getschedparam`: To access dynamic thread scheduling parameters

`pthread_attr_getdetachstate`: To get detachstate attributes

`pthread_attr_getstacksize`: To get stacksize attribute

`pthread_attr_init`: To initialize threads attribute object

`pthread_attr_setcpu_np`: To examine and change the CPU pthread attribute

`pthread_attr_setdetachstate`: To set detachstate attributes

`pthread_attr_setfp_np`: To set and get floating-point enable attribute

`pthread_attr_setschedparam`: To access dynamic thread scheduling parameters

`pthread_attr_setstacksize`: To set stacksize attribute

`pthread_cancel`: To stop or cancel a thread

pthread_create: To create a thread

pthread_condattr_destroy: To destroy condition variable attributes object

pthread_condattr_getshared: To get the process-shared condition variable attributes

pthread_condattr_init: To initialize condition variable attributes object

pthread_condattr_setpshared: To set the process-shared condition variable attributes

pthread_cond_broadcast: To broadcast a condition

pthread_cond_destroy: To destroy condition variable

pthread_cond_init: To initialize condition variable

pthread_cond_signal: To signal a condition

pthread_cond_timedwait: To wait on a condition variable

pthread_cond_wait: To wait on a condition variable

pthread_delete_np: To delete a real-time thread

pthread_exit: To terminate a thread

pthread_join: To terminate a thread

pthread_kill: To send a 'kill' signal to a thread

pthread_linux: To get the thread identifier of the Linux thread

pthread_make_periodic_np: To mark a real-time thread as periodic

pthread_mutexattr_destroy: To destroys a mutex attribute object.

pthread_mutexattr_getprioceiling: To get priority ceiling attribute of mutex attribute object.

pthread_mutexattr_getpshared: To obtain the process-shared setting of a mutex attribute object.

pthread_mutexattr_gettype: To get the mutex type

pthread_mutexattr_init: To initialize a mutex attribute object.

pthread_mutexattr_setprioceiling: To set priority ceiling attribute of mutex attribute object.

pthread_mutexattr_setpshared: To set the process-shared attribute of a mutex attribute object

pthread_mutexattr_settype: To set the mutex type

pthread_mutex_destroy: To destroy a mutex

pthread_mutex_init: To initialize a mutex with the attributes specified in the mutex attribute object.

pthread_mutex_lock: To lock an unlocked mutex. If you try to lock an already locked mutex, the calling thread blocks until the thread that currently holds the mutex releases it.

pthread_mutex_trylock: To try to lock a mutex. If the mutex is already locked, the calling thread returns without waiting for the mutex to be freed.

pthread_mutex_unlock: To unlock a mutex.

Pthread_getschedparam: To get schedparam attribute

pthread_self: To get the ID of the calling thread

`pthread_setcancelstate`: To set cancel state

`pthread_setschedparam`: To set schedparam attribute

`pthread_setfp_np`: To allow use of floating-point operations in a thread.

`pthread_suspend_np`: To suspend execution of a real-time thread.

`pthread_wait_np`: To suspend the current thread until the next period

`pthread_wakeup_np`: To wake up a real-time thread.

`rt_com`: Serial port driver for RTLinux

`rt_com_read`: To read data in real-time from a serial port

`rt_com_setup`: To dynamically change the parameters of each real-time serial port.

`rt_com_table`: An array of descriptions, one per serial port.

`rt_com_write`: To write data in real-time to a serial port

`rtf_create`: To create a real-time FIFO (First In First Out) buffer

`rtf_create_handler`: To install a handler for real-time FIFO data

`rtf_create_rt_handler`: To install a handler for real-time FIFO data

`rtf_destroy`: To remove a real-time FIFO created with rtf_create

`rtf_flush`: To empty a real-time FIFO

`rtf_get`: To read data from a real-time FIFO

`rtf_link_user_ioctl`: To install an ioctl (i/o control) handler for a real-time FIFO

`rtf_put`: To write data to a real-time FIFO

`rtf_make_user_pair`: To make a pair of receive-transmit FIFOs act like a bidirectional FIFO

`rtf_allow_interrupts`: To control the CPU interrupt state

`rtf_free_irq`: To install and remove real-time interrupt handlers

`rtf_free_soft_irq`: To install and remove software interrupt handlers

`rtf_get_soft_irq`: To install and remove software interrupt handlers

`rtf_getcpuid`: To get the current processor ID

`rtl_getschedclock`: To get the current scheduler clock

`rtl_global_pend_irq`: To schedule a Linux interrupt

`rtl_hard_disable_irq`: Interrupt control

`rtl_hard_enable_irg`: Interrupt control

`rtl_no_interrupts`: Control the CPU interrupt state

`rtl_printf`: For formatted print

`rtl_request_irq`: To install and remove real-time interrupt handlers

`rtl_restore_interrupts`: To control the CPU interrupt state

`rtl_setclockmode`: To set the RTLinux clock mode

rtl_stop_interrupts: To control the CPU interrupt state

rtlinux_sigaction: RTLinux v3 User-Level signal handling functions.

rtlinux_signal: List of available RTLinux User-Level signals

rtlinux_sigprocmask: RTLinux v3 User-Level signal handling functions.

rtlinux_sigsetops: RTLinux User-Level signal set operations.

sched_get_priority_max: Get maximum priority limits for the scheduling policy

sched_get_priority_min: Get minimum priority limits for the scheduling policy

sem_init: Initialize POSIX semaphore

sem_destroy: Destroy an unnamed POSIX semaphore

sem_getvalue: Get the value of a sempahore

sem_getvalue: To unlock a semaphore

sem_trywait: To lock a semaphore

sem_wait: To lock a semaphore

sigaction: RTLinux POSIX signal handling functions

sysconf: Get configurable system variables

time: Clock and timer functions

uname: Get name of the system

usleep: Suspend execution for an interval

rt_task_delete: Delete a real-time task

rt_task_init: Create a real-time task

rt_task_make_periodic: Mark a real-time task for execution.

rt_task_suspend: Suspend a real-time task.

In the following sections, we will study how to make use of these function calls for multi-threaded applications using semaphore and mutex for inter-task communication.

12.3 Program to Display a Message Periodically

In this section, we will study how to write an RTLinux module. The process of compiling and executing the program is also explained. This program sends a message (as usual, it is "hello world") to the receive buffer. To display the message on the Linux terminal, we have to give dmesg at the command prompt.

The files on the RTLinux machine are:

hello.c: This file is used to display "hello world" every 0.5 seconds in RTLinux System.

rtl.mk: This file makes the object file.

hello.o: This is the object file for hello.c.

Listing 12.1 gives the source code for hello.c which is to display a message periodically.

Listing 12.1: Source code for hello.c

```
#include <rtl.h>
#include <time.h>
#include <pthread.h>

pthread_t thread;

void *start_routine(void *arg)
{
        int i, count=0;
  struct sched_param p;
  p.sched_priority = 1;
  pthread_setschedparam (pthread_self(), SCHED_FIFO, &p);

  pthread_make_periodic_np (pthread_self(), gethrtime(), 500000000);

  while (1) {
        for(i=0;i<60;i++)
                {
      pthread_wait_np ();
                }
                count = count + 1;
        rtl_printf("%d hello world ",count);
  }
  return 0;
}

int init_module(void) {
  return pthread_create (&thread, NULL, start_routine, 0);
}

void cleanup_module(void) {
        pthread_cancel(thread);
        pthread_join(thread,NULL);
}
```

The hello function has three component—initialization, runtime and termination—with the first call to hello routine that is newly created thread. The initialization guides the scheduler to assign this thread a priority of 1. The pthread setschdedparam will set the scheduler behaviour to sched_fifo. The loop while (1) is an infinite loop, hence the thread executes forever. To stop the program, you have to remove it from the kernel with rm_mod(). The function call pthread_wait_np will make the thread wait for one second. The init_module() starts the entire program by creating an execution thread which exists in hello function. The cleanup_module function cancels the thread process and the CPU cycles allocated to the thread will be freed.

To execute this program, the steps are:

1. Compiling the source code and creating a module.
2. Locating and copying the rtl.mk file along side with hello.c file.
3. Inserting the module in RTLinux kernel.

2.3.1 Compiling and Executing the Program

Compile the source code and create a module: You can compile the source code by using the gcc compiler directly from the command line. A simpler way is to create a makefile. Then you need to just type "make" to compile the code.

Locate and copy the rtl.mk file: The rtl.mk file is an include file which contains all the flags needed to compile the code. For simplicity, you can copy it from the RTLinux source tree and place it in your home directory along with your file, i.e. hello.c.

Insert the module into the running RTLinux kernel: The object file obtained after compiling the source code has to be "plugged in" to the kernel, where it will be executed by RTLinux.

Let's look at these steps in more detail.

We begin by creating the makefile that will be used to compile hello.c program. Type the following lines in a file called makefile and put it in the same directory as your hello.c program:

```
hello.o: hello.c
gcc $(CFLAGS) hello.c
```

Locate the file rtl.mk and copy it into the same directory in which the files hello.c and makefile are available. The rtl.mk file can usually be found at /usr/include/rtlinux/rtl.mk. Use the following command to copy the rtl.mk file into your directory.

```
$cp /usr/include/rtlinux/rtl.mk
```

Now, type the following command:

```
$make -f rtl.mk hello.o
```

This compiles the hello.c program and produces an object file named hello.o.

We now need to load the RTLinux module. You can use the following command:

```
$rtlinux start hello
```

You can check the status of your module by typing the command:

```
$rtlinux status hello
```

You should now be able to see your hello.o program printing its message twice per second. Depending on the configuration of your machine, you should either be able to see it directly in your console, or by typing the command:

```
$dmesg
```

To stop the program, we need to remove it from the kernel. To do so, type the command:

```
$rtlinux stop hello
```

Now that you are familiar with creating and executing the RTLinux modules, we will study semaphore management calls in the next section.

12.4 Semaphore Management

When you use multiple threads, the threads need to synchronize with one another. Semaphore provides the mechanism for synchronization. The following program illustrates the semaphore management function calls in RTLinux.

Listing 12.2: semaphore.c

```
#include <rtl.h>
#include <time.h>
#include <pthread.h>
#include <semaphore.h>

#define No_Tasks 3

static pthread_t threads[No_Tasks];

static sem_t sem;

static void *sub_routine(void *arg)
{
   int i;
   int sleep = 500000000;
   int nthread = (int)arg;

   struct sched_param p;
   p.sched_priority = 1;
   pthread_setschedparam(pthread_self(), SCHED_FIFO, &p);
// pthread_make_periodic_np(pthread_self(),gethrtime(),sleep);
   rtl_printf("\nThread %d starts\n",nthread+1);
   sem_wait(&sem);
// while(1){
      for(i=0;i<10;i++){
         if(nthread == 0)
            rtl_printf("A ");
         else if(nthread == 1)
```

```
            rtl_printf("B ");
        else
            rtl_printf("C ");
        }
        rtl_printf("\nThread %d: Before sleep\n",nthread+1);
        nanosleep(hrt2ts(sleep),NULL);
        rtl_printf("Thread %d: After sleep\n",nthread+1);
        sem_post(&sem);
        //pthread_wait_np();
// }
    return 0;
}

int init_module(void)
{
    int ret;
    int i;

    sem_init(&sem,1,1);

    rtl_printf("Main thread starts \n");

    for(i=0;i<No_Tasks;i++)
    {
        ret = pthread_create(&threads[i], NULL, sub_routine,(void *) i);
        if(ret)
        {
            rtl_printf("Failed to create a thread \n");
            return ret;
        }
    }
 return 0;
}

void cleanup_module(void)
{
    int i;
    for(i=0;i<No_Tasks;i++)
    {
        pthread_cancel(threads[i]);
```

```
        pthread_join(threads[i],NULL);
    }
    sem_destroy(&sem);
}
```

In this program, we are creating three threads, the first thread prints "A", the second thread prints 'B' and the third thread prints "C"—each ten times. The first thread acquires a semaphore, prints 'A' ten times and then releases the semaphore. Then B will acquire the semaphore and does its job. And, then C will do the same. Note the syntax of the function calls and the function call for printing. You can see the output in the console windows. Note that some of the lines are commented. To start with, you can execute the program as it is so that you will understand the functionality of the program. Later on, you can uncomment the lines. When uncommented, the program executes in an infinite loop.

12.5 Mutex Management

Mutex is another mechanism for synchronization. The following program illustrates the use of mutex management function calls.

Listing 12.3: mutex.c

```
#include <rtl.h>
#include <time.h>
#include <pthread.h>

static pthread_t thread1,thread2;

static pthread_mutex_t mutex;

static void *sub_routine1(void *arg)
{
    int i,ret;
    int sleep = 500000000;
    int nthread = (int)arg;

    struct sched_param p;
    p.sched_priority = 1;
    pthread_setschedparam(pthread_self(), SCHED_FIFO, &p);
    pthread_make_periodic_np(pthread_self(),gethrtime(),sleep);
    rtl_printf("Thread %d starts\n",nthread);
    ret = pthread_mutex_lock(&mutex);
//  rtl_printf("thread1: lock  returns %d\n",ret);
//  while(1){
        //ret = pthread_mutex_lock(&mutex);
```

```
    //rtl_printf("thread1: lock returns %d\n",ret);
    for(i=0;i<10;i++){
      rtl_printf("A ");
    }
    rtl_printf("thread1: before sleep\n");
    nanosleep(hrt2ts(sleep),NULL);
    rtl_printf("thread1: after sleep\n");
    ret = pthread_mutex_unlock(&mutex);
//  rtl_printf("thread1: unlock returns %d \n",ret);
//  pthread_wait_np();
//}
  return 0;
}

static void *sub_routine2(void *arg)
{
  int i,ret;
  int sleep = 500000000;
  int nthread = (int)arg;
  hrtime_t itime;
  hrtime_t ftime;
  struct sched_param p;
  p.sched_priority = 1;
  pthread_setschedparam(pthread_self(), SCHED_FIFO, &p);
  pthread_make_periodic_np(pthread_self(),gethrtime(),sleep);
  rtl_printf("Thread %d starts\n",nthread);
  itime = gethrtime();
  ret = pthread_mutex_lock(&mutex);
// rtl_printf("thread2: lock returns %d",ret);
// while(1){
    //ret = pthread_mutex_lock(&mutex);
    //rtl_printf("thread2: lock returns %d",ret);
    ftime = gethrtime();
    rtl_printf("thread2 waits for %d ns \n",(ftime - itime));
    for(i=0;i<10;i++){
      rtl_printf("B ");
    }
    rtl_printf("thread2: before sleep\n");
    nanosleep(hrt2ts(sleep),NULL);
    rtl_printf("thread2: after sleep\n");
```

```
      ret = pthread_mutex_unlock(&mutex);
//    rtl_printf("thread2: unlock returns %d",ret);
//    pthread_wait_np();
// }
   return 0;
}

int init_module(void)
{
   int ret;

   pthread_mutex_init(&mutex,0);

   rtl_printf("Main thread starts \n");

   ret = pthread_create(&thread1, NULL, sub_routine1,(void *) 1);
   if(ret)
   {
      rtl_printf("Failed to create thread1 \n");
      return ret;
   }

   ret = pthread_create(&thread2, NULL, sub_routine2,(void *) 2);
   if(ret)
   {
      rtl_printf("Failed to create thread2 \n");
      return ret;
   }
  return 0;
}

void cleanup_module(void)
{
   pthread_cancel(thread1);
   pthread_join(thread1,NULL);

   pthread_cancel(thread2);
   pthread_join(thread2,NULL);

   pthread_mutex_destroy(&mutex);
}
```

In this program, we are creating two threads. One thread prints 'A' and the second thread prints 'B'. The first thread locks the mutex, prints the value of 'A' and then unlocks the mutex. Then the second thread locks the mutex. As in the previous program, first execute the program and observe the output. Later on, you can uncomment the commented lines so that the program executes in an infinite loop.

12.6 Case Study: Appliance Control by RTLinux System

In this section, we will develop a full-fledged application that uses a number of RTLinux API function calls. This project is to control an audio player by RTLinux system. An audio player program will be running on a Windows machine. You can control the audio player from an RTLinux system by issuing the commands Play, Pause and Stop. The tape recorder controls which exist on the Windows system will be accessed remotely from RTLinux application. To issue the commands for Play, Pause and Stop, we need to write separate modules in the RTLinux system.

To test the application given in this section, you need to have the following development environment:

- RTLinux installed on a Linux system
- A Windows 9x (or later) system to communicate with RTLinux system
- A null modem cable. Using this cable, you need to interconnect the RTLinux system and the Windows system.

On the RTLinux machine, the following files are required:

`rt_com.c`: This file is used for establishing the serial communication.

`rt_com.h, rt_comp.h`: These are the header files.

Notes...

[Note: These three files are available in the directory /usr/src/rtlinux-xxx/drivers/rt_com. xxx is the version number of your RTLinux. If these files are not found in this directory, they can be downloaded from www.rtlinux.org]

`play.c`: This file is used to send an instruction to the Windows machine to Play the audio file.

`stop.c`: This file is for sending an instruction to stop the audio play.

`pause.c`: This file is for sending an instruction for pause.

`rtl.mk`: This file makes object files.

`rtl_com.o, play.o, stop.o, pause.o` : These are the object files.

Listing 12.4 gives the program play.c which sends the 'Play' command to the audio player.

Listing 12.4: play.c

```
#include <rtl.h>
#include <rtl_fifo.h>

#include <time.h>
#include <pthread.h>
```

```
#include <asm/io.h>
#include "rt_com.h"

int period=100000000;
int fifo_size=4000;
pthread_t thread;
int fd_fifo;

char a[210]={};
void *play(void *t) {
  pthread_make_periodic_np (thread, gethrtime(), period);
  a[0]='2'; // send signal '2' to play
  rt_com_write(0, a, 1); // send 1 byte of array a through base port
0
  return 0;
}

int init_module(void)
{
  pthread_attr_t attr;
  struct sched_param sched_param;
  int thread_status;

  rt_com_setup(0, 9600, RT_COM_PARITY_NONE, 1, 8);

  pthread_attr_init (&attr);
  pthread_attr_setcpu_np(&attr, 0);
  sched_param.sched_priority = 1;
  pthread_attr_setschedparam (&attr, &sched_param);
  thread_status = pthread_create(&thread, &attr, play, (void *)1);
  if (thread_status != 0) {
    printk("failed to create RT-thread\n");
    return -1;
  } else {
    printk("created RT-thread\n");
  }
  return 0;
}

void cleanup_module(void)
{
```

```
   pthread_delete_np  (thread);
   rt_com_setup(0,  -1,  0,  0,  0);
}
```

Note the important function calls used in this program. pthread_make_periodic_np call is to make the real-time thread execute periodically. This function utilizes a structure called itimerspec. Its parameters are: it_interval and it_value, which specify the timer period and its expiry, respectively. The it_value parameter also specifies the time of its first invocation which will be passed to the structure itimerspec.

The function rt_com_write attempts to write one character, i.e. '2' for play from buffer pointer to real-time serial port.

The function rt_com_setup dynamically sets the parameters of the serial port: baud rate, parity type, stop bits and word length. Then we initialize the thread with its attribute object. Next we will take the default CPU cycles for the thread by sending 0 to the pthread_attr_setcpu_np(). Next, we will take the scheduling priority for the thread as 1 and set the schedule with pthread_attr_setschedparam(). Finally, we create the thread with all the selected parameters using the function call pthread_create. The status will be known from thread_status.

The cleanup_module function cancels the thread process on the pthread join and frees the CPU cycles.

Listing 12.5 gives the source code for stop.c

Listing 12.5: stop.c

```
#include  <rtl.h>
#include  <rtl_fifo.h>
#include  <time.h>
#include  <pthread.h>
#include  <asm/io.h>
#include  "rt_com.h"

int  period=100000000;
int  fifo_size=4000;
pthread_t  thread;
int  fd_fifo;
char  a[210]={};

void  *stop(void  *t)  {
   pthread_make_periodic_np  (thread,  gethrtime(),  period);
   a[0]='3';  //  send  signal  '3'  to  stop
   rt_com_write(0,  a,  1);
   return  0;
}

int  init_module(void)
```

```
{
  pthread_attr_t  attr;
  struct  sched_param  sched_param;
  int  thread_status;
  rt_com_setup(0,  9600,  RT_COM_PARITY_NONE,  1,  8);
  pthread_attr_init  (&attr);
  pthread_attr_setcpu_np(&attr,  0);
  sched_param.sched_priority  =  1;
  pthread_attr_setschedparam  (&attr,  &sched_param);
  thread_status  =  pthread_create(&thread,  &attr,  stop,  (void  *)1);
  if  (thread_status  !=  0)  {
     printk("failed  to  create  RT-thread\n");
     return  -1;
  }  else  {
     printk("created  RT-thread\n");
  }

  return  0;
}

void  cleanup_module(void)
{
  pthread_delete_np  (thread);
  rt_com_setup(0,  -1,  0,  0,  0);
}
```

The code in this file is almost same as that of play.c. Notice one important difference: while sending the command through the serial port, the function rt_com_write attempts to write one character, i.e. '3' from buffer pointer to serial port, for issuing the stop command.

Listing 12.6 gives the source code for pause.c

Listing 12.6: pause.c

```
#include  <rtl.h>
#include  <rtl_fifo.h>
#include  <time.h>
#include  <pthread.h>
#include  <asm/io.h>
#include  "rt_com.h"

int  period=100000000;
```

```
int fifo_size=4000;
pthread_t thread;
int fd_fifo;

char a[10]={};
void *pause(void *t) {
   pthread_make_periodic_np (thread, gethrtime(), period);
   a[0]='4'; // send signal '4' to pause
   rt_com_write(0, a, 1); // send 1 byte of array a through base port
0
   return 0;
}

int init_module(void)
{
   pthread_attr_t attr;
   struct sched_param sched_param;
   int thread_status;
   rt_com_setup(0, 9600, RT_COM_PARITY_NONE, 1, 8);
   pthread_attr_init (&attr);
   pthread_attr_setcpu_np(&attr, 0);
   sched_param.sched_priority = 1;
   pthread_attr_setschedparam (&attr, &sched_param);
   thread_status = pthread_create(&thread, &attr, pause, (void *)1);
   if (thread_status != 0) {
      printk("failed to create RT-thread\n");
      return -1;
   } else {
      printk("created RT-thread\n");
   }
   return 0;
}


void cleanup_module(void)
{
   pthread_delete_np (thread);
   rt_com_setup(0, -1, 0, 0, 0);
}
```

The code in this file is self-explanatory. However, note the important change: the function rt_com_write writes one character, i.e. '4' from buffer pointer to the serial port for issuing the 'pause' command.

On the Windows machine, we need to simulate an Audio player. The MviplayerDlg.cpp contains the source code for this project. The methods used for audio player simulation are given in the Listing 12.7. The complete project files for VC++ are given in the CDROM.

Listing 12.7: Mviplayer.cpp methods

OnBrowse method:

```
void CMviplayerDlg::OnBrowse()
{
   CFileDialog dlg(TRUE, NULL, NULL, OFN_HIDEREADONLY,
         _T("Wave files (*.wav)|*.wav|All Files (*.*)|*.*||"),
                 NULL);
   CString name;
   if(dlg.DoModal()==IDOK)
   {
      name=dlg.GetPathName();
      m_fname.SetWindowText(name);
      m_wavplay.SetFileName(name);
      m_MThread=AfxBeginThread(MonThread,this);
   }
}
```

MonThread method:

```
UINT MonThread(LPVOID lParam)
{
   CMviplayerDlg *dlg=(CMviplayerDlg*)lParam;
   char data[1];
   int value;
   while(1)
   {
      prt.ReadData(data,1); //read data from serial port
      if(data[0]=='2'||data[0]=='3'||data[0]=='4')
      {
         value=(int)data[0];
         switch(value)
         {
         case 50:   //ASCII value of 2 is 50
            {
               (dlg->m_wavplay).Play();
```

```
            }
            break;
        case 51:    //ASCII  value  of  3  is  51
            {
                (dlg->m_wavplay).Stop();
                (dlg->m_wavplay).SetCurrentPosition(0);
            }
            break;
        case 52:    //ASCII  value  of  4  is  52
            {
                (dlg->m_wavplay).Pause();
            }
            break;

        }
    }
  }
  return  0;
}
```

OnClose method:

```
void  CMviplayerDlg::OnClose()
{
  if(m_MThread!=NULL)  //if  the  thread  is  running  terminate  it
     TerminateThread(m_MThread->m_hThread,m_MThread->m_nThreadID);
  CDialog::OnClose();
}
```

Browse method: You can browse a .WAV file and on clicking OK button in the open dialog box, this method will set the filename to the edit box in the dialog. The .WAV file is set to the Windows Media Player and a thread for MonThread method is created.

MonThread method: This method keeps on monitoring the serial port of the Windows system. It will accept the signals given by the RTLinux system and respond accordingly.

OnClose method: This method is for terminating the thread (if it is running) and close the dialog.

12.6.1 Executing the Program

You need to execute the programs on the Windows machine as well as the RTLinux machine using the procedure given below.

To compile RTLinux Programs

Compile the RTLinux programs using the following commands:

$make –f rtl.mk rt_com.o

$make –f rtl.mk play.o

$make –f rtl.mk stop.o

$make –f rtl.mk repeat.o

Execution steps on RTLinux machine

For establishing the serial connection, use the following command:

$setserial /dev/ttyS0 uart none

Then the connection gets established.

To execute the project, give the following commands, based on the functionality you require. For example, to start the audio player, you have to give the command with the argument start.

$rtlinux start rt_com play

$rtlinux stop rt_com play

$rtlinux start rt_com pause

$rtlinux stop rt_com pause

$rtlinux start rt_com stop

$rtlinux stop rt_com stop

Execution Steps on Windows Machine

Source code for the player software project is given in the folder "Chapter 12" of the CDROM. Some of the important project files are as follows:

mediaplayer2.h

mediaplayer2.cpp

mediaplayerdvd.h

mediaplayerdvd.cpp

mviplayer.h

mviplayer.cpp

mviplayerDlg.h

mviplayerDlg.cpp

SerialComm.h

SerialComm.cpp

mviplayer.dsw

In the above list, the first four files are created automatically when the user adds the "Windows Media Player" component to the project. The last file is the project workspace file.

Output

When you execute the program on the Windows machine, the screen shown in Fig. 12.1 will appear. Depending on whether you are using COM1 or COM2, you need to make the necessary changes in the program. In the CDROM, two executable files are given for COM1 and COM2 ports.

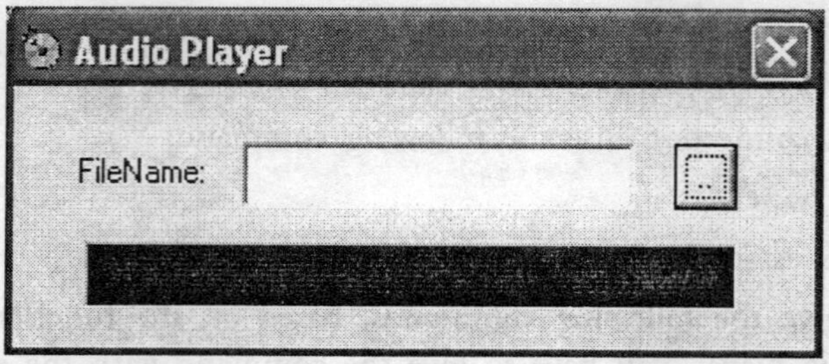

Fig: 12.1: Output screen for Audio Player Control Application

Now you can browse a .WAV file using the Browse button ('..'). The screenshot is shown in Fig. 12.2.

Fig: 12.2: Audio Player after Browsing a File

Now you can issue the commands from the RTLinux to Play, Stop or Pause as per the syntax given above in the section "Execution steps on RTLinux".

When you issue the Play command from the RTLinux system, the screen shown in Fig. 12.3 will be displayed.

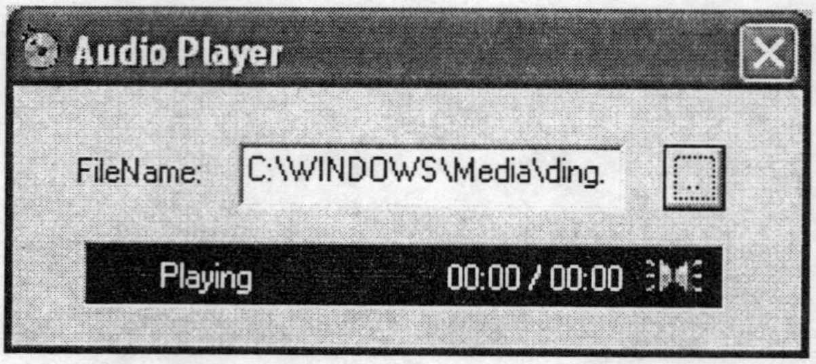

Fig: 12.3: Audio Player after Play Command is Received from the RTLinux System

When you issue the pause command from the RTLinux system, the screen shown in Fig. 12.4 will be displayed.

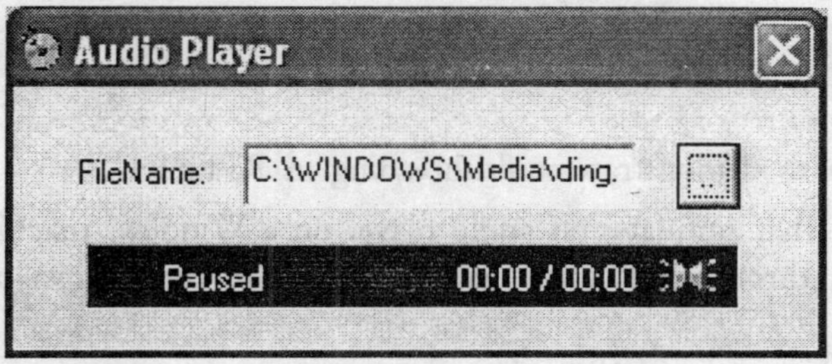

Fig: 12.4: Audio Player after Pause Command is Received from the RTLinux System

When you issue the stop command from the RTLinux system, the screen shown in Fig. 12.5 will be displayed.

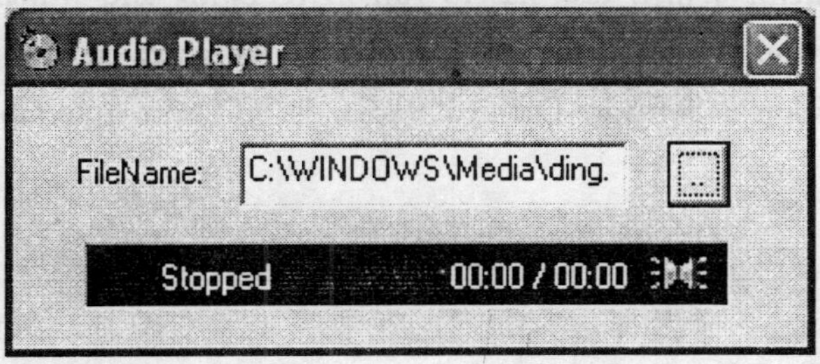

Fig: 12.5: Audio Player after Stop Command is Received from the RTLinux System

Summary

This chapter demonstrated software development in RTLinux environment. We can develop hard real-time applications using this operating system. We have also demonstrated how an embedded system can communicate to a host system using a serial communication link for applications such as process control, controlling consumer appliances etc. Since RTLinux is POSIX compliant, you can write applications in any other POSIX compliant real-time operating system easily based on the knowledge gained in this chapter.

Questions

1. What is an RTLinux module?
2. Explain the use of semaphore with an example.
3. Explain the use of mutex with an example.
4. What are the function calls provided for timer management in RTLinux?

5. List the function calls provided in RTLinux for mutex and semaphore management.
6. Study how to achieve communication between a process running in Linux and a process running in RTLinux.

Exercises

1. Write a program to demonstrate multithreading in RTLinux.
2. Write a program that simulates an audio player on a Windows machine. This audio player has to be controlled through RTLinux machine with the commands: play, pause, stop and fast forward.
3. Write a program that demonstrates the communication between two processes. One process is running as a Linux process and the other as an RTLinux process.
4. In an embedded system used for process control, the real-time data has to be collected through an RS232 port and the spectrum has to be displayed on the monitor. What are the different tasks for this system. Which task has to run in RTLinux and which task in Linux.
5. You need to develop an IP Phone. Study whether RTLinux can be used as the platform.
6. You need to develop a Software-Defined Radio. Is RTLinux a suitable choice? If not, explain why.

Chapter 13

Development of Navigation System

CHAPTER OBJECTIVES

After reading this chapter, you will be able to:

- Understand the format in which a GPS receiver sends location information
- Simulate a GPS receiver on a Linux system
- Develop a navigation system that displays the location on a map

To know where you are, is very important. You will realize the importance of this information when you are lost in an unknown city or when you are hitch-hiking or when you are driving long distance. Navigation systems come in handy in such cases. In this chapter, we will study the development of a navigation system.

13.1 Project Overview

A navigation system consists of a GPS receiver interfaced to an embedded system. The GPS receiver calculates the location information (longitude, latitude and altitude) and sends it over a serial communication link to the embedded system. On the LCD screen of the embedded system, the map of the area you are travelling is shown; and on this map, the place where you are will be highlighted. If you have a GPS receiver, you can directly interface it to the embedded system. Otherwise, you can write a GPS receiver simulator software that generates the location information and also updates it every one second to simulate movement of a vehicle.

13.2 Development Environment

You need the following tools to develop the navigation system:

- A GPS receiver such as the Conexant's GPS receiver (www.conexant.com). This receiver has an RS232 port through which the location information is given out. You need to read this serial data and then decode the values of longitude, latitude, altitude and also the time in GMT.

- If you do not have access to a GPS receiver, no problem. A simulator software source code is given in this chapter that simulates the GPS receiver. This software runs on a Linux system. The simulator changes the location parameters every one second and transmits the data on the serial port to another desktop computer.
- A desktop computer running Windows operating system receives the GPS simulator data from the Linux machine and shows the location on a digitized map.
- You need a digitized map on which you can show the position.
- You need a null modem cable to interconnect the Linux machine and the Windows machine.

13.3 GPS Receiver Packet Format

The GPS receiver sends the location information through the serial port in the form of a packet. As you can see from this format, the GPS receiver sends lot of information in addition to the longitude, latitude, altitude and time. These parameters include the longitude and latitude directions, the number of satellites visible at that location, quality of the received signal etc. However, for this project, we are mainly interested in the longitude and latitude parameters. The packet format is as follows:

$GPGGA, 222435, 3339,7334,N,11751,7598, W,2,06,1.33,27,0,M,-34.4,M,7,0000*41

The various fields in this packet are explained in Table 13.1.

Field	Field type	Example
Start of the packet		$GPGGA
Time	hhmmss	222435
Latitude	xxxx.xxxx	3333.7334
Latitude direction	A	N
Longitude	yyyyy.yy	11751.7598
Longitude direction	A	W
GPS Quality indicator	X	2
Number of satellites in use	xx	06
Horizontal dilution of precision	x.x	1.33
Altitude	x.x	27.0
Units of altitude	M	M
Geodetic separation	x.x	-34.4
Units of geodetic separation	M	M
Age of differential GPS data	x.x	7
Differential reference station ID	xxxx	0000
Checksum	*hh	*41

Table 13.1: GPS Receiver Packet Format

The information obtained from the GPS receiver's serial port is decoded using this format. If you do not have a GPS receiver, the program given in Listing 13.1 simulates the GPS receiver by generating a packet exactly in the above format. To simulate a moving vehicle, the longitude and latitude fields are changed every second and sent over the RS232 link.

13.4 Implementation

The CDROM that accompanies this book has the complete source code and the project files for this project. In "Chapter 13" folder of the CDROM, you find the following:

- GPSSimulator.c which gives the source code that runs on the Linux system. This program is to simulate the GPS receiver.
- "GPS" folder which contains the project files for the VC++ project that runs on the Windows machine. The readme file in this folder gives the complete details of the files in this folder. This folder also contains a digitized map (BITMAP3.bmp). GPS.exe is the executable file. You can run this program directly; COM2 port should be connected to the Linux system for this program to work.

Listing 13.1 gives the source code of the program GPSSimulator.c for simulating a GPS receiver.

Listing 13.1: GPSSimulator.c

```
#include <stdio.h>
#include <string.h>
#include <unistd.h>
#include <fcntl.h>
#include <errno.h>
#include <termios.h>
#include <time.h>

int open_port(void)
{
int fd;
fd = open("/dev/ttyS0",O_RDWR | O_NOCTTY | O_NDELAY);
if(fd == -1)
{
perror("Unable to open the port /dev/ttyS0");
}
else
{
```

```
fcntl(fd,F_SETFL,0);
}
return(fd);
}// end of open_port

void config_port(int fd)
{
struct termios options;

tcgetattr(fd,&options);

cfsetispeed(&options,B9600);
cfsetospeed(&options,B9600);

options.c_cflag |= (CLOCAL | CREAD);

options.c_cflag &= ~PARENB;
options.c_cflag &= ~CSTOPB;
options.c_cflag &= ~CSIZE;
options.c_cflag |= CS8;

tcsetattr(fd,TCSANOW,&options);
} // end of config_port

void write_data(int fd,char *c)
{
int n;
n = write(fd, c, strlen(c));
if(n<0)
{
fputs("write() of data failed! \n",stderr);
}
} // end of write_data
```

```
void SendSignals(int fd)
{
char array[100];
float longitude=11751.7598;
float latitude=3333.7334;
char buffer[10],h[3],m[3],s[3],buffer1[10];
struct tm *t;
time_t timer;
char h1,h2,m1,m2,s1,s2;
int hour,minute,second,hour1,hour2,min1,min2,sec1,sec2;
while(1)
{
array[0] = '$';
array[1] = 'G';
array[2] = 'P';
array[3] = 'G';
array[4] = 'G';
array[5] = 'A';
array[6] = ',';

timer=time(NULL);
t=localtime(&timer);
hour=t->tm_hour;
if(hour<10)
sprintf(h,"0%d",hour);
else
sprintf(h,"%d",hour);

minute=t->tm_min;
if(minute<10)
sprintf(m,"0%d",minute);
else
sprintf(m,"%d",minute);
```

```
second=t->tm_sec;
if(second<10)
sprintf(s,"0%d",second);
else
sprintf(s,"%d",second);

array[7] =h[0]; // Index 7 - 12 Time, hhmmss
array[8] =h[1];
array[9] =m[0];
array[10] =m[1];
array[11] =s[0];
array[12] =s[1];
array[13] = ',';
latitude=latitude+0.03;
sprintf(buffer1,"%f",latitude);
array[14] = buffer1[0]; // Index 14 - 22 Latitude, xxxx.xxxx
array[15] = buffer1[1];
array[16] = buffer1[2];
array[17] = buffer1[3];
array[18] = buffer1[4]; //
array[19] = buffer1[5]  ;
array[20] = buffer1[6];
array[21] = buffer1[7];
array[22] = buffer1[8];
array[23] = ',';
array[24] = 'N'; // Direction of Latitude
array[25] = ',';

longitude=longitude+0.03;
sprintf(buffer,"%f",longitude);
array[26] =  buffer[0];   //  Index  26  -  35  Longitude, xxxxx.xxxx
array[27] =  buffer[1];
array[28] =  buffer[2];
```

```
array[29] =  buffer[3];
array[30] =  buffer[4];
array[31] =  buffer[5];
array[32] =  buffer[6];
array[33] =  buffer[7];
array[34] =  buffer[8];
array[35] =  buffer[9];
array[36] = ‘,’;
array[37] = ‘W’;  // Direction of Longitude
array[38] = ‘,’;

array[39] = ‘2’;    // GPS quality indicator
array[40] = ‘,’;

array[41] = ‘0’;    // Number of Satellites in use
array[42] = ‘6’;
array[43] = ‘,’;

array[44] = ‘1’;  // Horizontal Dilution of Precision
array[45] = ‘.’;
array[46] = ‘3’;
array[47] = ‘3’;
array[48] = ‘,’;

array[49] = ‘2’;  // Altitude
array[50] = ‘7’;
array[51] = ‘.’;
array[52] = ‘0’;
array[53] = ‘,’;

array[54] = ‘M’;  // Units of Altitude
array[55] = ‘,’;

array[56] = ‘-’;  // Geodetic separation
```

```
array[57] = '3';
array[58] = '4';
array[59] = '.';
array[60] = '4';
array[61] = ',';

array[62] = 'M';  // Units of Geodetic separation
array[63] = ',';

array[64] = '7';  // Age of Differential GPS Data x.x
array[65] = ',';

array[66] = '0'; // Differential reference station ID xxxx

array[67] = '0';
array[68] = '0';
array[69] = '0';
array[70] = '*';
array[71] = '4';  // checksum *hh
array[72] = '1';

array[73] = '\0';

write_data(fd,array);
sleep(1);
} // end of while
} // end of SendSignals

void close_port(int fd)
{
close(fd);
} // end of close_port

int main(void)
```

```
160. {
161. int fd;
162. fd  = open_port();
163. config_port(fd);
164. SendSignals(fd);
165. close_port(fd);
166. return 0;
167. } // end of main
```

- Lines 1-7: Preprocessor directives
- Lines 8-21: open_port(void) function definition to open the serial port. /dev/ttyS0 is the serial port device file. For your Linux system, you need to use the appropriate filename as per the entry in /dev directory.
- Lines 22-34: config_port(void) function definition to configure the serial port parameters. The data rate, number of data bits, number of stop bits and parity are set here.
- Lines 35-43: write_data(int fd, char *c) function is to write data to the serial port.
- Lines 44-154: SendSignals(int fd) is the function that simulates the GPS receiver and also keeps changing the values of longitude and latitude. The simulated data is stored in an array to send it over the serial link. Note the important functionality of the following lines:
  - o Line 54: The simulator uses an infinite loop to continuously generate the data.
  - o Lines 63-85: To obtain the system time.
  - o Line 87: Latitude is changed by 0.03 to simulate movement.
  - o Line 101: Longitude is changed by 0.03 to simulate the movement.
  - o Line 151: Call to write_data (fd, array) function to write the array to serial port.
  - o Line 152: Sleep for one second
- Lines 155-158: close_port(int fd) call to close the serial port.
- Lines 159-167: main(void) function to open the port, configure the port parameters, call the SendSignals function and then close the port.

You can compile the program using the following command (Note that $ symbol is the system prompt):

```
$gcc -o GPSSimulator GPSSimulator.c
```

You can execute the program using the command:

```
$./GPSSimulator
```

On the Windows machine, you need to develop the navigation software that obtains the GPS data and shows the location on a digitized map. The file GPSDlg.cpp contains the following method that reads the data from the serial port and decodes the location parameters. The source code of this method is given in Listing 13.2.

Listing 13.2 Receiver method of GPSDlg.cpp

```
UINT Receiver(LPVOID lParam)
{
CGPSDlg* Dlg=(CGPSDlg*)lParam;
CString temp;
CPoint point;
CRect rect1;
CWindowDC dc1(Dlg->GetDlgItem(IDC_PLOTTER));
LOGBRUSH logBrush;
float ilat,ilon;
int incr=1;
float x=0.0,y=40.0;
unsigned char ch[1], Latitude[12], Longitude[13], Altitude[11],
str[60];
unsigned int i;
(Dlg->m_plotter).SetBitmap(::LoadBitmap(AfxGetInstanceHandle(),
MAKEINTRESOURCE(IDB_BITMAP3)));

logBrush.lbStyle =BS_SOLID;
logBrush.lbColor=RGB(255,0,0);

CPen pen(PS_GEOMETRIC | PS_JOIN_ROUND,1, &logBrush);
dc1.SelectObject(&pen);

(Dlg->m_plotter).GetClientRect(rect1);
dc1.MoveTo(x,y);

/* open the serial port 2 with settings of baudrate as 9600,
parity as None(n),databits as 8 and stopbits as 1;*/
if(!prt.Open(2,9600,'n',8,1))
AfxMessageBox("Unable To Open The Port");

while(1)
{
```

```
if(prt.ReadData(ch,1) > 0)
{
if((ch[0] == 'g') || (ch[0] == 'G'))
{

prt.ReadData(ch,1);
if((ch[0] == 'p') || (ch[0] == 'P'))
{
prt.ReadData(ch,1);
if((ch[0] == 'g') || (ch[0] == 'G'))
{
prt.ReadData(ch,1);
if((ch[0] == 'g') || (ch[0] == 'G'))
{
prt.ReadData(ch,1);

if((ch[0] == 'a') || (ch[0] == 'A'))
{
prt.ReadData(ch,1); //',' 
if(ch[0] != ',')
continue;
prt.ReadData(ch,1); //first char of time of
if(ch[0] == ',')
continue;
prt.ReadData(str,55); //remaining char of time
str[55] = '\0';

Latitude[0] = str[6];//latitude
Latitude[1] = str[7];
Latitude[2] = str[8];
Latitude[3] = str[9];
Latitude[4] = str[10];
Latitude[5] = str[11];
Latitude[6] = str[12];
```

```
Latitude[7] = str[13];
Latitude[8] = str[14];
Latitude[9] = ‘ ’;
Latitude[10] = str[16];//direction of latitude
Latitude[11] = ‘\0’;

Longitude[0] = str[18];//longitude
Longitude[1] = str[19];
Longitude[2] = str[20];
Longitude[3] = str[21];
Longitude[4] = str[22];
Longitude[5] = str[23];
Longitude[6] = str[24];
Longitude[7] = str[25];
Longitude[8] = str[26];
Longitude[9] = str[27];

Longitude[10] = ‘ ’;
Longitude[11] = str[29];//direction of longitude
Longitude[12] = ‘\0’;

for(i=0;i<10;i++)
{
Altitude[i] = str[41+i];//altitude
if(str[41+i] == ‘M’)
{
Altitude[41+i-1] = ‘ ’;
Altitude[41+i+1] = ‘\0’;
break;
}
}

Latitude[9] = ‘\0’;
Longitude[10] = ‘\0’;
```

```
86. temp.Format("%s",Latitude);
87. ilat = atof(temp);

88. temp.Format("%s",Longitude);
89. ilon = atof(temp);
90. x=(int)(incr+(ilon-11751.7598));
91. y=(int)( incr+(ilat-3333.7334));

92. _sleep(1100);
93. point.x=x;
94. point.y=y;
95. dc1.MoveTo(x,y);
96. dc1.Rectangle(x,y,x+4,y+4);
97. incr++;
98. continue;

99. }//end of if condition for 'a'
100. }//end of if condition for 'g'
101. }//end of if condition for 'g'
102. }//end of if condition for 'p'
103. }//end of if condition for 'g'
104. }//end of if condition (if any character in the port)
105. }//end of while loop

106. }
```

- Line 14: Loads the digitized map (BITMAP3.bmp)
- Line 21: Opens the COM2 serial port with bit rate 9600 bps, parity none, data bits 8 and 1 stop bit. If you are using a different COM port, you need to change this line appropriately.
- Line 23: The receiver uses an infinite loop to accept the data every second.
- Lines 24-38: Read the data from the serial port byte by byte and check for the start of packet.
- Lines 49-60: Assigning the values of latitude and latitude direction to the latitude array.
- Lines 61-73: Assigning the values of longitude and the longitude direction to the longitude array.

- Line 87: Converting the latitude value from string to floating point number.
- Line 89: Converting the longitude value from string to floating point number.
- Line 90: Longitude is on X-axis and origin is 11751.7598.
- Line 91: Latitude is on Y-axis and origin is 3333.7334.
- Line 92: Sleep for 1.1 second. Note that the Linux machine sends the data every one second and we need to read that data and then process it.
- Line 93-97: Plot the current location on the map.
- Line 97: Scaling the increment. The variations in longitude and latitude are very small, and hence we scale it up for one pixel.

You need to invoke this method using the following code in GPSDlg.cpp:

```
CwinThread *m_RThread;
m_RThread=AfxBeginThread(Receiver,this);
```

13.5 Executing the Program

When you execute the GPS simulator on the Linux machine and the navigation software on the Windows machine, you can see the screen shot shown in Fig. 13.1. On the top left corner, a thick line can be seen which shows the movement of the vehicle.

If you have a GPS receiver, you can interface it to a laptop and run the navigation software on the laptop. Alternatively, you can port the navigation software on to an Embedded NT or Windows XP embedded system without any changes in the source code presented here. However, you need to obtain an accurate digitized map for your city/town. For most of the cities, accurate maps are not available. You can create a digitized map your city yourself by carrying a laptop fitted with a GPS receiver. Take a city bus, and at each bus stop, note down the longitude and latitude. Then map these values on to the actual map—and you have the map for navigation. Well, you can also sell this map to many organizations and make some money!

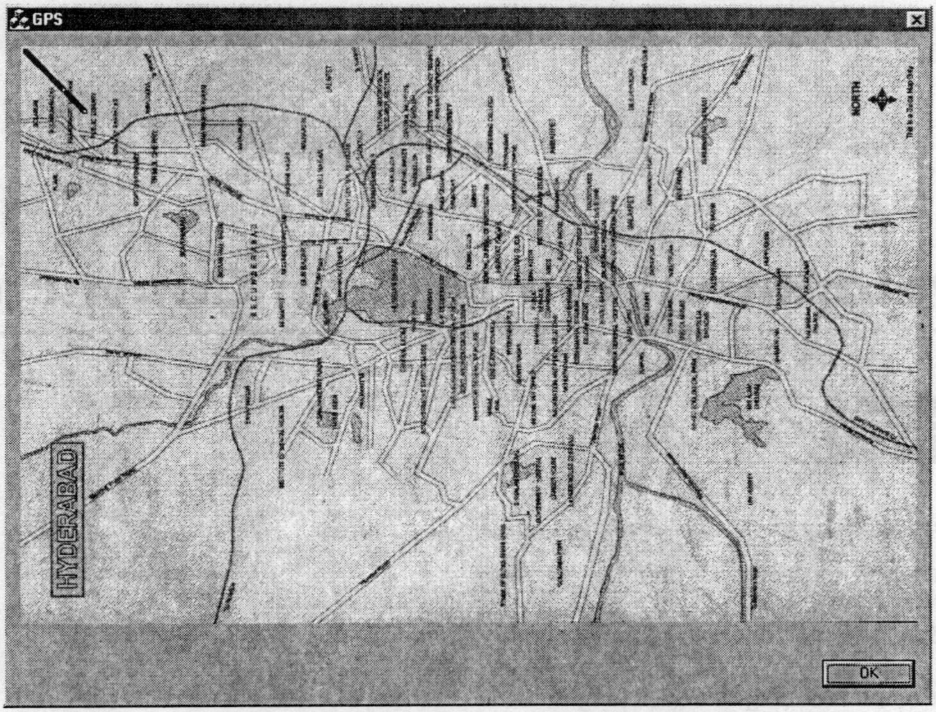

Fig. 13.1: Display of Location on the Digitized Map

Summary

This chapter presented the implementation details of a navigation system using a GPS receiver. The GPS receiver sends location information that contains longitude and latitude through an RS232 port. This data is sent in the form of a packet with predefined format for each field. The navigation software has to decode the packet and obtain the longitude and latitude, and then indicate the position on a digitized map. The software that simulates a GPS receiver is given here. This software generates the packet as per the format of the GPS receiver and keeps changing the longitude and latitude values every second to simulate a moving vehicle. A Windows machine receives the information through its RS232 port and displays the location on the map. The implementation details of the mapping software are also given. The software written on the Windows machine can be ported on to embedded NT or Windows XP embedded platform to create an embedded navigation system.

Chapter 14

Development of Protocol Converter

CHAPTER OBJECTIVES

After reading this chapter, you will be able to:

- Learn how to develop a protocol converter
- Understand the concepts of network programming
- Gain understanding of developing software to test your embedded software

In many data communication applications, a need arises to do conversion of protocols from one format to another. In this chapter, we will demonstrate how to develop the software to do protocol conversion from Ethernet format to RS232 serial format. Important aspects of network programming are also demonstrated using this case study.

14.1 Project Overview

In this project, we will develop software that takes Ethernet packets and converts them into serial packets for sending over an RS232 link. Fig. 14.1 shows the setup. PC1 and PC2 are connected over a Local Area Network. PC2 does the protocol conversion. It takes the Ethernet packets sent by PC1 and converts them into serial packets. These serial packets are sent over RS232 link to PC3. Though the software is developed on a desktop computer, it is written in such a way that you can port it on an embedded system. To demonstrate the intricacies of network programming using different programming languages, we will use a mix of C and Java. On PC1, a Java program will be running which transmits a file over Ethernet link to PC2. PC2 runs a C program that captures the Ethernet packets and converts them into serial format. PC3 is just to check whether your software is running correctly or not. It runs a C program that assembles the packets of the file transmitted by PC1. If the file transmitted by PC1 is same as the file received by PC3, then you can be assured that your protocol converter is doing a good job.

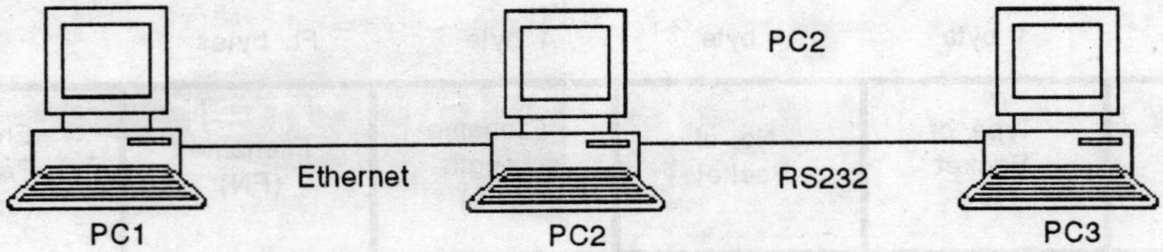

Fig. 14.1: Setup to Test the Protocol Converter Software

14.2 Design

To test the protocol converter, we need to develop a small file transfer program. On PC1, the file transfer program takes the filename as input. First it sends a packet which contains the filename. Then it sends a series of data packets which contain the contents of the file. There will be two types of packets: "Filename packet" (F packet) that sends the name of the file to be transmitted; and "Data packets" (D packets) that contain the actual contents of the file. F packets and D packets are inserted into the Ethernet frames and sent over the Ethernet link. The formats of F and D packets are shown in Fig. 14.2(a) and Fig. 14.2(b), respectively.

1 byte	1 byte	1 byte	FL bytes
Type of Packet (F)	Number of Packets	Length of File Name (FL)	File Name

Fig. 14.2(a): "Filename Packet" for Ethernet

1 byte	1 byte	1 byte	LD bytes
Type of Packet (D)	Packet Number	Length of Data (LD)	Data

Fig. 14.2(b): "Data Packet" for Ethernet

PC2 receives the Ethernet frames and converts the data into packets for transmission over the RS232 link. Again, we need to have two types of packets "Filename Packet" (F packet) and "Data Packets" (D packets) for serial communication. Fig. 14.3(a) and 14.3(b) give the F and D packet formats for serial communication. Note that we need to have additional fields for 'start of packet' and 'end of packet' for serial communication.

	1 byte	1 byte	1 byte	FL bytes	
Start of Packet (0x02)	Type of Packet (F)	No. of Packets	Filename Length (FL)	Filename (FN)	End of Packet (0x10)

Fig. 14.3(a): "Filename Packet" for Serial Communication

	1 byte	1 byte	1 byte	LD bytes	
Start of Packet (0x02)	Type of Packet (D)	Packet Number	Length of Data (LD)	Data	End of Packet (0x10)

Fig. 14.3(b): "Data Packet" for Serial Communication

In these packet formats, we did not include CRC field to make it a simple design.

14.3 Implementation and Testing

The details of the programs that will be running on different machines are as follows:

- UDPFileTx.java will be running on PC1, which is a Windows machine
- ProtocolConverter.c will be running on PC2 which is a Linux machine
- SerialRx.c will be running on PC3 which is a Linux machine.

For testing the software, first you need to execute SerialRx.c on PC3, ProtocolConverter.c on PC2 and then execute UDPFileTx.java on PC1.

Listing 14.1 gives the source code for UDPFileTx.java. This program takes a filename as input, generates the F and D packets and sends them over the Ethernet link. Since, we are not including any CRC for error checking, and since there are no acknowledgements in the reverse direction, we are effectively using a protocol similar to the UDP protocol for file transfer.

Listing 14.1: UDPFileTx.java

```
import java.net.*;
import java.util.*;
import java.io.*;

public class UDPFileTx
{
public static DatagramSocket ds;
```

```
public static int buffer_size=100;
public static int serverport=999;
public static int clientport=666;
public static byte buffer[]=new byte[buffer_size];

public static void FileTx(String FileName) throws Exception{
byte b[] = new byte[1500];
InetAddress iaddress = InetAddress.getByName(“131.200.2.10”);
int i=0;
int FileNameLen = FileName.length();
int pos;
int c;

File f1 = new File(FileName);
long file_length= f1.length();
double pcd = (file_length / 1450.0);
double pccd = Math.ceil(pcd);
Double pcdd = new Double(pccd);
int PacketCount = pcdd.intValue(); // Packet Count

/*  Filename Packet */
b[0] = ‘F’; // Type of Packet
b[1] = (byte)PacketCount;  // Packet count
b[2] = (byte)FileNameLen; // Length of the file name
for(i=0;i<FileNameLen;i++){
b[i+3] = (byte)FileName.charAt(i);
}
b[i+3] = ‘\r’;
b[i+4] = ‘\n’;
ds.send(new DatagramPacket(b,b.length,iaddress,clientport)); // Filename packet

/*  Data Packet */
FileInputStream fis = new FileInputStream(f1);
```

```
36) b[0] = 'D';
37) b[1] = (byte)(PacketCount);
38) pos = 3;
39) while((c=fis.read())!= -1){
40) b[pos++]=(byte)c;
41) }
42) fis.close();
43) b[2] = (byte)(pos-3);
44) b[pos++] = '\r';
45) b[pos++] = '\n';
46) ds.send(new DatagramPacket(b,b.length,iaddress,clientport)); //
    Data packet sending
47) } //end of FileTx

48) public static void main(String args[]){
49) try{
50)     if(args.length==1){
51)         System.out.println("Tx starts...... ");
52)         ds=new DatagramSocket(serverport);
53)          FileTx(args[0]);
54)         System.out.println("Tx ends");
55)     }
56)     else
57)       System.out.println("Usagae: java UDPFileTx test.txt\n");
58)     }catch(Exception e){ }
59) } // end of main
60) } //end of class, UDPFileTx
```

This program takes the file name as an argument. It generates the F and D packets for the file to be transmitted and then transmits them over the Ethernet LAN. Note that in Line 13, the destination machine IP address is to be given. The address (131.200.2.10) corresponds to the Linux machine's IP address. You need to change the address appropriately based on the configuration of your Linux machine.

This file can be compiled using the following command:

```
javac UDPFileTx.java
```

Execute the file using the following command. Note that test.txt is a text file which has to be transmitted to PC3.

```
java UDPFileTx test.txt
```

The source code for ProtocolConverter.c is given in Listing 14.2. This program captures the Ethernet packets, decodes the filename and file's contents, puts them into serial communication packets as per the format discussed above, and then sends these packets over the serial link.

Listing 14.2: ProtocolConverter.c

```
#include <stdio.h>
#include <string.h>
#include <fcntl.h>
#include <termios.h>
#include <sys/socket.h>
#include <net/ethernet.h>

#define MAXLINE 1024

char c[MAXLINE + 1],Data[MAXLINE*10],FileName[256];

int port_open(void)
{
int fd;
/* Open com port 1 (COM1) */
fd = open(“/dev/ttyS0”,O_RDWR | O_NOCTTY | O_NDELAY);
if(fd == -1)
{
perror(“Unable to open the port: /dev/ttyS0”);
}
else
{
fcntl(fd,F_SETFL,0);
}
return(fd);
} // end of port_open
```

```
void port_config(int fd)
{
struct termios settings;

/* Get the present port settings */
tcgetattr(fd,&settings);

/* Set the baud rates to 9600 */
cfsetispeed(&settings,B9600);
cfsetospeed(&settings,B9600);

/* Set local mode and enable the receiver */
settings.c_cflag |= (CLOCAL | CREAD);

/* Configure the port settings as No parity(8N1) */
settings.c_cflag &= ~PARENB; // Parity bit
settings.c_cflag &= ~CSTOPB; // Stop bit
settings.c_cflag &= ~CSIZE;  // Bit mask for data bits
settings.c_cflag |= CS8;           // 8 data bits

/* Set the above values to the port */
tcsetattr(fd,TCSANOW,&settings);
} //end of port_config

void write_data(int fd,char *c,int DataLength)
{
int n,i;
n = write(fd, c, DataLength);
if(n<0)
{
fputs("write() of data failed! \n",stderr);
}
}//end of write_data
```

```
void port_close(int fd)
{
close(fd);
}//end of port_close

void read_ethernet_data()
{
int sockfd, n, i, j, k;
int PacketCount;
int FileNameLength;
int PacketNumber;
int LOD1,LengthOfData;
char recvline[MAXLINE +1];

/* To receive packets from datalink layer, we create socket of type
    SOCK_PACKET. To do this, we must have super user privileges.
    The third argument specifying a protocol of ETH_P_ALL tells the
    data link layer which frame types to pass onto the socket */
if((sockfd = socket(AF_INET, SOCK_PACKET, htons(ETH_P_ALL))) <
0)
printf("Socket error\n");

/*
The following read statement returns frames for all protocols that
    the datalink layer receives. The result is in recvline array.

*/
while((n = read(sockfd, recvline, MAXLINE)) >0)
{
j = 0;
for(i=0;i < n;i++){
if(i > 41) //User data of the frame starts at 42 byte.
{
c[j] = recvline[i];
j++;
```

```
}
}
if(c[0] == 'F')  // Filename packet
{
PacketCount = c[1];
FileNameLength = c[2];
for(i=0;i < FileNameLength; i++){
FileName[i] = c[i+3];
}
FileName[i] = '\0';
k = 0;
} // end of Filename packet
if(c[0] == 'D') //Data packet
{
PacketNumber = c[1];
LOD1 = c[2];
LengthOfData = LOD1;
for(i=0;i < LengthOfData; i++){
Data[k] = c[i+3];
k++;
}
} //end of Data packet
if(PacketCount == PacketNumber)
break;
}
if(n < 0)
printf("Read error\n");
printf("FileName: %s \n",FileName);
printf("Data: ");
for(i=0;i<k;i++)
printf("%c",Data[i]);
printf("\n");
} //end of read_ethernet_data
```

```
void convert_data_send(char *EthernetData,char Packet,int fd)
{
int i;
char SerialComData[256];
int EthernetDataLength,Length;
int PacketCount,PacketNumber;
EthernetDataLength = strlen(EthernetData);
PacketCount = 1;
if(Packet == ‘F’)    //Filename packet
{
SerialComData[0] = 0x02;
SerialComData[1] = ‘F’;
SerialComData[2] = PacketCount;
SerialComData[3] = EthernetDataLength;
for(i=0;i < EthernetDataLength; i++)
SerialComData[i+4] = EthernetData[i];
SerialComData[i+4] = 0x10;
SerialComData[i+5] = 0x0d;
SerialComData[i+6] = ‘\0’;
PacketNumber = 0;
write_data(fd,SerialComData,EthernetDataLength+6);
} //End of Filename packet
if(Packet == ‘D’)   //Data packet
{
while(EthernetDataLength > 0)
{
SerialComData[0] = 0x02;
SerialComData[1] = ‘D’;
SerialComData[2] = PacketNumber+1;
SerialComData[3] = EthernetDataLength/256;
SerialComData[4] = EthernetDataLength%256;
if(EthernetDataLength > 1024)
Length = 1024;
else
```

```
134) Length = EthernetDataLength;

135) for(i=0;i < Length; i++){
136) SerialComData[i+5] = EthernetData[i];
137) }
138) SerialComData[i+5] = 0x10;
139) SerialComData[i+6] = 0x0d;
140) SerialComData[i+7] = '\0';

141) write_data(fd,SerialComData,Length+7);
142) EthernetDataLength -= Length;
143) PacketNumber++;
144) }  // end of while
145) }  // end of Data packet
146) }  // end of convert_data_send

147) int main(void)
148) {
149) int fd;
150) read_ethernet_data();
151) fd  = port_open();
152) port_config(fd);
153) convert_data_send(FileName,'F',fd);
154) convert_data_send(Data,'D',fd);
155) port_close(fd);
156) return 0;
157) } // end of main
```

- Lines 1-8: Preprocessor directives and declarations.
- Lines 9-22: port_open(void) function definition, to open the serial port. You may need to use the appropriate serial port device file based on the entry in /dev directory.
- Lines 23-35: port_config(int fd) function definition, to configure the serial port parameters.
- Lines 36-44: write_data(int fd, char *c, int DataLength) function definition, to write data to the serial port.

- Lines 45-48: port_close(fd) function definition to close the serial port.
- Lines 49-99: read_Ethernet_data() function definition to read the Ethernet frames. Note that in the Ethernet frame, the actual user data starts at 42nd byte. The earlier bytes contain Ethernet header.
- Lines 100-146: convert_data_send(char *c, EthernetData, char Packet, int fd) function definition to convert the Ethernet packets into serial packets and to send them to the serial port.
- Lines 147-157: main(void) function which calls the above functions to read the Ethernet data, open the serial port, configure the serial port parameters, convert the Ethernet data to serial packets and transmit to the serial port.

You can compile this program using the command:

```
$gcc -o ProtocolConverter ProtocolConverter.c
```

Execute the program using the command:

```
$./ProtocolConverter
```

Listing 14.3 gives the source code for SerialRx.c. This program is to receive the serial communication data and assemble the file.

Listing 14.3: SerialRx.c

```
1)  #include <stdio.h>
2)  #include <string.h>
3)  #include <unistd.h>
4)  #include <fcntl.h>
5)  #include <errno.h>
6)  #include <termios.h>

7)  int port_open(void)
8)  {
9)  int fd;
/* Open com port 1 (COM1) */
10) fd = open("/dev/ttyS0",O_RDWR | O_NOCTTY | O_NDELAY);
11) if(fd == -1)
12) {
13) perror("Unable to open the port: /dev/ttys0");
14) }
15) else
16) {
17) fcntl(fd,F_SETFL,0);
```

```
}
return(fd);
} // end of port_open

void port_config(int fd)
{
struct termios settings;

/* Get the present port settings */
tcgetattr(fd,&settings);

/* Set the baud rates to 9600 */
cfsetispeed(&settings,B9600);
cfsetospeed(&settings,B9600);

/* Set local mode and enable the receiver */
settings.c_cflag |= (CLOCAL | CREAD);

/* Configure the port as No parity(8N1) */
settings.c_cflag &= ~PARENB; // Parity bit
settings.c_cflag &= ~CSTOPB; // Stop bit
settings.c_cflag &= ~CSIZE;  // Bit mask for data bits
settings.c_cflag |= CS8;     // 8 data bits

/* Set the above values to the port */
tcsetattr(fd,TCSANOW,&settings);
} // end of port_config

char* read_data(int fd)
{
char array[256];
char *ptr;
int nbytes,i;
ptr = array;
```

```
while((nbytes = read(fd, ptr, array + sizeof(array) - ptr -1))
> 0)
{
ptr += nbytes;
if((ptr[-1] == '\n') || (ptr[-2] == 0x10))
break;
}
*ptr = '\0';
return (&array[0]);
} // end of read_data

void receive_packets(int fd)
{
char *str;
int i,j,k;
char FileName[256];
char Data[10240];
int PacketCount=1,PacketNumber,LengthOfData;
int FileNameLength;
FILE *fp;
char ch;

str = read_data(fd);
if(str[1] == 'F') // Filename packet
{
PacketCount = str[2] - 48; // Packet Count
FileNameLength = str[3] - 48; // Length of the file name
for(i=0;i<FileNameLength;i++)
FileName[i] = str[i+4];
FileName[i] = '\0';
k = 0;
printf("File Name: %s\n",FileName);
}
for(i=0;i<PacketCount;i++)
```

```
{
str = read_data(fd);
if(str[1] == ‘D’) // Data packet
{
PacketNumber = str[2] - 48;
LengthOfData = str[3] - 48;
for(j=0;j < LengthOfData;j++)
{
Data[k] = str[j+4];
k++;
}
} // end of data packet
}
Data[k] = ‘\0’;
printf(“Data: %s”,Data);
fp=fopen(FileName,”w”);
if(fp==NULL)
printf(“Unable to open file\n”);
else
{
for(j=0;j<k;j++)
{
ch=Data[j];
fputc(ch,fp);
}
fclose(fp);
}
} // end of receive_packets
void port_close(int fd)
{
close(fd);
} // end of port_close
int main(void)
{
```

```
105) int fd;
106) char *a;
107) fd   = port_open();
108) port_config(fd);
109) receive_packets(fd);
110) port_close(fd);
111) return 0;
112) } // end of main
```

- Lines 1-6: Preprocessor directives.
- Lines 7-20: port_open(void) function to open the serial port.
- Lines 21-33: port_config(int fd) to configure the port parameters.
- Lines 34-48: read_data(int fd) to read the data from the serial port.
- Lines 49-98: receive_packets(int fd) to receive the packets and form the file.
- Lines 99-102: port_close(fd) to close the port.
- Lines 103-112: main(void) function that calls the above functions.

Compile the program using the following command:

```
$gcc -o SerialRx SerialRx.c
```

Execute the program using the following command:

```
$./SerialRx
```

Instead of running SerialRx on PC3, you can also use the HyperTerminal program of Windows.

On PC1, when you execute the Java file, the file is sent over the Ethernet link. PC2 catches the Ethernet frames, converts them into serial packets and transmits them to PC3. PC3 displays the files sent from PC1.

You can port the program ProtocolConverter.c onto an embedded system very easily. Such embedded protocol converters are available commercially. You can develop converters for serial to parallel, parallel to serial, RS232 to USB, USB to RS232 interfaces based on the concepts discussed in this chapter.

Summary

In this chapter, development of a protocol converter is discussed in detail. This software captures the Ethernet frames, converts them into serial format, and sends them over a serial link. How to design simple packet formats for file transfer protocol is illustrated. The implementation details of network programming to capture Ethernet frames, conversion to serial packets and assembling the file are given. The details presented in this chapter reveal the intricacies of network programming. And, it is lot of fun! Also, note that just to test your protocol converter software, you need to develop a good amount of testing software. While developing embedded systems, you need to do lot of software development only for testing purposes.

Chapter 15

Embedded Database Application

CHAPTER OBJECTIVES

After reading this chapter, you will be able to:

- Understand Microsoft's eMbedded visual tools development environment
- Learn how to create an embedded database application

The handheld computer is now becoming a very useful gadget for many automation activities. Software developers who worked on client/server applications using Microsoft's Visual Studio can write powerful applications for handheld computers using eMbedded visual tools. In this chapter, we will study the eMbedded visual tools development environment and how to create an embedded database application using embedded Visual Basic. It is assumed that you are familiar with Visual Basic, even otherwise, it is not difficult to understand the code presented in this chapter.

15.1 Project Overview

Handheld computers can be used by field personnel to collect field data. For instance, field personnel doing a market survey can enter the data directly on the handheld computer instead of using paper forms. The data can be later transferred to the corporate database. The challenge for developers lies in creating a user-friendly interface to facilitate easy data entry on the handheld computer.

In this project, the field personnel will carry the Pocket PC to various software development organizations to conduct a survey. This survey involves collection of the following information:

- The area of focus of the organization (type of work) which can be one of the following: (a) database (b) embedded software (c) VLSI or (d) CRM or (e) Computer Networks.
- The size of the organization: small, medium or large.
- Annual turnover of the organization in dollars.

The objective is to develop a simple GUI to the database to facilitate data entry, browsing through the database records, deleting or modifying the records.

15.2 Development Environment

Microsoft's eMbedded Visual tools can be used to develop Graphical User Interfaces for handheld computers such as the Pocket PC. To create this application, you need the following development environment:

- eMbedded Visual Tools 3.0 (www.microsoft.com/mobile/downloads/emvt3.0) installed on Windows NT/2000 system. The project described in this chapter has been developed using embedded Visual Basic.
- Pocket PC hardware. If you do not have a Pocket PC, you can use the emulator provided with eMbedded visual tools to test the software.
- Database: Pocket Access.

15.3 Design

The database used in embedded visual tools is Pocket Access. Unlike MS Access that runs on the desktop computer, the database on the handheld computer will have limitations due to memory constraints. The following guidelines have to be followed while creating the database:

- The table name should not be longer than 31 characters
- Field names should not be longer than 64 characters
- Index name should not be longer than 64 characters
- System tables cannot be copied or converted
- If the system table MySysTables does not have an entry for your table, your table cannot be converted or copied

The data in the Pocket Access can be transferred to a desktop using ActiveSync, a utility for data synchronization.

The database consists of one table the details of which are given in Table 15.1.

Field Name	Field Type	Field Size	Constraints
Serial No.	int	3	Primary Key, Indexed
AreaOfWork	varchar	30	-
TypeOfOrg	varchar	30	-
TurnOver	varchar	10	-

Table 15.1: SoftwareIndustrySurvey Table

15.4 Implementation

The following four files are required for this project. These files are available on the CDROM that accompanies this book:

- SoftwareIndustrySurvey.ebp: Visual Basic Project file
- frmSoftwareIndustrySurvey.ebf : Visual Basic form file

- frmSoftwareIndustrySurvey.frx : frx file
- SoftwareIndustrySurvey.vbw : Visual Basic work file

The source code for the Visual Basic form file is given in Listing 15.1. Note that the line numbers are not a part of the code, they are included here only for referring to the lines in the explanation of the code.

Listing 15.1 frmSoftwareIndustrySurvey.ebf

```
1. Option Explicit
     'Form Global Declarations
2. Dim RSSoftwareIndustrySurvey As ADOCE.Recordset
3. Dim RSSoftwareIndustrySurveyModify As ADOCE.Recordset
4. Dim RSSoftwareIndustrySurveySave As ADOCE.Recordset
5. Dim CNSoftwareIndustrySurvey As ADOCE.Connection
6. Dim MyQuery As String
7. Dim MyQueryModify As String
8. Dim MyButtonAction As String
9. Dim ModifySerialNo As Integer
10. Dim MyFirstBookMark As Variant
11. Dim MyLastBookMark As Variant
12. Dim MyCurrentBookMark As Variant
     'This control event is to enter data for new record.
13. Private Sub cmdADD_Click()
14.      EnableFields
15.      ClearTextFields
16.      MyButtonAction = "New"
17.      cmdClose.Caption = "&Cancel"
18.      DisablecmdButtons
19.      txtSerialNo.SetFocus
20. End Sub
     'This control event is to cancel the operation or close the
   application.
21. Private Sub cmdClose_Click()
22.     If cmdClose.Caption = "E&xit" Then
23.           Form_OKClick
24.     Else
```

```
            EnablecmdButtons
        cmdClose.Caption = "E&xit"
           MyButtonAction = ""
           ClearTextFields
            Display
           DisableFields
   End If
End Sub
     'This procedure is to create database and tables
Private Sub CreateDBandTable()
   Dim SQl As String
     Set RSSoftwareIndustrySurvey
 =CreateObject("ADOCE.Recordset.3.0")
       'create database
   RSSoftwareIndustrySurvey.Open "CREATE DATABASE '\My
     Documents\SoftwareIndustrySurvey\SoftwareIndustrySurveyDB.cdb'"
        'create SoftwareIndustrySurvey Table
    SQl = "CREATE TABLE SoftwareIndustrySurvey ("
    SQl = SQl & "SerialNo int ,"
    SQl = SQl & "AreaOfWork varchar(30) ,"
    SQl = SQl & "TypeOfOrg varchar(30) ,"
    SQl = SQl & "TurnOver varchar(10)  )"
   RSSoftwareIndustrySurvey.Open SQl, "\My
    Documents\SoftwareIndustrySurvey\SoftwareIndustrySurveyDB.cdb"
     'Create Index for SoftwareIndustrySurvey Table
RSSoftwareIndustrySurvey.Open "CREATE INDEX PrimaryKey ON
          SoftwareIndustrySurvey(SerialNo)", _
"\My Documents\SoftwareIndustrySurvey\SoftwareIndustrySurveyDB.cdb"
  RSSoftwareIndustrySurvey.Close
   Set RSSoftwareIndustrySurvey = Nothing
End Sub
     'This control event is to delete a record.
Private Sub cmdDelete_Click()
     MyQuery = "Select * FROM SoftwareIndustrySurvey where
```

```
SerialNo='" &
      txtSerialNo.Text & "'"
Set RSSoftwareIndustrySurveyModify = CreateObject
("ADOCE.Recordset.3.0")
  RSSoftwareIndustrySurveyModify.Open MyQuery,
CNSoftwareIndustrySurvey,
     adOpenKeyset, adLockOptimistic
  If RSSoftwareIndustrySurveyModify.RecordCount > 0 Then
        Dim MyVar
        MyVar = MsgBox("Do You Want to Delete ?", 65,
"SoftwareIndustrySurvey")
        If MyVar = 1 Then
             RSSoftwareIndustrySurveyModify.Delete
             RSSoftwareIndustrySurveyModify.Close
             Set RSSoftwareIndustrySurveyModify = Nothing
             MyQuery = "SELECT * FROM
SoftwareIndustrySurvey"
            Set RSSoftwareIndustrySurveyModify =
                CreateObject("ADOCE.Recordset.3.0")
            RSSoftwareIndustrySurveyModify.Open MyQuery,
CNSoftwareIndustrySurvey, adOpenKeyset, adLockOptimistic
            If RSSoftwareIndustrySurveyModify.EOF Or
                RSSoftwareIndustrySurveyModify.BOF Then
                    MsgBox ("There are no Records")
                   RSSoftwareIndustrySurveyModify.Close
                Set RSSoftwareIndustrySurveyModify = Nothing
                    ClearTextFields
              Else
                   RSSoftwareIndustrySurveyModify.Close
                Set RSSoftwareIndustrySurveyModify = Nothing
                    RefreshDB
                   RSSoftwareIndustrySurvey.MoveFirst
                    EnableFields
                    ClearTextFields
```

```
                '     Display
                    DisableFields
                End If
            Else
                MsgBox "Record not Deleted"
                RSSoftwareIndustrySurveyModify.Close
                Set RSSoftwareIndustrySurveyModify = Nothing
            End If
    Else
        MsgBox "No Record to Delete"
        RSSoftwareIndustrySurveyModify.Close
        Set RSSoftwareIndustrySurveyModify = Nothing
    End If
End Sub
    This control event is to display the first record
Private Sub cmdFirst_Click()
    cmdSave.Enabled = False
    ClearTextFields
    RSSoftwareIndustrySurvey.MoveFirst
    Display
End Sub
    ' This control event is to display the last record
Private Sub cmdLast_Click()
    cmdSave.Enabled = False
    ClearTextFields
    RSSoftwareIndustrySurvey.MoveLast
    Display
End Sub
    ' This control event is to get the record to be modi-
fied
Private Sub cmdModify_Click()
    EnableFields
    MyQuery = "SELECT * FROM SoftwareIndustrySurvey where
SerialNo='" &
```

```
        txtSerialNo.Text & "'"
    Set RSSoftwareIndustrySurveyModify = CreateObject
("ADOCE.Recordset.3.0")
    RSSoftwareIndustrySurveyModify.Open MyQuery,
CNSoftwareIndustrySurvey,
        adOpenKeyset, adLockOptimistic
    If RSSoftwareIndustrySurveyModify.RecordCount > 0 Then
ModifySerialNo =
RSSoftwareIndustrySurveyModify.Fields("SerialNo")
        DisablecmdButtons
        cmdClose.Caption = "&Cancel"
        MyButtonAction = "Modify"
        txtSerialNo.SetFocus
    Else
        MsgBox "No Records in Database!"
    End If
    RSSoftwareIndustrySurveyModify.Close
    Set RSSoftwareIndustrySurveyModify = Nothing
End Sub
    'This control event is to display the next record
Private Sub cmdNext_Click()
    cmdSave.Enabled = False
    ClearTextFields
  If RSSoftwareIndustrySurvey.Bookmark = MyLastBookMark Then
        RSSoftwareIndustrySurvey.MoveLast
        MsgBox "Last Record"
    Else
        RSSoftwareIndustrySurvey.MoveNext
    End If
  Display
End Sub
    'This control event is to display the previous record
Private Sub cmdPrevious_Click()
    cmdSave.Enabled = False
```

```
        ClearTextFields
    If RSSoftwareIndustrySurvey.Bookmark = MyFirstBookMark Then
          RSSoftwareIndustrySurvey.MoveFirst
          MsgBox "First Record"
    Else
        RSSoftwareIndustrySurvey.MovePrevious
    End If
  Display
End Sub
'This control event is to add new record or update existing record
Private Sub cmdSave_Click()
    If MyButtonAction = "New" Then
      ' This condition is to validate text fields for null
          If txtSerialNo.Text = "" Then
                 MsgBox "Serial Number is mandatory"
               txtSerialNo.SetFocus
                 Exit Sub
        ElseIf txtTurnOver.Text = "" Then
                 MsgBox "Annual Turn Over is mandatory"
                 txtTurnOver.SetFocus
                 Exit Sub
        End If
MyQuery = "SELECT * FROM SoftwareIndustrySurvey where SerialNo='" &
                txtSerialNo.Text & "'"
                Set RSSoftwareIndustrySurveySave =
CreateObject("ADOCE.Recordset.3.0")
                RSSoftwareIndustrySurveySave.Open MyQuery,
CNSoftwareIndustrySurvey,
                adOpenKeyset, adLockOptimistic
        If RSSoftwareIndustrySurveySave.RecordCount > 0 Then
              MsgBox "With This SerialNo Record Already Exists"
                RSSoftwareIndustrySurveySave.Close
                Set RSSoftwareIndustrySurveySave = Nothing
```

```
                    txtSerialNo.SetFocus
               Else
                    RSSoftwareIndustrySurveySave.AddNew
                    AddDataFromFieldsToDB
                    RSSoftwareIndustrySurveySave.Update
                    RSSoftwareIndustrySurveySave.Close
                    Set RSSoftwareIndustrySurveySave = Nothing
                    EnablecmdButtons
                    cmdClose.Caption = "E&xit"
                    MyButtonAction = ""
                    RefreshDB
                    DisableFields
          End If
     ElseIf MyButtonAction = "Modify" Then
          ' This condition is to validate text fields for null
          If txtSerialNo.Text = "" Then
            MsgBox "Serial Number is mandatory"
                    txtSerialNo.SetFocus
                    Exit Sub
               ElseIf txtTurnOver.Text = "" Then
                    MsgBox "Annual Turn Over is mandatory"
                    txtTurnOver.SetFocus
                    Exit Sub
               End If
            MyQuery = "SELECT * FROM SoftwareIndustrySurvey where
SerialNo='" &
                    txtSerialNo.Text & "'"
            Set RSSoftwareIndustrySurveyModify =
                 CreateObject("ADOCE.Recordset.3.0")
                 RSSoftwareIndustrySurveyModify.Open MyQuery,
CNSoftwareIndustrySurvey,
                 adOpenKeyset, adLockOptimistic
          If RSSoftwareIndustrySurveyModify.RecordCount > 0 Then
             If CInt(Trim(txtSerialNo.Text)) = ModifySerialNo Then
```

```
MyQueryModify = "SELECT * FROM SoftwareIndustrySurvey where
 SerialNo='" & ModifySerialNo & "'"
            Set RSSoftwareIndustrySurveySave =
                 CreateObject("ADOCE.Recordset.3.0")
        RSSoftwareIndustrySurveySave.Open MyQueryModify,
CNSoftwareIndustrySurvey, adOpenKeyset, adLockOptimistic
          If RSSoftwareIndustrySurveySave.RecordCount
   > 0 Then
                AddDataFromFieldsToDB
                RSSoftwareIndustrySurveySave.Update
                RSSoftwareIndustrySurveySave.Close
           Set RSSoftwareIndustrySurveySave = Nothing
                EnablecmdButtons
                cmdClose.Caption = "E&xit"
                MyButtonAction = ""
MyCurrentBookMark = RSSoftwareIndustrySurvey.Bookmark
                RefreshDB
                RSSoftwareIndustrySurvey.Bookmark =
    MyCurrentBookMark
                DisableFields
             End If
            RSSoftwareIndustrySurveyModify.Close
         Set RSSoftwareIndustrySurveyModify = Nothing
        Else
           MsgBox "With This SerialNo Record Already
    Exists"
            RSSoftwareIndustrySurveyModify.Close
         Set RSSoftwareIndustrySurveyModify = Nothing
            txtSerialNo.SetFocus
       End If
    Else
    MyQueryModify = "SELECT * FROM SoftwareIndustrySurvey
    where
                SerialNo='" & ModifySerialNo & "'"
```

```
            Set RSSoftwareIndustrySurveySave =
                      CreateObject("ADOCE.Recordset.3.0")
          RSSoftwareIndustrySurveySave.Open MyQueryModify,
 CNSoftwareIndustrySurvey, adOpenKeyset, adLockOptimistic
          If RSSoftwareIndustrySurveySave.RecordCount > 0
   Then
                AddDataFromFieldsToDB
                RSSoftwareIndustrySurveySave.Update
                RSSoftwareIndustrySurveySave.Close
              Set RSSoftwareIndustrySurveySave = Nothing
                EnablecmdButtons
                cmdClose.Caption = "E&xit"
                MyButtonAction = ""
         MyCurrentBookMark = RSSoftwareIndustrySurvey.Bookmark
                RefreshDB
RSSoftwareIndustrySurvey.Bookmark = MyCurrentBookMark
                DisableFields
          End If
         RSSoftwareIndustrySurveyModify.Close
         Set RSSoftwareIndustrySurveyModify = Nothing
      End If
  End If
End Sub
     'This form event is to display first record while the
 application is loading.
Private Sub Form_Load()
     'CreateDBandTable
          Set CNSoftwareIndustrySurvey =
 CreateObject("ADOCE.Connection.3.0")
       CNSoftwareIndustrySurvey.Open "\My
   Documents\SoftwareIndustrySurvey\SoftwareIndustrySurveyDB.cdb"
  EnablecmdButtons
  ClearTextFields
  MyQuery = "SELECT * FROM SoftwareIndustrySurvey"
```

```
    Set RSSoftwareIndustrySurvey =
CreateObject("ADOCE.Recordset.3.0")
            RSSoftwareIndustrySurvey.Open MyQuery,
CNSoftwareIndustrySurvey,
        adOpenKeyset, adLockOptimistic
    If RSSoftwareIndustrySurvey.RecordCount > 0 Then
        RSSoftwareIndustrySurvey.MoveFirst
        MyFirstBookMark = RSSoftwareIndustrySurvey.Bookmark
        RSSoftwareIndustrySurvey.MoveLast
        MyLastBookMark = RSSoftwareIndustrySurvey.Bookmark
        RSSoftwareIndustrySurvey.MoveFirst
         Display
      Else
         MsgBox "No Records In Database!"
   End If
  DisableFields
End Sub
      'This control event is to close the record set, con-
nection and application
Private Sub Form_OKClick()
  RSSoftwareIndustrySurvey.Close
  Set RSSoftwareIndustrySurvey = Nothing
  CNSoftwareIndustrySurvey.Close
  Set CNSoftwareIndustrySurvey = Nothing
   App.End
End Sub
      'This procedure is to clear all the text boxes
Private Sub ClearTextFields()
    txtSerialNo.Text = ""
    txtTurnOver.Text = ""
End Sub
      'This procedure is to display the data
Private Sub Display()
    Dim i As Integer
```

```
   If RSSoftwareIndustrySurvey.RecordCount = 0 Then
    Else
          txtSerialNo.Text =
RSSoftwareIndustrySurvey.Fields("SerialNo")
              ' to display area of work
             For i = 0 To CboAreaOfWork.ListCount - 1
                   If CboAreaOfWork.List(i) =
                  RSSoftwareIndustrySurvey.Fields("AreaOfWork")
Then
                         CboAreaOfWork.ListIndex = i
                         Exit For
                   End If
             Next i
        To display type of organization
             For i = 0 To CboOrgType.ListCount - 1
        If CboOrgType.List(i) =
RSSoftwareIndustrySurvey.Fields("TypeOfOrg")
                         Then
             CboOrgType.ListIndex = i
                         Exit For
                   End If
             Next i
 txtTurnOver.Text = RSSoftwareIndustrySurvey.Fields("TurnOver")
     End If
    End Sub
        'This procedure is to disable all text fields
Private Sub DisableFields()
       txtSerialNo.Enabled = False
     CboAreaOfWork.Enabled = False
 CboOrgType.Enabled = False
 txtTurnOver.Enabled = False
End Sub
       'This procedure is to enable all text fields
Private Sub EnableFields()
```

```
    txtSerialNo.Enabled = True
    CboAreaOfWork.Enabled = True
    CboOrgType.Enabled = True
    txtTurnOver.Enabled = True
End Sub
    'This procedure is to enable the command buttons
Private Sub EnablecmdButtons()
    cmdSave.Enabled = False
    cmdADD.Enabled = True
    cmdModify.Enabled = True
    cmdDelete.Enabled = True
    cmdFirst.Enabled = True
    cmdLast.Enabled = True
    cmdNext.Enabled = True
    cmdPrevious.Enabled = True
End Sub
    'This procedure is to disable the command buttons
Private Sub DisablecmdButtons()
    cmdSave.Enabled = True
    cmdADD.Enabled = False
    cmdModify.Enabled = False
    cmdDelete.Enabled = False
    cmdFirst.Enabled = False
    cmdLast.Enabled = False
    cmdNext.Enabled = False
    cmdPrevious.Enabled = False
End Sub
    'This procedure is to read data from text fields and add
to database
Private Sub AddDataFromFieldsToDB()
        RSSoftwareIndustrySurveySave.Fields("SerialNo") =
Trim(txtSerialNo.Text)
    RSSoftwareIndustrySurveySave.Fields("AreaOfWork") =
            Trim(CboAreaOfWork.Text)
```

```
    RSSoftwareIndustrySurveySave.Fields("TypeOfOrg") =
Trim(CboOrgType.Text)
    RSSoftwareIndustrySurveySave.Fields("TurnOver") =
Trim(txtTurnOver.Text)
End Sub
      'This procedure is to refresh the database
Private Sub RefreshDB()
    RSSoftwareIndustrySurvey.Close
    Set RSSoftwareIndustrySurvey = Nothing
   MyQuery = "SELECT * FROM SoftwareIndustrySurvey"
    Set RSSoftwareIndustrySurvey =
CreateObject("ADOCE.Recordset.3.0")
RSSoftwareIndustrySurvey.Open MyQuery,
CNSoftwareIndustrySurvey,
      adOpenKeyset, adLockOptimistic
   RSSoftwareIndustrySurvey.MoveFirst
   MyFirstBookMark = RSSoftwareIndustrySurvey.Bookmark
   RSSoftwareIndustrySurvey.MoveLast
   MyLastBookMark = RSSoftwareIndustrySurvey.Bookmark
End Sub
      ' This event is to validate for numeric values
Private Sub txtTurnOver_KeyPress(ByVal KeyAscii As Integer)
    If KeyAscii = 8 Or KeyAscii = 46 Or KeyAscii >= 48
And KeyAscii <= 57 Then
    Else
        KeyAscii = 0
         MsgBox "Enter Numbers only"
    End If
End Sub
      ' This event is to validate for numeric values
Private Sub txtSerialNo_KeyPress(ByVal KeyAscii As Integer)
    'MsgBox KeyAscii
    If (KeyAscii = 8) Or (KeyAscii >= 48 And KeyAscii <=
57) Then
    Else
```

```
340.          KeyAscii = 0
341.          MsgBox "Enter Numbers only"
342.      End If
343. End Sub
```

If you are familiar with Visual Basic, you can easily understand the functionality of this code. If you are not familiar with Visual Basic, the source code details are explained below.

- Lines 1-12: Declaration of variables.
- Lines 13-20: Definition of the cmdADD_Click() event to enter data for a new record.
  - o Line 14: Calling the procedure EnableFields to enable all text fields.
  - o Line 15: Calling the procedure ClearTextFields to clear all the text boxes.
  - o Line 18: Calling the procedure DisablecmdButtons to disable the command buttons.
- Lines 21-32: Definition of the cmdClose_Click() event to cancel the operation or close the application.
  - o Line 23: Calling the procedure Form_OKClick event to close the application.
  - o Line 25: Calling the procedure EnablecmdButtons to enable command buttons.
  - o Line 28: Calling the procedure ClearTextFields to clear all the text boxes.
  - o Line 29: Calling the procedure Display to assign database field data to text fields.
  - o Line 30: Calling the procedure DisableFields to disable all text fields.
- Lines 33-46: Definition of the CreateDBandTable() procedure to create a database and table.
  - o Line 36: Creating a database with SoftwareIndustrySurveyDB.cdb and saving it in the specified location, '\MyDocuments\SoftwareIndustrySurvey\
  - o Lines 37-42: Creating a string named SQl. This string contains the table name and the field names. For each field, the type and size are also specified. Line 42 is for executing the SQL command that creates a table with the table name SoftwareIndustrySurvey; SerialNo., AreaOfWork, TypeOfOrg, TurnOver are the names of the fields.
  - o Line 43: Creating an index for the table on the field named SerialNo.
- Lines 47-86: Definition of the cmdDelete_Click() event to delete a record.
  - o Lines 48-51: Creating a recordset and finding the current record in the database.
  - o Line 55: Deleting a record from the database.
  - o Line 69: Calling the procedure RefreshDB to refresh the database.
- Lines 87–92: Definition of the cmdFirst_Click() event to display the first record.
- Lines 93–98: Definition of the cmdLast_Click() event to display the last record.
- Lines 99–115: Definition of the cmdModify_Click() event to get the record to be modified.
- Lines 116–125: Definition of the cmdNext_Click() event to display the next record.
  - o Line 119: Checking for the last record.
- Lines 126–136: Definition of the cmdPrevious_Click() event to display the previous record.

- Line 129: Checking for the first record.

- Lines 137–228: Definition of the cmdSave_Click() event, to add a new record or to update the existing record.
  - Line 151: Checking for a duplicate record.
  - Line 157: Adding a new record to the database.
  - Line 158: Calling the procedure AddDataFromFieldsToDB to assign text field data to database fields.
  - Line 181: Checking for a duplicate record.
  - Line 182: Checking whether the SerialNo is changed.
  - Line 186: Getting the record to be modified.
- Lines 229–247: Definition of the Form_Load() event to display the first record's data while the application is loading. Commented line is a call to the procedure CreateDBandTable. This procedure is given at Lines 33-46. Before executing this program, you need to create a database table using this procedure.
- Lines 248–254: Definition of the Form_OKClick() event to close the recordset, the connection, and the application.
- Lines 255–258: Definition of the ClearTextFields() procedure to clear all the text fields.
- Lines 259–279: Definition of the Display() procedure to assign database field data to text fields.
- Lines 280–285: Definition of the DisableFields() procedure to disable all text fields.
- Lines 286–291: Definition of the EnableFields() procedure to enable all text fields.
- Lines 292–301: Definition of the EnablecmdButtons() procedure to enable all command buttons
- Lines 302–311: Definition of the DisablecmdButtons() procedure to disable all command buttons.
- Lines 312–317: Definition of the AddDataFromFieldsToDB() procedure to assign text field data to database fields.
- Lines 318-328: Definition of the RefreshDB() procedure to refresh the database.
- Lines 329–335: Definition of the txtTurnOver_KeyPress event to validate for a numeric value.
- Lines 336–343: Definition of the txtSerialNo_KeyPress event to validate for a numeric value.

15.5 Executing the Program

You can execute the program and test it on the Pocket PC emulator using the following steps:

- Invoke the eMbedded Visual Basic 3.0 from the Start menu of your desktop. A window will open with tabs for Existing projects, New projects, and Recent Projects. Select the New Projects tab and choose Windows CE for the Pocket PC Project; the default form will be displayed.

- In the Project menu, select Project Properties and set the project name as "SoftwareIndustrySurvey". Save the form as frmSoftwareIndustrySurvey.ebf and save the project as SoftwareIndustrySurvey.ebp. Note that .ebf is the extension for eMbedded Visual Basic Form. The extension for Embedded Visual Basic Project is .ebp.
- Select the form and set the following form properties in the Properties window:

  Name: frmSoftwareIndustrySurvey

  Caption: Software Industry Survey

  Border Style:1- Fixed Single

  Height: 3990

  Width: 3705

Select the required controls from the Toolbox and set them as shown in Fig. 15.1.

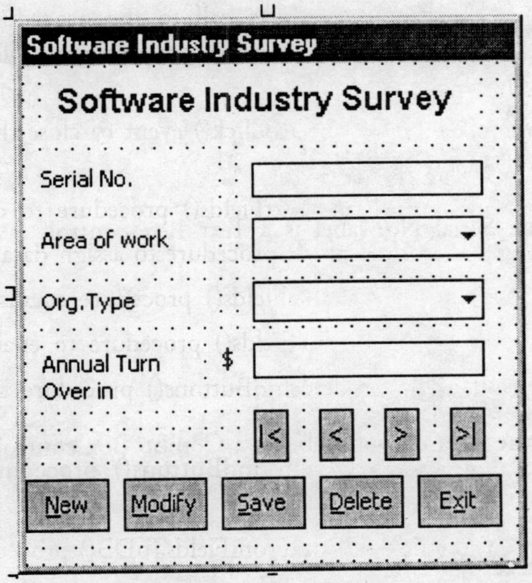

Fig. 15.1: SoftwareIndustrySurvey Form

The Software IndustrySurvey title shown in bold at the top of the form is a Label control. Set the label properties as follows:

Name: lblTitle

Caption: SoftwareIndustrySurvey

Font: Arial, Bold, font size 12

"Serial No." is a Label control. Set the label properties as follows:

Name: lblSerialNo

Caption: Serial No.

"Area of work" is a Label control. Set the label properties as follows:

Name: lblAreaOfWork

Caption: Area of work

"Org.Type" is a Label control. Set the label properties as follows:

Name: lblOrganization

Caption: Org.Type

"Annual Turn Over in" is a Label control. The label properties are to be set as follows:

Name: lblATurnOver

Caption: Annual Turn Over in

The character "$" is a Label control. Set the label properties as follows:

Name: lblDollar

Caption: $

The text box next to the Serial No. label is a Text Box control. Set the text box properties as follows:

Name: txtSerialNo.

MaxLength: 3

The combo box next to the Area of work label is a Combo Box control. The combo box properties are to be set as follows:

Name: cboAreaOfWork

Text: Clear the default text

Style: 2-VbComboDropdown

In the combo box properties window, select categorized tab and double click on custom property. The following screen will appear.

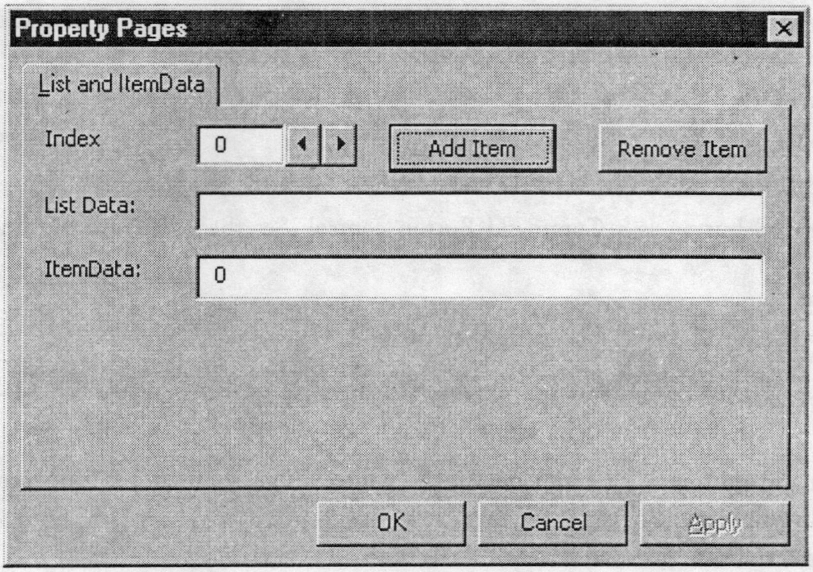

Fig. 15.2: Combo box Custom Property Window

List Data: eMbedded Systems

In list data text field, type the above text and click the Apply button. For adding next item click "Add Item button". Add the following items:

Database

VLSI

CRM

Computer Networks

The combo box next to the Org.Type label is a Combo Box control. Set the combo box properties as follows:

Name: cboOrgType

Text: Clear the default text

Style: 2-VbComboDropdown

In the combo box properties window, select categorized tab and double click on custom property. Enter text in Item Data text field using the same procedure as mentioned above.

Small

Medium

Large

The text-box next to the "Annual Turn Over in" label is a Text Box control. The text box properties are to be set as follows:

Name: txtTurnOver

MaxLength: 10

The |< command button is a Command Button control. Set the command button properties as follows:

Name: cmdFirst

Caption: |<

Functionality: When clicked, this button displays the first record available in the database.

The < command button is a Command Button control. The command button properties are to be set as follows:

Name: cmdPrevious

Caption: <

Functionality: When clicked, this button displays the previous record available in the database.

The > command button is a Command Button control. Set the command button properties as follows:

Name: cmdNext

Caption: >

Functionality: When clicked, this button displays the next record available in the database.

The >| button is a Command Button control. The command button properties are to be set as follows:

Name: cmdLast

Caption: >|

Functionality: When clicked, this button displays the last record available in the database.

The New command button is a Command Button control. Set the command button properties as follows:

Name: cmdADD

Caption: &New

Functionality: When clicked, this button clears all the text fields and enables the user to input data.

The Modify command button is a Command Button control. The command button properties are to be set as follows:

Name: cmdModify

Caption: &Modify

Functionality: When clicked, this button enables the user to modify the values of the currently displayed record.

The Save command button is a Command Button control. Set the command button properties as follows:

Name: cmdSave

Caption: &Save

Functionality: When clicked, this button saves the existing record; it may be either a new record or a modified record.

The Delete command button is a Command Button control. The command button properties are to be set as follows:

Name: cmdDelete

Caption: &Delete

Functionality: When clicked, this button deletes the existing record after asking for a confirmation.

The Exit command button is a Command Button control. Set the Command Button properties as follows:

Name: cmdClose

Caption: E&xit

Functionality: When clicked, this button unloads the application.

- In the Project menu, select References and select reference Microsoft CE ADO Control 3.0. This reference is used for database connectivity.
- In the Run menu, select Execute or click the Run button on the toolbar.

When you execute the program, the screen shot shown in Fig. 15.3 appears. The first record of the table will be displayed (if records are available in the database). Using the buttons provided, you can add, modify, delete the records or navigate through the records. Fig. 15.4 shows the screen shot when the "New" button is pressed and the data entered in fields. Fig. 15.5 shows the screen shot when the "Delete" button is pressed. Note that the "Save" button is enabled only when you click the "New" or "Modify" button.

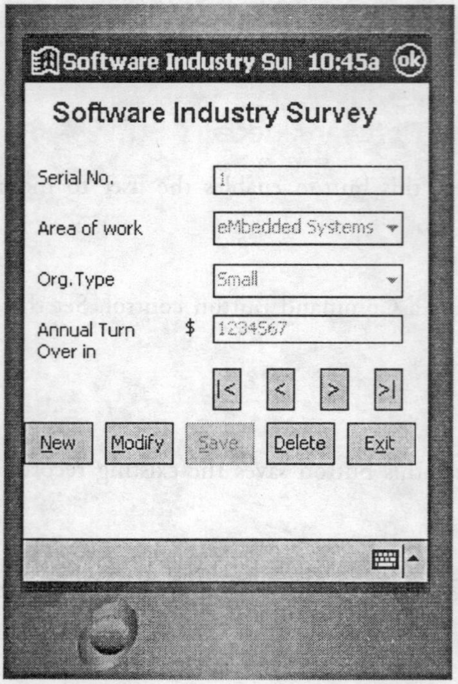

Fig. 15.3: Output Screen on a Pocket PC for the Software Industry Survey Project

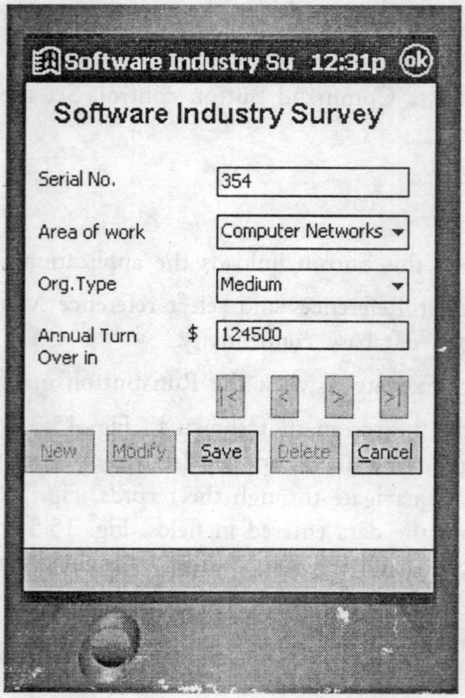

Fig. 15.4: Output Screen on a Pocket PC while adding new Record

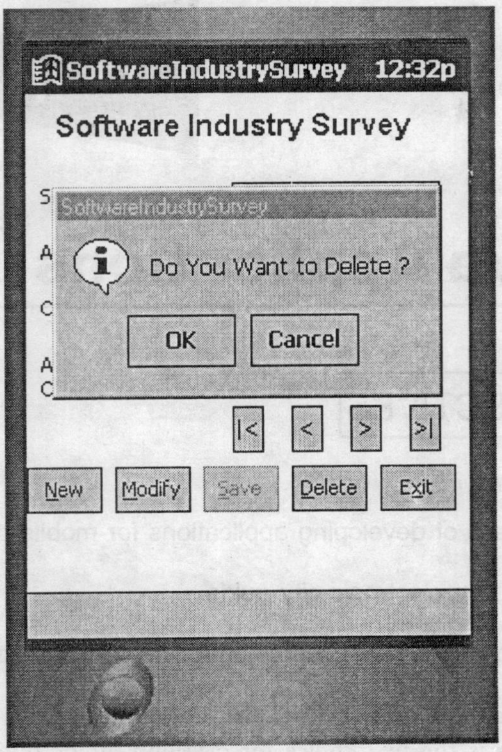

Fig. 15.5: Output Screen on a Pocket PC while deleting a Record

Summary

In this chapter, development of embedded database application has been demonstrated using eMbedded Visual Tools 3.0 for Pocket PC. Using eMbedded Visual Basic and Pocket Access database, Graphical User Interfaces can be developed for handheld computers. Such a GUI is useful for field personnel for carrying out database operations such as entry of data, searching for records, editing records, etc. The data collected in the field by the field personnel can be later on uploaded to the corporate database using ActiveSync.

This project demonstrates the simplicity of creating embedded databases even by those who have been doing application programming. Of course, because of the memory and size restrictions of handheld computers, the embedded databases have limitations in terms of the filed sizes, table sizes and the number of records that the database can hold.

If you are an application software developer and if you have been dreaming of getting on to the bandwagon of embedded software development, embedded database application development using embedded Visual Tools is the best way to start off!

Chapter 16

Mobile Java Applications

CHAPTER OBJECTIVES

After reading this chapter, you will be able to:

- Understand the process of developing applications for mobile devices
- Learn how to develop an electronic city guide
- Learn how to develop an Internet-based electronic voting application

Java programming language revolutionized the software development. Due to its most attractive feature—platform independence—Java is the best choice for development of Internet-enabled applications. In this chapter, we will study how to develop two applications for mobile devices—an electronic city guide application and an electronic voting application.

16.1 Development Environment

To develop these projects, you need a system with the following software installed:

- Windows XP Professional
- Windows NT 4.0 SP6, Windows 2000 SP2 system on which the following packages are installed:
    - o Java 2 Platform, Standard Edition, v 1.4.1 (J2SE 1.4.1)
    - o J2ME Toolkit Version 2.0 using MIDP, which can be downloaded from http://java.sun.com/products/j2mewtoolkit
    - o Sun ONE Studio, Mobile Edition, a Java Integrated Development Environment (IDE) for developing applications that can be deployed on Java-enabled mobile devices. Sun ONE Studio can be downloaded from http://wwws.sun.com/software/sundev/jde/studio4u1_me/index.html

  If you would like to use Sun ONE Studio with J2ME, first you need to install Sun ONE Studio and then install the Wireless Toolkit with the 'Option for Integrating' selected.
- A database engine such as MS-Access.

16.1.1 Invoking the Tool

You can first get a familiarity with the operation of the tool, using the following steps:

- Copy all the JSP Files in c:\javawebserver2.0\pubic_html.
- Start the JavaWebServer using the command c:\javawebserver2.0\bin\httpd.exe.
- After installing Sun ONE Studio, go to

All Programs-> Sun Microsystems-> Sun ONE Studio 4 ME-> Sun ONE Studio as shown in Fig. 16.1.

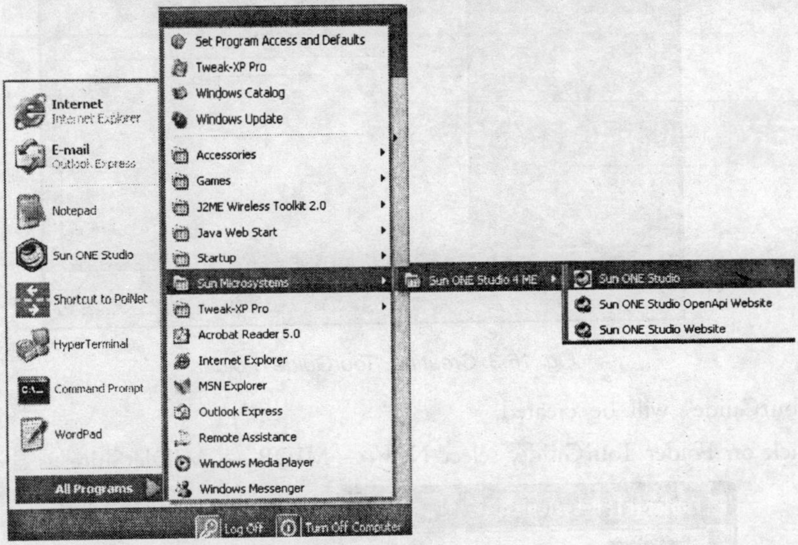

Fig 16.1: Invoking SUN ONE Studio

- The File System Explorer will open. Select "File" menu and select the item "Explorer". Select New Folder as shown in Fig. 16.2.

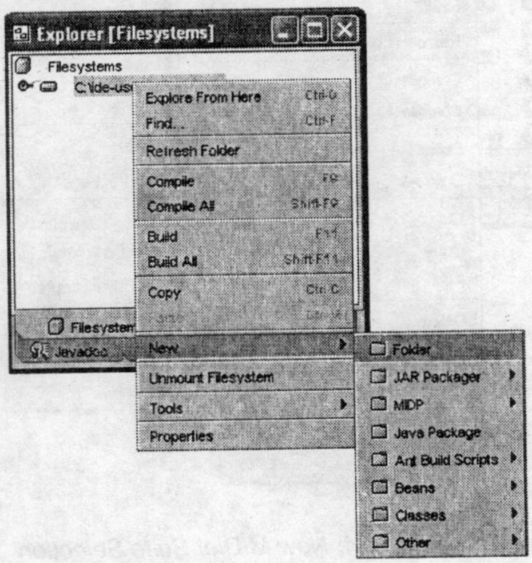

Fig 16.2: Creating the New Folder.

- Give Folder name as "TourGuide" in the TextField and then click Finish Button as shown in Fig 16.3.

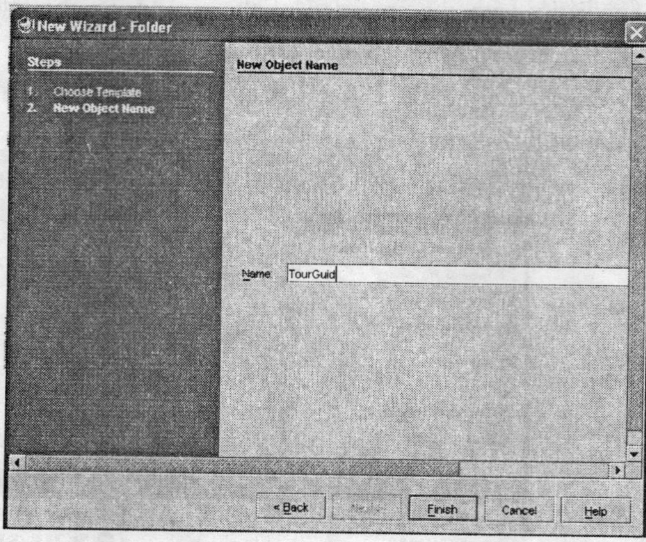

Fig. 16.3: Creating "TourGuide" Folder

The Folder "TourGuide" will be created.

- Right click on Folder TourGuide, select New ← MIDP → MIDletSuite as shown in Fig 16.4.

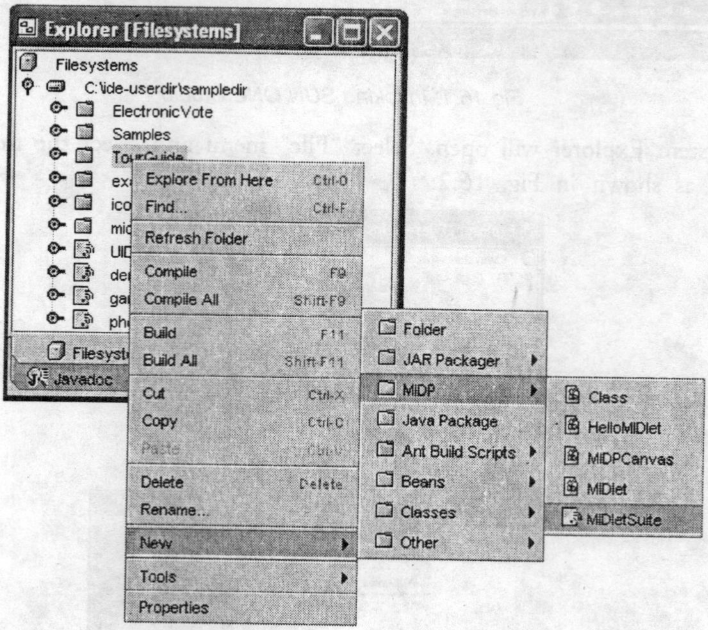

Fig. 16.4: New MIDlet Suite Selection

- Give name for MIDletSuite as CityGuide and click Next as shown in Fig. 16.5.

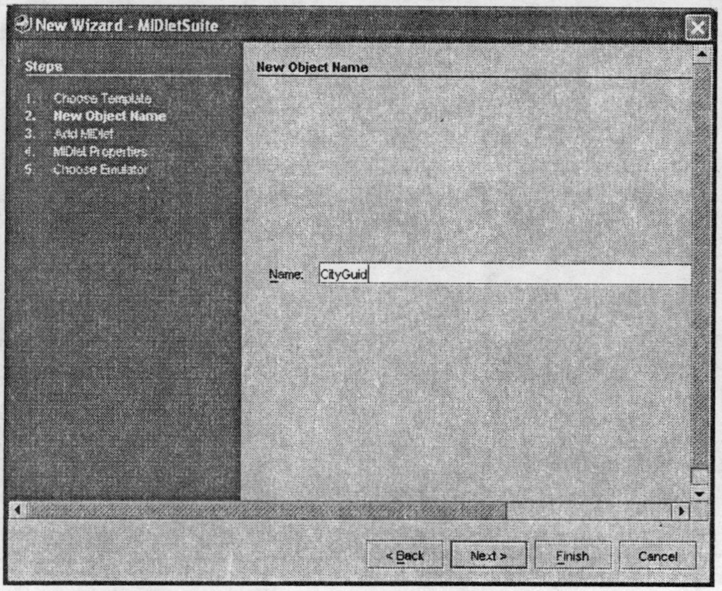

Fig. 16.5: MIDlet Suite CityGuide Creation

- Give Package & Class Name as CityGuide and click Next Button as shown in Fig. 16.6.

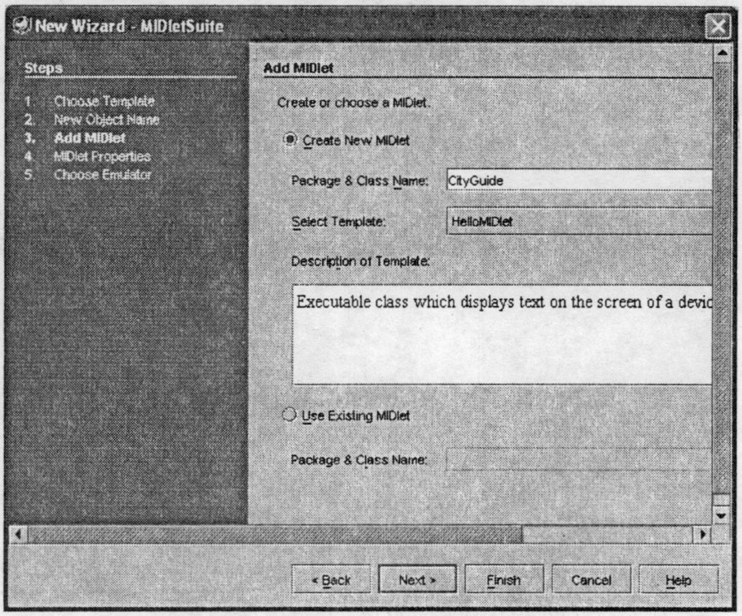

Fig. 16.6: Setting the CityGuide Package and Class Name

- Give MIDlet Displayable Name as CityGuide and Click Next Button as shown in Fig. 16.7.

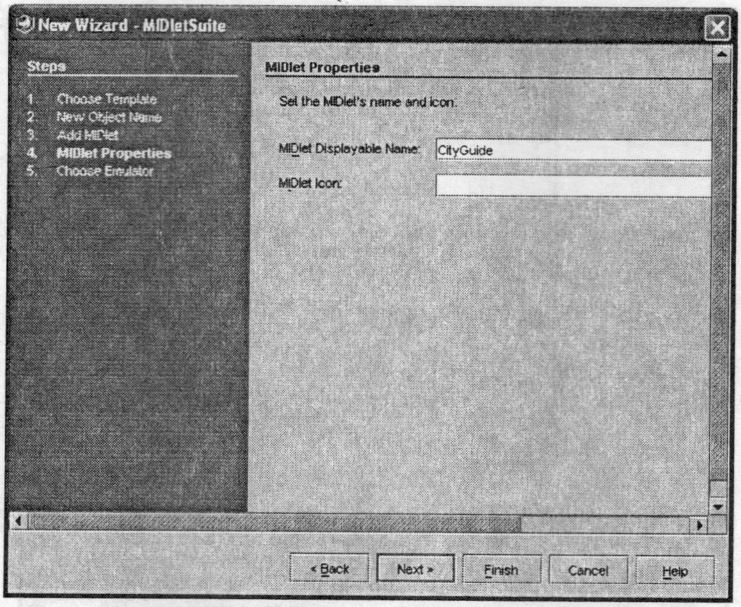

Fig. 16.7: Setting the MIDlet Name

- Select the Emulator Device and click Finish Button as shown in Fig. 16.8.

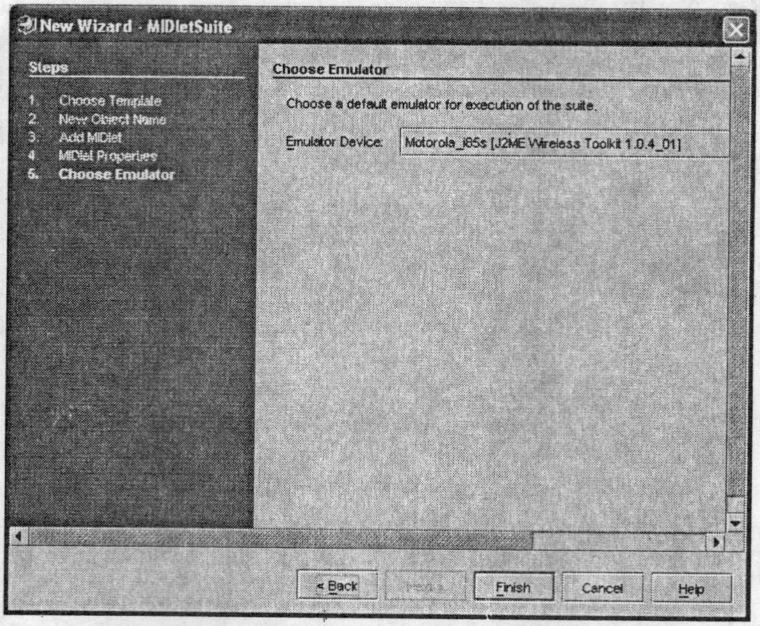

Fig: 16.8: Selection of Emulator Device

- Right click on CityGuide and select Compile as shown in Fig. 16.9.

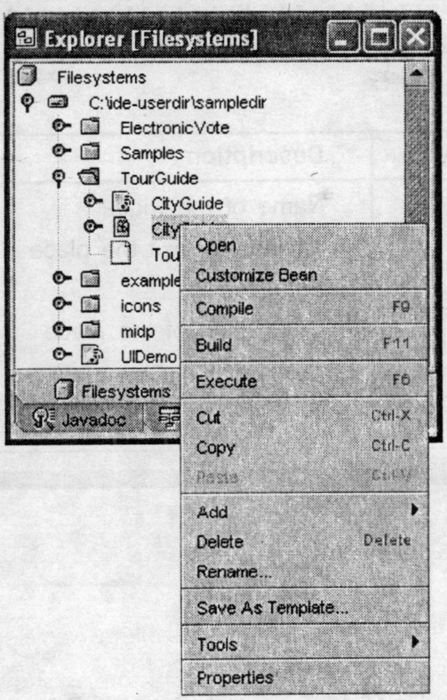

Fig: 16.9: Compiling the MIDlet

- After compilation is finished, again right click on CityGuide and select "Execute"

16.2 Project: Tour Guide

In the first project, we will develop an electronic city tour guide. Assume that you are visiting a new city. Instead of hiring a tourist guide, you can use your mobile phone to obtain the information about the tourist spots of that city. The database on the Internet server contains the information about cities, tourist places and description of these places.

You need to create a database containing the information and write a J2ME MIDlet. When the user gets connected to this server through a URL, the information will be passed on to the user on his mobile phone.

This application has the following modules:

- A database created in MS Access (TourGuide.mdb)
- CityGuide.java
- Cities.jsp
- Citydetails.jsp
- NameCategory.jsp

The complete source code and the explanation are given in the following sections.

16.2.1 Database Design

You have to create a database as per the following details.

Table Name: TourDetails

Field Name	Field Type	Description	Length
Name	Text	Name of the Place	50
Timings	Text	Timings to visit the place	50
EntryFee	Text	Entry fee	50
Description	Memo	Description of the place	up to 65,535 Char
City	Text	Name of the City	50

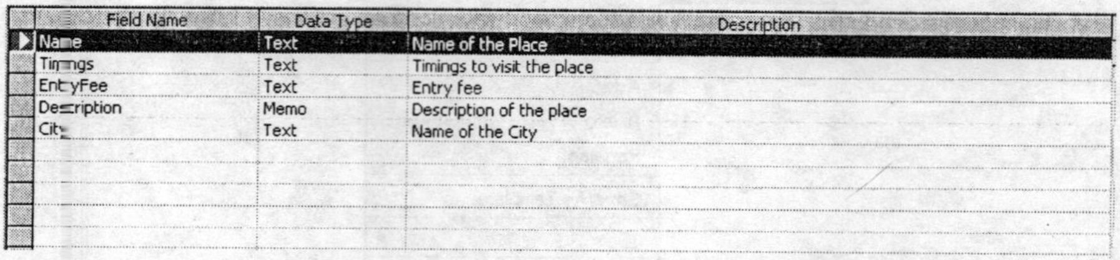

Field Name	Data Type	Description
Name	Text	Name of the Place
Timings	Text	Timings to visit the place
EntryFee	Text	Entry fee
Description	Memo	Description of the place
City	Text	Name of the City

Fig 16.10: TourDetails Database Table

After creating the table, populate the fields with information about a few cities, tourist spots, timings, entry fee and description of the places.

16.2.2 Source Code Listing of Java Program

Listing 16.1 gives the source code of CityGuide.java, which is for creating the user interface and giving the output to the user on the mobile device. Using a HTTP connection, the data on the server is retrieved and presented to the user.

Listing 16.1: CityGuide.java

```
/*
 * CityGuide.java
 * This application is for Tour Guide
 *i.e to visit the places of Visitor's
 *interest in a particular City and know
 *the details of that place.
 */
package TourGuide;
import javax.microedition.midlet.*;
import javax.microedition.lcdui.*;
import javax.microedition.io.*;
```

```
import java.io.*;
public class CityGuide extends MIDlet implements CommandListener
{
/* This HttpConnection object connects to the web server and
   retrieves from the Data base */
HttpConnection hc = null;
/* Declaring variable for Display class. */
private Display display = null;
/* Declaration of Commands */
 Command quit = null;
 Command ok = null;
 Command details=null;
 Command inform=null;
 Command back1 = null;
/* Declaration of Form */
 Form frm = null;
 Ticker t =null;
/* Declaration of Lists */
 List menu = null;
 List menud = null;
 List menui=null;
 String url, temp, str, item, tempp, tempm;
 StringItem cityname;
 StringItem st1=null,st2=null,st3=null,st4=null,st5=null,st6=null;
// Initialize the Display and place system controls in the Constructor..
 public CityGuide() {
/* This will get the Display Object */
 display = Display.getDisplay(this);
 quit = new Command ("Quit",Command.SCREEN,1);
 ok = new Command ("OK",Command.OK,2);
 details = new Command ("SELECT",Command.SCREEN,2);
 inform = new Command ("CLICK",Command.SCREEN,2);
 back1 = new Command ("BACK",Command.BACK,2);
 t = new Ticker("Welcome To Electronic City Guide" );
 }
/**
  This method is called when the application starts ..
*/
 public void startApp()
 {
     try {
```

```
                System.out.println("StartedApplication");
            cityDetails(str);
    }catch(IOException ie)      {
     System.out.println("Start Application Exception:  "+ie);
    }
   } // end of startApp()
/**   This method is to retrieve Cities from Database using JSP   */
  private void cityDetails(String str) throws IOException
   {
   StringBuffer sb=new StringBuffer();
/* This InputStream Object is used to read data from the InputStream
   opened on a URL */
   InputStream is = null;
 /* HttpConnection Object */
    HttpConnection hc = null;
try{
        long len = 0;
        int ch = 0;
        String name="";
/* Connecting to the given url.The url String contains a url pointing
   to jsp which will retrieve from the database */
  hc=(HttpConnection)Connector.open  ("http://localhost:8080/
  Cities.jsp");
/* An inputstream is opened to read from that connection */
  is = hc.openInputStream();
  len = hc.getLength();
    if(len !=-1){
        for(int i=0;i<len;i++){
           if((ch = is.read()) !=-1)            {
                     sb.append((char)ch);
        }
      }
        }
     else{
       while(( ch = is.read()) !=-1){
         len = is.available() ;
          sb.append((char)ch);
         }
      }
     String str1 = sb.toString();
     str1.trim();
```

```
/* Initializing a List to select cities  from the List.*/
      menu = new List("Please Select a City",List.IMPLICIT);
      menu.setTicker(t);
      int index = str1.indexOf("#");
      while(index != -1)
      {
            index = str1.indexOf("#");
         if(index != -1)      {
      String item = str1.substring(0,str1.indexOf("#"));
      str1 = str1.substring (str1.indexOf("#")+1);
        item=item.trim();
/* Append Item to a menu(List) */
      menu.append(item,null);
 }
 }
/* menu is registered for OK command */
   menu.addCommand(ok);
   menu.addCommand(quit);
/* Menu registered for receiving command*/
   menu.setCommandListener(this);
/*This will set the current display to List containing the items,
   ie Cities */
 display.setCurrent(menu);
 }catch(Exception e)    {
 System.out.println(e+"Exception In Menu");
       }
     finally{
        try{
                   is.close();
                   hc.close();
             }catch(Exception e)
        {   System.out.println(e+"Exception in Finally");
  }
 }
 }
       // end of cityDetails(String str)
/**This is a method to retrieve Details when a particular city is
   clicked */
private void cityClicked(){
    List down = (List)display.getCurrent();
     temp = down.getString (down.getSelectedIndex());
```

```
 if(temp.equals("New Delhi")){
              informationDetails(temp);
 }
else  if(temp.equals("Hyderabad"))
{
 informationDetails(temp);
}
else  if  (temp.equals("Bangalore"))
{
 informationDetails(temp);
}
}
  //end of cityClicked()
/**
This is a method for Action Performed, i.e when a Command is clicked,
i.e. Event handling routine..
*/
  public void commandAction(Command c,Displayable d){
     if(c == quit) {
     destroyApp(true);
  } else if(c==ok) {
  cityClicked();
  } else if(c==details) {
  List down = (List)display.getCurrent();
  String cname=cityname.getText();
  tempp = down.getString(down.getSelectedIndex());
   informationDetails(cname);
 } else if(c==inform) {
     List down = (List)display.getCurrent();
     String cname=cityname.getText();
     tempm = down.getString(down.getSelectedIndex());
     informationCategory(cname,tempm);
     } else if(c==back1) {
  try{
     String cname=cityname.getText();
     cityDetails(cname);
  }catch(Exception p) {
     System.out.println("Exception in back "+p);
     }
    }
```

```
    }  //end of commandAction(Command c,Displayable d)
/**
   This is a method to retrieve information when a particular City
   and Name of the category are clicked */
   private void informationCategory(String cname,String tempm){
   StringBuffer sbc = new StringBuffer();
   InputStream isc = null;
   HttpConnection hcc = null;
        int count = 1;
   try{
   long lenc = 0;
   int ch = 0;
   String name=" ";
   cname = cname.replace(' ','_');
   tempm=tempm.replace(' ','_');
   String param=cname+" & name="+tempm;
   param = param.replace(' ','_');
        String   url   ="http://localhost:8080/NameCategory.jsp?city="+param;
   hcc = (HttpConnection)Connector.open(url);
   isc = hcc.openInputStream();
    lenc = hcc.getLength();
   if(lenc !=-1){
   for(int i=0;i<lenc;i++){
  if((ch = isc.read()) !=-1)
   {
   sbc.append((char)ch);
   }
   }
   }else{
   while(( ch = isc.read()) !=-1){
   lenc = isc.available() ;
   sbc.append((char)ch);
   }
   }
   String str1 = sbc.toString();
   str1.trim();
   menui = new List("Information ",List.IMPLICIT);
   int index = str1.indexOf("#");
  while(index != -1){
   index = str1.indexOf("#");
```

```
    if(index != -1){
    String item = str1.substring(0,str1.indexOf("#"));
    str1 = str1.substring(str1.indexOf("#")+1);
    item=item.trim();
 if(count == 1){
/*The str is passed as an argument to the Constructor of StringItem
   which will display the value in str */
    st1 = new StringItem("Description : ",item);
    }
    if(count == 2){
    st2 = new StringItem("Timing : ",item);
    }
 if(count == 3){
    st3 = new StringItem("Entry : ",item);
    }
 count++;
    }
    }
/* Initializing a Form */
    frm =new Form("Details");
/* Append StringItem's to a Form */
    frm.append(st1);
    frm.append(st2);
    frm.append(st3);
/*form is registered for quit command*/
    frm.addCommand(quit);
    frm.addCommand(back1);
/*frm registered for receiving command*/
    frm.setCommandListener(this);
    display.setCurrent(frm);
    }catch(Exception e) {
        System.out.println(e+"Exception In Menu city clicked");
    }
    finally{
 try{
          isc.close();
          hcc.close();
    }catch(Exception e){
    System.out.println(e+"Exception in Finally in city clicked");
    }
    }
```

```
   System.out.println("information category"+tempm);
   }
/*end of informationCategory(String cname,String tempm)*/
/**
 This is a method to retrieve names
 of a particular Category
 when a particular City and Category are clicked */
 private void informationDetails(String cname)
   {
      StringBuffer sbd = new StringBuffer();
      InputStream isd = null;
      HttpConnection hcd = null;
     try{
     long lend = 0;
     int ch = 0;
     String name=" ";
     cname = cname.replace(' ','_');
     String param=cname;
     param = param.replace(' ','_');
           String url ="http://localhost:8080/
  CityDetails.jsp?city="+param;
     hcd = (HttpConnection)Connector.open(url);
     isd = hcd.openInputStream();
     lend = hcd.getLength();
     if(lend !=-1){
       for(int i=0;i<lend;i++){
          if((ch = isd.read()) !=-1){
     sbd.append((char)ch);
       }
     }
     }else{
    while(( ch = isd.read()) !=-1){
     lend = isd.available() ;
     sbd.append((char)ch);
     }
    }
    String str1 = sbd.toString();
    str1.trim();
    cityname=new StringItem("Select",temp);
    menud = new List("Please Select an Option",List.IMPLICIT);
    int index = str1.indexOf("#");
```

```
      while(index  !=  -1){
         index  =  str1.indexOf("#");
       if(index  !=  -1){
         String  item  =  str1.substring(0,str1.indexOf("#"));
                  str1  =  str1.substring(str1.indexOf("#")+1);
                       item=item.trim();
                       menud.append(item,null);
       }
          }
       menud.addCommand(inform);
       menud.addCommand(back1);
       menud.setCommandListener(this);
       display.setCurrent(menud);
       }catch(Exception  e)        {
         System.out.println(e+"Exception  In  Menu  city  clicked");
        }
     finally{
       try{
                        isd.close();
                        hcd.close();
     }catch(Exception  e)     {
                System.out.println(e+"Exception  in  Finally  in  city
  clicked");
        }    //catch(Exception  e)
     }   //finally
     }
 /* End  of  informationDetails(String  cname,String  tempp)  */
/* This  method  is  called  when  the  application  is  paused*/
 public  void  pauseApp()
 {
      menu  =  null;
    menud  =  null;
  }
 //  end  of  pauseApp()
/* This  method  is  called  when  the  application  is  terminated.  This
   is  the  ideal  method  to  free  resources  */
 public  void  destroyApp(boolean  unconditional)
 {
        menu  =  null;
        menud  =  null;
           notifyDestroyed();
```

```
277. }
   /* end of destroyApp(boolean unconditional) */
278. }
```

- Lines 1-5: Importing of the various packages required for the program. These statements import various GUI components, Http Connection classes like Http Connection and Connector class, and Input Stream class for communication.
- Line 6: Declaration of the class CityGuide.
- Lines 7-22: Declaration of objects for User Interface Classes like the List, Form and several Command objects.
- Lines 23-31: Constructor for the class CityGuide. This code initializes different command objects. The commands are generated when the user presses any button on the mobile phone.
- Lines 32-40: Declaration of the startApp() method, which is called when the MIDlet starts. Line 36 is for invoking the cityDetails() method within the try catch block.
- Lines 41-96: Implementation of cityDetails method.
    - o Line 43: Instantiate the StringBuffer Object.
    - o Lines 44-49: Declaration and initialization of the variables.
    - o Lines 51-65: Inputstream is opened to read from the connection, get the length and process the data.
    - o Line 67: Removes white space from both ends of the string.
    - o Line 70: Returns the index within this string of the first occurrence of the specified substring (#).
    - o Line 75: City Name will be assigned to the String Item.
- Lines 97-111: Implementation of cityClicked method.
    - o Line 98: Current Displayable object of MIDlet is assigned to the list.
    - o Line 99: Selected string of the list is assigned to the string temp.
    - o Lines 100-110: If the string is NewDelhi or Hyderabad or Bangalore, invoke the method informationDetails.
- Lines 112-135: Definition of commandAction method, which performs the action when the user presses a button.
    - o Lines 113-114: If Quit button is clicked, destroyApp method will be invoked.
    - o Lines 115-116: If OK button is clicked, cityClicked method will be invoked.
    - o Lines 117-121: If Details button is clicked, informationDetails method will be invoked.
    - o Lines 122-126: If Inform button is clicked, informationCategory method will be invoked.
    - o Lines 127-130: If Back command is clicked, cityDetails method will be invoked.
- Lines 136-208: Implementation of informationCategory method.

- o Line 145: Replace the spaces with underscore in the cname string, which contains the City name.
- o Line 146: Replace the spaces with underscore in the tempm string, which contains the Name of the Place.
- o Line 147: Concatenate cname and tempm string and assign it to another string param.
- o Line 148: Replace the spaces with underscore in the param string.
- o Lines 170-187: Within the while loop, value will be assigned to the string item.
- o Lines 176-186: Instantiate the StringItem with parameter String (item).
- o Lines 188-193: Instantiate the form object and append the StringItem and commands to the form.

- Lines 209-266: This is an implementation of informationDetails method. The code here is same as that in the other methods and is self-explanatory.
- Lines 267-271: This is an implementation of pauseApp method. When the application is paused, this method will be invoked.
- Lines 272-277: Implementation of destroyApp method. When the application is terminated, this method will be invoked to free the resources.

16.2.3 Source Code Listings of JSP Programs

Listing 16.2 gives the source code of Cities.jsp. This program retrieves the names of the cities from the database.

Listing 16.2: Cities.jsp

```
<%— This is a JSP File to retrieve Cities from the Database —
    %>
<%@ page import="java.sql.*,java.util.*" %>
<%! Connection conn; %>
<%! Statement stmt; %>
<%! ResultSet rs; %>
<%! String str1; %>
<%
try{
/* Connecting to the Data Base */
Class.forName("sun.jdbc.odbc.JdbcOdbcDriver");
conn = DriverManager.getConnection("jdbc:odbc:ETour");
    stmt = conn.createStatement();
/* Information of Cities from Database*/
    rs = stmt.executeQuery("select Distinct(City) from TourDetails
    ");
    str1 = "";
```

```
13.  while(rs.next())
14.  {
15.  str1  +=  rs.getString(1)   +"#";
16.  }
17.  out.println(str1);
18.  System.out.println(str1);
19.  rs.close();
20.  stmt.close();
21.  conn.close();
22.  }catch(Exception  e)  {
23.  System.out.print(e);
24.  }
25.%>
```

- Line 1: Importing the packages.
- Line 2-5: Declaring the variables.
- Line 8: To indicate the Class object associated with the class or interface with the given string name, sun.jdbc.odbc.JdbcOdbcDriver to initialize the driver.
- Line 9: To create an object of Connection.
- Line 10: To create an instance of Statement.
- Line 11: To retrieve the distinct cities from the table TourDetails.
- Lines 13-16: To select the city and add it to the string until end of the Resultset.
- Line 19: Close the Resultset.
- Line 20: Close the Statement.
- Line 21: Close the Connection.
- Lines 22-24: To catch any exception.

Listing 16.3 gives the source code for Citydetails.jsp. This program retrieves the information from the database using the information of city and name of the place selected.

Listing 16.3: Citydetails.jsp

<%— This is a JSP File to retrieve Names based on name of the Place and City from the Database —%>

```
<%@ page import="java.sql.*,java.util.*"  %>
<%! Connection conn; %>
<%! Statement stmt; %>
<%! ResultSet rs; %>
<%! String str1,category,city,cityname;
String param; %>
<%
try{
```

```
9. city = request.getQueryString();
10.   city = city.replace('_',' ');
11.   cityname = city.substring(city.indexOf("=")+1);
12.   param="select Name from TourDetails where City='"+cityname+"'";
/* Connecting to the Data Base */
13.   Class.forName("sun.jdbc.odbc.JdbcOdbcDriver");
14.   conn = DriverManager.getConnection("jdbc:odbc:ETour");
15.   stmt = conn.createStatement();
16.   rs = stmt.executeQuery(param);
17.   str1 = "";
18.   while(rs.next())
19.   {
20.   str1 += rs.getString(1)  +"#";
21.   }
22.   out.println(str1);
23.   System.out.println(str1);
24.   rs.close();
25.   stmt.close();
26.   conn.close();
27.   }catch(Exception e)  {
28.   System.out.print(e);
29.   }
30.   %>
```

- Line 1: Importing the packages.
- Lines 2-6: Declaring the variables.
- Line 9: QueryString will be assigned to the string city.
- Line 10: Replace the underscore with the space.
- Line 11: Get the substring of the string cityname to the specified index and assign it to the string cityname.
- Line 12: Assign the Select query to the string param.
- Line 13: To indicate the Class object associated with the class or interface with the given string name, sun.jdbc.odbc.JdbcOdbcDriver for initializing the driver.
- Line 14: To create an object of Connection.
- Line 15: To create an instance of Statement.
- Line 16: To retrieve the Name from the table TourDetails for the corresponding City.
- Lines 18-21: To select the Place, add it to the string until end of the Resultset.
- Line 24: Close the Resultset.
- Line 25: Close the Statement.
- Line 26: Close the Connection.

Listing 16.4 gives the source code for NameCategory.jsp. This program retrieves the information of a particular category for the selected city.

Listing 16.4: NameCategory.jsp.

<%— This is a JSP File to retrieve Infromation of Particular Category of a particular City from the Database —%>

```
<%@ page import="java.sql.*,java.util.*" %>
<%! Connection conn; %>
<%! Statement stmt; %>
<%! ResultSet rs; %>
<%! String str1,category,city,cityname;
String param; %>
<%
try{
city = request.getQueryString();
   city = city.replace('_',' ');
   cityname = city.substring(city.indexOf("=")+1,city.indexOf("&"));
   category=city.substring(city.lastIndexOf("=")+1);
   param="select Description,Timings,EntryFee,City,Name from
TourDetails where City='"+cityname+"' and Name='"+category+"'";
/* Connecting to the Data Base */
   Class.forName("sun.jdbc.odbc.JdbcOdbcDriver");
   conn = DriverManager.getConnection("jdbc:odbc:ETour");
   stmt = conn.createStatement();
   System.out.println(param);
   rs = stmt.executeQuery(param);
   str1 = "";
   while(rs.next())
   {
   str1 = rs.getString(1) +"#";
   str1 += rs.getString(2) +"#";
   str1 += rs.getString(3) +"#";
   str1 += rs.getString(4) +"#";
   }
   out.println(str1);
   System.out.println(str1);
   rs.close();
   stmt.close();
   conn.close();
   }catch(Exception e) {
   System.out.print(e);
   }
   %>
```

- Line 1: Importing the packages.
- Lines 2-6: Declaring the variables.
- Line 9: QueryString will be assigned to string city.
- Line 10: Replace the underscore with the space.
- Line 11: Get the substring starting after equal to (=) and upto the symbol & but not including &; assign it to the string cityname.
- Line 12: Get the substring of the string city to the specified index and assign it to the string Category.
- Line 14: Mention the Class object associated with the class or interface with the given string name, sun.jdbc.odbc.JdbcOdbcDriver for initializing the driver.
- Line 15: To create an object of Connection.
- Line 16: To create an instance of Statement.
- Line 18: To retrieve the Description, Timings, EntryFee, City, Name from the table TourDetails for the corresponding City and Place.
- Lines 20-26: To select the fields and add them to the string until end of the Resultset.
- Line 29: Close the Resultset.
- Line 30: Close the Statement.
- Line 31: Close the Connection.
- Lines 32-34: To catch exceptions, if any.

16.2.4 Output

When you execute this application using the steps given in Section 16.1, the output will be displayed on the emulator as shown in Fig. 16.11(a) and (b).

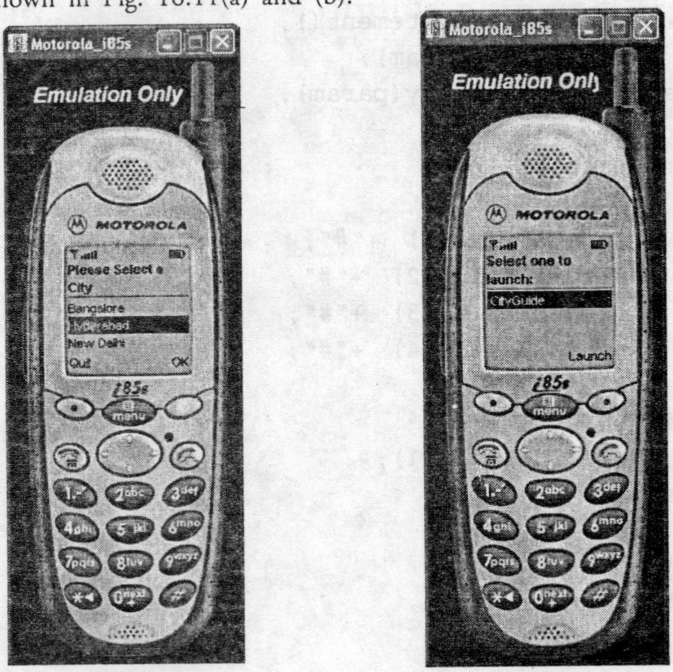

Fig. 16.11(a): CityGuide Application on the Emulator

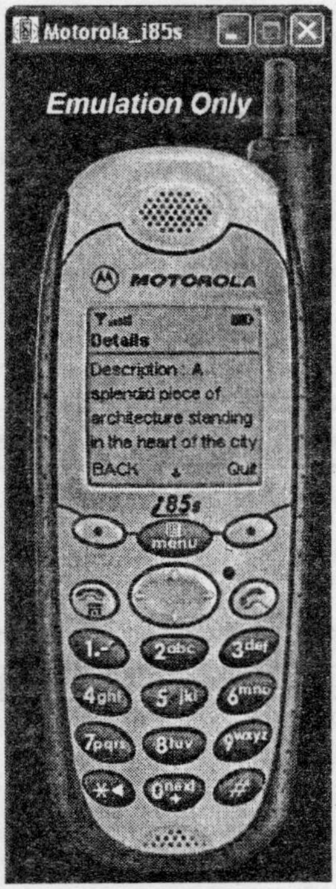

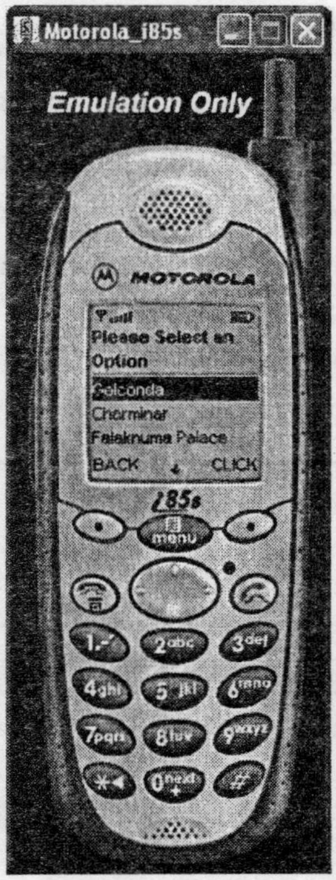

Fig. 16.11(b): CityGuide Application on the Emulator

16.3 Project: Electronic Voting

Why do we need to go to a polling booth for voting? In the not too distant future, we can use our mobile phones to do the voting. Anywhere-anytime voting! As of now, security is a major issue and hence electronic voting is yet to become popular. Some politicians may not like it as it is not possible to do rigging! In this project, we will demonstrate how to develop an electronic voting application for a professional body (for example, IEEE student chapter of your college). You need to give your membership number and password to vote. You need to elect President, Secretary and Treasurer.

As in the above example, we need to write Java programs and JSP programs to do the job.

This project consists of the following modules:

- A database consisting of two tables (vote.mdb)
- ElectionVote.java
- ValidateMember.jsp
- UpdateContestant.jsp
- UpdateVoter.jsp
- DisplayContestant.jsp
- DisplayResults.java
- DisplayResults.jsp

16.3.1 Database Design

First let us create the database that consists of two tables:

- Voters table that contains the membership number, password and status (whether voted or not).
- Contest table that contains the votes obtained by the contestants.

The details of the tables are as shown in Fig. 16.12 and Fig. 16.13. The field names, field types, description and length are as follows:

Table Name: Voters

Field Name	Field Type	Description	Length
Membershipno	Text	Membership Number	8
Pwd	Text	Password	8
Status	Number	Status	

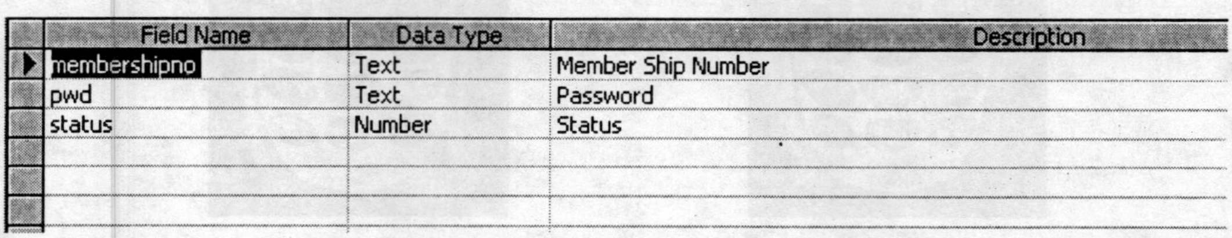

Field Name	Data Type	Description
membershipno	Text	Member Ship Number
pwd	Text	Password
status	Number	Status

Fig 16.12: Electronic Voting Database Table "Voters"

Table Name: Contest

Field Name	Field Type	Description	Length
PersonName	Text	Name of the Person	50
Votes	Number	Number of Votes	8
Post	Text	Name of the Post	50

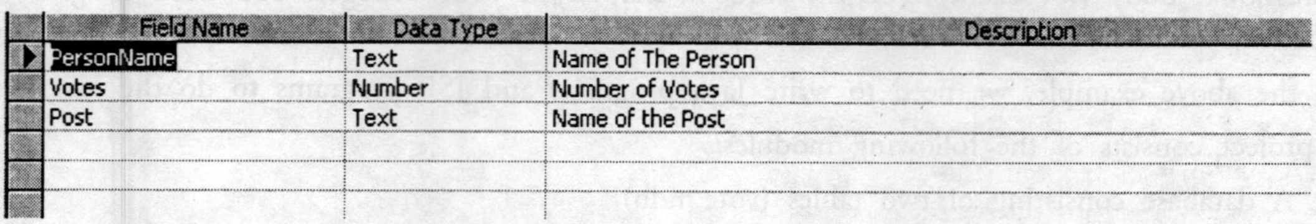

Field Name	Data Type	Description
PersonName	Text	Name of The Person
Votes	Number	Number of Votes
Post	Text	Name of the Post

Fig 16.13: Database Table "Contest"

After creating these tables, you need to populate the Voters table with some data to test your application.

16.3.2 Source Code Listing of Java Program

The source code of the Java program ElectionVote.java is given in Listing 16.5. This program is to create the user interface and give the output to the user on the mobile device. Using a HTTP connection, the data on the server is retrieved and presented to the user.

Listing 16.5: ElectionVote.java

```
/**
  * An Application for Electronic voting
  * Refer to ElectionVote, PostDetails,ContestantDetails Methods
  * Refer to the startApp, pauseApp, and destroyApp
  * methods so see how each handles the requested transition.
*/
package ElectronicVote;
import javax.microedition.midlet.*;
import javax.microedition.lcdui.*;
import javax.microedition.io.*;
import java.io.*;
 public class ElectionVote extends MIDlet implements CommandListener
{
     private Command okCommand,exitCommand; // The exit command
     private Command nextcommand,quitcommand,msgcommand;
    private Display display;      // The display for this MIDlet
     private Form MainFrm;
     StringItem memsname;
       TextField tf1,tf2;
       List list;
       HttpConnection hc = null;
       InputStream isc = null,isccont=null;
       HttpConnection hc2 = null;
       HttpConnection hcupdate1=null,hcupdate2=null;
       InputStream isc2 = null,isctest=null;
       StringBuffer sb2;
       StringBuffer contestants=new StringBuffer();
       String[] options;
       long len=0;
       int flag=0;
       String mno,psd;
       public ElectionVote() {
               display = Display.getDisplay(this);
               MainFrm=new Form("Electronic Voting");
```

```
            tf1=new TextField("MS No","",10,TextField.NUMERIC);
           tf2=new TextField("Password","",10,TextField.PASSWORD);
            MainFrm.append(tf1);
            MainFrm.append(tf2);
            okCommand = new Command("OK", Command.OK, 1);
            exitCommand = new Command("Exit", Command.EXIT, 1);
            MainFrm.addCommand(okCommand);
            MainFrm.addCommand(exitCommand);
            MainFrm.setCommandListener(this);
            display.setCurrent(MainFrm);
        }
    /**
    * Start up the MIDlet by creating the TextBox and associating
      * the exit command and listener.
      */
public void startApp() {
        System.out.println("Application Started");
    }
   /**
     * Pause is a no-op since there are no background activities
 or
      * record stores that need to be closed.
      */
public void pauseApp() {
    }

     /** * Destroy must cleanup everything not handled by the
 garbage collector.
      * In this case there is nothing to cleanup.
      */
public void destroyApp(boolean unconditional) {
            hc=null;
            hc2=null;
            isc=null;
            isc2=null;
            hcupdate1=null;
            hcupdate2=null;
            flag=0;
        }
```

```
    /*
     * Respond to commands, including exit
     * On the exit command, cleanup and notify that the MIDlet
   has been destroyed.
     */
public void commandAction(Command c, Displayable s) {
        if (c == okCommand) {
            mno=tf1.getString();
            psd=tf2.getString();
            if ( (mno.equals("")) || (psd.equals("")) )
            {
                Alert error=new Alert("Error","Fields are
                        mandatory",null,AlertType.ERROR);
        error.setTimeout(Alert.FOREVER);
                display.setCurrent(error,MainFrm);
            }
            else                              //first else
            {
                StringBuffer sb=new StringBuffer();
                String param=mno+"&pwd="+psd;
                param = param.replace(' ','_');
          String url=
"http://localhost:8080/Electionvote/ValidateMember.jsp?membershipno
 ="+param;
                try{
          hc = (HttpConnection)Connector.open(url);

                int ch=0;
    /* An inputstream is opened to read from that connection */
                isc = hc.openInputStream();
                len = hc.getLength();
                if(len !=-1){
                    for(int i=0;i<len;i++){
                      if((ch = isc.read()) !=-1)
                      {
                        sb.append((char)ch);
                      }
                    }
                }
              else{
              while(( ch = isc.read()) !=-1){
```

```
                len = isc.available()  ;
                sb.append((char)ch);
                  }
              }
            String  str1  =  sb.toString();
            String  item="";
              str1.trim();
              int  index  =  str1.indexOf("#");
             if(index  !=  -1)
             {
              item  =  str1.substring(0,str1.indexOf("#"));
               item=item.trim();
             }
              item.trim();
    if(item.equals("0"))  {          //  If  voter  not  participated  in  election
                      PostDetails("President");
                    }    //if(item.equals("0"))
                            else  if(item.equals("1"))   {  //If  voter  already  voted
                                 Alert  info=new  Alert("Information","Already  Voted",null,AlertType.INFO);
                          info.setTimeout(Alert.FOREVER);
                          display.setCurrent(info,MainFrm);
                          tf1.setString("");
                          tf2.setString("");
                    }
                  else
                    {
 Alert  error=new  Alert("Error","Please  Check  Membership  Number  &  Password",null,  AlertType.ERROR);
                          error.setTimeout(Alert.FOREVER);
                          display.setCurrent(error,MainFrm);
                    }
                        }catch(Exception  e)     {
     System.out.println(e+"Exception  catch");
                        }
                       finally{
                            try{
                                   hc.close();
                                   isc.close();
```

```
                                        }catch(Exception e){
    System.out.println(e+"Exception in Finally ");
                                            }
                                    }
                                } // first else
                        } //if (c==okCommand)
                        if (c==exitCommand){
                            destroyApp(false);
                            notifyDestroyed();
                        }
                        if(c==quitcommand){
                                destroyApp(false);
                                notifyDestroyed();
                        }
                        if(c==msgcommand){
                                destroyApp(false);
                                notifyDestroyed();
                        }
                        if(c==nextcommand){
                            try{
                                    String listitem;
                                    if(flag==1)
                                    {
  listitem=list.getString(list.getSelectedIndex())+"#";
                                        contestants.append(listitem);
                                        PostDetails("Secretary");
                                    }
                                    else if(flag==2){
  listitem=list.getString(list.getSelectedIndex())+"#";
                                        contestants.append(listitem);
                                        PostDetails("Treasurer");
                                    }
                                    else if(flag >2){
  listitem=list.getString(list.getSelectedIndex())+"#";
                            contestants.append(listitem);
                            // dividing the contestents
      int pos=0;
                                    int p=0;
                                        String[] conteststr;
                                        conteststr=new String[3];
```

```
String pcont=contestants.toString();
while(pos != -1) {
pos = pcont.indexOf("#");
if(pos != -1)
{ conteststr[p] = pcont.substring(0,pcont.indexOf("#"));
pcont = pcont.substring (pcont.indexOf("#")+1);
conteststr[p]=conteststr[p].replace(' ','_');
}
p=p+1;
} //dividing the contestents
String pname=conteststr[0]+"&"+conteststr[1] +"&"+conteststr[2];
String contesturl=
"http://localhost:8080/Electionvote/UpdateContestant.jsp?PersonName="+pname;
String voter=mno+"&pwd="+psd;
String voterurl=
"http://localhost:8080/Electionvote/UpdateVoter.jsp?membershipno="+voter;
try{
hcupdate1 = (HttpConnection)Connector.open(contesturl);
//to update number of votes of contestents jsp page
isccont=hcupdate1.openInputStream();
hcupdate2=(HttpConnection)Connector.open(voterurl); //To update status of voter jsp page
isctest = hcupdate2.openInputStream();
}
catch(Exception e){
System.out.println("Exception in Update:"+e);
}
finally{
try{
hcupdate1.close();
hcupdate2.close();
isctest.close();
isccont.close();
}catch(Exception e){
System.out.println(e+"Exception in Finally update");
}
} //finally
```

```
String [] text={"Thanks for participating in Electronic Voting"};
List msglist=new List("Thank You",List.IMPLICIT,text,null);
            msgcommand=new Command("OK",Command.OK,1);
            msglist.addCommand(msgcommand);
            msglist.setCommandListener(this);
            display.setCurrent(msglist);
        }
            }
                catch(Exception e){
System.out.println("exception in secretary"+e);
            }
        }
    } // end of public void commandAction(Command c, Displayable s)
    public void ContestantDetails(String[] a,String b) throws IOException
    {
            list=new List(b,list.EXCLUSIVE,a,null);
nextcommand = new Command("NEXT", Command.SCREEN, 1);
          quitcommand = new Command("EXIT", Command.EXIT, 1);
            list.addCommand(nextcommand);
            list.addCommand(quitcommand);
            list.setCommandListener(this);
            display.setCurrent(list);
}//end of public void ContestantDetails(String[] a,String b)
     public void PostDetails(String post) throws IOException
     {
        sb2=new StringBuffer();
         String url2="http://localhost:8080/Electionvote/DisplayContestant.jsp? Post=" +post;
try{
             hc2 = (HttpConnection)Connector.open(url2);
             long len2=0;
             int ch2=0;
  /* An inputstream is opened to read from that connection */
             isc2 = hc2.openInputStream();
             len2 = hc2.getLength();
                if(len2 !=-1) {
                    for(int i=0;i<len;i++){
                      if((ch2 = isc2.read()) !=-1){
                      sb2.append((char)ch2);
```

```
                    }
                  }
                } //if(len2!=-1)
              else{
                while(( ch2 = isc2.read()) !=-1){
                  len2 = isc2.available() ;
                  sb2.append((char)ch2);
                  }
                }
              String str2 = sb2.toString();
              String str3=sb2.toString();
              String item2="";
                str3.trim();
                str2.trim();
            int index2 = str2.indexOf("#");
int i=0;                                    //to count the members
                    while(index2 != -1)
                  {
                        index2 = str2.indexOf("#");
 str2 = str2.substring (str2.indexOf("#")+1);
    if(index2== -1)
                        {
                            break;
                        }
                        i=i+1;
      }                 //to count the members
            options=new String[i];
             i=0;
             index2 = str3.indexOf("#");
             while(index2 != -1)
             {
                  index2 = str3.indexOf("#");
               if(index2 != -1)
               {
      item2 = str3.substring(0,str3.indexOf("#"));
 str3 = str3.substring (str3.indexOf("#")+1);
                   item2=item2.trim();
                   options[i]=item2;
               }
                i=i+1;
             }
```

```
272.                 ContestentDetails(options,post);
273.                           }catch(Exception e) {
274.             System.out.println(e+"Exception catch");
275.                           }
276.                           finally{
277.                               try{
278.                                       hc2.close();
279.                                       isc2.close();
280.                               }catch(Exception e){
281.          System.out.println(e+"Exception in Finally ");
282.                                   }
283.     }
284.          flag=flag+1;
285.     }// end of public void PostDetails(String post)
286. }
```

- Lines 1-5: Importing of the various packages required for the program. These statements import various GUI components, HTTP Connection classes like HttpConnection and Connector class, and Input Stream class for communication.
- Line 6: Declaration of the class ElectionVote.
- Lines 8-25: Declaration of objects. Objects for User Interface Classes such as List, Form and several Command objects.
- Lines 26-39: Constructor for the class ElectionVote. This code initializes different command objects. The commands are generated when the user presses any button on the mobile phone.
- Lines 40-42: Declaration of the startApp() method, which is called when the MIDlet starts.
- Lines 43-44: This is an implementation of pauseApp method. When the application is paused, this method will be invoked.
- Lines 45-53: Implementation of destroyApp method. When the application is terminated, this method will be invoked to free the resources.
- Lines 54-204: Definition of commandAction method, which performs the action when the user presses a button.
  - o Lines 55-127: If OK command button is clicked
  - o Line 56: Get the Membership number from the textfield tf1.
  - o Line 57: Get the Password from the textfield tf2.
  - o Line 58-63: If any one of the textfeilds is null, display the error message "Fields are mandatory".
  - o Line 66-98: Get the status of voter for a particular membership number and password i.e., it is stored in item string.

- o Lines 99-101: If voter has not participated in election, PostDetails method will be invoked with parameter President.
- o Lines 102-108: If voter already participated, display the message "Already Voted".
- o Lines 109-114: If membership number and password are incorrect, display the message "Please Check Membership Number and Password".
- o Lines 128-131: If exit command button is clicked, destroyApp method will be invoked.
- o Lines 132-135: If quit command button is clicked, destroyApp method will be invoked.
- o Lines 136-139: If msgcommand button is clicked, destroyApp method will be invoked.
- o Lines 140-202: If next command button is clicked, the following code is executed.
- o Lines 143-148: When the user selects the President, the name will be appended to the StringBuffer contestants. The method PostDetails will be called to display Secretary candidates.
- o Lines 149-153: When the user selects the Secretary, the name will be appended to the StringBuffer contestants and calls the method PostDetails to display Treasurer candidates.
- o Lines 154-156: When the user selects the Treasurer, the name will be appended to the StringBuffer contestants.
- o Lines 157-170: The StringBuffer contestants is divided to get names of the candidates.
- o Lines 171-193: The status of voter and are updated the votes of the candidates by calling the server pages.
- o Lines 194-199: Displaying the message "Thanks for participating in Electronic Voting".

- Lines 207-216: Implementation of ContestantDetails method.
  - o Lines 209-215: List and Commands are created and added to the form.
- Lines 217-285: Implementation of PostDetails method.
  - o Line 219: The StringBuffer Object is instantiated.
  - o Lines 260-271: Within the while loop, assign the contestants to the string array options.

16.3.3 Source Code Listings of JSP Programs

Listing 16.6 gives the source code of ValidateMember.jsp. This program retrieves the status of voter from the database.

Listing 16.6: ValidateMember.jsp

```
<%— This is a JSP File to retrieve Status of a Voter from the Database —%>
<%@ page import="java.sql.*,java.util.*" %>
<%! Connection conn; %>
<%! Statement stmt; %>
<%! ResultSet rs; %>
<%! String memname,pwd,member,param,str1;
%>
```

```
7.<%
8.try{
9. member = request.getQueryString();
10.member = member.replace('_',' ');
11.memname                                                          =
   member.substring(member.indexOf("=")+1,member.indexOf("&"));
12.pwd=member.substring(member.lastIndexOf("=")+1);
13.param="select * from voters where membershipno='"+memname+"' and
   pwd='"+pwd+"'";
/* Connecting to the Data Base */
14.Class.forName("sun.jdbc.odbc.JdbcOdbcDriver");
15.conn = DriverManager.getConnection("jdbc:odbc:vote");
16.stmt = conn.createStatement();
17.rs = stmt.executeQuery(param);
18. if(rs.next())
19.{
20.   str1 = rs.getString(3)+"#";;
21.   out.println(str1);
22.   }
23.   else
24.   {
25.      str1="-1"+"#";
26.out.println("Please check Membership Number and Password Correctly");
27.   }
28.   System.out.println(str1);
29.   rs.close();
30.   stmt.close();
31.   conn.close();
32.   }catch(Exception e) {
33.   System.out.print(e);
34.   }
35.   %>
```

- Line 1: Importing the packages.
- Lines 2-5: Declaring the variables.
- Line 9: QueryString will be assigned to the string member.
- Line 10: Replace the underscore with the space.
- Line 11: Get the substring starting after equal to (=) and upto the symbol & but not including &; assign it to the string memname.

- Line 12: Get the substring of the string member to the specified index and assign it to the string pwd.
- Line 14: To indicate the Class object associated with the class or interface with the given string name, sun.jdbc.odbc.JdbcOdbcDriver for initializing the driver.
- Line 15: To create an object of Connection.
- Line 16: To create an instance of Statement
- Line 17: To retrieve the status of voter from the table voters for the corresponding membershipno and password.
- Lines 18-27: To find the status of voter and add it to the string until end of the Resultset.
- Line 29: Close the Resultset.
- Line 30: Close the Statement.
- Line 31: Close the Connection.

Listing 16.7 gives the source code of UpdateContestant.jsp. This program is to update the votes of a contestant and store in the database.

Listing 16.7: UpdateContestant.jsp

```
<%— This is a JSP File to update the votes of a contestent —%>
1.<%@ page import="java.sql.*,java.util.*" %>
2.<%! Connection conn; %>
3.<%! Statement stmt; %>
4.<%! String members,param,member1,member2,member3;
5.int i;
6.%>
7.<%
8.try{
9.members = request.getQueryString();
10.members=members.replace('_',' ');
11.member1 =
   members.substring(members.indexOf("=")+1,members.indexOf("&"));
12.members=members.substring(members.indexOf("&")+1);
13.member2=members.substring(0,members.indexOf("&"));
14.member3=members.substring(members.lastIndexOf("&")+1);
15.param="update Contest set votes=votes+1 where PersonName
   in('"+member1+"','"+member2+"','"+member3+"')";
/* Connecting to the Data Base */
16.Class.forName("sun.jdbc.odbc.JdbcOdbcDriver");
17.conn = DriverManager.getConnection("jdbc:odbc:vote");
18.stmt = conn.createStatement();
19.i=stmt.executeUpdate(param);
```

```
20.if  (i==0)
21.System.out.println("Not  Updated");
22.else
23.System.out.println("Updated");
24.stmt.close();
25.conn.close();
26.}catch(Exception  e)  {
27.System.out.print(e);
28.}
29.%>
```

- Line 1: Importing the packages.
- Lines 2-5: Declaring the variables.
- Line 9: QueryString will be assigned to string members.
- Line 11: Get the substring starting after equal to (=) and up to the symbol & but not including &; and assign it to the string member1.
- Line 13: Get the substring of the string members to the specified index and assign it to the string member2.
- Line 14: Get the substring of the string members to the specified index and assign it to the string member3.
- Line 16: To indicate the Class object associated with the class or interface with the given string name, sun.jdbc.odbc.JdbcOdbcDriver for initializing the driver.
- Line 17: To create an object of Connection.
- Line 18: To create an instance of Statement.
- Line 19: Update the votes of the candidates to the table Contest for the selected person.
- Line 24: Close the Statement.
- Line 25: Close the Connection.

Listing 16.8 gives the source code of UpdateVoter.jsp. This program is to update the status of a voter

Listing 16.8: UpdateVoter.jsp

```
<%— This is a JSP File to update Status of a Voter —%>
1.<%@  page  import="java.sql.*,java.util.*"  %>
2.<%!  Connection  conn;  %>
3.<%!  Statement  stmt;  %>
4.<%!  String  memname,pwd,member,param;
5.int  i;
6.%>
7.<%
8.try{
```

```
9.member = request.getQueryString();
10.memname =
   member.substring(member.indexOf("=")+1,member.indexOf("&"));
11.pwd=member.substring(member.lastIndexOf("=")+1);
12.param="update voters set status=status+1 where
   membershipno='"+memname+"' and pwd='"+pwd+"'";
/* Connecting to the Data Base */
13.Class.forName("sun.jdbc.odbc.JdbcOdbcDriver");
14.conn = DriverManager.getConnection("jdbc:odbc:vote");
15.stmt = conn.createStatement();
16.i=stmt.executeUpdate(param);
17.if (i==0)
18.System.out.println("Not Updated");
19.else
20.System.out.println("Updated");
21.stmt.close();
22.conn.close();
23.}catch(Exception e) {
24.System.out.print(e);
25.}
26.%>
```

- Line 1: Importing the packages.
- Lines 2-5: Declaring the variables.
- Line 9: QueryString will be assigned to the string member.
- Line 11: Get the substring starting after equal to (=) and up to the symbol & but not including &; and assign it to the string memname.
- Line 13: To indicate the Class object associated with the class or interface with the given string name, sun.jdbc.odbc.JdbcOdbcDriver for initializing the driver.
- Line 14: To create an object of Connection.
- Line 15: To create an instance of Statement
- Line 16: Update the status of voter to the table Voters.
- Line 21: Close the Statement.
- Line 22: Close the Connection.

Listing 16.9 gives the source code of DisplayContestant.jsp. This program retrieves the candidate's name from the database for the corresponding post.

Listing 16.9: DisplayContestant.jsp

```
<%— This is a JSP File to retrieve person name from the Database for the corresponding Post
  —%>
1.<%@ page import="java.sql.*,java.util.*" %>
2.<%! Connection conn; %>
3.<%! Statement stmt; %>
4.<%! ResultSet rs; %>
5.<%! String str1,str,contest;
6.%>
7.<%
8.try{
9.contest=request.getQueryString();
10.contest=contest.substring(contest.lastIndexOf("=")+1);
/* Connecting to the Data Base */
11.Class.forName("sun.jdbc.odbc.JdbcOdbcDriver");
12.conn = DriverManager.getConnection("jdbc:odbc:vote");
13.stmt = conn.createStatement();
/* Information of contest from    Database*/
14.str="select * from Contest where Post='"+contest+"'";
15.rs = stmt.executeQuery(str);
16.str1 = "";
17.while(rs.next())
18.{
19.str1 += rs.getString(1) +"#";
20.}
21.out.println(str1);
22.System.out.println(str1);
23.rs.close();
24.stmt.close();
25.conn.close();
26.}catch(Exception e) {
27.System.out.print(e);
28.}
29.%>
```

- Line 1: Importing the packages.
- Lines 2-5: Declaring the variables.
- Line 9: QueryString will be assigned to the string contest.
- Line 10: Get the substring of the string contest to the specified index and assign it to the string contest.

- Line 11: To indicate the Class object associated with the class or interface with the given string name, sun.jdbc.odbc.JdbcOdbcDriver for initializing the driver.
- Line 12: To create an object of Connection.
- Line 13: To create an instance of Statement.
- Line 15: To retrieve the person names from the table contest for the corresponding post.
- Lines 17-20: To retrieve the person name for the specified post and add it to the string until end of the Resultset.
- Line 23: Close the Resultset.
- Line 24: Close the Statement.
- Line 25: Close the Connection.

16.3.4 Output of Electronic Voting Application

When you execute the programs using the steps given in Section 16.1, the output will be displayed on the emulator as shown in Fig. 16.14(a), (b) and (c).

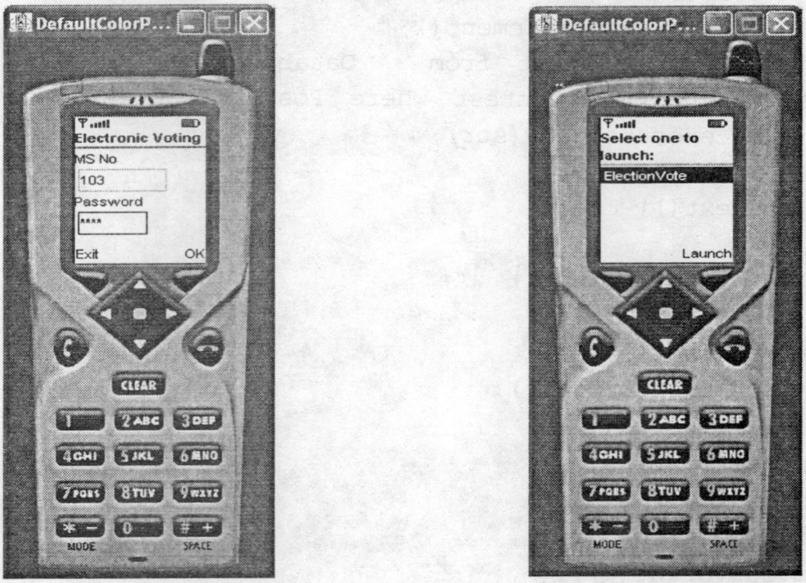

Fig. 16.14(a): Electronic voting application on the Emulator

Fig. 16.14(b): Electronic voting application on the Emulator

Fig. 16.14(c):Electronic Voting Application on the Emulator

16.3.5 Programs for Displaying Election Results

The following programs are to display the voting results. Listing 16.10 gives the source code for DisplayResults.java.

Listing 16.10: DisplayResults.java

```
/**
  * An Application for Displaying Election Results
  * Refer to DisplayResults,commandAction Methods
  * Refer to the startApp, pauseApp, and destroyApp
  * methods so see how each handles the requested transition.
*/
package ElectronicVote.Results;
import javax.microedition.midlet.*;
import javax.microedition.lcdui.*;
import javax.microedition.io.*;
import java.io.*;
public class DisplayResults extends MIDlet implements CommandListener
{
    private Command exitCommand; // The exit command
    private Display display;     // The display for this MIDlet
HttpConnection hc=null;
  InputStream isc=null;
      Command okcommand;
      public DisplayResults() {
            display = Display.getDisplay(this);
exitCommand = new Command(“Exit”, Command.SCREEN, 2);
String url =”http://localhost:8080/ElectionVote/DisplayResults.jsp”;
                   try{
   StringBuffer sb=new StringBuffer();
                                    String[] numconts;
numconts=new String[6];
hc = (HttpConnection)Connector.open(url);
 /* An inputstream is opened to read from that connection */
                           isc = hc.openInputStream();
                           long len=0;
                           int ch=0;
                           len = hc.getLength();
                           if(len !=-1){
                               for(int i=0;i<len;i++){
                                if((ch = isc.read()) !=-1)]
```

```
                    {
                        sb.append((char)ch);
                    }
                 }
              }
              else{
                 while(( ch = isc.read()) !=-1)
                 {
                   len = isc.available() ;
                   sb.append((char)ch);
                 }
     }
              String str1 = sb.toString();
              String item="";
                 str1.trim();
                 int index = str1.indexOf("#");
                 String strname,strvote;
                 int n=0;
            while(index != -1)
            {
                          index = str1.indexOf("#");
                       if(index != -1)
                       {
  item = str1.substring(0,str1.indexOf("#"));
    str1 = str1.substring (str1.indexOf("#")+1);
                              item=item.trim();
                              int pos=0;
                              pos=item.indexOf("@");
                              if (pos!=-1)
                              {
                              strname=item.substring(0,pos);
                              strvote=item.substring(pos+1);
      numconts[n]=strname+" got "+strvote+" votes.";
                              }
                       }
 n=n+1;
        }
 //Displaying Results in List
List result=new List("ELECTION RESULTS",List.
IMPLICIT,numconts,null);
```

```
        okcommand=new Command("OK",Command.OK,1);
        result.addCommand(okcommand);
        result.setCommandListener(this);
        display.setCurrent(result);
                    //Displaying Results in List
    }catch(Exception e)    {
System.out.println(e+"Exception catch");
}
    }

  /**
    * Start up the Hello MIDlet by creating the TextBox and
  associating
    * the exit command and listener.
    */
      public void startApp() {
      }

  /**
    * Pause is a no-op since there are no background
  activities or
    * record stores that need to be closed.
    */
 public void pauseApp() {
      }

  /**
    * Destroy must cleanup everything not handled by the
  garbage collector.
    * In this case there is nothing to cleanup.
    */
 public void destroyApp(boolean unconditional) {
      }

  /*
    * Respond to commands, including exit
    * On the exit command, cleanup and notify that the MIDlet
  has been destroyed.
    */
 public void commandAction(Command c, Displayable s) {
  if (c == exitCommand) {
```

```
82.                     destroyApp(false);
83.                     notifyDestroyed();
84.                 }
85.                 if(c==okcommand){
86.                     destroyApp(false);
87.                     notifyDestroyed();
88.                 }
89.         } //public void commandAction(Command c,Displayable s)
90.     } // end of public class DisplayResults
```

- Lines 1-5: Importing of the various packages required for the program. These statements import various GUI components, Http Connection classes like HttpConnection and Connector class, and Input Stream class for communication.
- Line 6: Declaration of the class DisplayResults.
- Lines 7-11: Declaration of Objects for User Interface Classes like the List, Form and several Command objects.
- Lines 12-73: Constructor for the class DisplayResults through HttpConnection, calls the server page, retrieves the information and stores it in the string array numconts; displays the results in the List result.
- Lines 74-75: Declaration of the startApp() method which is called when the MIDlet starts.
- Lines 76-77: This is an implementation of pauseApp method. When the application is paused, this method will be invoked.
- Lines 78-79: Implementation of destroyApp method. When the application is terminated, this method will be invoked to free the resources.

Listing 16.11 gives the source code of DisplayResults.jsp. This program retrieves the number of votes of contestants from the database.

Listing 16.11: DisplayResults.jsp

```
<%— This is a JSP File to Display Results of contestants from the Database—%>
1.<%@ page import="java.sql.*,java.util.*" %>
2.<%! Connection conn; %>
3.<%! Statement stmt; %>
4.<%! ResultSet rs; %>
5.<%! String str1,str,contest;%>
6.<%
7.try{
/* Connecting to the Data Base */
8.Class.forName("sun.jdbc.odbc.JdbcOdbcDriver");
9.conn = DriverManager.getConnection("jdbc:odbc:vote");
```

```
10.stmt  =  conn.createStatement();
/*  Information  of  contest  from    Database*/
11.str="select  *  from Contest";
12.rs  =  stmt.executeQuery(str);
13.str1  =  "";
14.while(rs.next())  {
15.str1  +=  rs.getString(1)  +"@"+rs.getString(2)+"#";
16.}
17.  out.println(str1);
18.  rs.close();
19.  stmt.close();
20.  conn.close();
21.  }catch(Exception e)  {
22.              System.out.print(e);
23.}
24.%>
```

- Line 1: Importing the packages.
- Lines 2-5: Declaring the variables.
- Line 8: To indicate the Class object associated with the class or interface with the given string name, sun.jdbc.odbc.JdbcOdbcDriver for initializing the driver.
- Line 9: To create an object of Connection.
- Line 10: To create an instance of Statement.
- Line 12: To retrieve the person names and total votes polled from the table contest.
- Lines 14-16: To retrieve the person name and votes and add it to the string until end of the Resultset.
- Line 18: Close the Resultset.
- Line 19: Close the Statement.
- Line 20: Close the Connection.

16.3.6 Voting Results Display

The election results are displayed when you execute the above programs. The output on the emulator is shown in Fig. 16.15.

Fig.16.15: Display of Election Results on the Emulator

Summary

In this chapter, we studied how to develop mobile applications in Java. Sun Microsystems released the Java 2 Micro Edition (J2ME) to address the consumer and embedded devices market. CDC and CLDC devices use J2ME for downloading the MIDlets for execution on the mobile device. The first application, City Guide, demonstrated how you can obtain information about the various places of a selected city on your mobile phone. The second application demonstrated the use of mobile phones for electronic voting. Even though the display size is very small on mobile phones, very user-friendly interfaces can be developed using J2ME. Java is the most attractive language for developing mobile applications as demonstrated through these two projects.

Chapter 17

Embedded Software Development on 89C51 Micro-Controller Platform

CHAPTER OBJECTIVES

After reading this chapter, you will be able to:

- Understand the usage of cross-development tools for 8051 family processors
- Learn the process of porting the embedded software onto the target hardware
- Gain knowledge of programming the 89C51 micro-controller development board for various applications

Intel 8051 family micro-controllers are simple yet powerful processors used extensively in embedded systems. In this chapter, we will study programming of this family of processors using 89C51-based development board.

17.1 Development Environment

In Chapter 5, we studied the hardware architecture of 89C51-based development board. In this chapter, we will study programming on this development board. To work on these projects, you need the following development tools:

- 89C51 development board. You can assemble the development board based on the circuit details given in Chapter 5. Alternatively, you can procure this development board from Innovation Communication Systems Ltd., Hyderabad (www.iseeyes.com)
- 10-15V DC, 500 mA Power Supply
- A Flash programmer
- A host system with the following minimal configuration:
  - Pentium processor
  - 16 MB RAM
  - 12 MB free Hard-Disk space (for cross-platform development tools)

    - Windows 95/98/2000 operating system
- Cross-platform development tools:
    - Keil C51 suite of development tools which can be obtained from www.keil.com
- Small Device C Compiler (SDCC), which is available under GPL
- 8051Sim, a code simulator

17.2 Cross-Platform Development Tools

If you want to develop software for industry-applications using 8051 family processors, you need to obtain a commercial cross-platform development suite. Keil C51 is one such suite. This suite includes an Integrated Development Environment (IDE) with editor, compiler, assembler, debugger and simulator. You can obtain a demo version of the software from www.keil.com. The demo version compiles code of size 8KB only.

Small Device C Compiler (SDCC) is an open source software available under GPL. It is a retargetable ANSI C Compiler for Intel 8051, Z80 and Dallas 80C390 micro-controllers. You can download this compiler from www.sourceforge.net.

8051Sim is a code simulator. In other words, it is a software implementation of 8051 family processors. So, even if you do not have the hardware, you can test your software. This is an ideal tool to debug the software before the executable image is transferred to the memory chip. You can obtain the code from www.dontronics.com/8051sim.html. Or, write to Steve Nolan, the author of this software at stevenolan@ukonline.co.uk

17.2.1 Using SDCC

To install the SDCC on your system, copy the SDCC.zip file into a directory and unzip the file. Extract the contents of the zip file to c:\SDCC folder.

For using SDCC, edit the C source Program using any Text Editor (for example, notepad). Save the source with extension .c in the target directory. Run the command prompt and change the directory to the target directory. Set the path to the BIN directory of SDCC using the following command:

```
path =   c:\sdcc\bin;
```

To compile the source file, type the following command:

```
sdcc filename.c
```

If compilation is successful, the following files will be created:

- filename.ihx
- filename.asm
- filename.lsm
- filename.rel
- filename.sym
- filename.map
- filename.rst

To program the Flash, remove the Flash with the help of a plucker and program it with the help of a Flash programmer. Load the ihx file into the Flash. After programming, again insert the flash into the base, give power supply to the development board and observe the output.

17.2.2 Using 8051Sim

The 8051Sim is a code simulator that can be used for debugging the software before it is transferred to the ROM. To run 8051Sim, click on 8051Sim.exe file. The user interface will be as shown in Fig. 17.1.

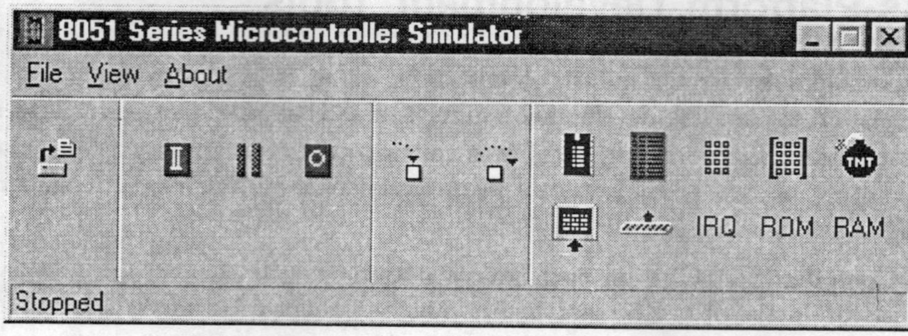

Fig. 17.1: 8051Sim User Interface

To simulate the code, click on the File option and select the Hex file. To run the program, click on the green button (highlighted in Fig. 17.2 below). Note that if you have used SDCC to compile the program, the .ihx file has to be renamed as .hex file.

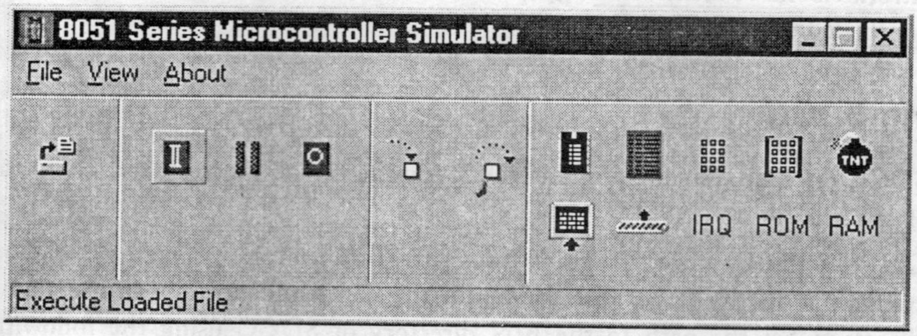

Fig. 17.2: Execution of the Loaded File

To halt the program execution, click on the blue button (highlighted in Fig. 17.3).

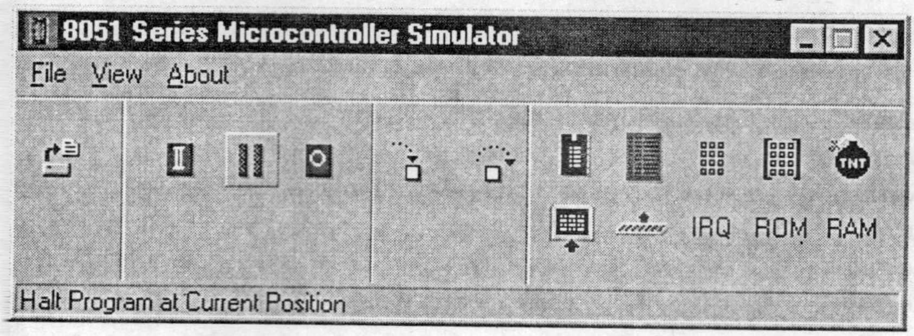

Fig. 17.3: To Halt the Program at Current Position

To stop the program execution, click on the red button (highlighted in Fig. 17.4).

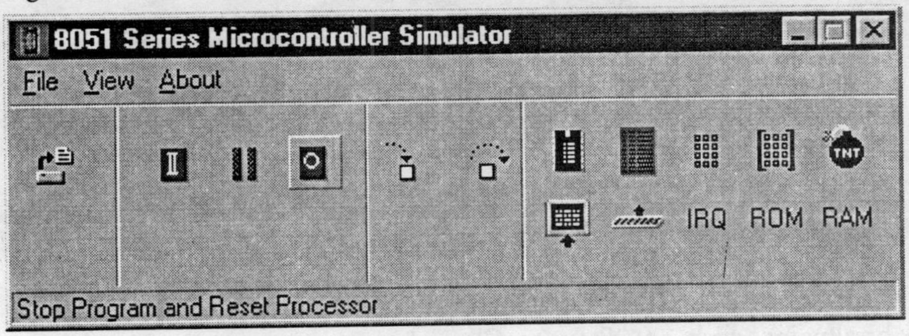

Fig. 17.4: To Stop the Program and Reset the Processor

For single-step execution, click on the highlighted button shown in Fig. 17.5.

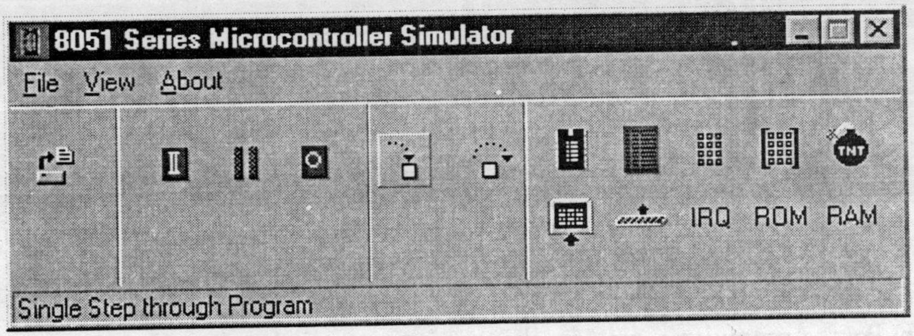

Fig. 17.5: Single-step Execution

To run the program to next instruction, click on the highlighted button shown in Fig. 17.6.

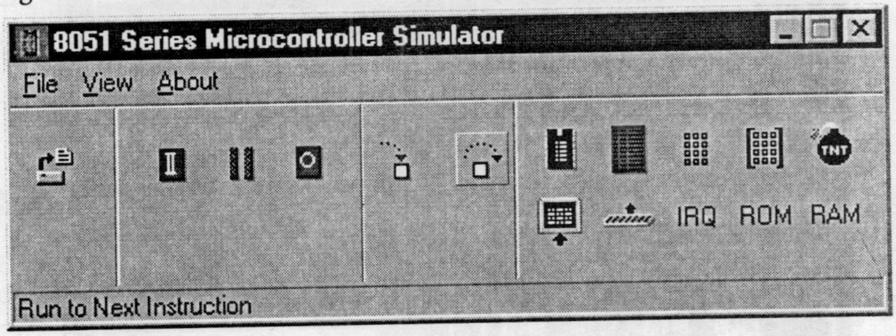

Fig. 17.6: Run to Next Instruction

To set a breakpoint, click on the View option and select the Breakpoints option as shown in Fig. 17.7. Write the address where you want to keep breakpoint and click on "Press to Set" button.

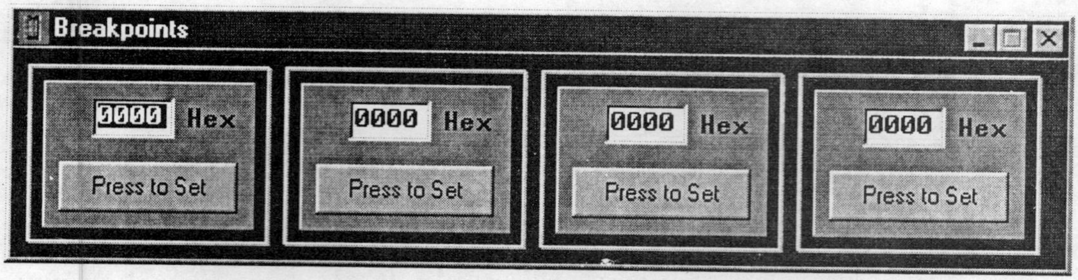

Fig. 17.7: To Set Breakpoints

To remove the breakpoint, click on "Press to Clear" button as shown in Fig. 17.8.

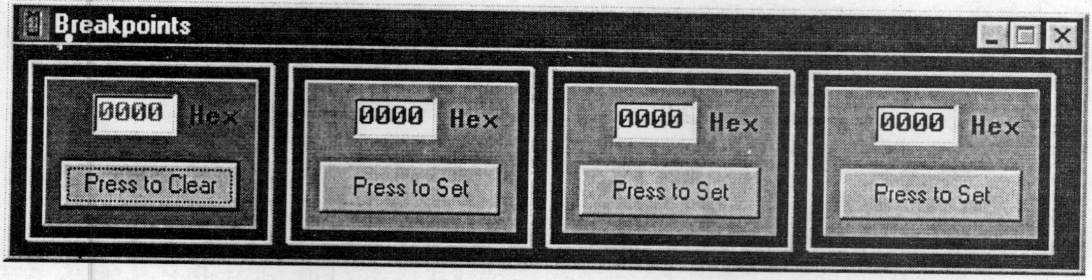

Fig. 17.8: To Remove Breakpoints

You can view the Processor Core by clicking on the View and selecting Core option. The status of Internal register, Port, Accumulator etc., in the runtime are displayed as shown in Fig. 17.9.

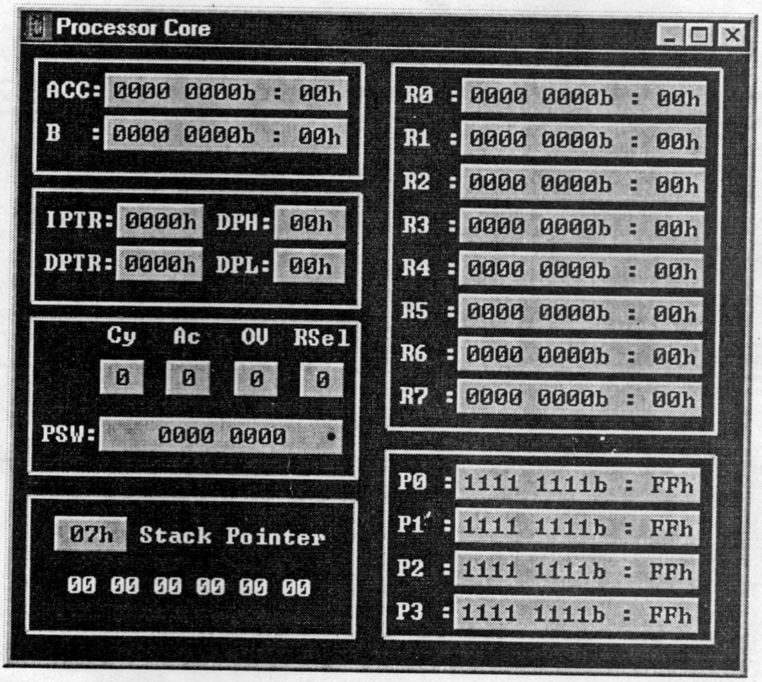

Fig. 17.9: To View the Processor Core

To view the source code, click on View and select the Listing option. The assembly code with the address location will be displayed on the screen, as shown in Fig. 17.10.

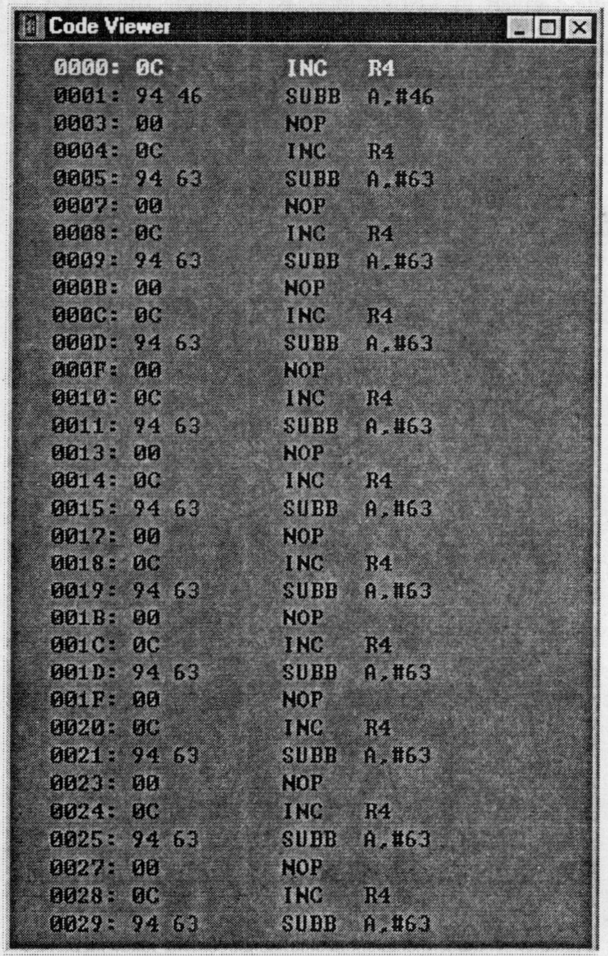

Fig. 17.10: To View the Source Code

17.3 Application Development

Once you are familiar with the development tools, you can start working on simple programs given in this section. Now, we will study three applications which can be compiled using SDCC and the executable image can be transferred to the 89C51 development board. You can also experiment with 8051Sim for these programs to do the debugging.

17.3.1 To Toggle the LEDs

The program LED_Toggle.c given in Listing 17.1 is to toggle the LEDs with a given delay.

Listing 17.1: LED_Toggle.c

```
/* Files generated By SDCC   : Assembly,List,Rel,SYM,Map,MEM,RST */
/*            ihex                      */
/* Purpose        : Toggles the LED at the given delay */
/* Registers used     : PORT1 :- Connected to LED N/W  */
/*              R0,R1 :- Delay                     */
/* Result         : LEDs connected to the PORT1 will  blink */
#Include<8051.h>
int delay(void); //this function generates the delay
/* The main routine writes the Value on the PORT1 after delay  */
int main(void)
{

  while(1)      //Infinite Loop

  {
    delay();    // Call the delay function

    P1 = 0xff;    // Write 0xFF in PORT1

    delay();    // Call the delay function

    P1 = 0x00;    // Write 0x00 in PORT1

  }

    return 1;

}

/*Generates the delay */

int delay(void)
{
  unsigned char count;
  for(count=0;count<=10;count++)
```

```
   {
                //Inline assembly
      _asm
      mov  R0,255     //Copy 255 in register R0
      0002$:   mov R1,255 //Copy 255 in register R1
      0001$:   djnz R1,0001$
      djnz R0,0002$
      _endasm ;

   }

   return 1;
}

/*END*/
```

In this program, observe the first preprocessor directive. The header file <8051.h> contains the register declarations for the 8051 family micro-controllers. You can go through this file to obtain the details of the registers in 8051 micro-controller.

You can also go through the following header files given along with SDCC. Some important files you need to study are:

- limits.h
- math.h
- serial.h
- stdio.h
- stdlib.h
- string.h
- time.h
- typedef.h

Another point to be observed in this program is inclusion of assembly code. This is known as inline assembly. Most of the compilers allow inline assembly code. Manipulation of registers is done through assembly. Also, if you want a faster execution, you may like to convert some portions of the C code into assembly.

17.3.2 To Glow a LED when a Switch is Pressed

Listing 17.2 gives the program SWITCH.c that glows a LED when a switch is pressed.

Listing 17.2 SWITCH.c

```
/* Compiler      : SDCC */
/* Files generated By SDCC : Assembly,List,Rel,SYM,Map,MEM,RST     */
/*                      ihex */
/* Purpose : corresponding LED will glow with      */
/*   respect of the switch     */
/* Ports used  : PORT1 :- Connected to LED N/W         */
/* PORT1 :- Connected to Switch N/W              */
/*Result : LEDs connected to the PORT1 will */
/*   blink when the corresponding switch is
*/
/*   pressed                                   */
/* PROGRAM FOR INPUTING DATA THROUGH SWITCH AND VIEW ON LED'S */

#include<8051.h>                                //HEADER FILE

unsigned char SW;                              //INITIALISING SW AS CHAR

/* The switches are connected to PORT0 and LEDs connected to PORT1
When you press a switch , the corresponding register gets updated, in
this case P0. This value is written onto another port register where
LEDs are connected, in this case P1 and the corresponding LED will glow
*/

int main(void)
{
        while(1)
                {
                 SW = P0;

                 P1 = SW;
                }
          return 1;
}

/*END*/
```

17.3.3 Communication through UART Port

Listing 17.3 gives the program TXD.c for serial communication between the host and the 89C51 development board.

Listing 17.3: TXD.c

```
/* Compiler: SDCC */
/* Files generated By SDCC : Assembly,List,Rel,SYM,Map,MEM,RST
*/        /*                    ihex      */
/* Purpose : UART Transmission   */ */
/* Registers used :SCON :- SERIAL PORT CONTROL SPECIAL */
    FUNCTION REGISTER                  */
/* :PCON :- POWER MODE CONTROL SPECIAL
FUNCTION REGISTER                        */
/* :TMOD :- TIMER MODE CONTROL SPECIAL
FUNCTION REGISTER                         */
/* :SBUF :- SERIAL PORT DATA BUFFER  */
/* :TH1   :- TIMER1 IS USED TO GENERATE
BAUD RATES FOR MODE1                     */

/* Result  : The corresponding value of "55"
which is "U", we can see on the
serial comm output of simulator
*/
/*PROGRAM FOR SERIAL DATA TRANSMISSION*/

#include<8051.h>
int main(void)
{

    unsigned char dat;
SCON = 0x40; //Setting the SCON for mode1,8 bit UART
PCON = 0x00;//Setting the SMOD bit in PCON to 0

TMOD =0x10; //Set timer1

TH1 =0xFD;  //To get standard baud rate 9600 hertz for timer1

SBUF =0x55; //Assigning "55" i.e. "U" to the SBUF for
//serial data transmission
        while(1)
  {
lab:  dat = SCON; //When 1 byte is transmitted SCON 2nd bit will
//become        1
dat = dat & 0x02; //Till that time it keeps transmitting bit by bit
```

```
if(dat !=0x00) //If transmitted this condition is true and again
{        //assigning SBUF to data and disabling SCON 2nd bit to 0
                              SCON = 0x00;
                              SBUF = 0x55;
                           }
                        else
                        goto lab;
            }

    return 1;
}

/*END*/
```

17.3.4 Further Experimentation

The C programs presented in Chapter 3 can be ported onto this development board. You can try out the following experiments:

- To transfer a file from the host system to the development board through UART.
- To obtain a string from the host system, calculate the CRC and send the CRC value back to the host system.
- To encrypt a string received from the serial port using a simple encryption algorithm and transfer the encrypted string back to the host system. The encryption algorithm can be, to start with, very simple: replace a by b, b by c and so on and finally replace z by a.

To avoid code repetition, the program listings are not included here. The 89C51 development board is the best way to start off your journey of working on embedded system hardware platforms. Embedded system programming is not as complicated as what many people perceive, thanks to the cross-platform development tools.

Summary

The objective of this chapter is to give headstart for embedded software development using one of the simplest development boards based on 89C51. The use of Small Device C Compiler (SDCC) and 8051Sim is explained. As demonstrated in this chapter, these cross-platform development tools are so sophisticated that the programmer's productivity is increased manifold. Simple applications such as making LEDs blink, giving inputs to the board through switches and communication through UART port are demonstrated. These are the fundamental building modules of any embedded software. These programs also give insight into the functioning of the hardware as well as programming the hardware.

Chapter 18

Embedded Software Development on AVR Micro-controller Platform

CHAPTER OBJECTIVES

After reading this chapter, you will be able to:

- Understand the cross-platform development tools usage for AVR micro-controllers.
- Gain knowledge of in-system programming
- Learn the details of programming the development board for different applications

AVR family of micro-controllers is yet another family that is used widely for embedded system development. In this chapter, we will study the programming aspects of the development board. We will also discuss how the target image is transferred to the embedded system.

18.1 Development Environment

The AVR ATmega128 micro-controller development board, the details of which are given in Chapter 5, is used to illustrate the software development on AVR micro-controllers. For cross-platform development, AVR Studio and AVRGCC together give you the ability to do advanced application development. You can create, compile, assemble, debug and link programs written in C, C++ and AVR assembly language.

To work on the applications presented in this chapter, you need the following development environment:

- AVR ATmega128 development board the hardware details of which are given in Chapter 5. Using the circuit details given in Chapter 5, you can develop the board yourself. Alternatively, you can procure the board from Innovation Communications Systems Ltd., Hyderabad (www.iseeyes.com)
- 12 Volts DC power supply
- Host system with the following minimum configuration for installing and running the AVR Studio and AVRGCC software:
  - o Pentium processor

- o 50MB free on hard drive
- o 64 MB RAM
- o One COM Port
- o One USB Port.

18.2 Cross-Platform Development Tools

AVR Studio and AVRGCC together can be used for cross-platform development. AVR Studio can be obtained from www.atmel.com. It is an Integrated Development Environment (IDE) for AVR micro-controllers. It provides the complete development suite consisting of editor, compiler, assembler, debugger, simulator and is also the interface for using emulators.

After downloading the AVRstudio, execute the "AVRstudio.exe" file. It is a self-extracting file that will extract all the required files to the current directory. Execute the "Setup.exe" file and you will be guided through the setup process.

AVRGCC is available under GNU GPL. You can obtain the software from www.avrfreaks.net. It contains C/C++ compiler, assembler, standard libraries, debugger and ELF to COFF converter. After downloading AVRGCC, execute the "AVRGCC" file. It is a self-extracting file that will extract all the required files to the current directory. Execute the "Setup.exe" file and it will guide you through the setup process.

18.2.1 Using the Tools

The step-by-step process for running assembly code and C code is as follows:

Assembly Code

Run the AVRStudio4.exe. The present List of Projects will be displayed. Click on the Create New Project, as shown in Fig. 18.1.

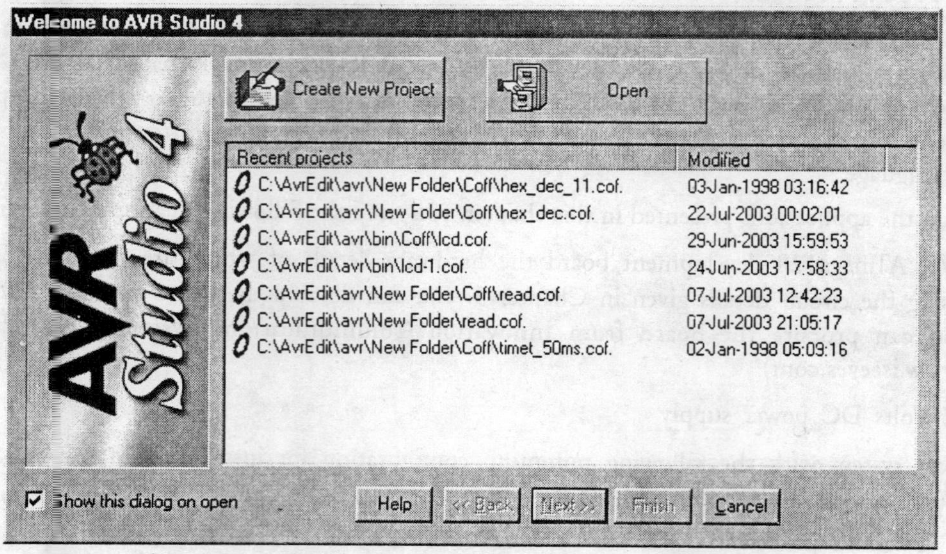

Fig. 18.1: Invoking AVR Studio

Edit the Project name and the name of assembly file in the Edit box and click on Next button, as shown in Fig. 18.2.

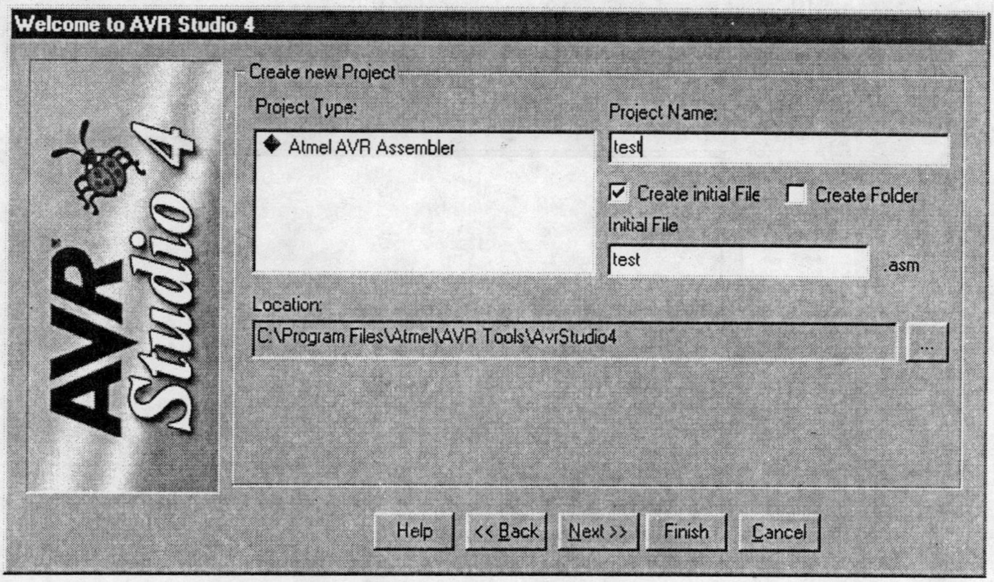

Fig.18.2: Creating a New Project

Select the Target device as ATmega128 and AVR simulator option. Click on the Finish button, as shown in Fig. 18.3.

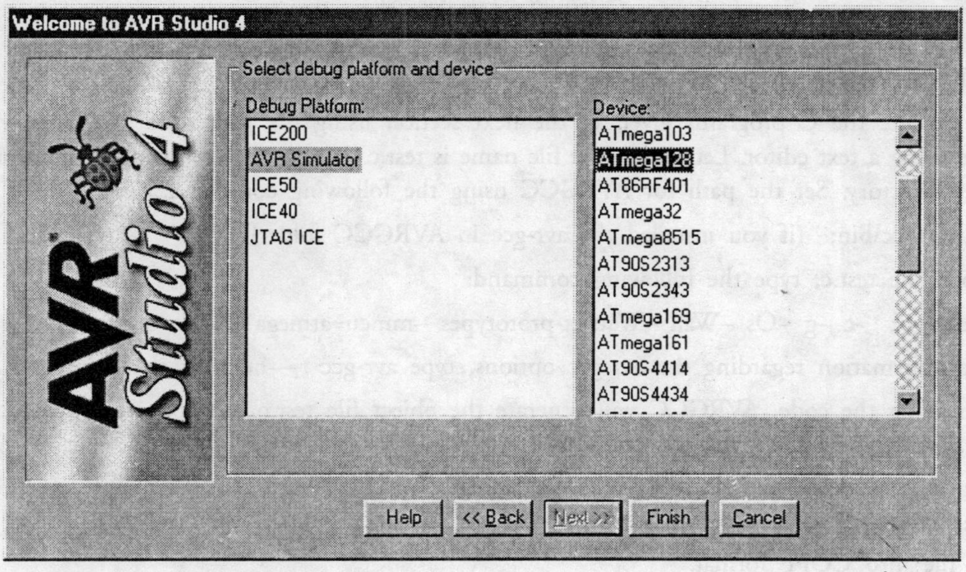

Fig. 18.3: Selection of Debug Platform and Target Device

Write the assembly code in the blank Edit window. After writing the code, click on the Build (F7) option to generate Hex file. If there are no errors in the code, the Build will be successful. Click on the Debug option to debug the code. Fig. 18.4 shows the Edit window.

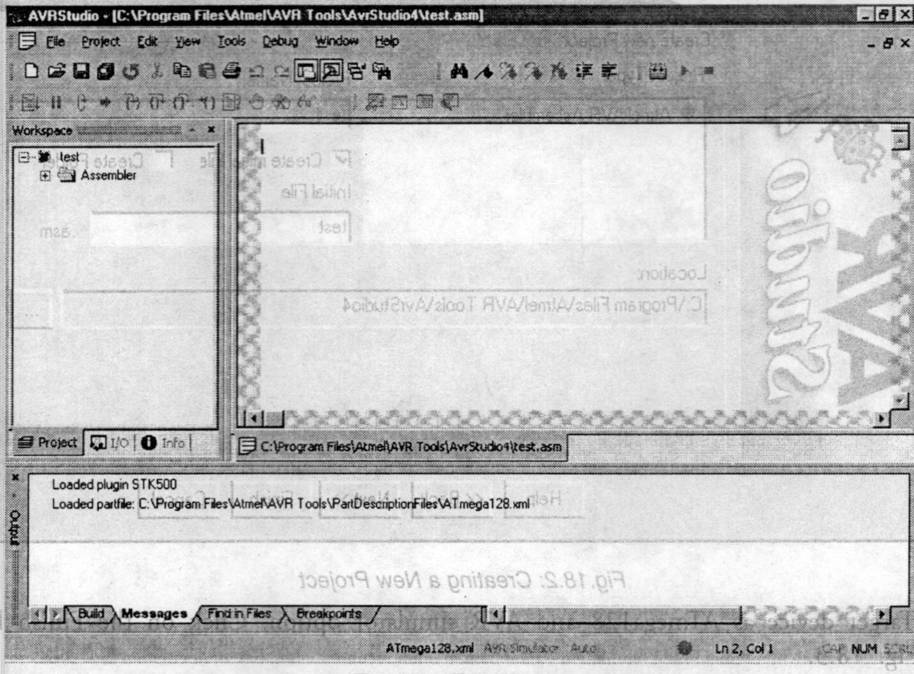

Fig. 18.4: Edit Window

C Programming

You can execute the C programs given in the next section using the procedure given below. Create the C file using a text editor. Let us say, the file name is test.c. Invoke the command prompt and open the target directory. Set the path for AVRGCC using the following command:

path = c:\avrgcc\bin; (if you installed the avr-gcc in AVRGCC folder)

To compile the test.c, type the following command:

c:\test\ avr-gcc -c –g –Os –Wall –Wstrict-prototypes –mmcu=atmega128 –o test.o test.c

For more information regarding the avr-gcc options, type avr-gcc —help on the command prompt.

After compiling the code, AVRGCC will generate the object file test.o. To convert the object file to the ELF format, type the following command:

c:\test\ avr-gcc test.o –mmcu=atmega128 –o test.elf

The ELF file is used to generate the Hex file. If you want to simulate the C code, you need to convert the ELF file into COFF format.

Simulation

To simulate the C Code, convert the ELF file to COFF format using the following command:

```
c:\test\elfcoff   test.elf  COFF  test.cof
```

Run the AVR Studio.EXE and click on the Open button of Menu. Select the test.cof file and select the Device and Debug Platform as shown in Fig. 18.5.

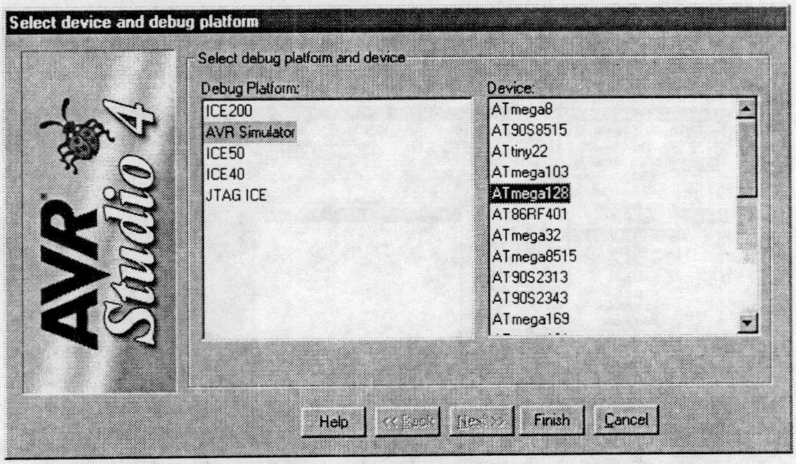

Fig. 18.5: Selection of Device and Debug Platform for C Program

Click on the Finish button. AVR studio will configure the parameters and you can simulate the code with breakpoints with single-stepping. You can see the Register values or status of each register value while simulating the code. Fig.18.6 shows the Debug window.

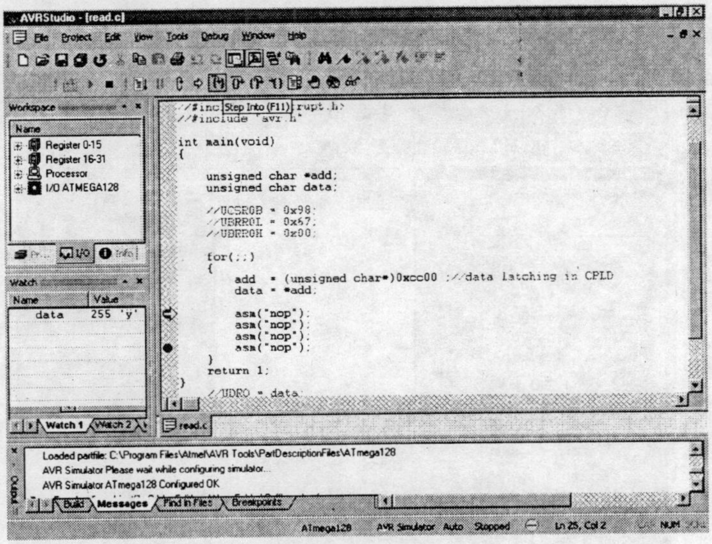

Fig. 18.6: Debug Window

Generation of Hex File

To generate the Hex file, type the following command.

c:\test\ avr-objcopy –O ihex –R eeprom test.elf test.hex

The test.hex is Intel Hex file. The following section gives the details of programming the Flash memory.

18.2.2 Parallel In-System Programming

Run the Serial Device Programmer (Pony-Prog2000), and select the Target device as ATmega128, as shown in Fig. 18.7.

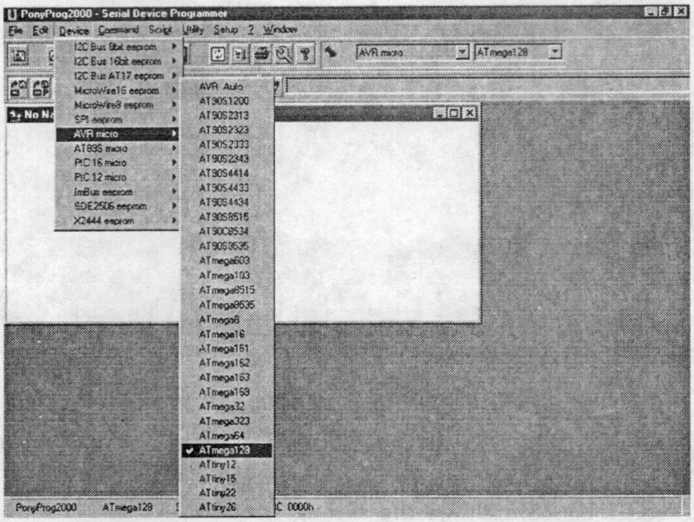

Fig. 18.7: Running the Serial Device Programmer

Set the I/O parameters as Parallel Port with AVRISP API, as shown in Fig. 18.8.

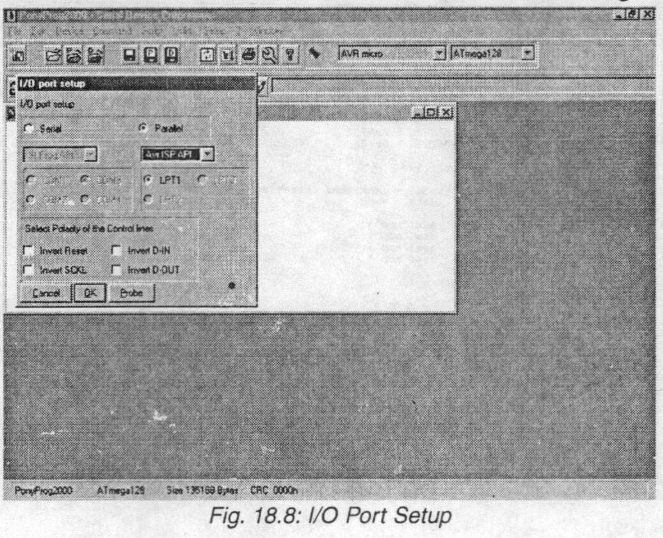

Fig. 18.8: I/O Port Setup

Click on the Open button of main Menu to select the Hex file as shown in Fig. 18.9.

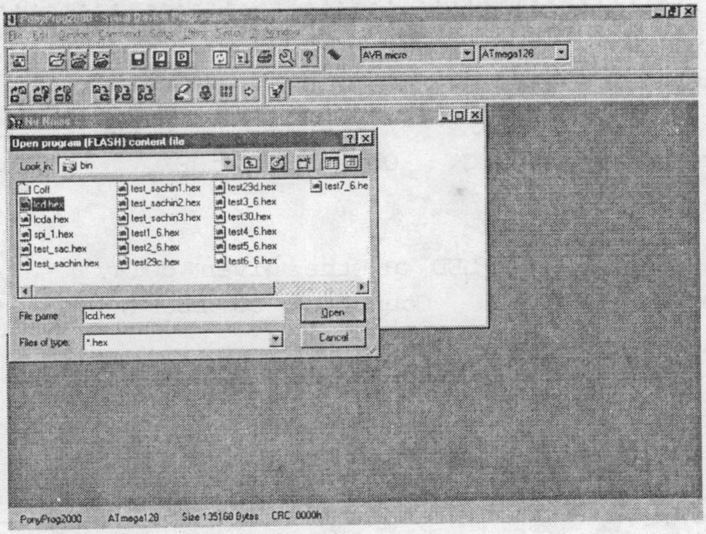

Fig. 18.9: Flash Content File Selection

Select the Erase option from the command Button to erase the Internal Flash of ATmega128. After erasing, select the Program option to program the device, as shown in Fig. 18.10.

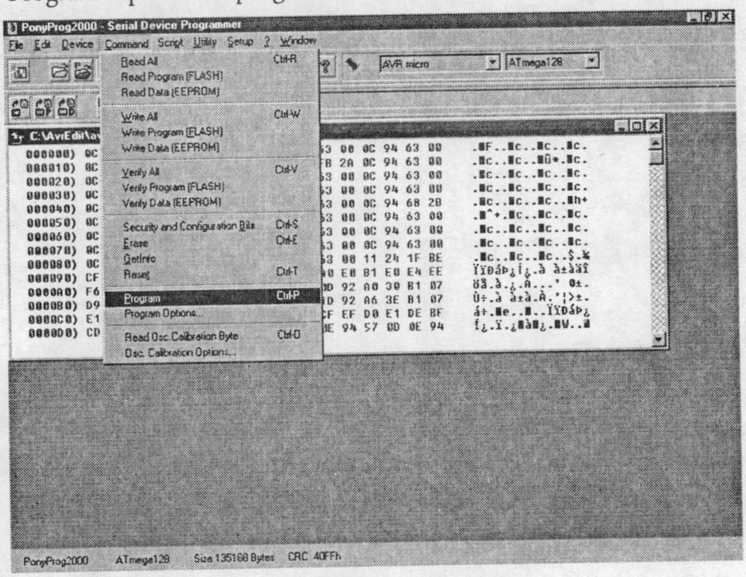

Fig.18.10: Programming the Flash

18.3 Application Development

In this section, we will study three programs to illustrate programming the development board using the above tools.

18.3.1 To Toggle the LEDs

Listing 18.1 gives the program LED_Toggle.c to toggle LEDs.

Listing 18.1 LED_Toggle.c

```
/* Compiler             : AVRGCC    */
/* Files generated by AVRGCC : Object,ELF,iHEX
*/
/*                                                    */
/* Purpose   : Toggles the LED at the given delay     */
/* Registers used : PORTA :- Connected to LED N/W     */
/*                                              */
/* Result    : LEDs connected to the PORTA will  blink */
#include "iom128.h"
#include<sfr_defs.h>

int delay (void);
//this function generates the delay

/* The main routine writes the Value on the PORTA then delay*/

int main (void)
{

   outp(0xFF,SPL);
   outp(0x0A,SPH);

   outp(0xFF,DDRA);

      for(;;)
      {
      outp(0x55,PORTA);
      delay();
      delay();
      outp(0xAA,PORTA);
      delay();
      delay();
      }
      return 1;
}

/*Generates the delay */
```

```
int delay(void)
{
  {
  unsigned int count;

  for(count=0;count<=5000;count++)
  {
     asm("nop");          //Inline assembly
     asm("nop");
     asm("nop");
     asm("nop");
  }
  return 1;
}
```

This listing shows how to include inline assembly code in the C program. You also need to study the following header files:

- eeprom.h (EEPROM access functions)
- interrupt.h
- math.h
- sig_avr.h (AVR signals and interrupt handling)
- stdlib.h
- string.h
- time.h
- wdt.h (watchdog timer functions)

18.3.2 To Glow LED based on the Input through a Switch

Listing 18.2 gives the program that glows a LED when a switch is pressed.

Listing 18.2 SWITCH.c

```
/* Compiler : AVRGCC                    */
/* Files generated By AVRGCC  : Object,ELF,iHEX   */
/* Purpose : corresponding led will glow with */
/*   respect of the switch
*/
/* Registers used : DDRA,PORTA,DDRB,PORTB          */
/* Ports used  : PORTA :- Connected to LED N/W        */
```

```
/*                  PORTB  :- Connected to Switch N/W       */
/*Result   : LEDs connected to the PORTA will              */
/*                  blink when corresponding switch is     */
/*         pressed                                          */

/* PROGRAM FOR INPUTING DATA THROUGH SWITCH AND VIEW ON LED'S */

#include "iom128.h"                          //HEADER FILE
#include<sfr_defs.h>

/* The switches are connected to PORTB and LEDs are connected to PORTA.
When you press a switch corresponding register gets updated, in this
case, PORTB. This value is written onto another port register where LEDs
are connected, in this case PORTA and corresponding LED will glow. */

int main(void)
{
   unsigned char data ;
   outp(0xFF,SPL);
   outp(0x0A,SPH);

   outp(0xFF,PORTA);
   outp(0x00,PORTB);

      for(;;)
      {
      data = inp(PORTB);

      outp(data,PORTA);
   }
      return 1;

}

/*END*/
```

18.3.3 Serial Communication Programming

Listing 18.3 gives the program UART.c for communication through UART port.

Listing 18.3 UART.c

```
/* Compiler            : AVRGCC
*/      /* Files generated By AVRGCC : Object,ELF,iHEX    */
/* Purpose             :                                    UART
*/
/* Registers used          : DDRD,PORTB,DDRB,PORTB    */
        :UCSROB,UBRROL,UBRROH,UDRO                   */
/*Result  : Transmitting the value "55"in UDRO */
/*      while receiving updating the register UDRO      */

#include "iom128.h"
#include<sfr_defs.h>
#include "signal.h"
#include <interrupt.h>

int main(void)
{

SPL  =  0xff  ;
SPH  =  0x0b  ;

 /*******************************UART**********************************/

UCSR0B  =  0x98;
UBRR0L  =  0x67;
UBRR0H  =  0x00;
UDR0  =  0x55;
sei();

for(;;)
{

DDRB  =  0xff;
DDRD  =  0xff;
PORTD  =  0xff;

}
return 1;
```

```
}

SIGNAL(SIG_UART0_RECV)
{

unsigned char dar;
dar = UDR0;
UDR0 = dar;

}

SIGNAL(SIG_UART0_TRANS)
{
UDR0 = 0x55;
}
```

18.3.4 Further Experimentation

In addition to the above programs, you can port the various programs given in Chapter 3 onto the development board. You can try the following programs on this board:

- Store voice in a file through the microphone input and play the voice file through the speakers.
- Transfer a file between the development board and the host system using USB interface.
- Transfer a file from the host system to the development board.
- Calculate the CRC of the received file on the development board.
- Use the development board as an encryption device. The data received from RS232 port should be encrypted and sent over USB interface.
- Send a file from the host system and display the file line by line on the LCD display.
- Port an operating system such as MicroC/OS-II on the development board.

Summary

In this chapter, we studied the cross-platform development tools for AVR family of micro-controllers. AVR Studio in conjunction with AVRGCC provides an excellent environment for developing applications on AVR-based development boards. How to develop applications on the ATmega128-based development board is also illustrated in this chapter. You can use this board to develop a variety of applications and also to port a real-time operating system.

Chapter 19

Embedded Systems Applications Using Intel® StrongARM Platform

CHAPTER OBJECTIVES

After reading this chapter, you will be able to:

- Understand the architecture of Intel StrongARM development board
- Learn how to program the Flash memory
- Gain knowledge of development of a number of applications such as parallel communication, interfacing stepper motor, JPEG encoder, MP3 decoder, file transfer and interfacing IrDA card.

This chapter presents a detailed description of an embedded reference board, Prayog™ developed by Aspire Communications Pvt. Ltd. This description will enable you to understand the actual composition of the hardware which is essential for developing hardware applications. The operating system used is LINUX. You can contact the company, for any further information on the Prayog board. Some important applications that can be developed using this development board are described in this chapter. The CDROM given with book contains complete source code for these applications. The CDROM also contains the details of a few other projects that can be done using this board.

19.1 Architecture of Prayog

Prayog is an embedded reference board based on Intel® StrongARM Processor. StrongARM processors are being used in many products such as PDA, handheld devices, cell phones, etc. The main reasons for wide usage of StrongARM processors include their high MIPS rate, low power consumption and availability of library functions under Linux operating system. Prayog board is a multi-function development platform under embedded Linux operating System. The peripherals provide wide-ranging options to design suitable hardware and interface them for realizing many applications irrespective of the fields of interest.

The material presented in this chapter serves two purposes, namely:

(1) It provides an insight to the reader about the actual composition of an embedded development system which supports all applications.

(2) It provides a good amount of knowledge about development of various applications on embedded development platforms. The applications have been carefully selected so that the reader should be able to easily understand them.

Prayog is based on Intel® StrongARM Microprocessor that incorporates a 32-bit StrongARM processor core, system control module, multiple communication channels, an LCD controller, general-purpose I/O ports, and a memory and PCMCIA control module. It provides various interfaces such as LCD, PCI, IrDA, PCMCIA, USB, AC'97 audio codec interface, along with other interfaces like PS/2, Serial, Parallel, FDD, HDD, and CDROM and an optional Ethernet interface.

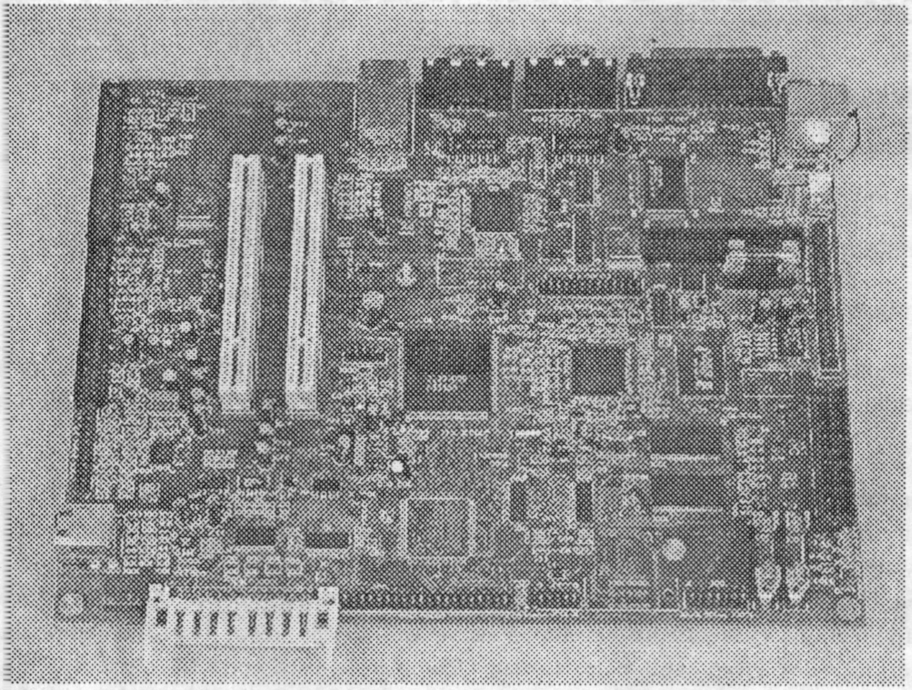

PRAYOG : Embedded reference board

19.1.1 Prayog Features

The important features of Prayog are listed below.

1. Highly integrated StrongARM processor featuring a 100 MHz memory bus and a flexible memory controller that provides high-bandwidth support for SDRAM, Flash, and variable-latency I/O devices.
2. Support for maximum of 64 MB SDRAM in a 54-pin TSOP footprint. System partitioning enables the system to support up to 103 MHz SDRAM.
3. On-board flash memory support for maximum of 16 MB, fast-page mode, 3V, 56-pin TSOP footprint Intel Strata Flash memory.
4. Multiple probe points for access to key signals.

5. Extremely flexible circuit routing employing complex programmable logic devices (CPLDs). User-designed daughter cards can be interfaced to the CPU local bus with the interface logic incorporated into the CPLD.

19.1.2 Peripherals

1. USB host controller interface that supports both low speed (1.5Mbps) and high speed (12Mbps) USB devices
2. Audio interface that can be directly interfaced to AC' 97 CODEC for controlling voice data to the speaker or from the microphone
3. Standard serial port (16C550 UART)
4. PCMCIA interface
5. IEEE 1284 Parallel Port
6. Floppy Disk Controller
7. IrDA port and transceiver capable of transfers up to 4 MB/sec
8. PS/2 for Keyboard and mouse
9. 10/100 Ethernet interface (RJ45)
10. Hard Disk Drive (2 HDD interface)
11. The two PCI slots provide option to include PCI-compliant devices to the development platform.

19.1.3 Prayog Software

The Prayog software consists of the following:

a. Boot loader

b. Linux OS

c. ARM-Linux GNU GCC Cross-Compiler tool chain

d. Application software on both hardware and software projects

The following figure shows the position of various IO facilities on the reference board.

19.1.4 Prayog Block Diagram

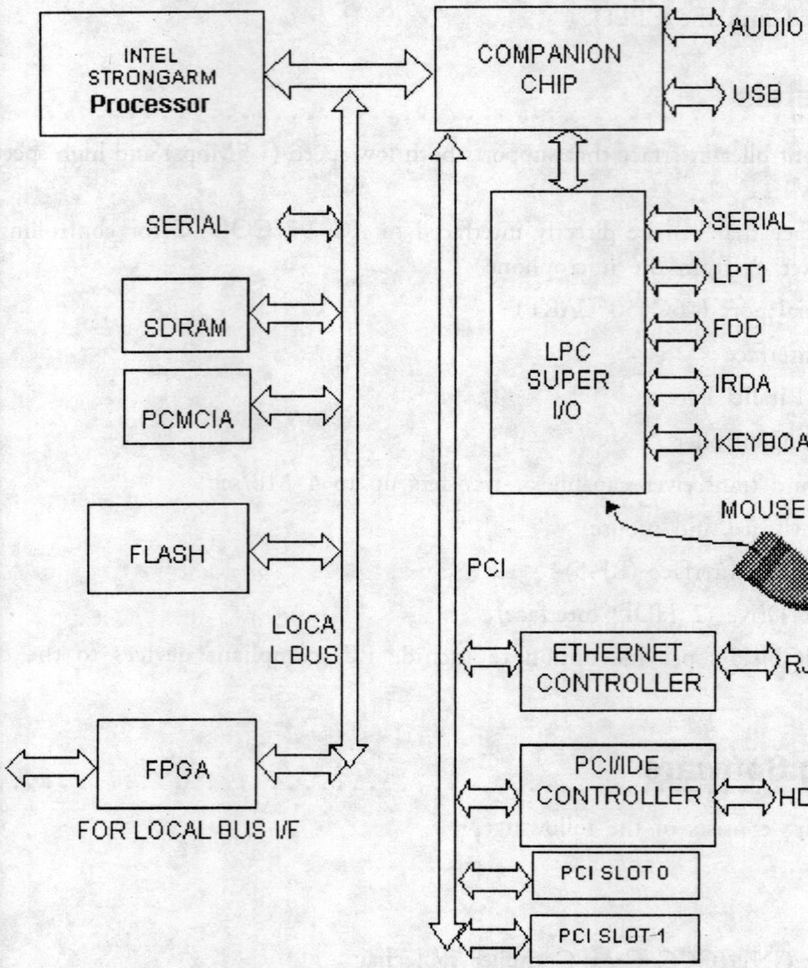

The above block diagram shows the simplified architecture of the embedded reference board. LPC super IO and companion chips have been used to provide the necessary IO facility for StrongARM processor. The processor itself can directly connect to Flash, SDRAM, FPGA and PCMCIA. Besides it gives out many IO lines.

19.2 Applications

This section presents applications on the embedded platform. The applications are carefully selected and presented to enable the user learn them systematically. Enough emphasis is given to theory part as most embedded systems are application-specific. The following applications are described in this section:

1. StrongARM device ID detection using JTAG
2. Programming the Flash Memory using JTAG

3. Parallel communication on reference board
4. Interfacing the stepper motor
5. Working with audio codecs
6. JPEG encoder
7. MP3 decoder
8. File Transfer between two embedded boards
9. Interfacing IrDA card with Prayog

The StrongARM microprocessor Device ID

The processor's "Device Identification code register" is a 32-bit "read-only" register. This register which is part of the JTAG circuitry is used to read the 32-bit device identification code. No programmable supplementary identification code is provided. The IDCODE (00110) instruction is used to read the ID register contents.

The program to read the device ID begins by having the Test-Access-Port Controller state machine of the JTAG in "Test-Logic Reset" state, then transitioning into the "Run-Test/Idle" state. Next is to have the state machine in the IR-Scan mode and hence pass the IDCODE (Binary code—00110) instruction, followed by updating the IR and looping back to "Run-Test/Idle" state. Next step is to transition the TAP Controller state to DR-Scan. The data hence obtained from the TDO is the device ID.

The TDI and TMS are sampled on the rising edge of TCK, and all output transitions on TDO occur as a result of the falling edge of TCK.

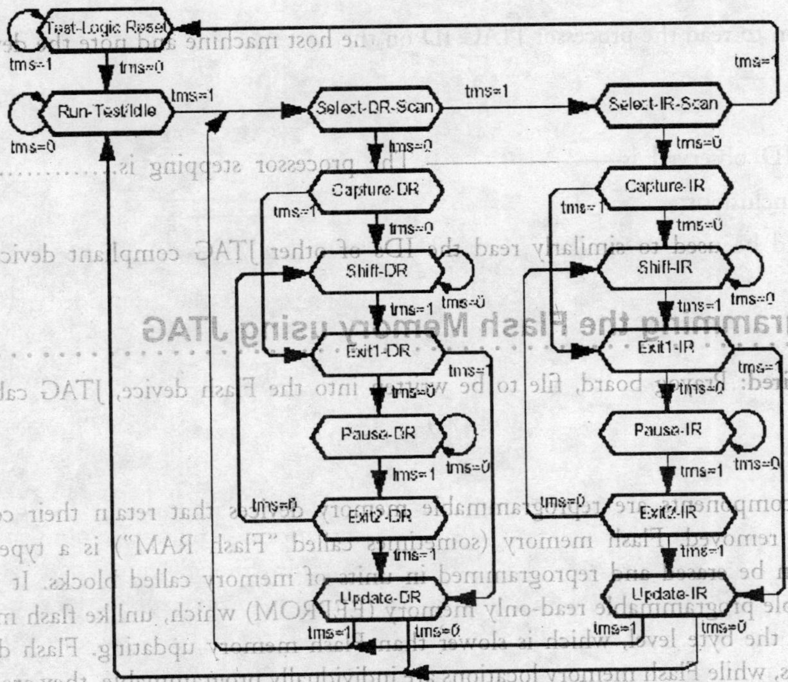

Test Access Port (TAP) Controller State Transitions

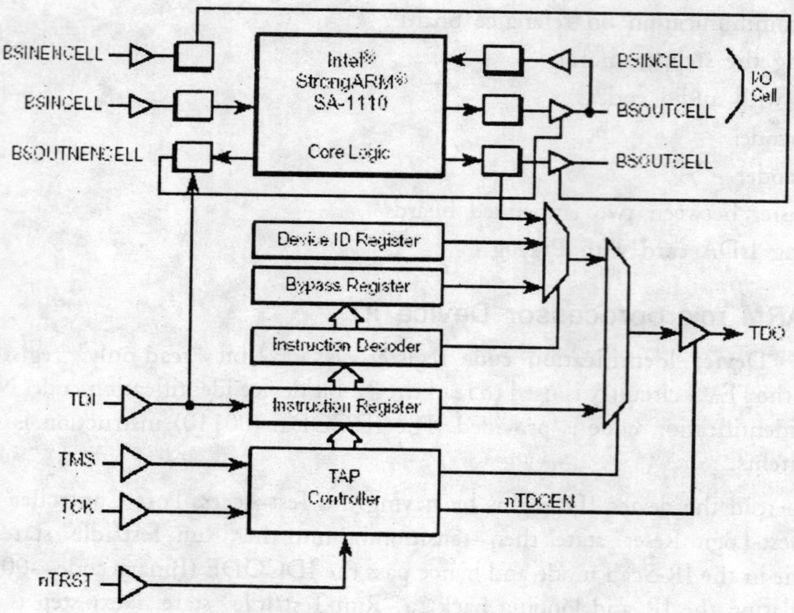

Boundary scan Block Diagram

Procedure:

Connect the Prayog board to the host system via the JTAG cable.

Power-up the board

Run the program to read the processor JTAG ID on the host machine and note the device ID displayed on the host.

Observations:

The processor ID observed is————————— The processor stepping is..............

Results and Conclusions:

The JTAG could be used to similarly read the IDs of other JTAG compliant devices.

19.2.2 Programming the Flash Memory using JTAG

Resources Required: Prayog board, file to be written into the Flash device, JTAG cable, host system.

Theory

Flash memory components are reprogrammable memory devices that retain their content after the power source is removed. Flash memory (sometimes called "Flash RAM") is a type of non-volatile memory that can be erased and reprogrammed in units of memory called blocks. It is a variation of electrically erasable programmable read-only memory (EEPROM) which, unlike flash memory, is erased and rewritten at the byte level, which is slower than Flash memory updating. Flash devices are block structured; that is, while Flash memory locations are individually programmable, they are not individually erasable the way they are with EEPROM. Instead, Flash memory is erased in sections whose sizes and locations in the chip are defined by the part's manufacturer. As a result, once a Flash memory location is programmed, the entire section containing the location must be erased before that location can be programmed again.

We will study how to program Flash memory via JTAG port.

We will use the JTAG Test Access Port (TAP) for programming the Flash memory. JTAG communicates serially (one bit at a time) with the PCB application. JTAG is a viable programming alternative in a manufacturing environment if your PCB application contains a JTAG-compliant microprocessor and you can tolerate somewhat longer programming times than those spent in other OBP methods. Alternatively, JTAG can be used to program boot code into the flash memory, with the remainder of the device programmed via in-system write. By using the JTAG cable to connect to the host and the target's JTAG port, you send commands and data through the JTAG TAP to the microprocessor. These commands and data instruct the microprocessor to program the Flash memory. You create the software to program Flash memory. A JTAG-compliant microprocessor has the following four pins included in its pin architecture:

TCK – Test Clock Input. A free running clock separate from the system clock.

TDI – Test Data In. Data is shifted into the JTAG-compliant device via TDI.

TDO – Test Data Out. Data is shifted out of the JTAG-compliant device via TDO.

TMS – Test Mode Select. TMS commands select test modes as defined in the JTAG specification.

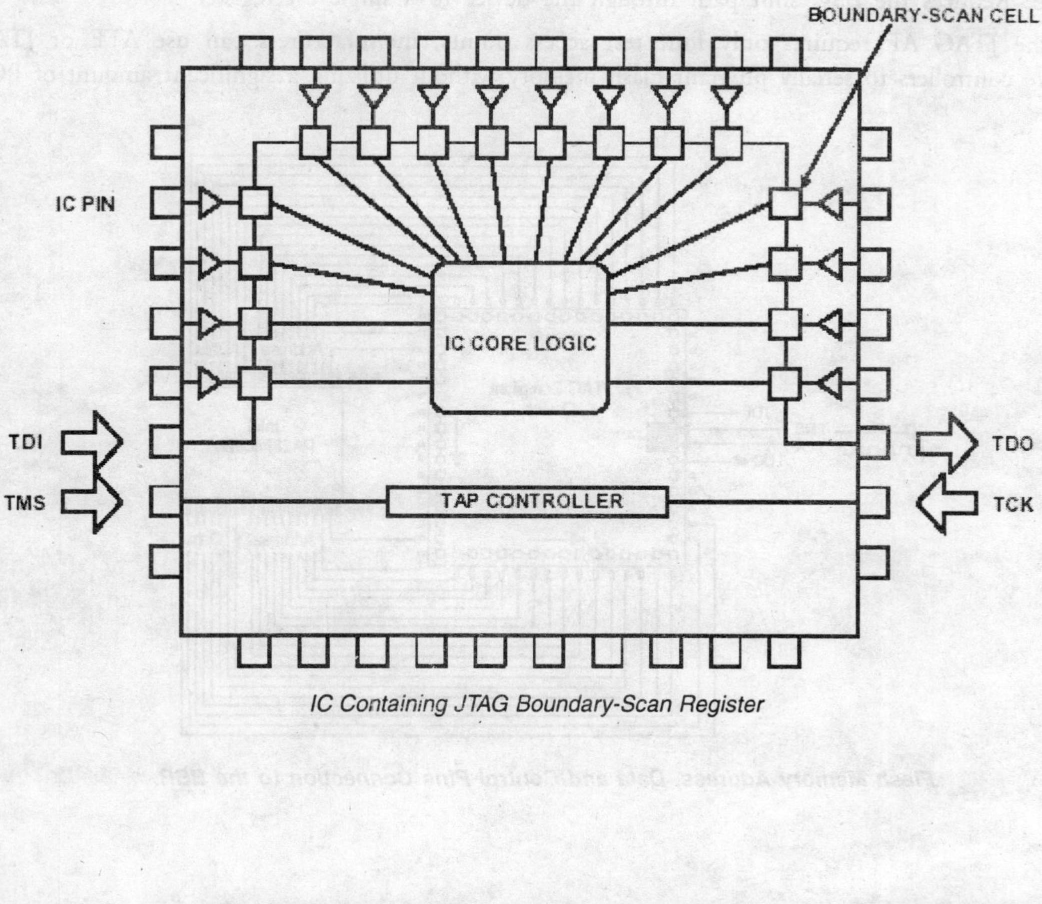

IC Containing JTAG Boundary-Scan Register

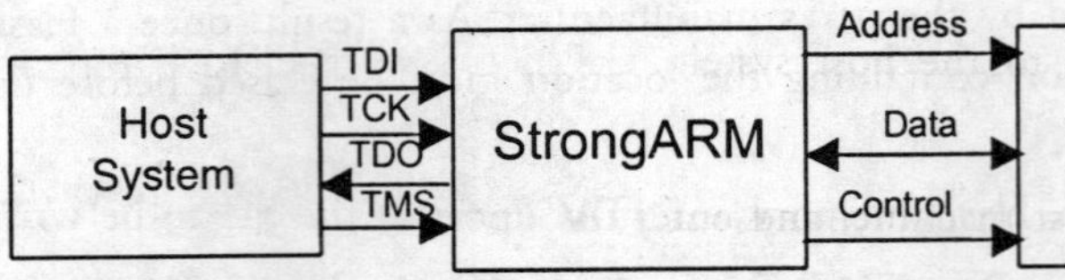

The StrongARM's JTAG Test Access Port provides an interface to Program Flash Memory. The flash memory need not be JTAG-compliant for this programming method to function. The JTAG hardware controller sends commands and data to the JTAG-compliant device, then propagates the data to the Flash memory for programming. The JTAG-compliant device(s) must connect to all Flash memory address, data and control signals. You create the software to perform the "On-Board" programming functions.

The hardware controller communicates serially with the JTAG-compliant device through the TAP controller. You must use the TCK and TMS inputs to clock in state-machine commands. Three TAP instructions, described below, manipulate the data:

SAMPLE/PRELOAD: Use this instruction to either SAMPLE the data currently contained in the BSCs, or to PRELOAD data into the BSCs.

EXTEST: When EXTEST is performed, the BSCs attached to the JTAG-compliant device input pins act as sensors while the BSCs attached to output pins propagate data to interconnecting devices. The interconnecting devices may or may not be JTAG-compliant.

BYPASS: Reduces the BSC shift path through the device to a single bit register.

Since the JTAG AP requires only four test access points, manufacturers can use ATE or JTAG hardware controllers to serially program Flash memory without utilizing a significant amount of PCB space.

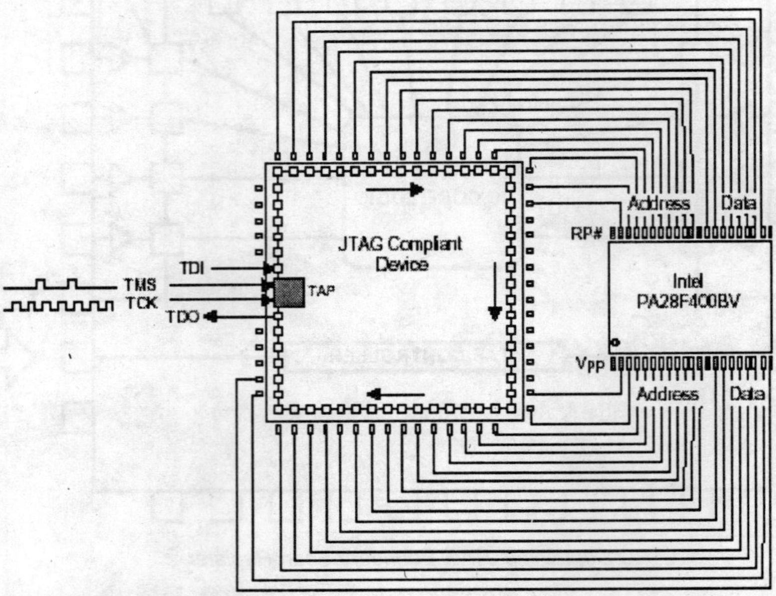

Flash Memory Address, Data and Control Pins Connection to the BSR.

Procedure:

Connect the StrongARM board to the host system via the JTAG cable.

Power-up the board

Run the JFlash utility on the host machine, and enter the name of the file to be written into the Flash memory.

Observations:

Note on the host machine the messages received from the board via the JTAG port

19.2.3 Parallel Communication on Prayog

Aim

To demonstrate the communication between two Prayog systems through the parallel port interface.

Theory

The following diagram shows various pins and their bit position in the corresponding port.

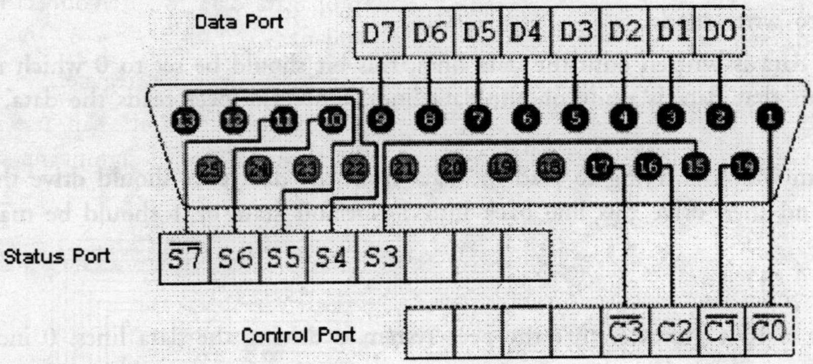

Various ports have the following port addresses:

Data Port:	Base address (0x378)
Status Port:	(Base + 1)
Control Port:	(Base +2)

Protocol Used for Bi-directional data transfer:

It can be observed that the parallel cable is crossed for bi-directional data transfer purpose and the cross connection is as follows.

A	B
INIT ——>	——— BUSY
STB ——>	——— SLCT
ACK ——>	——— AFD

BUSY ————   <———— INIT

SLCT ————   <———— STB

AFD ————   <———— ACK

The first set of lines is used for data transfer from System A to System B. The second set is used for data transfer from System B to System A.

The INIT – BUSY pair is used to indicate whether the system is driving the data lines (PPDIR set to 0).

The STB - SLCT pair is used to indicate to the peer system that the data on the data lines are valid.

The AFD – ACK pair is used to indicate to the sender that the data has been read by the system.

The status of the pins is explained below.

Control Port

INIT: Before writing data onto the data port, this pin should be set to 0. Once data writing cycle is complete, this should be set to 1.

Writing 0 to this bit indicates to the peer system that this system is writing data (driving the data lines) onto the data lines of parallel port. When one system is writing data, the other system should not set its PPDIR bit to write mode.

STB: Once the data is written onto the data lines, this bit should be set to 0 which indicates to the other peer system that data is ready on the data lines. Once the peer reads the data, this should be reset to 1.

AFD: The system which is trying to read the data from the data port should drive this pin to, then read the data, and then drive this line back into 1. Default state of 1 should be maintained.

Status Port

Busy: If this bit is 1, it indicates that the peer system is driving the data lines. 0 indicates that the peer system is in read mode.

SLCT: If this bit is 0, it indicates that the peer system is writing the data onto the data lines and the data is valid. 0 indicates data on the data lines are not valid.

ACK: This bit going from 1 to 0 and then back 1 indicates that the peer system has read the data written onto the data lines.

Signal diagram

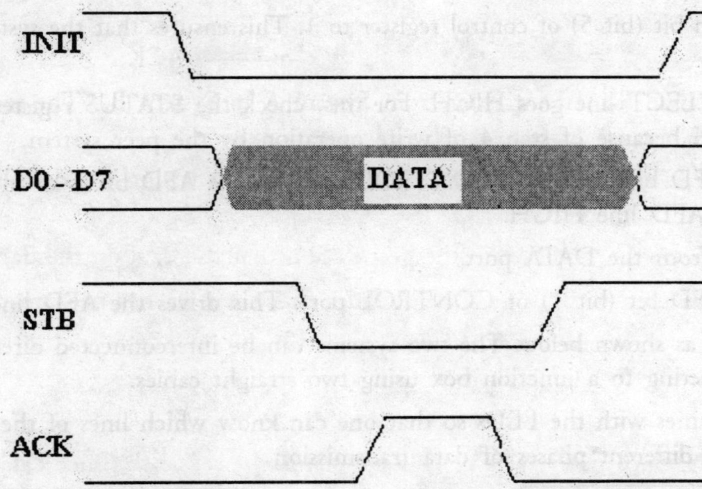

Various Signals at the system writing Data

The above figure indicates the signal at the system which is writing data. Note that the signals INIT, D0 – D7 and STB are the Controls port signals to which it can write whereas ACK is the status port signal which is driven by the peer system reading the data.

At the peer system which is reading the data, only the data lines are not inverted, and the signal pins are according to the cross connection described earlier.

Steps for writing a byte of data onto Parallel Port

1 Read the status register. If BUSY (bit 7) is HIGH, return –1 which indicates peer system is in write mode, and hence driving the D0-D7 data lines.

2 Set the INIT bit of control register to 0 which indicates to the peer system that this system is driving the D0-D7 data lines. Also ensure STB line is high.

3 Write the data onto DATA PORT.

4 Write 0 into STROBE bit of CONTROL port which drives strobe line HIGH (STROBE bit is inverted logic). This indicates to the peer system (through his SELECT pin and bit 4 of his STATUS register) that a valid data is ready on the data lines and should be read.

5 Wait for the ACK line to go HIGH and then LOW. For this, read the STATUS registers bit 6. This cycle indicates that the peer system read the data from the data lines.

6 Write 1 into STROBE bit of CONTROL port which drives strobe line high. This indicates to the peer system that the data is not valid any more.

7 Set the direction bit (bit 5) of control register to 1. This stops driving the data lines.

8 Write 1 into STROBE bit of CONTROL port which drives strobe line high. This indicates to the peer system that the data is not valid any more.

9 Set the INIT bit of control register to 1 which indicates to the peer system that this system is not driving the D0-D7 data lines.

Steps for reading a byte of data from Parallel Port

1 Set the direction bit (bit 5) of control register to 1. This ensures that the system is not driving the data lines.

2 Wait till the SELECT line goes HIGH. For this, check the STATUS register bit 4. SELECT line goes HIGH because of step 4 of write operation by the peer system.

3 Write 0 into AFD bit (bit 1) of CONTROL port. As the AFD bit is of inverted logic type, this drives the AFD line HIGH.

4 Read the data from the DATA port.

5 Write 1 into AFD bit (bit 1) of CONTROL port. This drives the AFD line LOW.

The hardware setup is as shown below. The two systems can be interconnected directly using a cross parallel cable or connecting to a junction box using two straight cables.

The Interface board comes with the LEDs so that one can know which lines of the parallel interface are being used during different phases of data transmission.

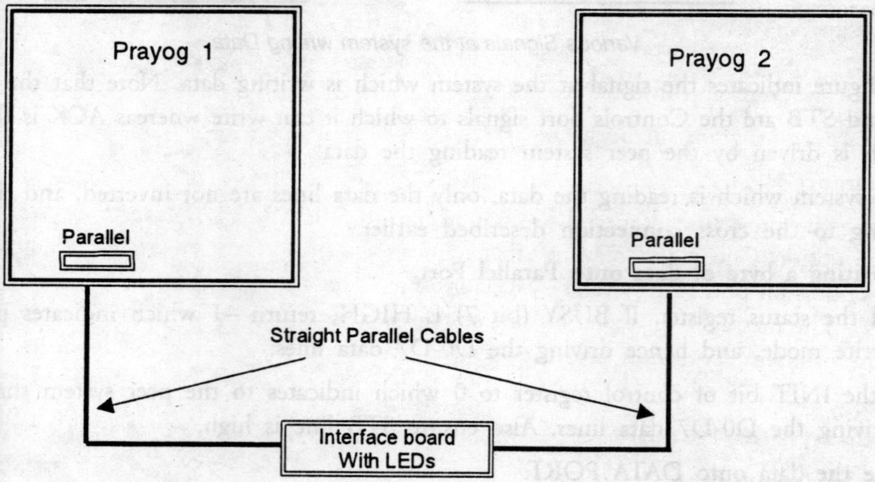

Software Setup

Type the following command.

ash2.0# su - ↵

If this command is typed earlier, skip it.

Install the parallel port driver by using following commands

ash2.0# insmod pport.o ↵

This installs the parallel port driver onto the system, through which the program can access the parallel interface related ports.

Procedure

Bi-directional parallel communication through parallel cable can be tested with a sample program which can send and receive the data. Sample program on parallel communications is available as the source file parport.c under the directory /CCN/Part-2/Parallel. This program in a loop reads a message from the peer system displays it and then asks the user to type a message and sends it to the peer system. The quit message stops the program. For simplicity, the reading and writing procedures used are blocking, i.e. the system writing the data waits till the other system reads it. The same is true with the reading also. The program provides an option to the user to choose the role: client or server. In client option, the program starts with sending the messages whereas in server option, the program begins with receiving the message. For program to run successfully, the user should choose the Client option on one system, and the Server option on the other.

Follow the procedures given below on both the Prayog systems.

Compile and build the executable using the following commands

ash2.0# gcc –o <output filename> <source filename>

For the parport.c file this can be

ash2.0# gcc –o parport parport.c ↵

This creates an executable file named parport

Run the parport program on both the systems Prayog1 and Prayog2.

ash2.0# parport ↵

On running the program, it queries the user to choose the option: Client or Server. On one system, choose the option Client and on the other, choose the option Server. Ensure that you don't choose the same option on both the systems. When prompted for the message to send, type a line of message and type ↵. The message you typed on one system would appear on the other system. When you want to quit the program, type quit and then type ↵. Both the programs would quit.

Observation and Results

With the above setup of parallel interface, it is possible to achieve 8-bit bi-directional data transmission. As the data lines in a parallel port can be driven by one end only, we can achieve half-duplex transmission. Handshaking is achieved by crossing 3 lines connected to the Control and Status port. Because it is possible to transmit 8 bits at a time, it is much faster than the serial port in which only 1 bit is transmitted at a time. However, parallel interface involves more number of pins, which are dedicated for control and status purpose.

19.2.4 Interfacing Stepper Motor to Prayog

The Intel StrongARM processor has 28 GPIO pins which could be configured as either inputs or outputs. The stepper motor forms a very important component in a plethora of electro-mechanical applications. With their burgeoning use in robotics, aviation, automobile and other such industries and applications, design engineers have a challenge to understand the interfacing of stepper motors to processors. This application note aims to demonstrate the design methodology to successfully build such systems.

Resources Required

Prayog board, one Stepper Motor Interface Card (Part number: ASP-SBD-STEP), one ATX power Supply, one 2 pin flat ribbon cable, one stepper motor (in this example, we have used a stepper motor which has a rating of 12V DC & 0.67 A/Phase as input voltage, 3 Kg-com torque).

The stepper motor by virtue of its being a direct digital actuator has become an important element of a control system. Well known applications include watches, floppy and hard disk drives, printers, etc.

What is a Stepper Motor?

A stepper motor is a special kind of motor that moves in individual steps which are usually .9 degrees each. Each step is controlled by energizing one or more of the coils inside the motor which then interacts with the permanent magnets attached to the shaft. Turning these coils on and off in sequence will cause the motor to rotate forward or reverse. The time delay between each step determines the motor's speed. Steppers can be moved to any desired position reliably by sending them the proper number of step pulses. Unlike servomotors, steppers can be used "open-loop" without the need for expensive encoders to check their position. Stepper motors are much more cost-effective than servo systems due to their simplified control and drive circuitry. There are no brushes to replace in a stepper motor, eliminating the need for maintenance. Even though a stepper motor system cannot achieve the speed of a servo motor system, its ease of use allows it to be the preferred solution for many of today's computerized motion control systems.

Using the Stepper Motor Controller Card in stand-alone mode

Before powering on or making connections:

(a) Ensure that the SW1 switch matrix on the stepper motor controller card has only the first switch in OFF position. The rest of the switches are used for stepper motor control.

(b) The two pins of the J3 header first are shorted.

Interfacing Stepper Motor Controller Card to Prayog

Before powering on or making connections:

(a) Ensure that the SW1 switch matrix on the stepper motor controller card has all the switches in OFF position

(b) To use the on-board timer circuit for motor speed control, short the pins of the header J3. Then by varying R4, motor speed can be controlled (frequency variations obtained by varying R4 are between 937 Hz and 2.7 KHz).

Notes...

The reason for providing on-board timer circuit is to ensure that the stepper motor controller IC is not damaged due to inadvertent supply of high frequencies from Prayog. We therefore advise beginners to use the on-board timer circuit for motor speed control.

(c) If the speed of the motor has to be controlled by Prayog then the pins of the header J3 are left open.

Notes...

It is safe to supply a frequency of 940Hz when you are providing the speed control option from Prayog

Mapping of GPIOs of Prayog to stepper motor controller pins

The following maps the GPIOs used in our experiment. The user is free and encouraged to experiment with different GPIOs

Stepper motor controller pins available at J4 header	GPIOs of StrongARM	Remarks
OE#	GPIO 20	Available at JP17 header
Direction	GPIO 19	Available at JP17 header
STEP input	—	Can be mapped to any available GPIO
Half STEP input	—	Can be mapped to any available GPIO
One Phase	—	Can be mapped to any available GPIO

Connecting the pins available at J4 to GPIOs at JP17

Connect the DIR and OE pins available at J4 header on Stepper motor controller interface card to pin 5 and pin 6 of the JP17 header of Prayog using the flat ribbon cable given, as shown in the figure below.

Connecting the 2 pin ribbon cable from J4 header of interface card to PRAYOG

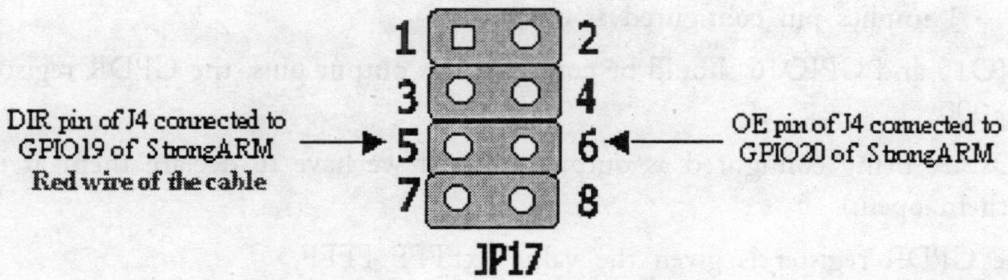

Power Supply to Stepper Motor Controller card and Prayog

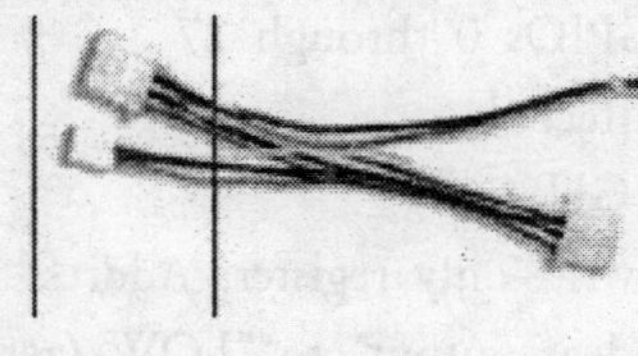

A single ATX power supply is sufficient to provide power supply to Stepper motor controller card and Prayog

After connections are made as described earlier, undertake the following steps:

1. Connect the 4-pin connector of ATX power supply to the power supply connector of Stepper motor controller card.

Notes...

The 4-pin connector's yellow cable is the +12V line, the two black cables are the GND lines, and the red cable is the +5V line. Connect them to the corresponding pins of the power supply header of stepper motor controller card.

2. Power up Prayog as described in section 2.2 of Prayog user guide.

Writing a program to control the stepper motor (direction only) Algorithm

Step 1: Define GPIO15 and GPIO16 as output pins of Prayog

Step 2: Enable the stepper motor controller IC

Step 3: Toggle the DIR signal of stepper motor controller IC to change the direction of rotation.

Step 4: Disable the stepper motor controller IC to stop the stepper motor controller IC.

StrongARM Register Settings for using the GPIOs

{Positive logic convention is implied unless specified otherwise}

GPDR (GPIO Pin Direction Register)—read/write; Address = 0x 9004 0004

This register configures the GPIO pins either as inputs or outputs

Bits 0 thro 27 correspond to the GPIOs 0 thro 27.

Bit value = 0 implies pin configured as input

Bit value = 1 implies pin configured as output

Since the GPIO15 and GPIO16 should be configured as output pins, the GPDR register will take the value 0x00018000.

Unused GPIOs are being configured as output pins. (If we have to declare them as inputs then we cannot keep them open.)

Therefore, the GPDR register is given the value 0xFFFF FFFF

GPSR (GPIO Pin SET Register)—write-only register; Address = 0x 9004 0008

This register sets GPIO pins (configured as output) to "HIGH " level

Bits 0 thro 27 correspond to the GPIOs 0 through 27

Bit value = 0 implies pin level unaffected

Bit value = 1 implies pin level "HIGH (one)"

GPCR (GPIO Pin CLEAR Register)—write-only register; Address = 0x 9004 000C

This register sets GPIO pins (configured as output) to "LOW (zero)" level

Bits 0 thro 27 correspond to the GPIOs 0 thro 27

Bit value = 0 implies pin level unaffected

Bit value = 1 implies pin level "LOW (zero)"

GPCR and GPSR will be used to change the values of GPIO15 and 16 only

GPLR (GPIO Pin-Level Register)—read-only register; Address = 0x 9004 0000

The state of each of the GPIO pins is visible thro GPLR, and is used to determine the current level of a particular GPIO pin

Bits 0 thro 27 corresponds to the GPIOs 0 thro 27.

GPLR will not be used in the current experiment

Flowchart

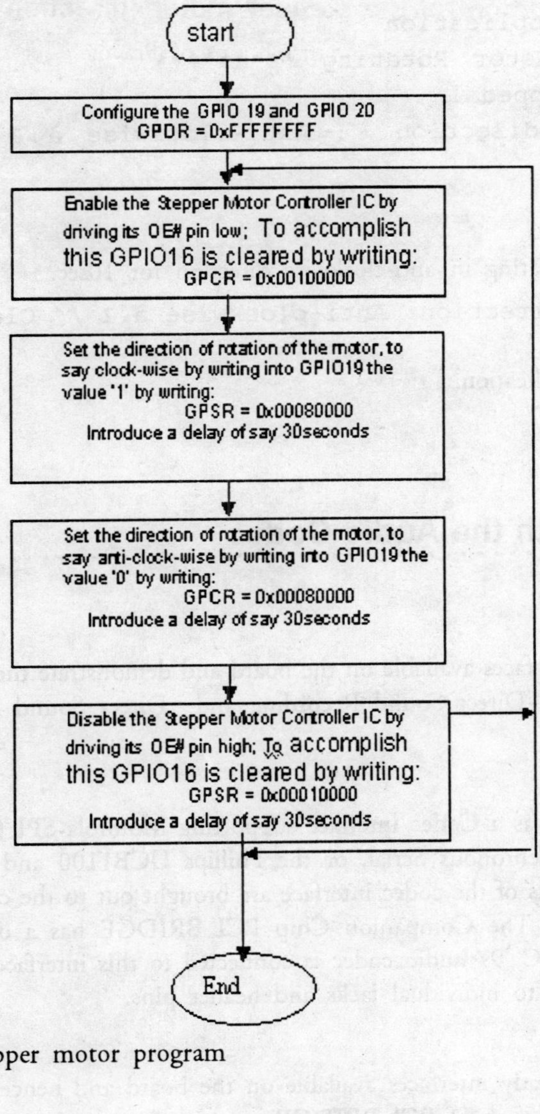

Steps to execute the Stepper motor program

```
sh-2.04#
```

Type the following commands:

```
ash-2.04# su -
ash-2.04# cd  /hw
ash-2.04# insmod   intdriver.o
ash-2.04#cd stepper
ash-2.04#gcc -o step stepper.c
```

To execute the program step, type the following command

```
ash-2.04# ./step
```

On running the above programme, you see the following messages:

```
  Stepper Motor Application
****** Watch the Motor Rotating *********
Motor rotating stopped....
Please choose the direction  : Anti-clockwise à 1 /  Clockwise à 2
/  Exit à 3
1
```

You can see the motor rotating in anti-clockwise direction for 10sec.

```
Please choose the direction: Anti-clockwise à 1 / Clockwise à 2 / Exit
à 3
```

You will exit from the application.

```
ash-2.04#
ash-2.04#
```

19.2.5 Working with the Audio Codec

Aim

To work with the ready interfaces available on the board and demonstrate the working of AC '97 codec interface of PCI BRIDGE—Direct Sound Recording and Direct Sound Playback.

Theory

The StrongARM processor has a Codec interface supporting Motorola SPI (Serial Peripheral Interface, National Microwire, TI Synchronous Serial, or the Phillips UCB1100 and UCB1200 protocols. On the board, the individual pins of the codec interface are brought out to the common header along with other serial peripheral pins. The Companion Chip PCI BRIDGE has a direct interface to AC '97 Codec. On the board, an AC '97 audio codec is connected to this interface. The inputs and outputs of this IC are brought out to individual jacks and header pins.

This application includes:

- Working with the ready interfaces available on the board and hence demonstrate the working of AC '97 codec interface of PCI BRIDGE

- Design our own interface circuit and interface it to the relevant port pins of StrongARM brought out to the header.
- Design our own Modem codec circuit and interface it to the relevant port pins of StrongARM brought out to the header.

What is a Codec?

In communications engineering, the term codec is used in reference to integrated circuits or chips that perform data conversion. The term is an acronym for "COder/DECoder". This device codes in one direction of transmission and decodes in another direction of transmission. The term codec is also an acronym that stands for "COmpression/DECompression". A codec is an algorithm, or specialized computer program, that reduces the number of bytes consumed by large files and programs.

What is AC '97 Codec?

The AC '97 (where AC stands for Audio Codec) is a specification that defines the Audio Codec '97 Architecture and Digital Interface (AC-Link) specifically designed for implementing audio and modem I/O functionality in mainstream PC systems.

Typical AC '97 devices include:

Audio Codec (often referred/abbreviated as AC '97 or just AC)

Modem Codec (often referred/abbreviated as MC '97 or just MC)

Combined Audio/Modem Codec (often referred/abbreviated as AMC '97 or just AMC)

More details about the AC '97 devices are available in AC '97 Specifications.

Direct Sound Recording

1. Program the Capture Channel Data Length Register (0x16~0x17) and the Capture Channel Buffer I & II System Starting Address Registers (0x18~0x1F) with the proper value.
2. Set Recording WAVE format by setting Stereo or Mono, 8-bit or 16-bit and the sampling rate at the Capture Channel Control Register (0x14~15).
3. Set the bit 5 of the Capture Channel Control Register (0x14~15) to "1" to start the PCI bus-master transfer for recording.
4. Capture current address can be read from the Capture Channel Buffer I or II System Starting Address Register (0x18~0x1B or 0x1C~0x1F). The Capture current remaining count can be read from the Capture Channel Current Count Register (0x16~0x17) to determine where the Hw pointer is. The interrupt status will be generated when the current count reaches "0".
5. When the current count reaches "0", Hw will switch to buffer 2 starting address to transfer the data (pingpong buffers scheme) and the current count will be re-loaded and starts from the data length again. In the meantime, the driver has to move the data in the buffer 1 to the system.
6. To pause the recording, set the bit 6 of the Capture Channel Control Register (0x14~15) to "1". To resume, just restore "0" to the bit 6.
7. To stop/finish Recording, set the bit 7 of the Capture Channel Control Register (0x14~15) to "1" and the bit 5 to "0".

Direct Sound Playback

1. Program the Playback Channel Data Length Register (0x0A~0x0B) and Playback Buffer I & II System Starting Address Registers (0x0C~0x13) with the proper value.
2. Set playback WAVE format by setting Stereo or Mono, 8-bit or 16-bit and the sampling rate at the Playback Channel Control Register (0x08~09).
3. Fill the buffer 1 and buffer 2 with the playback data. Set the bit 5 of the Playback Channel Control Register (0x08~09) to "1" to start the PCI bus-master transfer for playback.
4. Playback current address can be read from the Playback Channel Buffer Address Register (0x0C~0x0F or 0x10~0x13). Playback current remaining count can be read from the Playback Channel Current Count Register (0x0A~0x0B) to determine where the Hw pointer is. The interrupt status will be generated when the current count reaches "0".
5. When the current count reaches "0", Hw will switch to buffer 2 starting address to transfer the data (pingpong buffers scheme) and the current count will be re-loaded and starts from data length again. In the meantime, the driver has to start filling the data in buffer 1.
6. To pause the playback operations, set the bit 6 of the Playback Channel Control Register (0x08~09) to "1". To resume, just restore "0" to the bit 6.
7. To stop/finish playback, set the bit 7 of the Playback Channel Control Register (0x08~09) to "1" and the bit 5 to "0".

Audio Signal Processing using Intel IPPs

Resources Required:

Prayog, head phone set, Mic, signal sources for corresponding input, mono speaker

Procedure:

- Use the microphone as input source and head phone as output source
- Power up the SDB after the mic and headphone are connected to it.
- From the mic, record the audio signals and store them in the HDD/FDD in a suitable format
- Using IPPs, implement relevant signal processing to the audio collected signals collected
- Playback the audio processed through the head phone.
- Repeat the above procedure for other audio sources
- Using other signal processing techniques and algorithms, repeat the above procedure.

Observations:

Bring out the performance difference when IPP is used and when other algorithms are used.

Results and Conclusion:

The AC '97 interface on the board was tested for its features and performance. The lab manual gives more details on experimentation with Audio Codecs.

19.2.6 JPEG ENCODER

This application aims at converting an image file to its compressed format by developing an encoder called JPEG Encoder. This is accomplished by using a set of primitives. These primitives are meant to process an image through various steps, resulting in an image file which is compressed by nearly 10 times the original image size. JPEG details are given in the lab manual given in the CDROM.

JPEG Encoder Implementation

The JPEG encoder is implemented in C using Intel's IPP for StrongARM Microprocessor.

Intel Integrated Performance Primitives for Intel StrongARM Microprocessor

The Intel Integrated Performance Primitives (IPP) provide a rich and powerful set of general and multimedia signal processing functions optimized for the Intel StrongARM microprocessor. IPP offers application developers a number of significant advantages:

- The primitives are optimized for maximum performance on the processor. Therefore, IPP enables migration to the StrongARM of many computationally intensive applications that have traditionally required special-purpose DSP hardware.
- IPP drastically reduces development costs and profoundly accelerates time-to-market by eliminating the need for hand optimization of routines commonly used for multimedia signal processing. Developers are provided with an "off-the-shelf" optimized solution.
- IPP is compatible with popular real-time embedded operating systems that run on the StrongARM. The primitives are low-level and have been carefully designed to avoid host Operating System (OS) dependencies.
- IPP supports application porting across certain Intel platforms. A consistent API is defined for those StrongARM processors that are supported by IPP, and therefore applications can be ported easily without sacrificing performance.

Intel IPPs include primitives to support imaging codecs that are compliant with the ISO/IEC International Standard 10918 or so-called JPEG codec. Like all the other primitives, the JPEG primitives focus on well defined and the computationally expensive operations in JPEG codec.

IPP JPEG primitives support the following features:

- Interleave and non-interleave
- DCT (Discrete Cosine Transform)-based sequential
- Entropy coding based on Huffman coding algorithm
- Processing of a Rectangle of Interest (ROI).

To compile and Run the Code

To compile the code, you need to have the Makefile in the directory in which the source code is available. Along with the source code Makefile has also been provided. This Makefile is meant to compile JPEG source code on x86 processor and the platform is Linux.

Example:

$ make

This results in a binary file called jpegencoder. This is included in the folder /JPEG/sampleimages. To run this binary, you have to specify the input and output image file names. You can find sample images in the directory /JPEG/sampleimages. Example to run this binary on Prayog board is as follows

Example:

ash-04 # jpegencoder beanflower.bmp beanflower.jpg

Image File Name: beanflower.bmp

Image size before compression: 900000 bytes

Image size after compression: 21000 bytes

Successful execution results in a compressed image file called beanflower.jpg.

19.2.7 MP3 Decoder

This application note aims to provide the description of compression and decompression algorithms of audio data with decompression algorithm implementation using the DSP library primitives. This section assumes that the user has the basic knowledge of compression techniques.

The MP3 decoder is a software, which converts audio data in compressed format (say .mp3 format) to an uncompressed format (say PCM format). Uncompressed data is then played back through an audio device.

In the past few years, huge progress has been made in the field of video compression. The most popular of these compression is those developed by the Moving Picture Experts Group (MPEG). Their goal was to provide a worldwide standard for moving images, audio, and images combined with audio. The MPEG compression system includes a subsystem to compress sound, called MPEG Audio Layer-3, abbreviated MP3. MPEG is the international standard for multimedia. It incorporates both audio and video encoding at a range of data rates. MPEG audio and video are the standard formats used on Video CDs and DVDs. There are three types of MPEG audio encoding, layer I, layer II and layer III in increasing order of sound quality and encoding time. MPEG-2 provides broadcast quality audio and video at higher data rates and MPEG-3 has been absorbed into MPEG-2.

Interestingly enough, the MP3 specification (ISO 11172-3) does not specify exactly how the encoding is to be accomplished. Rather, it outlines techniques and specifies a level of conformance; in other words, it tells developers that their resulting MP3 files must meet certain structural criteria. The specification only serves to guarantee a baseline consensus in the community regarding how certain things will operate. An encoder developed according to the MP3 specification will be capable of outputting a "compliant bit stream" that can be played successfully with any MP3 player.

The MP3 format uses characteristics of the human ear to design the compression algorithm. For example, there are certain sounds that the human ear cannot hear; there are certain sounds that the human ear hears much better than others; if there are two sounds playing simultaneously, we hear the louder one but cannot hear the softer one. Using there characteristics of the human ear, certain parts of a song can be eliminated without significantly hurting the quality of the song for the listener.

Compressing the rest of the song with well-known compression techniques shrinks the song considerably — by a factor of 10 at least. The MP3 version of the song does not sound exactly the same as the original CD song because some of it has been removed, but it's very close.

Compression Algorithm

The steps in creating an MP3 are heavily math intensive. The compression algorithm for MPEG1 has a common basic structure. What changes is the calculation of the psycho-acoustic model and the sub-bands from one layer to the next.

The block diagram for the MPEG encoding algorithm is shown in the following figure:

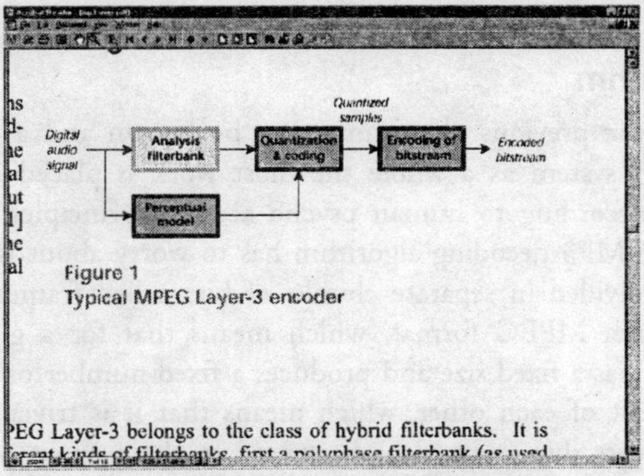

MP3 Compression Algorithm

The compression is divided into stages as follows:

1. The first stage consists of dividing the sampled signal into sub-bands. This procedure is known as time-frequency mapping. These sampled pieces are called frames.
2. The second stage consists of implementing the psycho-acoustic model using FFT (Fast Fourier Transform), which provides detailed information about the signal, which is divided into tonal and non-tonal signals. The tonal and non-tonal sound masks are then identified and the perceptibility thresholds of the individual masks are then combined to generate a global masking threshold. This is then related to the maximum signal level detected in the sub-bands, obtaining a signal-to-masker ratio (SMR), which constitutes the point of departure for quantifying the data to be compressed.
3. The third stage consists in quantifying and encoding each sample of each sub-band by calculating a coefficient required to represent, in scale, the signal-to-noise ratio.
4. The last stage is to generate the compressed file. Here much more traditional means of compression is used. This process in known as Huffman coding, which compresses redundant information throughout the sample.

With the above steps an MPEG1 is achieved. The Fraunhofer Institute took the above algorithm and added these additional steps:

In step 3 and 4 as well as the FFT, another transform (DCTF = Discrete Cosine Transform Filter) is added to implement a psycho-acoustic model which is much more faithful and gives better performance.

In step 4, a sophisticated algorithm is added to vary the size of the frames. A reserve bit is also added, similar to the one used in MPEG encoding. This bit is used to solve critical situations and distortions that might affect the encoding of the sample.

When using the above algorithm, the most important consideration is the bit-rate. The bit rate refers to the number of bits per second that should be devoted to storing the final product. The current default standard for encoding MP3s is 128 Kilo-bits-per-second (kbps). The codec takes the bit rate into consideration as it writes each frame to the bit stream. If the bit rate is low, the code will be much more harsh on the signal leading to a lower-quality product. The higher the bit rate, the more lenient the codec will be resulting in higher-quality. MP3s created at different bit rates will result in different file sizes.

Decompression Algorithm

When building a decoder, the previous algorithm must be known and a reverse algorithm must be made. However, in an MP3 system as a whole the most work is placed on encoding. Decoders do not need to store or work according to human psycho acoustic principles, nor do they require a bit allocation procedure. All the MP3 decoding algorithm has to worry about is examining the bit stream. All MPEG bit streams are divided in separate chunks of bits called frames. There is a fixed number of frames per second for each MPEG format, which means that for a given bit rate and sampling frequency, each input frame has a fixed size and produces a fixed number of output samples. In MPEG audio, frames are independent of each other, which means that it is trivial to fast-forward and back-up in a bit stream — you just skip forward or backward to the next or previous frame. Each frame is processed as depicted in the following figure.

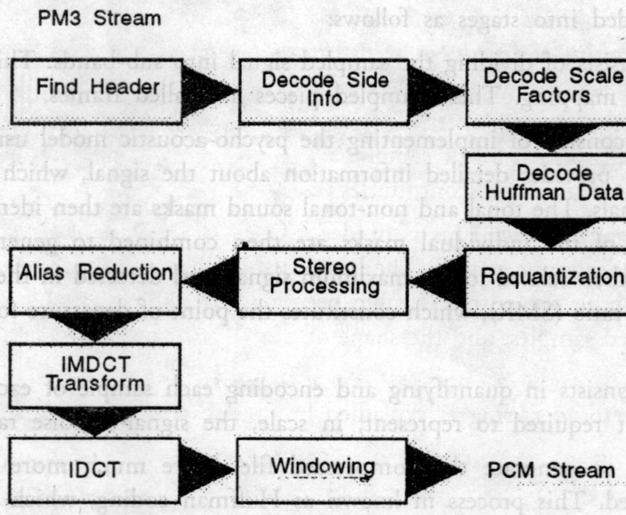

MP3 decompression algorithm

First step in the decoding process is to find the beginning of a frame. This is done by searching for a synchronization bit-pattern.

After this is found, the frame header and side-information can be read. This contains information on how the frame was encoded, so the decoder knows what to do with the data contained in the frame, which is read after the side-information. The first data transmitted after the header, is the scale factors. They control the gain for each frequency band. After this, come the actual frequency energies, quantized and Huffman-encoded.

The decoders task is to

Huffman-decode,

Re-quantize,

Transform the energies into the time-domain so a sample-output can be made.

The Huffman encoding in the encoder selectively uses many different Huffman trees, according to the data contents, to minimize the total bit-length. The Huffman decoder has to select the appropriate Huffman tree, and then traverse the tree for each energy-symbol in the frame data, to arrive at the decoded value. When the Huffman-decoder has decoded the values, they have to be re-scaled using the scale factors into real spectral energy values.

If the stream is encoding a stereo signal, each channel can be transmitted separately in every frame, but often the encoder chooses to utilize redundancies between the two channels by transmitting the sum and the difference instead. If this is the case, the decoder has to perform stereo-processing to recover the original two channels.

After the stereo recovery, the frequency values in each frequency band are symmetrically added together to smooth out aliasing distortions that appear due to quantizing.

A transform is applied that is the reverse of the time-to-frequency transform used in the encoder. In layer-3, two transforms are done after each other to get better frequency resolution than in the other layers. Both transforms are essentially critically sampled Discrete Cosine Transforms (DCT's). This means that if no quantizing had been done, the decoder would have reconstructed the original signal perfectly. To avoid discontinuities between transformed blocks, which would result in very perceptible noise and clicks, the transforms use a 50 percent overlap. This means that if the block size is X, the encoder only advances the input pointer X/2 samples for each transformed block. The decoder does the reverse. Every re-transformed block sample is overlapped with half of the previous block sample. This process smoothens out any discontinuities.

The final step is low-pass filtering. This is needed to reconstruct the original signal, which was low-pass filtered at the encoder input as well. The low-pass filtering is realized by convolution with a sync-shaped wave. Technically, every output sample becomes a weighted average of the surrounding 512 time-domain transformed samples, and the shape of the 512 weights is predefined in the MPEG-audio standard.

The detailed procedure for decoding is explained in the lab manual given in the CDROM.

The flowchart for MP3 decompression is give below:

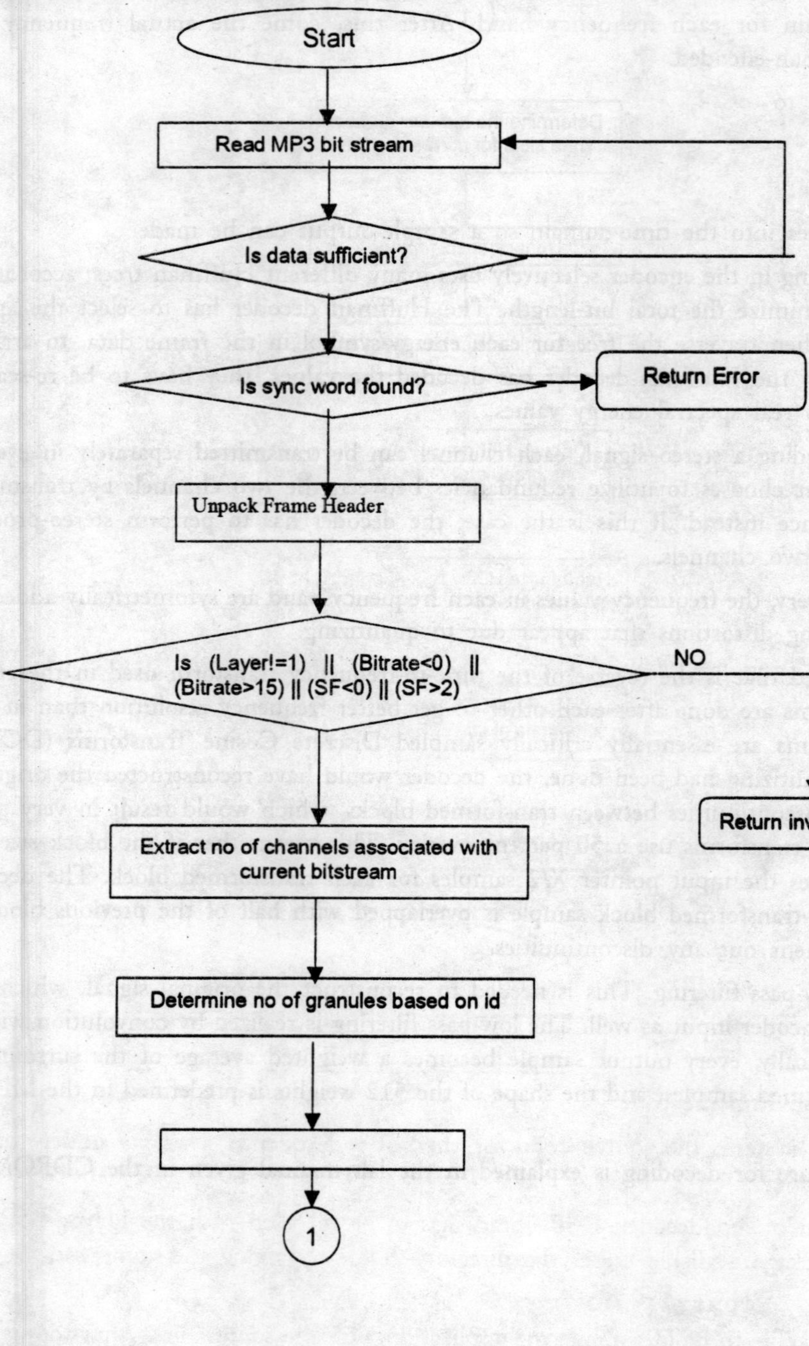

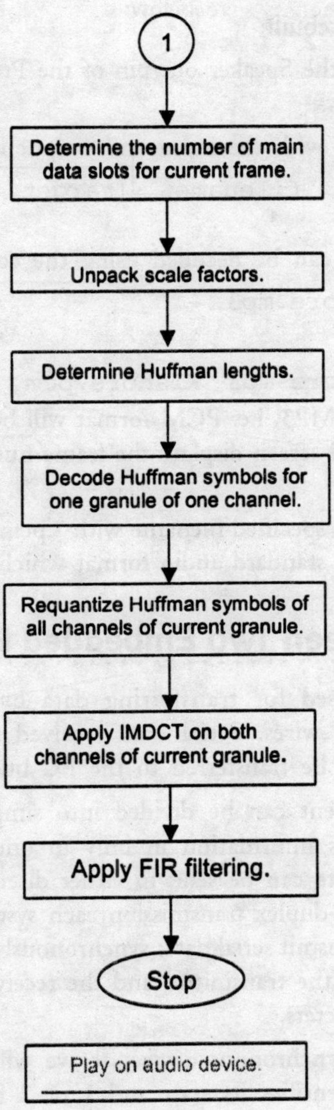

How to Compile and Run the code

On the **Linux host system,** the source code for the MP3 decoder is available under the directory **/data/DSP/MP3decoder**

For any modification of mp3decoder, DSP library has to be installed with the Prayog-BSP. Instal the ippsal1_lnx.rpm package available under the directory **/DSP** by giving the command

```
ash2.04# rpm -i ippsall_lnx.rpm
```

Find the sample Makefile to build/compile the application with the source files. After the modifications to source file, build the application by giving the command as (be in the same folder)

```
ash2.04# make
```

The binary "mp3decoder" will be rebuilt.

Connect headphone or speakers to the Speaker out pin of the Prayog (See the Prayog User document to locate Speaker out pin)

Run the binary with the command with the input and output filename. Output file is optional

```
ash2.04# mp3decoder <MP3 filename> [target filename- *.pcm]-> click enter
```

For example, the file Kishore.mp3 can be decoded using the command:

```
ash2.04# mp3decoder kishore.mp3
```

Or

```
ash2.04# mp3decoder kishore.mp3 Kishore.pcm
```

Note: Decompressed format of the MP3, i.e. PCM format will be stored in the target file if specified. The song selected will be played and screen displays the frame numbers while decoding until it reaches the end of stream.

On completion, find the copy of the specified filename with *.pcm extension which is the decompressed or decoded version of MP3. This is standard audio format which can be played on any audio device.

19.2.8 File Transfer between Two Embedded Reference Boards

The serial communications are used for transferring data over long distances, because parallel communications require too many wires. Serial data received from a modem or other devices is converted to parallel so that it can be transferred to the PC bus.

The serial communications equipment can be divided into simplex, half-duplex and full-duplex. A simplex serial communication sends information in only in one direction (i.e. a commercial radio station). Half-duplex means that data can be send in either direction between two systems, but only in one direction at a time. In a full-duplex transmission each system can send and receive data at the same time. There are two ways to transmit serial data: synchronously or asynchronously. In a synchronous transmission, data is sent in blocks, the transmitter and the receiver are synchronized by one or more special characters called sync characters.

The serial port of the PC is an asynchronous device, so we will describe this kind of systems. For asynchronous transmission, a bit identifies its start and 1 or 2 bits identify its end; it doesn't need any synchronization. The data bits are sent to the receiver after the start bit. The least significant bit is transmitted first. A data character usually consists of 7 or 8 bits. Depending on the configuration of the transmission, a parity bit is sent after each data bit. It is used to check errors in the data characters. Finally 1 or 2 stop bits are sent.

Steps

Get the file name to transfer and send it across serial port

Open the file

Get the file size and send the file size

Read the file data and send it across serial port.

Close the file

At receiving end, decode the file name and file size

Create the file with the received filename

Write the received file data into created file

Close the file.

Requirements

Two Prayog boards

An RS232 cable cross-wired null modem cable

Hardware Setup

An RS232 cable cross-wired null modem cable is connected to the serial port 2 (identified as VB2 on PCB) of both the boards. Please refer to Prayog user manual to check for serial port2.

Software Setup

Switch on both Prayog broards. On successful boot up, you can see the

`ash# prompt`

Get the super user mode by typing

`Ash2.0# su - ↵`

Change to the CCN directory available at **/CCN** by typing the command

`Ash2.0# cd /CCN ↵`

Procedure

File transfer through RS232 media can be tested with a set of client server programs. The client will receive the file sent by the server. Both client and server programs can be run on any of the two Prayog boards.

Sample programs on file transfer through RS232 are available in the source files file_send.c and file_recv.c under the directory **/CCN/Part-2/PC2PC/FileTransfer**

Compile and build the object files by giving the command

Ash2.0# gcc –o <object name><source filename>

Example:

Ash2.0# gcc –o file_send file_send.c

Ash2.0# gcc –o file_recv file_recv.c

Run the object files by typing the object filename.

Example:

Ash2.0# file_send

Ash2.0# file_recv

Run file_recv first on one board, say Prayog1, and dile_send on other board, say Prayog2
Enter the input file name (**only .txt files**) after receiving the message to "FileName:"
The file will be transferred to Prayog2 through the RS232 media

Observation and Results

On Prayog1:
ash-2.04# file_send
Select file :new.txt

File Name : new.txt
Filesize : 121
File Sent

On Prayog2:
ash-2.04# file_recv
Filename :new.txt
Filesize : 121

File received.

Conclusion

File new.txt is transferred from Prayog1 to Prayog2. This can tested in reverse also. The text file should be of size less than 1Kbytes.

19.2.9 Interfacing IrDA Card with Prayog

Aim

The aim of this experiment is to interface IrDA and with Prayog board and transfer data over the infared link.

Theory

The pictorial representation of the IrDA – 7 Segment Display Interface card (code ASP-SDB-DISP) is shown below. This card actually has two applications—viz 7 segment display Interface and IrDA interface.

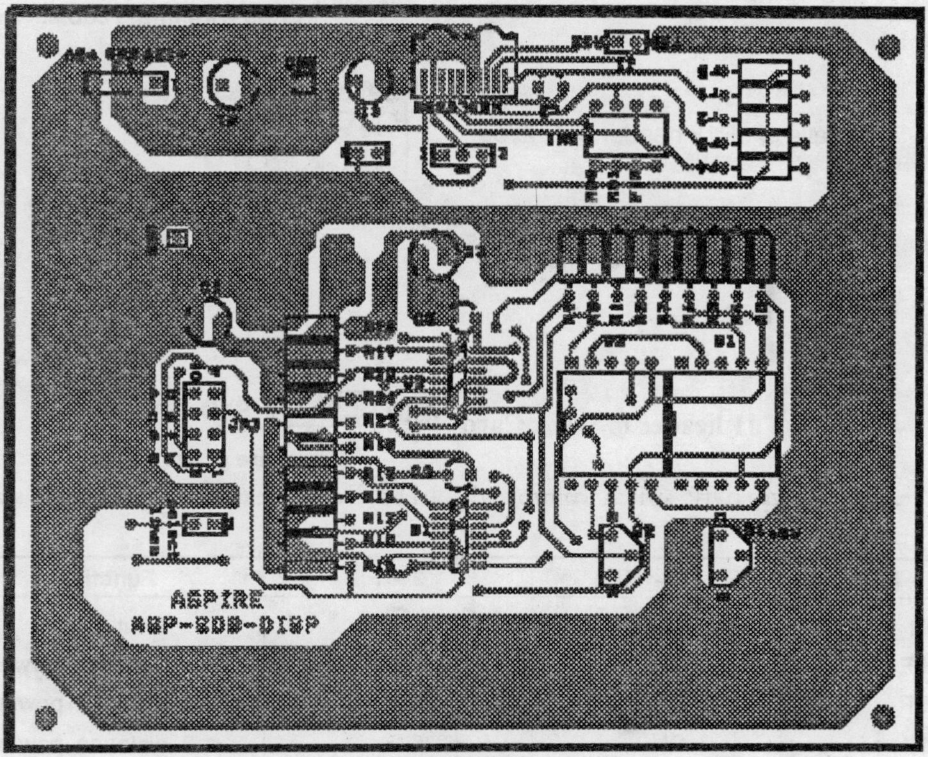

IrDA Interface card layout

Connection Setup

Connect the Power cable to the power-header of the card.

In order to power up the IrDA application short the 2 pin header (1) present just behind c1which is near to the IrDA transceiver (Please note that it is c1 and not C1).

On the Interface Card, there are 2 pins adjacent to IrDA Transceiver, with name TXD and RXD (header J1). These are the Transmit and Receive lines respectively for the IrDA module. These lines have to be driven by the StrongARM IrDA of Prayog. The data to be transmitted appears on JP18.6 (i.e. pin no 6 in JP18 header). The data received by the IrDA module is sent to Prayog through JP18.5 (i.e. pin no 5 in JP18 header)

Connect one end of the 2 pin flat ribbon cable to J1 header pins on IrDA Interface card. The other end of the cable is connected to pins 5 and 6 available at JP18 header of Prayog as shown in the Table and Figure below:

IrDA lines on J1 header of IrDA Card	Corresponding signal	PrayogPins	Remarks
1	TXD	JP18.6	This line is available at **pin6** of header **JP18**
2	RXD	JP18.5	This line is available at **pin5** of header **JP18**

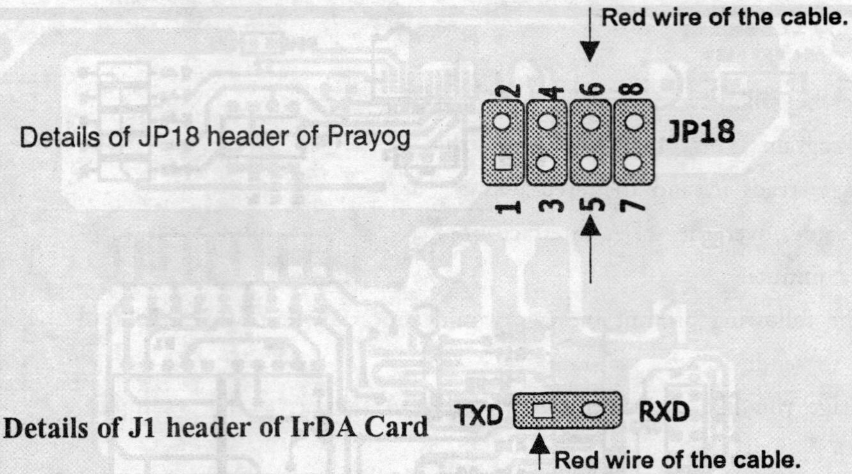

On IrDA card, a 4 way DIP switch controls the IrDA Transceiver. The DIP switch states are as follows.

1 - MD0	2 - MD1	3 - FIR	Function
ON	OFF	ON	Shut down
OFF	**OFF**	**ON**	**Full distance power**
OFF	ON	ON	2/3 distance power
ON	ON	ON	1/3 distance power

For the best performance, maintain the lines MD0, MD1 and the FIR lines as mentioned for **Full Distance Power,** in the table above.

Running the demo program

Make the connection setup as described above. Then, switch on the power supply to Prayog. Wait till you get the following prompt on the screen.

```
sh-2.04#
```

Type the following commands:

```
ash-2.04# su  -
ash-2.04# cd   /hw/irda
ash-2.04# insmod     irda.o
ash-2.04# rxvt   &
```

After executing the last command, you would get an additional terminal. You can switch between the two terminals using either the mouse or using the **<Alt– tab>** keys. [Press **Alt** and **Tab** simultaneously.]

On one of the terminals type the following command, which starts transmitting the data through the IrDA transceiver of the card.

```
ash-2.04#  ./irsend
```

You would see the following message

IrDA Demo Program. This program prompts the user for message, reads it, and then repeatedly transmits the same, over the IrDA interface of the card, for a minute.

At the end, the following prompt message would appear requesting you to type the message.

Type message to send:

Type the message you like to transmit over the IrDA transceiver. For example:

IrDA demo programme. abc 123 xyz

Now switch to the other terminal either by using the mouse or by pressing **Alt - Tab** keys simultaneously. You would see the following prompt.

```
ash-2.04#
```

Type the following commands.

```
ash-2.04
ash-2.04# stty   istrip -F   /dev/ttyS0
ash-2.04# cat      /dev/ttyS0
```

After the last command, you should see the message you typed earlier appearing on the screen repeatedly for a minute.

Type **Ctrl-C** when you want to stop this.

Notes...

You should ensure that the IrDA transceiver present on the IrDA card and the IrDA transceiver present on the Prayog are in the line of sight, without any obstacles in between. Ideal distance is 1 foot.

19.3 ADVANCED APPLICATIONS

In addition to the projects described above, the details of the following projects are given in the CDROM that accompanies this book:

1. Implementation of error detection codes between two boards
2. Implementation of cryptographic algorithms

The following list is an indication of many other possible applications that can be developed using the Prayog development board:

1. Design of Smart card interface
2. Interfacing video camera with USB port

3. Interfacing digital Camera with USB port
4. Wireless communication through IrDA
5. Wireless communication through Bluetooth
6. Using PCMCIA for networking, storage and removable media
7. Building Storage area networks
8. Embedded system for fault monitoring and diagnosis in communication systems.

Summary

This chapter dealt with the various applications developed using Prayog, Intel StrongARM-based development board. Implementation details of the following projects are also presented: Flash memory programming, parallel communication programming, interfacing a stepper motor, audio codec usage, JPEG encoder, MP3 decoder, file transfer between two boards and interfacing IrDA card with the board.

Chapter 20

RFID Systems

CHAPTER OBJECTIVES

After reading this chapter, you will be able to:

- Understand the importance and applications of RFID technology
- Learn how to develop applications using RFID in C++
- Appreciate the importance of object oriented programming for developing embedded software
- Understand the main features of Embedded C++ language

In the last few years, Radio Frequency Identification (RFID) technology has become very popular. This technology gives a glimpse of the future of embedded systems—how a small electronic device can be attached to any item of your choice making "system on chip" a very low cost commodity. In this chapter, we will study about RFID technology and also demonstrate how to develop applications using this technology.

Object oriented programming has gained a lot of importance for application software development due to its main attraction of reusability. However, for many years, the use of C++ for embedded software development did not take off mainly because it is considered less efficient as compared to C. However with the development of ANSI standard for Embedded C++ (EC++), nowadays, many embedded software developers are using this language for development. In this chapter, we will study the importance of object-oriented programming and the important features of embedded C++.

20.1 RFID System

To uniquely identify assets—whether it is a small item in a shopping mall, or a book, or a large container—bar code system is widely used. For example, at Point of Sale terminals, the bar code on an item to be purchased is read by a bar code scanner. However, bar code system has many disadvantages:

- The bar code is fixed at the time of printing and it cannot be changed.

- For the bar code to be read by the scanner, there should be a clear optical line of sight and in many practical applications, it is difficult to achieve this.
- It is very easy to deface the bar code.
- With just a laser printer, it is very easy to duplicate bar code causing security violations.

To overcome these problems, RFID technology can be effectively used for materials management and asset tracking. In the last few years, Radio Frequency Identification (RFID) technology has gained a lot of importance and many innovative applications are being developed using this technology. RFID technology is going to revolutionize the businesses all over the world in coming years.

An RFID system is shown in Fig. 20.1. The system consists of

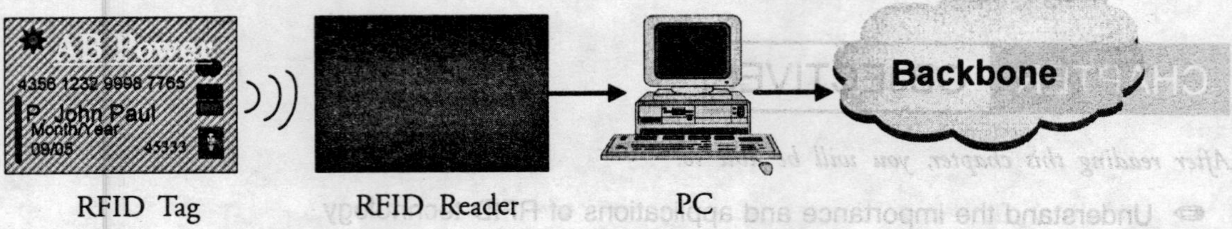

Fig 20.1: RFID System

- RFID tag (also called "Transponder")
- RFID reader attached to a PC
- Backbone network

Commercial RFID tags are shown in Fig. 20.2 and an RFID reader is shown in Fig. 20.3. RFID tags are of two types (a) passive and (b) active. A Passive tag does not have any battery and the power required by the tag is obtained from the RFID reader. An Active tag contains a battery.

Notes...

When active RFID tags are used, the range of the system becomes much more compared to when passive tags are used. However, the cost of active tag is higher.

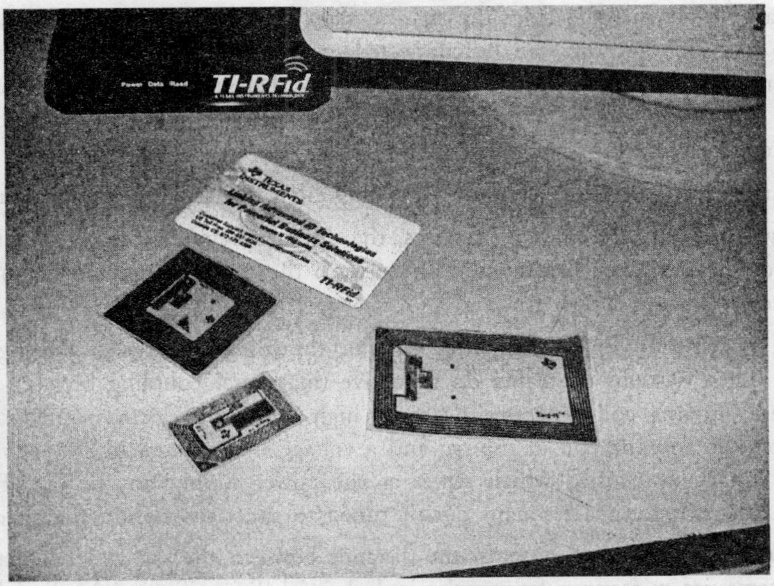

Fig. 20.2: RFID Tags

Fig. 20.3: RFID Reader

The RFID tag is a compact "system on chip" with a micro-controller, memory, modem circuitry and radio module along with an antenna. Data can be written into the memory of the tag from the RFID reader. The communication between the reader and the tag is through radio frequencies and hence there is no need for a physical contact between the tag and the reader. As a result, all the drawbacks listed for bar code system do not exist for RFID systems. The RFID reader reads the data from the RFID tag and, is also capable of writing data onto the tag. When the tag is in the radio vicinity of the reader, the reader reads the data from the tag and then the data can be transferred through RS232 or USB interface to a PC. The PC can be connected to a backbone network (which can be a LAN or a WAN or even the Internet). It is the backbone network that gives the power to the RFID systems. The data on the tag can be made accessible anywhere in the world leading to global supply chain management systems.

RFID systems can be categorized as follows depending on their capabilities and functionalities:

Close coupling systems: In close coupling systems, the distance between the tag and the reader is less than 1 cm. In such a system, the communication between the tag and reader does not depend on the radiation of the electromagnetic waves.

Remote coupling systems: In remote coupling systems, the distance between the tag and the reader is up to 1 meter. These systems are based on inductive (magnetic) coupling between the tag and the reader. The reader's antenna coil generates a strong, high frequency electromagnetic field. A part of this field penetrates the antenna coil of the tag and a voltage is generated in the tag's antenna coil by inductance. This voltage is rectified which serves as the power supply for the tag. The antenna coil of the tag and a capacitor form a resonant circuit tuned to the transmission frequency of the reader.

Long range systems: In long range systems, the distance between the tag and the reader is up to 10 meters. These systems use microwave frequencies in Industrial, Scientific and Medical (ISM) and Ultra High Frequency (UHF) bands.

Read-only systems versus read-write systems: In read only systems, the tag has a unique ID which is read by the reader. The data transfer is unidirectional and the tag sends the data to the reader. The unique ID is set at the factory at the time of manufacturing. Data is read at a time and the reader cannot interrogate the tag. In the case of read-write systems, the reader is capable of writing data on to the tag as well as reading the data from the tag.

Frequency bands of operation: The frequency of operation differs to some extent from country to country. In the US and Canada, the frequency bands used are: 125 KHz, 13.56 MHz and 902-928 MHz. In Europe, the frequency bands used are: 125 KHz, 13.56 MHz, 868-870 MHz. In Japan, the frequency bands of operation are: 125 KHz, 13.56 MHz, 950-956 MHz. In addition, 2.4 GHz ISM band is also used for RFID systems. Note that ISM band is a free band and hence no government approvals are required for making use of this band.

Though RFID technology appears very promising, practical implementation calls for careful designing. Some of the important design issues are:

Anti-collision: When more than one tag responds to the command from the reader, then there is a collision of data. Suppose each book in a library is attached with an RFID tag. When a set bunch of 5 books is brought near the reader, there will be collision of data. So, the RFID protocol between the reader and the tag should take care of the collision.

Speed of reading: The speed with which the reader can read the data from the tags is another important design consideration. This speed is measured in terms of number of tags that can be read per second by the reader.

Memory capacity of the tag: The amount of data that can be held by the tag is another important issue. The memory required for any specific application has to be calculated first and then a suitable tag to be identified.

> **In Brief...**
>
> The important design issues for RFID systems are: speed of reading, frequency of operation, range of the system, anti-collision protocol, memory capacity of the tag and security.

Security: Security is a major concern in RFID systems. Unauthorized access, denial of service, fraud, forgery, location privacy are the important security issues. The protocol between the reader and the tag should be such that these security issues are addressed.

20.2 RFID Applications

RFID technology has immense potential in every market segment—it is not surprising what the market surveys indicate that it will be a US$ 10 billion industry by the year 2010. However, for RFID to penetrate the market on a large scale, the cost of the tag should be very low—about 5 cents per tag would be ideal. Though the cost of the tag is coming down, it is still on the higher side for a large-scale penetration.

Each and every product/item can be attached with an RFID tag. And, when the tag comes in the vicinity of the reader, the contents of the tag can be read by him and then processed/sent over a network. The power of the RFID technology comes in integrating this information with the corporate network or even the global Internet. Some important applications are listed below.

Asset tracking: Every valuable asset can be tracked using RFID. Computers, instruments, machinery etc. in an organization can be attached with tags to make asset verification easier. When assets are moved from one place to another (say, from one office location to another location), their movement can be tracked easily. RFID tags are used for tracking of animals also. The Point of Sale (POS) terminals can now be based on RFID rather than on the old bar codes. Shop-lifting can be curbed to a great extent using this technology. In European countries, car theft has been reduced to the minimum using this technology. The ignition key is fitted with an RFID tag with a security feature. When a thief tries to start the car using a duplicate key, an alarm is raised.

As RFID tags can be used in harsh industrial environment (with high temperatures, humidity etc.) and as there is no need for contact between the tag and the reader, asset tracking through RFID tags will become very easy and efficient.

Inventory management: Manufacturing organizations can use RFID technology for efficient inventory management. Automobile industry uses this technology in the production facilities. Each manufactured part of the car is attached with a tag—the tag stores the details of the part. In the production line, the reader reads this information to ensure that the correct part is being integrated. This also leads to an efficient warehouse management system. When the inventory management system is integrated into the supply chain management system, an efficient supply chain management system can be developed.

Transport management: Transport organizations have been the greatest beneficiaries of RFID technology. In public transport systems, a lot of money is spent on ticketing. Ticketing can be automated completely using RFID systems. Each bus can have an RFID reader and the public can be given debit cards. The fare will be automatically deducted from the card—at the time of entry into the bus, the reader will write into the tag the point of entry and when the user alights from the bus, the fare will be calculated and deducted from the card.

Sensor networks: The RFID tags can be integrated with sensors such as temperature sensors, pressure sensors etc. so that the sensor information can be transferred to the reader and from the reader to another controlling device. Such sensor networks are extensively used in industrial environments for process control, industrial automation etc.

These are just a few commercial applications of RFID technology—imagination is the limit for finding new innovative applications of this technology.

20.3 RFID Tag

Development of an RFID tag is a very challenging task of engineering. The tag consists of

- Controller circuitry
- Non-volatile memory
- Modem
- Oscillator that generates the necessary clock for the entire circuitry
- Rectifier that converts the incident RF energy into DC voltage required to power up the tag
- Radio module and antenna

The memory capacity of the tag is an important design parameter. The application decides the memory requirement. For asset tracking, the unique identity has to be stored in this memory. The Electronic Product Code (EPC) is a standard that has been developed to uniquely identify the products. 64 bit, 96 bit and 256 bit codes are defined. The number of bits used for different purposes is shown in Table 20.1

Standard	Version Number	EPC Manager	Product class	Serial number
EPC-64 Type I	2	21	17	24
EPC-64Type II	2	15	13	34
EPC-64 Type III	2	26	13	23
EPC-96Type I	8	28	24	36
EPC-256Type I	8	32	56	192
EPC-256Type II	8	64	56	128
EPC-256Type III	8	128	56	64

Table 22.1 Electronic Product Code (EPC) Standards

20.4 RFID Reader

Though generally referred to as reader, the RFID reader is both a reader and a writer. It is capable of writing data on to the tag as well as reading the data from the tag. The protocol between the reader and the tag is defined by ISO standards. ISO 18000-6A and ISO 18000 6-B standards specify the protocols in the UHF band. The important specifications as per this standard are:

- Frequency of operation: 860 – 930 MHz
- Tag read speed: 100 tags per second
- Memory type: User programmable
- Memory organization: Organized as 256 blocks. (each block of 8 bits or 256 bits)
- Security: No strict security, reader broadcasts the ID. However, it is possible to lock a tag so that data cannot be written onto it by another reader.
- Tag capacity: 300[4]

20.5 Application Development using RFID

In this section, we will demonstrate application development using RFID. You need an RFID reader and RFID tags to work on application development. The RFID reader from Texas Instruments has been used for application development. This reader has a RS 232 interface to connect to the PC. To create an RFID application, you need to write application software that puts data into the transponder and also reads the data from the transponder. The following description illustrates how these are done.

Application 1: RFID Tag ID creation (for ID Card Application)

In this application, we will demonstrate how to make use of RFID system for developing an attendance system in an organization. To start with, we need to create a utility that will generate "ID cards" which RFID tags. We need to create tags that will store the employee information and also verify whether the data was written correctly by reading back the written data.

The screen shot given in Fig. 20.4 gives the application main menu for creating an ID card application.

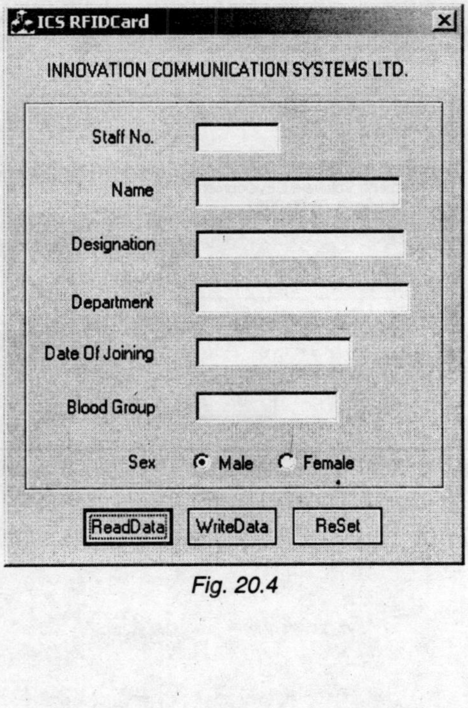

Fig. 20.4

The GUI gives the provision to write the data by clicking on "WriteData" button after filling all the fields Staff No, Name, Designation, Department, Date of Joining, Blood group and Sex.

Fig. 20.5 shows the screen after the employee information is written.

Fig. 20.5

After the data is written into the RFID tag, it has to checked whether the correct data is stored in the tag. By clicking "ReadData" button, we can verify that the card data is successfully written or not, as shown in Fig. 20.6.

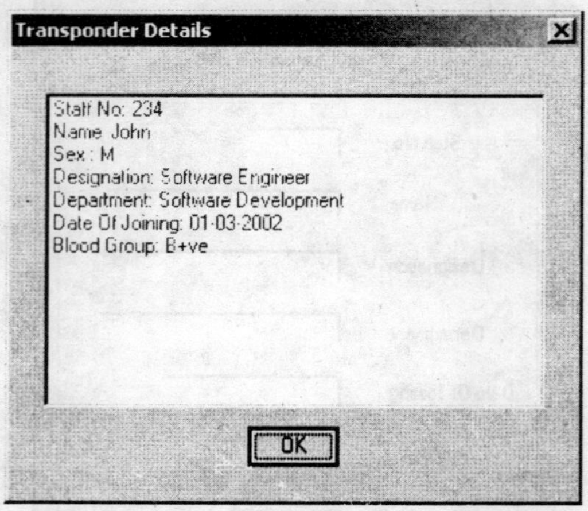

Fig. 20.6

Application 2: RFID (ID Card) Tag Attendance register

In this application, we will use the RFID (ID card) to log the attendance of the employees. The reader can be placed at the entrance and whenever an employee walks in, the in-time will be automatically noted down. Similarly, when the employee goes out, the out-time will be automatically noted down. Fig. 20.7 shows the main screen of the attendance application using RFID system.

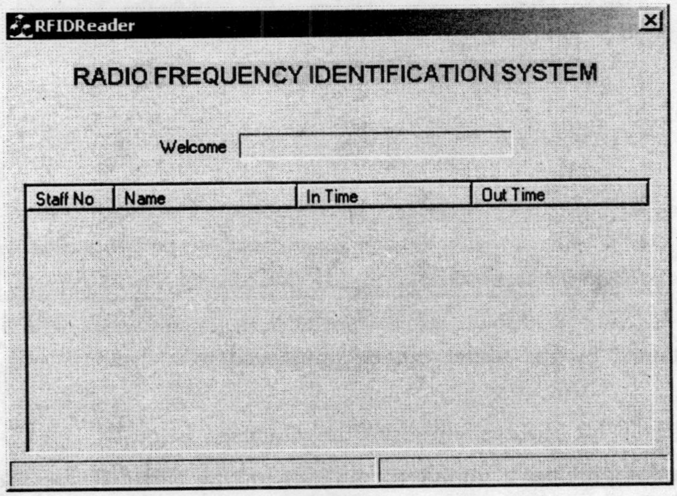

Fig. 20.7

When the employee comes in the vicinity of the reader, automatically, the reader obtains the employee data from the tag and sends it to the PC. The information is stored in a database table. Fig. 20.8 shows the screen that records the in-time.

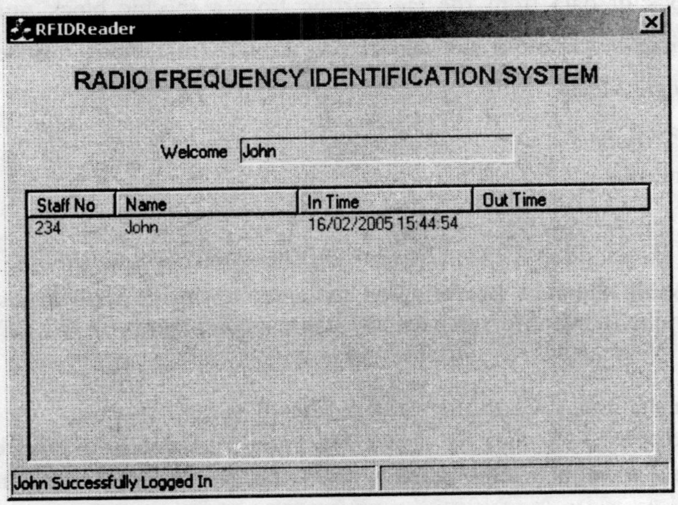

Fig 20.8

Similarly, when the employee leaves the premises, the out-time will be recorded and updated in the database. Fig. 20.9 shows the screen that displays both in-time and out-time.

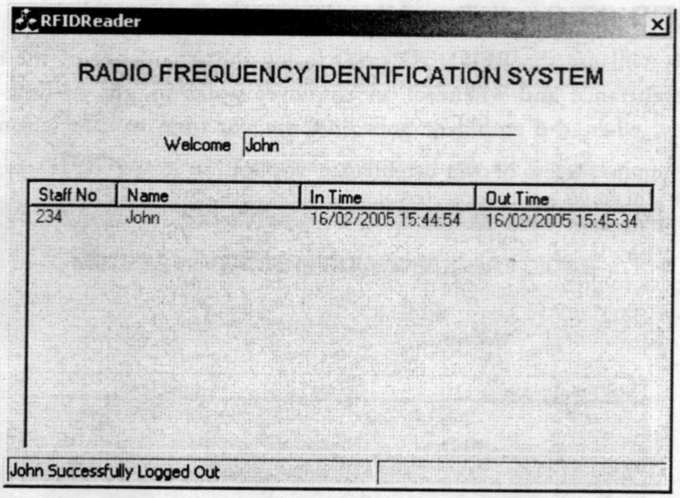

Fig. 20.9

The information obtained by the reader can be transferred to a database and necessary reports can be generated.

The programming details for these applications are discussed below.

The RFID reader vendor provides a number of utilities for the RFID Reader. Some of the important utilities are listed below. Note that the RF tag has to be compliant with ISO 15693 standard.

- To display the version of the RFID reader
- To display the unique ID of the tag
- To read a block of data from the tag starting from a specific block number
- To read multiple blocks from the tag starting at a specific block number.
- To write a single block
- To lock a block
- To turn off the tag

Notes...

Texas Instruments' S6350 Midrange Reader, used for development of applications in this chapter, complies with the standard RF interface and transmission protocol of ISO/IEC 15693-2, -3.

The data packet from the host (PC) to the reader is known as the request and the reply from the reader to the host as the response. The host is always the primary station and initiates all communication sequences. These consist of request/response pairs where the host waits for a response before continuing. ISO 15693-3 transmission protocol commands have been used for reading data from and writing data to the tag.

In Brief...

The communication between the reader and the tag is through command-response packets. Each packet will have a checksum. Commands to read the unique ID, read a block, read consecutive blocks, write data blocks etc. use a standard structure defined by the standard.

The tags are called "Tag-it ISO Transponder Inlays". These transponders are ISO/IEC 15693 complaint and are of 2k bit memory in 64x32-bit blocks (Total 256 bytes of memory). Each block contains 4 bytes of memory.

In ISO 15693-3 transmission protocol commands, each packet format requires Packet Length of 2 bytes. In these two bytes first byte should be LSB and second byte should be MSB of packet length. Also each packet requires reader Command byte that the reader executes. For ISO 15693-3 commands, this value is always 0x60.

Notes...

The following code listings are available on the CDROM that accompanies the book. Note that you need to install the RFID reader and the associated driver software to execute these applications. Otherwise, error messages will be displayed.

Listing 20.1 gives some member functions from RFIDCard Dlg.cpp file. This listing illustrates the programming of the RFID application.

Listing 20. 1. Some member functions from **RFIDCardDlg.cpp** file:

```
BOOL CRFIDCardDlg::OnInitDialog()
{
   CDialog::OnInitDialog();

   // Add "About..." menu item to system menu.

   // IDM_ABOUTBOX must be in the system command range.
   ASSERT((IDM_ABOUTBOX & 0xFFF0) == IDM_ABOUTBOX);
   ASSERT(IDM_ABOUTBOX < 0xF000);

   CMenu* pSysMenu = GetSystemMenu(FALSE);
   if (pSysMenu != NULL)
   {
      CString strAboutMenu;
      strAboutMenu.LoadString(IDS_ABOUTBOX);
      if (!strAboutMenu.IsEmpty())
      {
         pSysMenu->AppendMenu(MF_SEPARATOR);
         pSysMenu->AppendMenu(MF_STRING, IDM_ABOUTBOX, strAboutMenu);
      }
   }
```

```
  // Set the icon for this dialog.  The framework does this automatically
  //   when the application's main window is not a dialog
  SetIcon(m_hIcon, TRUE);         // Set big icon
  SetIcon(m_hIcon, FALSE);        // Set small icon

  m_sex = 0;
  UpdateData(0);
  char cPortNr[4];
  itoa(1, cPortNr, 10);// Convert Integer to Char

  //open port (COM1)
  iPortHandle = FECOM_OpenPort(cPortNr);
  if(iPortHandle < 0)
    AfxMessageBox("port cannot be opened");
  else
  {
    /* Configuring the COM port with the following values:
          Baudrate : 57600
          Data bits  : 8
          Parity     : None (N)
          Stop bit : 1
          Timeout   : 600    */
    FECOM_SetPortPara(iPortHandle, "Baud", "57600");
    FECOM_SetPortPara(iPortHandle, "Frame", "8N1");
    FECOM_SetPortPara(iPortHandle, "Timeout", "600");
    FECOM_SetPortPara(iPortHandle, "TxTimeControl", "1");
    FECOM_SetPortPara(iPortHandle, "TxDelayTime", "50");
  }

  return TRUE;  // return TRUE  unless you set the focus to a control
}

/* To close the COM port, while closing the application */

void CRFIDCardDlg::OnClose()
{
  CString status;

  if(FECOM_ClosePort(iPortHandle) == 0)
  {
    status.Format("Port : %d Closed Successfully",iPortHandle);
```

```
    }
    else if(FECOM_ClosePort(iPortHandle) < 0)
    {
        AfxMessageBox("PortHandle is -ve, cannot close Port");
    }
    CDialog::OnClose();
}
/*
Function for:
Writing the data into transponder using ISO Write Single Block commands.
While writing the data into blocks of transponder, write data in the
reverse order and in ASCII format, in order to put data correctly.
After data is successfully written into transponder, data will be
inserted into database.
*/
void CRFIDCardDlg::OnBtnWritedata()
{
    UpdateData();

    int datalen;
    datalen = m_edt_staffno.GetLength() + m_edt_name.GetLength() +
m_edt_desg.GetLength() + m_edt_dept.GetLength() + 8 +
m_edt_bgroup.GetLength() + 1;

    if(datalen > 256)
    {
        AfxMessageBox("data overflow: cannot write data");
        return;
    }

    if( (m_edt_staffno == "") || (m_edt_name == "") || (m_edt_desg ==
"") || (m_edt_dept == "") || (m_edt_doj == "") || (m_edt_bgroup == ""))
    {
        AfxMessageBox("All Fields are mandatory!");
        return;
    }

    //variables for database connectivity
    CBDTest empDB;
    _RecordsetPtr pRst;
```

```
    empDB.OpenDBConnection();
    char szSQl[250];
    CString tmp, data;

    int staffno = atoi(m_edt_staffno);

    //checking whether staffno already exists in the database or not
    sprintf(szSQl,"Select * from EmpDetails where StaffNo=%d",staffno);
    pRst = empDB.GetRecordset(szSQl);

    if(pRst->RecordCount > 0)
    {
      tmp.Format("StaffNo: %d data already exists!",staffno);
      AfxMessageBox(tmp);
      empDB.CloseDBConnection();
      return;
    }

    EnableCtrls(FALSE);
    //AfxMessageBox("new entry");

    unsigned char WSB_Buff[17]; //buffer to store write single block
request
    BYTE CHS = 0, bData;
    int p = 0, namelen, desglen,deptlen, bglen, iErr;
    CString bFlag = "StNo",doj, sx;

    namelen = m_edt_name.GetLength();
    desglen = m_edt_desg.GetLength();
    deptlen = m_edt_dept.GetLength();
    bglen = m_edt_bgroup.GetLength();

    if(m_sex == 0)
      sx = "M";
    else
      sx = "F";

    doj = m_edt_doj; //storing original doj value to store in the
database
    if(m_edt_doj.Find("/") > 0)
      m_edt_doj.Remove('/');
```

```
else if(m_edt_doj.Find("-") > 0)
   m_edt_doj.Remove('-');

int i = 0, lcnt = 0;
while(bFlag != "NONE")
{
   WSB_Buff[0] = 0x01; //write single block request header
   WSB_Buff[1] = 0x11; //2 bytes for packet length
   WSB_Buff[2] = 0x00; //
   WSB_Buff[3] = 0x00; // 2 bytes for node address
   WSB_Buff[4] = 0x00; //
   WSB_Buff[5] = 0x00; // cmd flag : will be set if node address
is set other wise will be clear(0)
   WSB_Buff[6] = 0x60; //ISO command always 0x60
   WSB_Buff[7] = 0x11; //configuration byte
   WSB_Buff[8] = 0x43; //option_flag : always 0x43 for write and
lock single block request
   WSB_Buff[9] = 0x21; //write single block command code
   WSB_Buff[10] = p;   //block no. to which data to be written

   //each block ocuupies 4 bytes
   //insert data into buffer in reverse order and in ascii format

   if(bFlag == "StNo") //1 block for staff no
   {
      for(i=1; i<=4; i++)
      {
         if(i <= m_edt_staffno.GetLength())
         {
tmp.Format("%d",m_edt_staffno.GetAt(m_edt_staffno.GetLength()-i));
            bData = atoi(tmp);
            WSB_Buff[10+i] = bData;
         }
         else
            WSB_Buff[10+i] = 0x00;
      }

      p += 1;
      bFlag = "NLen";
   }
```

```
else if(bFlag == "NLen") //1 block for name len
{
  data.Format("%d", namelen);

  for(i=1; i<=4; i++)
  {
    if(i <= data.GetLength())
    {
       tmp.Format("%d",data.GetAt(data.GetLength()-i));
       bData = atoi(tmp);
       WSB_Buff[10+i] = bData;
    }
    else
       WSB_Buff[10+i] = 0x00;
  }

  p += 1;
  bFlag = "Name";
}
else if(bFlag == "Name") //for name
{
  while(lcnt <= namelen)
  {
    data = m_edt_name.Mid(lcnt,4);

    for(i=1; i<=4; i++)
    {
      if(i <= data.GetLength())
      {
        tmp.Format("%d",data.GetAt(data.GetLength()-i));
        bData = atoi(tmp);
        WSB_Buff[10+i] = bData;
      }
      else
        WSB_Buff[10+i] = 0x00;
    }

    p += 1;
    lcnt += 4;
    break;
  }
```

```
    if(lcnt >= namelen)
    {
       bFlag = "Sex";
       lcnt = 0;
    }
 }
 else if(bFlag == "Sex")  //1 block for m/f
 {

    for(i=1; i<=4; i++)
    {
       if(i <= sx.GetLength())
       {
          tmp.Format("%d",sx.GetAt(sx.GetLength()-i));
          bData = atoi(tmp);
          WSB_Buff[10+i] = bData;
       }
       else
          WSB_Buff[10+i] = 0x00;
    }

    p += 1;

    bFlag = "DesgLen";
 }
 else if(bFlag == "DesgLen") //1 block for desglen
 {
    data.Format("%d",desglen);

    for(i=1; i<=4; i++)
    {
       if(i <= data.GetLength())
       {
          tmp.Format("%d",data.GetAt(data.GetLength()-i));
          bData = atoi(tmp);
          WSB_Buff[10+i] = bData;
       }
       else
          WSB_Buff[10+i] = 0x00;
    }
```

```
  p += 1;
  bFlag = "Desg";
 }
 else if(bFlag == "Desg") //for desg
 {
  while(lcnt <= desglen)
  {
    data = m_edt_desg.Mid(lcnt,4);

    for(i=1; i<=4; i++)
    {
      if(i <= data.GetLength())
      {
        tmp.Format("%d",data.GetAt(data.GetLength()-i));
        bData = atoi(tmp);
        WSB_Buff[10+i] = bData;
      }
      else
        WSB_Buff[10+i] = 0x00;
    }

    p += 1;
    lcnt += 4;
    break;
  }

  if(lcnt >= desglen)
  {
    bFlag = "DeptLen";
    lcnt = 0;
  }
 }
 else if(bFlag == "DeptLen") //1 block for deptlen
 {
  data.Format("%d",deptlen);

  for(i=1; i<=4; i++)
  {
    if(i <= data.GetLength())
    {
      tmp.Format("%d",data.GetAt(data.GetLength()-i));
```

```
            bData = atoi(tmp);
            WSB_Buff[10+i] = bData;
         }
         else
            WSB_Buff[10+i] = 0x00;
      }

      p += 1;
      bFlag = "Dept";
   }
   else if(bFlag == "Dept") //for dept
   {
      while(lcnt <= deptlen)
      {
         data = m_edt_dept.Mid(lcnt,4);

         for(i=1; i<=4; i++)
         {
            if(i <= data.GetLength())
            {
               tmp.Format("%d",data.GetAt(data.GetLength()-i));
               bData = atoi(tmp);
               WSB_Buff[10+i] = bData;
            }
            else
               WSB_Buff[10+i] = 0x00;
         }

         p += 1;
         lcnt += 4;
         break;
      }

      if(lcnt >= deptlen)
      {
         bFlag = "DOJ";
         lcnt = 0;
      }
   }
   else if(bFlag == "DOJ")  //for Date of Joining
   {
```

```
        while(lcnt <= m_edt_doj.GetLength())
        {
            data = m_edt_doj.Mid(lcnt,4);

            for(i=1; i<=4; i++)
            {
                if(i <= data.GetLength())
                {
                    tmp.Format("%d",data.GetAt(data.GetLength()-i));
                    bData = atoi(tmp);
                    WSB_Buff[10+i] = bData;
                }
                else
                    WSB_Buff[10+i] = 0x00;
            }

            p += 1;
            lcnt += 4;
            break;
        }
        if(lcnt >= m_edt_doj.GetLength())
        {
            bFlag = "BGLen";
            lcnt = 0;
        }
    }
    else if(bFlag == "BGLen") //1 block for bglen
    {
        data.Format("%d", bglen);

        for(i=1; i<=4; i++)
        {
            if(i <= data.GetLength())
            {
                tmp.Format("%d",data.GetAt(data.GetLength()-i));
                bData = atoi(tmp);
                WSB_Buff[10+i] = bData;
            }
            else
                WSB_Buff[10+i] = 0x00;
```

```
    }

    p += 1;
    bFlag = "BG";
  }
  else if(bFlag == "BG")
  {
    while(lcnt <= bglen)
    {
      data = m_edt_bgroup.Mid(lcnt,4);

      for(i=1; i<=4; i++)
      {
        if(i <= data.GetLength())
        {
          tmp.Format("%d",data.GetAt(data.GetLength()-i));
          bData = atoi(tmp);
          WSB_Buff[10+i] = bData;
        }
        else
          WSB_Buff[10+i] = 0x00;
      }

      p += 1;
      lcnt += 4;
      break;
    }

    if(lcnt >= bglen)
    {
      bFlag = "NONE";
      lcnt = 0;
    }
  }
  //CRC value, 2 bytes - 1 byte for chksum and other byte is 0xFF
XOR chksum
  CHS = 0;
  for(i=0; i<15; i++)
    CHS = CHS ^ WSB_Buff[i];
  WSB_Buff[15] = CHS;
  WSB_Buff[16] = 0xFF ^ CHS;
```

```
if(iPortHandle > 0) //valid port
{
  iErr = FECOM_Transmit(iPortHandle, WSB_Buff, 17);
  //if FECOM_Transmit fails
  if(iErr < 0)
  {
    char error[100];
    FECOM_GetErrorText(iErr, error);
    tmp.Format("%d %s", iErr,error);
    AfxMessageBox(tmp);
    EnableCtrls(TRUE);
    return;
  }
  else
  {
    int recd;
    unsigned char recvBuff[20];

    recd = FECOM_Receive(iPortHandle, recvBuff, 20);
    if(recd > 0)
    {
      if(recvBuff[7] == 0)  //if response is success
      {
        tmp.Format("data in block %d is written",p-1);
        //AfxMessageBox(tmp);
      }
      else
      {
        if(recvBuff[7] == 1)  //if error code is 1
          AfxMessageBox("Write Failed: Transponder not found");
        else if(recvBuff[7] == 2) //if error code is 2
          AfxMessageBox("Write Failed: Command not supported");
        else if(recvBuff[7] == 4) //if error code is 4
          AfxMessageBox("Write Failed: Invalid Flags");

        EnableCtrls(TRUE);
        return;
      }
    }
    else
    {
```

```
            char  error[100];
            FECOM_GetErrorText(recd,  error);
            tmp.Format("%d  %s", recd,error);
            AfxMessageBox(tmp);
            EnableCtrls(TRUE);
            return;
         }
      }
   }
   else
   {
      char  error[100];
      FECOM_GetErrorText(iPortHandle,  error);
      tmp.Format("%d  %s",  iPortHandle,error);
      AfxMessageBox(tmp);
      EnableCtrls(TRUE);
      return;
   }

   memset(WSB_Buff,0,17);
 }  //end  of  while

 AfxMessageBox("writing  data  completed");

 sprintf(szSQl,"Select  *  from  EmpDetails");
 pRst  =  empDB.GetRecordset(szSQl);
 if(pRst->GetRecordCount()  >  0)
    pRst->MoveLast();

 sprintf(szSQl,"Insert  into  EmpDetails  values(%d,\'%s\',\'%s\',\'%s\',
\'%s\',\'%s\',\'%s\')",staffno,m_edt_name,sx,m_edt_desg,m_edt_dept,doj,m_edt_bgroup);

 empDB.ExecuteSQLStatement(szSQl);

 AfxMessageBox("data  inserted  into  database");

 EnableCtrls(TRUE);
}

/*  To  reset  the  fields  */
```

```
void CRFIDCardDlg::OnBtnReset()
{
   m_edt_staffno = "";
   m_edt_name = "";
   m_edt_desg = "";
   m_edt_dept = "";
   m_edt_doj = "";
   m_edt_bgroup = "";
   m_sex = 0;
   UpdateData(0);
}

/* To read data from the Transponder */

void CRFIDCardDlg::OnBtnReaddata()
{
   CReadDetails rDlg;
   rDlg.DoModal();
}

/* To enable or disable the buttons, write, read and reset */

void CRFIDCardDlg::EnableCtrls(BOOL enable)
{
   if(enable)
   {
      m_btn_writedata.EnableWindow(1);
      m_btn_readdata.EnableWindow(1);
      m_btn_reset.EnableWindow(1);
   }
   else
   {
      m_btn_writedata.EnableWindow(0);
      m_btn_readdata.EnableWindow(0);
      m_btn_reset.EnableWindow(0);
   }
}

/* To restrict all characters other than numbers for staffno edit
control */
```

```
void CRFIDCardDlg::OnChangeEditStaffno()
{
   UpdateData();
   CString str;

   if(m_edt_staffno.GetLength() > 0)
   {
      str.Format("%d",m_edt_staffno.GetAt(m_edt_staffno.GetLength()-1));

      if((atoi(str) < 48) || (atoi(str) > 57))
      {
m_edt_staffno.Replace(m_edt_staffno.Mid(m_edt_staffno.GetLength()-1),"");

         UpdateData(0);
         ((CEdit*)GetDlgItem(IDC_EDIT_STAFFNO))-
>SetSel(m_edt_staffno.GetLength(),-1);
      }
   }
}
```

Listing 20.2 gives the important functions from ReadDetails.cpp file:

Listing 20.2 Some functions from ReadDetails.cpp

```
BOOL CReadDetails::OnInitDialog()
{
   CDialog::OnInitDialog();

   CString read;
   int sob, nob, staffnum;

   m_lst_details.EnableWindow(0);

   //read data from transponder

   read = ReadBlocks(0, 0); //read StaffNo
   if(read == "Error")
      EndDialog(1);
   else
   {
      staffnum = atoi(read);
      m_lst_details.AddString("Staff No: "+read);
```

```
read = ReadBlocks(1, 0); //read Name Length
nob =  atoi(read);
if((nob % 4) != 0)
   nob = (nob/4) + 1;
else
   nob = nob/4;

sob = 2;
read = ReadBlocks(sob, nob); //read name
m_lst_details.AddString("Name: "+read);

sob = sob + nob;
read = ReadBlocks(sob, 0);  //read m/f
m_lst_details.AddString("Sex : "+read);

sob = sob + 1;
read = ReadBlocks(sob, 0);  //read desglen
nob =  atoi(read);
if((nob % 4) != 0)
   nob = (nob/4) + 1;
else
   nob = nob/4;

sob = sob + 1;
read = ReadBlocks(sob, nob); //read designation
m_lst_details.AddString("Designation: "+read);

sob = sob + nob;
read = ReadBlocks(sob, 0);  //read deptlen
nob =  atoi(read);
if((nob % 4) != 0)
   nob = (nob/4) + 1;
else
   nob = nob/4;

sob = sob + 1;
read = ReadBlocks(sob, nob); //read department
m_lst_details.AddString("Department: "+read);

sob = sob + nob;
read = ReadBlocks(sob, 2);  //read date of joining
```

```
    read.Insert(2,"-");
    read.Insert(5,"-");
    m_lst_details.AddString("Date Of Joining: "+read);

    sob = sob + 2;
    read = ReadBlocks(sob, 0);  //read blood group len
    nob =  atoi(read);
    if((nob % 4) != 0)
       nob = (nob/4) + 1;
    else
       nob = nob/4;

    sob = sob + 1;
    read = ReadBlocks(sob, nob); //read blood group
    m_lst_details.AddString("Blood Group: "+read);

  }
  return TRUE;  // return TRUE unless you set the focus to a control
                                // EXCEPTION: OCX Property Pages should return
FALSE
}

/*
Function For:
Reading single or multiple blocks of data from transponder using ISO
Read Single/Multiple block request.
While reading blocks of data from transponder, in order to retrieve data
correctly, read data in the reverse order and character by character.
*/

CString CReadDetails::ReadBlocks(int SBlock, int NumBlocks)
{
  unsigned char RSB_Buff[14];
  BYTE CHS = 0;
  int recd, iErr, handle;
  unsigned char recvBuff[256];
  CString str, rstr;
  CStringArray tidArray;

  handle = FECOM_GetPortHnd("1");
```

```
if(NumBlocks == 0) //Read Single Block
{
    RSB_Buff[0] = 0x01; //read single block request header
    RSB_Buff[1] = 0x0D; // 2 bytes for packet length
    RSB_Buff[2] = 0x00; //
    RSB_Buff[3] = 0x00; // 2 bytes for block address
    RSB_Buff[4] = 0x00; //
    RSB_Buff[5] = 0x00; // cmd flag : will be set if block address
is set other wise will be clear(0)
    RSB_Buff[6] = 0x60; //ISO command always 0x60
    RSB_Buff[7] = 0x11; //configuration byte
    RSB_Buff[8] = 0x03; //option_flag : always 0x03 for read single
block
    RSB_Buff[9] = 0x20; //read single block command code
    RSB_Buff[10] = SBlock; //block number to be read
    //chs value, 2 bytes - 1 byte for chksum and other byte for ~
of chksum
    CHS = 0;
    for(int i=0; i<11; i++)
        CHS = CHS ^ RSB_Buff[i];
    RSB_Buff[11] = CHS;
    RSB_Buff[12] = 0xFF ^ CHS;

    iErr = FECOM_Transmit(handle, RSB_Buff, 13);
    //if FECOM_Transmit fails
    if(iErr < 0)
    {
        //AfxMessageBox("Error in sending request for ReadSingleBlock");
        char error[100];
        FECOM_GetErrorText(iErr, error);
        str.Format("%d %s", iErr,error);
        AfxMessageBox(str);
        return "Error";
    }
    else
    {
        recd = FECOM_Receive(handle, recvBuff, 256);
        if(recd > 0)
        {
            if(recvBuff[7] == 0)   //if response is success
            {
```

```
            for(int k=11; k>=8; k—)
            {
               str.Format("%c",recvBuff[k]);
               if(!str.IsEmpty())
                  rstr += str;
            }
         }
         else
         {
            if(recvBuff[7] == 1)  //if error code is 1
               AfxMessageBox("Read Failed: Transponder not found");
            else if(recvBuff[7] == 2) //if error code is 2
               AfxMessageBox("Read Failed: Command not supported");
            else if(recvBuff[7] == 4) //if error code is 4
               AfxMessageBox("Read Failed: Invalid Flags");

            return "Error";
         }
      }
      else
      {
         char error[100];
         FECOM_GetErrorText(recd, error);
         str.Format("%d %s", recd,error);
         AfxMessageBox(str);
         return "Error";
      }
   }

}
else //Read Multiple Blocks
{
   RSB_Buff[0] = 0x01; //read single block request header
   RSB_Buff[1] = 0x0E; // 2 bytes for packet length
   RSB_Buff[2] = 0x00; //
   RSB_Buff[3] = 0x00; // 2 bytes for node address
   RSB_Buff[4] = 0x00; //
   RSB_Buff[5] = 0x00; // cmd flag : will be set if node address
is set other wise will be clear(0)
   RSB_Buff[6] = 0x60; //ISO command always 0x60
   RSB_Buff[7] = 0x11; //configuration byte
```

```
    RSB_Buff[8] = 0x03; //option_flag : always 0x03 for read single/
multiple block
    RSB_Buff[9] = 0x23; //read multiple block command code
    RSB_Buff[10] = SBlock; //starting block no
    RSB_Buff[11] = NumBlocks; //no. of blocks to be read
    //chs value, 2 bytes - 1 byte for chksum and other byte for ~
of chksum
    CHS = 0;
    for(int i=0; i<12; i++)
        CHS = CHS ^ RSB_Buff[i];
    RSB_Buff[12] = CHS;
    RSB_Buff[13] = 0xFF ^ CHS;
    iErr = FECOM_Transmit(handle, RSB_Buff, 14);
    //if FECOM_Transmit fails
    if(iErr < 0)
    {
        char error[100];
        FECOM_GetErrorText(iErr, error);
        str.Format("%d %s", iErr,error);
        AfxMessageBox(str);
        return "Error";
    }
    else
    {
        recd = FECOM_Receive(handle, recvBuff, 256);
        if(recd > 0)
        {
            if(recvBuff[7] == 0)   //if response is success
            {
                for(i=0; i<NumBlocks*4; i+=4)
                {
                    for(int k=11+i; k>=8+i; k—)
                    {
                        str.Format("%c",recvBuff[k]);
                        if(!str.IsEmpty())
                            rstr += str;
                    }
                    //AfxMessageBox(rstr);
                }
            }
```

```
        else
        {
            if(recvBuff[7] == 1)  //if error code is 1
                AfxMessageBox("Read Failed: Transponder not found");
            else if(recvBuff[7] == 2)//if error code is 2
                AfxMessageBox("Read Failed: Command not supported");
            else if(recvBuff[7] == 4) //if error code is 4
                AfxMessageBox("Read Failed: Invalid Flags");
            return "Error";
        }
      }
      else
      {
        char error[100];
        FECOM_GetErrorText(recd, error);
        str.Format("%d %s", recd,error);
        AfxMessageBox(str);
        return "Error";
      }

    }
  }

  return rstr;
}
```

20.6 Object-Oriented Programming for Embedded Systems

As can be seen from the previous section, it is very easy and productive to do programming in C++. Though C++ is extensively used for application programming on desktop computers, its use in embedded software development is yet to take off. In this section, we will study the important features of OOP. OOP is now catching up very fast and a good understanding of the OOP concepts is very important.

In OOP languages, objects are identified which are closer to real life and the software is built around these objects. For instance, to build library automation software, the book and the library user can be considered as objects. Each object can interact with the other objects and the rest of the program only through specified interface..

In OOP, key element is an object—an entity closer to real life. Object is an autonomous part of a program which will have a controlled interface with the rest of the program. This feature makes software modification easier, as only the interface portion needs redefinition in case there are changes in the software. Objects are created through the mechanism of class. An object is an instance of a class. Class is a data type containing public and private sections. A class definition consists of member variables (called instance variables) and methods (functions to be performed). Instance variables and methods can be private or public. Private members are available only within the class whereas public members are available to other parts of the program. So, through public members (generally, public methods), interface is provided to the class.

The three important features of OOP are:

- Design encapsulation
- Polymorphism
- Inheritance

Design encapsulation enhances the modularity of the program through classes. A class interfaces with the rest of the program only through its public members, other members are protected and not available to the rest of the program.

Use of the same name symbol for more than one action is known as polymorphism. For example consider a C program in which you have to find the maximum value of two numbers. If the numbers are integers, you have to write a function int maxi(int x, int y) which will take two integer arguments and will return an integer. If the numbers are floating point numbers, you have to write another function float maxf(float x, float y). However, in OOP languages, you can use the same function name for both the functions int max (int x, int y) and float max(float x, float y). This is called function overloading. Function overloading is one example of polymorphism. Similarly operator overloading is possible. The operator + can be used for addition, and also for string concatenation. This makes programming flexible and closer to real life.

Inheritance is creation of new classes based on existing classes. New class inherits all the properties of the parent class (called super class). In addition, derived class can have its own additional properties. There is a special class called abstract class for which there can be no objects, but new classes can be derived from the abstract class. When a subclass inherits methods of a parent class, inherited methods can behave exactly as the parent class or they can behave differently i.e., they can be polymorphic. So, polymorphism happens when a method behaves differently and has varying effects for classes in an object hierarchy.

Due to these reasons, OOP for embedded software development is catching up very fast. However, due to the overheads of classes and objects, the C++ compilers are slower. To overcome this problem, Embedded C++ has been developed.

20.7 Embedded C++

Embedded C++ is a scaled-down version of the standards C++ developed by American National Standards Institute (ANSI). In ANSI C++, the following features have been omitted:

- Multiple inheritance and virtual base class
- Runtime type identification
- Exception handling
- Templates

- Namespaces
- New-style casts

Due to this scaled down features, Embedded C++ gives the best of both worlds of C and C++. It is very fast and at the same time provides the advantages of Object Oriented Programming.

Summary

This chapter gives the details of RFID technology. RFID-based systems will replace the bar code based systems because of their flexibility in use and operation as well as their advantage of developing identification systems without the need for a contact between the item and the reader. The RFID tags can be either active or passive. The active tag has a battery whereas the passive tag obtains its power from the RF radiation. The RFID systems operate in different bands, UHF and ISM bands being the most predominant. The RFID tag and the reader need to be chosen keeping in view the various issues such as memory capacity of the tag, range of the system, security features etc. The power of RFID system is in the capability of the reader being networked. The information stored in the tag can be made available over a network, paving way for a global asset tracking or global supply chain management.

In this chapter, we demonstrated how to program the RFID tag, using C++. As C++ provides the facility of reuse, it is now being used for embedded software development as well. Embedded C++ is a scaled down version of ANSI C++ optimized for embedded software development.

Questions

1. Explain the functioning of an RFID system.
2. What is the difference between a passive tag and an active tag?
3. What is EPC? Explain the format of EPC and the various standards for the EPC.
4. What are the different frequency bands used for RFID?
5. What are the advantages of using RFID tags over using bar codes for product identification?
6. What are the advantages of C++ over C? List the important features of Embedded C++.

Exercises

1. Carry out a survey of manufacturers of RFID tags/readers and reader ICs.
2. RFID tags can be used by universities to issue tamper-proof marks lists to the students. Design the format for storing of the marks list for a semester. Using an RFID reader, develop the software for such a system.
3. Design an RFID system for library automation if (a) each book is attached with an RFID tag and (b) each library user is given an RFID tag.

Chapter 21

DSP-based Embedded Systems

CHAPTER OBJECTIVES

After reading this chapter, you will be able to:

- Understand the importance and applications of DSP-based embedded systems
- Learn the fundamentals of digital signal processing
- Understand the process of design and development of DSP-based embedded systems
- Know the various application areas in which DSP is extensively used
- Learn how to implement DSP algorithms in MATLAB

In recent years, Digital Signal Processing (DSP) has taken center-stage in embedded systems development. More than 50% of the DSP market is driven by mobile communications because of the intense signal processing involved to process audio and video signals. In this chapter, we will study the DSP-based embedded systems in detail and their various applications. After a quick review of fundamentals of digital signal processing, we will study the architecture of digital signal processors. We will also discuss the design process for developing DSP-based systems. How to implement DSP algorithms in MATLAB is discussed in detail.

21.1 Need for DSP-based Embedded Systems

Embedded systems that use General Purpose Processors do very simple data processing. For instance, the embedded system for process control collects some inputs and uses some logic to produce/control some outputs. The logic that is implemented in the processor does not involve much of mathematical manipulation.

On the other hand, consider an MP3 player. This embedded system has to process the audio signals and convert them into MP3 format using very complex mathematical algorithms. The General Purpose Processor (GPP) is not well-suited for such highly mathematical operations. In such a case, it is more appropriate to design the embedded system around a Digital Signal Processor (DSP).

In Brief...

General Purpose Processors (GPPs) are not well suited for complex mathematical calculations. Digital Signal Processors (DSPs) are optimized for fast repetitive mathematical operations for filtering, spectal analysis etc.

To process voice, music, video, fax, and many types of communication signals, the embedded systems are built around DSPs. The DSP architecture is such that it can do signal processing—spectral analysis, filtering etc.—much more efficiently than a GPP.

Notes...

General Purpose Processors (GPPs) can be divided into micro-controllers and microprocessors. Micro-controllers have in-built peripherals whereas microprocessors need lot of external circuitry.

21.2 An Overview of Digital Signal Processing

The foundation for Digital Signal Processing was laid by the 18th and 19th century mathematicians. However, with the advent of digital computers in the 1950's only, the DSP emerged as a strong engineering field. During the last decade of the 20th century, particularly with the tremendous growth in wireless technologies, applications of DSP have grown rapidly. In this section, we will present an overview of the digital signal processing. Our focus will be on getting a conceptual understanding of DSP and its applications.

To transmit a message or information, the message/information is converted into a signal. The real world signals such as voice, video etc., are analog signals i.e., their signal amplitude varies continuously with respect to time. We also convert real-world physical quantities such as pressure, temperature etc., into analog signals using sensors and then process these signals. This processing is done to extract useful information, or to remove unwanted signals that get added to the desired signal (such as noise etc.). Processing of signals is done to:

- Extract useful information from the signal (the information may be contained in the amplitude, frequency, phase etc.)
- Remove unwanted portions from the signal such as removal of noise, removal of undesired signals etc.)
- To reformat the signal for telecommunication (for example multiplexing, multiple access)
- To compress the signal without any sizeable degradation in their quality so that the signal can be transmitted with a reduced bandwidth, or stored with less storage requirement.

Traditionally, the processing was done in analog domain using amplifiers, filters etc. These systems are known as Analog Signal Processing (ASP). However, with the advent of digital electronics, processing the signals using digital techniques is catchig up. This is known as Digital Signal Processing. However, the world is analog and we need to convert an analog signal into a digital signal. The output of sensors, transducers etc. is analog and not digital. We need to carry out signal conditioning (such as amplification, filtering, isolation etc.) which is done in analog domain. If the processing is done in both analog and digital domains, it is called mixed signal processing.

In Brief...

The real-world signals are anolog signals. For digital signal processing, the first step is to convert the analog signal into digital format.

Digital Signal Processing (DSP) is now an integral part of many embedded systems such as mobile phones, electronic instruments, modems, etc. As discussed in the previous chapters, many embedded systems use both DSP and a GPP (General Purpose Processor).

21.2.1 Signals and Systems

When you speak into a microphone, the output of the microphone is an electrical signal which represents the speech. The speech signal shows how the amplitude varies with respect to time. Similarly, the real-world physical quantities such as temperature, pressure, velocity etc. can be represented as electrical signals. A sensor or a transducer converts this physical quantity into its equivalent electrical signal. "Signal processing" deals with analyzing these signals either for understanding the signal characteristics or to process the signals to obtain a desired effect. Here are some examples of signals:

- Speech
- Music
- Electrocardiogram (ECG)
- Electroencephalogram (EEG)
- Image
- Video

Systems

A hardware device or a software routine that processes a signal is defined as a signal processing system. A system may carry out functions such as:

- Amplify the signal
- Attenuate the signal
- Filter out the unwanted frequency components
- Multiply two signals
- Extract some important characteristics of the signals

Signal processing systems can be classified as analog processing systems and digital signal processing systems.

Notes...

For digital signal processing, mathematical analysis is very important. However, as math becomes complex for non-linear systems, in DSP, systems are generally assumed to be "Linear Time Invariant (LTI)" systems.

21.2.2 Analog Signal Processing

If you speak into a microphone and observe the output of the microphone in an oscilloscope, you will observe a waveform in which the amplitude of the signal varies continuously with respect to time. Such a signal is called the analog signal. All the real-world signals are analog in nature—for example, speech signal, music signal, electrocardiogram signal, electroencephalogram signal etc. In good old days, before the digital computers were invented, the signals were processed using analog computers. Nowadays, you can find these analog computers only in science and technology museums. Analog signals are also called continuous-time signals.

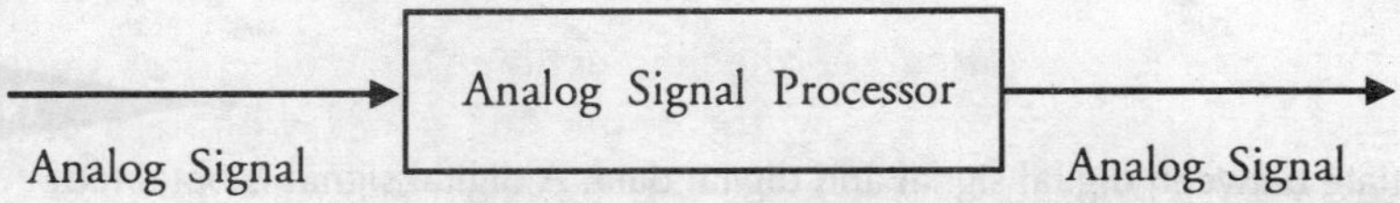

Fig. 21.1 Analog Signal Processing

As shown in Fig. 21.1, analog signal processing systems take analog signal as input and process the signal in analog domain to produce the desired output. Examples include: analog amplifiers, analog filters, modulators etc.

Even today, analog signal processing systems are widely used. Particularly, high frequency radio signals are processed in the analog domain only.

For example, consider an analog system, a low pass filter, which takes an analog speech signal as input. If the low pass filter has a 'cutoff frequency' of 2 KHz, the output of the filter is a speech signal which will not have frequency components above 2 KHz.

Notes...

Analog signal processing is used for processing frequency radio signals. However, digital signal processing is slowly replacing analog signal processing.

21.2.3 Digital Signal Processing

A signal whose amplitude values are defined only at discrete-time intervals is called discrete-time signal. Each amplitude value is called a sample value. The time period between two successive samples is called the sampling period.

Discrete-time signals are obtained by measuring the amplitude values at regular intervals. For instance, we can measure the value of temperature every half-an-hour and then obtain the discrete signal. The stock price of a company at the closing time of the stock market everyday, the number of bouquets sold by a shop every day are some other examples of such discrete signals. Another way of obtaining the discrete signal is by taking the analog signal and then finding out its amplitude values at regular intervals.

Hence, a discrete-time signal can be obtained in one of the following ways:

- By taking the analog signal and taking its amplitude values at regular intervals
- By measuring the amplitude values at regular intervals

Note that in a discrete-time signal, the amplitude values can be any value within a range. For instance, if the amplitude represents the voltage level, the sample values can be 4.23145 volts, 3.2123344 volts etc. Hence, the amplitude values are still analog, though the time scale is now discrete.

In the discrete-time signal, if we limit the amplitude values to pre-defined values, then the signal becomes digital. In other words, we can round-off the amplitude values to obtain the digital signal. Hence, a digital signal is characterized by fixed number of amplitude values at fixed time intervals.

When we process signals using a digital computer, the amplitude values can be represented using the internal registers which have finite length and hence digital signal processing involves processing of the digital signals which have fixed number of amplitude values at fixed time intervals.

Notes...

It is important to differentiate between digital signal and digital data. A digital signal is obtained by quantizing the amplitude values obtained at fixed time intervals. On the other hand, digital data is the data generated by a computer for example, the ASCII values of the characters.

21.2.4 Advantages of Digital Processing of Signals

Anyone who has ever worked on analog system design, at some point or the other, hs felt frustrated because of their erratic behaviour. Sometimes, the system works and suddenly it stops working! And, you don't know what has gone wrong! It happens many a times that you successfully develop one system but when you try to assemble another using the same design it does not work. The problem is that analog components have

a. **stability problems:** components age (become old), as they are sensitive to environmental conditions such as temperature and thermal aging.

b. **predictability problems:** component to component variations are common and

c. **accuracy problems** due to internally generated noise.

Digital processing of signals has many advantages:

- Components used in analog systems are less reliable as compared to digital Integrated Circuits. Analog components are more susceptible to temperature variations, tuning of analog components is difficult.
- Digital processing provides lot of flexibility. We can implement the algorithm using software and hence programming is easier and the programs can be modified easily if required.
- Reconfiguration of the digital systems is possible because by simply changing the programming, new systems can be developed.
- With the advent of system-on-chip technology, very low cost compact digital signal processing systems can be developed.
- It is easier to store digital signals (in a floppy, CDROM, hard disk etc.)

In Brief...

Advantages of DSP are: reliability, flexibility, repeatability and reconfigurability. It is also easy and efficient to store digital data than analog data.

Due to all these advantages, DSP has now gained a lot of importance in all information, communication and entertainment technologies.

21.2.5 Types of Signals

Signals, whether analog or digital, are of different types depending on their characteristics. Some important types of signals are described below.

Deterministic Signal

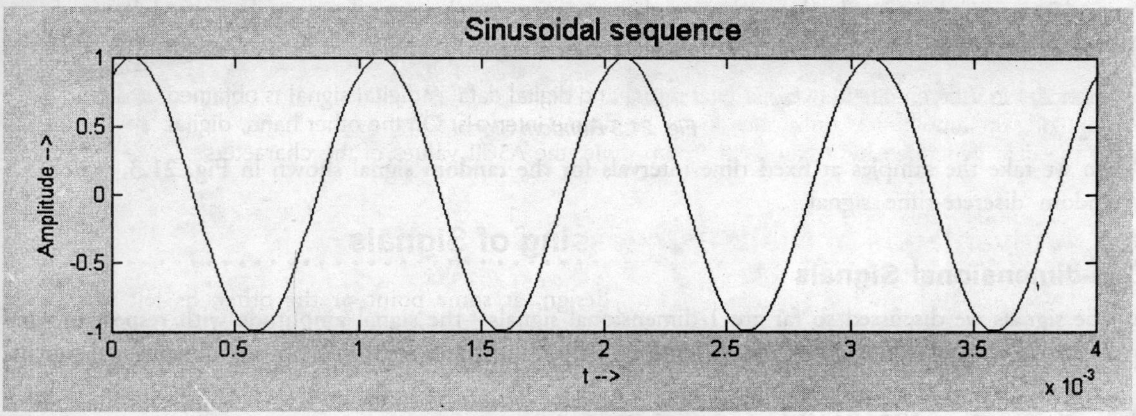

Fig. 21.2 Deterministic Signal

A signal, which can be represented mathematically, is called a deterministic signal. For instance, consider a sine wave shown in Fig. 21.2. It can be represented mathematically and hence we can precisely estimate its amplitude value at a particular instant of time. However, note that it is very difficult to represent real-world signals (such as the speech signal) mathematically. But then, deterministic signals are useful for carrying out the analysis.

Periodic Signal

A signal is periodic if the waveform repeats after a fixed amount of time. Fig. 21.2 is a periodic signal.

Aperiodic Signal

A signal that does not repeat is called aperiodic signal.

Random Signal

A signal whose amplitude value changes in a random fashion is called a random signal. The amplitude value is not deterministic and hence it is a random signal. The noise generated by resistors and the noise added to the signal when the signal passes through a transmission medium are examples of random signals. In signal processing, it is necessary to understand the characteristics of random signals as one of the important signal processing activities is to remove the noise that gets added to the signal.

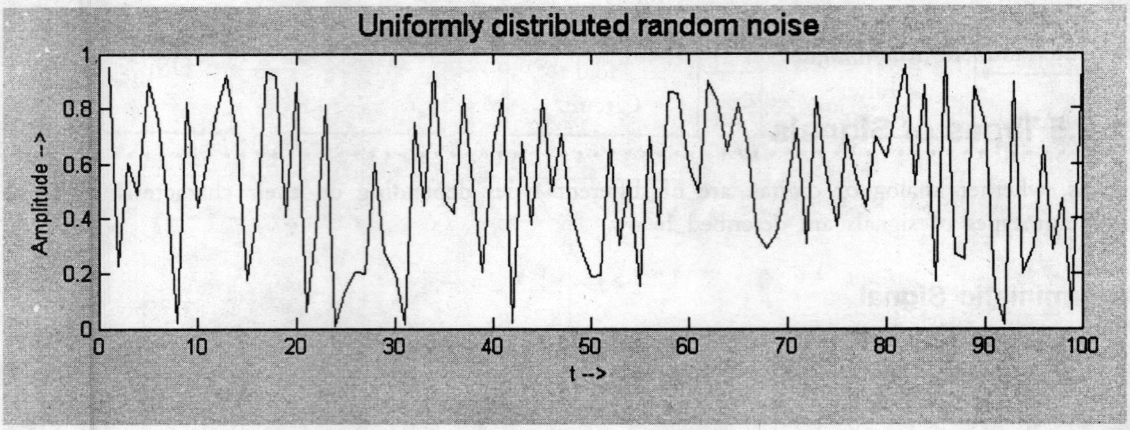

Fig. 21.3 Random Signal

When we take the samples at fixed time intervals for the random signal shown in Fig. 21.3, we obtain a random discrete-time signal.

One-dimensional Signals

All the signals we discussed so far are 1-dimensional signals—the signal amplitude with respect to time is plotted in all the figures given above. In this chapter, our focus is mainly on one-dimensional signals.

Two-dimensional/Multi-dimensional Signals

An image can be represented as a two-dimensional signal. The image can be divided into small grids called pixels. Each pixel will have x-coordinate, y-coordinate and a pixel value which represents the gray scale value. This is a two dimensional signal.

In Brief...

A signal can be deterministic or non-deterministic, periodic or aperiodic or completely random. It is difficult to carry out mathematical analysis of random signals.

Video signal is a function of three variables—two spatial coordinates (x and y) and time. A video can be considered as a series of images. Color video is a three dimensional, three channel signal, the three channels corresponding to red, blue and green colors.

ECG, seismic signal are examples of multi-channel signals. For instance, for ECG, a number of probes are kept on the human body, and the signals are recorded.

21.2.6 Digital Signal Processing Systems

With the developments in digital electronics, analog signal processing is paving way for digital signal processing systems. The block diagram of a digital signal processing system is shown in Fig. 21.7.

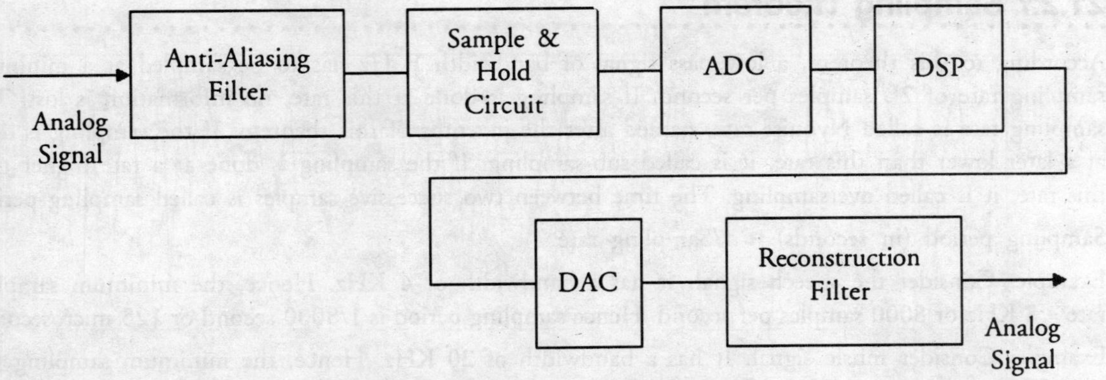

Fig. 21.4 Digital Processing of Analog Signal

The input analog signal is converted into digital signal and the processing is done completely in the digital domain and then finally, the signal is converted back to analog domain. Hence, in digital signal processing, the signals are represented as a sequence of numbers and these numbers are processed either using hardware or software.

Notes...

Signal processing deals with the mathematical concepts and algorithms. Digital Signal Processor is a device/system that does signal processing in digital domain. However, note that both are abbreviated as DSP.

To process the signal completely in digital domain, we need a special device called Analog to Digital Converter (ADC). The ADC takes the analog input and gives out the equivalent digital signal (i.e., a series of samples). The input analog signal is sampled and that samle value is converted into a digital number. Now, either using hardware or software, the samples are processed and the processed samples are again converted back to analog form using a device called Digital to Analog Converter (DAC). As shown in Fig. 21.4, before the ADC, an anti-aliasing filter is placed, which is an analog filter. The function of sample and hold circuit is to hold the analog signal at specific intervals so that the amplitude level can be measured. The output of the DAC is again passed through an analog filter called reconstruction filter to obain an accurate analog output.

As an example, consider a speech processing system. The input signal from a microphone is converted into digital format using an ADC and then the processing is done either on a digital computer or on a digital signal processor and then the processed output is passed through a DAC to get back the analog speech signal which is passed through speakers for listening. The processing can be to filter the noise, or to carry out special effects such as introducing echo etc.

For digital signal processing, the most important requirement is to convert the analog signal into digital signal. This conversion has to be done in such a way that important information is not lost. To achieve this, the sampling theorem is used.

21.2.7 Sampling Theorem

According to this theorem, a low pass signal of bandwidth B Hz has to be sampled at a minimum sampling rate of 2B samples per second. If sampling is done at this rate, no information is lost. This sampling rate is called Nyquist rate, named after the inventor of this theorem. If the sampling is done at a later lower than this rate, it is called sub-sampling. If the sampling is done at a rate higher than this rate, it is called oversampling. The time between two successive samples is called sampling period.

Sampling period (in seconds) = 1/Sampling rate

Example: Consider the speech signal. It has a bandwidth of 4 KHz. Hence, the minimum sampling rate = 8 KHz or 8000 samples per second. Hence sampling period is 1/8000 second or 125 microseconds.

Example: Consider music signal. It has a bandwidth of 20 KHz. Hence, the minimum sampling rate = 40 KHz or 40,000 samples per second. Hence, sampling period is 1/40000 second or 25 microseconds.

Once sampling is done, the amplitude values are still in analog form. Since, we cannot represent these values in a computer due to the finite length of the registers, we need to round off these amplitude values. This rounding off process is called quantization. For example, the amplitude values can be represented by numbers 0 to 255. So, we have 256 quantization levels to represent the amplitude values. Hence, each sample can be represented by 8 bits.

In Brief...

According to sampling theorem, a signal of bandwidth B Hz has to be sampled at a rate at least 2B samples/second to ensure that no information present in the signal is lost.

In the case of speech signals, we sampled the signal at 8000 samples per second. We can represent each sample by 8 bits. Hence, speech signal of 1 second can be represented by 8000 * 8 = 64000 bits.

Note that by rounding off the numbers, we are introducing an error in the sampled values. This error is known as quantization error (or quantization noise). If we increase the number of quantization levels, we can decrease the quantization noise. For example, in the case of speech signal, instead of using 8 bits, if we use 16 bits, the quantization noise will be much less.

21.2.8 Time Domain Analysis of Digital Signals

To obtain the information present in the signal, we need to analyze the signal. The signal analysis can be done either in

- Time domain
- Frequency domain

For time-domain analysis, we take the digital signal (the sample values at different sampling times) and extract some parameters.

The basic operations that can be done on a signal in the time-domain are:

Scaling: The signal can be amplified or attenuated.

Delay: A delayed version of the signal

Addition: Two or more signals can be added.

Product: Two signals can be multiplied.

In Brief...

In time-domain analysis of signals, parameters such as energy, power, zero crossing rate etc. can be obtained.

When we analyze the signal in the time domain, we get some useful information—whether the signal is periodic or not, whether it has high amplitude variations or not, whether the signal is deterministic or random etc.

We can analyze the time-domain signal further and arrive at some additional conclusions. Some of the parameters that can be obtained from the time-domain waveform are: energy, power, zero-crossing rate etc.

Notes...

When a signal with a bandwidth of f_a is sampled with a sampling rate of f_s, the ideal sampler has images (aliases) at $| \pm Kf_s \pm f_a|$ where K = 1,2,3,...

21.2.9 Frequency-domain Analysis of Signals

Though analyzing a signal in time-domain gives some useful information, analysis of the signal in frequency-domain gives a good insight into the signal characteristics. In DSP, frequency-domain representation is studied extensively. A spectrum analyzer is used to display a signal in frequency domain.

Fourier, a French mathematician, formulated the mathematics for frequency-domain reprsentation of signals. He gave Fourier series which says that any complex signal can be broken down into a sine wave and its harmonics. Fourier series and Fourier transform are important in signal processing.

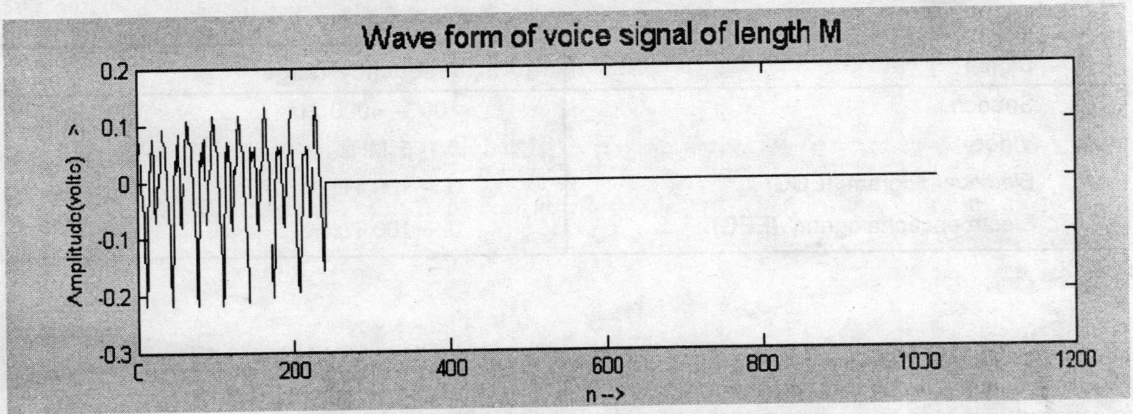

Fig. 21.5 Time-Domain Waveform of a Voice Signal

Consider a signal whose time-domain representation is shown in Fig. 21.5. We get very little information from this waveform. This signal represents a small portion of voice waverom.

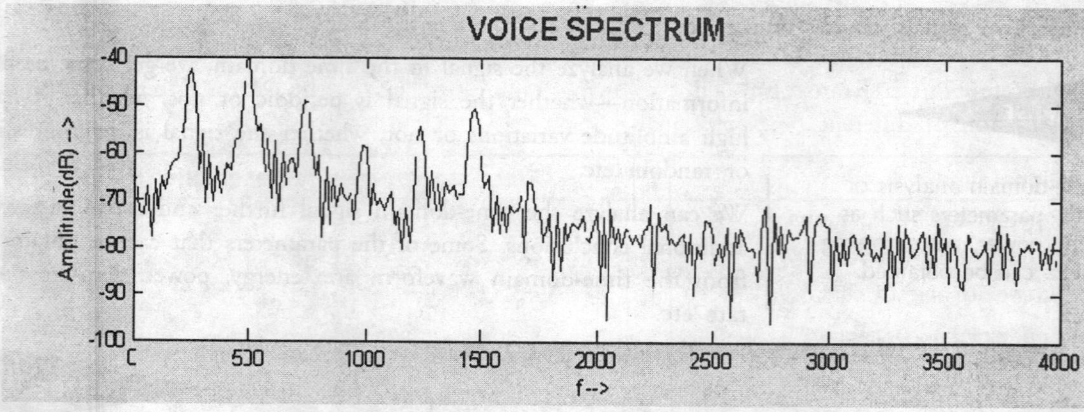

Fig. 21.6 Frequency-Domain Representation of Voice Signal.

The frequency-domain representation of the signal shown in Fig. 21.6 reveals very useful information. Up to about 1.5 KHz, the frequency components are siginificant. The peaks of the spectrum are also very useful for analysis of voice signal. This information is not evident when we look at the time-domain representation of the signal. The frequency-domain representation of a signal is called the spectrum.

Once such information is available to us, we can carry out the desired signal processing—for example, we can remove the frequency comoponents above 2 KHz by applying a filter.

In signal processing, we need to analyze the signal in both time domain and frequency domain. Frequency-domain analysis gives very useful information about the signal. For example, every signal will consist of only some frequency components which are significant (have high amplitude values). The highest significant frequency component present in a signal is called its bandwidth. The range of frequency components present in some representative signals are given below:

Signal	Frequency range
Speech	100 – 4000 Hz
Video	0 – 5 MHz
Electocardiogram (ECG)	0 – 100 Hz
Electroencephalogram (EEG)	0 – 100 Hz

Notes...

Normally human speech signals have a bandwidth of 4 KHz. However, people with speech impairments are able to produce signals which have bandwidth of about 2 KHz only.

Fourier Analysis

The entire digital signal processing is based on a paper published in 1807. Fourier laid the foundation for frequency domain analysis of signals. According to Fourier, any continuous periodic signal can be represented as a sum of sine waves. This is known as Fourier series. However, real-life signals are not necessarily periodic. But when we have to analyze these signals in the frequency domain, we take a small portion of the signal (called frame) and assume that this frame repeats. Such an analysis results in Discrete Fourier Transform. The following table summarizes the various frequency-domain representation of different types of signals.

Signal type	Frequency domain representation
Periodic and Continuous	Fourier Series
Periodic and Discrete	Discrete Fourier Transform
Aperiodic and Continuous	Fourier Transform
Aperioidic and Discrete	Discrete-time Fourier Series

In Brief...

For DSP, we assume that the signal is periodic and discrete and hence our interest is in Discrete Fourier Transform. Fast Fourier Transform is just a method of calculating DFT in an efficient manner.

In Brief...

Direct computation of N-point DFT of a discrete-time sequence requires $4N^2$ real multiplications and (4N-2)/N real additions.FFT reduces the multiplications and additions.

No. of FFT Points and Spectral Resolution

Spectral analysis will give useful information about the signal if the resolution of the spectrum is high. For example, 512-point FFT gives a much better resolution spectrum as compared to 256-point FFT. However, the computation time required for 512-point FFT is much higher. Depending on the application requirement, the number of FFT points has to be chosen.

The resolution of the spectrum is obtained using the formula

Resolution of the spectrum (in Hz) = Sampling rate / Number of FFT points.

Fig. 21.7 shows the waveform of voice signal and Fig. 21.8 shows the corresponding spectrum plotted using 512-point FFT analysis.

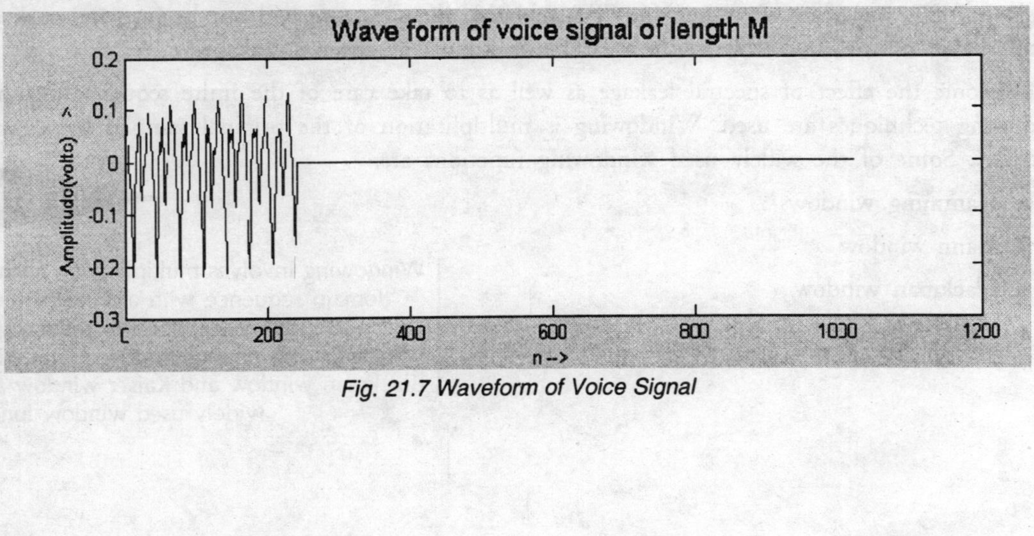

Fig. 21.7 Waveform of Voice Signal

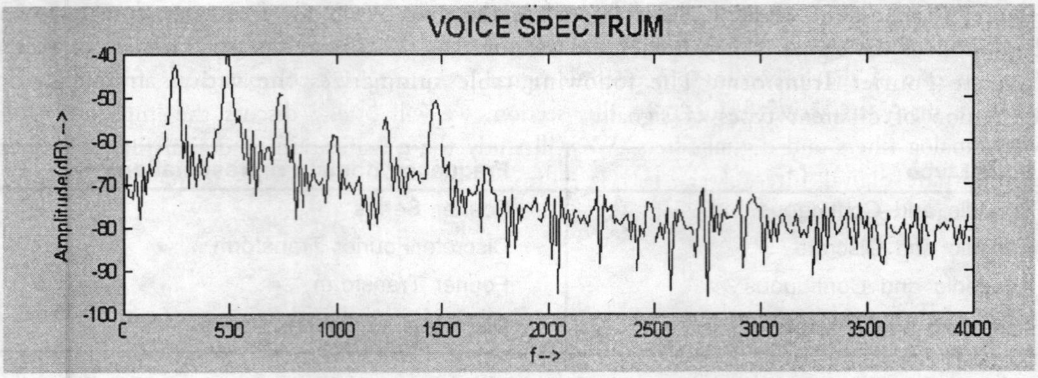

Fig. 21.8 Voice Spectrum: 512 FFT

Zero padding

Suppose the number of samples to be analyzed for FFT is 200. Since this number is not an integral power of 2, zero valued samples are added to the original sequence. Hence, from samples 201 to 256, zero sampled values are added to obtain 256 samples and then 256-point FFT analysis is carried out. If the number of samples is 1600 and we need to do 2048-point FFT, zeros are appended from 1601 to 2048 sample values.

In Brief...

The higher the number of FFT points, the better will be the resolution of the spectrum. The number of FFT points is caculated from the formula N = Sampling rate/Resolution in Hz.

In Brief...

For carrying out FFT analysis, zero padding of the time domain sequence is done to make the number of samples an integral power of two.

Spectral Leakage and Windowing

While doing FFT analysis on a signal, we take only a finite number of samples and then do the analysis. For example, we can take 256 sample values and do 256 point FFT analysis. This analysis is done with the assumption that before and after the samples of the sequence being analyzed, there are a large number of similar sequences, which is a wrong assumption.

Even if you take a sine wave, which has discontinuities at the two ends of the sequence (ie., an integral number of sine waves are not taken for FFT analysis), the spectrum will not be just one peak at one specific value of the sine wave frequency. This is known as spectral leakage.

To overcome the effect of spectral leakage as well as to take care of the finite sequence assumption, windowing techniques are used. Windowing is multiplication of the original samples by a "window function". Some of the widely used windowing functions are:

- Hamming windows
- Hann window
- Blackman window
- Kaiser window

In Brief...

Windowing involves multiplication of the time domain sequence with a window function. Windowing is done to reduce spectral leakage. Hamming window, Hann window, Blackman window and Kaiser window are the widely used window functions.

21.2.10 Filters

Filtering is one of the important processes in signal processing. As compared to analog filters, digital filters have many attractive features. In this section, we will briefly discuss the important differences between analog filters and digital filters. We will study the classification of digital filters and study the two important digital filter categories viz., Finite Importance Response (FIR) filters and Infinite Impulse Response (IIR) filters. We will also discuss the important differences between the two categories of filters.

Classification of Filters

A filter removes the unwanted portions of a signal or extract the desired portions of a signal. As shown in Fig. 21.9, the input to the filter consists of both wanted and unwanted signal and the output of the filter is only the wanted signal.

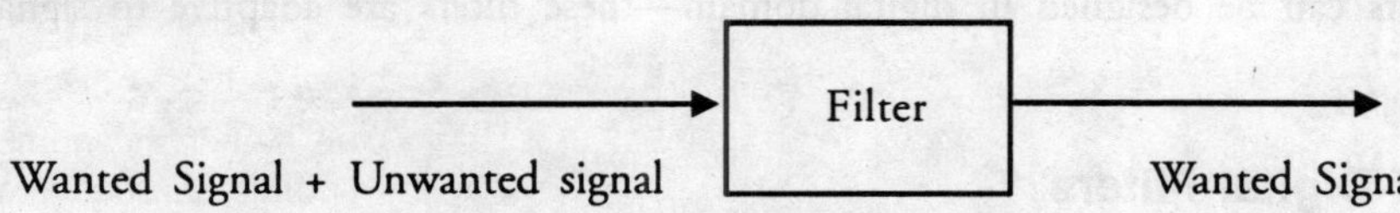

Fig. 21.9 Filter

Types of filters

Low Pass Filter (LPF): Passes frequency-components below a frequency (f_c) and blocks frequency components above f_c.

High Pass Filter (HPF): Passes frequency-components above a frequency (f_c) and blocks frequency components below f_c.

Band Pass Filter (BPF): Passes frequency-components in the range f_{c1} and f_{c2} and blocks all frequency components below f_{c1} and above f_{c2}.

Band Stop Filter (BSF): Blocks all frequency components in the range f_{c1} and f_{c2} and passes all frequency components below f_{c1} and above f_{c2}.

Notch filter: A band stop filter that blocks a single frequency component.

Comb filter: Blocks frequency components that are integral multiples of a low frequency.

In Brief...

Depending on the characteristics, filters can be divided into Low Pass Filters, High Pass Filters, Band Pass Filters, Band Stop Filters, notch filters and comb filters.

Analog Filters

A filter can be an analog filter or a digital filter. An analog filter is implemented using analog circuits using resistors, capacitors and operational amplifiers.

Digital Filters

Digital filters are implemented through a processor-based circuit. The processor can be either a DSP or a GPP. The input to the digital filter is the sampled values of the signal containing wanted and unwanted portions; and the output is the sampled values of the wanted signal.

As compared to analog filters, digital filters have the following advantages:

- Programmability is the main advantage. The processor can be programmed to change the filter characteristics.
- Digital filters are very easy to design, implement and test as compared to analog filters.
- A digital filter can be designed to operate for a wider range of frequencies.
- Digital filters are stable as compared to analog filters with respect to time and temperature.
- Digital filters are more reliable as compared to analog filters.
- Adaptive filters can be designed in digital domain—these filters are adaptive to signal characteristics.

Classification of Digital Filters

Digital filters are broadly classified as

- Finite Impulse response filters (or non-recursive filters)
- Infinite Impulse Response filters (or recursive filters)

Finite Impulse Response (FIR) Filters

FIR filters are also referred to as non-recursive filters.

A filter whose current output is calculated based on current and previous inputs only is called a non-recursive filter or FIR filter. In other words, in FIR filters,the output sample values are calculated from the input sample values only.

For example, assume that we are giving an input sequence to a filter. This input time domain sequence can be represented by X(i) where X(i) are the sample values at different values of i.

Assume that the output from the filter is the sequence Y(i).

Here are some examples of FIR filters:

Pure Delay filter

The output samples and input samples are related as follows:

$$Y(0) = X(-1)$$

$$Y(1) = X(0)$$

$$Y(2) = X(1)$$

In general,

$$Y(i) = X(i-1)$$

In this case, the signal is delayed by sampling one sample or one sampling period.

Note that we can assume the value of X(-1) as zero.

2-Term difference filter

The output and input sequences are related as follows:

$$Y(0) = X(0) - X(-1)$$

$$Y(1) = X(1) - X(0)$$

$$Y(2) = X(2) - X(1)$$

In general,

$$Y(i) = X(i) - X(i-1)$$

In this filter, the output sample is the difference between two successive input samples. This digital filter is an equivalent of analog differentiation circuit.

3-Term Average filter

The input sequence and output sequence are related as follows:

$$Y(0) = \{ X(0) + X(-1) + X(-2) \} / 3$$

$$Y(1) = \{ X(1) + X(0) + X(-1) \} / 3$$

$$Y(2) = \{ X(2) + X(1) + X(0) \} / 3$$

In general,

$$Y(i) = \{ X(i) + X(i-1) + X(i-2) \} / 3$$

This filter can be used to smoothen the high frequency variations in a signal and hence it is a low pass filter.

In Brief...

A filter whose current output is calculated based on current and previous inputs only is called a finit impulse response filter or non-recursive filter.

Order of the digital filter

The number of previous inputs stored in the memory of the processor to calculate the current value of the output is called the order of the digital filter.

$Y(i) = X(i-1)$ 1st order digital filter as we need to store one previous input value

$Y(i) = X(i) - X(i-1)$ is also a 1st order digital filter

$Y(i) = \{ X(i) + X(i-1) + X(i-2) \} / 3$ is a 2nd order digital filter

In general, the filters can be represented by the following equations:

0th order filter: $Y(i) = A_0 X(i)$

1st order filter: $Y(i) = A_0 X(i) + A_1 X(i-1)$

2nd order filter: $Y(i) = A_0 X(i) + A_1 X(i-1) + A_2 X(i-2)$

A0, A1 and A2 etc. are called the filter coefficients. The values of these filter coefficients determine the characteristics of the filter. Designing a filter is to find out these coefficients for the desired characteristiscs.

Infinite Impulse Response (IIR) Filters

IIR filters are also known as recursive filters.

A filter whose current output is calculated based on current and previous inputs as well as previous output values is called a recursive filter.

In other words, the value of Y(i) depends on Y(i-1), Y(i-2) etc. in addition to X(i), X(i-1), X(i-2) etc.

Here is an example of a recursive filter:

$Y(i) = X(i) + Y(i-1)$

$Y(0) = X(0) + Y(-1) = X(0)$

$Y(1) = X(1) + Y(0) = X(1) + X(0) + Y(-1) = X(1) + X(0)$

$Y(2) = X(2) + Y(1) = X(2) + X(1) + X(0)$

$Y(3) = X(3) + X(2) + X(1) + X(0)$

In this case, the filter sums or integrates the input values and hence it has the same effect as the analog integrator circuit.

As you can see from this example, using the past output values reduces the computation and hence IIR filters are more computationally efficient.

Suppose you want to find out the output value at 20T,

In IIR filter, $Y(20) = X(20) + Y(19)$

In FIR filter, $Y(2) = X(20) + X(19) + X(18)+ X(0)$

Hence, FIR filter requires more computation and more storage space.

Order of IIR Filters

The order of an IIR filter is defined as the largest number of previous input values or output values required to calculate the current output.

If $Y(i) = X(i) - Y(i-1)$, it is a 1st order IIR filter.

In practice, the IIR filter requires the same number of previous input and previous output values.

1st order IIR filter requires x(i-1) and Y(i-1)

2nd order IIR filter requires X(i-1), X(i-2), Y(i-1) and Y(i-2) i.e., two previous inputs and two previous outputs.

The general form of 1st order IIR filter is

$B_0 Y(i) + B_1 Y(i-1) = A_0 X(i) + A_1 X(i-1)$

The general form of 2nd order digital filter is

$B_0 Y(i) + B_1 Y(i-1) + B_2 Y(i-2) = A_0 X(i) + A_1 X(i-1) + A_2 X(i-2)$

Comparison of FIR and IIR Filters

Computation time: FIR filter requires more computation time as compared to IIR filter.

Phase: FIR filters have linear phase whereas IIR filters have non-linear phase.

Sensitivity to quantization of filter coefficients: Since the filter coefficients have to be represented in a register with finite word length (16 bit or 32 bit depending on the processors), the filter coefficients are rounded off. This may lead to unstable filter. IIR filters are more sensitive to quantization of filter coefficients as compared to FIR filters.

The following table summarizes the comparison between FIR and IIR filters.

FIR versus IIR filters: a comparison

Characteristic	FIR filter	IIR filter
Design complexity	Low	High
Linear phase	Yes	No
Stability	Yes	To be taken care in design
Memory requirement	High	Low
Number of multiplications	High	Low
Sensitivity to quantization of filter coefficients	Low	High
Quantization noise analysis	Easy	difficult

A number of design techniques are available for designing FIR and IIR filters. We will demonstrate the desing using MATLAB programs in a later section.

21.3 Applications of DSP

DSP technology is now used extensively in many application domains. To become a good DSP engineer, in additon to the knowledge of DSP technology, a good understanding of the application domain is equally important. Gaining expertise in one application domain itself will take lot of time and effort. For example, there are engineers who spent their entire lives working only on DSP applications for speech processing. In this section, we will give an overview of the various application domains and some illustrative applications.

21.3.1 Communications

The filed of communication driven by Digital Signal Processing. Particularly, multimedia communication over the Internet and mobile networks has been made possible only because of the advances in DSP. In fact, nearly 50% of the DSP market is due to mobile communications. Here are some important applications:

- The subscriber equipment such as the digital phones, IP phone, video camera, video conferencing equipment, cellular mobile phones, modems etc. use DSP.
- The network infrastructure equipment such as the cellular mobile communication base stations, satellite modems etc. are DSP-based systems.
- Global Positioning System (GPS) technology is used to obtain the location of a person or a device. A GPS receiver obtains information from GPS satellites and displays the longitude, latitude and altitude of the receiver. This involves processing of the signals received from the satellites and performing complex mathematical computations to find out the location.

- The line modems we use for accessing the Internet are powered by digital signal processors. It is the modem technology that is constantly increasing the Internet access speeds.
- RADAR and SONAR which are used to identify the flying objects either in the air or under the water use DSP technology extensively.
- All communication systems used in civilian and military applications use DSP technology.
- Due to the flexibility provided by DSP through programming, 'Software Defined Radio' (SDR) systems are now becoming widely used. SDR facilitates reconfigurable radio systems wherein you can use the same hardware to develop different types of communication systems, simply by changing the software. For instance, we use different mobile phones for accessing GSM network and CDMA network. However, with SDR, we can buy one hardware module and run one software package to make it a GSM phone and another software package to make it a CDMA phone.

The block diagram of a generic communiation system is shown in Fig. 21.10. The information produced by the information source is passed through a source coder, channel coder and modulator and the upconverted radio signal is sent over the channel. At the receiving end, the corresponding reverse operations are performed viz., demodulation, channel decoding and source decoding. Each of the blocks can be implemented through DSP.

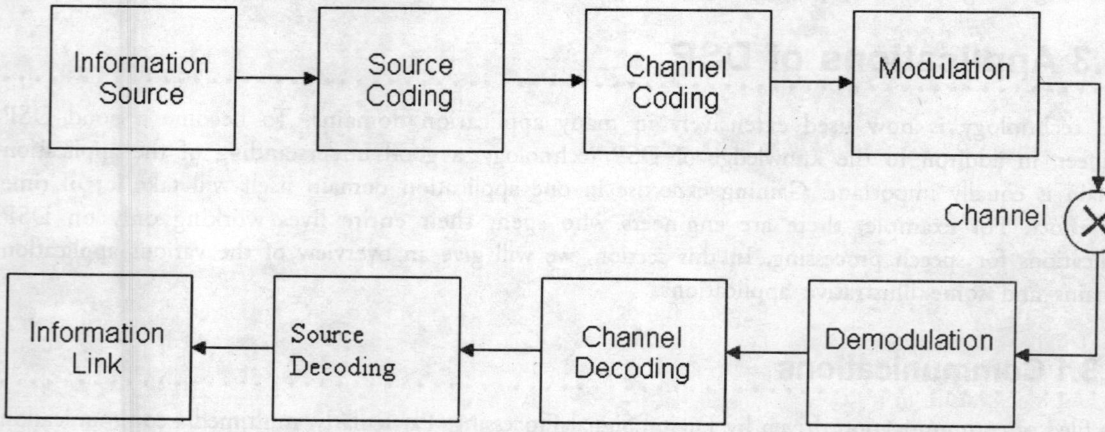

Fig. 21.10 Block Diagram Of A Generic Communication System

As a simple example, let us consider DTMF signaling in telephone communication. When you dial a digit on your telephone keypad, a combination of two tones is produced and sent over the medium. These tone values differ from digit to digit. As shown in Fig. 21.11, when you dial the digit 1, a combination of 697 and 1209 Hz is produced. This dialing is very efficient as compared to pulse dialing. At the telephone exchange, the dialed digit has to be recognized. An obvious way to do this is to do a spectral analysis of the signal. For the digit 1, there will be spectral peaks at the two specific frequencies viz., 697 and 1209 Hz. We will illustrate DTMF generation and detection algorithm using MATLAB in the next section.

	1209 Hz	1336 Hz	1477 Hz	1633 Hz
697 Hz	1	2	3	A
770 Hz	4	5	6	B
850 Hz	7	8	9	C
941 Hz	*	0	#	D

DTMF Digit = Row Tone + Column Tone

Fig. 21.11 DTMF Signaling

In Brief...

Dual Tone Multi Frequency (DTMF) signaling is an efficient signaling mechanism. In this signaling scheme, when you dial a digit on your telephone keypad, a combination of two tones is produced. At the exchange, the digit is recognized using spectral analysis.

Notes...

In good old days, "pulse dialing" was used in the place of DTMF signaling. In pulse dialing, when the digit 1 is dialed, one pulse is sent, when digit 2 is dialed, two pulses are sent and so on. When digit 0 is dialed, 10 pulses are sent. As the pulses get distorted over the medium, it is difficult to recognize the digits accurately at the telephone exchange resulting in wrong calls.

21.3.2 Audio Coding

One of the most commercially successful applications of DSP is in audio coding. In the telephone network, Pulse Code Modulation (PCM) technique is used to convert speech into digital format and transmit it over the channel. In PCM, to store/transmit one second of speech, we need 64 Kbits. This is a very high data rate. In radio systems and satellite communication where the bandwidth is very costly, we need to reduce this data rate so that we can make use of the bandwidth more efficiently. Low bit rate coding of audio and music signals without degrading the quality is done through DSP. Some offshoot applications of this are:

- Professional audio systems for recording, audio broadcasting, dubbing etc. Low bit rate coding of speech is done in almost all communication systems including mobile communication systems and radio communication systems.
- Coding of music signals such as MP3, Ogg Vorbis using which the data rate can be reduced to about 10-20% without degrading the quality of the music.
- Speech synthesis systems such as talking toys, talking cameras etc.
- Automatic text to speech conversion
- Automatic speech recognition

Fig. 21.12 shows the voice coding mechanism in a mobile communication system. The mobile communication network consists of Base Transceiver Subsystem (BTS) which is a radio module, Base Station Controller (BSC) and Mobile Switching Center (MSC). The Public Switched Telephone Network (PSTN) is connected to the mobile network at the MSC.

It is not advisable to transmit voice signals using 64 KBps PCM coding scheme because this data rate calls for very large radio bandwidth. However, the PSTN uses on 64 Kbps PCM. Hence the low bit rate coding scheme shown in Fig. 21.12 is used in mobile communication systems based on Global System for Mobile Communications (GSM) standard.

When you speak into the microphone of your mobile phone, the voice is coded at 13 Kbps and transmitted over the radio channel, to reduce the radio bandwidth. At the Base Station Controller (BSC), the voice is again coded at 64 Kbps and sent to the Mobile Switching Center (MSC). The MSC sends the voice using PCM over to the PSTN.

The mobile phone carries out the voice coding at 13 Kbps using DSP techniques. This can be achieved either using a Digital Signal Processor (DSP) or through an Application Specific Integrated Circuit.

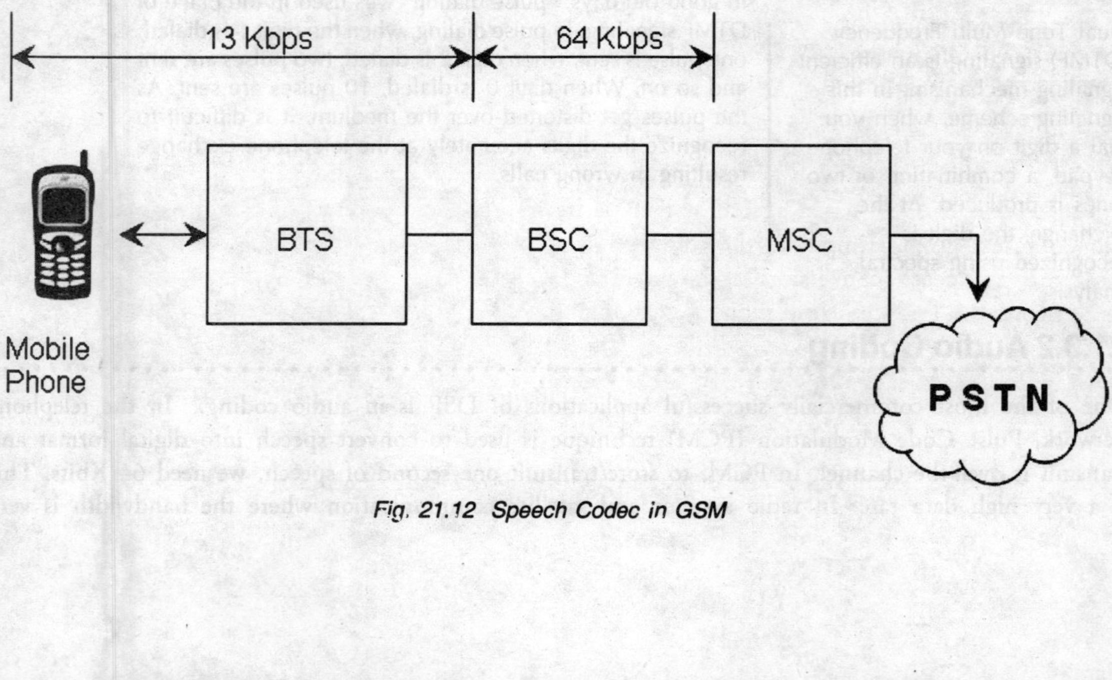

Fig. 21.12 Speech Codec in GSM

Coding of audio (music or voice) signals is one of the major applications of DSP. In low bit rate coding of voice, the aim is to reduce the data rate to the maximum possible extent without appreciable change in the quality of the speech. However, when the data rate is reduced drastically, the quality of voice degrades. For example, the voice quality on mobile phones is not as good as the voice quality on the fixed tephones. This is mainly due to the low bit rate coding of voice signals to reduce the bandwidth requirement over the radio channel.

For low bit rate voice coding, "speech production model" shown in Fig. 21.13 is used. The human vocal tract is modeled as a filter. This filter is excited by a pulse generator to produce voiced sounds (such as vowels) and by a noise generator to produce unvoiced sounds (such as consonants). The output of the vocal tract filter is passed through a filter to produce synthesized speech. For good quality speech to be synthesized using this model, the vocal tract filter coefficients have to be calculated every 10 milliseconds and these new coefficients have to be used to synthsize 10 milliseconds of the speech signal. Using this model, many low bit rate coding techniques have been developed to reduce the data rate to as low as 1.2 Kbps. However, below about 4.8 Kbps data rate, the quality of the speech output will not be good.

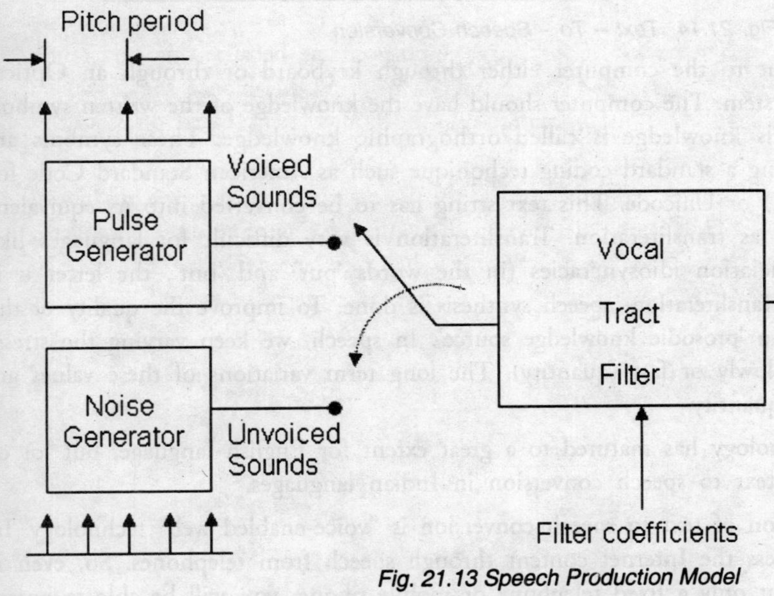

Fig. 21.13 Speech Production Model

Another application of DSP based speech systems is in text to speech conversion. In text to speech conversion, the text given as input to the computer is automatically converted into speech form. The process of text to speech conversion is shown in Fig. 21.14. DSP in conjunction with Artificial Intellligence concepts leads to conversion of text into speech.

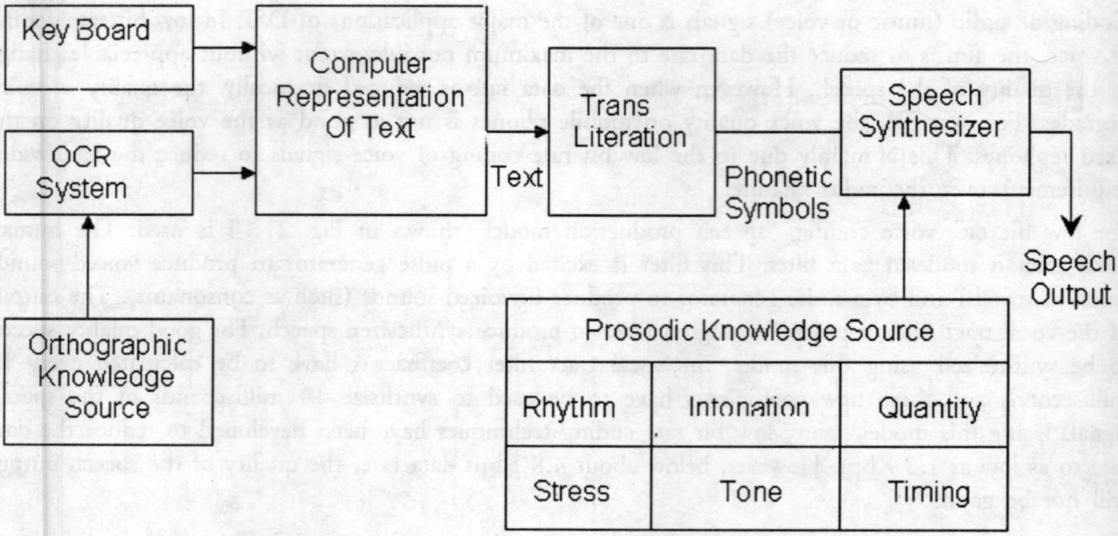

Fig. 21.14 Text – To – Speech Conversion

The text can be given as input to the computer either through keyboard or through an Optical Character Recongiton (OCR) system. The computer should have the knowledge of the written symbols to recognize these symbols.This knowledge is called orthographic knowledge. These symbols are represented in the computer using a standard coding techqnique such as American Standard Code for Information Interchange (ASCII) or Unicode. This text string has to be converted into its equivalent pronunciation which is known as transliteration. Transliteration is very difficult for languages like English because of the pronunciation idiosyncracies (in the words 'put' and 'but', the letter u is pronounced differently!). After transliteration, speech synthesis is done. To improve the quality of the speech output, we need to use a 'prosodic knowledge source'. In speech, we keep varying the stress, tone or pitch, and also speak slowly or fast (quantity). The long term variations of these values are called rhythm, intonation and quantity.

Text to speech conversion technology has matured to a great extent for English language, but lot of research needs to be done for text to speech conversion in Indian languages.

An important practical application of text to speech conversion is "voice-enabled web" technology. In voice-enabled web, you can access the Internet content through speech from telephones. So, even if you do not have a computer but only a fixed telephone or mobile phone, you will be able to access the content from the web servers. The mechanism of voice-enabled web is shown in Fig. 21.15. A language called VoiceXML is developed to add voice capability to the web. As shown in Fig. 21.15, you access the telephone network (fixed telphone network PSTN or mobile telephone network PLMN) which interprets your voice commands and sends that information over the Internet to the web server from which you want to access the web page.

Voice-enabled web provides the Internet access facilities to the rural/remote area people, who do not have access to a computer, but only a telephone.

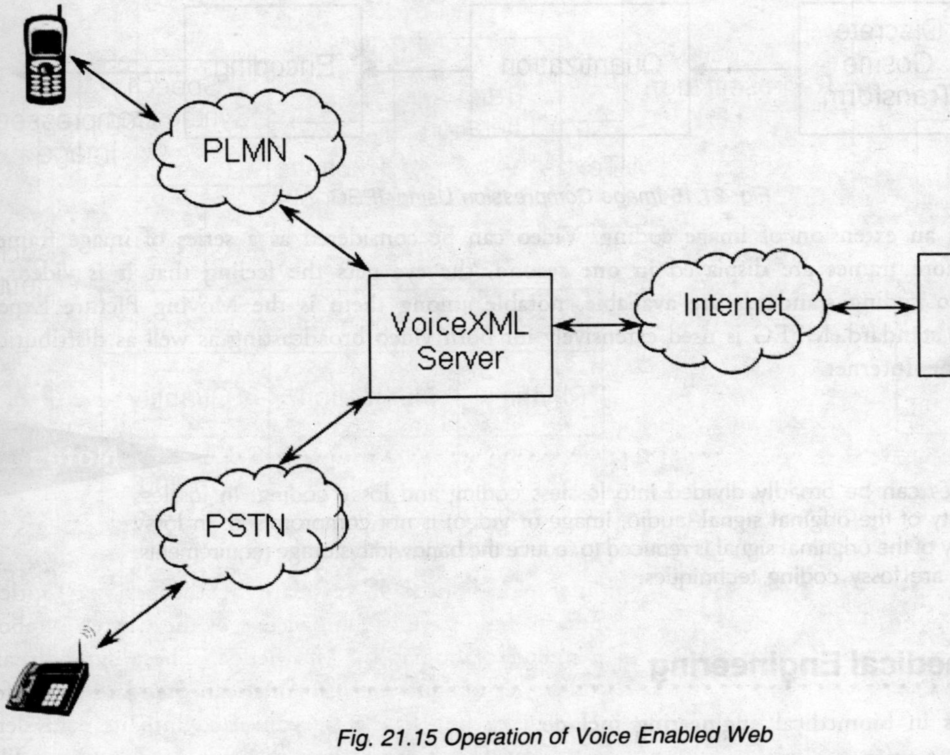

Fig. 21.15 Operation of Voice Enabled Web

21.3.3 Image/Video Processing

Processing of image signals and video signals is another important application area of DSP. Some application are:

- X-ray enhancement
- Remote sensing
- Analysis of weather photographs
- Analysis of biomedical charts
- Low bit rate coding of images such as JPEG coding
- Low bit rate coding of video such as MPEG coding

In image coding, the image is divided into pixels and each pixel is quantized. For example, consider an image of size 300 pixels by 400 pixels. The total number of pixels is 120000 or 120 Kpixels. If each pixel is coded with 8 bits, the image has to be coded at 960 Kbits. This can be reduced to a great extent using coding techniques such as Joint Photographic Expert Group (JPEG) standard. Image compression using JPEG is shown in Fig. 21.16. The original image is passed through Discrete Cosine Transform (similar to Fast Fourier Tranform) and then quantized and encoded.

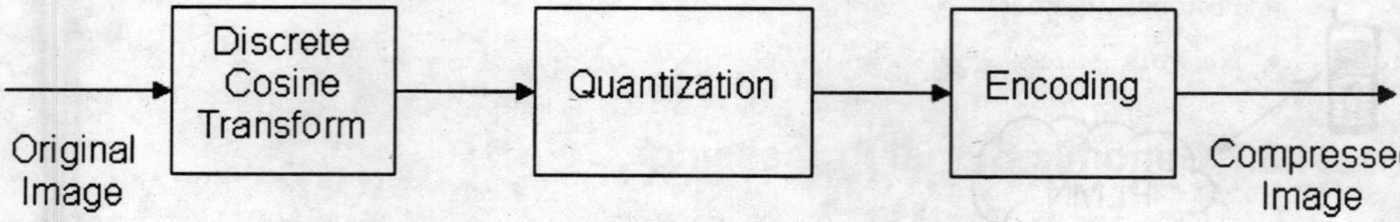

Fig. 21.16 Image Compression Using JPEG

Video coding is an extension of image coding. Video can be considered as a series of image frames. When 10 or more frames are displayed in one second, the eye gets the feeling that it is video. A number of video coding standards are available, notable among them is the Moving Picture Expert Group (MPEG) standard. MPEG is used extensively for both video broadcasting as well as distribution of video over the Internet.

Notes...

Coding techniques can be broadly divided into lossless coding and lossy coding. In lossless coding, the quality of the original signal (audio, image or video) is not compromised. In lossy coding, the quality of the origninal signal is reduced to reduce the bandwidth/storage requirements. JPEG and MPEG are lossy coding techniques.

21.3.4 Biomedical Engineering

The applications in biomedical engineering include:

- Analysis of EEG signals
- Analysis of ECG signals
- Development of artificial organs such as e-eye, e-nose etc.

The advances in medical diagnosis is the result of the application of DSP techniques for applications such as the above.

21.3.5 Seismology

The applications in this area include:

- Earthquake measurements
- Oil exploration

For example, earthquakes produce very low frequency signals. Capturing and analysing these signals is a very involving and challenging task.

21.3.6 Instrumentation

Many instruments are powered by DSP. These include:

- Oscilloscopes
- Spectrum analyzers

- Protocol analyzer
- Network testers

21.3.7 Genomic Signal Processing

In the fields of Astrophysics and Cosmology, the scientists need to analyze the radiation maps. The cosmic microwave background radiation provide information about the early universe shortly after big bang,. The signals received are non-stationary, non-Gaussian and corrupted with noise. There are also non-linearities in the measurment process. Hence genomic signal processing is a very complex activity, but at the same time provides important information about the origin of universe and the evolution. The various activities include: feature extraction, compression of signals, data mining and restoration of astrophysical images.

In addition, DSP technology has been used for many decades in process control and industrial automation. Entertainmnet appliances such as CD players, DVD players, MP3 players, digital cameras use DSP extensively.

21.4 Digital Signal Processor Architecture

The architecture of a Digital Signal Processor is different from that of a General Purpose Processor such as a micro-controller or a microprocessor. As shown in Fig. 21.17, the Harvard architecture is used in DSPs. In this architecture, there will be two pairs of buses—one pair of buses for program memory and one pair of buses for data memory. As program memory contains only instructions and data memory contains only data, both data and program can be fetched to the CPU fast and mathematical computations can be done very fast.

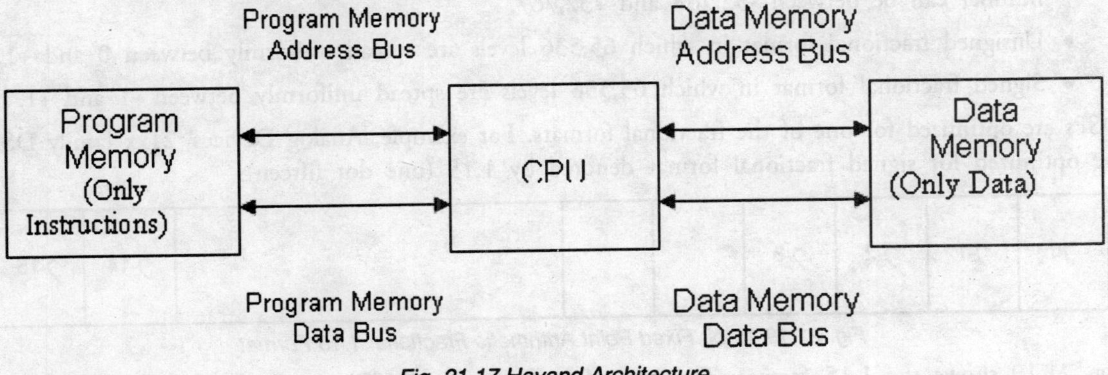

Fig. 21.17 Havand Architecture

This architecture has been slightly modified by Analog Devices, as shown in Fig. 21.18. In this architecture, both instructions and data can be stored in the program memory. The advantage is that in a single cycle both instruction and data can be fetched (as the case of a digital filter). This makes the DSP much more efficient. The CPU also contains a cache memory in which the instructions can be cached and the data can be fetched from the program memory or data memory.

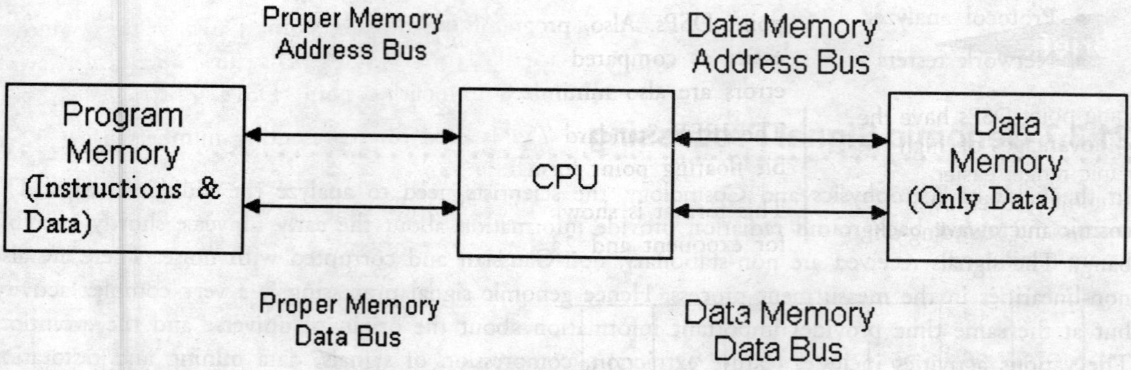

Fig. 21.18 ADI Modified Harvard Architecture

DSPs can be divided into

- Fixed Point DSPs
- Floating Point DSPs

This division refers to the format used to store the numbers in the DSP.

21.4.1 Fixed Point DSP

Consider a 16 bit fixed point DSP. Here each number is represented using 16 bits. There are four possible ways of representing these numbers:

- Unsigned integer format in which each number is between 0 and 65,536.
- Signed integer format in which each number is represented by 2's complement so that each number can be between -32,768 and +32,767.
- Unsigned fractional format in which 65,536 levels are spread uniformly between 0 and +1.
- Signed fractional format in which 65,536 levels are spread uniformly between -1 and +1.

DSPs are optimized for one of the fractional formats. For example, Analog Devices' 21xx family DSPs are optimized for signed fractional format denoted by 1.15 (one dot fifteen).

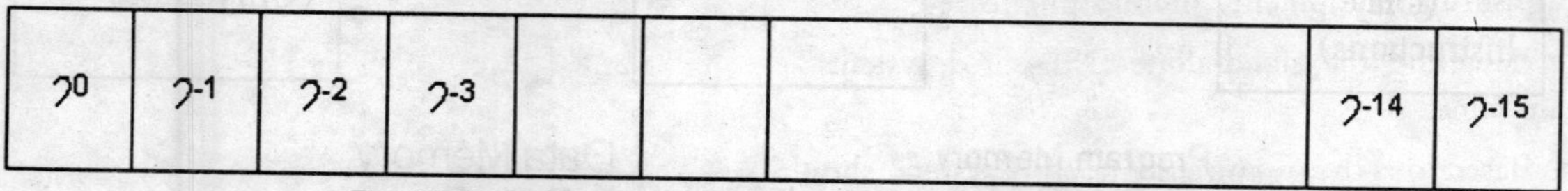

Fig. 21.19 16-bit Fixed Point Arithmetic Fractional 1.15 Format

Fig. 21.19 shows the 1.15 format. The Most Significant Bit (MSB) represents the sign bit. This is followed by 15 fractional bits as denoted by 2^{-1}, 2^{-2} etc. in the figure.

21.4.2 Floating Point DSP

In floating point DSPs which are generally 32-bit DSPs, each number is represented by 32 bits and hence the possible numbers that can be represetend in these DSPs is much more than 16-bit fixed

In Brief...

Floating point DSPs have the main advantages of: high dynamic range, easier programming; overflow, underflow and rounding-off errors are minimized.

point DSPs. Also, programming floating point DSPs is much more easier as compared to fixed point DSPs. Overflow and underflow errors are also minimized in floating point DSPs.

The IEEE Standard 754 is used for representing numbers using 32 bit floating point format.

This format is shown in Fig. 21.20. One bit is used for sign, 8 bits for exponent and 23 bits for mantissa.

0/1	2^7	2^6	2^5	2^4	2^3	2^2	2^1	2^0	2^{-1}	2^{-2}	2^{-3}		2^{-23}

Fig. 21.20 Single Precision 32 bit Fractional Point Format (IEEE754)

21.5 DSP-based Embedded System Design Process

The process of designing DSP-based embedded systems is similar to that of designing GPP-based embedded systems. However, there are some differences because of the architecture of the digital signal processors. In this section, we will discuss the important issues to be dealt with while designing DSP-based embedded systems.

21.5.1 Types of DSP-based Systems

DSP-based systems can be broadly divided into three categories:

- Stand-alone systems
- PC add-on cards
- Networked systems

Stand-alone systems: These systems can operate in isolation. Examples include field instruments, test and measuring equipment, mobile phones etc.

While designing the stand-alone DSP-based systems, the following design considerations need to be kept in mind:

- Based on the requirements, the system should have the necessary input devices such as a function keypad or a keyboard; output devices such as LED display or LCD display.
- Necessary communication interfaces may need to be provided to interface with the host system such as a PC. For example, the DSP system may collect some data, process the data and send the output periodically to a PC. In such a case, a communication interface such as RS232, USB, Ethernet, IEEE 802.11, CAN interface needs to be provided.
- As it is a stand-alone system, the necessary power supply unit needs to be designed keeping in view the power consumption of the system.
- There may be a need to interconnect the stand-alone system to a PC or workstation. For

example, an instrument may have to be connected to a PC for data logging. In such a case, the necessary interface has to be worked out—it can be RS232 or USB or HPIB or GPIB etc.

PC add-on cards: Data acquisition systems, software defined radio, virtual instruments etc. are examples of DSP-based systems which are designed as PC add-on cards. The PC add-on card is plugged into the motherboard of the PC. The interface can be either PCI or compact PCI or PC104 interface.

The following guidelines need to be kept in mind while designing DSP-based PC add-on cards:

- No separate power supply is required as the PC add-on card will obtain the power from the PC. However, the power rating of the SMPS used in the PC should cater to the extra currents drawn by the add-on card.
- The processed information needs to be sent to the PC for display purposes. However, note that if the PC runs an operating system such as Windows, it is not possible to obtain real time performance. Hence, the real time processing needs to be performed on the PC add-on card itself, and only non-time critical application such as display of the data etc. needs to be done on the PC platform. Alternatively, you can port an operating system such as Linux and RTLinux on to the desktop computer to achieve the real time performance.

Networked systems: In the case of networked systems, the DSP based system will be interconnected through a network to other systems. Examples include sensor networks, networked information appliances etc. In such systems, the DSP based system will support the following requirements:

- The DSP based system will run a real time operating system and also the TCP/IP protocol stack to make it network-enabled.
- If the DSP system also has to be accessed through the Internet or Intranet, it is necessary to run a web server software on the DSP system.
- The DSP system should have the necessary network interface such as Ethernet or IEEE 802.11 interface.

In all the three types of DSP-based systems, the system may have a single processor or multiple processors depending on the application. In case of multiple DSP based systems, inter-processor communication needs to be handled carefully.

In Brief...

DSP-based embedded systems can be stand-alone systems, PC addon cards or networked systems.

21.5.2 The Development Process

The process of development of DSP based system can be divided into the following phases:

- Requirements engineering
- Simulation studies
- Design
- Implementation
- Testing

These phases are same for any type of software development. However, since both hardware development and software development are involved in the development of DSP based systems, we will study these phases in more detail with focus on the important activities to be carried out in each of the phases.

Requirements Engineering: To start with, your marketing team will get an inquiry for the development of a DSP based system, or your management will initiate development of a product. In either case, the first step is to gather the requirements. In this phase, you need to carry out a detailed study and arrive at the detailed specifications of the proposed DSP based system.

- You need to obtain the inputs to the system and outputs of the system. The details of the input signals need to be obtained which include: the type of signals, the bandwidth of the signal, the input signal level etc. Similarly, you need to obtain the details of the output signals.
- You need to find out the processing involved such as time domain analysis and frequency domain analysis.
- You need to obtain the communication interfaces to be provided such as RS232, USB, PCI, IEEE 802.11, IrDA etc.
- You need to obtain the power supply input requirements—whether the system has to operate on 230 V AC, or a battery, or the power supply has to be derived from a host PC etc.
- You need to obtain the performance requirements such as whether real time operation is required. The real time systems are divided into hard real time systems and soft real time systems. In hard real time systems, the timing constraints are stringent, if the deadline is not met, then it results in a catastrophe. In the case of soft real time systems, the deadlines are imposed but not meeting these deadlines once in a while does not result in a catastrophe. Note that obtaining the performance requirements at this stage is very important; if the performance requirements are not specified at this stage but introduced at a later stage, the total design may need to be redone, leading to many problems.
- You need to obtain the size of the system. There will be size restrictions for systems used in industrial, airborne and military applications.
- You need to obtain the environmental specifications and EMI/EMC specifications that need to be met for the system. For systems that are used in military applications, airborne systems etc., the environmental and EMI/EMC specifications are stringent. Systems used in industrial environments also need to work in very harsh environments.

Obtaining the requirements is an iterative process. You need to interact with the client, study whether the requirements are 'enough' to start the design work, and if you need more clarity, again interact with the client. After obtaining all the requirements, you need to prepare System Requirements Specifications document and then get this document validated by the client.

Simulation Studies: After obtaining the requirements, you need to carry out simulation studies if necessary. You can use tools such as MATLAB and SIMULINK (www.mathworks.com) to develop the algorithms and also study the memory and processing power requirements. Obviously, the simulation to be carried out differs from application to application.

- If you have to develop a speech codec, you can develop the complete algorithm using C language and test it on a desktop computer.
- If you are developing a modem, you can simulate the modulation and demodulation algorithms using MATLAB and SIMULINK.

- If you are developing a software defined radio, the complete system can be simulated on a PC.

Design: In this phase of development, the validated SRS document is converted into a design document. The design document needs to address the details of the hardware and software. While doing the design, the following aspects need to be kept in mind:

- Work out the design alternatives: for a given system, there are a number of alternative solutions. It is necessary to study each alternative and choose the best alternative keeping in view the design goals such as reduction in cost, reliability etc.
- Design for testability: The design should be such that testing the system is easy. You need to provide the necessary test points and also a JTAG port for testing.
- Hardware design: the issues in hardware design are selection of the right processor, program memory and data memory, choosing the right peripherals such as ADC, DAC, communication interfaces etc.
- Software Design: design of algorithms, data structures etc.

Selection of DSP

The selection of a DSP is based on the following criteria:

- Fixed point versus floating point DSP
- On-board memory (program memory and data memory)
- On-chip peripherals (such as ADC, DAC, communication interfaces)
- Clock frequency and MIPS rating
- Support for development tools
- Support for JTAG
- Packaging of the DSP
- Benchmark results for FFT analysis, filter implementation etc.

In Brief...

Selection of the DSP has to be done carefully keeping in view the computational requirements. The benchmark results given by the vendor is a good starting point to approximately find out the timing requirements. Floating point DSPs are costlier than fixed point DSPs but provide lot of flexibility and higher processing power.

Notes...

For real time processing of signals, the processing of a sample has to be completed by the time the next sample arrives. Hence, No. of instructions per sample = Sampling Period/instruction cycle time. If 125 microseconds is the sampling period and 100 nanoseconds is the instruction cycle time, then 1,250 instructions per sample are required. If 10 nanoseconds is the instruction cycle time, then 12,500 instructions per sample are required.

Selection of ADC

The following specifications have to be kept in mind while selecting an ADC:

- The resolution of the ADC determines the dynamic range. For every one bit of resolution, the dynamic range is about 6 dB. For example, for a 14 bit ADC, the dynamic range is 14 * 6 = 84 dB.

- Input sensitivity: the minimum signal strength of the ADC
- Serial or parallel interface
- Spurious free dynamic range
- Sampling rate variability which is determined by programmable clock
- The maximum clock speed which determines the highest sampling rate that can be achieved with the ADC

In Brief...

The most important specifications of the ADC are the sampling rate and the resolution. The resolution determines the dynamic range of the signal.

Implementation: Implementation involves converting the design into a working model. Both hardware and software are developed independently then integrated gradually.

Testing: Testing is a very tedious and iterative process. Sometimes it is very difficult to detect whether the fault is in hardware or software. Hence, a very rigorous co-verification process has to be defined.

21.5.3 Development Environmet

After you decide on the DSP to be used, you need to have the necessary development tools for that DSP. These tools are:

- Development board supplied by the DSP vendor
- PC based Integrated Development Environment (IDE) consisting of Cross compiler, assembler, debugger etc. The IDE is specific to the DSP vendor. For example, Analog Devices supplies Visual DSP Tools for its DSPs.
- Emulator
- Test instruments specific to the application such as oscilloscope, spectrum analyzer, logic analyzer etc.
- MATLAB and Simulink for simulation.

21.6 DSP Algorithm Implementation using MATLAB

In this section, we will discuss DSP algorithm implementation using MATLAB. MATLAB is a very powerful programming language and is very easy to learn. Programming through MATLAB is the best way of learning DSP. You can obtain MATLAB from www.mathworks.com.

We will discuss generation of waveforms, different modulations and filter design in this section. For each program the ".m file" is given along with output results. It is assumed that you are familiar with the basics of MATLAB. You can master DSP techniques without dwelling into the deep mathematics using MATLAB.

Notes...

The program listings are available in the CDROM that accompanies this book.

Listing 21.1 unitsamplesequence.m

This program is for generation of unit sample sequence, a fundamental sequence used in digital signal processing. Fig. 21.1 shows the unit sample sequence.

%Program Title: Generation of unit sample sequence of length N and its delayed sequence by k samples.

%Filename: unitsamplesequence.m

```
clc;
clear all;
N = input ('Enter the no. of samples in the sequence N = ');
n = 0:N-1;
y = [ones(1,1) zeros(1,N-1)];
k = input('Enter the delay k such that k<N, k = ');
yd = [zeros(1,k) y];
figure(1)
subplot(211)
stem(n,y)
title('Unit sample sequence of length N','fontsize',14);
xlabel('n ->')
ylabel('Amplitude ->')
subplot(212)
stem((0:length(yd)-1),yd)
title('Delayed unit sample sequence by k samples','fontsize',14);
xlabel('n ->')
ylabel('Amplitude ->')
```

Results:

Enter the no. of samples in the sequence N = 20

Enter the delay k such that k<N, k = 8

Output Plots:

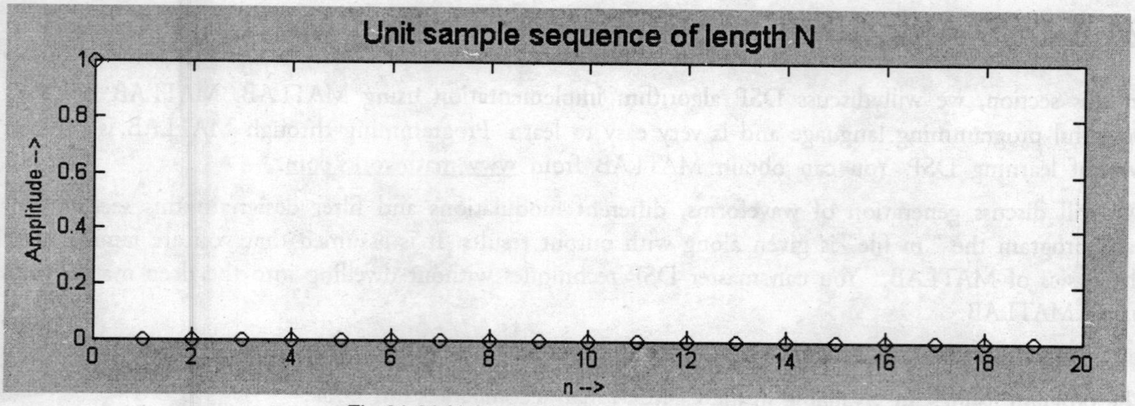

Fig.21.21 Unit sample sequence of length N

Notes...

The response of a system to the unit sample sequence (also called the unt impulse) is called impulse response of the system.

Listing 21.2 unitstepsequence

This program generates unit step sequence of given length, and also delayed sequence. Fig. 21.22 shows the unit step sequence and Fig. 21.23 shows the delayed sequence.

%Program Title: Generation of unit step sequence of length N and its delayed sequence by k samples

%Filename: unitstepsequence.m

```
clc;
clear all;
N = input('Enter the no. of samples in the sequence N =      ');
n = 0:N-1;
y = ones(1,N);
k = input('Enter the delay k such that k<N, k =      ');
yd = [zeros(1,k) y];
figure(1)
subplot(211)
stem(n,y)
title('Unit step sequence of length N','fontsize',14);
xlabel('n ->')
ylabel('Amplitude ->')
subplot(212)
stem((0:length(yd)-1),yd)
title('Delayed unit step sequence by k samples','fontsize',14);
xlabel('n ->')
ylabel('Amplitude ->')
```

Results:

Enter the no. of samples in the sequence N =10

Enter the delay k such that k<N, k = 3

Output Plot:

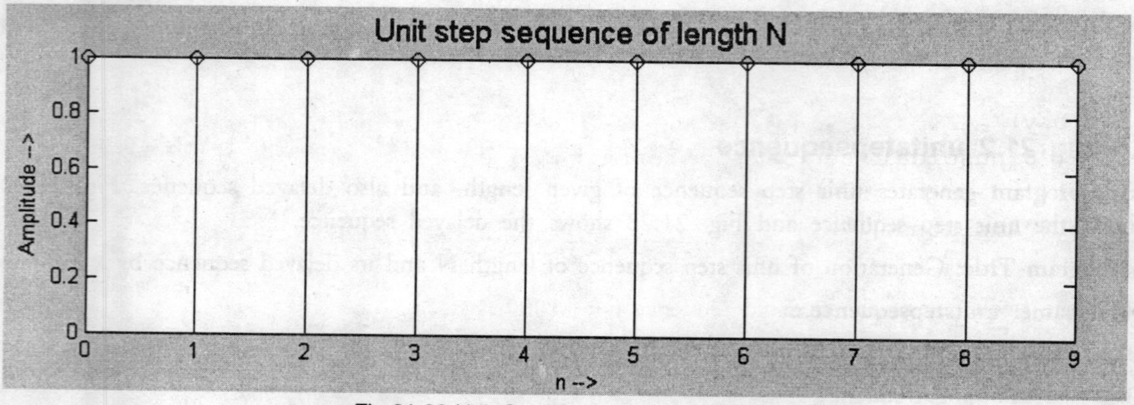

Fig.21.22 Unit Step Sequence of Length N

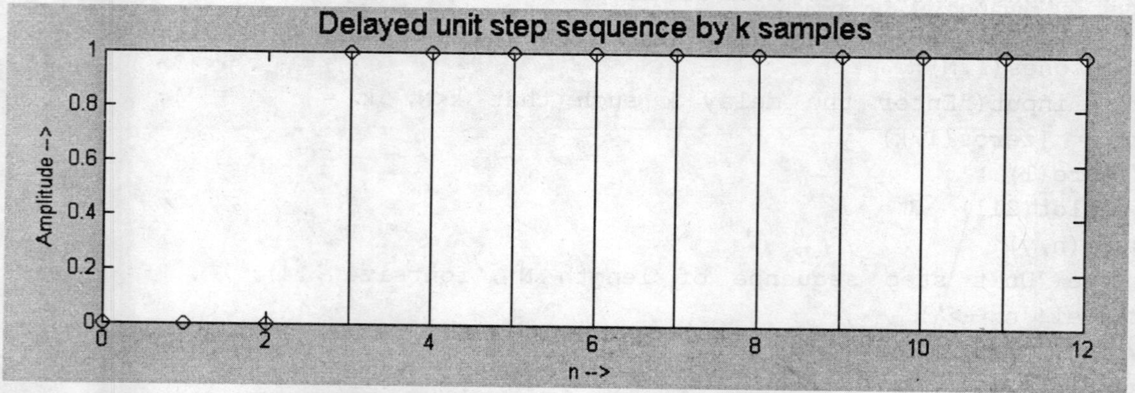

Fig. 21.23 Delayed Unit Step Sequence, delayed by K Samples

Listing 21.3 sinudioalsequence.m

This program generates a sine wave of given frequency and phase. Note that you need to specify the sampling frequency which should be much higher than the frequency of the sine wave. This program is useful for generation of DTMF signals, generation of modulating signal, generation of carrier in a radio system etc. You can generate sine wave in the audio band and then pass it through the sound card of your system as you listen to the tone. Fig. 21.24 shows the sine wave.

%Program Title: Generation of Sinusoidal sequence of f HZ and phase phi

%Filename: sinusoidalsequence.m

```
clc;
clear all;
f = input('Enter the frequency of the sinusoid sequence f = ');
phi = input('Enter the phase of the sinusoid sequence phi = ');
fs = input('Enter the sampling frequency  fs = ');
T = input('Enter the duration of the sequence T = ');
```

```
dt = 1/fs;
t = 0:dt:T;
y = sin(2*pi*f*t + phi);
figure(1);
plot(t,y)
title('Sinusoidal sequence','fontsize',14);
xlabel('t ->')
ylabel('Amplitude ->')
```

Results:

Enter the frequency of the sinusoid sequence f = 1000

Enter the phase of the sinusoid sequence phi = pi/3

Enter the sampling frequency fs = 50000

Enter the duration of the sequence T = 4e-3

Output Plot:

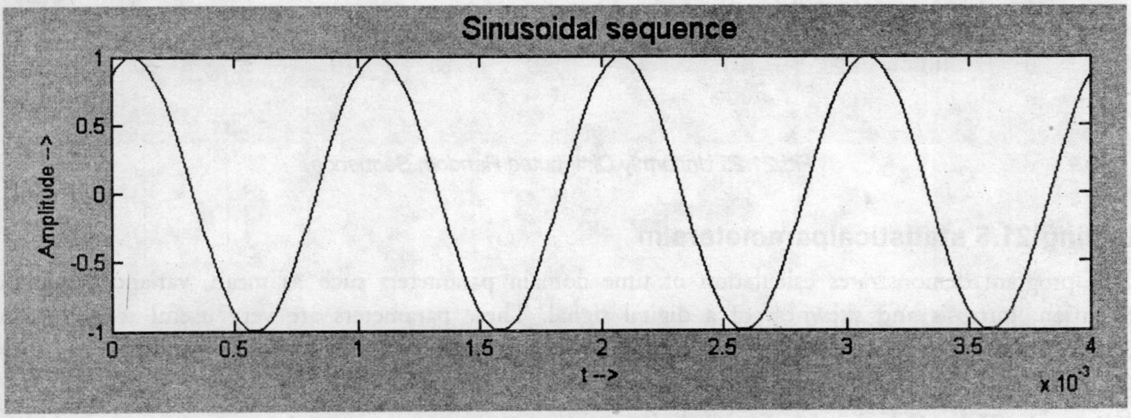

Fig.21.24 Sinusoidal Sequence

Listing 21.4 uniformrandomseqeunce.m

This program demonstrates how to generate uniformly distributed random sequence. Such a sequence is very useful for simulation of communication systems where the noise is modeled as a random sequence. For instance, to generate a noisy sine wave, you can generate sine wave samples and add them to the random sequence. Fig. 21.25 shows the plot of the random sequence.

%Program Title: Generation of uniformly distributed random sequence in the interval (0,1)

%Filename: uniformrandomsequence.m

```
clc;
clear all;
N = input('Enter the no. of samples in the sequence N = ');
y = rand(1,N);
figure(1)
```

```
plot(y)
xlabel('t ->')
ylabel('Amplitude ->')
title('Uniformly distributed random noise','fontsize',14);
```

Results:

Enter the no. of samples in the sequence N = 100

Output Plot:

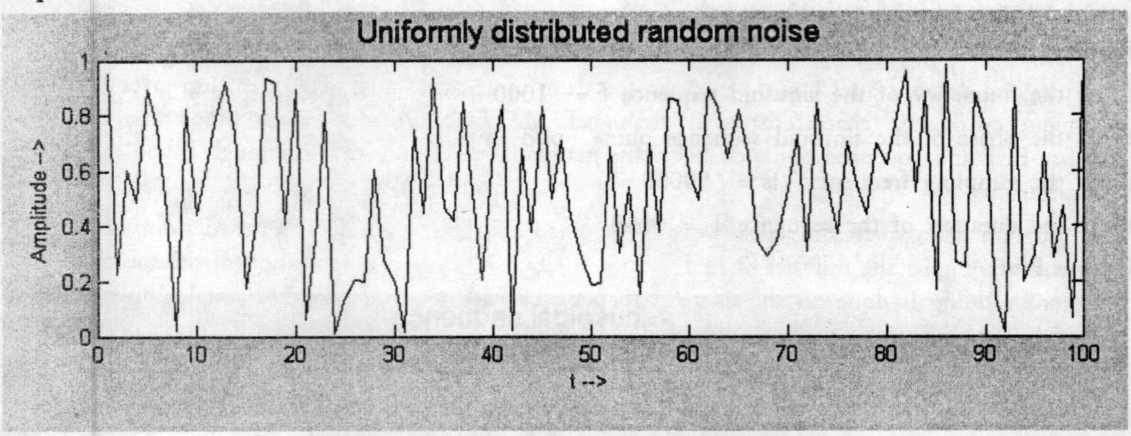

Fig.21.25 Uniformly Distributed Random Sequence

Listing 21.5 statisticalparameters.m

This program demonstrates calculation of time domain parameters such as mean, variance, standard deviation, kurtosis and skewness of a digital signal. These parameters are very useful to get useful information about the signal. For instance, if the input signal type is not known, you can use these parameters, in conjunction with frequency domain analysis, to identify the type of signal.

%Program Title: Calculation of statistical parameters such as mean, variance, standarad deviation, kurtosis and skewness of the time domain sequence

%Filename: Statisticalparameters.m

```
clc;
clear;
N = input('Enter the length of time domain sequence      N =  ');
x = rand(1,N);
mu = mean(x);
variance = var(x);
st_dev = std(x);
ku=kurtosis(x);
ske=skewness(x);
```

Results:

Enter the length of time domain sequence N = 100

Output:

mu= -0.127

variance=0.8924

st_dev=0.9447

ku=2.4775

ske=0.3141

Listing 21.6 voicespectrum.m

This program demonstrates how to plot the spectrum of a voice signal. The spectrum gives insight into the frequency domain characteristics of the signal. MATLAB provides a very simple function call to calculate FFT and you need not even know the mathematics behind it. It is enough if you can interpret the spectrum.

This program takes voice samples and plots N-point FFT. The value of N is varied from 128 to 1024. Note that the higher the number of FFT points, the better will be the resolution of the spectrum. Study how zero padding is done on the data to calculate FFT. When you take 512 data sample values and do 1024-point FFT, you need to do the zero padding.

Fig. 21.26 to Fig. 21.33 show the voice signal in time domain and frequency domain. Note that the resolution of the spectrum becomes better and better as the number of FFT points increase.

Notes...

The higher the number of FFT points, the better would be the resolution of the spectrum. The spectrm resolution is given by the formula Resolution (in Hz) = fs/N where fs is the sampling rate and N is the number of FFT points. Depending on the application and computation time requirements, value of N has to be chosen.

%Program Title: Wave and spectrum plot for different number of FFT points of voice Signal

%Filename: voicespectrum.m

```
clc;
clear;
file = input('enter voice file name =        ','s');
[u,fs,bits] = wavread(file);
M = length(u);
n=0:M-1;
N = input('Enter the no. of FFT points        N =       ');
ms=u(1:240);
for i=241:1024
      ms(i)=0;
end
dt=1/fs;
nmax=length(ms);
```

```
T=nmax*(1/fs);
t=dt:dt:T;
spect=(1/(nmax))*abs(fft(ms,N));
nmax1=length(spect);
f  =  fs*(0:round(nmax1/2))/nmax1;
f  =  f(1:round(nmax1/2));
voicespec=spect(1:(nmax1/2));
voicespectrum=20*log10(voicespec);
subplot(211)
n1=n(1:1024);
plot(n1,ms);
xlabel('n ->')
ylabel('Amplitude(volts)  ->')
title('Wave form of voice signal of length M','fontsize',14);
subplot(212)
plot(f,voicespectrum)
xlabel('f ->')
ylabel('Amplitude(dB)  ->')
title('VOICE  SPECTRUM','fontsize',14);
```

Result1:

Enter voice file name = C:\WINDOWS\Desktop\New Folder (2)\welcome.wav

'Enter the no. of FFT points N = 128

Output Plot:

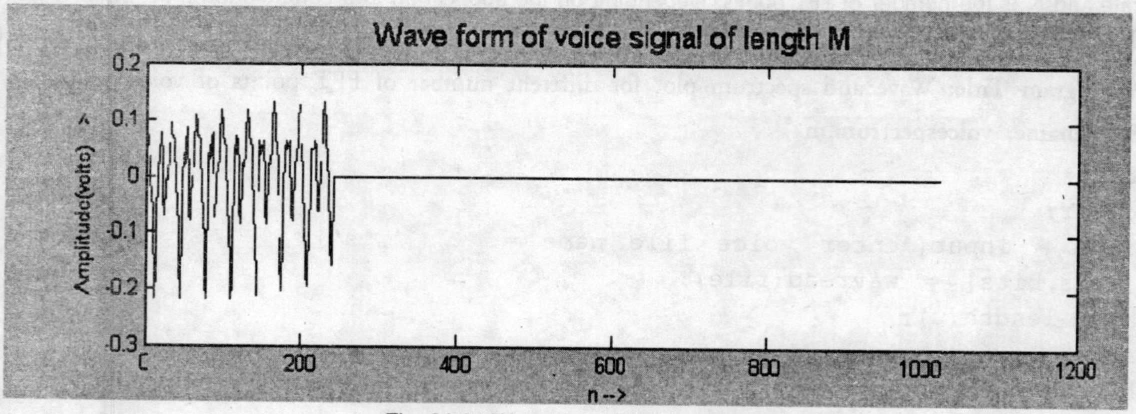

Fig. 21.26 Waveform of Voice Signal

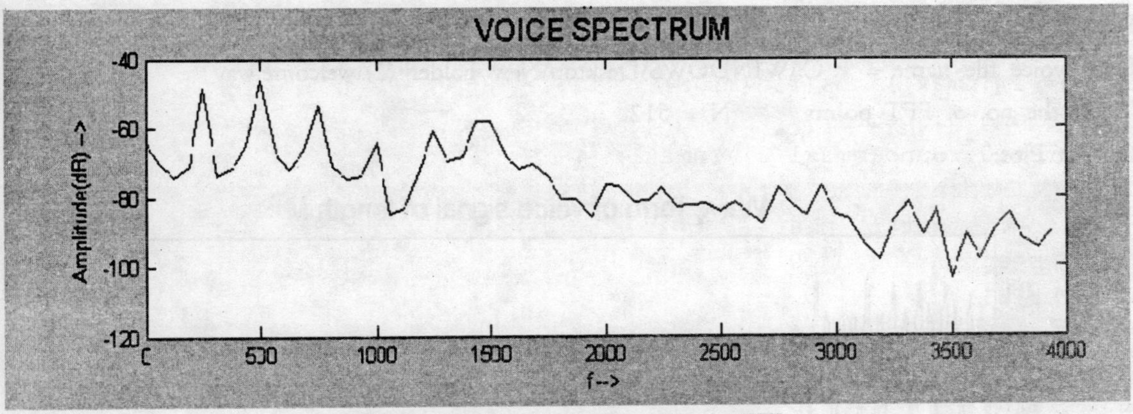

Fig. 21.27 Voice Spectrum: 128-point FFT

Result2:

Enter voice file name = C:\WINDOWS\Desktop\New Folder (2)\welcome.wav

'Enter the no. of FFT points N = 256

Output Plot:

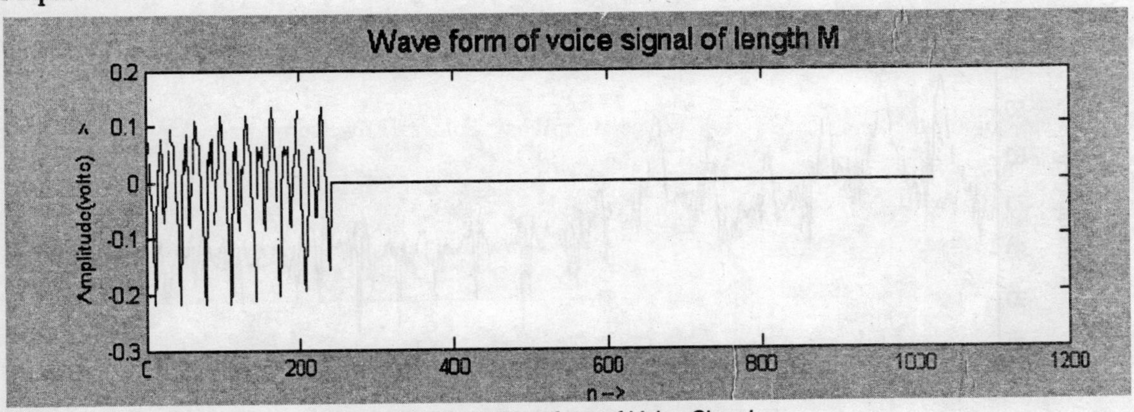

Fig. 21.28.Waveform of Voice Signal

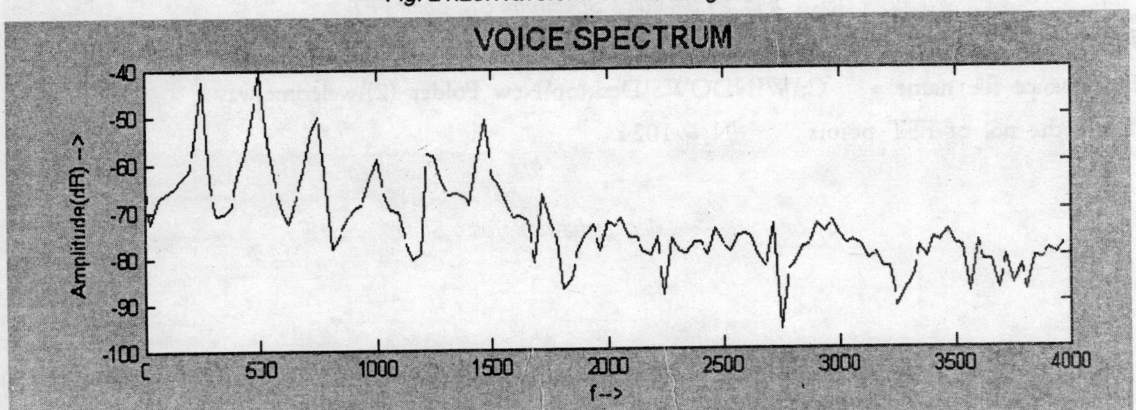

Fig. 21.29 Voice Spectrum: 256-point FFT

Result3:

Enter voice file name = C:\WINDOWS\Desktop\New Folder (2)\welcome.wav

'Enter the no. of FFT points N = 512

Output Plot:

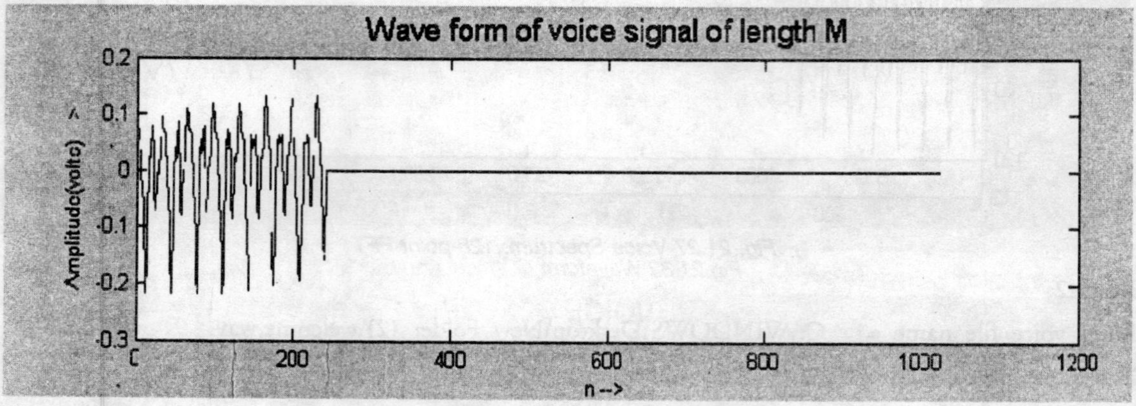

Fig. 21.30 Waveform of Voice Signal

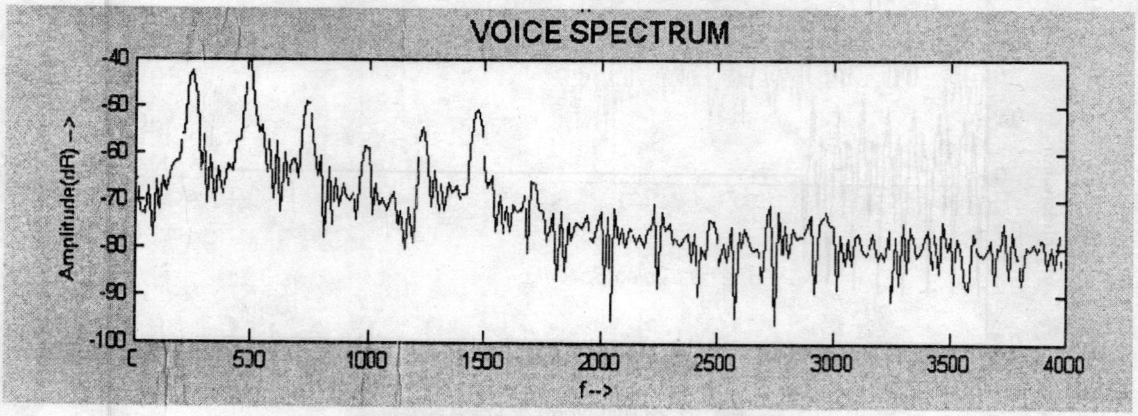

Fig. 21.31 Voice Spectrum: 512-point FFT

Result4:

Enter voice file name = C:\WINDOWS\Desktop\New Folder (2)\welcome.wav

'Enter the no. of FFT points N = 1024

Output Plot:

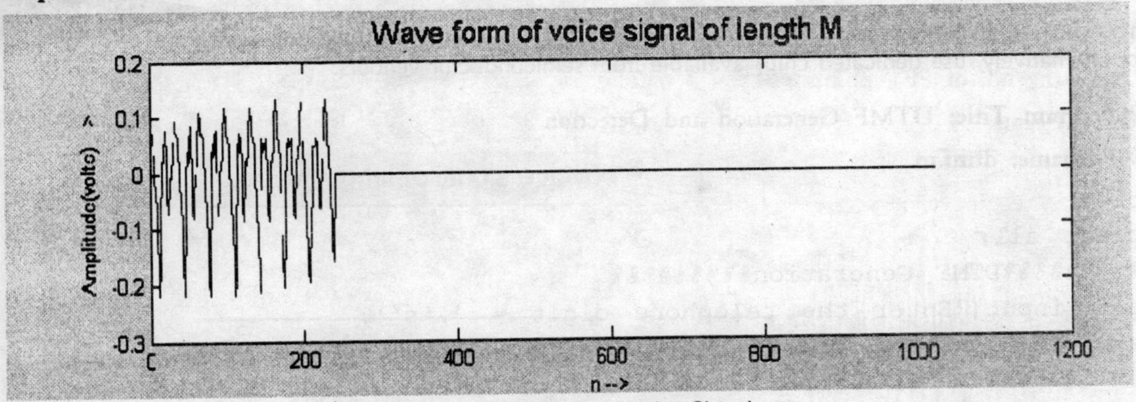

Fig.21.32 Waveform of Voice Signal

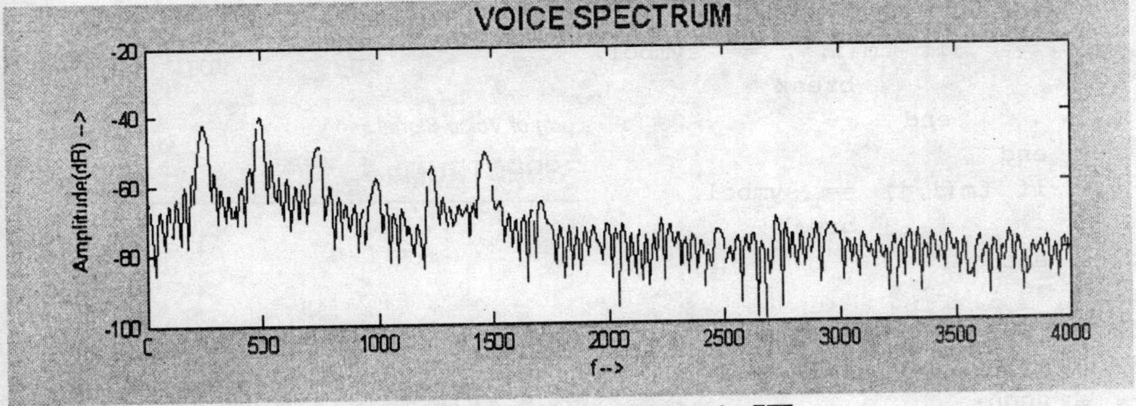

Fig. 21.33 Voice Spectrum: 1024-point FFT

Notes...

For analysis of voice signals, it is advisable to plot the spectrum with at least 10 Hz resolution. If the sampling rate is 8000 samples/second, the number of FFT points should be at least 1024. Note the peaks up to 2000 Hz in spectrum shown in Fig. 21.33. These peaks are called format frequencies and these values are useful for speaker recognition.

Listing 21.7 dtmf.m

This program demonstrates generation of DTMF and then recognition of the digits. When you dial a number on your telephone keypad, a combination of two sine waves is produced. At the exchange, the digit is recognized by carrying out a spectral analysis. The spectrum will show two distinct peaks at different frequencies depending on the digit dialed. Fig. 21.34 shows the DTMF signal in the time domain and Fig. 21.35 shows the spectrum corresponding to this signal.

Notes...

You can use a very low cost DSP to implement DTMF generation and recognition algorithms, or alternatively, use dedicated chips available from semiconductor vendors.

%Program Title: DTMF Generation and Detection

%Filename: dtmf.m

```
clc;
clear all;
%%%%%%%%DTMF Generation%%%%%%%%
d = input('Enter the telephone digit = ','s');
symbol = abs(d);
tm = [49 50 51 65;52 53 54 66;55 56 57 67;42 48 35 68];
for i = 1:4
    for j = 1:4
        if tm(i,j) == symbol,
            break
        end
    end
    if tm(i,j) == symbol,
            break
    end
end
f1 = [697 770 852 941];
f2 = [1209 1336 1477 1633];
fs = 8000;
dt = 1/fs;
t = 0:dt:1023/fs;
N = length(t);
x = sin(2*pi*f1(i)*t) + sin(2*pi*f2(j)*t);
xf = 1/N*abs(fft(x,N));
f = fs*(0:round(N/2))/N;
f = f(1:round(N/2));
figure(1);
subplot(211)
plot(t,x)
subplot(212)
stem(f,xf(1:round(N/2)))
%%%%%%%%DTMF Detection%%%%%%%%
xfs = fliplr(sort(xf(1:round(N/2))));
fd = [];
```

```
for k = 1:N/2
    if((xf(k) == xfs(1))|(xf(k) == xfs(2)))
        fd   = [fd k];
    end
end
fd =sort(fd);
dtmf1 = round(f(fd(1)));
dtmf2 = round(f(fd(2)));
for p = 1:4
    if ((dtmf1 > f1(p)-5)&(dtmf1 < f1(p)+5))
        dtmf1 = f1(p);
        break
    end
end
for q = 1:4
    if ((dtmf2 > f2(q)-5)&(dtmf2 < f2(q)+5))
        dtmf2 = f2(q);
        break
    end
end
disp('The tone frequencies are');
dtmf1
dtmf2
```

Results:

```
Enter the telephone digit = 3
The tone frequencies are
dtmf1 =

    697

dtmf2 =

    1477
```

Output Plot:

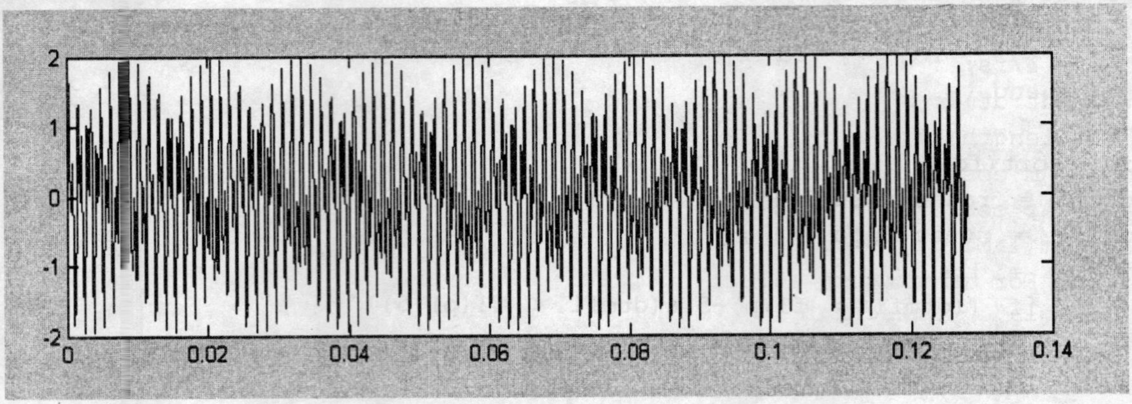

Fig.21.34 DTMF Signal

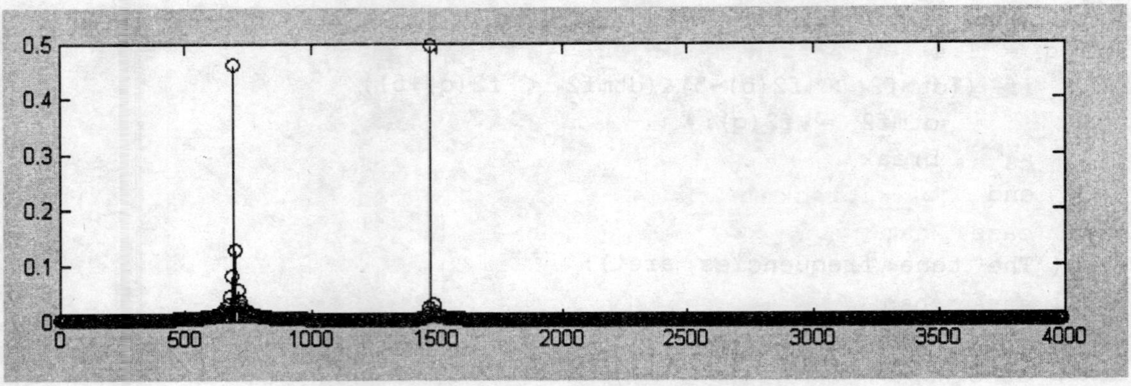

Fig.21.35 DTMF Spectrum

Listing 21.8 amdsb.m

This program is for generation of Amplitude Modulation Double Side Band (AM DSB) signal. It takes the message signal and a carrier signal as input and produces modulated signal with two side bands. Fig. 21.36 and Fig. 21.37 show the waveform and spectrum of the modulating signal. Fig. 21.38 and Fig. 21.39 show the waveform and spectrum of the modulated signal. Note the two side bands in the spectrum.

%Program Title: AM-DSB signal generation and its spectrum

%Filename: amdsb.m

```
clc;
clear;
Am = input('Enter the message amplitude                    Am =      ');
fm = input('Enter the modulating frequency                 fm =      ');
Ac = input('Enter carrier Amplitude                   Ac = ');
Fc = input('Enter carrier frequency                   Fc = ');
```

```
fs = input('Enter the sampling frequency                    fs =     ');
T = input('Enter the duration of the signal in seconds   T =     ');
dt = 1/fs;
t = dt:dt:T;
M = length(t);
m = Am*cos(2*pi*fm*t);
c = Ac*cos(2*pi*Fc*t);
s = m(1:M).*c;
disp('For windowing select    "rec" - rectangular / "bart" - bartlett
/  "bla" - blackman   /   "ham" - hamming / "han" - hanning ');
window_type = input('Enter the type of the window required for spectrum
','s');
switch window_type
     case 'rec'
          w = rectwin(M);
     case 'bart'
          w = bartlett(M);
     case 'bla'
          w = blackman(M);
     case 'ham'
          w = hamming(M);
     case 'han'
           w = hann(M);
     otherwise
          disp('window is not available');
end
w = w';
ms = m(1:M).*w;
sp = s(1:M).*w;
N = input('Enter the no. of FFT points                 N =     ');
if M<N,
     ms = [ms zeros(1,N-M)];
     sp = [sp zeros(1,N-M)];
     L = M;
else
     ms = ms(1:N);
     sp = sp(1:N);
     L = N;
end
msp = 1/N*abs(fft(ms));
msp=20*log10(msp);
```

```
f  =  fs*(0:round(N/2))/N;
f  =  f(1:round(N/2));
sp1  =  1/N*abs(fft(sp));
sp1=20*log10(sp1);
figure(1);
subplot(211);
plot(t(1:L),m(1:L));
title('MESSAGE  SIGNAL');
subplot(212);
plot(f,msp(1:round(N/2)));
title('MESSAGE  SPECTRUM');
%axis([0,  fs/10,  0,  1.5*max(msp)]);
figure(2);
subplot(211);
plot(t(1:L),s(1:L));
title('MODULATED  SIGNAL');
subplot(212);
plot(f,sp1(1:round(N/2)));
title('SPECTRUM  OF  MODULATED  SIGNAL');
```

Result1:

Enter the message amplitude Am = 1

Enter the modulating frequency fm = 1000

Enter carrier Amplitude Ac =1

Enter carrier frequency Fc =15000

Enter the sampling frequency fs = 150000

Enter the duration of the signal in seconds T = 4e-3

Enter the type of SSB modulation usb

For windowing select "rec" - rectangular / "bart" - bartlett / "bla" - blackman / "ham" - hamming / "han" – hanning

Enter the type of the window required for spectrum rec

Enter the no. of FFT points N = M

Output Plot:

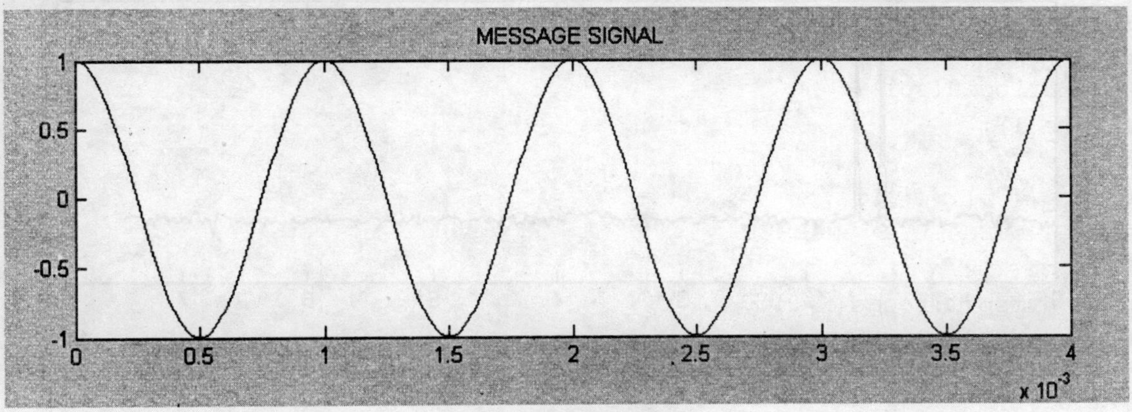

Fig.21.36 Message Signal

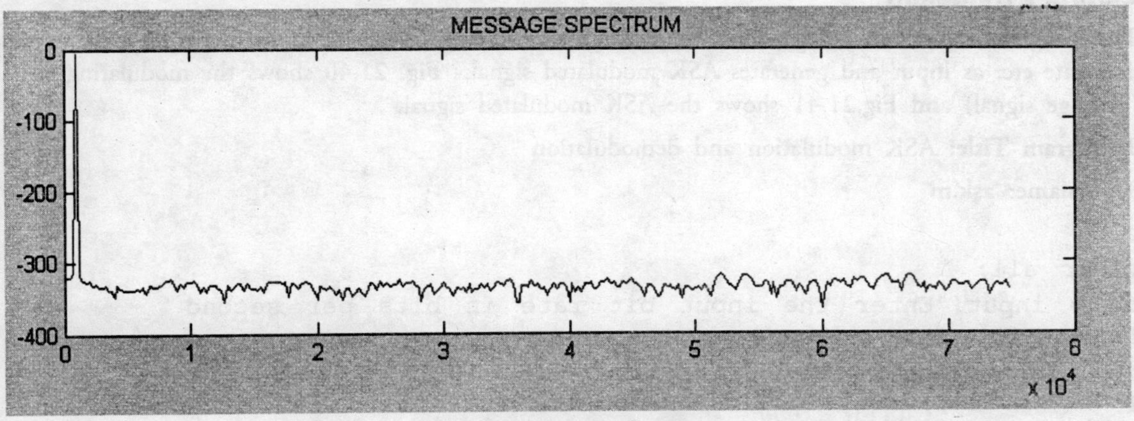

Fig. 21.37 Message Spectrum

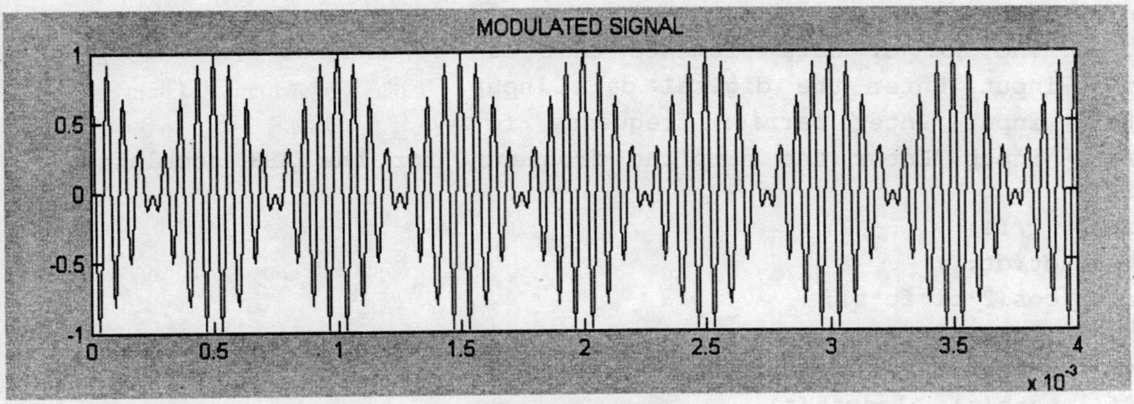

Fig. 21.38 Modulated Signal

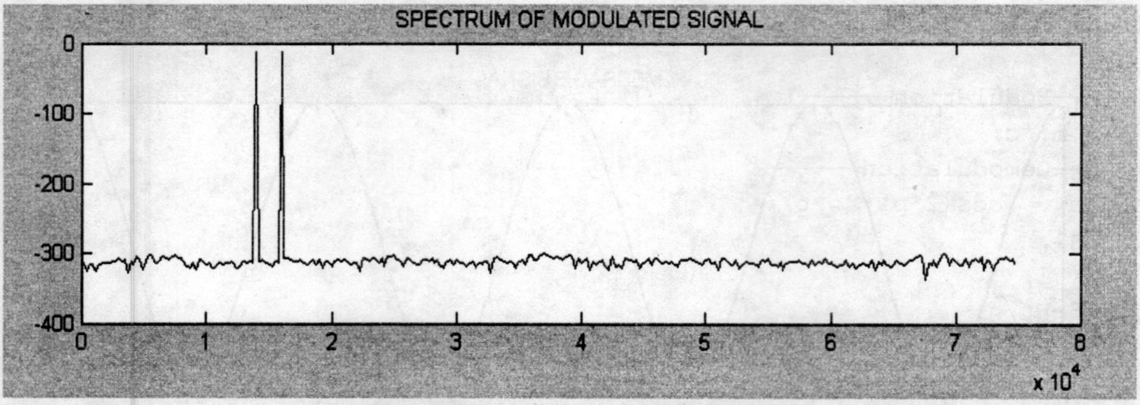

Fig. 21.39 Spectrum of the Modulated Signal

Listing 21.9 ask.m

This program shows how to generate Amplitude Shift Keying (ASK). It takes the input data stream, data rate etc. as input and generates ASK modulated signal. Fig. 21.40 shows the modulating signal (message signal) and Fig.21.41 shows the ASK modulated signal.

%Program Title: ASK modulation and demodulation

%Filename: ask.m

```
clc;
clear all;
fb = input('Enter the input bit rate in bits per second
fb =        ');      %baud rate
T = input('Enter the duration of the signal to generate
T =        ');
Tb = 1/fb;           %one bit period
n = T/Tb;
disp('The no. of data elements that can be entered');n
m = input('Enter the digital data input          m = ');
fc = input('Enter carrier frequency  fc =       ');
fs = input('Enter the sampling frequency for the ASK modulation
fs =       ');
dt = 1/fs;
t = dt:dt:T;
c = cos(2*pi*fc*t);
Nt = length(t);
m = kron(m,ones(1,round(Nt/n)));
if(length(m) >length(t))
     m = m(1:length(t));
else
```

```
      t = t(1:length(m));
end
%———Modulation————%
s = m.*c;
%———Demodulation————%
qdmod = cos(2*pi*fc*t);
i = 1;
T1 = 1;
T2 = Nt/n;
md = [];
while i<=n
      md = [md trapz(s(T1:T2).*qdmod(T1:T2))];
      if md(i) == 0
           md(i) = 0;
      elseif md(i)>0
           md(i) = 1;
      end
      T1 = 1+T2;
      T2 = T2+Nt/n;
      i = i+1;
end
disp('Demodulated message signal');md
figure(1)
subplot(211)
plot(t,m);
xlabel('t ->')
ylabel('Amplitude ->')
title('Message Signal','fontsize',14);
subplot(212)
plot(t,s);
title('Modulated Signal','fontsize',14);
xlabel('t ->')
ylabel('Amplitude ->')
```

Results:

Enter the input bit rate in bits per second fb = 600

Enter the duration of the signal to generate T = 5/fb

Enter the digital data input m =[1 1 0 0 1]

Enter carrier frequency fc = 15000

Enter the sampling frequency for the ASK modulation fs = 150000

Output Plot:

Demodulated message signal

md = 1 0 1 0 1

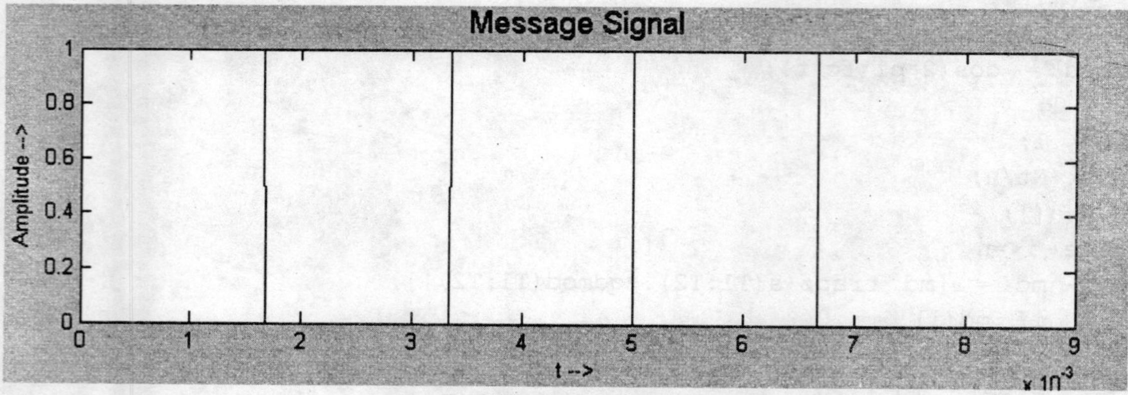

Fig.21.40 Message Signal

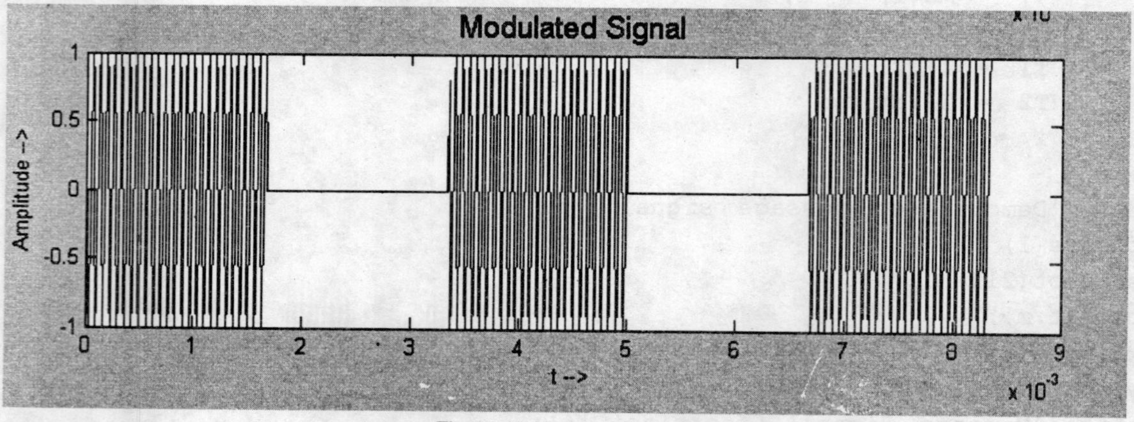

Fig.21.41 Modulated Signal

Listing 21.10 decimation.m

This program demonstrates decimation. To reduce the sampling rate of the input digital signal, decimation is used. The important input parameter to this program is the factor by which the sampling rate has to be reduced. Fig. 21.42 shows the original sequence and Fig. 21.43 shows the decimated sequence.

%Program Title: Decimation of sequence

%Filename: decimation.m

```
clc;
clear all;
disp('Let us take a sinusoidal sequence which has to be decimated');
fm = input('Enter the signal frequency                    fm =        ');
```

```
fs = input('Enter the sampling frequency                    fs =      ');
T = input('Enter the duration of the signal in seconds   T =      ');
dt  =  1/fs;
t  =  dt:dt:T;         % Defines time variable
M  =  length(t);
m  =  cos(2*pi*fm*t);
r = input('Enter the factor by which the sampling frequency has to be
reduced   r =  ');
md  =  decimate(m,r);
figure(1)
subplot(211)
stem(m);
xlabel('t ->')
ylabel('Amplitude ->')
title('Sinusoidal  Signal  before  decimation','fontsize',14);
subplot(212)
stem(md);
title('Sinusoidal  Signal  after  decimation','fontsize',14);
xlabel('t ->')
ylabel('Amplitude ->')
```

Results:

Let us take a sinusoidal sequence which has to be decimated

Enter the signal frequency fm = 1000

Enter the sampling frequency fs = 50000

Enter the duration of the signal in seconds T = 4e-3

Enter the factor by which the sampling frequency has to be reduced r = 5

Output Plot:

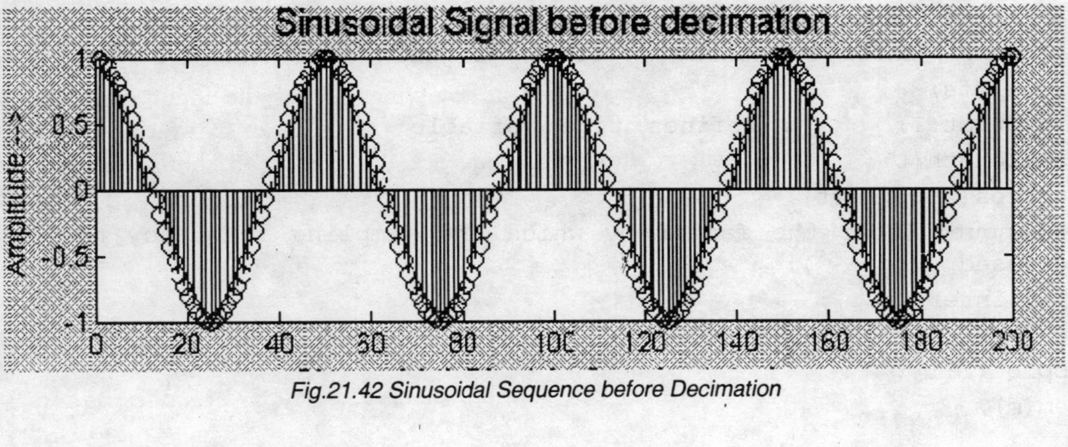

Fig.21.42 Sinusoidal Sequence before Decimation

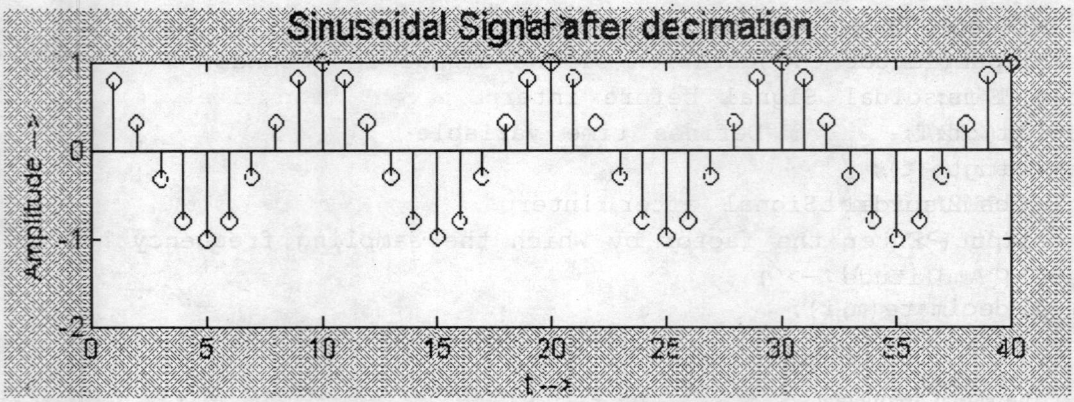

Fig. 21.43 Sinusoidal Sequence after Decimation

In Brief...

Decimation is used to reduce the sampling rate of the original sequence. However, the reduced rate should still be above the Nyquist rate to avoid aliasing.

Listing 21.11 interpolation.m

This program demonstrates interpolation of a sequence. In interpolation, additional samples are added to the sequence. To start with, additional zero-valued samples are inserted in the original sequence and then the samples are filtered. An important input parameter to this program is the factor by which the sampling frequency of the signal has to be increased. Fig. 21.44 shows the original sequence and Fig. 21.45 shows the interpolated sequence.

%Program Title: Interpolation of sequence

%Filename: interpolation.m

```
clc;
clear all;
disp('Let us take a sinusoidal sequence which has to be interpolated');
fm = input('Enter the signal frequency                   fm =      ');
fs = input('Enter the sampling frequency                  fs =      ');
T = input('Enter the duration of the signal in seconds  T =      ');
dt = 1/fs;
t = dt:dt:T;      % Defines time variable
M = length(t);
m = cos(2*pi*fm*t);
r = input('Enter the factor by which the sampling frequency has to be
increased  r = ');
md = interp(m,r);
figure(1)
subplot(211)
stem(m);
```

```
xlabel('t ->')
ylabel('Amplitude ->')
title('Sinusoidal Signal before interpolation','fontsize',14);
subplot(212)
stem(md);
title('Sinusoidal Signal after interpolation','fontsize',14);
xlabel('t ->')
ylabel('Amplitude ->')
```

Results:

Let us take a sinusoidal sequence which has to be interpolated

Enter the signal frequency fm = 1000

Enter the sampling frequency fs = 20000

Enter the duration of the signal in seconds T = 4E-3

Enter the factor by which the sampling frequency has to be increased r = 4

Output Plot:

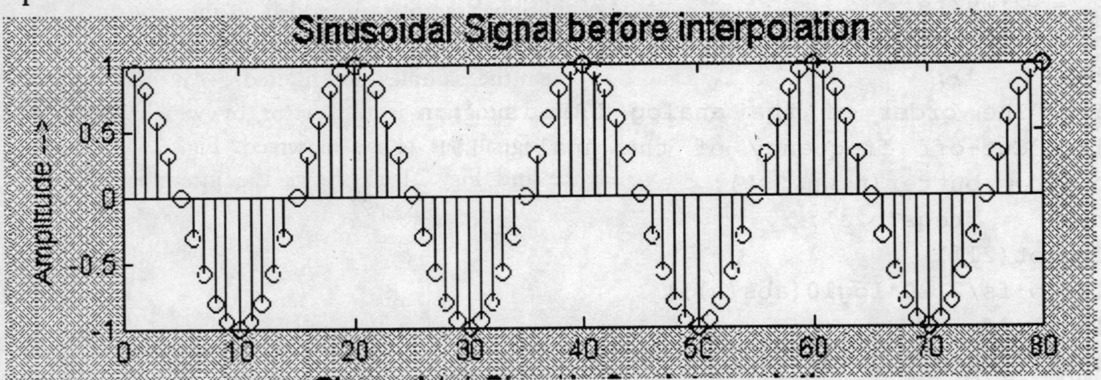

Fig.21.44 Sinusoidal Signal Before Interpolation

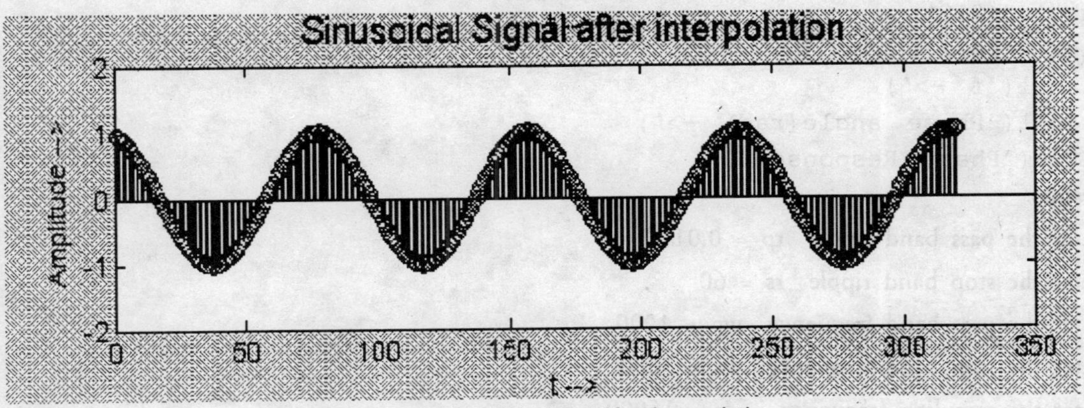

Fig. 21.45 Sinusoidal Signal After Interpolation

Listing 21.12 firlpf.m

This program demonstrates how to design an FIR Low Pass Filter. Study how the LPF specifications are given as input to the program. Fig. 21.46 shows the magnitude response of the filter and Fig. 21.47 shows the phase response of the filter. Note that the phase response is linear.

%Program Title: : Design of analog butterwoth low pass filter

%Filename:firlpf.m

```
clc
clear
%% Specifications %%
rp = input('Enter the pass band ripple   rp = ');
rs = input('Enter the stop band ripple   rs = ');
wp = input('Enter the pass band frequency   wp = ');
ws = input('Enter the stop band frequency   ws = ');
fs = input('Enter the sampling frequency    fs = ');
w1 = 2*wp/fs;
w2 = 2*ws/fs;
[n,wn] = buttord(w1,w2,rp,rs,'s');
disp('   ');
disp('The order of the analog LPF is ');n
disp('Cut-off frequency of the analog LPF is ');wn
[b,a] = butter(n,wn,'s');
[h,w] = freqs(b,a);
subplot(211)
plot(w*fs/2,20*log10(abs(h)))
xlabel('f ->')
ylabel('Magnitude(dB) ->')
title('Magnitude Response')
subplot(212)
plot(w*fs/2,angle(h));
xlabel('f ->')
ylabel('Phase angle(rad) ->')
title('Phase Response')
```

Results:

Enter the pass band ripple rp = 0.01

Enter the stop band ripple rs = 60

Enter the pass band frequency wp = 1000

Enter the stop band frequency ws = 3000

Enter the sampling frequency fs = 15000

The order of the analog LPF is

n =

    10

Cut-off frequency of the analog LPF is

wn =

    0.2005

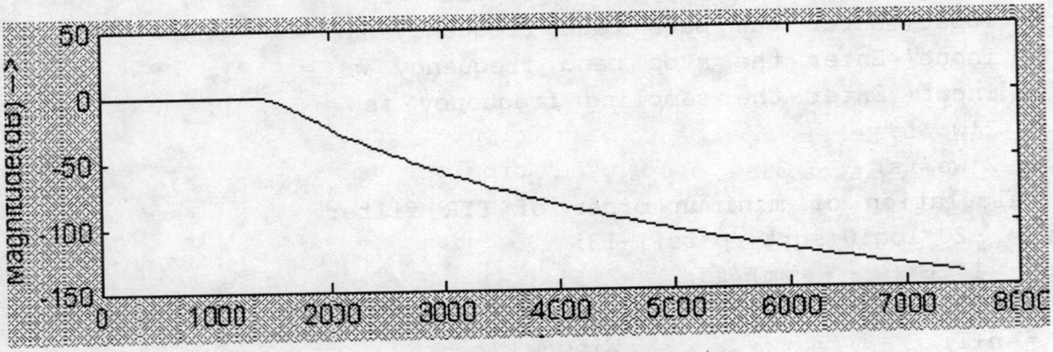

Fig.21.46 Magnitude Response of LPF

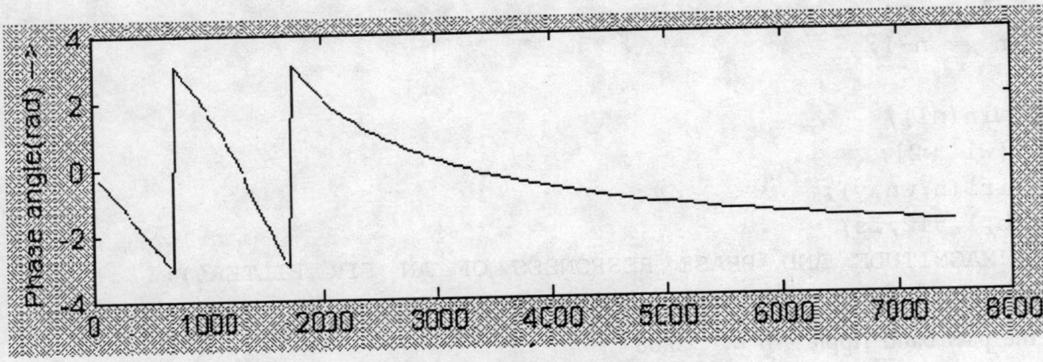

Fig. 21.47 Phase Response of LPF

Notes...

A number of design techniques are available to design digital filers. Using windowing techniques is one of the simplest and efficient methods.

Listing 21.13 firbpf.m

This program illustrates design of FIR Band Pass Filter. Note how the BPF is specified. Fig. 21.48 and Fig. 21.49 show the magnitude response and the phase response of the BPF respectively.

```
%Program Title: Design of FIRBPF
%Filename: firbpf.m
clc;
clear all;
%% Filter specifications %%
rp = input('Enter the pass band ripple   rp =       ');
rs = input('Enter the stop band ripple   rs =       ');
wp = input('Enter the pass band frequency wp =     ');
ws = input('Enter the stop band frequency ws =     ');
fs = input('Enter the sampling frequency fs =      ');
w1 = 2*wp/fs;
w2 = 2*ws/fs;
%% Calculation of minimun order of FIR filter
num = -20*log10(sqrt(rp*rs))-13;
den = 14.6*(ws - wp)/fs;
n = ceil(num/den);
n1 = n+1;                          %% Window length
if(rem(n,2) ~= 0)          %% In the case of odd value of n
     n1 = n;
     n = n-1;
end
y=rectwin(n1);
wn = [w1 w2];
b = fir1(n,wn,y);
freqz(b,1,512,fs)
title('MAGNITUDE AND PHASE RESPONSES OF AN FIR FILTER');
```

Results:

Enter the pass band ripple rp = 0.08

Enter the stop band ripple rs = 0.01

Enter the pass band frequency wp = 3000

Enter the stop band frequency ws = 5000

Enter the sampling frequency fs = 20000

Output Plot:

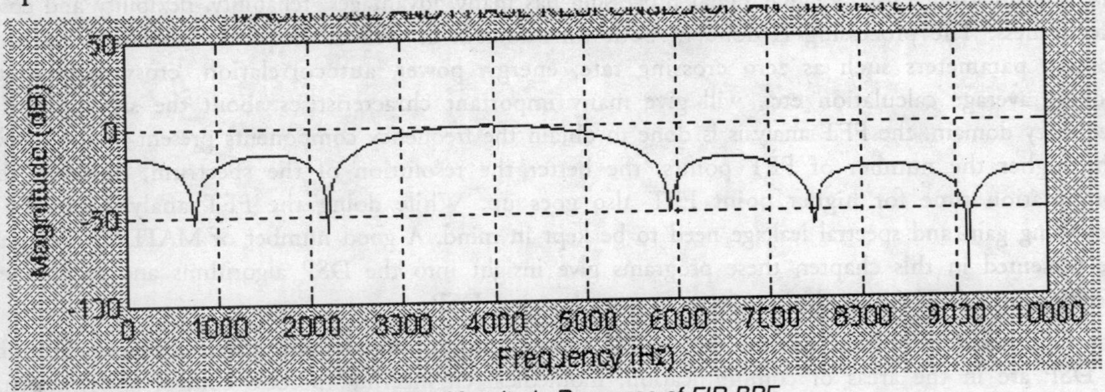

Fig. 21.48 Magnitude Response of FIR BPF

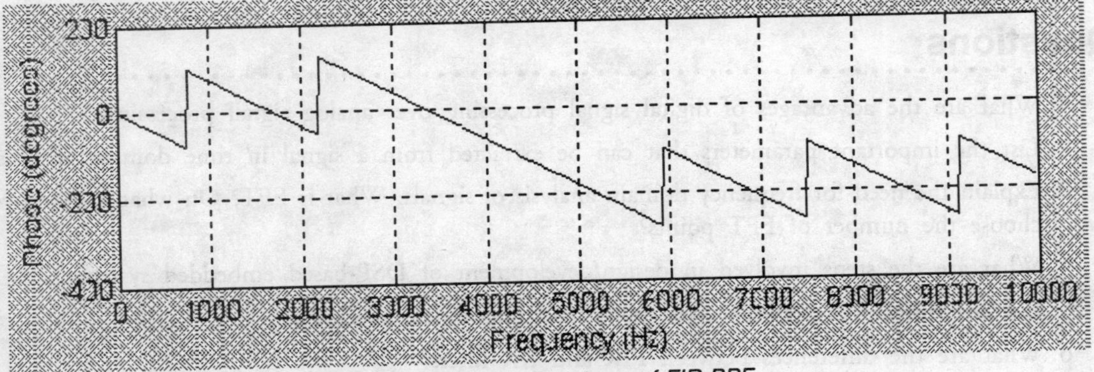

Fig. 21.49 Phase Response of FIR BPF

Notes...

Design of IIR filters is very tricky as the filter may become unstable. Also, the finite word length effects of the Digital Signal Processor affects the stability of the filter. These aspects have to be taken into consideration while designing the IIR filters.

Summary

This chapter presented an overview of Digital Signal Processing and its importance in embedded systems. As processing of signals such as voice, image, video, data, fax, biomedical signals etc., has become very important, embedded systems are now driven by Digital Signal Processing technology. This chapter presented the important concepts of DSP without dwelling too much on the mathematics. Physical interpretation of the mathematics is very important to appreciate the practical aspects of DSP.

The world is analog—the signals such as voice, video etc. are analog signals. These analog signals are converted into digital signals using an Analog to Digital Converter and then processed in the digital domain using either General Purpose Prcesssor or a Digial Signal Processor. As DSPs are tailor-made for handling complex mathematical calculations, DSP is the preferred choice. The digital signal processing is done through hardware and software, and the processed digital signal is converted into analog form using DAC. Digital signal processing has many advantages: reliability, flexibility and cost-effectiveness. The processing is done in both time-domain as well as frequency domain. The time domain parameters such as zero crossing rate, energy, power, autocorrelation, cross correlation, moving average calculation etc., will give many important chracteristiscs about the signal. In the frequency domain, the FFT analysis is done to obtain the frequency components present in the signal. The higher the number of FFT points, the better the resolution of the spectrum, however, the computation time for higher point FFT also goes up. While doing the FFT analysis, the FFT processing gain and spectral leakage need to be kept in mind. A good number of MATLAB programs are presented in this chapter, these programs give insight into the DSP algorithms and techniques. Working on MATLAB is the best way to start learning DSP.

The DSP-based embedded systems can be PC add-on cards or stand-alone systems. The applications of DSP are in the areas of communication, biomedical engineering, process control and industrial automation instrumentation, astrophysics and cosmology, and communication.

Questions

1. What are the advantages of digital signal processing over analog signal processing?
2. List the important parameters that can be extracted from a signal in time domain analysis.
3. Explain the need for frequency domain analysis of signals. What is FFT? On what basis do you choose the number of FFT points?
4. What are the steps involved in design/development of DSP-based embedded systems?
5. List the differences between fixed point and floating point DSPs.
6. What are the differences between FIR and IIR filters?

Exercises

1. Study the various processor families of Analog Devices and the benchmark results for these processors.
2. Study GoldWave application software and how it can be used for voice file editing.
3. Study Java Media Framework (JMF) architecture and develop a voice/video over IP application using JMF.
4. Study Microsoft's NetMeeting SDK and develop voice/video over IP application using this SDK.
5. Write a MATLAB program to generate normally distributed random noise samples.
6. Write a MATLAB program to do FFT analysis on a noise sequence.
7. Write a MATLAB program to generate AM SSB signal.
8. Write a MATLAB program to design an IIR Low Pass Filter.
9. Write a MATLAB program to design an IIR Band Pass Filter.
10. Prepare a technical report on Software Defined Radio.

Chapter 22

Future Trends

CHAPTER OBJECTIVES

After reading this chapter, you will be able to:

- Gain an understanding of the emerging technologies
- Learn about the new applications of these technologies

The landscape of embedded system technology is changing rapidly. Developments in microelectronics are paving way for miniaturized, powerful computing devices. And, these devices can be used for a variety of purposes bringing in revolutionary changes in all walks of human life. In this chapter, we will peep into these futuristic technologies and their applications.

22.1 Emerging Technologies

The presence of desktop computer can be felt wherever you go—its size and shape makes its presence significant. Thanks to the developments in microelectronics, the computing power of the desktop computers is now becoming available on the palmtops. This handheld computing technology, in conjunction with wireless communication technology, is leading to anywhere-anytime multimedia communication. These developments are in turn paving way for making the dream of 'global village' a reality.

Research in developing powerful embedded systems to carry out intelligent tasks is leading to the important technologies of "pervasive computing" and "ubiquitous computing". Emergence of language-independent and platform-independent software development tools will make development even faster and the software more reliable. We will briefly review these developments in this section.

22.1.1 Pervasive/Ubiquitous Computing

During 1990's, many researchers envisioned a world where the computers do their jobs silently without their presence being noticed. Pervasive computing and ubiquitous computing are the two catchphrases that emerged out of this vision.

Today, the computers appear significant—their shapes and sizes make us feel their presence wherever we go. Embedded systems, on the other hand, do their job silently and in many cases their presence is not even known to us.

"Embeddedness" and "mobility" are the two characteristics used for categorizing a system as a pervasive computer or ubiquitous computer. Pervasive computers have high embeddedness but low mobility; ubiquitous computers have high embeddedness and high mobility.

Consider the case of a smart card that acts as an electronic wallet. It has high embeddedness and high mobility and hence it can be considered as a ubiquitous computer. On the other hand, a smart card reader that can act also as a web server has high embeddedness but low mobility, and hence it can be considered as a pervasive computer.

Pervasive computers and ubiquitous computers will have a tremendous impact on all walks of life. Here are some typical applications of such computers:

Electronic Personal Assistant: Every individual can have a device (we need not call it a computer, any longer!) that will assist him/her on all aspects such as the next appointment, next trip for a medical checkup, time when the next dose of the medicine has to be taken etc.

Electronic wallet: A smart card can act as an electronic wallet. The smart card ultimately can obviate the need for cash or cheque transactions completely.

Wearable computers: Lot of research is going on in many academic institutions and research laboratories to develop wearable computers that can be placed on say, the frame of the spectacles or it can be tucked to your belt. The wearable computer can be programmed to do any work of your choice—when you are walking in a park, it can recognize the faces of the persons who are around, get connected to the Internet and obtain information about them, and then tell you (through the voice synthesizer) the details of these persons.

Invisible computing: Computing devices that are not visible can be used for a variety of applications such as in surveillance, security etc. An invisible computer can be attached to a person whom you want to track, and the location of that person will be transmitted to you continuously. This computing and communication device can be attached to say, the shoe of the person, and it cannot be even noticed. Certainly, this technology leads to a debate on privacy of individuals, but then technology provides us immense possibilities.

A number of projects have been initiated to work on various aspects of pervasive/ubiquitous computing. Some of these projects are:

- "Personal Information aura" of Carnegie Mellon University.

  www-2.cs.cmu.edu/~aura/

- "Endeavour" of University of California, Berkeley

  endeavour.cs.Berkeley.edu/

- "Oxygen" of Massachusetts Institute of Technology

  www.oxygen.lcs.mit.edu/. The objective is to make computing available everywhere, like Oxygen.

In Brief...

Pervasive computers have high 'embeddedness' and low mobility. Ubiquitous computers have high embeddedness and high mobility.

22.1.2 Java for Embedded Systems

Development of software is still in its primitive stages. Every software development is essentially a development from the scratch. Though the object-oriented programming languages have brought in reuse in the application software arena; the reuse is yet to become an accepted practice in embedded systems software. In spite of the standardization activities in C/C++ programming languages, porting is still a major issue.

In Brief...

Real Time Java Specifications (RTSJ) enable use of Java for embedded real-time applications. Platform independence coupled with real-time performance will make Java the ideal programming language for developing mobile applications as well as embedded applications.

Java programming language made a great impact on Internet computing to start with and then on mobile computing. In the near future, Java will have a profound impact on embedded systems arena as well. With the release of Real Time Specifications for Java (RTSJ), use of Java in embedded/real-time applications will increase many fold. Porting will be confined to history once Java is used for embedded systems because of its 'write once run anywhere' capability.

22.1.3 Security of Embedded Systems

In Brief...

As the embedded systems get network-enabled, their security will be a major issue. The security protocols such as SSL/TLS need to be incorporated in the TCP/IP protocol stack.

As more and more embedded systems are network-enabled, security of these systems will be a major issue just as the security of Internet servers is a major issue presently. The security-related protocols such as Secure Socket Layer (SSL)/Transport Layer Security (TSL) need to be integrated along with the TCP/IP protocol stack. The computational complexity of the cryptographic algorithms is very high and the present embedded systems cannot handle such a high complexity. However, the future embedded systems certainly will have the processing power to implement complex cryptographic algorithms for developing highly secure embedded systems.

22.1.4 Embedding Intelligence

Developments in Artificial Intelligence (AI) have led to deployment of intelligent systems for a variety of applications. Automatic speech recognition and automatic speech generation are the two technologies that have matured to a great extent in recent years. Now it is possible to make the computer speak in a natural language such as English. The computers are also capable of recognizing the speech if they are trained for a particular person's voice. This software can be integrated into the embedded system. As a result, embedded systems will be capable of speaking to us in a language of our choice, say English, or they can be made to understand our speech. So, we can communicate with the embedded systems just as we communicate with fellow human beings. Similarly, developments are taking place in the area of computer vision, and embedded systems can be made to recognize objects. These developments will provide impetus to developments in robotics and development of humanoids.

In Brief...

Using the Artificial Intelligence (AI) concepts, embedded systems can be made intelligent. Embedded systems can be made to talk to us in speech and also understand our speech.

22.2 Emerging Applications

Technology development is not an end in itself; we need to focus on applying the technology for making the quality of life better. The developments in pervasive/ubiquitous computers will have profound impact on all aspects of human life. Here are their few applications.

Digital cash: The whole world revolves around money and financial transaction is one of the most fundamental activities of human beings. Present financial transactions are through cash, cheque or credit cards. These mechanisms are very inefficient as cash is prone to theft and the credit cards are prone to fraud. To eliminate the need to carry cash, end-to-end digital payment systems can be developed using the smart card technology. Smart card technology has an immense potential to eliminate the cash transactions completely. Soon, every person will carry a smart card that can be used for making any payment—howsoever small the amount may be. All the shops, business establishments, banks and credit card organizations will be networked together so that there is no need for any cash/cheque transactions at all, the entire financial transactions can be carried out only through smart cards and smart card readers/writers. This digital cash will usher in a "cashless" society.

In Brief...

In end-to-end digital payment systems, a smart card will be used to make all the payments. All the office establishments and banks will be networked so that the financial transactions are done only through 'digital cash'.

Citizen cards for e-governance: To comply with government regulations, we need to keep a number of papers/documents—passport, driving license, voter identity card, vehicle registration papers and so on. Now, under e-governance projects, many governments are planning to bring out "citizen cards". A citizen card is a smart card that will have the complete information about the citizen. The citizen card can replace all the documents listed above. Multi-purpose citizen cards can be used for storing information such as the medical history of the person, fingerprints etc.

Real smart phones: The future mobile phones will be powerful devices with high computing and communicating power. These mobile phones—the real smart phones—will be based on Software-Defined Radio and hence would be highly configurable. They will be capable of receiving signals from different wireless networks running different protocols. These smart phones can be used not just for voice and data calls, but also for multi-party video conferencing when all the participants are travelling, for receiving location information, music programs from broadcast networks etc.

Electronic aids to the physically handicapped: Artificial organs such as electronic nose (e-nose), e-eye etc. are being developed which will be of immense use to the physically handicapped persons. Powerful sensors in conjunction with computing power can take the place of the human organs effectively. Although technology is available for electronic ear, electronic larynx etc., it is not being put to good use.

Well, as they say, imagination is the limit for the applications of future embedded systems.

In Brief...

Applications which will have profound impact on all of us in the coming years are: end-to-end digital payment systems that can eliminate the need for cash transactions; multi-purpose citizen cards for e-governance; aids to the physically handicapped and very smart mobile devices providing anywhere-anytime multimedia communication.

22.3 "The Greatest Songs are still Unsung"

In spite of the tremendous progress in the field of computer science and engineering, the computers are still dumb and they are still not intelligent enough. Developments in nanotechnology, artificial intelligence, etc. will lead to many unforeseen developments in the coming years. Yes, "the greatest songs are still unsung" even in the field of computer science. It is today's students of the embedded systems who can 'sing' those songs.

Today's young embedded professionals will have a great opportunity to contribute to these exciting developments. But then, as the field is changing very fast, it is necessary to be always in touch with the latest developments through professional journals and trade magazines. To maintain the professional vitality is a must to survive in this era of fast-changing technology.

Summary

This chapter presented a brief overview of the emerging technologies and applications in the field of embedded systems. "Pervasive computing" and "ubiquitous computing" are the two catchphrases for the next decade. Powerful embedded systems with high mobility will pave way for their extensive applications in all walks of life. These systems have the capability of ushering in a cashless society. We can totally do away with cash/cheque transactions and develop end-to-end digital payment systems. These technologies will also have a wide range of applications in wireless communication, e-governance and as a great aid to the physically handicapped.

Appendix A

Glossary

2G: Second Generation. 2G wireless networks support data services up to 28.8 Kbps data rates.

2.5G: Two-and-a-half Generation. 2.5G wireless networks support data rates up to 144 Kbps.

3G: Third Generation. 3G wireless networks support data rates up to 2.048 Mbps. Multimedia services such as video conferencing can be offered on these networks.

4004: World's first general purpose microprocessor. Developed by Intel in 1971.

555: An IC used to generate periodic clock signal. Usually referred to as 555 timer.

680x0: The family of 68000-series processors of Motorola. 68000 was the first 16-bit microprocessor, followed by 68010, 68020, 68030, 68040 etc.

68HCxx: The family of 8-bit and 16-bit micro-controllers from Motorola such as 68HC05, 68HC11, 68HC12 etc.

Address bus: A set of wires using which a processor communicates with the peripheral to select a memory location or a register of a peripheral. If the address bus has n lines, the processor can address 2^n unique memory locations.

Address space: The maximum memory size that can be addressed by a processor. CPU with 16 address lines can address 2^{16} bytes of address space.

Algorithm: A step-by-step procedure to solve a problem.

Anti-aliasing filter: A filter that removes the frequency components above the Nyquist frequency. For example, to process voice signals, the bandwidth of the voice signals is limited to 4 KHz if the sampling is done at 8000 samples per second. So, an anti-aliasing filter of 4 KHz bandwidth is used before sampling is done.

Application Programming Interface (API): A set of function calls using which applications can be developed over an operating system or a software development tool. IEEE standardized the operating system API in the Portable Operating System Interface (POSIX) standard.

Assembler: Software tool which converts assembly language program into object code.

Big-endian: In Big-endian data representation, the most significant byte of a multi-byte value is stored at the lowest memory address. Sun SPARC, Motorola 68000 and Power PC family processors; Java Virtual Machine, TCP/IP protocols use big-endian format.

Bill of Materials: List of parts/components needed to build a system.

Binary semaphore: A special type of semaphore with only two states.

Bit rate: The number of bits transmitted per second over a communication channel.

Blocked state: One of the states of a task. In blocked state, the task is waiting for an external event to occur. When a task is in blocked state, it does not use any CPU cycles. Also referred as waiting state.

Bootable image: The executable code that is transferred to the target hardware of the embedded system. Bootable image, executable image, runtime image and target image are used interchangeably to refer to the executable code that resides in the program memory of the embedded system.

Bootloader: A small piece of software stored in ROM. This software initializes the hardware and downloads the application software to the embedded system.

Bulk Storage Segment (BSS): A segment in an object file that contains uninitialized data.

Bytecode: The code produced by a Java compiler. The bytecode is interpreted by the Java Virtual Machine to give the program output. Bytecode is independent of the platform and hence Java is a platform-independent programming language.

C99: International standard for C programming language, updated in the year 1999 and specified in the standard document ISO/IEC 9899. Standard names for 8,16,32 signed/unsigned integers, C++ like commenting (//) are some of the important features of this latest revision.

Cache memory: A very high-speed memory between the RAM/ROM and the CPU. Cache memory is used to supply the most recently used instructions/data to the CPU. Cache memory is much faster to access than the RAM/ROM, but is very costly.

Chip Select: A signal that enables an input/output device or a memory device.

Co-design: The process of partitioning the system into hardware and software.

Co-verification: The process of identifying the problem—whether it is in hardware or software.

Compiler: A software development tool that converts the source code of a high level language into an object file/executable file.

Complex Instruction Set Computer (CISC): Processors with variable length instructions and multiple addressing formats. Intel 80x86 family is an example of CISC processors.

Configuration Management: The process of making changes to various work products (such as requirements specifications document, design document, source code etc.) in a systematic way. Every proposed change is analyzed for its impact and then only a decision is taken whether the change can be incorporated. The change is communicated to all the engineers working on the project.

Connected Device Configuration (CDC): One of the two configurations addressed by Java 2 Micro Edition (J2ME). These devices get connected to a high-bandwidth network and run the TCP/IP protocol stack. They have a memory capacity in the range 2 to 16 MB. Examples are Set Top Box and Internet TV.

Connected Limited Device Configuration (CLDC): One of the two configurations addressed by Java 2 Micro Edition (J2ME). These devices have limited capabilities such as low memory (128 KB to 512 KB) and small display; they get connected to low-speed networks such as second Generation (2G) wireless networks. These devices contain a K Virtual Machine which occupies few Kilobytes of memory. Examples are mobile phone, pager and Personal Digital Assistant.

Context: The current state of the processor's registers and flags. When the operating system decides to run a new task, the context of the current task has to be saved.

Context switch: The process of switching from one task to another task in a multitasking operating system. The context of the presently running task is saved and the context of the new task is loaded.

Controller Area Network (CAN): Network of controllers/processors. CAN is used in industrial control, cars, ship navigation and control to interconnect embedded systems. Processors have a CAN module using which the processors communicate using communication protocol layers. CAN can be used in noisy environments for real-time communication up to 1 Mbps over 2-wire serial link. Philips' PCA82C250T is an example of CAN controller.

Cooperative multitasking: A scheduling algorithm in which there is no pre-emptive mechanism, but a task yields to other tasks so that every task gets a fair share of the CPU time.

Copyleft: Opposite of copyright. Copyleft software can be freely modified and distributed. The modified versions should be made available free of cost.

Counting semaphore: A semaphore with more than two states.

Critical section: The portion of the program that must be executed without interruption.

Cross-Compiler: A software development tool that runs on one platform (say, PC) and produces object code for a different platform (say, embedded system with a micro-controller).

Cyclic Redundancy Check (CRC): Additional bits added to the information bits for error checking. Normally 16 or 32 bits are added to the information bits at the transmitting side. At the receiving side, the received CRC bits are compared with the re-calculated CRC. If the two match, the information bits are received correctly. CRC-16, CRC-32 and CRC-CCITT are the three standard algorithms to calculate CRC.

Data segment: The segment in an object file that contains initialized data.

Data sheet: The sheet containing the complete technical details of a component or Integrated Circuit. The collection of data sheets of a manufacturer is called data book. These data books are now being supplied in the form of CDROMs. Surprisingly, many electronics engineers graduate without having seen a data sheet.

Datagram: Another word for 'packet'. In Internet Protocol version 4, the packet is known as datagram. The UDP packet is known as user datagram.

Deadlock: A situation in which all the tasks are blocked. Solution is to reset the system!

Development life cycle models: Models used to develop software in a systematic way. Waterfall model, prototyping model, spiral model, evolutionary development model and synchronize-and-stabilize model are the widely used development life cycle models.

Device driver: A software module that interfaces between the input/output device and the application program. The data is read from the device or written onto the device through the device driver.

Dual Port RAM (DPRAM): RAM that can be accessed by two or more processors simultaneously. For example, a micro-controller can write data into the DPRAM which can be read by another processor.

Dual Tone Multi Frequency (DTMF): In telephone networks, the signaling between the subscriber and the switch is done through DTMF signaling. Each digit pressed on the keypad is transmitted using a pair of tones. For example, 1 is a combination of 697 Hz and 1209 Hz tones, 5 is a combination of 770 Hz and 1336 Hz tones.

Dual UART: An Integrated Circuit that contains two UARTs.

Dynamic Memory Access (DMA): A mechanism to transfer data directly between the memory and an input/output device. A DMA controller is used for this mechanism. DMA controller shares the memory bus with the processor.

Dynamic Random Access Memory (DRAM): A type of RAM which retains the contents if the data is refreshed at regular intervals. It is cheaper than SRAM, but slower, i.e. has longer access time.

eCOS: embedded Configurable Operating System, an open source operating system available under GPL.

Electrically Erasable Programmable ROM (EEPROM): One type of programmable ROM that can be erased electrically by applying a voltage to one of the pins of the IC. In EEPROM, individual bytes can be erased.

Electro-Magnetic Interference (EMI): Interference caused by nearby radio systems. Radio transmitters, electric generators etc. generate radio frequencies which interfere with the operation of the embedded system. Special precautions need to be taken to reduce the effect of EMI.

Engineering Change Note (ECN): A note issued by the project manager informing about any changes to a work product such as requirements specifications document, design document, source code, acceptance test plan etc.

Erasable Programmable Read Only Memory (EPROM): EPROM is programmed using an EPROM programmer. For erasing the contents of the EPROM, EPROM eraser is used. The eraser uses ultraviolet radiation to erase the data on the EPROM.

Execute In Place (XIP): When a program is executed directly from the memory chip such as EPROM or Flash, it is said to be execute-in-place. Generally, a program is transferred to RAM and then executed. Such programs are not XIP programs.

Frequency Hopping (FH): A spread spectrum multiple access technique. In FH, each packet is sent on a separate frequency and the sequence of hopping is pre-decided between the sender and the receiver. Though FH consumes high bandwidth, secrecy is ensured. Bluetooth, 802.11 LAN and GSM systems use FH.

Firmware: Executable software that resides in the ROM of an embedded system. Also, called embedded software.

First-Come-First-Served: A scheduler algorithm in which tasks are executed in the order in which they become ready to run.

Five-nines: A measure of availability of a system. A system has 99.999% uptime (five nines), if its downtime is just five minutes in a year.

Flash file system: A file system stored in Flash memory. Data can be accessed using filenames rather than using memory addresses.

Global Positioning System (GPS): The system developed by Department of Defence, USA to provide location information (longitude, latitude, altitude and time). The system consists of space segment with a set of 24 NAVSTAR satellites, earth stations to control and monitor the satellites and GPS receivers which are now embedded into many consumer items such as wrist watches, cell phones, PDAs etc.

GNU: A project launched in 1984 to create a free Unix-like operating system. This project gave birth to free software revolution.

GNU Public License (GPL): GPL gives the guidelines for usage and distribution of free software. You can use the GNU tools to write your applications and commercialize them. But you need to supply the source code of the modifications done.

Handheld Operating System: An operating system ported on the handheld computers. Palm OS, Symbian OS, Windows CE and Embedded Linux are the most widely used handheld operating systems.

Hard real-time system: A system in which tasks have to be completed within strict deadlines. If a task is not completed within the stipulated time, it may lead to a catastrophe.

Hardware-in-the-loop (HIL) simulation: A simulation technique in which the target hardware (or a part of the target hardware) and software are integrated for laboratory testing. HIL simulation is done when the full-fledged testing cannot be done in the laboratory (for example, to test a missile guidance system, satellite subsystems etc.)

Harvard architecture: Processor architecture in which two pairs of buses are used to access program memory and data memory. This architecture is used in Digital Signal Processors extensively.

Host system: In embedded software development, the machine on which the software is initially developed. The software development tools hosted on this machine are used to develop an executable image of the embedded software. This executable image is later transferred to the target processor board (target system) through a communication link such as RS232, USB, Ethernet or JTAG port.

HP-IB bus: Hewlett-Packard Interface Bus. A bus to control instruments such as oscilloscopes, logic analyzers, signal analyzers and also data acquisition boards. A maximum of 15 devices can be connected to the bus. This bus has been renamed by IEEE as GPIB bus (General Purpose Interface Bus) and the standard is specified in IEEE 488.2-1987.

In-Circuit Emulator (ICE): A tool to debug embedded software. ICE emulates (takes the place of) a processor on the target board.

Instruction cycle: Time required to fetch and execute one opcode.

Instruction Pointer: A register in the processor that contains the address of the next instruction that has to be executed.

Instruction Set: The complete list of opcodes recognized by a processor.

Intel Hex format: An ASCII format for binary image to be loaded into ROM. The format is developed by Intel Corporation.

Intellectual Property core: The vendor-proprietary core or hardware object that can be purchased and included in your FPGA design. DSP core, Micro-controller core etc. are available to develop ASICs.

Internet appliance: An appliance connected to the Internet. In future, many embedded systems will be connected to the Internet. Your door-lock can be an Internet appliance that can be accessed through the browser of your office desktop—you can open it sitting at you office. Your refrigerator can in an

Internet appliance that can order for milk packets.

Interrupt: A signal from a peripheral to the processor. On occurrence of an interrupt, the processor executes an ISR and then goes back to the previously running task.

Interrupt controller: A device that controls multiple interrupts. The interrupt controller's job is to accept and assign priorities to the interrupts and inform the requests to the processor.

Interrupt latency: The delay between interrupt assert signal and the start of the ISR.

Interrupt priority: The priority given to the interrupt. The order of execution of the ISR depends on this priority.

Interrupt Service Routine (ISR): The code that gets executed in response to an interrupt.

Interrupt vector: The address of an Interrupt Service Routine.

Interrupt vector table: The table containing the interrupt vectors.

IP address: The unique identification given to a device on the Internet. In future, many embedded systems including mobile phones, PDAs, web cameras etc. will be given unique IP addresses. In IP version 4, the IP address length is 32 bits and in IP version 6, the address length is 128 bits.

IP Phone: A phone that uses the TCP/IP protocols for voice communication. IP phone can be connected to a data network such as the Ethernet, and the voice transmission takes place in the form of packets.

IP version 4: The version of IP protocol that is presently running. In this version, the IP address is 32 bits. The limited number of addresses, lack of support for real-time applications, lack of security are the main drawbacks of this version.

IP version 6: The next version of Internet Protocol that will be deployed after IP version 4. In this version, the IP address length is 128 bits. Support for real-time applications, increased security features and modified IP headers for fast processing are the main attractions of IP version 6.

ISM band: Industrial, Scientific and Medical band. Radio systems operating in these frequency bands do not need any prior government approval, i.e. ISM band is a free band. IEEE 802.11 Local Area Networks and Bluetooth operate in this band.

Java 2 Micro Edition (J2ME): Java class libraries for developing applications for devices with limited capabilities such as mobile phones, PDAs etc.

Java Virtual Machine (JVM): Software that converts the Java bytecode into machine code and executes it.

Jini: Jini connection technology, developed by Sun Microsystems, facilitates development of dynamic distributed systems. Any device can be Jini-enabled by running a small piece of code. Jini-enabled devices can form a network to share services. The network can be formed automatically when two or more devices come near to each other.

Kernel: The 'heart' of an operating system. Kernel is responsible for task scheduling, inter-task communication, interrupt handling, providing timer service, device management and memory management.

K Virtual Machine (KVM): Java virtual machine that occupies very little memory—just a few Kilobytes. It is used in small devices such as mobile phones and pagers.

Linear Predictive Coding (LPC): A coding technique extensively used for low bit rate coding of voice signals. In LPC, each sample is predicted as a linear combination of past samples. Variations of this coding technique are used in GSM phones and Internet telephony.

Linker: A software tool that combines a number of object files into a single object file, which is a relocatable program.

Lint: Unix utility to check the portability of a C program.

Lithium battery: Battery used extensively in embedded systems due to its lightweight and long life.

Little-endian format: A data representation format in which the least significant byte of a multi-byte value is stored at the lowest memory address. Intel 80x86 processors use this format.

Locator: A software tool that assigns physical memory addresses to a relocatable program. The resultant file is called the executable code.

Lookup table: A table from which you can pick up the desired values. For instance, instead of writing a program to calculate factorial of say 20 numbers, you can create a lookup table containing the numbers and their factorials. For a given number, you can look up and pick up its factorial fast.

Mean Time Between Failures (MTBF): The average time between two failures of a system. MTBF is a measure of reliability of the system.

Memory cycle time: The total time required for a memory device to start and complete an access.

Message queue: A data structure used in an operating system to pass data between two or more threads.

Metrics: Measures used for product quality and process quality. Time, effort and budget required to carry out different phases of software development, MTBF, MTTR, MTTF, number of changes proposed/accepted in different documents such as requirements document, design document etc. are the important metrics to be collected during the development of the embedded system.

Micro-controller: A processor along with RAM, ROM and other peripherals such as UART, ADC, DAC etc. on the same silicon. Microchip's PIC, Intel 8051, Motorola 68HCxx are examples.

MicroC/OS-II: A real-time operating system for micro-controllers. Developed by Jean Labrosse.

Multitasking: Execution of multiple tasks or threads concurrently or pseudo-simultaneously.

Mutex: Short for mutual exclusion. A binary flag used for managing shared resources. A mutex prevents different tasks to access shared resources simultaneously. The shared resource can be a block of memory, a global variable, a register or a peripheral.

Nibble: four bits.

Non-maskable interrupt: An interrupt which cannot be disabled.

Non-preemptive scheduling: A scheduling algorithm in which a task cannot be stopped from running till it is completed e.g., DOS (Disk Operating System) uses non-preemptive scheduling.

Non-reentrant function: A function in which data will be corrupted if more than one task uses it. If you use global variables in a function, it is a non-reentrant function.

Non-volatile memory: A memory device which retains its data even if power is switched off, e.g. PROM, EPROM, NVRAM.

Null modem cable: A cable used to interconnect two data terminal equipments such as PCs for serial communication using RS232 standard.

Nyquist rate: The rate at which sampling has to be done. If a signal has a bandwidth of B Hz, according to Nyquist theorem, the minimum sampling rate is 2B samples/second. This is a fundamental theorem using which analog signal is converted into digital format.

Object-Oriented Design (OOD): A design methodology wherein the objects are used to represent real-life models. Encapsulation, polymorphism and inheritance are the three important concepts of object-oriented design.

Open source software: A revolutionary movement that makes software free. The complete source code will be made available by the developer.

Oscilloscope: An instrument to view the time domain waveforms.

OSI reference model: Open System Interconnection reference model. The protocol architecture developed for computer communication by International Organization for Standardization (ISO). In this model, there are seven layers of protocols: physical, data link, network, transport, session, presentation and application layers. Though networks based on OSI protocol suite did not become popular (due to the competition from the TCP/IP networks), OSI model is considered a "reference model".

Parity bit: Extra bit added for error detection. Parity can be even, odd or none. If the data to be transmitted is 1010111, an additional bit is added which is called the parity bit. For even parity, the parity bit will make the total number of 1's even. So, the bits transmitted are 10101111. In the case of odd parity, the parity bit will make the number of 1's odd. So, the bits transmitted will be 10101110.

PC/104: A standard for interconnecting computer boards. A number of computer boards can be stacked instead of using a motherboard.

PCI bus: A high-speed bus used in PCs. PCI replaced the ISA bus.

Peripheral: An input/output device connected to the processor. The peripherals can be on the same silicon as the processor as in the case of micro-controllers or, they can be connected externally to the processor.

Peripheral Interface Controller (PIC): PIC processors of Microchip are powerful processors for small embedded applications. Example: PIC 12C508, PIC16C73.

Personal Area Network (PAN): A network of devices in a small area of about 10 meters. Devices such as desktop, laptop, palmtop, mobile phone, fax machine, digital camera etc. can form a network to make it a PAN. Bluetooth and IEEE 802.11b are the popular PAN technologies.

Personal Software Process (PSP): A software development process to be followed by software engineers. It was developed by Watts Humphrey at Software Engineering Institute, Carnegie Mellon University. The philosophy of PSP is simple: plan your work, track your work and do a postmortem analysis—this approach leads to a better plan, better product and better person. Advice of a great sage—wish every software developer follows it.

Polling: To read a status register periodically to check whether a device reached the desired state. Polling and interrupt driven mechanisms are used to interface a peripheral to a processor.

Porting: The process of modifying the software developed on one platform to another platform.

Portability: The characteristic of a software package that can run on different platforms. If the platform-dependent features are not used while writing the code, the software is portable.

Portable Operating System Interface (POSIX): IEEE Standard for API for Unix and Unix-like like operating systems. Many commercial and open source operating systems are now POSIX-compliant. POSIX standards are available for C, ADA and FORTRAN.

Pulse Code Modulation (PCM): A coding technique to convert analog signals into digital format. Used extensively for conversion of voice signals into digital format. Voice signals band-limited to 4 KHz are sampled at 8000 samples per second and each sample is quantized using 8 bits to obtain 64 Kbps data rate. ITU-T recommendation G.711 gives the specifications for PCM coding of voice signals.

Real-Time System: A system in which strict deadlines are imposed to complete specific tasks.

Recursive function: A function that calls itself. To calculate factorial of a number, Fibonacci number, to solve Towers of Hanoi problem etc., recursion is used. Recursive functions have to be avoided in embedded software.

Reduced Instruction Set Computer (RISC): A processor with fixed length opcodes, load-store memory architecture and large number of registers.

Reentrant function: A function that can be used by more than one task without data corruption.

Regression testing: A testing methodology which specifies that whenever you modify the software, you need to test the complete functionality to ensure that the modifications do not have adverse impact on other parts of the program.

Round-robin: A scheduling algorithm in which all the tasks get the CPU share one after the other.

Royalty: A fee to be paid to the vendor/author of a software package when it is sold. If you use a commercial operating system for your embedded system, the operating system vendor may ask for a royalty for each copy of the runtime operating system code bundled with your firmware.

RS232: Electronic Industries Association (EIA) standard for serial communication. Very widely used in embedded systems. Data rates up to 115.2 Kbps can be supported by RS232 with a distance up to 100 meters. Likely to be replaced by Universal Serial Bus (USB) in coming years.

RS422: EIA standard for serial data communication over large distances in noisy environments. Maximum data rate is 10 Mbps and distance 1200 meters. four wires are used—2 for transmission and two for reception.

RS485: EIA standard for serial data communication over large distances in noisy environments, in multi-drop mode. Up to 32 devices can be connected. Data rate up to 10 Mbps and distances up to 1200 meters are supported.

Peripheral: Device connected to the processor. Memory, UART, ADC, DAC etc. are the peripherals.

Protocol analyzer: An instrument to analyze communication protocols such as X.25, Ethernet, ISDN, ATM, Frame Relay etc.

Protocol stack: The layers of protocols used for communication between two or more devices. TCP/IP and ISO/OSI protocol stacks are the most widely known stacks. Also referred to as protocol suite.

Pseudocode: A simple representation of an algorithm—looks like code, but not really.

Pseudorandom number generator: A software/hardware component that generates numbers which appear random. The C functions srand() and rand() are used to generate pseudorandom numbers. srand() function initializes the sequence. A call to rand() generates a random number.

Preemption: To stop or suspend a running task. A low priority task is preempted to run a high priority task.

Preemptive scheduling: A scheduling algorithm in which tasks are preempted based on their priority levels. Such a scheduling is a must in real-time systems.

Priority Queue: A data structure in which the queue is formed based on priority. Unlike the normal queue in which First In First Out (FIFO)/Last In First Out (LIFO) is done, jumping a queue is possible in priority queue.

Process: In a multi-user system, the "job" to be done. Each process will have its own virtual memory space. One or more threads can run in the memory space of each process.

Process ID: The unique identification given to each process.

Process ID table: The table that contains the details of the process along with the process ID. Also called Process Control Block or Task Control Block.

Processor: Generic word used for a micro-controller, micro-processor, digital signal processor.

Profiler: Software utility that gives the statistics of the software in terms of number of calls to a function, the time taken for each function execution etc.

QNX Neutrino: QNX Software System's real-time operating system.

Quality Assurance: The mechanism to ensure quality in each and every phase of development. QA addresses technical and managerial issues involved in the development.

Queue: Data structure in which the first element inserted is taken out first. Also called FIFO data structure. Variations of queue are: (a) priority queue in which each element is given a priority, and an element with a higher priority can jump the queue; (b) circular queue in which the tail of the queue merges with the front of the queue; (c) double-ended queue in which the elements can be inserted at front and rear of the queue.

Radio Frequency Interference (RFI): Unwanted radio frequency components in the desired frequency band. RFI is caused by nearby radio transmitters, electric generators etc.

Revision Control System: GNU's software utility for version and release control. Equivalent of SCCS (Source Code Control System) of Unix.

Real Time Clock (RTC): A hardware device for maintaining the time of the day information.

Real-Time Operating System (RTOS): An operating system that is deterministic. To implement real-time embedded systems, RTOS is required.

Sampling rate: The rate at which the amplitudes of the time-domain signals are measured. The minimum sampling rate is twice the bandwidth of the time-domain signal. For example, voice signal has a bandwidth of 4 KHz and hence the minimum sampling rate is 8000 samples per second or one sample every 125 microseconds.

Single Board Computer (SBC): A computer with all the peripheral devices on the same Printed Circuit Board as the processor. SBC is used in embedded systems.

Scheduler: One module of the operating system kernel that decides which task has to run next, based on the scheduling algorithm, priorities of the tasks etc.

Scheduling algorithm: The algorithm based on which the scheduling is done. Shortest job first, earliest deadline first, run-to-completion and preemptive priority-based scheduling are some of the algorithms.

Semaphore: A data structure used for inter-task synchronization. Two types of semaphores are: binary semaphores and counting semaphores. Semaphore is like a key to access a resource. The task that wants to access the resource acquires the semaphore, uses the resource and then releases the semaphore.

Shared memory: A block of memory that can be written/read by two or more processors.

Shortest job first: A scheduling algorithm in which the task that requires the least time will be executed first. This is a non-preemptive scheduling algorithm. Not a good choice for embedded systems. Maximum number of users will be satisfied using this algorithm, though.

Significant lines of code: In a source code, the number of lines excluding the blank lines, comments etc.

Smart card: A card with an in-built micro-controller and memory. Smart card is of the size of a credit card. The data in the smart card can be read by a smart card reader. The applications include payment cards, SIM card in mobile phones, digital security, electronic voting, patient information storage etc.

Smart phone: Phones integrated with palmtop computers. These phones are built around powerful processors. An operating system such as Palm OS, Symbian OS, Windows CE is ported on to it.

Soft deadline: If a deadline is missed and nothing catastrophic happens, the deadline is called soft deadline. CD players, IP phones etc. are examples of systems that will have soft deadlines.

Soft key: Software defined input.

Soft real-time system: An embedded system in which even if deadlines are missed occasionally, nothing catastrophic happens.

Software engineering: The discipline which gives the guidelines for systematic development of software. Software engineering addresses the technical, managerial and administrative issues related to development of software. It is "A disciplined, systematic and quantitative approach to software development' as defined in IEEE standards.

Software interrupt: Interrupt issued by a software routine.

Software prototyping: Development of a small working model. Note that software prototyping is done to obtain the user requirements whereas hardware prototyping is done to prove the design concepts.

SourceSafe: The version and release control software of Microsoft.

Spectrum analyzer: Test instrument that analyzes and displays the signals in frequency domain.

Spread Spectrum Multiple Access (SSMA): A multiple access technique used in radio systems. Frequency Hopping (FH) and Direct Sequence Code Division Multiple Access (DS-CDMA) are the two types of SSMA.

Stack: Data structure in which the last element inserted is taken out first. Also called Last In First Out data structure.

Status bit: The bit that indicates the status of a processor or a peripheral. Also called status flag.

Stop bits: The bits that are appended to the information bits to indicate the end of a character.

Symbol table: The data structure implemented as part of the compiler that keeps a list of all the variables and their data types.

Synchronous bus: A bus with clock in the control lines.

Synchronous communication: Communication in which a clock signal is used in addition to data. Transitions in the clock signals indicate the presence of data. Synchronous communication is more efficient than asynchronous communication.

System-on-Chip (SOC): A single Integrated Circuit that houses a processor, memory and input/output devices. It can be an FPGA or an ASIC.

Task: A job that has to be performed by an operating system. These jobs are referred as processes on desktop operating systems and as tasks in embedded systems. Task and process are similar in the sense that both compete for CPU time independently. The subtle difference is that processes have better memory management capability. Task/process is a divided into different threads. The different threads in a task can run independently but they share variables.

Task ID: A unique identification given to each task by the operating system.

Task states: The states in which a task can be. Ready-to-run, running and waiting (or blocked) states are the three task states.

TCP/IP: Transmission Control Protocol/Internet Protocol stack is the protocol suite that runs on each and every machine connected to the Internet. Above the TCP, application layer software will be running, such as SMTP and MIME for email, FTP for file transfer, HTTP for web access.

Test cases: A set of input parameters/conditions identified to test the software.

Test jig: A custom-built hardware to test an embedded system.

Test point: A specific point on the Printed Circuit Board to test the hardware.

Timeout: Expiry of a timer set for a particular value.

Timing diagram: A graphical representation of a circuit's timing. Timing diagrams are used to study the response times and to check whether the embedded system meets the time constraints.

Transducer: A device that converts the physical phenomena into equivalent electrical signal and vice versa. A microphone converts the acoustic waves into electrical signal. The speakers convert the electrical waves into acoustic waves.

Trivial File Transfer Protocol (TFTP): A file transfer protocol that can be implemented on embedded systems to upgrade the software in the field, through a communication interface such as RS232, USB or Ethernet.

"Trust but Verify": Famous words of the former US President Ronald Reagan after he signed the Inter-Continental Ballistic Missile treaty with the erstwhile USSR. Remember these words when your colleague says "my software/hardware module is working fine, and the problem is only with your module".

Unicode: 16-bit representation of characters in the computer. Any character of any world language can be represented by Unicode. Java, C99 and XML support Unicode.

Unified Modeling Language (UML): A graphical notation to represent specifications and design.

Universal Asynchronous Receive/Transmit (UART): A device that transmits and receives asynchronous data.

Universal Serial Bus USB): A standard serial bus that supports higher data rates than RS232. Up to 127 devices can be connected to a USB host. USB 2.0 supports 480 Mbps data rate.

Universal Plug and Play (UpnP): A concept for creating dynamic networking environment. The concept is to create administration-free networking. Just plug in the device, and it starts working.

UV Eraser: A device that radiates Ultra Violet (UV) rays to erase data in the EPROM.

Verilog: A Hardware Description Language

Version and Release Control Software: A software utility that facilitates keeping track of various versions of a software package. SCCS, CVS, RCS, Visual SourceSafe are the popular version and release control software utilities.

Virtual Instrument: Instrument developed using PC or workstation as the hardware platform. National Instruments' Labview is the one of the popular lab instrumentation development tools. Oscilloscopes, spectrum analyzers, signal analyzers etc. can be developed using such development tools.

Voice over IP (VoIP): Voice communication over IP-based packet networks. In the telephone network, voice communication is achieved through circuit switching whereas in VoIP, it is done through packet switching.

VxWorks: The Real Time Operating System of Wind River Systems.

Watchdog Timer: A timer used to reset the processor in an embedded system. A timer is set to a large value and is counted down. When the timer value reaches zero, the processor is reset. If everything is fine with the processor, the timer is reset to the large value before it reaches zero.

Waterfall model: A software development life cycle model in which the development process is divided into the following stages: requirements engineering, design, implementation, testing and maintenance.

Web Server: A server that provides the web service. To access a web page, the client gives a URL and the resource corresponding to the URL that resides on the web server is downloaded to the client in the form of HTML pages. IIS, Apache WebServer, IBM WebSphere are some of the popular web servers.

White noise: A noise signal in which all the frequency components are present. The spectrum of white noise is flat.

Wireless Application Protocol (WAP): The protocol stack used to provide wireless Internet access from mobile devices such as mobile phones, PDAs etc. WAP is a light-weight protocol as compared to TCP/IP, i.e. it has less protocol overhead.

Wireless LAN: A Local Area Network in which the nodes communicate using free space as transmission medium using radio technology. IEEE 802.11 and HiperLAN are the two popular wireless LAN technologies.

Wireless Markup Language (WML): A markup language used in Wireless Application Protocol (WAP) to provide wireless Internet access. WML is based on XML but supports only limited number of tags as compared to HTML.

Write-only Memory: A memory device onto which you can write, but you cannot read the contents. Can you think of some applications for such a device?

Xilinx: A popular semiconductor vendor known for the FPGA and ASIC technology.

XML: Extensible Markup Language. A meta-language using which you can develop your own markup language. XHTML, WML, VoiceXML etc. have been developed based on XML. Just as Java achieves code portability, XML achieves data portability.

Y2K: Short for the year 2000. During 1997-1999, it was expected that most of the embedded systems would crash due to the change of date to the new millennium on 1st Jan 2000. Nothing drastic happened, the only beneficiary of the so-called Y2K problem was the Indian software community that made big bucks fixing the Y2K bug.

Yacc: yet another compiler compiler. A utility in the Unix and its variants. Using lex and yacc, you can develop new programming languages. Lex is a lexical analyzer and yacc is a parser for a defined grammar.

Yield: A task will 'yield' to another task in a multitasking operating system.

ZIF Socket: Zero Insertion Force Socket. An IC socket designed in such a way that insertion and removal of an IC is very easy with zero insertion force.

Appendix B

Acronyms and Abbreviations

2G	2nd Generation (wireless networks)
3G	3rd Generation (wireless networks)
ACK	Acknowledgement
ACL	Asynchronous Connection Less (link)
ACM	Association for Computing Machinery
ADC	Analog-to-Digital Converter
ADSL	Asymmetric Digital Subscriber Line
ALE	Address Latch Enable
ALU	Arithmetic Logic Unit
AM	Amplitude Modulation
ANSI	American National Standards Institute
API	Application Programming Interface
ARM	Advanced RISC Machine
ASCII	American Standard Code for Information Interchange
ASIC	Application Specific Integrated Circuit
ASK	Amplitude Shift Keying
ATE	Automatic Test Equipment
BCD	Binary Coded Decimal
BDM	Background Debug Mode
BER	Bit Error Rate
BGA	Ball Grid Array
BIOS	Basic Input/Output System
BIST	Built-In Self Test
BOM	Bill of Materials
bps	Bits Per Second

BREW	Binary Runtime Environment for Wireless
BSD	Berkeley Standard Distribution
CAN	Controller Area Network
CASE	Computer Aided Software Engineering
CCD	Charge Coupled Device
CCITT	International Telegraph and Telephone Consultative Committee
CDC	Connected Device Configuration
CISC	Complex Instruction Set Computer
CLB	Configurable Logic Block
CLDC	Connected, Limited Device Configuration
CLID	Calling Line Identification Device
CMOS	Complementary Metal-Oxide Silicon
COFF	Common Object File Format
COTS	Commercial Off The Shelf (equipment)
CPLD	Complex Programmable Logic Device
CPU	Central Processing Unit
CRC	Cyclic Redundancy Check
CR/LF	Carriage Return/Line Feed
CS	Chip Select
CTS	Clear To Send
CVSD	Continuously Variable Slope Delta (modulation)
DAC	Digital-to-Analog Converter
DC	Direct Current
DDK	Device Driver Kit
DDS	Direct Digital Synthesizer
DIMM	Dual Inline Memory Module
DIP	Dual Inline Plastic
DLL	Dynamically Linked Library
DMA	Dynamic Memory Access
DOS	Disk Operating System
DPRAM	Dual Port Random Access Memory
DRAM	Dynamic Random Access Memory
DSL	Digital Subscriber Line
DSO	Digital Storage Oscilloscope

DSP	Digital Signal Processor
DTE	Data Terminal Equipment
DTR	Data Terminal Ready
DVM	Digital Volt Meter
ECL	Emitter Coupled Logic
ECN	Engineering Change Note
eCOS	Embedded Configurable Operating System
EEMBC	EDN Embedded Microprocessor Benchmarking Consortium
EEPLD	Electrically Erasable Programmable Logic Device
EEPROM	Electrically Erasable Programmable Read Only Memory
ELCPS	Embedded Linux Consortium Platform Specifications
ELF	Executable and Linking Format
EMI	Electro-Magnetic Interference
EMV	Europay, MasterCard, Visa
EOF	End Of File
EPLD	Erasable Programmable Logic Device
EPROM	Erasable Programmable Read Only Memory
FCC	Federal Communications Commission
FFS	Flash File System
FIFO	First In First Out
FM	Frequency Modulation
FPGA	Field Programmable Gate Array
FPU	Floating Point Unit
GAL	Generic Array Logic
GB	GigaBytes
GFSK	Gaussian Frequency Shift Keying
GIGO	Garbage In Garbage Out
GMT	Greenwich Mean Time
GNU	Gnu's Not Unix
GNUCC	GNU Compiler Collection
GPIB	General Purpose Interface Bus
GPL	GNU Public License
GPOS	General Purpose Operating System
GPP	General Purpose Processor

GPS	Global Positioning System
GUI	Graphical User Interface
HDL	Hardware Description Language
HILS	Hardware In the Loop Simulation
HPIB	Hewlett Packard Interface Bus
HTML	Hyper Text Markup Language
HTTP	Hyper Text Transfer Protocol
I/O	Input/Output
I^2C	Inter-Integrated Circuit (bus)
IC	Integrated Circuit
ICE	In-Circuit Emulator
ICP	In-Circuit Programming
IDE	Integrated Development Environment
IEEE	Institute of Electrical and Electronics Engineers
IETF	Internet Engineering Task Force
INT	Interrupt
IP	Internet Protocol/Instruction Pointer
IPC	Inter-Process Communication
IrDA	Infrared Data Association
IRQ	Interrupt Request
ISM	Industrial, Scientific and Medical (band)
ISO	International Organization for Standardization
ISR	Interrupt Service Routine
ISS	Instruction Set Simulator
ITU	International Telecommunications Union
IVR	Interactive Voice Response
J2EE	Java2 Enterprise Edition
J2ME	Java 2 Micro Edition
J2SE	Java 2 Standard Edition
JAR	Java Archive
JCWS	Java Card Web Servlet
JDK	Java Development Kit
JIT	Just In Time (compiler)
JNI	Java Native Interface

JTAG	Joint Test Action Group
JVM	Java Virtual Machine
KB	Kilo Bytes
Kbps	Kilo bits per second
KVM	Kilobytes Virtual Machine
LAN	Local Area Network
LCD	Liquid Crystal Display
LED	Light Emitting Diode
LIFO	Last In First Out
LOC	Lines of Code
LSB	Least Significant Bit
LSI	Large Scale Integration
LUT	Look Up Table
MAC	Multiply And Accumulate/Medium Access Control
MAN	Metropolitan Area Network
MEMS	Micro-Electro-Mechanical Systems
MIPS	Millions of Instructions Per Second
MISRA	Motor Industry Software Reliability Association
MMU	Memory Management Unit
MOS	Metal Oxide Semiconductor
MP3	MPEG Layer 3
MSB	Most Significant Bit
MSI	Medium Scale Integration
MSPS	Mega Samples Per Second
MTBF	Mean Time Between Failures
MTTF	Mean Time To Fail
MTTR	Mean Time To Repair
mW	milliWatt
NMI	Non-Maskable Interrupt
NVRAM	Non-Volatile Random Access Memory
OCD	On-Chip Debugging
OLED	Organic Light Emitting Diode
OOD	Object-Oriented Design
OOP	Object-Oriented Programming

OS	Operating System
OSI	Open System Interconnection
OTP	One Time Programmable
PAL	Programmable Array Logic
PAN	Personal Area Network
PC	Personal Computer/Program Counter
PCB	Printed Circuit Board
PCI	Peripheral Component Interconnect
PCM	Pulse Code Modulation
PDA	Personal Digital Assistant
PDU	Protocol Data Unit
PIC	Peripheral Interface Controller/Programmable Interrupt Controller
PLC	Programmable Logic Controller
PLCC	Plastic Leadless Chip Carrier
PLD	Programmable Logic Device
POSIX	Portable Operating System Interface
POST	Power On Self-Test
PROM	Programmable Read Only Memory
PSU	Power Supply Unit
QA	Quality Assurance
QPSK	Quadrature Phase Shift Keying
RAM	Random Access Memory
RCS	Revision Control System
RF	Radio Frequency
RFI	Radio Frequency Interference
RISC	Reduced Instruction Set Computer
RMI	Remote Method Invocation
ROM	Read Only Memory
RTC	Real Time Clock
RTOS	Real Time Operating System
RTSJ	Real-Time Specification for Java
SBC	Single Board Computer
SCO	Synchronous Connection Oriented (link)
SDK	Software Development Kit
SHARC	Super-Harvard Architecture
SIM	Subscriber Identity Module

SIMM	Single Inline Memory Module
SNR	Signal to Noise Ratio
SOC	System on Chip
SP	Stack Pointer
SRAM	Static Random Access Memory
SRS	Software Requirements Specifications
STB	Set Top Box
TAP	Test Access Port
TAPI	Telephony Application Programming Interface
TCP	Transmission Control Protocol
TDD	Time Division Duplex
TDM	Time Division Multiplexing
TDMA	Time Division Multiple Access
TFTP	Trivial File Transfer Protocol
TTL	Transistor Transistor Logic
UART	Universal Asynchronous Receiver Transmitter
UDP	User Datagram Protocol
UML	Unified Modeling Language
UPnP	Universal Plug and Play
UPS	Uninterrupted Power Supply
USB	Universal Serial Bus
UV	Ultra Violet (radiation)
UWB	Ultra Wide Band
VHDL	VHSIC Hardware Design Language
VHSIC	Very High Speed Integrated Circuit
VLIW	Very Long Instruction Word
VLSI	Very Large Scale Integration
VME	Versa Module Euro-card
VoIP	Voice over Internet Protocol
WAP	Wireless Application Protocol
WDT	Watch Dog Timer
WiFi	Wireless Fidelity
WLAN	Wireless Local Area Network
WML	Wireless Markup Language
XIP	Execute In Place
XML	Extensible Markup Language
ZIF	Zero Insertion Force (socket)

Appendix C

Solutions to Selected Exercises

Chapter 1

1. Mobile devices such as the mobile phone, pager, digital dairy are embedded systems because they do a focused, specific job and the software is fixed for the application. However, devices such as handheld computers can be used to do many general-purpose tasks such as word processing, playing games etc. It is also possible to download a new software package onto the handheld computer from the desktop. However, they are also considered as embedded systems, as designing these systems is akin to designing any other embedded system due to limited resources, limited input/output device capabilities, need for low power consumption etc.
2. Military applications of embedded systems are quite many. Radars have embedded systems that do the signal processing to identify the flying objects such as aircraft and missiles. Tankers and missiles use navigation systems for location finding. Surveillance aircraft contain embedded systems that send video data of the enemy territory. Night vision equipment used by soldiers is an embedded system. Communication systems used to intercept enemy signals are embedded systems. Jamming and anti-jamming communication systems are built around embedded systems.
3. The major manufacturers of micro-controllers and microprocessors are: AMD, ARM, Atmel, Hitachi, IBM, Intel, Microchip, Mitsubishi, Motorola, National Semiconductors, NEC, Philips, Samsung, Sun Microsystems, Texas Instruments, Toshiba and Zilog. You can obtain the details of their products from their websites.
4. The major manufacturers of digital signal processors are Analog Devices, Lucent Technologies, Motorola and Texas Instruments.
5. Because of the small size of a palmtop computer, there is no full-fledged keyboard and hence it is difficult to input text. The options provided are: (a) you can attach a full-fledged keyboard while working in the office; (b) you can use Graffiti for writing the alphabets and digits, which will be recognized by the software and the corresponding character is displayed; you need to learn how to write letters and digits in Graffiti so that the computer can recognize accurately; and (c) you can use the soft keypad and stylus to enter the text. A new technology is emerging wherein the full keyboard layout is projected onto your table from the palmtop and when you type on this layout, the software will recognize which key is pressed. A sensor on the palmtop computer will sense the key pressed and the software will identify the key. An optical system is used to project the keyboard on any surface.

Chapter 2

1. The temperature varies from –20 degrees to +60 degrees and hence the range is 80 degrees. Since the resolution is 0.1 degree, the number of quantization levels is 800. Hence, a 10-bit ADC is a required. A 12-bit ADC chip can be used because, 10-bit ADC is not commonly available.
2. To process music signals, a high-resolution ADC is required. The music signals have a bandwidth of 20 KHz. Hence, the minimum sampling rate is 40 KHz. An ADC of 40 KHz sampling rate and 16-bit resolution is required to process music signals.
3. Though the desktop computers use multi-tasking operating systems, they cannot meet real-time performance because a particular process cannot be locked in the memory to meet a specified deadline. The task scheduling algorithm does not permit the mechanism of a task obtaining the CPU time to complete its time-critical work. Of course, they can be used for soft real-time applications but not hard real-time applications.
4. Unix, in its original flavour, is not a real-time operating system. It is a multitasking operating system, but a user cannot give a high priority to a task and get it executed at the cost of other processes. The nice command in Unix permits priority assignment, but you can make your process a lower priority. Unix is based on cooperative multitasking scheduling. Of course, there are now many variations of Unix that are tailored to meet real-time requirements.
5. The desktop computers we use for regular office work for applications such as word processing, spreadsheets, games, Internet access etc., do not need a real-time operating system. For applications such as IP telephony or desktop video conferencing, soft real-time operating system will suffice and the desktop operating systems meet this soft real-time performance requirement.
6. The embedded/real-time operating systems can be compared using the following criteria:
   - The memory occupied by the operating system (called the footprint)
   - Portability (what percentage of the code is written in assembly language and what percentage in a portable high-level language such as C).
   - Scalability—whether the operating system can be ported to 8-bit, 16-bit, 32-bit and 64-bit processors.
   - Application Programming Interface: Every operating system vendor gives a Graphical User Interface (GUI) based Integrated Development Environment consisting of editor, compiler, debugger etc. The API should be based on a standard called Portable Operating System Interface (POSIX) developed by IEEE.
   - The OS features such as the availability of different task schedulers, number of tasks that can be created.
   - Support for C, C++ and Java
   - Support for protocol stacks such as TCP/IP, Bluetooth, Infrared and IEEE 802.11 wireless interface.
   - Cost of the development system and the cost of the runtime copy.

7. Palm OS, Symbian OS, Windows CE, Windows CE.NET are the most widely used mobile/handheld operating systems. Embedded Linux and Real-time operating systems such as VxWorks, OS/9, QNX Neutrino are also being ported on handheld computers.
8. Here are some embedded systems that are hard real-time systems:
   (a) Navigation system used in aircraft and missiles.
   (b) Process control systems that are used to control valves, or drive stepper motors or servomotors in process industry.
   (c) A software-defined radio system which has to generate a specified radio signal within the stipulated time.

   In all these systems, a hard real-time operating system such as RTLinux, OS/9, VXWorks, QNX Neutrino, MicroC/OS-II or VRTX is used.
9. ROM is read-only memory. RAM is read-write memory. WOM is a write-only memory but you cannot read what is written. A chip from which you cannot read what is written is not of any use in many practical applications. If you are angry with your boss or your spouse, you can create a WOM chip that contains all sorts of abuses, and then present it to your boss or spouse. You got rid of your anger and you are safe, too!

Chapter 3

1. The program to calculate the CRC-16 for a fie is given below:

   Listing C.1: CRC16file.c

```
/*
   This program is for calculating crc16 for a file.
*/

#include <stdlib.h>
#include <stdio.h>
#include <string.h>

unsigned int CRCfor16(int initialCRC, char *String, int length);

unsigned int CRCLookupTable[16] = {
  0x0000, 0xCC01, 0xD801, 0x1400, 0xF001, 0x3C00, 0x2800, 0xE401,
  0xA001, 0x6C00, 0x7800, 0xB401, 0x5000, 0x9C01, 0x8801, 0x4400
};
int main(int argc,char *argv[])
{
   unsigned int FinalCRC;
   int initialCRC = 0x00,i=0;
   char ch;
```

```
char String[1024],*filename;
FILE *fp;

if(argc > 1)
{
filename=argv[1];
   fp=fopen(filename,"r");
   if(fp==NULL){
      printf("File doesn't exist \n");
      return 1;
   }
   else
   {
      do
      {
         ch=fgetc(fp);
         //printf("%c\n",ch);
         if(ch != EOF)
            String[i++]=ch;
      }while(ch!=EOF);
      //String[i]='\0';
      FinalCRC = CRCfor16(initialCRC,&String[0],(i-1)/
*strlen(String)*/);
      printf("CRC: 0x%x \n",FinalCRC);
      fclose(fp);
   }

}
else
   printf("Usage: ./a.out temp.txt\n");
return 0;
}
unsigned int CRCfor16(int initialCRC, char *String, int length)
{
unsigned int CRCVALUE =initialCRC ;
int temp;
int i;
for(i=0;i<length;i++)
{
   //checksum for lower 4 bits
   temp = CRCLookupTable[CRCVALUE & 0xF];
```

```
    CRCVALUE = (CRCVALUE >> 4) & 0x0FFF;
   CRCVALUE = CRCVALUE ^ temp ^ CRCLookupTable[*String & 0xF];

    //checksum for upper 4 bits
    temp = CRCLookupTable[CRCVALUE & 0xF];
    CRCVALUE = (CRCVALUE >> 4) & 0x0FFF;
   CRCVALUE = CRCVALUE ^ temp ^ CRCLookupTable[(*String >> 4)
& 0xF];
    String++;
  }
  return(CRCVALUE);
}
```

2. You can modify the program CRC16.c to implement CRC-CCITT algorithm.
3. You can modify the RS232 software given in Chapter 6 for file transfer.
4. C program to count the number of characters in a file is given below:

Listing C.2: nocharfile.c

```
/*
  This program is for counting number of characters in a file.
*/

#include <stdlib.h>
#include <stdio.h>
#include <string.h>

int main(int argc,char *argv[])
{
   int i;
   char ch;
   char String[1024],*filename;
   FILE *fp;

   if(argc > 1)
   {
      filename=argv[1];
      fp=fopen(filename,"r");
      if(fp==NULL){
         printf("File doesn't exist \n");
         return 1;
```

```
        }
        else
        {
            i=0;
            do
            {
                ch=fgetc(fp);
                if(ch != EOF)
                    String[i++]=ch;
            }while(ch!=EOF);
            printf("No of Characters: %d \n",(i-1));
            fclose(fp);
        }
    }
    else
        printf("Usage: ./a.out temp.txt\n");
    return 0;
}
```

5. An embedded system sends data (one character) every 20 seconds to a PC through an RS 232 link. The C program on the PC that receives and transfers the data to a file is given below:

Listing C.3: scread.c

```
#include <stdio.h>
#include <string.h>
#include <unistd.h>
#include <fcntl.h>
#include <errno.h>
#include <termios.h>

int open_port(void)
{
    int fd;
    fd = open("/dev/ttyS0",O_RDWR | O_NOCTTY | O_NDELAY);
    if(fd == -1)
    {
        perror("Unable to open the port /dev/ttyS0");
    }
    else
    {
```

```
        fcntl(fd,F_SETFL,0);
    }
    return(fd);
}

void config_port(int fd)
{
    struct termios options;

    tcgetattr(fd,&options);

    cfsetispeed(&options,B9600);
    cfsetospeed(&options,B9600);

    options.c_cflag |= (CLOCAL | CREAD);

    options.c_cflag &= ~PARENB;
    options.c_cflag &= ~CSTOPB;
    options.c_cflag &= ~CSIZE;
    options.c_cflag |= CS8;

    tcsetattr(fd,TCSANOW,&options);
}

char* read_data(int fd)
{
    char array[255];
    char *ptr;
    int nbytes;

    ptr = array;
    while((nbytes = read(fd, ptr, array + sizeof(array) - ptr -
1)) > 0)
    {
        ptr += nbytes;
        if((ptr[-1] == '\n') || (ptr[-1] == '\r'))
            break;
    }
    *ptr = '\0';
    return &array[0];
}
```

```
void scdata(int fd)
{
    int i,j=0;
    char *c,filename[20];
    FILE *fp;
    while(1){
        j++;
        sprintf(filename,"temp%d",j);
        fp = fopen(filename,"w");
        for(i=0;i<9;i++){     /* Since 1 character for every 20
seconds, in 3 minutes it has to accept 9 characters. */
            c = read_data(fd);
            fputc(c[0],fp);
        }
        fclose(fp);
    }
}

void close_port(int fd)
{
    close(fd);
}

int main(void)
{
    int fd;
    fd   = open_port();
    config_port(fd);
    scdata(fd);
    close_port(fd);
    return 0;
}
```

6. C program in Linux that displays a character every 10 seconds is given below:

Listing C.4: every10.c

```
#include <stdio.h>
#include <stdlib.h>
#include <time.h>
#include <math.h>
int main()
```

```
{
    int i=0;
    time_t t0;
    while(1)
    {
        t0=time(NULL);
        printf("Time: %ld ",t0);
        printf("Iteration: %d \n",++i);
        sleep(10);
    }
    return 0;
}
```

7. C program which generates packets of 32 bits is given below. The first bit of the packet indicates whether the packet is a control packet or a data packet. You need to set the first bit to 0 to indicate it is control packet and to 1 to indicate that it is data packet.

Listing C.5: packet32bit.c

```
#include <stdio.h>
#include <stdlib.h>
#include <time.h>

int main()
{
    int res;
    unsigned int packet=0;
    time_t t;

    srand((unsigned)time(&t));
    while(1){
        res = rand() % 2;
        if(res == 0){
            printf("Control packet ");
            packet = packet | (1 << 31);
            // User can set the remaining bits ......
            printf("value: %u \n",packet);
        }
        else
        {
            printf("Data packet ");
            packet = packet & ~(1 << 31);
```

```
        // User can set the remaining bits ......
        printf("value: %u \n",packet);
      }
      sleep(5);
    }
    return 0;
  }
```

8. C program that takes a file name as input and generates packets of 100 bytes is given below:

Listing: C.6: packet100.c

```
#include "stdio.h"
#include "string.h"
int main(int argc ,char *argv[])
{
FILE *fp;
char ch,file[255],data1[10240],data[10240];
int i=0,count=0,tpackets,flen,j=0,k=0,c=0,l=0,f=100;
char *name;
if(argc>1)
{
   name=argv[1];
   fp=fopen(name,"r");

   if(fp==NULL)
      printf("Unable to open the file");
   else

     while(1)
     {
        ch=fgetc(fp);
        data[i++]=ch;
        if(ch==EOF)
        break;
     }
     data[i]='\0';
     count=strlen(data);
              file[0]='F';
              tpackets=count/100;
```

```
                    if(tpackets*100<count)
                         tpackets=tpackets+1;

                    file[1]=tpackets;
                    flen=strlen(name);
                    file[2]=flen;

                    for(j=0;j<flen;j++)
                   file[j+3]=name[j];

          file[flen+3]='\0';
               /*printf("File Packet: ");
          for(i=0;i<flen+3;i++)
          printf("%d ",file[i]);
          printf("\n Data packets: "); */
          for (j=0;j<tpackets;j++)
          {
                              l=3;
          c=0;
          data1[0]='D';
          data1[1]=j+1;
          for(k=j*100;k<f;k++)
          {
            data1[l++]=data[k];
            c++;
          }
          data1[2]=c;
          data1[c+4]='\0';
          for(i=0;i<c+4;i++)
          {
          ch=data1[i];
       // printf("%c",ch);
          }
          f=k+100;
       }
       fclose(fp);
       }
    }else
       printf("Usage: ./a.out temp\n");
       return 0;
    }
```

Chapter 4

1. The input requirement of a handheld device to collect field data is: provision to enter alphanumeric characters to enter the data; and the output requirement is to display the records in the database. The handheld computers achieve this using a soft keyboard and LCD. The soft keyboard is displayed on the LCD and the desired key is pressed using a stylus. To facilitate easy entry of field data, a GUI has to be developed for the handheld computers. Implementation of embedded databases and development of GUI for handheld computers is discussed in Chapter 15.
2. To develop a system that is capable of recording telephone conversations, you need to develop a processor-based system. This system has to be connected in parallel to the telephone. Hence, the input is through a telephone jack (RJ11 jack). The voice signals have to be converted into digital format using an ADC or a PCM codec. The voice converted into digital format is then transferred to a memory chip. You need to develop a processor-based hardware with all the necessary interfaces to the telephone network. This hardware should have a communication interface such as the USB to transfer the recorded conversations to the PC. If two engineers work on this project, they can complete the work in about three months. Hence, the time required is three months, effort is six person months and accordingly, the budget can be estimated. If you assume that per month, each engineer will work for about 200 hours, the total effort spent on the project is 1200 person hours. Assuming an hourly rate of US$ 5, the manpower cost is US$6,000. In addition, you need to spend on the components, obtaining the PCBs etc. for which you need to spend another US$4,000. Hence, the total project cost is about US$10,000.
3. A navigation system used in cars obtains the location information from a GPS receiver. This location information is sent to the processor every one second. The processor has to decode the GPS data and then show the location on a map. Certainly a real-time operating system is a requirement. However, there is no time criticality and hence a soft real-time operating system will do the job.
4. To develop a software-defined radio that generates various types of modulations such as Amplitude Modulation, Frequency Modulation, Amplitude Shift Keying, Frequency Shift Keying and Phase Shift Keying etc., a Digital Signal Processor would be a good choice as the signal generation is much more efficient on a DSP than a GPP. The SDR generally contains a DSP and a GPP. The GPP is used to obtain the information from the user (type of modulation to be generated, the modulation parameters such as modulation index for AM, mark and space frequency for FSK etc.) and also for providing the user interface. The information obtained from the user is given to the DSP for generation of appropriate signals. The details of the SDR are discussed in Chapter 10.
5. To track a person's movement, the person has to be given a tiny embedded system that has a GPS receiver and a radio transmitter. The radio transmitter sends the location data to a central location from where the person is tracked. The important requirements for this product are (a) very small size; (b) low power consumption and it has to be operated through a battery; (c) light weight; (d) the power of the radio transmitter is dependent on the range to be covered,

a range of about two miles can be assumed; and (e) the frequency of operation has to be obtained from the customer as prior approvals are required for radio operation, generally 800 MHz band is used for this application. At the central location, there should be a radio receiver that is interfaced to a computer on which the location of the person is displayed. There are no restrictions on the size, weight or power consumption of the system at the central location. It takes about three months for four engineers to develop this system. You need to have a good knowledge of GPS receiver, radio transmitter/receiver design to take up this work.

6. The most important requirement of a product is that it should meet the requirements of the customer. In addition to the customer requirements, the manager may put additional requirements to ensure that the product is developed at low cost and also the product can be maintained at low cost. Accordingly, the quality characteristics of a product are divided into:

- Operational characteristics, which specify the requirements of the product during its operation. These characteristics are: reliability, safety, security, correctness, usability and efficiency.
- Revision characteristics, which reflect the ease with which the software can be modified. These characteristics are: testability, maintainability, scalability and modularity.
- Transition characteristics, which reflect the ease with which the software can be used on other platforms. These characteristics include portability, reusability and interoperability.

Chapter 5

1 to 4: Application program development using 89C51 development board is covered in Chapter 17. The programs for AVR development board are given in Chapter 18. Based on the hardware details given in this chapter, you can develop your own board or procure the boards from ICS Ltd. (www.iseeyes.com).

6. Porting an operating system on AVR micro-controller based hardware is explained in Chapter 9.
7. You can study the data sheet of CS8900A of Cirrus Logic for Ethernet chip details.
8. You can obtain any RTOS along with the TCP/IP stack from the site www.ethernut.de/en/download.html. The RTOS, AVR-nut can be ported onto an AVR micro-controller based board which has the Ethernet interface. You can use the API of the RTOS to do socket programming to access network services.
9. The TCP/IP protocol stack is a software implementation and is generally integrated with the operating system software and supplied to us. Windows and Unix have full-fledged stack implemented in software. Software implementation has the advantage that you can modify the code if required, i.e. flexibility. However, it results in slower processing of the packets. On the other hand, an ASIC implementation will result in faster processing, but lacks flexibility. For example, if IP version 4 has to be replaced by IP version 6, the ASIC has to be replaced. But then, a Korean entrepreneur developed an ASIC for TCP/IP implementation and made lots of money.
10. You can obtain the details of Single Board Computer's from www.mpl.ch. www.arcom.com, www.iar.com,
11. You can obtain the information on PCI controllers from www.pcisig.com.

Chapter 6

1. To network-enable an embedded system, you need to port the TCP/IP protocol stack. The hex file of the stack will occupy just around 16 KB.
2. Ericsson gives a Bluetooth development kit which can be interfaced to a PC using RS232 or USB port. The API provided with the protocol stack can be used to develop Bluetooth applications. You can obtain the details from www.ericsson.com. The cost of Bluetooth module can be reduced by developing a single chip solution, i.e. an ASIC.
3. Data synchronization is done to make the data in two devices the same. For instance, you have an address book on your laptop. You also have an address book on your palmtop. Sometimes you update the one on the laptop and sometimes the one on the palmtop. After a few days, the address books are not the same and you have to search both the address books to locate a telephone number. Using data synchronization, you can make the contents of the two address books same. Every palmtop computer vendor gives a data synchronization software. For instance, Palm gives a software called HotSync. HotSync will be running on the laptop and the palmtop and through this utility, data is synchronized.
4. You can develop a Bluetooth-based solution to provide location information in the exhibition ground of the size of 5 square kilometers. All along the corridors, you need to keep a number of Bluetooth base stations every 10 meters. All these Bluetooth base stations are networked to a server which has the complete database of the various stalls, the items displayed by the stalls, stall number etc. Bluetooth-enabled handheld computer gets connected to the nearest base station and the server sends the information. A Java application can be developed to provide the user interface for selection of stall number, item etc. which are demonstrated in Chapter 16.
5. There are 20 sensors, each sensor samples signals at 10 KHz and resolution of ADC is 16 bits. 20 * 10 K * 16, i.e. 3200 Kbits or 400 Kbytes/second, is the aggregate data rate. RS232 will not be able to support this data rate. USB is the best choice.
6. If the voice coding is done using Pulse Code Modulation at 64 Kbps, the storage requirement is 8 KB for one second or 0.48 MB per minute for one channel. So, for two channels for one minute, it is approximately 1 MB. If we want to store the telephone conversations for one hour, the memory capacity of the embedded system should be 60 MB. Every hour, we can transfer the memory contents to the PC and reset the memory of the embedded system.

Chapter 7

1. The various tasks in this system are: (a) store the ADC data in a buffer; (b) read the data from the buffer and form into packets and put each packet in a buffer; and (c) take each packet from the buffer and send it to the network port. These are the three application level tasks. As the storing of data and reading the data have to be completed in real-time, these two tasks are given the high priority. The ADC operation is given top-most priority and then the buffer has to be cleared fast so that it does not overflow. A real-time operating system will make the development very fast.

2. Whether priority inheritance is an important feature of an operating system is a debatable issue. RTLinux does not support it; VxWorks supports it. Those who do not like this feature argue that you can always design your real-time systems without the need for such a feature.
3. You cannot use the desktop computer for real-time data logging. Even voice and video conferencing applications will not work very well if you are carrying out some other activities simultaneously.
4. Semaphores can be used for data communication. Such applications include:
   - Implementation of a packet switch. The packet switch accepts packets from the incoming lines, puts them in a buffer, analyzes each packet for its destination address and keeps the packet in the outgoing buffer. The tasks for writing on to the buffer and reading from the buffer have to synchronize themselves, which can be done using semaphore.
   - A semaphore can be used for sharing the buffers.
5. When you run the program

```
int main(void)
{
     printf("Hello\n");
     if(fork())  = =  0)
          printf("World\n");
}
```

   The output will be:

   Hello

   World
6. When the above program's output is redirected to a file, the output will be:

   Hello

   Hello

   World

Chapter 8

1. Some of the embedded/real-time operating systems not covered in this chapter are: eCOS (embedded Configurable Operating System); Microware's OS/9; Microtec's VRTX, Kodak's AMX, Accelerated Technology's Nucleus.
2. Data synchronization is presently done through proprietary protocols. For example, Palm uses HotSync, Symbian uses Symbian Connect, Windows CE uses ActiveSync. A markup language called SyncML (Synchronization Markup Language) has been standardized to bring interoperability of software for data synchronization. A number of mobile handheld computer manufacturers and mobile phone manufacturers support this standardization activity and hence proprietary protocols are no longer required for data synchronization.

3. Software development on Pocket PC is discussed in Chapter 15.
4. The operating systems required for various applications are as follows:
   a. An Internet kiosk installed in a rural area: Embedded XP or Embedded Linux.
   b. A navigation system used in an aircraft: A hard real-time operating system such as QNX Neutrino, VxWorks or MicroC/OS-II.
   c. A navigation system used in a car: A soft real-time operating system such as Embedded Linux or a handheld operating system such as Palm OS, Symbian OS or Windows CE.
   d. A DVD player: A soft real-time operating system.
   e. A desktop computer to be used as a process control system with hard real-time requirements: A hard-real time operating system.
   f. An electronic toy helicopter: A small footprint OS such as MicroC/OS—II.

Chapter 9

1. If you anticipate problems in the software when it is working in the field, it is not a bad idea to leave some important debugging code in the software, if the memory is enough. Recall Mars Pathfinder problem.
2. You can download the software from www.qnx.com and port it on your desktop.
3. Many operating system ports for 8-bit micro-controllers are available. You can try out MicroC/OS-II.
4. DSP vendors give OS that can be ported on to the DSP boards. You can get the details from www.analogdevices.com, www.ti.com, www.lucent.com, www.motorola.com.
5. The additional memory requirement to network-enable an embedded system by porting TCP/IP stack is around 16 KB.
6. Web server software requires less than 16 KB of additional memory.

Chapter 10

1. The various embedded systems required for the smart-card based payment system are: the blank smart cards that can be programmed by you and smart card readers/writers to be installed at various places such as college administrative office, hostel admn office, library etc.
2. To develop a system for your college library that will track the library books through RF tags, an RF tag can be attached to each book in the library. The RF tag can be a passive tag without any battery and it will send the data stored in it when it comes near the RF tag reader. Each RF tag has to store the information about the book, i.e. title of the book, names of the authors, ISBN number, accession number, publisher name, year of publication and the price of the book. This information can be stored in about 256 characters. So, each RF tag should have a memory of about 256 bytes. When the book is near the RF tag reader located at the issue counter, the reader reads this information and transfers it to a PC by attaching the date/time

stamp. This reader should have the communication interface (RS232 or USB) to connect to the PC.

3. To develop a Calling Line Identification Device (CLID), a micro-controller such as 8051 or AVR ATmega128 will suffice. When you dial a number, just before the actual ringing of the telephone, the calling party's number will be sent which is in the form of FSK (Frequency Shift Keying) signals. CLID has to decode the calling line number by decoding the FSK signals. Hence, the processing requirement is very low. The CLID should have the provision to display the calling number on a small LCD screen of one line by 16 characters. Though not a must, a good amount of memory is required to store the previously received calls.
4. To develop a signal generator, you need to develop a system built around a DSP. There should be a function keypad that can be used to input the parameters and also control the display. The display should be of the size at least 6.4 inches for display of the prompts to enter data. You can study the user interface on a commercial signal generator to work out the details of the user interface.
5. BREW (Binary Runtime Environment for Wireless) of Qualcomm is used for developing mobile data applications. You can download the BREW Development kit from www.qualcomm.com. Using C++ or Java, you can develop mobile applications. The applications can be tested on the desktop using the emulators provided in the development kit. The software can then be converted into DLLs and ported to the mobile device running an ARM processor.
6. HP Chai Appliance Platform (www.hp.com/go/embedded) can be used to develop networked information appliances. It has the following components:

- Chai VM: A virtual machine for the information appliance.
- Chai AWT: A GUI for the information appliance
- Chai Server: A web server on which the applications are written for access by the mobile device or desktop browser
- ChaiFarer: A web browser for embedded devices

In addition to these components, the platform provides components such as Micro ChaiVM, a virtual machine for very small devices; and Oracle 8iLite, a mobile extension for Oracle 8i for database applications.

An embedded system can run a Chai server. It includes a home page, in which data generated by the appliance is kept—which can be static, or change dynamically. This home page can be accessed by any desktop connected to the Internet or a mobile device running ChaiFarer. You can refer to the book "Programming for Embedded Systems: Cracking the Code" by Dreamtech Press for application development on HP's Chai Platform.

Chapter 11

1. You can create a shell script "test" which contains the line:

```
echo  "How are you?"
```

When the shell script is given execution permission and is executed using the following command:

$test

nothing will be displayed and the system prompt will appear again. Note that when a command is given, the shell looks for this command in /bin and then /usr/bin. There is already a shell command 'test' in /bin which is to test the type of the file. When you give the shell command as above, always it executes the bin command without any arguments; the shell is not executing your shell script. To force the shell to skip searching for /bin, you need to give the shell command as below:

$./test

And, you will get the desired output.

2. Shell script to find single letter, two-letter and three-letter words in a text file is:

   $grep "^.$" textfile; grep "^..$" textfile; grep "^...$" textfile

3. The shell command to find the number of users logged in

   $who | wc -l

4. The shell command to find all the executable files in your home directory is:

   $ls –l $HOME | grep "^-..x"

5. The shell script to obtain the word frequency counts in English text sorted in alphabetical order and numerical order:

   $cat textfile | tr –d [:punct:] | tr "[ ]" "[\012]" | sort | uniq -c

6. The shell script to count occurrences of single letter, two-letter and three-letter words in English text (assume 26 letters and space character only):

   echo "Single letter words"

   cat text | tr –d [:punct:] | tr "[ ]" "[\012]" | sort | grep "^.$" | wc –l

   echo "Two letter words"

   cat text | tr –d [:punct:] | tr "[ ]" "[\012]" | sort | grep "^..$" | wc –l

   echo "Three letter words"

   cat text | tr –d [:punct:] | tr "[ ]" "[\012]" | sort | grep "^...$" | wc –l

7. The shell script that displays the number of readable, writable and executable files in a specified directory is:

   ls –l $1 | grep "^-rwx" | wc -l

8. The C program that takes input from the keyboard, converts the characters to upper case and prints them, is given below. The program will exit when you press ^c.

Listing C.7: prgs.c

```
#include <stdio.h>
#include <ctype.h>
#include <string.h>

#define LEN 1024

int main()
{
   int i,len;
   char str[LEN];
   while(1){
      printf("Enter text: ");
      fgets(str,LEN,stdin);
      len = strlen(str);
      printf("Converted text: ");
      for(i=0;i<len;i++)
         printf("%c",toupper(str[i]));
   }
   return 0;
}
```

9. The C program that takes a string input from keyboard and displays the length of the string is given below.

Listing C.8: multhd.c

```
#include<stdio.h>
#include<unistd.h>
#include<stdlib.h>
#include<string.h>
#include<ctype.h>
#include<pthread.h>
#include<semaphore.h>

#define BUFFER_SIZE 1024

sem_t sem;

char buffer[BUFFER_SIZE];

void *read_thread(void *arg) {
```

```
    while(strncmp("stop",buffer,4) != 0){
        printf("Enter text: ");
        fgets(buffer, BUFFER_SIZE, stdin);
        sem_post(&sem);
    }
    pthread_exit("read_thread exit successful");
}

void *length_thread() {
    int i;
    sem_wait(&sem);
    while(strncmp("stop", buffer, 4) != 0) {
        printf("Length of entered text: %d\n",strlen(buffer)-1);
        sem_wait(&sem);
    }
    pthread_exit("length_thread exit successful");
}

int main()
{
    int result;
    pthread_t rthread,lthread;
    void *thread_result;

    result = sem_init(&sem, 0, 0);

    if(result != 0){
        printf("Semaphore initialization failed");
        exit(1);
    }

    printf("Enter text, the program will display the length of the
string,
        To stop enter 'stop'\n");

    result = pthread_create(&lthread, NULL, length_thread, NULL);
    if(result != 0){
        printf("length_thread creation failed");
        exit(1);
    }
```

```
    result = pthread_create(&rthread, NULL, read_thread, NULL);
    if(result != 0){
       printf("read_thread creation failed");
       exit(1);
    }

    result = pthread_join(rthread, &thread_result);
    if(result != 0){
       printf("read_thread join failed");
       exit(1);
    }
    printf("read_thread joined, %s\n",thread_result);

    result = pthread_join(lthread, &thread_result);
    if(result != 0){
       printf("length_thread join failed");
       exit(1);
    }
    printf("length_thread joined, %s\n",thread_result);

    sem_destroy(&sem);
    exit(0);
 }
```

10. The C programs that take a string input from keyboard and display the length of the string, using message queues, are given below:

Listing C.9: input.c

```
#include <stdio.h>
#include <stdlib.h>
#include <unistd.h>
#include <string.h>
#include <sys/msg.h>
#include <sys/ipc.h>
#include <sys/types.h>

#define TEXT_SIZE 1024

struct data_struct {
  char text_to_convert[TEXT_SIZE];
};
```

```
int main()
{
   int flag = 1;
   int msgqid;
   char buffer[TEXT_SIZE];
   struct data_struct user_data;

   msgqid = msgget((key_t)2377, 0666 | IPC_CREAT);

   if(msgqid == -1){
      printf("An error occurred: msgget failed\n");
      return 1;
   }

   printf("Enter text, to put it in a message queue,
               To exit enter 'stop' \n");

   while(flag) {
      printf("Enter text: ");
      fgets(buffer, TEXT_SIZE, stdin);
      strcpy(user_data.text_to_convert, buffer);
      if(msgsnd(msgqid, (void *)&user_data, TEXT_SIZE, 0) == -1)
{
         printf("An error occurred: msgsnd failed\n");
         return 1;
      }

      if(strncmp(buffer, "stop", 4) == 0 ) {
         flag = 0;
      }
   }
   return 0;
}
```

Listing C.10: strlength.c

```
#include <stdio.h>
#include <stdlib.h>
#include <unistd.h>
#include <string.h>
#include <ctype.h>
```

```
#include <sys/msg.h>
#include <sys/ipc.h>
#include <sys/types.h>

#define TEXT_SIZE 1024

struct data_struct {
  char text_to_convert[TEXT_SIZE];
};

int main()
{
   int flag = 1;
   int msgqid;
   int i, result, len;
   struct data_struct convert_data;

   msgqid = msgget((key_t)2377, 0666 | IPC_CREAT);

   if(msgqid == -1){
      printf("An error occurred: msgget failed\n");
      return 1;
   }

   while(flag) {
      if(msgrcv(msgqid,(void *)&convert_data,TEXT_SIZE,0,0) == -1)
{
         printf("An error occurred: msgrcv failed\n");
         return 1;
      }
      len = strlen(convert_data.text_to_convert);
      printf("Length of the entered text: %d\n",len-1);
      if(strncmp(convert_data.text_to_convert, "stop", 4) == 0 )
{
         flag = 0;
      }
   }
   result = msgctl(msgqid, IPC_RMID, 0);
   if(result == -1) {
      printf("An error occurred: msgctl(IPC_RMID) failed \n");
      return 1;
```

```
    }
    return 0;
}
```

11. The C programs that take a string input from keyboard and display the length of the string, using shared memory, are given below.

    Listing C.11: common.h

```
#define BUFFER_SIZE 1024

struct common_struct {
   int something_is_there;
   char buffer[BUFFER_SIZE];
};
```

Listing C.12: prg1.c

```
#include <stdio.h>
#include <stdlib.h>
#include <unistd.h>
#include <ctype.h>
#include <string.h>
#include <sys/shm.h>
#include <sys/ipc.h>
#include <sys/types.h>
#include "common.h"
int main()
{
   int flag = 1;
   void *shrd_memory = (void *)0;
   struct common_struct *shm_block;
   int smemid,i,result,len;

   smemid = shmget((key_t)2377, sizeof(struct common_struct), 0666
| IPC_CREAT);
   if(smemid == -1) {
      printf("An error occurred: shmget failed\n");
      return 1;
   }

   shrd_memory = shmat(smemid, (void *)0, 0);
   if(shrd_memory == (void *) -1) {
```

```
        printf("An error occurred: shmat failed\n");
        return 1;
    }
    printf("Shared Memory at %X\n", (int)shrd_memory);

    shm_block = (struct common_struct *)shrd_memory;
    shm_block->something_is_there = 0;
    while(flag == 1) {
        if(shm_block->something_is_there) {
            len = strlen(shm_block->buffer);
            printf("Length of entered text: %d\n",len-1);
            sleep(1);
            shm_block->something_is_there = 0;
            if(strncmp(shm_block->buffer, "stop", 4) == 0) {
                flag = 0;
            }
        }
    }

    result = shmdt(shrd_memory);
    if(result == -1) {
        printf("An error occurred: shmdt failed \n");
        return 1;
    }

    result = shmctl(smemid, IPC_RMID, 0);
    if(result == -1) {
        printf("An error occurred: shmctl(IPC_RMID) failed\n");
        return 1;
    }
    return 0;
}
```

Listing C.13: prg2.c

```
#include <stdio.h>
#include <stdlib.h>
#include <unistd.h>
#include <string.h>
#include <sys/shm.h>
#include <sys/types.h>
```

```
#include <sys/ipc.h>
#include "common.h"

int main()
{
    int flag = 1;
    void *shrd_memory = (void *)0;
    struct common_struct *shm_block;
    char buffer[BUFFER_SIZE];
    int smemid,result;

    smemid = shmget((key_t)2377, sizeof(struct common_struct), 0666
| IPC_CREAT);
    if(smemid == -1) {
      printf("An error occurred: shmget failed \n");
      return 1;
    }

    shrd_memory = shmat(smemid, (void *)0, 0);
    if(shrd_memory == (void *) -1) {
      printf("An error occurred: shmat failed \n");
      return 1;
    }
    printf("Shared Memory at %X\n", (int) shrd_memory);

    shm_block = (struct common_struct *)shrd_memory;
    printf("Enter text, the other program, prg1 will display the
length of entered text \n, To stop the execution of these programs
enter 'stop'\n");
    while(flag) {
      while(shm_block->something_is_there == 1) {
        sleep(1);
        printf("waiting .... \n");
      }
      printf("Enter text: ");
      fgets(buffer, BUFFER_SIZE, stdin);

      strncpy(shm_block->buffer, buffer, BUFFER_SIZE);
      shm_block->something_is_there = 1;

      if(strncmp(buffer, "stop", 4) == 0) {
```

```
            flag = 0;
        }
    }

    result = shmdt(shrd_memory);
    if(result == -1) {
        printf("An error occurred: shmdt failed \n");
        return 1;
    }
    return 0;
}
```

Chapter 12

1. The following program illustrates the implementation of multithreading in RTLinux. Compare it with the multithreading in Linux.

Listing C.14:multithreading.c

```
#include <rtl.h>
#include <time.h>
#include <pthread.h>

static pthread_t thread1,thread2;
static void *sub_routine1(void *arg)
{
    int i;
    int sleep = 500000000;
    int nthread = (int)arg;

    struct sched_param p;
    p.sched_priority = 1;
    pthread_setschedparam(pthread_self(), SCHED_FIFO, &p);
    pthread_make_periodic_np(pthread_self(),gethrtime(),sleep);
    rtl_printf("Thread %d starts\n",nthread);
//  while(1){
        for(i=0;i<10;i++){
            rtl_printf("A ");
        }
        rtl_printf("thread1: before sleep\n");
        nanosleep(hrt2ts(sleep),NULL);
        rtl_printf("thread1: after sleep\n");
```

```
//      pthread_wait_np();
//  }
    return 0;
}

static void *sub_routine2(void *arg)
{
    int i;
    int sleep = 500000000;
    int nthread = (int)arg;

    struct sched_param p;
    p.sched_priority = 1;
    pthread_setschedparam(pthread_self(), SCHED_FIFO, &p);
    pthread_make_periodic_np(pthread_self(),gethrtime(),sleep);
    rtl_printf("Thread %d starts\n",nthread);
//  while(1){
       for(i=0;i<10;i++){
          rtl_printf("B ");
       }
       rtl_printf("thread2: before sleep\n");
       nanosleep(hrt2ts(sleep),NULL);
       rtl_printf("thread2: after sleep\n");
//     pthread_wait_np();
//  }
    return 0;
}

int init_module(void)
{
    int ret;

    rtl_printf("Main thread starts \n");

    ret = pthread_create(&thread1, NULL, sub_routine1,(void *) 1);
    if(ret)
    {
       rtl_printf("Failed to create thread1 \n");
       return ret;
    }
```

```
    ret = pthread_create(&thread2, NULL, sub_routine2,(void *) 2);
    if(ret)
    {
      rtl_printf("Failed to create thread2 \n");
      return ret;
    }
  return 0;
}

void cleanup_module(void)
{
    pthread_cancel(thread1);
    pthread_join(thread1,NULL);

    pthread_cancel(thread2);
    pthread_join(thread2,NULL).
}
```

2. You can modify the programs given in the appliance control project of this chapter, to add fast forward button.
3. The following programs demonstrate the communication between two processes. One process is running as a Linux process and the other as an RTLinux process.

Listing C.15: control.h

```
#define COMMAND_FIFO 3
#define START_TASK 1
#define STOP_TASK 2
struct my_msg_struct {
  int command,
  int task;
  int period;
};
```

Listing C.16: RTLinux_ps.c

```
#include <linux/errno.h>
#include <rtl.h>
#include <time.h>
#include <rtl_sched.h>
#include <rtl_fifo.h>
#include "control.h"
pthread_t tasks[2];
```

```
static char data[2][2];
#define TASK_CONTROL_FIFO_OFFSET 4

void *thread_code(void *t)
{
    int count1,count2;
    int fifo = (int) t;
    int taskno = fifo - 1;
    struct my_msg_struct msg;
    count1 = 65; // ASCII value of upper case alphabet, A
    count2 = 97; // ASCII value of lower case alphabet, a
    while (1)
    {
        int ret;
        int err;
        ret = pthread_wait_np();
        if ((err = rtf_get (taskno + TASK_CONTROL_FIFO_OFFSET, &msg,
sizeof(msg))) == sizeof(msg))
        {
            switch (msg.command) {
                case START_TASK:
                    pthread_make_periodic_np(pthread_self(), gethrtime()
msg.period * 1000);
                break;
                case STOP_TASK:
                    pthread_suspend_np(pthread_self());
                    break;
                default:
                    rtl_printf("RTLinux task: bad command\n");
                return 0;
            }
        }
        if(fifo == 1){
            data[0][0] = (char)count1; // Upper case alphabets
            count1++;
        }
        else if (fifo == 2){
            data[0][0] = (char)count2; // Lower case alphabets
            count2++;
        }
        data[0][1] = '\0';
```

```
    rtf_put(fifo, data[0], 3);
  }
  return 0;
}

int my_handler(unsigned int fifo)
{
  struct my_msg_struct msg;
  int err;
  while ((err = rtf_get(COMMAND_FIFO, &msg, sizeof(msg))) ==
sizeof(msg))
  {
    rtf_put(msg.task + TASK_CONTROL_FIFO_OFFSET,&msg, sizeof(msg));
    pthread_wakeup_np (tasks [msg.task]);
  }
  if (err != 0) {
    return -EINVAL;
  }
  return 0;
}

int init_module(void)
{
  int c[5];
  pthread_attr_t attr;
  struct sched_param sched_param;
  int ret;
  rtf_destroy(1);
  rtf_destroy(2);
  rtf_destroy(3);
  rtf_destroy(4);
  rtf_destroy(5);
  c[0] = rtf_create(1, 4000);
  c[1] = rtf_create(2, 4000);
  c[2] = rtf_create(3, 200); /* input control channel */
  c[3] = rtf_create(4, 100); /* input control channel */
  c[4] = rtf_create(5, 100); /* input control channel */
  pthread_attr_init (&attr);
  sched_param.sched_priority = 4;
  pthread_attr_setschedparam (&attr, &sched_param);
  ret = pthread_create (&tasks[0], &attr, thread_code, (void
```

```
*)1);
    pthread_attr_init (&attr);
    sched_param.sched_priority = 5;
    pthread_attr_setschedparam (&attr, &sched_param);
    ret = pthread_create (&tasks[1], &attr, thread_code, (void
*)2);
    rtf_create_handler(3, &my_handler);
    return 0;
}
void cleanup_module(void)
{
    #ifdef DEBUG
    printk("%d\n", rtf_destroy(1));
    printk("%d\n", rtf_destroy(2));
    printk("%d\n", rtf_destroy(3));
    printk("%d\n", rtf_destroy(4));
    printk("%d\n", rtf_destroy(5));
    #else
    rtf_destroy(1);
    rtf_destroy(2);
    rtf_destroy(3);
    rtf_destroy(4);
    rtf_destroy(5);
    #endif
    pthread_cancel (tasks[0]);
    pthread_join (tasks[0], NULL);
    pthread_cancel (tasks[1]);
    pthread_join (tasks[1], NULL);
}
```

Listing C.17: Linux_ps.c

```
#include <stdio.h>
#include <errno.h>
#include <sys/time.h>
#include <sys/types.h>
#include <fcntl.h>
#include <unistd.h>
#include <sys/ioctl.h>
#include "rtl_fifo.h"
#include "rtl_time.h"
```

```
#include "control.h"
#define BUFSIZE 70
char buf[BUFSIZE];

int main()
{
   fd_set rfds;
   struct timeval tv;
   int retval;
   int fd0, fd1, ctl;
   int n;
   int i;
   struct my_msg_struct msg;
   if ((fd0 = open("/dev/rtf1", O_RDONLY)) < 0) {
      fprintf(stderr, "Error opening /dev/rtf1\n");
      exit(1);
   }
   if ((fd1 = open("/dev/rtf2", O_RDONLY)) < 0) {
      fprintf(stderr, "Error opening /dev/rtf2\n");
      exit(1);
   }
   if ((ctl = open("/dev/rtf3", O_WRONLY)) < 0) {
      fprintf(stderr, "Error opening /dev/rtf3\n");
      exit(1);
   }
   /* now start the tasks */
   msg.command = START_TASK;
   msg.task = 0;
   msg.period = 200000;
   if (write(ctl, &msg, sizeof(msg)) < 0) {
      fprintf(stderr, "Can't send a command to RT-task\n");
      exit(1);
   }
   msg.task = 1;
   msg.period = 200000;
   if (write(ctl, &msg, sizeof(msg)) < 0) {
      fprintf(stderr, "Can't send a command to RT-task\n");
      exit(1);
   }
   for (i = 0; i < 26; i++) {
```

```
    FD_ZERO(&rfds);
    FD_SET(fd0, &rfds);
    FD_SET(fd1, &rfds);
    tv.tv_sec = 1;
    tv.tv_usec = 0;
    retval = select(FD_SETSIZE, &rfds, NULL, NULL, &tv);
    if (retval > 0) {
       if (FD_ISSET(fd0, &rfds)) {
          n = read(fd0, buf, BUFSIZE - 1);
          buf[n] = 0;
          printf("FIFO 1: %s \n", buf);
       }
       if (FD_ISSET(fd1, &rfds)) {
          n = read(fd1, buf, BUFSIZE - 1);
          buf[n] = 0;
          printf("FIFO 2: %s \n", buf);
       }
    }
 }
 fprintf(stderr,"Linux_ps: Sending commands to stop RT-tasks\n");
 /* stop the tasks */
 msg.command = STOP_TASK;
 msg.task = 0;
 if (write(ctl, &msg, sizeof(msg)) < 0) {
    fprintf(stderr,"Can't send a command to RT-task\n");
    exit(1);
 }
 msg.task = 1;
 if (write(ctl, &msg, sizeof(msg)) < 0) {
    fprintf(stderr, "Can't send a command to RT-task\n");
    exit(1);
 }
 return 0;
}
```

4. The tasks are: (a) real-time collection of data and transferring to a buffer; (b) reading the buffer contents and calculation of spectral coefficients; and (c) drawing the spectrum. Only the task (a) is time-critical and hence it can run as an RTLinux task. The other two tasks can run as normal Linux tasks.

5. IP Phone is generally based on a 32-bit processor. The real-time operations of capturing the data packets and playing them can be done through the RTLinux and the less time-critical tasks such as dialing the digits etc. can be done through the Linux tasks. In fact, a number of IP Phones use RTLinux.
6. If the Software-Defined Radio is based on a micro-controller, you can port an operating system such as VxWorks, QNX Nutrino or MicroC/OS-II. If the SDR uses Pentium-based hardware built around a Single Board Computer, certainly RTLinux is a good choice.

Chapter 20

1. Major semiconductor manufacturers such as Texas Instruments, Philips etc. supply RFID tags and reader ICs. You can check their web sites to obtain the latest information. The range, the frequency of operation, and of course, the cost are the major considerations for selection of a reader. For the tag, compliance to ISO standard, the memory capacity of the tag (how many characters the tag can hold), active or passive and the cost are the major specifications.
2. Every marks list issued to a student can have an RFID tag. This tag contains the marks in electronic form. The data to be stored is: roll number of the student (8 digits), name of the student (50 characters), semester number (2 digits), marks in each of the 8 subjects along with subject names (20 characters each). Additionally, the name of the university, college and other details can be stored. Hence the total capacity of the tag should be 256 characters at least. This has to be a passive tag.
3. When each book is attached with an RFID tag, the tag should contain the following information: ISBN of the book, accession number of the book, title, author(s), year of publication, publisher's name, edition number and price of the book. As the book is issued to a library user, this information (to whom the book is issued) should also be written to the tag at the time of issue. Hence the additional information to be written is: user id of the person to whom the book is issued, issue date and due date of return.

When each library user is given an RFID reader, the user information is stored in the tag. At the time of the issue of the book, the book information is also transferred to the tag through the reader.

Chapter 21

1. You can get the latest information on Analog Devices' DSP families—218x, 219x, BlackFin, SHARC, TigerSHARC etc. and their benchmark results from the site www.analog.com .
2. You can download the trial version of GoldWave application software from www.goldwave.com. It is a powerful software package for editing of voice files. You can remove unwanted portions, remove noise and also incorporate special effects using this software.
3. You can download Java Media Framework (JMF) API from Sun Microsystems' web site. Please refer to the book " Programming for Embedded Systems: Cracking the Code" by Dreamtech Software Team for code that implements Voice/video over IP application using JMF.
4. You can download the NetMeeting SDK from Microsoft's web site. Please refer to the book

"Programming for embedded systems: Cracking the Code" by Dreamtech Software Team for development of voice/video over IP application using this SDK.

5. MATLAB program to generate normally distributed random noise samples is given in Listing C.18.

Listing C.18 Normallydistributedrandomsequence.m

%Program Title: Generation of Normally distributed random sequence with zero mean and unity variance

```
clc;
clear all;
N = input('Enter the no. of samples in the sequence N =    ');
y  = randn(1,N);
figure(1)
plot(y)
xlabel('n  ->')
ylabel('Amplitude  ->')
title('Normally  Distributed Noise','fontsize',14);
```

Results:

Enter the no. of samples in the sequence N =   100

Output Plot:

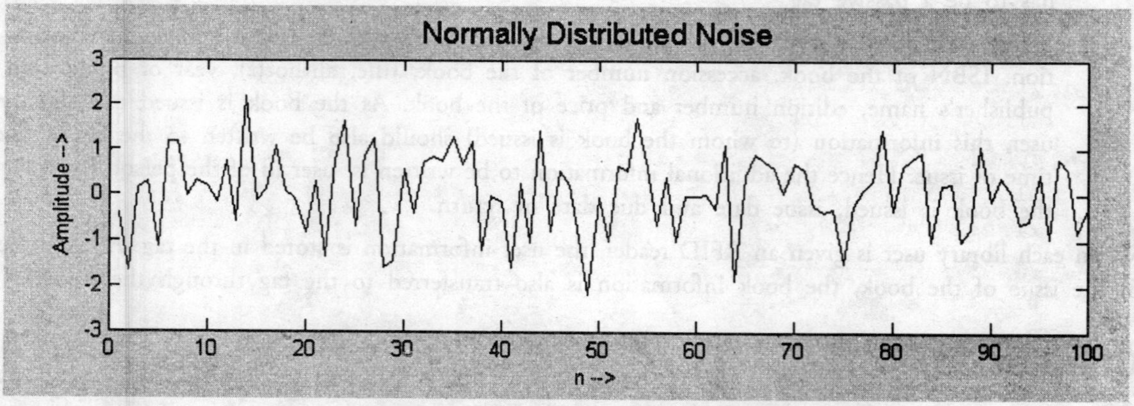

Fig. C.1. Normally Distributed Noise

6. MATLAB program to do FFT analysis on a noise sequence is given in Listing C.19. Note that zero padding is done wherever necessary to do the FFT analysis. Higher point FFT gives a better resolution spectrum.

Listing C.19 noisespectrum.m

%Program Title: Wave and spectrum plot for different number of FFT points of noise signal

```
clc;
clear;
u=randn(1,1024);
```

```
fs=8000;
M = length(u);
n=0:M-1;
N = input('Enter the no. of FFT points    N =        ');
ms=u(1:240);
for i=241:1024
   ms(i)=0;
end
dt=1/fs;
nmax=length(ms);
T=nmax*(1/fs);
t=dt:dt:T;
spect=(1/(nmax))*abs(fft(ms,N));
nmax1=length(spect);
f = fs*(0:round(nmax1/2))/nmax1;
f = f(1:round(nmax1/2));
noisespec=spect(1:(nmax1/2));
noisespectrum=20*log10(noisespec);
subplot(211)
n1=n(1:1024);
plot(n1,ms);
xlabel('n ->')
ylabel('Amplitude(volts) ->')
title('Wave form of noise signal of length M','fontsize',14);
subplot(212)
plot(f,noisespectrum)
xlabel('f ->')
ylabel('Amplitude(dB) ->')
title('NOISE SPECTRUM','fontsize',14);
```

Result1:

'Enter the no. of FFT points   N = 128

Output Plot:

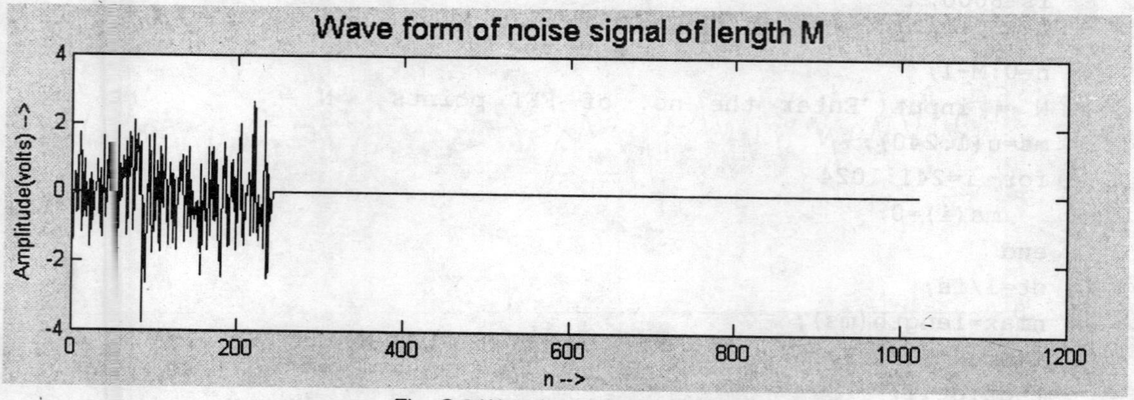

Fig. C.2 Waveform of Noise Signal

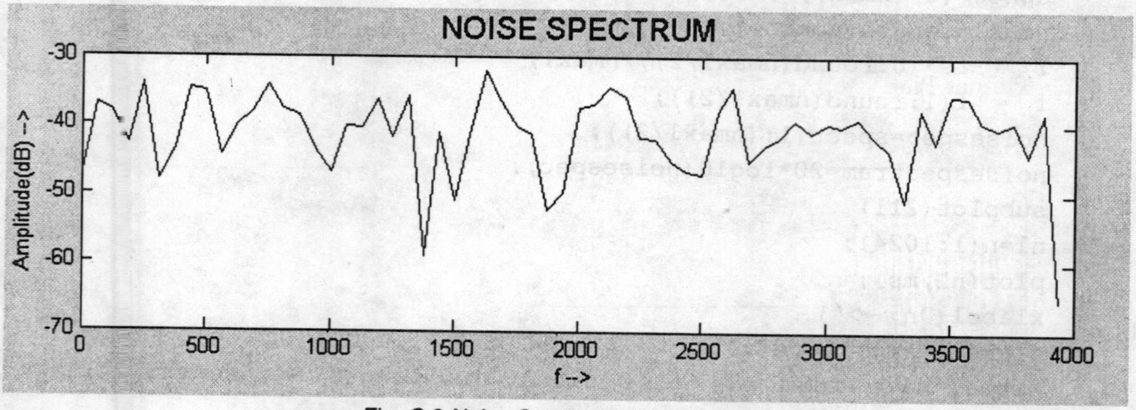

Fig. C.3 Noise Spectrum: 128 Point FFT

Result2:

'Enter the no. of FFT points N = 256

Output Plot:

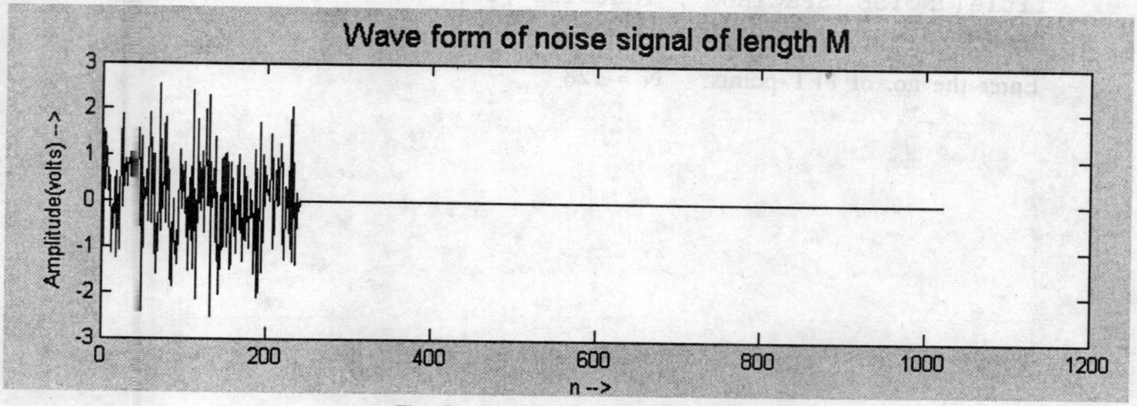

Fig. C.4 Waveform of Noise Signal

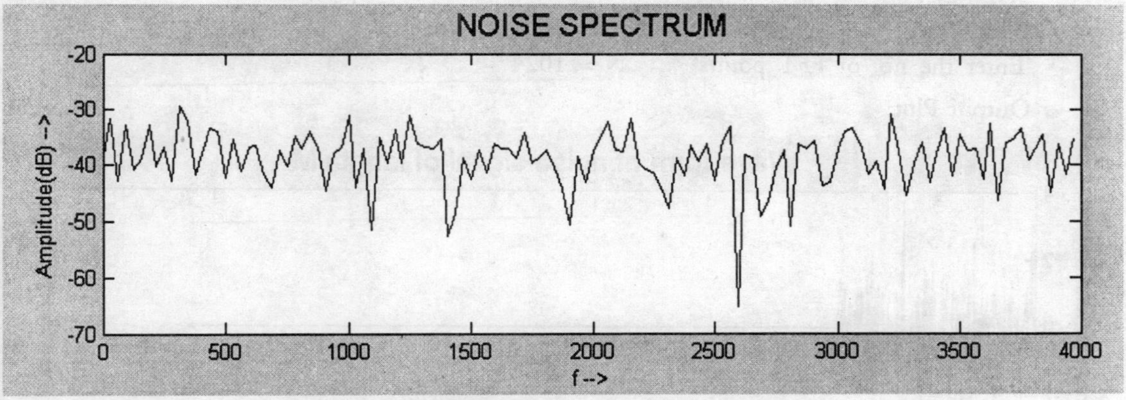

Fig. C.5 Noise Spectrum: 256 Point FFT

Result3:

'Enter the no. of FFT points N = 512

Output Plot:

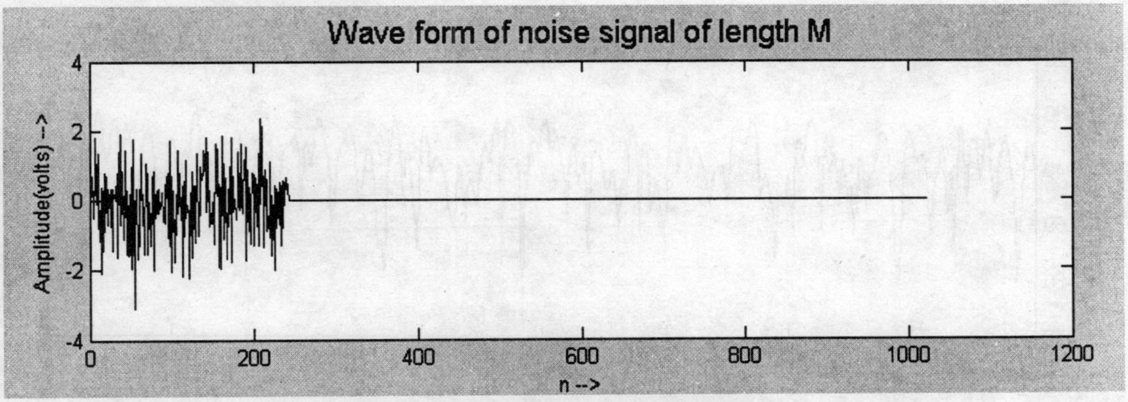

Fig. C.6 Waveform of Noise Signal

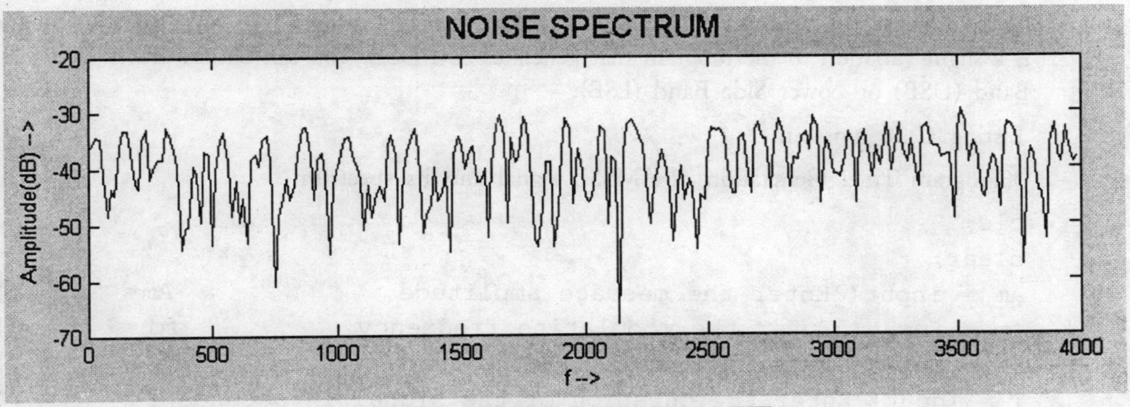

Fig. C.7 Noise spectrum: 512 Point FFT

Result4:

'Enter the no. of FFT points N = 1024

Output Plot:

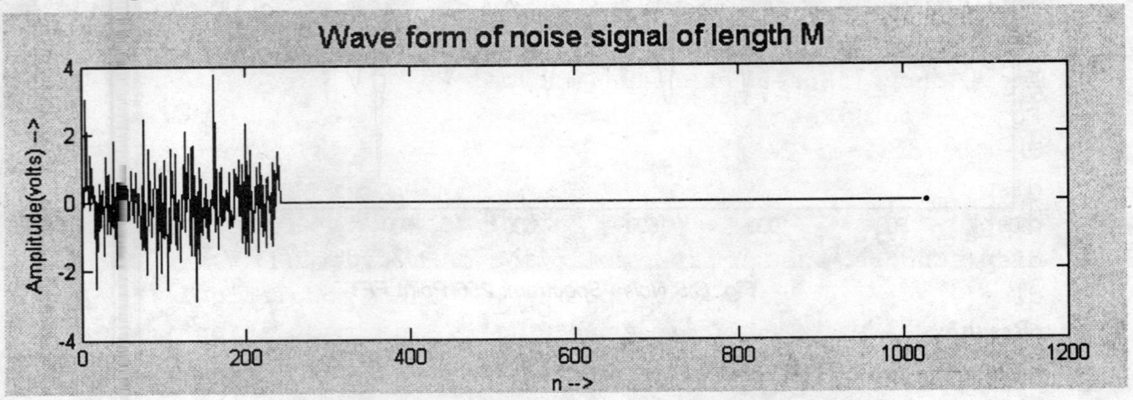

Fig. C.8 Waveform of Noise Signal

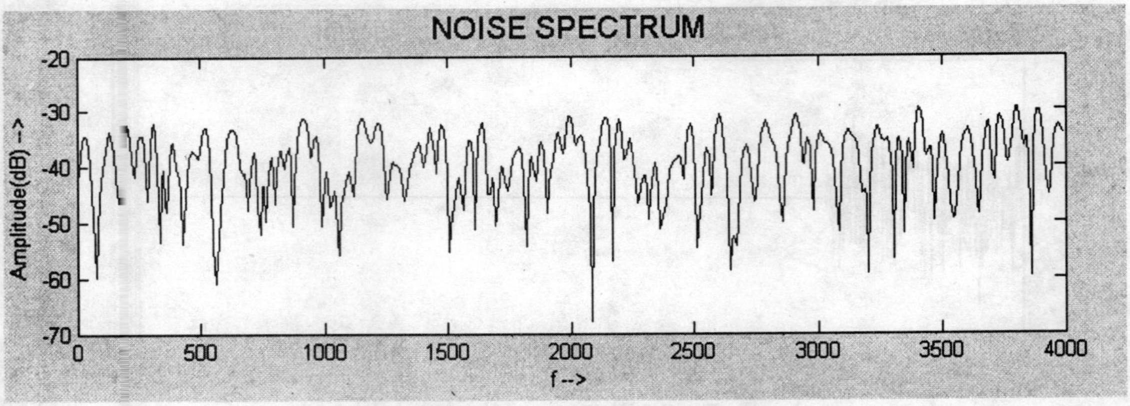

Fig. C.9 Noise Spectrum: 1024 Point FFT

7. MATLAB program to generate AM SSB signal is given in Listing C.20. Note that this program is a slight variation to the program that generates AM DSB. You can choose either Upper Side Band (USB) or Lower Side Band (LSB).

Listing C.20 amssb.m

```
%Program Title: Generation of AMSSB signal and its spectrum
clc;
clear;
Am = input('Enter the message amplitude                    Am=       ');
fm = input('Enter the modulating frequency                 fm =      ');
fs = input('Enter the sampling frequency                   fs =      ');
T = input('Enter the duration of the signal in seconds T =          ');
dt  =  1/fs;
```

```
t = dt:dt:T;      %% Time variable
M = length(t);
m = Am*cos(2*pi*fm*t);
mh = hilbert(m(1:M));
mh = imag(mh);
Ac = input('Enter carrier Amplitude               Ac = ');
Fc = input('Enter carrier frequency               Fc = ');
c =Ac*cos(2*pi*Fc*t);
disp('                                              ');
disp('                                              ');
disp('Choose one of the following SSB types');
disp('          "usb" for Upper Side Band modulation');
disp('          "lsb" for Lower Side Band modulation');
disp('                                              ');
disp('                                              ');
ssb_type = input('Enter the type of SSB modulation       ','s');
switch ssb_type
   case 'usb'
   s = .5*Ac*(m(1:M).*cos(2*pi*Fc*t) - mh.*sin(2*pi*Fc*t));
   case 'lsb'
   s = .5*Ac*(m(1:M).*cos(2*pi*Fc*t) + mh.*sin(2*pi*Fc*t));
   otherwise
   disp('There is no such SSB modulation');
end
disp('For windowing select  "rec" - rectangular / "bart" -
bartlett / "bla" - blackman / "ham" - hamming / "han" -
hanning ');
window_type = input('Enter the type of the window required for
spectrum            ','s');
switch window_type
   case 'rec'
      w = rectwin(M);
   case 'bart'
      w = bartlett(M);
   case 'bla'
      w = blackman(M);
   case 'ham'
      w = hamming(M);
   case 'han'
      w = hann(M);
   otherwise
```

```
    disp('window is not available');
end
w = w';
ms = m(1:M).*w;
sp = s(1:M).*w;
N = input('Enter the no. of FFT points       N =      ');
if M<N,
    ms = [ms zeros(1,N-M)];
    sp = [sp zeros(1,N-M)];
    L = M;
else
    ms = ms(1:N);
    sp = sp(1:N);
    L = N;
end
msp = 1/N*abs(fft(ms));
msp=20*log10(msp);
f = fs*(0:round(N/2))/N;
f = f(1:round(N/2));
F1 = Fc;
sp1 = 1/N*abs(fft(sp));
sp1=20*log10(sp1);
figure(1);
subplot(211);
plot(t(1:L),m(1:L));
title('MESSAGE SIGNAL');
subplot(212);
plot(f,msp(1:round(N/2)));
title('MESSAGE SPECTRUM');
figure(2);
subplot(211);
plot(t(1:L),s(1:L));
title('MODULATED SIGNAL');
subplot(212);
plot(f,sp1(1:round(N/2)));
title('SPECTRUM OF MODULATED SIGNAL');
```

Results:

Enter the message amplitude Am = 1

Enter the modulating frequency fm = 1000

Enter carrier Amplitude Ac =1

Enter carrier frequency Fc =15000

Enter the sampling frequency fs = 150000

Enter the duration of the signal in seconds T = 4e-3

For windowing select "rec" - rectangular / "bart" - bartlett / "bla" - blackman / "ham" - hamming / "han" – hanning

Enter the type of the window required for spectrum rec

Enter the no. of FFT points N = M

Output Plot:

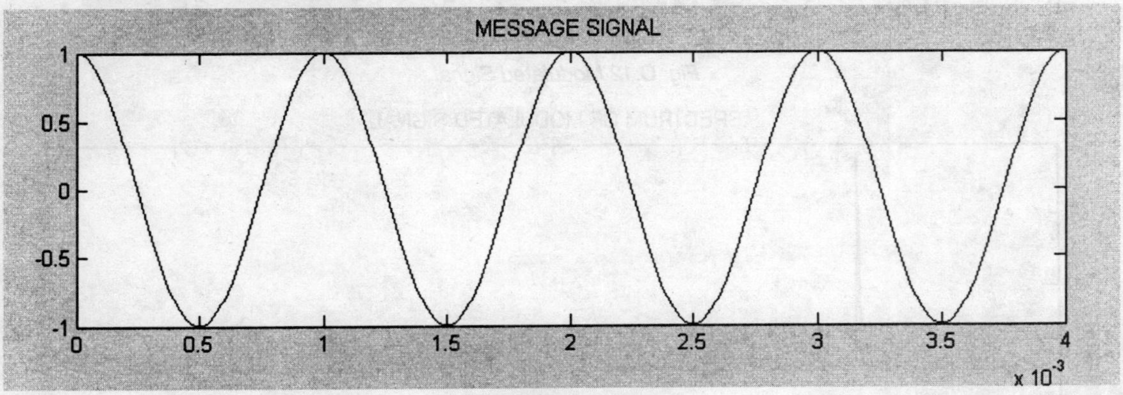

Fig.C.10 Message Signal

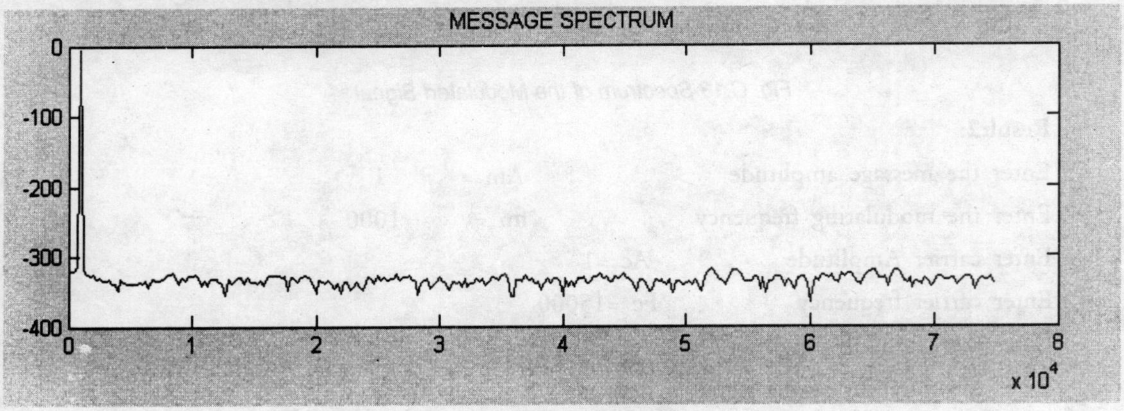

Fig. C.11 Message Spectrum

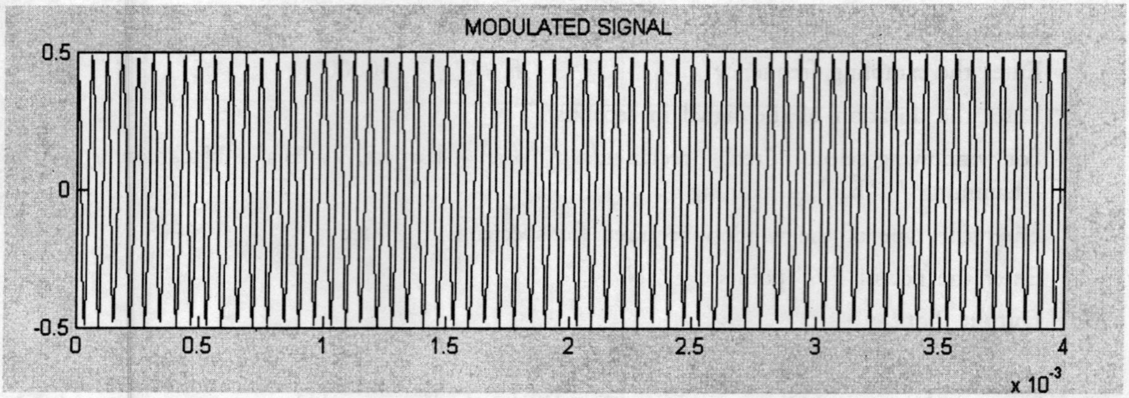

Fig. C.12 Modulated Signal

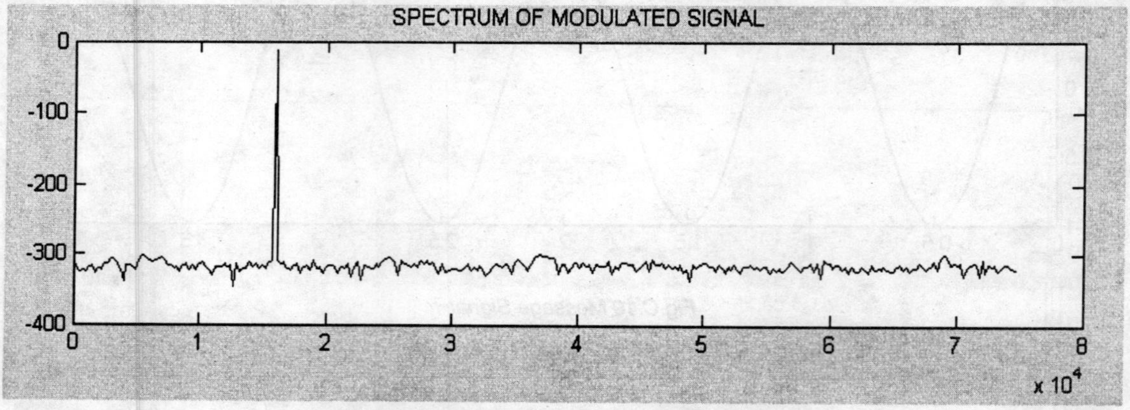

Fig. C.13 Spectrum of the Modulated Signal

Result2:

Enter the message amplitude Am = 1

Enter the modulating frequency fm = 1000

Enter carrier Amplitude Ac =1

Enter carrier frequency Fc =15000

Enter the sampling frequency fs = 150000

Enter the duration of the signal in seconds T = 4e-3

For windowing select "rec" - rectangular / "bart" - bartlett / "bla" - blackman / "ham" - hamming / "han" – hanning

Enter the type of the window required for spectrum rec

Enter the no. of FFT points N = M

Output Plot:

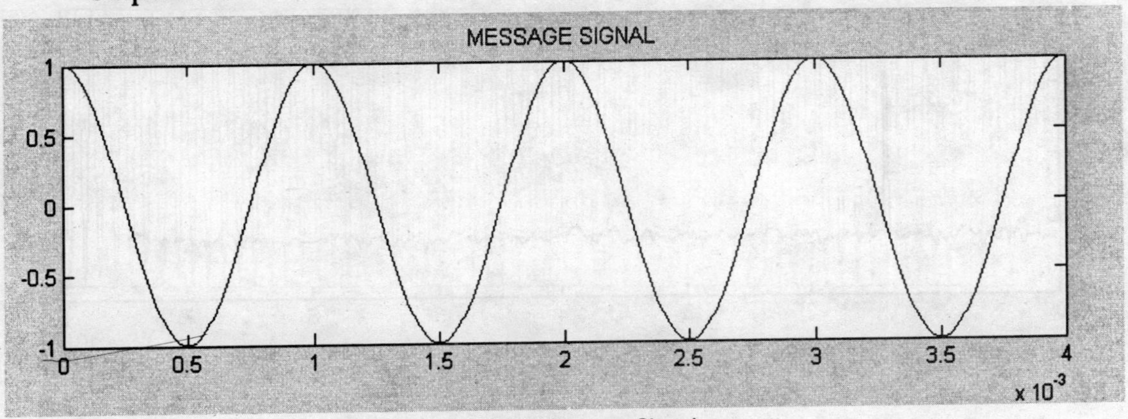

Fig. C.14 Message Signal

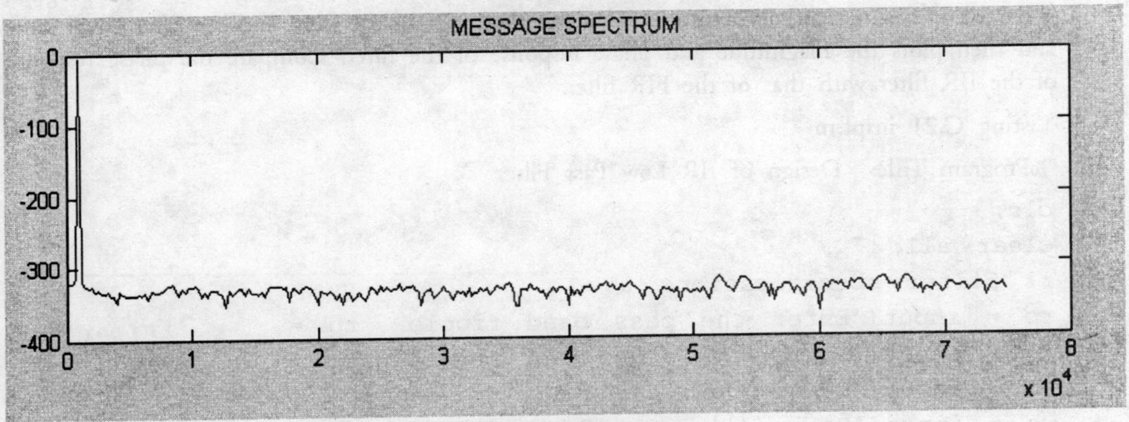

Fig. C.15 Message Spectrum

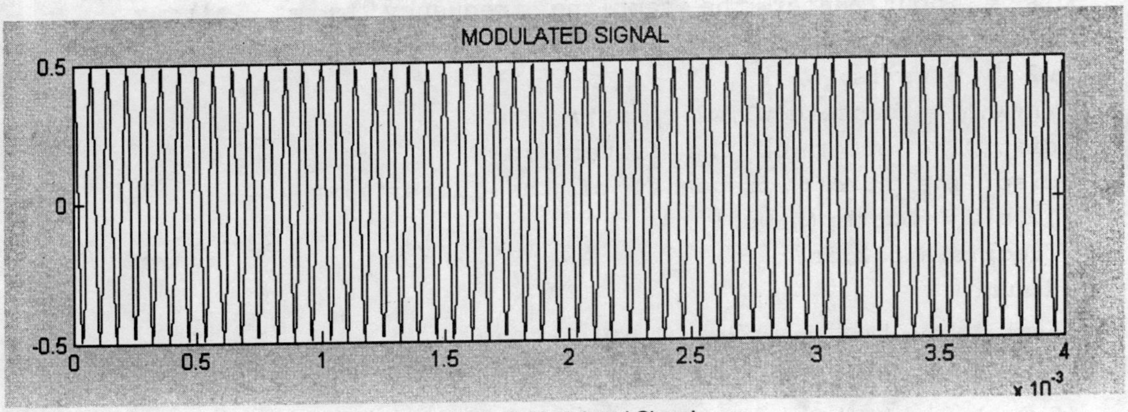

Fig.C.16 Modulated Signal

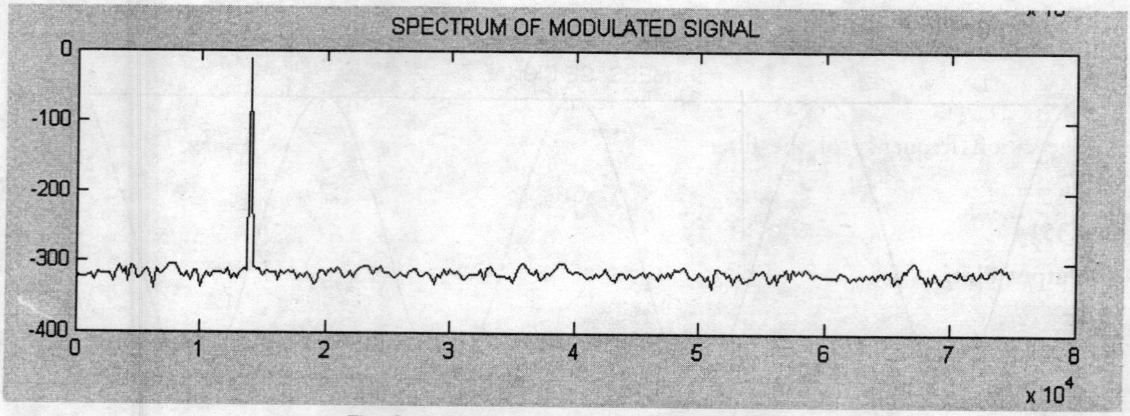

Fig. C.17 Spectrum of the Modulated Signal

8. MATLAB program to design an IIR Low Pass Filter is given in Listing C.21. The program takes the LPF specifications as input, calculates the order of the filter and the filter coefficients and then plots the magnitude and phase response of the filter. Compare the phase response of the IIR filter with that of the FIR filter.

Listing C.21 iirlpf.m

```
%Program Title:  Design of IIR Low Pass Filter
clc;
clear all;
%% Filter specifications %%
rp = input('Enter the pass band ripple    rp =      ');
rs = input('Enter the stop band ripple    rs =      ');
wp = input('Enter the pass band frequency wp =    ');
ws = input('Enter the stop band frequency ws =    ');
fs = input('Enter the sampling frequency fs =     ');
w1 = 2*wp/fs;
w2 = 2*ws/fs;
[n,wn] = buttord(w1,w2,rp,rs);
disp('The order of the filter');n
disp('The cutoff frequency of the filter');wn
[b,a] = butter(n,wn);
freqz(b,a,512,fs)
```

Results:

Enter the pass band ripple rp = 0.01

Enter the stop band ripple rs = 80

Enter the pass band frequency wp = 3000

Enter the stop band frequency ws = 5000

Enter the sampling frequency fs = 20000

The order of the filter

n =

19

The cutoff frequency of the filter

wn =

0.3514

Output Plot:

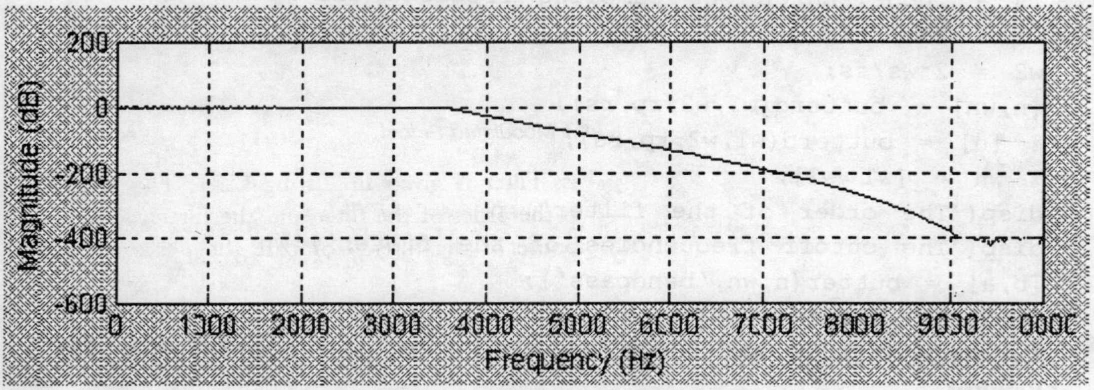

Fig. C.18 Magnitude Response of IIR LPF

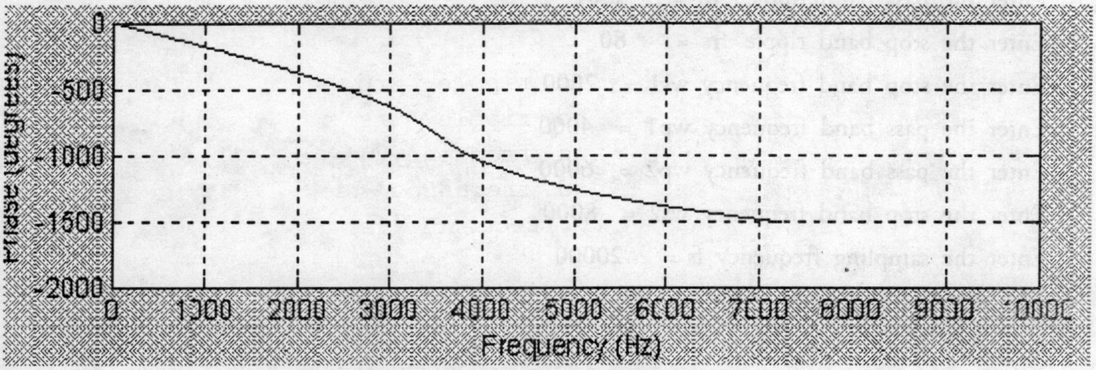

Fig. C.19 Phase Response of IIR LPF

9. MATLAB program to design an IIR Band Pass Filter is given in Listing C.22. The program takes the specifications of the BPF as input, calculates the filter coefficients and then plots the magnitude and phase response of the filter.

   Listing C.22 iirbpf.m

   %Program Title: Design of IIR BPF

```
clc;
clear all;
%% Filter specifications %%
```

```
rp = input('Enter the pass band ripple   rp =   ');
rs = input('Enter the stop band ripple   rs =   ');
% wp = input('Enter the pass band frequency wp =   ');
% ws = input('Enter the stop band frequency ws =   ');
ws(1) = input('Enter the stop band frequency ws1 = ');
wp(1) = input('Enter the pass band frequency wp1 =   ');
wp(2) = input('Enter the pass band frequency wp2 =   ');
ws(2) = input('Enter the stop band frequency ws2 =   ');
fs = input('Enter the sampling frequency fs =   ');
w1 = 2*wp/fs;
w2 = 2*ws/fs;
[n,wn] = buttord(w1,w2,rp,rs);
% [n] = buttord(w1,w2,rp,rs);
% wn = [w1 w2];
disp('The order of the filter');n
disp('The cutoff frequencies of the filter');wn
[b,a] = butter(n,wn,'bandpass');
freqz(b,a,512,fs)
title('MAGNITUDE AND PHASE RESPONSES OF IIR BUTTERWORTH BPF');
```

Results:

Enter the pass band ripple rp = 0.01

Enter the stop band ripple rs = 80

Enter the stop band frequency ws1 = 2000

Enter the pass band frequency wp1 = 4000

Enter the pass band frequency wp2 = 6000

Enter the stop band frequency ws2 = 8000

Enter the sampling frequency fs = 20000

The order of the filter

n =

9

The cutoff frequencies of the filter

wn =

0.3538 0.6462

Output Plot:

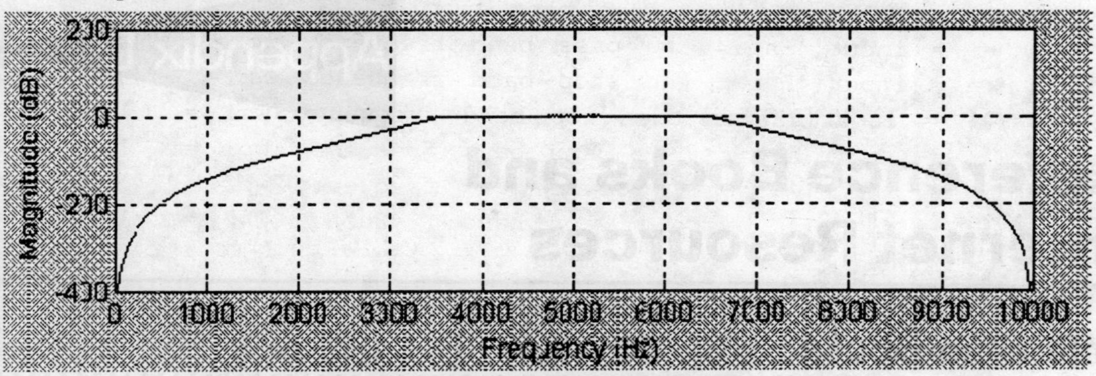

Fig. C.20 Magnitude Response of IIRBPF

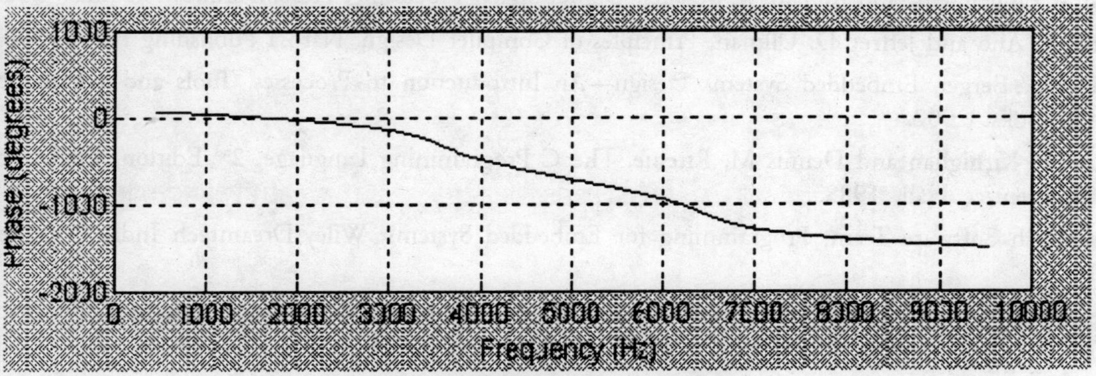

Fig. C.21 Phase Response of IIRBPF

10. "Software Defined Radio" is a hot DSP technology. Also referred to as software radio or reconfigurable radio, this field deals with the development of DSP-driven radio systems. Unlike the conventional radio systems that are dedicated to a set of communication parameters (such as type of modulation, multiple access technique, bandwidth etc.), software defined radio systems can be configured to receive and demodulate communication signals of different parameters. You can get a wealth of information on this from the Internet. www.sdrforum.org is the official site of Software Defined Radio Forum.

Appendix D

Reference Books and Internet Resources

Reference Books

Alan V. Oppenheim and Ronald W. Schafer, Digital Signal Processing, Pearson Education India, 2002.

Alfred V. Aho and Jeffrey D. Ullman, Principles of Compiler Design, Narosa Publishing House, 1987.

Arnold S. Berger, Embedded Systems Design—An Introduction to Processes, Tools and Techniques, CMP Books. 2002.

Brain W. Kirnighan and Dennis M. Ritchie, The C Programming Language, 2nd Edition, Englewood Cliffs, Prentice Hall, 1988.

Dreamtech Software Team, Programming for Embedded Systems, Wiley-Dreamtech India Pvt. Ltd., 2002.

Dreamtech Software Team, WAP, Bluetooth and 3G Programming, Wiley-Dreamtech India Pvt. Ltd., 2001.

Ed Sutter, Embedded Systems Firmware Demystified, CMP Books, 2002.

IEEE, IEEE Software Engineering Standards Collection, IEEE Press, 1994.

Jack Ganssle and Michael Barr, Embedded Systems Dictionary, CMP Books. 2003.

Jean J. Labrosse, MicroC/OS—II The Real-Time Kernel, CMP Books, 2002.

John Catsoulis, Designing Embedded Hardware, O'Reilly & Associates Inc. 2003.

K.V.K.K. Prasad, Principles of Digital Communication Systems and Computer Networks, Dreamtech Press, 2003.

K.V.K.K. Prasad, The Roadmap for a Successful Career in Software Development, ICS Ltd., 1999.

Miro Samek, Practical Statecharts in C/C++, CMP Books, 2002.

Qing Li with Caroline Yao, Real-Time Concepts for Embedded Systems, CMP Books, 2003.

Software Engineering Institute, CMU, The Capability Maturity Model, Guidelines for Improving the Software Process, Addison Wesley, 1994.

Watts S. Humphrey, Introduction to Personal Software Process, Addison Wesley Longman Inc., 1997.

Internet Resources

www.3com.com	3COM
www.3gpp.org	3G Partnership Program. (For GSM, 2.5G, 3G wireless standards)
www.acm.org	Association for Computing Machinery
www.agere.com	Agere Systems
www.agilent.com	Agilent Technologies
www.altera.com	Altera
www.analogdevices.com	Analog Devices
www.ansi.org	American National Standards Institute
www.apsca.org	Asia Pacific Smart Card Association Online
www.aspirecommunication.com	Aspire Communications Pvt. Ltd. (for Intel StrongARM development board)
www.atmel.com	ATMEL
www.bluetooth.com	Bluetooth Special Interest Group
www.cirrus.com	Cirrus Logic Corporation
www.computer.org	IEEE Computer Society
www.conexant.com/cnxt	Conexant GPS receiver
www.eg3.com	Embedded software resources
www.elearn.cdacindia.com	E-learning portal of CDAC
www.embedded.com	On-line resources for embedded software development.
www.Embedded-Control-Europe.com	Embedded Control Europe (ECE), ICC Media, Germany
www.embedded-linux.org	Embedded Linux Consortium
www.fairchild.com	Fairchild Corporation
www.fsf.org	Free Software Foundation
www.gnu.org	The GNU Free Software Foundation
gcc.gnu.org	GNU Compiler Collection
www.gemplus.com	Gemplus, Smart card manufacturer
www.hitachi.com	Hitachi
www.hp.com/go/embedded	HP's Chai platform for development of embedded/mobile applications.
www.ieee.org	Institute of Electrical and Electronics Engineers
www.ietf.org	Internet Engineering Task Force
www.intel.com/design/intarch	Intel Processors architecture
www.irda.org	Infrared Data Association
www.iseeyes.com	Innovation Communications Systems Ltd. (for 89C51 and AVR development boards)

www.iso.org	International Organization for Standardization
www.itu.int	International Telecommunications Union
www.javasoft.com/products/jini	Jini Technology of Sun Microsystems
www.Jboss.org	Open Source Java Development Products suite Jboss
www.lucent.com	Lucent Technologies
www.maxim-ic.com	Maxim (Dallas Semiconductors)
www.microsoft.com/embedded	Microsoft's embedded operating systems and tools
www.motorola.com/PowerPC	Motorola PowerPC
www.national.com	National Semiconductor
www.palmos.com	Palm OS
qdn.qnx.com	QNX Neutrino OS
www.redhat.com/embedded	Redhat Embedded Linux
ftp.rtlinux.org	RTLinux
www.sdcc.sourceforge.net	SDCC compiler for 8051
www.st.com	ST Microelectronics
standards.ieee.org	IEEE Standards
www.symbian.com	Symbian OS
java.sun.com/products/j2metoolkit	J2ME Toolkit
www.pc104.org	PC/104 standard
www.pcisig.org	PCI Special Interest Group
www.qualcomm.com/Brew	Qualcomm's BREW development kit
www.rtj.org	Real Time Java
www.sei.cmu.edu	Software Engineering Institute, Carnegie Mellon University
www.tagsys.net	RF tag systems
www.techonline.com	E-learning portal on embedded systems and Digital Signal Processing
www.ti.com	Texas Instruments
www.microsoft.com/mobile/downloads	Embedded visual tools
www.uCOS-II.com	MicroC/OS-II Operating System
www.usb.org	Universal Serial Bus
www.wapforum.org	WAP Forum
www.wileydreamtech.com	Wiley Dreamtech Pvt. Ltd.
www.xilinx.com	Xilinx
www.zilog.com	Zilog

Appendix E

About Online Content

The online content contains the complete source code listings given in the book and software folder. Various code listings are provided in the **CodeFile** folder. For each Chapter, there is a separate sub-folder with the Chapter number. For example, the sub-folder "Chapter 11" contains all the source code listings given in Chapter 11. Apart from code listings of the book, an additional sub-folder Appendix C is provided along with code listings. The Appendix C folder contains additional programs related to the selected chapters, which you can use to implement solutions on various platforms discussed in the book. The **Software** folder contains tool kits for developing embedded applications on Java, RTLinux environment and software for 89C51 Micro-Controller Platform. Please note that:

- If you want to open the Linux files on a Windows machine, you can select the file, write-click and in the option "Open with", select "WORDPAD".
- To open the project files of VC++ and VB, you need to open the files on a system in which the Visual Studio is installed.
- For projects which involve serial communication, you need to have a null modem cable to interconnect two computers. The instructions to make a null modem cable are given in Chapter 6.
- To run the VB programs given in Chapter 15, you need to copy them on a system in which eMbedded Visual tools are installed.
- To run the Java programs given in Chapter 16, you need to copy the files given in the folder "Chapter 16" in a system in which JDK and Java Web Server are installed. Ensure that the path is set correctly as instructed in Chapter 16.
- The programs given in Chapters 3, 11, 12 and **Appendix** C run on a Linux system. For programs in Chapter 12 and some programs in Appendix C, you need to install RTLinux also.

About Appendix C Sub-folder

As mentioned earlier, the Appendix C sub-folder contains some additional programs for Linux and RTlinux. For better understanding, a brief description of programs is provided. You can use these programs to develop your skills for the Linux environment.

Listing	Program Name	Description
C.1	CRC16file.c	Calculates the CRC-16 for a file.
C.2	nocharfile.c	Counts the number of characters in a file
C.3	scread.c	Receives data from an embedded system and transfer the data to the file.
C.4	every10.c	Displays a character on Linux machine at every 10 seconds.
C.5	packet32bit.c	Generates packets of 32 bits and checks whether the packet is control packet or data packet.
C.6	packet100.c	Generates packets of 100 bytes for a given file.
C.7	prgs.c	Takes an input from the user, converts into uppercase and send them for printing.
C.8	multhd.c	Calculates and displays the length of a given string.
C.9, C.10	input.c, strlength.c,	These programs calculate and display the length of a given string using message queues in Linux.
C.11, C.12, C.13	common.h, prg1.c, prg2.c	These programs calculate and display the length of a given string using shared memory in Linux.
C.14	multithreading.c	Implements multi-threading in RTLinux
C.15, C.16	control.h, RTLinux_ps.c, Linux_ps.c	These programs demonstares inter-process communication between Linux and RTLinux.

About code listings provided in the book

Chapter 3: Programming for Embedded Systems

- Due to memory constraints, bit manipulation is quite an important aspect of embedded programming. Various C programs that you can use for *bit manipulation* are listed below:

Listing	Name of the program
3.1	bitwise.c
3.2	checkbit1.c
3.3	checkbit2.c
3.4	setbit1.c
3.5	setbit2.c
3.6	clearbit.c

- C programs that can be used to *calculate CRC* on the basis of standard algorithms (CRC-16, CRC-32 and CRC-CCITT) are as follows:

Listing	Name of the program
3.7	crc16.c
3.8	crc32.c

- C programs that can be used for *memory management* and to calculate *time taken by a program* are as follows:

Listing	Name of the program
3.9	memalloc.c
3.10	ttiming.c
3.11	ctiming.c

- C programs that can be used to *read and write data*, in Linux/Unix environment, with the help of various system calls are as follows:

Listing	Name of the program
3.12	syscall.c
3.13	fileops.c
3.14	readwrite.c

- C programs illustrating the usage of *Makefile* utility are listed below:

Listing	Name of the program
3.15	Makefile
3.16	hello.h
3.17	hello.c
3.18	world.h
3.19	world.c
3.20	main.c

Chapter 6: Communication Interfaces

- The C program for *Serial Communication* is as follows:

Listing	Name of the program
6.1	serailcom.c

Chapter 11: Programming in Linux

- Various C programs that can be used in *creating a new shell* and handling of the *fork()* function are as follows:

Listing	Name of the program
11.1	cproc.c
11.2	forkdemao.c
11.3	forkwait.c

- C programs illustrating the *event handling* and *multithreading* in Linux environment are listed below:

Listing	Name of the program
11.4	sendsignal.c
11.5	multithreading.c

- The following programs display the usage of *semaphore* and *mutex* functions:

Listing	Name of the program
11.6	sema.c
11.7	mutex.c·

- The following programs display the concept of *shared memory* and the way of using it under Linux environment:

Listing	Name of the program
11.8	common.h
11.9	prg1.c
11.10	prg2.c·

- An efficient way of message queuing can be learned with the help of the following programs. The following programs uses various function calls for *message queuing*.

Listing	Name of the program
11.11	converter.c
11.12	input.c
11.13	generator.c
11.14	monitor.c

Chapter 12: Programming in RTLinux

- The following program provides the source code to *display a message periodically* in the RTLinux environment

Listing	Name of the program
12.1	Hello.c·

- The following programs provide source code for *threads synchronization* using the semaphore and mutex function calls

Listing	Name of the program
12.2	semaphore.c
12.3	mutex.c

- The following programs provides the source code to *control the working of an audio player*. With the help of the following programs, you can control the working of the audio player running on Windows, from the RTLinux system.

Listing	Name of the program
12.4	Playc
12.5	Stop.c
12.6	Pause.c
12.7	MviplayerDlg.cpp

- Apart from the above-listed programs, the executable files AudioPlayer1 and AudioPlayer2 for Windows COM1 and COM2 port respectively are given in the sub-folder. Various project files are provided in the Player folder.

Chapter 13: Development of Navigation System

- The following program provides the source code for the *GPS receiver.*

Listing	Name of the program
13.1	GPSSimulator.c
13.2	GPSDlg.cpp

The chapter folder contains the project files in sub-folder GPS.

Chapter 14: Development of Protocol Converter

- The following programs provide the source code for the *protocol converter* application, which is implemented on three computers. Computer A runs a Java program, which transmits the file over the Ethernet link to computer B. Computer B receives the file (Ethernet Packet) and converts it into the serial format with the help of a C program. Computer C runs another C program to assemble packets of computer A and checks whether the program is running correctly or not. The following programs illustrate this procedure.

Listing	Name of the program
14.1	UDPFileTx.java
14.2	ProtocolConverter.c
14.3	SerailRx.c

Chapter 15: Embedded Database Application

- The following programs provide the source code for an embedded database application using eMbedded Visual Tools 3.0 for Pocket PCs. The application allows the user to easily add, modify or delete records in a Pocket PC. The GUI interface for handheld PC is developed using eMbedded Visual Basic while the Pocket Access database is used at the backend.

Listing	Name of the program
15.1	frmSoftwareIndustrySurvey.ebf
SoftwareIndustrySurvey.ebp	VB Project file
frmSoftwareIndustrySurvey.frx	frx file
SoftwareIndustrySurvey.vbw	VB work file

Chapter 16: Mobile Java Applications

- This chapter provides the source code for two Java applications running on the Windows platform. The two applications are Electronic City Guide for mobile devices and Internet - based electronic voting machine. Both applications are designed with special focus on mobile phone. Both applications use HTTP connection between the client and server ends. The code listings for the two applications are categorized between two folders: CityGuide and E-Voting. Let us briefly discuss the code listing provided in the two folders for theese applications.

Electronic City Guide

The Electronic City Guide application works as a tourist guide for you. The application provides a GUI interface that a user can use to obtain the details of a selected city.

The folder CityGuide provides the entire source code and database for the application Electronic City Guide. The details of various cities reside on the Access database TourGuide.mbd. The following program generates the user interface for the application and delivers the output to the user on a mobile device.

Listing	Name of the program
16.1	CityGuide.java

The following programs fetch the selected city details from the database and display that to the user.

16.2	Cities.jsp
16.3	Citydetails.jsp
16.4	NameCategory.jsp

Electronic Voting

Electronic voting application provides an interface for the user to cast his vote directly from the mobile phone. The application provides a list of contesting candidates. The user can select a candidate and cast his vote. The application maintains the validity of the voter and updates votes obtained by the candidate. To ensure security and unbiased voting, the application provides authentication measures such as user ID and password. Once the voting is complete, the application displays the result on the mobile phone.

The folder E-Voting provides both the entire source code and the database for the application Electronic voting on mobile phone. The source code is categorized between two sub-folders : ForVote and DisplayResults. Let us briefly discuss the listings provided in the two sub-folders. To start with, let us look at the listings provided in the ForVote sub-folder. The following program creates the interface for the user to cast his vote.

Listing	Name of the program
16.5	ElectionVote.java

The following programs display the list of candidates using which the user can use to cast his vote. The application validates the status of the voter in the database as well as updates the total votes obtained by a contestant and stores in the database.

Listing	Name of the program
16.6	ValidateMember.jsp
16.7	UpdateContestant.jsp
16.8	UpdateVoter.jsp
16.9	DisplayContestants.jsp

The sub-folder DisplayResults contains the source code for displaying the voting results. Here is a brief description of the listings provided in the DisplayResults sub-folder. These programs add up and produce the display of the numbers of votes gotten by each contestant.

Listing	Name of the program
16.10	DisplayResults.java
16.11	DisplayResults.jsp

Chapter 17: Embedded Software Development on 89C51 Micro-Controller Platform

- The following C programs provide the source code to *toggle the LED with a specified delay* and *glow an LED* when a switch is pressed, respectively.

Listing	Name of the program
17.1	LED_Toggle.c
17.2	switch.c

- The following program can be used for *serial communication* between the host and the 89C51 development board on a UART port.

Listing	Name of the program
17.3	TDX.c

Apart from these programs, the chapter's folder contains a Small Device C Compiler in SDCC sub-folder and 8051Sim software in 8051Sim sub-folder.

Chapter 18: Embedded Software Development on AVR Micro-controller Platform

- The following programs provide the source code to develop *cross platform application* using AVR studio and AVRGCC together. The following programs can be used to toggle an LED and glow an LED when an input is received through a switch.

Listing	Name of the program
18.1	LED_Toggle.c
18.2	SWITCH.c

- The following program provides the source code for *communication through UART port* in the AVR platform.

Listing	Name of the program
18.3	UART.c

Apart from these programs, the chapter's folder contains a sub-folder AVRGCC. This sub-folder provides all the necessary files required for developing the embedded software on AVR platform.

Chapter 20: RFID Systems

The following folders give the complete project files (in VC++) for the two applications described in this chapter. The 'readme' file in each of the folders gives the complete description of the files in that folder. Note that for these projects to work, you need to have the Texas Instruments' S6350 Midrange Reader Module and Tag-it ISO Transponder Inlays. You need to install the driver software supplied by the RFID reader vendor for the program to execute successfully.

Folder Name	Description
RFIDCard	Project files for creation of Employee ID card application
RFIDReader	Project files for reading data from the tag and updating the database in the PC for recording of in and out times.

Chapter 21: DSP-based Embedded Systems

The following files give the complete source code for the MATLAB programs. This folder also contains the MATLAB programs of the exercises given in this chapter. Note that for executing these programs on your system, you need to install MATLAB 6.5 or later version.

Listing	Name of the program
Listing 21.1	unitsamplesequence.m
Listing 21.2	unitstepsequence.m
Listing 21.3	sinusoidalsequence.m
Listing 21.4	uniformrandomsequence.m
Listing 21.5	statisticalparameters.m

Listing	Name of the program
Listing 21.6	voicespectrum.m
Listing 21.7	dtmf.m
Listing 21.8	amdsb.m
Listing 21.9	ask.m
Listing 21.10	decimation.m
Listing 21.11	interpolation.m
Listing 21.12	firlpf.m
Listing 21.13	firbpf.m
Listing C.18	normallydistributed randomsequence.m
Listing C.19	noisespectrum.m
Listing C.20	amssb.m
Listing C.21	iirlpf.m
Listing C.22	iirbpf.m

Software

Apart from the CodeFile sub-folder, the online content has another Software sub-folder. The Softwar sub-folder contains:

Java 2 Wireless Toolkit

j2me_wireless_toolkit-1_0_3_win.exe exe file of the J2ME Software

RTLinux

rtlinux-3[1].2-pre2.tar.bz2 File of the RTLinux Software

8051

8051Sim Contain the software 8051Sim

Lab Manual

The Chapter 19 subfolder carries a file in the PDF format that can be treated as an e-book. This e-book provides a detailed courseware to understand the architecture of Intel StrongARM development board for embedded applications. Strong ARM processors are used in mobile devices such as PDA, hand held devices, cell phones, etc. The reader can use the e-book as a knowledge bank as well as a lab manual. The material in the e-book will enable the reader to understand the actual composition of the hardware required for developing hardware applications on Linux. Part B of the book introduces the reader to communication, encoding and encryption techniques. Part provides ideas to the reader to develop projects based on the Strong ARM-based processors.

The reader benefits from the e-book in two ways:

1. It provides an in-depth knowledge about the actual composition of an embedded development system, that supports all applications.
2. It provides enough information for the user to understand applications on embedded development platforms.

Note: **The content of CD is available online.**

To access the Online Resources:

1. Visit http://www.dreamtechpress.com/embedded-real-time-systems.html
2. Click the Companion Content tab.
3. Enter the Download code: **ERTS-0461-BB-600.**
4. Click the Download button.